Second Generation
Expert Systems

Jean-Marc David
Jean-Paul Krivine
Reid Simmons
(Editors)

Second Generation Expert Systems

With 212 Figures and 12 Tables

Springer-Verlag
Berlin Heidelberg New York
London Paris Tokyo
Hong Kong Barcelona
Budapest

Editors

Jean-Marc David
Renault
Service Systèmes Experts
860 Quai Stalingrad
92109 Boulogne-Billancourt
France

Jean-Paul Krivine
Electricité de France
Direction des Etudes et Recherches
1, Av. du Général de Gaulle
92141 Clamart Cedex
France

Reid Simmons
Carnegie Mellon University
School of Computer Science
5000 Forbes Avenue
Pittsburgh, PA 15213-3890
USA

ISBN-13: 978-3-642-77929-9   e-ISBN-13: 978-3-642-77927-5
DOI: 10.1007/ 978-3-642-77927-5

Library of Congress Cataloging-in-Publication Data
Second generation expert systems/J.-M. David, J.-P. Krivine, R. Simmons, eds. p. cm. Includes
bibliographical references and index.
1. Expert systems (Computer science) I. David, J.-M. (Jean Marc) II. Krivine, J.-P. (Jean Paul) III.
Simmons, R. (Richard) QA76.76.E95S43 1993   006.3'3–dc20   93-19194 CIP

© Springer-Verlag Berlin Heidelberg 1993
Softcover reprint of the hardcover 1st edition 1993

Cover Design: H. Lopka, Ilvesheim
Typesetting: Camera ready by the editors

33/3140 - 5 4 3 2 1 0 - Printed on acid-free paper

Foreword

This book results from a series of workshops and conferences that were organized in France between 1988 and 1991.

A workshop entitled "Second Generation Expert Systems: Combining Heuristic and Deep Reasoning" was organized during the IMACS Congress in Paris in July 1988. About fifty researchers gathered for that workshop, which can be considered the first meeting devoted explicitly to second generation expert systems.

The Avignon Conference on Artificial Intelligence, Knowledge-Based Systems and Natural Language then hosted a separate conference on this topic from 1989 to 1991. More than 200 papers were submitted during this period, and about 60 of them were published in the proceedings. Subsequent to 1991, the second generation expert system conference was integrated into the main scientific conference.

These gatherings played a major role in bringing researchers together, defining the field, and in the exchange of ideas. During those years, they were the prime forum for presenting research on second generation expert systems. Most of the contributors to this book were involved in one or more of the proceedings.

As chairman and co-chairs of these workshops and conferences, we would like to thank those who enabled these events. We are especially indebted to the authors and to those who acted in the different program committees for their invaluable contribution to the overall success of these meetings.

The Editors

Table of Contents

Part I

Introduction

Second Generation Expert Systems: A Step Forward in Knowledge Engineering

Jean-Marc David[1] and Jean-Paul Krivine[2] and Reid Simmons[3]

[1] Service Systemes Experts, Renault, Boulogne Billancourt, France
[2] Direction des Etudes et Recherches, Electricite de France, Clamart, France
[3] School of Computer Science, Carnegie Mellon University, Pittsburgh, PA

Abstract. Second generation expert systems are characterized by two approaches: combining multiple models and reasoning techniques, and using knowledge-level approaches for designing systems. These approaches are complementary ways to overcome drawbacks of first generation expert systems. This paper describes these approaches and reviews how they benefit knowledge-based systems with respect to knowledge acquisition, explanation, robustness and efficiency, and reuse of models, knowledge bases and problem-solving code. Many of the points are illustrated with examples taken from papers in this volume.

1 Introduction

This book contains a collection of articles about knowledge-based systems that are collectively known as "second generation expert systems." This term is somewhat fuzzy: there is not a clear distinction between "first" and "second" generation systems; it is more of an evolution of ideas, styles, and techniques for constructing knowledge-based systems. The ideas, as evidenced by the diversity of papers in this volume, in many cases arose independently as researchers saw both the potential in knowledge-based systems and the limitations of the then state of the art in technology.

While we cannot give a precise definition of "second generation expert systems," they have certain common characteristics. First and foremost is the acknowledgement that knowledge is central in problem solving and that the explicit modeling of knowledge is important for creating understandable and maintainable systems. Different models and problem-solving methods are needed for different aspects of the process, and the choice of models and methods to be used has a large impact on the efficiency and competence of the knowledge-based system. Another common characteristic is in distinguishing between what knowledge is used and how it is implemented (the distinction between the "knowledge level" and the "symbol level" [48]). In particular, second generation expert systems demonstrate the importance of using the appropriate knowledge for given problems, and representing that knowledge in appropriate ways. Such systems often combine multiple representations, problem solving strategies, and learning methods within a single system.

In short, the field is characterized by an increased understanding of what knowledge it takes to solve problems and how best to encode that knowledge so that a computer can make use of it.

Research in these "second generation" topics is still progressing and new systems continue to be developed. It is one of the main motivations of this volume to contribute to the dissemination and cross-fertilization of these ideas and to accelerate advancement of the field. The current state of the art, as reflected by this volume, is just a snapshot of an ongoing process. Yet it is valuable, at this point in time, to show where the field is and where it has yet to go to achieve truly "expert" systems.

Before discussing the promises and problems of second generation expert systems, we briefly review the development of the field of knowledge-based systems.

Solving complex problems has always been the hallmark of Artificial Intelligence. Early work in AI concentrated on developing general techniques for solving problems [32, 49]. In the late 1970's and early 1980's, however, researchers came to the realization that knowledge about tasks and problems, rather than clever search techniques, was a main source of power in problem solving. Even more importantly, they realized that this knowledge could be acquired from experts and represented in a form that computers could use. Expert systems were developed for quite complex domains, including medical diagnosis [56], geology [28, 31], computer layout [45], etc.

The knowledge in these early expert systems was often obtained by inquiring from experts how they solved particular problems. The "knowledge engineer" then encoded the experts' advice in the form of *associational* (also referred to as *heuristic* or *empirical*) rules-of-thumb that mapped from observable features of the problem to conclusions. For example, MYCIN has rules of the form "if given symptoms are observed, then there is evidence for a particular infection." These systems solved problems by chaining the rules together, either forward (from premises to conclusions) or backwards (from goal to initial conditions).

Thus, early expert systems typically had a simple control structure and uniform representation of knowledge, in the form of associational production rules. The knowledge was typically represented at a single level of abstraction and implicitly combined knowledge about "how" to perform a task, "what" is in the domain, and "why" things work. While it was initially thought that this would make systems fairly easy to develop, in fact it leads to several problems related to knowledge acquisition, explanation, brittleness, and maintainability [12, 26].

Knowledge acquisition can be difficult because experts often are unable to adequately explain how they solve problems, or they provide rationalizations that in practice do not lead to effective problem-solving behavior. While experts may be quite adept at describing why something works, they often have much more difficulty explaining how to diagnose malfunctions, such as indicating what information is relevant or how to match symptoms and causes.

Creating readily understandable explanations was often difficult for these early systems, in part because the absence of explicit "how", "what", or "why" knowledge limited their explanations to traces of how the problem was solved.

More generally, it has been shown that adequate explanations can be obtained either by using reconstructions of the task, such as those involving causal, functional or behavioral explanations, or by utilizing more abstract terms than that used to solve the original problem [70].

A third difficulty with associational, rule-based expert systems is that they tend to be *brittle* in that they do not work well outside their limited area of expertise. In particular, unlike true experts, the systems have no knowledge of their own limitations, and so tend to give nonsensical answers rather than degrading gracefully with a simple "don't know" when confronted with problems beyond their expertise. Another cause of brittleness is due to interactions amongst the rules. Initially, this was seen as a feature of rule-based systems: one could increase system competence merely by adding more associational rules and the correct problem-solving behavior would emerge [56]. In fact, this notion of rule independence is a myth [38]: there are often negative interactions (conflicts) between rules that cause performance to grade. In particular, adding new rules may cause the system to be unable to solve certain problems that it could before.

The first generation approach also affects system maintainability [62]. For example, validation of knowledge bases is difficult because knowledge about the domain is scattered throughout the rule base: while many rules might refer to features of a particular mechanism or process, nowhere is that whole represented, along with what it does or why it works. Validation is important because, as discussed above, adding additional associations often makes a rule-based system inconsistent. In addition, the task-specific associations tend to preclude effective reuse of knowledge and problem-solving methods.

In moving beyond first generation expert systems, researchers have focused on delineating and explicitly encoding more types of knowledge. This has involved two main issues: 1) developing multiple representations for knowledge and multiple methods for utilizing that knowledge, and 2) clearly distinguishing between what knowledge a system has and what mechanisms are used to encode that knowledge (these issues are discussed more fully in Sects. 2 and 3). Researchers have investigated the separation of control ("how") and domain knowledge [12, 66], the encoding of functional ("what") and causal ("why") knowledge [26, 55], and have developed representations for time and space, mechanisms and processes [74]. Different problem-solving methods have been developed to complement and extend one another [5, 52]. Many researchers have concentrated on combining associational and causal reasoning [18, 41, 60] to produce systems that are both efficient and robust. Another stream of research has focused on describing problem solving at a more abstract, knowledge level [9, 79].

All of these ideas make knowledge-based systems more competent, reusable, and explainable. First, competence is increased by incorporating more general models of the domain and task, along with more powerful problem solving techniques. The techniques can combine the more general knowledge in novel ways to solve new or particularly difficult tasks. Second, reusability is increased because the knowledge is partitioned into subareas that have relevance to multiple problem domains. Such diverse tasks as design, monitoring and diagnosis can all reuse explicit models of how a particular mechanism or process works. For example, the description of a chemical reaction may be used in designing a chemical process plant, monitoring its operation, or diagnosing why an excess amount of a chemical product is produced. Similarly, the diagnostic process can be broken into subtasks, such as data gathering, hypothesis generation, evaluation, etc. Many of these tasks are relevant for solving other problems as well. Finally, explanatory capability is increased because justification of answers can be given in more abstract terms or in terms relevant to the domain, not just by recapitulating the search process used to solve the problem.

The next two sections discuss in more detail the issues of domain modeling and knowledge-level problem solving. Section 4 describes how second generation approaches deal with some of the drawbacks cited earlier, namely with respect to knowledge acquisition, explanation, brittleness, and maintainability. As will be seen from the papers in this volume, these issues impact all aspect of knowledge-based systems: problem solving, knowledge acquisition, maintenance, explanation, and learning.

2   The Use of Multiple Models and Methods

Explicitly modeling different types of knowledge is a defining characteristic of second generation expert systems. In addition, many such systems utilize a variety of problem solving methods geared toward particular subtasks. These models and methods combine to produce systems that are more capable and/or more efficient than if any single model or method alone were used [61].

The use of different models and methods occurred to a limited extent in some early knowledge-based systems. For example, PROSPECTOR [31] used rules to represent associational knowledge and frames to represent taxonomic knowledge. R1 [45] used a specialized search procedure to solve the subproblem of laying out components on backplanes. However, these examples were typically seen as exceptions to the general paradigm of associational rule-based expert systems.

After the first wave of rule-based systems were developed, researchers began analyzing their strengths and shortcomings. One problem noted early was that the simple control structure of such systems (pattern matching and chaining) was often inadequate, especially in handling conflicting or competing rules. Various researchers advocated approaches such as partitioning the rules into related subsets, or using "meta" control knowledge to guide the search [25]. The utility of the latter approach was further recognized when it was shown that associational systems often inextricably combine domain and control knowledge, and that by separating them the systems can be more extensible, reusable and understandable [12, 69]. This led to the development of many system that separately represent domain and control knowledge [12, 66, 80].

2.1   Multiple Models

In addition to separating domain and control knowledge, researchers began focusing on the content of the domain knowledge itself. It was realized that associational rules-of-thumb are only one component of an expert's knowledge. Experts also have vast knowledge about how things work in their domain of expertise, at least at some level of abstraction [26]. Thus, for instance, doctors not only can diagnose diseases, they also understand (to some extent) the physiological processes of the human body.

The idea was to capture this domain knowledge and use it directly to solve problems from "first principles" [26]. In fact, the terms "first principles" and "deep" knowledge [7] are really misnomers, since the knowledge typically is not the most basic, nor is it necessarily more sophisticated or at a more detailed level than the associational rules [26]. Nevertheless the fundamental idea of understanding and modeling the domain, rather than just encoding rules for solving the problem, is sound. Thus, a more apt term to describe this work might be "model-based reasoning," since explicit models that detail how the domain works are being represented and reasoned about. Prime examples of this line of research is the development of systems to perform model-based diagnosis, and its associated theoretical framework [27, 29, 30, 36].

A related strand of research is in modeling domains at more abstract or "commonsense" levels. The guiding principle is that some problems can be solved using fairly abstract, qualitative models of the domain — quantitative information is often both unnecessary and difficult to obtain. The rationale is that by representing domains at the "appropriate" level of abstraction, one can minimize the amount of reasoning needed to solve problems.

Research in qualitative reasoning has led to the development of specialized models and reasoning methods for representing the physical world. In particular, models of time, space, causality, mechanisms, and processes have been developed [55, 74]. These models have been used for tasks such as diagnosis [5, 18, 39, 41], analysis [36], planning and data interpretation [50, 60], and design [35].

Often, however, modeling at a single level is insufficient for solving complex problems: detailed information may be needed for some parts of the problem, while trying to solve the whole problem at the most detailed level may be intractable. Researchers have developed systems that can solve problems at multiple levels of abstraction. Perhaps the earliest such system was ABEL [51], which performed medical diagnosis using models of diseases, anatomy, physiology, and pathophysiology. The system solved subproblems at whichever level had sufficient information, propagating information between levels to keep them consistent. Davis [27] developed a diagnostic system that represented circuits as a hierarchy of components. It first tried to localize a fault to a particular component, then examined its subcomponents to isolate the fault more exactly. These, and similar, efforts demonstrate that second generation expert systems can scale to handle complex problems by utilizing a hierarchy of abstract models.

For some problems, it is useful consider the domain from different points of view. For example, a piece of equipment can be viewed in terms of its mechanical, electrical or thermal properties. Similarly, an engineered entity can be viewed in both structural and functional terms [27, 35, 39]. Often, the different viewpoints are best modeled using different representations. This can result because certain representations are either more expressive or more efficient than others in modeling particular aspects of a problem. For example, representing causal relationships between objects as arcs in a directed graph is a very natural and effective means for reasoning about how one entity influences another [18]. On the other hand, for some problems using qualitative representations is both sufficient and more efficient than using more detailed, quantitative representations [5, 50]. Such systems, while time-consuming to develop, are often capable of efficiently solving fairly complex problems.

2.2 Multiple Methods

Along with representing multiple models, second generation expert systems often incorporate multiple problem-solving methods. Sometimes these methods are specialized to a particular representation [58]; sometimes the methods are specialized for particular subtasks [5, 9, 52]. A relatively common approach is to use a combination of associational (pattern-matching) and causal (model-based) reasoning [18, 60]. Others have combined causal and case-based reasoning [41], causal and probabilistic reasoning [36], and qualitative and quantitative methods [50]. One critical issue is understanding the roles the different methods play in the overall problem solving process [52, 59]. For example, in the GTD paradigm [60], associational reasoning is initially used because it is efficient, and usually produces correct answers, while causal reasoning is used to deal with problems that are too difficult for the associational methods.

It is desirable to combine multiple methods and models with a problem-solving architecture that provides flexibility and efficiency in combining models and methods. Some systems provide a set way for determining when to use which methods [41, 60], some provide for great flexibility in choosing which methods to use [9, 52], and some allow multiple methods to work on the same part of the problem simultaneously [37, 57].

There are many criteria for choosing a problem-solving architecture [19, 37], and no single architecture is best for all domains. The decision about which models and methods to use, and how to combine them, is very much an open problem. In general, though, the choice depends on the particular problem being solved and characteristics of the domain. To intelligently choose the architecture (methods and models), one needs to analyze the domain and problem in informational terms — in other words, at the knowledge level. Dealing with expert systems at this level is the subject of the next section.

3 The Knowledge Level Approach

First generation expert systems are built from a collection of rules; their intended behavior is supposed to emerge from the interactions of the rules. It is thus possible to characterize these systems only in terms of the application domain (e.g. diagnosis of blood infection) or in terms of the implementation language (pattern matching, backward chaining, etc). Neither of these characterizations is satisfactory for understanding what the system is doing and how it achieves a particular behavior.

A major advance of second generation expert systems has been to emphasize the distinction between the "knowledge level" and the implementation level, and to describe knowledge-based systems at the "right" level of abstraction. Describing knowledge-based systems in terms of rules, frames, backward or forward chaining, as was done in first generation systems, obscures their real nature. On the other hand, describing the problem-solving process in more abstract terms, such as classification, data abstraction, abduction, etc., provides a better characterization of how the system behaves.

The motivation for designing knowledge-based systems at the knowledge level, however, is not just to provide a more accurate description. Such an approach also enables a more principled design (emphasizing how the problem should be solved rather than how the system will be implemented), provides guidance in knowledge acquisition (what knowledge should be acquired, and what its role will be), enables the reuse of generic constructs, and enables more abstract explanations (the explanation is based on an explicit representation of the model instead of a trace of rules). These points will be discussed in Sect. 4.

We will briefly define the term "knowledge level," and then describe several significant approaches that use this concept, and their impact on knowledge engineering.

3.1 The Knowledge Level

The term "knowledge level" was introduced by Newell [48] to describe a system/agent as if it possesses certain knowledge, without making commitments about representation or implementation issues. More precisely, a knowledge-level model, according to Newell, is a model of behavior in terms of the knowledge and goals the agent has and the actions the agent can perform. The agent is driven by the *principle of rationality*, that is, it selects actions that it expects will lead to the satisfaction of its goals. Such a knowledge-level model is essentially aimed at explaining *why* the agent behaves in certain ways.

Since then, the expression "knowledge level" has become well accepted by AI practitioners. Part of the reason for its acceptance comes from the fact that Newell's paper described and amplified an emerging notion that the content of knowledge-based systems should be distinguished from the form used to represent the knowledge. The knowledge level rapidly became synonymous with a more abstract level for describing knowledge-based systems, independently from the implementation constructs. Van de Velde and Sticklen [68, 73] attempt to better characterize the knowledge level and propose possible evolutions of Newell's initial definition.

A well accepted paradigm for modeling knowledge-based systems at the knowledge level relies on a triad of components: tasks, methods and domain models. Tasks describe *what* should be done (the goals and sub-goals of the system). Problem solving methods describe *how* goals can be achieved. Domain models describe knowledge that is required by the methods.

In addition, we note that implementation issues are also somewhat relevant in knowledge-level modeling. In fact, researchers are trying to make explicit in the implementation the structure and knowledge that has been exhibited at the knowledge level. Clancey's work on NEOMYCIN is the first attempt to do that: he proposed a description of MYCIN in terms of *heuristic classification* [13], thus presenting a knowledge-level description of the system. Clancey then designed NEOMYCIN to represent this heuristic classification method explicitly [14].

3.2   Different Approaches

It is difficult to account for more than a decade of exciting, intensive work in a few lines. However, we can characterize the different approaches to knowledge-level modeling according to several viewpoints. Among the criteria that distinguishes these approaches, we cite the decision to put emphasis on either methods, on tasks, or on models. There are also approaches that provide general modeling languages, and ones that are based on a primitive set of "building blocks."

McDermott's work on *role limiting methods* is a good example of putting emphasis on methods [44]. The Generic Task approach, despite its name, can also be characterized as a method-oriented approach [6, 9]. CSRL, for example, is a classification method that can be applied to other interpretation tasks, as well as diagnosis. KADS, on the other hand, places emphasis on tasks: a task is decomposed into subtasks until basic inferences can be applied to execute them [78, 79]. While none of these approaches emphasize domain models as the primary perspective for modeling, there has been important work on model-based reasoning (see Sect. 2). Such work starts from a description of how a particular system behaves or has been built, and selects methods for a particular task (e.g., diagnostic methods used depend on the kind of models that have been defined: models of structure and behavior, causal models, functional models, etc). As the term "model-based" indicates, the construction of the knowledge-level model is in this case largely driven by the domain model.

Depending on the kind of problem, each of these three perspectives can in turn be the most effective one to start with. Actually, it is profitable consider the three perspective together, and support the modeling process by shifting from one point of view to another. For instance, the designer may first think about a task, then move to a model perspective to work out some of the models involved in the task, then think about the methods to achieve the tasks (which typically involves introducing additional models and subtasks) [43, 65].

Knowledge-level modeling approaches also differ in that some provide general modeling languages while others are rather based on a limited set of primitive constructs (building blocks). KADS [79] and COMMET [65] are examples of the former; Chandrasekaran's Generic Tasks (GT) [9], in its initial definition at least, is a prototypical example of the latter.

Building block approaches are appealing since they can associate a shell with each generic model. This facilitate the operationalization of the knowledge-level model. But pure building blocks approaches have some limitations. First, while such approaches provide ready-to-use constructs, in practice, one must often adapt or modify the generic constructs. For instance, the GT Toolset provides one primitive for classification, namely CSRL [4], while there are actually numerous ways to do classification, depending on available domain knowledge. However, in the GT framework, one cannot easily modify or adapt the generic CSRL to suit a particular need. A related problem is that it is impossible, both practically and theoretically, to come up with a complete set of building blocks for all tasks. Thus, in designing a particular application, one must often augment the components provided with task-specific code. This is also true, to a lesser extent, for the "glue" that is needed to connect building blocks. Chandrasekaran discusses these problems in [9]; proposals for ways to overcome some of the problems are discussed in [20, 52].

On the other hand, general modeling languages are much more flexible, since they tend to be more complete. Operationalization of knowledge, however, is not as direct, since the languages are typically at a finer granularity. Thus, a series of transformation is often required to go from a knowledge-level to symbol-level model. Actually, building block and general modeling language approaches are complementary, and could profitably be combined: building block approaches could benefit from a finer grain of components, and more general modeling languages could provide libraries of generic, ready-to-use, models.

3.3 Ongoing Work and Open Issues

An important issue concerns the *operationalization* of the model, that is, its transformation into an running system. This is especially true for general modeling languages. Mapping the knowledge-level model onto a computational framework has first been considered as the result of a *design* phase where a succession of transformations lead to the operational model [78]. However, explanation of reasoning, validation, and part of the knowledge acquisition process requires mappings from the operational behavior back to the knowledge-level model, in order to interpret symbol-level behavior in knowledge-level terms. Thus, it is desirable that the operationalization of knowledge and the architecture of the system should preserve the structure of the corresponding conceptual level. Model-K [40] and Omos [43] are two examples of languages in the KADS framework that attempt to maintain this correspondence, while at the same time providing a computational (as opposed to purely conceptual) framework.

Many of the approaches presented in this volume have been evolving and cross-fertilizing for years. For instance, Chandrasekaran describes the evolution of the Generic Tasks theory from the late seventies to the present [9]. KADS II [79] is an attempt to unify the KADS I framework and Steel's Componential Methodology [65]. While these approaches seem to be converging (or, at least, it is now possible to compare them in a common framework [17]), there remain many open issues. Several of these, relating to knowledge acquisition, explanation, performance, and reusability, will be discussed in the next section.

4 Second Generation Expert Systems

Combining multiple models and methods and adopting a knowledge-level approach for designing knowledge-based systems are complementary ways to overcome the drawbacks of first generation expert systems. These two avenues of research have mainly evolved in a parallel way, each one addressing its own issues. However, they both put emphasis on better modeling of the application domain, the role a particular piece of knowledge plays (and how different kinds of knowledge should cooperate), and better models of problem solving. We now survey and discuss the benefits these approaches have in second generation expert systems, and what open issues remain.

4.1 Knowledge Acquisition

Improving the process of knowledge acquisition has been an important motivation in developing second generation expert systems. It is thus not surprising it has been a very active field of research during the last decade. In first generation systems, knowledge acquisition was seen as a problem of transferring knowledge: extracting the expert's discourse and translating it into the implementation language constructs (rules). Knowledge acquisition is now considered to be a modeling task, composed of at least two distinct phases: building a model of the knowledge-based system (*modeling*) and filling the model with domain knowledge (*instantiation*).

Every knowledge engineer has a *mental* model of how his system behaves and why it behaves so. All knowledge-based systems (including first generation systems) contain at least an implicit model of the world they are reasoning/acting on, of the tasks they are supposed to achieve, etc. A major innovation of second generation expert systems has been to make these models explicit. This has provoked a major shift in the nature of knowledge acquisition and an emphasis on models and modeling [3, 15].

We now discuss how second generation expert systems facilitate knowledge acquisition with respect to modeling and instantiating the model. We will also address the issue of validation, since the validation of both the problem-solving model and its content can be considered as being part of the knowledge acquisition process.

Modeling: Knowledge-level models are useful for knowledge acquisition since they can fill the gap between the expert's discourse and implementation. Modeling, however, is rarely done from scratch; on the contrary, new models are often created by adapting and refining generic, or at least previously developed, models. As discussed in Sect. 3, different approaches have been used to built knowledge-level models. In the *building blocks* approach, the model is constructed from a library of primitive terms or elementary, generic models [9, 44]. For example, the GT Toolset [6] provides models for hierarchical classification, abductive assembly, hypothesis matching, etc. Similarly, general modeling languages can provide a basis for building task-specific models [65, 79].

Problems remain, however, in mapping problem features onto models and methods, in order to select the most appropriate one. Even with using knowledge-level approaches, modeling is still far from being a routine task; rather it still often requires a great deal of expertise and creativity [46].

Instantiating the model: The second phase of the knowledge acquisition process is driven by the model built in the first phase. This model indicates what knowledge should be acquired and clearly defines the role each piece of knowledge will play in the problem solving process. Using models to guide the knowledge acquisition process has proven to be a very powerful technique. Many of the tools that support the knowledge acquisition process can be classified as dedicated to a particular model: typical examples include ROGET (classification) [1], MOLE (cover and differentiate) and SALT (propose and revise) [44].

SALT, for instance, is knowledge acquisition tool dedicated to constraint satisfaction problems that can be solved by the "propose and revise" method. This method starts with an initial plan (propose) which is described in terms of values assigned to parameters. Then, *constraint violations* are detected and modifications are proposed to overcome them (revise). Since not all constraint satisfaction problems can be solved by this method, McDermott has proposed a set of criteria to assess the suitability of the "propose and revise" method [44]. Assuming the method is well suited to the problem, SALT dictates exactly what should be acquired: a set of parameters and attributes that describe a solution, the procedure to compute these values, the set of constraints that have to be checked, and modification procedures in case of constraint violation. SALT provides a dedicated knowledge editor to assist in acquiring this knowledge. In addition, since the role of each piece of knowledge in the problem solving process is clearly defined, SALT may also help in identifying incoherent or missing knowledge (for instance, a constraint that has no associated modification procedure). Thus, SALT illustrates how models can guide the knowledge acquisition process, by clearly assessing what knowledge is to be acquired and how this knowledge will be used by the solver.

Knowledge acquisition to instantiate the model can also benefit from the use of explicit domain models. In particular, causal models can support the refinement of the knowledge base, through a validation/explanation/acquisition loop [10, 54].

Validation: The validation of a knowledge base involves validating both the model itself and the acquired knowledge. Both can benefit from a knowledge-level approach. Knowledge-level models act as a functional specification of the system that can be discussed with the experts. They also provide a precise, unambiguous meaning to the acquired knowledge. David and Krivine have discussed the use of such an approach to debug the knowledge base by tracing the problem solving tasks that are performed [24]. Tracing the tasks, at various levels of details, appears to be much more efficient than using more classical debugging facilities (at the symbol level).

The use of a domain model can also be used to validate heuristic knowledge. For instance, Reynaud uses causal models to justify associational rules, as if these rules were the result of a compilation of causal knowledge [54]. The difficulty is then to map these different knowledge sources when they correspond to different points of view [11].

Open issues and ongoing work: The distinction between modeling and instantiating the model is a useful one. These two steps are often performed sequentially: initial interviews are used to construct the model, and domain knowledge is elicited only when the model is stable enough. However, development of the model and acquisition of domain knowledge may be interleaved: while the model is being progressively refined, domain knowledge may be acquired and used, in turn, to refine the model. This is the approach facilitated by the KEW workbench from the ACKnowledge project [72].

It must be emphasized again that dealing with libraries of generic models is not the panacea. On the one hand, generic models are a good communication medium: describing MYCIN as a classification system performing data abstraction, hypothesis matching and hypothesis refinement is certainly a good way to describe what the system is actually doing. However, designing a classification system by selecting a generic method appears to be more complex. Selecting the "right" model may not be that easy: selecting a too abstract model may be of little guidance while selecting a "wrong" (inadequate) model may lead to difficulties [53]. Indexing and retrieving models is not that obvious: what are their characteristics? in which case do they apply? Relationships between problems features and methods or models characteristics remains largely implicit in libraries. It should be acknowledged that these relationships are not yet well understood, and remain open areas for research.

4.2   Explanations

As Swartout and Moore point out [70], explanation is a process of constructing a coherent story that relates the expert system's concepts and results to things the user understands and accepts. First generation expert systems fail to meet this goal for two main reasons. First, most of the knowledge required to provide explanations is implicit in the knowledge base and is thus not accessible to the explanation module. Second, first generation systems build explanations essentially by paraphrasing the rules that are used in solving the problem. This is often considered unnatural and difficult to understand by users.

Second generation expert systems aim at overcoming these limitations. We discuss two different approaches that have been used to enhance explanations. The first approach relies on a more abstract representation of the knowledge used by the system to explain its behavior. The second approach, often called *reconstructive explanation* makes use of a different kind of knowledge to explain, with a different perspective, conclusions that have been reached.

Explaining at the right level of abstraction: Historically, NEOMYCIN [16] was the first example of this approach. In NEOMYCIN, the tasks achieved by MYCIN [56], such as gathering information, differentiate, etc., were made explicit. These tasks were implicit in MYCIN and supposed to emerge from the interaction of many specific rules [70]. Thus, MYCIN was unable to refer to these abstract terms when producing explanations. On the contrary, the task structure in NEOMYCIN provides the basis for more abstract explanations.

A similar idea has been used in the DIVA system [23, 24] and in the GT framework [8, 71]. The task structure and the domain models form the basis for more abstract explanations of the behavior of the system and its problem-solving strategy. The main difference between NEOMYCIN and these efforts is that NEOMYCIN uses a general explanation mechanism that directly interpret the task structure to build explanations: a modification in the task structure is then directly propagated into the explanations. On the contrary, the explanation module of DIVA and GT are task specific: modifying the task structure necessitates modification of the explanation module. The task-specific approach, however, has the advantage that global explanations can be built, while in NEOMYCIN only local, step by step, explanations are possible.

In the Explainable Expert System Framework (EES), system builders construct a high-level knowledge base that captures facts about the domain (domain models), its terminology, and general problem-solving strategies [70]. An automatic programming system use this knowledge base as an abstract specification of the knowledge-based system to be built. Design decisions are recorded in a *design history* that is used to construct explanations.

Other similar work is ongoing. Sprenger is exploring explanation strategies for KADS-based expert systems [63]. Greboval and Kassel have developed the AIDE shell with a particular concern for explanations of reasoning [34]. These systems all share the same basic principle: they provide better explanations through an abstraction of the problem-solving process. In addition, enhanced explanations are created by making explicit information about domain models, task structures, strategies, and rationales for design decisions.

Reconstructive explanations: It has often been observed that we do not explain a diagnosis, the demonstration of a mathematical theorem, or the solution of a detective story in the same way that we discovered the solution in the first place. Reconstructive explanations build on this principle: one knowledge-based system (the performance system) is used to solve the problem, then the conclusions of this system are passed to a second system (the explanation system) that justifies (and thus explains) the conclusions.

The DIVA project has experimented with such an approach [21, 22, 24]. DIVA initially produces a diagnosis using associational knowledge. This diagnosis, together with the observations collected during the reasoning, are then passed to the explanation module. This module builds a causal scenario of what has probably happened and shows how this scenario can account for observed phenomena. Two different kinds of reasoning are thus used: a kind of heuristic classification infers the diagnosis, and abduction on a causal model derives the story of what happened. The assumption that underlines this approach is twofold: first, that it is much more efficient to rely on the available associational expertise to diagnose faults; second, that the users understand and trust causal explanations of faults more than explanations of how diagnoses have been reached.

Tanner and Keuneke describe a similar approach using a functional reasoning approach [71]. In this case, justifications are based on knowledge that, at least in principle, could be used to compile the diagnostic problem solver. This is less true for David and Krivine's work: some difficulties may arise from the fact that not all the diagnostic knowledge can be derived from the knowledge used in justifying the conclusions [22].

Wick and Thompson have made significant contributions to reconstructive explanations [76, 75]. The REX (Reconstructive Explainer) system they developed maps the results of an expert system onto a representation of prototypical explanation patterns. This represents what knowledge is required to solve the problem at a more abstract level, without many of the implementation concerns. A search is then conducted in this knowledge base to build the explanation. An interesting feature of REX is that it can control the degree of coupling between the expert system's path and the explanation, in other words, what has to be taken into account from this path into the reconstructed explanation.

Conclusions and open issues: Second generation expert systems have enabled a step forward in explanation. In particular, it is now generally acknowledged that explaining reasoning is a complex problem solving activity on its own, requiring particular expertise, and that the modeling approaches used can facilitate this process.

However, there still remain many issues to be addressed [70]. We have already cited the trade-off between local, task structure independent explanations and global, task structure dependent explanations. Other open issues, less related to the knowledge-level content of the explanations, are no less important. Such issues include producing explanations in a natural form (natural language or other computer-based media), adapting the explanations to the user's needs and skills, managing the dialogue, using references to, or analogies with, previous explanations, etc. Suffice it to say that most of these issues can also benefit from the way second generation expert systems are built.

4.3 Robustness and Efficiency

It has long been observed that first generation expert systems are *brittle*, not performing well outside a narrow range of expertise [26, 60]. While it was initially thought that adding more knowledge (in the form of additional rules) would overcome the brittleness, this was not the case due to interactions between rules. In this section, we discuss how the use of multiple models and multiple representations can increase the overall robustness (competence) and efficiency of knowledge-based systems.

Multiple knowledge sources: The types of knowledge used in a system can dramatically affect its robustness [61]. By representing many different types of knowledge, coverage of a system can be improved. Researchers have demonstrated the utility of combining structural and functional knowledge [35, 39], qualitative and quantitative knowledge [50], and causal and empirical knowledge [5, 36]. Each of these knowledge sources provide reasoning capabilities that the others lack, and so together lead to more robust systems.

Another way to increase performance is to provide more structure to the problem-solving process. This underlies the knowledge-level modeling approach [73], where the appropriate knowledge at the right level of abstraction is encoded in systems. This can improve both the robustness and efficiency: robustness of a system is increased because sufficient knowledge is represented; efficiency is increased because only the necessary knowledge is processed.

Multiple representations: Efficiency is primarily affected by the way knowledge is represented and the methods used to solve problems. Specialized representations, tuned to particular types of knowledge, can make certain inferences very tractable [61]. The MIDAS modeling package, for instance, can perform complex qualitative and symbolic analyses by utilizing specialized representations for time, space, objects and causality [58].

The problem-solving methods used also have a big influence on efficiency. Many systems, such as GTD [60] and CASEY [41] use associational reasoning to solve commonly occurring problems. The associational reasoning, by directly matching observations with solutions, can solve problems very efficiently; causal reasoning is used to handle more difficult problems, therefore ensuring robustness. Other systems use associational methods to focus the search in a causal domain [5, 18]. In those systems, efficiency is gained by pruning the enormous (causal) search space. Still other systems gain efficiency by utilizing multiple methods simultaneously: the method with the fastest (or best) answer is utilized [37, 57].

The systems described above combine different models/methods in a static way. To provide even greater degrees of robustness and efficiency, systems need to dynamically modify the way they solve problems, depending on characteristics of the problem or of the problem solving process. TIPS, described in this volume, proposes an architecture that can dynamically select methods for the tasks at hand [52]. The KADS strategic layer is another way to describe the dynamic adaptation of a knowledge-based system to a particular problem [77]. In such cases, the problem-solving characteristics arise from the ability to opportunistically combine different knowledge and methods.

Open issues: While such heterogeneous systems provide increased robustness and efficiency (and flexibility), they have a few difficulties. For one, such systems are more difficult to implement, due to the variety of representations that must be developed. While generic models and general modeling languages can sometimes help, there is still a lot of effort involved in choosing the right models and representations.

More fundamentally, it is difficult to integrate diverse knowledge sources and representations [61]. In particular, one must be concerned with mapping between differing ontologies [35, 39] and maintaining consistency between representations. Typically, the latter is accomplished by propagating information between representations [35, 36, 58], but this can adversely impact problem-solving efficiency if not intelligently controlled. Sometimes this problem can be minimized by having one primary representation/knowledge source into which all others map. For example, Hunt uses a functional model as an integration framework [39] and Simmons uses a logic-based language to translate between diverse representations [58].

4.4 Reusability

Reusing previously developed components is a major concern in any business or industry. The benefits of reusability are particularly important when components are expensive or take time to design and validate. The identification of reusable components has been a recurrent activity in knowledge engineering. In particular, reusing knowledge bases or "inference structures" has long ago been considered as a way to overcome the knowledge acquisition bottleneck [2, 26, 33].

Reusability in second generation expert systems is present in each stage of development: creating knowledge-level models, instantiating a knowledge-level model for a particular domain to form knowledge bases, and encoding the application into symbol-level components.

Reusing knowledge-level models: Several years ago, Clancey showed that the same knowledge-level model (*heuristic classification*) can be used for many different tasks [13]. Since then, several other common models have been identified. Among the most successful are *data abstraction, cover and differentiate, abduction, generate test and debug*, and *propose and revise*. Although many variations of these generic models exist (indeed they often differ slightly from one application to another), they have proven to be generic enough to become part of the knowledge engineer's know how. The registration of models used in applications, their analysis and comparison, and the search for new generic models, have become a vast enterprise for the community. Attempts are currently being undertaken to design structured libraries that more or less completely cover certain domains.

While many projects have attempted to produced their own libraries, as yet there is no standardization of these libraries. This is due, in part, because there are many ways to describe and decompose a particular model and the primitive models used may differ in their granularity. This gives rise to many different libraries of models and methods, each with its own vocabulary and point of view. While a standardization effort is undoubtly desirable, one can nevertheless wonder if it will be possible to come up with one standard library/vocabulary.

In the end, local libraries, shared by a particular community or company, might prove to be practically easier to built and more efficient to use [65].

Reusing knowledge bases: The clear distinction introduced by second generation expert systems between domain models, tasks to be achieved, and problem-solving methods should, in principle, facilitate the reuse of parts of an existing knowledge base. However, to date there have been few attempts to do so, and fewer successful experiments.

Among the initial motivations for model-based diagnosis was the desire to reuse design knowledge for diagnostic purposes [26, 33]. The knowledge acquisition task would then be considerably reduced, if not totally eliminated. This approach has faced a lot of problems, however, and now appears to be a bit naive. Model-based reasoning requires much expertise to be put in the model, expertise that is usually not present in design models (mainly because the goals of designing and diagnosing a device are very different). This does not mean, however, that design knowledge cannot be reused: it is just part of the knowledge to be used, playing a role in structuring the knowledge acquisition phase.

There have also been attempts to develop large sharable knowledge bases [42] and formalisms to support knowledge base exchange [47]. These efforts try to provide effective means to reuse parts of previously developed knowledge bases in other contexts.

Reusing symbol-level components: Reuse of code or shells that implement generic models is an important step in the development of second generation expert systems. For example, Chandrasekaran has completed his Generic Tasks with the GT Toolset: for each generic task (e.g., classification, abduction, routine design) there is a corresponding shell (CSRL, PIERCE, DSPL, respectively) [6]. These shells have been used to build several applications from the high-level "building blocks" [9, 67].

This approach is appealing since it supports both the modeling and implementation phases. However, as discussed earlier, it faces several difficulties, mainly in adapting and refining generic models to fit specific problems.

More recently, Steels has developed the COMMET Workbench [65], which builds on the Componential Methodology approach [64]. COMMET requires one to define classes of domain models, methods, and knowledge acquisition methods that are encapsulated into *applications kits*. From these, and the hypothesis of a one-to-one mapping between knowledge-level objects and symbol-level components, the Workbench is able to generate an application directly from the knowledge-level model.

5 Conclusions

This paper has described two important avenues of research that have contributed to a new generation of knowledge-based systems: combining multiple models and reasoning techniques, and adopting knowledge-level approaches for designing knowledge-based systems. These two approaches were developed over the years in efforts to overcome some of the problems faced by early rule-based expert systems, including problems of brittleness, difficulty of developing, maintaining and validating large knowledge bases, and problems of understanding what a system was doing or why it was doing it.

In particular, the modeling and representation approaches used in second generation expert systems have had great impact in the areas of knowledge acquisition and reuse, generating explanations, and overall system competence and performance. While open issues remain, particularly in choosing appropriate models, integrating them effectively, and adapting generic models to fit specific tasks, the field has advanced to the point where practical systems, both academic and commercial, have proliferated.

The variety of approaches used in building second generation expert systems, as well as the benefits of such approaches, are the subject of the papers in this volume. These papers help to demonstrate that second generation expert systems are a major step forward in the field of knowledge engineering.

References

1. Bennett, J.: ROGET: Acquiring the conceptual structure of a diagnostic expert system. IEEE Workshop on Principles of Knowledge-Based Systems; Denver, Colorado (1984)
2. Bennett, J. and Engelmore, R.: SACON: A knowledge-based consultant for structural analysis. Proc. 6th IJCAI, Tokyo (1979)
3. Breuker, J. and Wielenga, B.: Models of expertise in knowledge acquisition. in Topics in Expert System Design : Methodologies and Tools. Guida and Tasso (eds.), North Holland Publishing Company (1989)
4. Bylander, T. and Mittal, S.: CSRL: A language for classificatory problem solving and uncertainty handling. AI Magazine **7:3** (1986) 66–77
5. Bylander, T., Wientraub, M. and Simon, S.: QUAWDS: Diagnosis using different models for different subtasks. *this volume*
6. Chandrasekaran, B.: Towards a functional architecture for intelligence based on generic information processing tasks. Proc. 10th IJCAI, Milano, Italy (1987)
7. Chandrasekaran, B., Mittal, S.: Deep versus compiled knowledge approaches to diagnostic problem-solving. Int. J. Man-Machine Studies **19** (1983) 425–436
8. Chandrasekaran, B., Tanner, M. and Josephson, J.: Explaining control strategies in problem solving. IEEE Expert; Spring (1989)
9. Chandrasekaran, B. and Johnson, T.: Generic tasks and task structures: history, critique and new directions. *this volume*
10. Charlet, J.: ACTE: A causal model-based knowledge acquisition tool. *this volume*
11. Charlet, J., Krivine, J-P. and Reynaud, C.: Causal model-based knowledge acquisition tools: Discussion of experiments. in Current Developments in Knowledge Acquisition, EKAW 92, Wetter, Althoff, Boose, Gaines, Linster and Schmalhofer (eds.), LNAI, Springer Verlag (1992)
12. Clancey, W.: The epistemology of a rule-based expert system: A framework for explanation. Artificial Intelligence **20:3** (1983) 215–251

13. Clancey, W.: Heuristic classification. Artificial Intelligence **27** (1985)

14. Clancey, W.: From GUIDON to NEOMYCIN and HERACLES in twenty short lessons. AI Magazine, Summer (1986)

15. Clancey, W.: Viewing knowledge bases as qualitative models. IEEE Expert (1989)

16. Clancey, W. and Letsinger, R.: NEOMYCIN: Reconfiguring a rule-based expert system for application to teaching. in Readings in Medical Artificial Intelligence: The First Decade, Clancey and Shortliffe (eds.) Addison-Wesley (1984)

17. Clancey, W. and Barbanson, M.: Using the system-model-operator metaphor for knowledge acquisition. *this volume*

18. Console, L., Portinale, L., Theseider Dupre, D. and Torasso P.: Combining heuristic reasoning with causal reasoning in diagnostic problem solving. *this volume*

19. Cuena, J.: Knowledge architectures for real time decision support. *this volume*

20. David J-M.: Functional architectures and the generic task approach. The Knowledge Engineering Review **3:3** (1988)

21. David J-M. and Krivine J-P.: What happened? Causal reasoning in DIVA. Proc. First European Workshop on Fault Diagnostics, Rhodes, Greece, (1986)

22. David J-M. and Krivine J-P.: Augmenting experience-based diagnosis with causal reasoning. Applied AI Journal, Special Issue on Causal Modelling (1989)

23. David J-M. and Krivine J-P.: Explaining reasoning from knowledge level models. Proc. ECAI 90 (1990)

24. David, J-M., Krivine, J-P. and Ricard, B.: Building and maintaining a large knowledge-based system from a "knowledge level" perspective: The DIVA experiment. *this volume*

25. Davis, R.: Meta-rules: Reasoning about control. Artificial Intelligence **15** (1980) 179–222

26. Davis, R.: Expert systems: Where are we and where do we go from here. AI Magazine **3:2** (1982) 3–22

27. Davis, R.: Diagnostic reasoning based on structure and behavior. Artificial Intelligence **24** (1984) 347–410

28. Davis, R. *et. al.*: The DIPmeter advisor: Interpretation of Geologic Signals. Proc. 7th IJCAI, Vancouver, Canada (1981)

29. Davis, R. and Hamscher, W.: Model-based reasoning: Troubleshooting, in Exploring Artificial Intelligence, Howard Shrobe (ed.) Morgan Kaufman, (1988) 297–346

30. deKleer, J. and Williams, B.: Diagnosing multiple faults. Artificial Intelligence **32** (1987) 97–130

31. Duda, R., Gaschnig, J, Hart, P.: Model design in the Prospector consultant system for mineral exploration. in Expert Systems in the Microelectronic Age, D. Michie (ed.), Edinburgh University Press (1980)

32. Fikes, R. and Nilsson N.: STRIPS: A new approach to the application of theorem proving to problem solving. Artificial Intelligence **2** (1971) 189–208

33. Genesereth, M.: Diagnosis using hierarchical design models. Proc. National Conference on AI (1982)

34. Greboval, C. and Kassel, G.: Modelling at the knowledge level: The shell AIDE. Proc. 12th International Conference on Artificial Intelligence, Expert Systems and Natural Language, Avignon, France, (1992)

35. Guida, G. and Zanella, M.: Knowledge-based design using the multi-modeling approach. *this volume*

36. Hamscher, W.: The business analyzer: A second generation approach to financial decision support. *this volume*

37. Hayes-Roth, B.: Architectural foundations for real-time performance in intelligent agents. *this volume*

38. Heckerman, D. and Horvitz, E.: The myth of modularity in rule-based systems. KSL Memo **86-33**, Stanford University (1986)

39. Hunt, J. and Price, C.: Integrating functional models and structural domain models for diagnostic applications. *this volume*

40. Karbach, W. and Voß, A.: MODEL-K for prototyping and strategic reasoning at the knowledge level. *this volume*

41. Koton, P.: Combining causal models and case-based reasoning. *this volume*

42. Lenat, D. and Guha, R.: Building Large Knowledge-Based Systems. Addison-Wesley (1990)

43. Linster, M.: Explicit and operational models as a basis for second generation knowledge acquisition tools. *this volume*

44. Marcus, S. (ed.): Automating Knowledge Acquisition for Expert Systems. Kluwer Academic Publishers (1988)

45. McDermott, J.: R1: A rule-based configurer of computer systems. Artificial Intelligence **19:1** (1982) 39–88

46. Musen, M.: An overview of knowledge acquisition. *this volume*

47. Neches, R., Fikes, R., Finin, T., Gruber, T., Patil, R., Senator, T. and Swartout W.: Enabling technology for knowledge sharing. AI Magazine, Fall (1991)

48. Newell, A.: The knowledge level. Artificial Intelligence, **18** (1982) 87–127

49. Newell, A. and Simon, H.: GPS: A program that simulates human thought. in Computers and Thought, Feigenbaum and Feldman (eds.) (1963)

50. Paillet, O.: Multiple models for emergency planning. *this volume*

51. Patil, R.: Causal representation of patient illness for electrolyte and acid-base diagnosis. Technical Report **267** Laboratory for Computer Science, Massachusetts Institute of Technology (1981)

52. Punch, W. and Chandrasekaran, B.: An investigation of the roles of problem-solving methods in diagnosis. *this volume*

53. Rademakers, P. and Vanwelkenhuysen, J.: Generic models and their support in modeling problem solving behavior. *this volume*

54. Reynaud, C.: Acquisition and validation of expert knowledge by using causal models. *this volume*

55. Shoham, Y.: Reasoning About Change: Time and Causation from the Standpoint of Artificial Intelligence. MIT Press (1988)

56. Shortliffe, E.: Computer Based Medical Consultations: MYCIN. American Elsevier (1976)

57. Silver, B., Vittal, J., Frawley, W., Iba, G., Fawcett, T., Dusseault, S. and Doleac, J.: A framework for integrating multiple heterogeneous learning agents. *this volume*

58. Simmons, R.: Integrating Multiple Representations for Incremental, Causal Simulation. Proc. Conference on AI, Simulation, and Planning, Cocoa Beach, FL (1991) 88–96

59. Simmons, R.: The Roles of Associational and Causal Reasoning in Problem Solving. Artificial Intelligence **53:2–3** (1992) 159–208

60. Simmons, R.: Generate, test and debug: A paradigm for combining associational and causal reasoning. *this volume*

61. Simmons, R. and Davis, R.: The roles of knowledge and representation in problem solving. *this volume*

62. Soloway, E., Bachant, J. and Jensen, K.: Assessing the maintainability of XCON-in-RIME: Coping with the problems of a VERY large rule-base. Proc. National Conference on AI, Seattle, Washington (1987)
63. Sprenger, M.: Explanation strategies for KADS-based expert systems. DIAMOD report 10 GMD, Germany (1991)
64. Steels, L.: Components of expertise. AI Magazine 11:2 (1990)
65. Steels, L.: The componential framework and its role in reusability. *this volume*
66. Stefik, M.: Planning and meta-planning (MOLGEN: part 2). Artificial Intelligence 16 (1981) 141–170
67. Sticklen, J.: MDX2: An integrated medical diagnostic system. PhD Dissertation, The Ohio State University (1987)
68. Sticklen, J. and Wallingford, E.: On the relationship between knowledge-based systems theory and application programs: Leveraging task specific approaches. *this volume*
69. Swartout, W.: XPLAIN: A system for creating and explaining expert consulting systems. Artificial Intelligence 21:3 (1983) 285–325
70. Swartout, W. and Moore, J.: Explanation in second generation expert systems. *this volume*
71. Tanner, M., Keuneke, A. and Chandrasekaran, B.: Explanation in knowledge systems: The roles of the task structure and domain functional models. *this volume*
72. Terpstra, P., van Heijst, G., Shadbolt, N. and Wielinga, B.: Knowledge acquisition process support through generalised directive models. *this volume*
73. van de Velde, W.: Issues in knowledge level modelling. *this volume*
74. Weld, D. and deKleer, J. (eds.): Readings in Qualitative Reasoning About Physical Systems, Morgan Kauffman (1990)
75. Wick, M.: Second generation expert system explanation. *this volume*
76. Wick, M. and Thomson, W.: Reconstructive expert system explanation. Artificial Intelligence 54 (1992)
77. Wielinga, B., Breuker, J.: Models of expertise. Proc. ECAI 86, Brighton, UK (1986)
78. Wielinga, B., Schreiber, G. and Breuker J.: KADS: A modelling approach to knowledge engineering. Knowledge Acquisition 4:1 (1992)
79. Wielinga, B., van de Velde, W., Schreiber, G. and Akkermans, H.: Towards a unification of knowledge modelling approaches. *this volume*
80. Wilensky, R.: Planning and Understanding. Addison-Wesley (1983)

Part II

Combining Multiple Models

& Reasoning Techniques

The Roles of Knowledge and Representation in Problem Solving

Reid Simmons and Randall Davis

[1] School of Computer Science, Carnegie Mellon University, Pittsburgh, PA
[2] Artificial Intelligence Laboratory, Massachusetts Institute of Technology, Cambridge, MA

Abstract. Knowledge and representation are separate, but equally important, concepts for designing and analyzing knowledge-based systems: knowledge describes what systems do, and representations are how they do it. Knowledge-based systems can be designed that utilize multiple knowledge sources (partitioned into different types or levels of abstraction) and multiple representations (specialized for particular inferences). This paper argues for the importance of distinguishing between the concepts of knowledge and representation, and describes advantages and pitfalls of using multiple knowledge sources and representations. Examples are presented of systems that use various combinations of knowledge and representation as their main sources of problem-solving power.

1 Introduction

Knowledge and representation are distinct entities that play central but distinguishable roles in knowledge-based systems. Knowledge is a description of the world. It determines a system's competence in solving problems: a system's depth and breadth of problem solving power is determined by what it knows. Representation is the way knowledge is encoded. It defines the performance of a system in solving problems: speed and efficiency of problem solving are determined to a significant degree by the choice of representation.

This paper demonstrates the importance of distinguishing between knowledge and representation, and illustrates how the use of multiple sources of knowledge and multiple representations can lead to more powerful systems. We attempt in particular to explain what benefits arise from the use of multiple knowledge sources and multiple representations, how, when and why they can be used, and what practical problems remain in combining them.

The distinction between knowledge and representation is important both in designing and in analyzing systems. In design, the distinction corresponds to two stages in the development process that are usefully distinguished: 1) acquiring sufficient knowledge to solve the required problem and 2) designing a computer system to encode and process that knowledge. These are largely sequential (though interrelated) stages: given knowledge about the domain and how to solve problems, the representation should be chosen to make the necessary operations on the knowledge (inference and access) transparent and easily computable.

For analysis, the distinction is an important tool in determining the origins of the bulk of a system's power: its knowledge, its representations, or both. Understanding the origins of a system's power is relevant in determining how features of a system contribute to its problem-solving performance and competence, and which aspects are transferable to other problems and domains. Unfortunately, all too often the power of a knowledge-based system is mis-ascribed. Too many descriptions focus on how a system uses its representation (rules, frames, etc.), rather than explaining what knowledge makes the problem tractable, and far more often it is that knowledge rather than the chosen representation that provides the important power.

Understanding the distinction between knowledge and representation is especially important in second generation expert systems, which typically use multiple sources of knowledge and/or multiple representations. As we will see in detail below, multiple knowledge sources and representations provide powerful ways to structure knowledge-based systems.

Knowledge can usefully be partitioned into multiple sources in several ways, including by level of abstraction and by type. The work of [11, 41], for example, illustrates how multiple levels of abstraction enable systems to work at the knowledge level most appropriate to the task at hand. The work of [5, 7, 23] illustrates the utility of distinguishing between knowledge that describes task requirements, problem-solving methods to be used, and domain models.

Separating knowledge in this way often makes it easier to acquire and update, and provides ways to structure the problem-solving process. For example, keeping structural and functional knowledge separate in circuit diagnosis facilitates reasoning about problems that arise from component malfunctions independently from those that arise due to faulty manufacturing [10].

Specialized representations also play a significant role in solving complex problems. Different representations make different types of inferences apparent. This principle has been put to use in developing specific representations for reasoning about space, time, causality, taxonomies, etc. [1, 13, 48]. However, in exchange for increased efficiency at performing certain sets of inferences, these specialized representations often make it difficult to express or reason about other types of knowledge. As a result, systems often need to use *multiple* specialized representations, in order to encode all the necessary knowledge.

The developer of a knowledge based system is thus faced with at least two important choices: whether to use single or multiple representations and whether to use a monolithic knowledge source or partition it into multiple, loosely coupled sources. All combinations are possible: we may represent different types of knowledge using the same, or different representations, or may even represent the same knowledge in different ways. The choices made can have significant impact on the ease of development, efficiency, understandability, and modifiability of the resulting system. This paper examines some of the issues that influence these tradeoffs.

The following section discusses in more detail the distinction between knowledge and representation and why it is important to maintain the distinction.

Section 3 describes the rationales for using multiple knowledge sources and multiple representations. Specific examples of how knowledge and representation may be combined are presented in Sect. 4.

2 Knowledge and Representation

Despite both past and recent attempts to present the distinctions between knowledge and representation and to define their roles in problem-solving [12, 16, 36, 40], the concepts are often not clearly delineated in the knowledge-based systems literature. In this section we try to make that distinction clear and argue why it is useful in designing and understanding knowledge-based systems.

Part of the confusion is doubtless due the vagueness of the concept of knowledge. In AI practice the key element of knowledge is description: knowledge is a description of the what, how, and why of the world — what constitutes tasks or problems, how to solve them, and why the world behaves as it does. Knowledge enables one to talk about the way mechanisms, circuits, or people behave, how a power network is connected, methods for decomposing goals into subgoals, etc. Knowledge is not something physical that can be examined, like a computer circuit or even a symbolic representation — it is instead something that we, as observers, ascribe to a system to explain its behavior [4, 40].

Representation is an easier concept to define: it is the formal encoding of knowledge, where by "formal" we mean that the encoding is composed of a set of primitive symbols, combined via well-defined syntactic rules, along with a semantic interpretation of the syntactic structure. We refer to the symbols and syntax as the *representation language*; the semantic interpretation is accomplished through algorithms that access and infer information. This combination of language and interpretation is fundamental to a representation — they cannot usefully be separated. For example, when we represent knowledge using production rules, we are asserting, implicitly at least, that the left-hand side is to be interpreted as the antecedent and the right-hand side as the consequent of a plausible inference (entailment). Any other interpretation of the rule, such as a disjunction of facts (arising from the equivalence $A \Rightarrow B$ and $\neg A \lor B$), would violate the spirit of the representation.

Maintaining the distinction between knowledge and representation is important both in designing and in analyzing knowledge-based systems. In designing systems, we can determine what knowledge is needed to achieve a desired competence without having to commit to any particular representation. Knowledge level descriptions permit "predicting and understanding behavior without having an operational model of the processing" [40, p. 108]. We can, for example, indicate that a system to perform medical diagnosis must have knowledge of diseases and their symptoms, and must have methods for classifying symptoms and/or understanding the causal pathways that give rise to symptoms. Knowing what knowledge is needed also aids in acquiring the relevant information.

Once system designers have determined what knowledge is needed, representations can be chosen to encode it. Where the focus in acquiring knowledge is

system competence, the main issue in choosing representations is performance —
how the necessary inferences can be produced efficiently. This is critical because
representations, even those with the same expressive power (e.g., rules, frames
and logic), typically differ in how efficient they perform certain classes of inferences. For example, rules are good at performing entailment; frames are more
suited to taxonomic matching. Depending on the types of inferences needed, a
designer might prefer one representation over another.

In analyzing knowledge-based systems, the distinction between knowledge
and representation is important in identifying the main sources of power in the
systems. For example, it is clear that for MYCIN [46] and R1 [37] their knowledge is more important to their success than is the simple (production rule)
representation and match algorithm used. Knowledge level descriptions can be
used to compare the competence of systems that use different representations
for the same types of knowledge (e.g., the extent of medical knowledge contained in CADUCEUS [42] vs. MYCIN [46]). Conversely, many systems that do
qualitative reasoning [15, 19, 30] get significant amounts of their power from specialized representations that encode some straightforward, but very important,
commonsense concepts about the physical world (e.g., continuity [62]). Accurately determining the sources of power in systems is important because of the
assistance it provides in deciding what elements of a system can be reused in
solving other problems.

Maintaining the distinction between knowledge (what a system can do) and
representation (how it does it) is thus critical for properly designing and analyzing knowledge-based systems. The distinction is particularly important when
describing why it is useful to partition knowledge into multiple sources and to
encode knowledge using multiple specialized representations. This is the subject
of the next section.

3   Multiple Knowledge Sources and Representations

Second generation expert systems are characterized by their use of multiple
knowledge sources and/or multiple representations. In this section, we describe
the uses and benefits of this multiplicity. In particular, we argue that 1) using
multiple knowledge sources can make systems easier to develop and more understandable, because it modularizes knowledge into more manageable packages
and adds structure to the way knowledge is combined, and 2) using multiple,
specialized representations tuned to particular tasks can make problem solving
more efficient, thereby making more complex problems tractable.

3.1   Multiple Knowledge Sources

This section explores two dimensions along which knowledge can be partitioned:
by type and by level of abstraction. We explain how these partitionings produce
significant benefits in constructing, extending, and understanding knowledge-
based systems, and indicate some of the difficulties associated with using multiple
knowledge sources.

Partitioning by type: Problem solving often requires different types of knowledge. Commonly needed types include knowledge about tasks (what defines a problem), methods (how to solve problems), and models (why things behave as they do). The last of these is often referred to as domain knowledge, while the other two are typically referred to as control knowledge. Knowledge-based systems invariably have all of these types of knowledge, though they do not necessarily represent them explicitly. Medical diagnostic systems, for example, have knowledge about disease and physiology (domain knowledge) and about diagnostic search (control knowledge) [7].

Each of these types of knowledge can, in turn, be further partitioned. For example, search control knowledge can be partitioned into adversarial and non-adversarial types of search [3]. Similarly, different subareas of domain knowledge can be distinguished and acquired relatively independently of each other. Much of the work in qualitative reasoning, for example, has involved attempts to elucidate the domain knowledge needed to reason about different aspects of the physical world, including time [1, 14, 63], space [18, 20], causality [19, 25, 45], and specific domains, such as electronic and mechanical devices [22, 26, 29]. Partitioning of domain knowledge is important since it is difficult (perhaps impossible) to develop a single ontology that encompasses every aspect of the world that a system might need to model. Rather, the world can be profitably divided into distinct domains of knowledge that are loosely connected to one another.

Explicitly separating different types of knowledge can provide benefits in the areas of knowledge acquisition, system extensibility, reuse, and understandability. It can help focus the knowledge acquisition effort by making apparent exactly what knowledge is needed to perform the given task. One can separately acquire the knowledge needed for the task (e.g., domain knowledge, problem-solving knowledge, and knowledge about task requirements), then combine the knowledge sources to solve the required problems. For example, domain knowledge about electronic devices can be combined with search control knowledge for localizing faults to produce a system that performs fault diagnosis.

Modular knowledge sources also facilitate extending a system to handle new tasks, or to handle tasks more reliably. When knowledge sources are loosely coupled, the competence of the system can be increased by incremental addition of knowledge sources, without modifying other parts of the system. The advantages of modularity are supported by system architectures that explicitly partition knowledge sources. One such example is the blackboard architecture, which encourages the use of multiple, loosely coupled knowledge sources that communicate via a centralized knowledge base [17, 23].

Maintaining separate types of knowledge also promotes reuse. This is particularly apparent in the utility of general search and problem-solving techniques that encode control knowledge about particular classes of problems. For instance, knowledge about solving problems for adversarial game playing is captured in algorithms such as mini-max and alpha-beta [3], while "domain-independent" planners [6, 61] incorporate knowledge about such things as the frame problem [45] and how to construct plans effectively (using means-ends analysis, hierarchical decomposition, etc.). Capturing this type of knowledge separate from its use for a particular task allows it to be reused in multiple domains.

Finally, partitioning knowledge into different types makes systems more understandable, particularly when domain and control knowledge are kept distinct [7, 54, 60]. This is primarily because it is easier to predict how knowledge will combine and interact when it is kept modularized, with well-defined interfaces between the sources of knowledge. It has also been demonstrated that such a separation leads to better explanations: the explanation for a system's conclusions can reflect the fundamental causal and problem-solving knowledge that underlies the conclusions, rather than merely reflecting the inferential mechanisms used by the representation [9, 55].

Partitioning by level of abstraction: Knowledge can also be partitioned into multiple levels of abstraction. Each level of abstraction provides increasing detail about some aspect of the world. For example, knowledge about physics can be described at qualitative, semi-quantitative, or quantitative levels. At the qualitative level, physical phenomena are described in discrete, relative terms, which can be used to reason about general trends (such as whether the velocity of an object is increasing, decreasing, or constant) [58]; the semi-quantitative level distinguishes between important and negligible effects [31, 43]; at the quantitative level, numeric information is used to model the physics precisely.

Different levels of knowledge often utilize different ontologies for describing the world. The ontology used for a particular level depends on the knowledge that level focuses on. In ABEL [41], for instance, disease, physiology and pathophysiology levels are each used to model patient illness. While the disease level has terms describing diseases and their symptoms, the ontology of the physiology and pathophysiology levels involve human organs, biology and biochemical processes. The use of different ontologies is useful in making the relevant knowledge at each level explicit, but it can also make it difficult to combine knowledge sources and to propagate inferences between them (see Sect. 3.1).

The two primary benefits of using multiple abstraction levels are that different sub-domains can be modeled to the level they are understood, and different sub-problems can be solved at the appropriate level. For many complex problems, all the domain knowledge needed may not be understood down to the same level of detail. In medicine, for example, the actions of some organs are understood quite well, while the biochemistry of others can currently be described in only qualitative or semi-quantitative terms. The use of multiple levels of knowledge enables system designers to model only what is understood about each sub-domain of knowledge.

The other benefit of using knowledge at multiple levels of abstraction is that problems can be solved at the appropriate level of detail. The idea is to bring to bear sufficient, but not excessive, knowledge for each task. For example, in diagnosis qualitative information may suffice to localize all possible faults, while quantitative information is necessary to compute the likelihood of the various faults occurring [22, 52]. By solving problems at the appropriate level of detail, the task can be solved more efficiently and the solution is often more understandable, in both cases because extraneous details need not be considered.

Difficulties with using multiple knowledge sources: There are several difficulties with using multiple knowledge sources. First, there is the problem of deciding how to partition the knowledge. While sometimes the choice is obvious, as is often the case in deciding how to separate domain and control knowledge, in many cases the decision is not clear cut, particularly in determining what levels of abstraction are needed. This choice, which is very task-specific, often involves subtle trade offs between the difficulty of acquiring and utilizing detailed knowledge vs. the increased accuracy of inferences gained by using more detailed knowledge.

The partitioning process is helped some by the availability of standard types of knowledge sources, such as general problem-solving methods (e.g., classification, generate and test) and general domain models (such as models of time, space, causality, etc.). These knowledge sources can sometimes be used as primitive building blocks for constructing more complex knowledge-based systems [53, 59]. At present, however, the availability of such generic knowledge sources is quite limited.

A second difficulty with multiple knowledge sources arises in combining them. The problems here are in propagating inferences between knowledge sources and maintaining consistency between them. These can pose significant challenges, particularly if the knowledge sources have very different ontologies. The accepted solution is to create narrow, well-defined interfaces between the knowledge sources, using common terms and concepts as "landmarks" to connect them. For example, GORDIUS [49] uses the concepts of rock-units, boundaries, and topological relationships as the interface between its causal and diagrammatic models of geology [51]. When the causal knowledge infers the existence of new geological entities, this propagates to the diagrammatic knowledge, which adds corresponding faces and edges in the diagram. Similarly, when spatial relationships are inferred from the diagrammatic knowledge, topological information is added to the causal knowledge.

While this approach preserves the modularization of knowledge sources, it also produces artificial boundaries: information can be transferred only through the interfaces, and if they are not chosen carefully it may not be possible for one KS to take advantage of conclusions made by another. In addition, for knowledge sources that describe the same aspects of the world (as is the case with multiple levels of abstraction), it is often desirable to keep these views consistent. Unfortunately, maintaining this consistency can often consume a significant amount of the problem-solving time [41].

One way of handling the problem of limited interfaces between knowledge sources is to employ machine learning techniques to transfer knowledge. For example, the SOAR architecture [32] solves problems using multiple knowledge sources, called *problem spaces*. When SOAR does not have enough knowledge to solve a subgoal in one problem space, it tries solving it in another, more detailed, space and then transfers an abstraction of the knowledge used (called a *chunk*) back up to the original problem space. In this way, information needed in one knowledge source can be acquired and utilized.

3.2 Multiple Representations

The case for using multiple representations is based on the observation that while a "good" representation must satisfy various criteria, including completeness, conciseness, transparency and computational efficiency [64], some of these criteria conflict. In particular, it can be difficult to find a representation that is expressive enough (able to encode and access all the knowledge relevant for a task) and also permits efficient inferences. One approach is to use multiple specialized representations, each of which is efficient and concise for a limited set of reasoning tasks. This section describes characteristics of specialized representations, and discusses some difficulties associated with combining multiple representations.

Representations may be specialized either for efficiently encoding particular types of knowledge, or for supporting specific types of inferences. For example, representations have been developed specifically to encode temporal [1, 63, 14], spatial [20, 51], and causal [13, 48]) knowledge. While these representations have narrowly limited expressive power, they tend to be quite efficient for problems in their particular domain.

There are also representations that differ, not in the inferences they are capable of (their *sanctioned* inferences), but in the ones that are most natural in the representation (the *recommended* inferences) [12]. Recommended inferences provide guidance on how best to use a representation. For example, while rules and frames have approximately the same expressive power, they are most useful for different types of problem-solving tasks: rules are suited for reasoning about plausible chains of entailment; frames are suited for taxonomic classification and inheritance of default values. For a given problem, one or the other representation may be more suitable depending on the types of inferences needed.

Promoting efficiency: There are several ways to make a representation efficient for a particular reasoning task, including: limiting expressiveness, having the syntax of the representation language expose relevant constraints, and embedding task-specific assumptions in the inference algorithms. We examine each of these in turn.

Limiting the expressive power of a representation sometimes produces improvements in worst-case performance, hence providing an improved guarantee of minimal performance. For example, the presence of disjunction and negation in a representation language often means that the running time of inference algorithms for that representation will be exponential in the worst case. By suitably restricting the representation (e.g., in this case removing disjunction and negation), one may trade off expressive power for efficiency [34, 16]. Then, by combining multiple representations one might get the best of both worlds: using more restricted representations for simpler problems and using more expressives ones (with correspondingly more expensive inference algorithms) only when necessary [49].

A second technique for creating specialized representations that support efficiency is to select a representation language that exposes features of the domain relevant to the reasoning task. These are often termed *analogical* representations [3, vol I, pp. 200–206] because objects that are closely related in the world have close syntactic relationships in the representation, and hence these relationships can often be easily inferred. For example, specialized spatial representations encode topological and geometric relationships, such as adjacency and containment, using direct links between objects [20, 51]. Determining spatial properties, such as whether two objects are near, can be performed efficiently simply by traversing links in the representation.

A third way to specialize representations for efficiency is to use inference algorithms that embody special assumptions about the domain, assumptions that would have to be explicitly encoded and reasoned about if more general representations were used. For example, many algorithms for qualitative reasoning use the concept of *continuity* to efficiently constrain the legal inferences [30, 62]. Similarly, many planning and temporal reasoning systems utilize special mechanisms to reason about the *persistence* of objects (those things that do not change when actions occur) [13, 49]. While predicate logic-based representations can be used to encode persistence assumptions [45], it is often quite cumbersome to use such representations to reason about persistence, primarily because it is a non-monotonic assumption.

Promoting conciseness and transparency: While efficiency is the major rationale for utilizing specialized representations, another significant reason is that a specialized representation can often encode a particular type of knowledge more concisely and naturally. Consider, for instance, the difference between encoding the knowledge that "everyone has exactly two parents" in a general logic-based and specialized set-based representation. The statement in first-order logic would look something like:
$$\forall(p:person) \; \exists(x,y:person) \; Parent(x,p) \wedge Parent(y,p) \wedge x \neq y \wedge$$
$$\forall(z:person) \; Parent(z,p) \Rightarrow (z=x) \vee (z=y)$$
By representing the parents of a person as a set, the corresponding statement is: $Cardinality(Parents(z)) = 2$ [57].

There are several benefits with using representations that promote concise and transparent encodings of knowledge. First, system development is facilitated, since the mappings from knowledge to symbols is simplified. Second, the encoded knowledge is often easier to modify. For example, while it is simple to modify the set-based statement to declare that "everyone has at most two parents" ($Cardinality(Parents(z)) \geq 2$), the change needed in the logic-based representation is not so apparent. The third benefit is that transparent representations aid in understanding how knowledge-based systems will behave, since the recommended inferences of such representations are more easily reproducible by humans. For example, knowledge encoded in semantic nets is often readily understandable, especially when the nets are presented pictorially, because the associated inference algorithm (graph traversal) is an easy concept for humans to grasp.

Similar arguments hold for representing control knowledge. While control and domain knowledge can be encoded using the same representation [32, 21], they are sufficiently different in character to warrant specialized representations for control knowledge. In particular, since control is primarily procedural (describing how to do things) it makes sense to encode such knowledge using procedural representations that have explicit constructs for encoding sequential, conditional, iterative and recursive behavior. Such constructs make the flow of control readily apparent, leading to more natural explanations of how the system works.

Difficulties with using multiple representations: There are several difficulties inherent in using multiple specialized representations. The problems are similar to those inherent in using multiple knowledge sources: deciding which representation to use and how to combine representations.

The choice of which representations to use for which types of knowledge is a fundamental and often very difficult decision in designing knowledge-based systems. While some choices are obvious (e.g., use a temporal representation for encoding knowledge about time), in general the mappings from knowledge to representation are not clear cut, since typically there is not a one-to-one relationship between knowledge sources and representations. A related difficulty is deciding when to use which representation. Although such decisions can sometimes be hard-coded, in many cases the decision must be made dynamically, based, for instance, on the amount of knowledge one has available and the types of inferences needed.

A more pragmatic difficulty is the need to transmit information effectively between multiple representations. This is particularly critical if different representations are used to solve different parts of a problem. A solution adopted by several researchers is to create an intermediate representation language in which all interfaces between representations are encoded [44, 48]. The intermediate language, which often has a simple predicate-based syntax, has associated procedures to translate to the different specialized representation languages. Thus, each representation needs to be defined only in relationship to one other representation, rather than all possible pairs, and all information is transmitted through this common representation. This makes it easier to add new representations and to change the definitions and interfaces of existing ones, since the changes only affect the relationship with the intermediate language.

4   Combinations in Knowledge-Based Systems

Given that knowledge and representation are distinct, one can imagine that knowledge-based systems could encode either single (monolithic) or multiple (partitioned) sources of knowledge, and might do so using either a single or multiple representations. Table 1 presents a few existing systems that illustrate each of the four possible combinations.

Where a given system belongs in the matrix is not always clear. In particular, almost no knowledge-based system exclusively uses a single knowledge source. Invariably, systems will utilize separate control knowledge and procedural representations to encode that knowledge. Thus, in labeling a system "single knowledge/single representation," we are actually indicating that that is the main source of problem-solving power, and that the other knowledge and associated representations are secondary in importance. This is clearly the case in production-rule systems, such as MYCIN, where the search control knowledge is not emphasized because it is so straightforward.

| | | KNOWLEDGE | |
		Single	Multiple
	Single	MYCIN R1 DENDRAL	ABEL NEOMYCIN HEARSAY
REPR.	Multiple	MACSYMA	GORDIUS CASEY Generic Tasks

Table 1. Combinations of Knowledge and Representation

The next four sections discuss examples of each combination. For each, we briefly discuss the relative merits and associated difficulties.

4.1 Single Knowledge and Representation

MYCIN [46], which diagnoses bacterial infections, offers a prototypical example of using a single representational framework to encode a single (unstructured) knowledge source. The knowledge used in MYCIN consists of empirical associations that map observable features (symptoms) to possible diagnoses, together with measures of confidence in the conclusions. MYCIN represents its knowledge using production rules, for which entailment is the recommended inference mechanism. The rule-based representation provides a fairly natural and concise mapping for the associational knowledge used in MYCIN.

Note it has been shown that the associational knowledge in MYCIN really combines both domain knowledge (e.g., medicine and physiology) and control knowledge (e.g., how to do diagnosis) [7]. While this means that a knowledge-level account of MYCIN would contain descriptions of different types of knowledge, in the MYCIN system the knowledge was in fact actually acquired, represented, and utilized as a single, monolithic source. Describing the system in terms of multiple knowledge sources is just a post-hoc reconstruction [8].

An initial impetus for developing such single knowledge/single representation systems was that it would facilitate developing and extending complex knowledge-based systems. The idea was that the knowledge engineer would not have to decide *a priori* how the knowledge would be used. By throwing the knowledge into one big, uniform "pot" there was the potential for it to get combined in novel ways to solve problems that were not originally anticipated. It was also expected that it would be easier to acquire knowledge from experts, if the knowledge could all be encoded and processed uniformly.

In fact, these expectations were rarely met in practice. The problem is that, while letting knowledge combine and interact freely may sometimes produce novel, useful results, it more often results in undesired interactions. It is now well known that, contrary to initial expectations, adding new knowledge in the form of unstructured collections of production rules is often difficult because the rules are not really independent, which can lead to unanticipated interactions [24]. In particular, as the knowledge base grows the system becomes less predictable and understandable, since it becomes more and more difficult to determine how the knowledge will interact. One solution to this problem is to structure the rules into loosely coupled sets; if the rules are partitioned appropriately, this can be a way of introducing multiple knowledge sources.

One advantage of this paradigm is that one does not have to worry about translating and propagating information between representations. In addition, system developers need to learn only a single representational syntax and interpretation. The main difficulty is finding a representation that is both expressive enough and facilitates concise encoding of the knowledge. An example of the difficulty of finding such a representation is illustrated by R1 [37] which, although it primarily uses production rules, also uses a specialized representation to solve the board placement problem because the rule-based paradigm is an inappropriate match for this particular subtask. In practice, such cases become more and more prevalent as task and domain complexity increase.

In general, single knowledge/single representation systems provide a simple method for acquiring and encoding knowledge. The paradigm tends to be useful for relatively simple tasks where the types of inferences needed are fairly limited and uniform.

4.2 Multiple Knowledge and Single Representation

ABEL [41], which was used to diagnose kidney problems, was one of the earliest systems to solve problems using knowledge at multiple levels of abstraction. ABEL had a multi-level hierarchy of knowledge sources, including knowledge about disease, anatomy, physiology and pathophysiology. All the knowledge was represented uniformly, using a causal network, with constraint propagation as the inference mechanism.

Whenever ABEL had sufficient information to propagate constraints, it did so. The propagation was primarily intra-level through the causal network, but there was transmission between levels, as well. Information was passed between "landmarks," common terms that appeared in adjacent levels of the hierarchy. The inter-level flow of information is needed both to propagate partial results needed by levels and to maintain consistency between common terms represented at different levels.

This type of flow within and between knowledge sources is typical of systems using this paradigm. Many systems using this paradigm have found it useful to explicitly control the flow of information between levels. For example, work in hardware troubleshooting has shown the importance of diagnosing complex circuits starting at the highest level of abstraction and descending as more detailed knowledge must be applied [11, 22].

The basic advantages of using multiple knowledge sources have been described in Sect. 3, namely ease of acquiring, modifying and understanding the knowledge. Advantages of a single representation have been discussed in Sect. 4.1, namely ease of implementation since only a single representation needs to be mastered. The major difficulty of this approach is in finding a single representation that efficiently encodes all the different types of knowledge needed.

For this particular paradigm, the single representational framework offers some additional advantages. First, a single representation facilitates propagating information between knowledge sources because there is no need to translate between representations (although one still needs to define interfaces between the knowledge sources). Second, a common representation can facilitate machine learning. In particular, many systems learn new knowledge by abstracting combinations of domain and control knowledge from other sources [32, 38]. Transfer of knowledge between sources is greatly facilitated by encoding them all using the same representation, since the interpretation of what a term "means" in one knowledge source can be easily maintained when the learning system transfers that knowledge to another source.

In general, multiple knowledge/single representation systems provide a good balance between taking advantage of the inherent structure in the knowledge needed to solve problems and ease of encoding that knowledge. While any given source of knowledge may not be encoded very concisely, and certain inferences may not be easily obtained, a single representation does facilitate defining interfaces and transferring information between multiple sources of knowledge.

4.3   Single Knowledge and Multiple Representations

At first glance, this combination might seem odd: since it is usually difficult enough to encode knowledge adequately, why try to create multiple encodings of the same knowledge? This approach does make sense if we need to ask different types of questions about the same, single body of knowledge, questions that can be most efficiently answered using different representations.

The MACSYMA symbolic algebra system, for example, uses different algebraic representations, depending on the information content and the transformations needed. For example, MACSYMA uses a recursive representation of polynomials (polynomials with polynomial coefficients) as a canonical representation for general simplification problems, and specialized representations (such as leaving integer powers of sums unexpanded) for dealing with problems such as factorization and solving certain types of linear equations [39].

The crucial point of this paradigm is that by choosing representations tuned to the types of inferences needed, seemingly difficult inferences can be made quite efficiently. This was illustrated quite graphically by Amarel, who presented different representations of the "cannibals and missionaries" problem [2]. The work clearly showed how the choice of representation can sometimes eliminate the need for expensive search in problem solving. Other work has demonstrated that, for certain problems at least, using specialized representations can be cost-effective, even taking into account the added expense of translating from a canonical representation to the specialized representation, and back again [35, 57].

The single knowledge/multiple representation paradigm also gives rise to some novel problem-solving strategies. One strategy is to use multiple methods in parallel, choosing either the first answer or the most reliable answer that is returned [27, 47]. This assumes that different inference methods have different problem-solving characteristics for the same knowledge, but that one cannot tell which will be best *a priori*. A similar strategy is to start with the least computationally expensive method; if it does not produce an acceptable answer, the next most expensive method is tried, and so on [33]. This strategy enables a system to devote resources to a problem based on the time available to solve it. While these strategies are fairly difficult to implement, since one needs to develop multiple inference methods for the same problem, they may be useful in time-critical situations where it is important to get the best possible answer in a given amount of time.

In general, the single knowledge/multiple representation paradigm is useful when different types of questions need to be answered based on the same underlying knowledge. By making multiple representations (languages and inference algorithms) available for the same knowledge, one can choose to solve problems using the most effective representation for the task.

4.4   Multiple Knowledge and Representations

The GORDIUS system [49] illustrates the use of both multiple knowledge sources and multiple representations. The system uses the Generate, Test and Debug (GTD) paradigm to solve geologic data interpretation and planning problems [50]. It uses associational (heuristic) knowledge to generate initial hypotheses, and tests and debugs them using causal (model-based) knowledge.

The associational knowledge of GORDIUS connects features of the problem with partial solutions. For example, the observation that one piece of sedimentary rock is laying on top of another is associated with the interpretation that the overlying rock was formed later. The associational knowledge is quite task-specific, combining domain and control knowledge in ways that are geared specifically toward solving interpretation and planning problems (in the example above, geologic interpretation). In GORDIUS, the associational knowledge is encoded using a rule-based representation. This representation provides efficiency through its use of relatively simple inferences and control structures, which is sufficient since much of the relevant control knowledge is already embedded within the associations.

The causal knowledge used in GORDIUS describes how the world works, enabling predictions to be made about the effects of actions and events. For example, the model of sedimentation states that deposition occurs from above, hence the system can infer that new sedimentary rocks are deposited onto the surface of existing, older rocks. GORDIUS uses multiple representations to encode the causal domain knowledge, including specialized representations for time, space, and changes to objects [48]. These representations enable GORDIUS to effectively encode and reason about complex domains, including geology [50] and semiconductor fabrication [52].

The associational and causal knowledge play distinct roles in the GTD paradigm. The associational knowledge is used first to generate hypotheses that are typically correct, or nearly so. The causal knowledge is used to test hypotheses (sequences of events), producing causal explanations of discrepancies for incorrect hypotheses. These explanations, together with the causal knowledge, are used to debug the hypothesis until a correct solution is produced. This combination of knowledge produces a system that is both efficient and robust: the associational knowledge, which is used most of the time, is efficient because it simply combines partial solutions as if they were independent; the causal knowledge makes the system robust because it can check for, and correct, negative interactions between hypothesized events.

By this point, the strengths and weaknesses of the multiple knowledge source/ multiple representation paradigm should be evident. Multiple knowledge sources provide modularity and add structure to a system; multiple specialized representations are utilized to concisely encode and efficiently reason about the different knowledge sources. Such systems are currently time-consuming to implement, however, due to the difficulties of combining diverse knowledge sources and representations, getting information to propagate correctly, and maintaining consistency between different levels of knowledge and between different representations.

With such a multiplicity of knowledge sources and representations, a critical problem is when to use what knowledge and which representation. Many systems delineate particular roles for the different sources of knowledge. As described above, the associational knowledge in GORDIUS is used to generate initial hypotheses, which are then debugged, if necessary, using the more detailed causal knowledge. CASEY [28] uses a similar strategy for the task of medical diagnosis. Other systems, such as CHECK [56], use the associational knowledge to prune the search space of the causal knowledge. Still other researchers advocate a more task-oriented approach, using whatever knowledge and representations are most suited for the particular subtask being considered [5]. As argued elsewhere [49, 50], the important idea is to match the characteristics of the knowledge sources and representations to the needs of the task being solved.

In general, the multiple knowledge/multiple representation approach can result in knowledge-based systems that combine the often conflicting criteria of competence, efficiency, extensibility and understandability. Using specialized representations for each of the different knowledge sources can result in a well-structured, modular system. The paradigm is most useful for complex tasks, where a wide range of knowledge at different levels of abstraction may be needed.

5 Conclusions

Knowledge and representation are separate, and equally important, concepts needed to build competent, efficient knowledge-based systems. Knowledge is needed to describe how the world works, what effects actions will have, how to solve problems, etc. Representation is the way the knowledge is encoded. Representations consist of a syntax (representation language) and a semantic interpretation (the access and inference algorithms); both are needed to fully describe a representation. A knowledge-based system can be effectively described at either the knowledge or representation level: the knowledge level description indicates what the system does, the representation level description tells how it does that. Maintaining this distinction has benefits both in designing and analyzing (ascribing sources of power to) a system.

Second generation expert systems use multiple knowledge sources and/or multiple representations to produce more capable, efficient systems. Multiple knowledge sources are used to structure the problem-solving process so that it is more modular, which has advantages for knowledge acquisition, system extensibility, reuse, and understandability. Multiple representations are used to increase problem-solving efficiency, by using representations specialized for particular inferences, and to increase transparency, by making the encoding of knowledge more concise and making the recommended inferences more apparent.

Knowledge-based systems can be created with any combination of single or multiple knowledge sources and representations. These systems have different strengths and weaknesses:

1. Single knowledge/single representation systems are the easiest to develop, but the least flexible.
2. Multiple knowledge/single representation systems can solve problems at multiple levels of abstraction and can bring to bear different types of knowledge, such as separate domain and control knowledge. The single representational framework makes it easier to implement such systems, but it is often difficult to find a single representation that is both expressive and efficient enough.
3. Single knowledge/multiple representation systems are useful when the same basic knowledge is needed to answer different types of questions. The advantage is that one can choose to use the representation best suited to the task at hand. Difficulties with such systems arise in translating and propagating information among the representations.
4. Multiple knowledge/multiple representation systems are the most flexible, being well-suited for efficiently and robustly tackling fairly complex tasks, but they are also the most complicated systems to design and implement. Difficulties include determining when to use which sources of knowledge, how to map from knowledge sources to representations, and how to combine representations.

In conclusion, there is not a single "correct" architecture for knowledge-based systems. The preferred design very much depends on what types of problems are being solved, what kinds and how much knowledge is available to the system, and the types of inferences that are needed to solve the problem. These concerns are at the heart of designing effective knowledge-based systems, and should be kept in mind when analyzing existing systems. While knowledge and representation are the sources of power in knowledge-based systems, they need to be used judiciously, matched to the concerns of one's tasks.

References

1. J. Allen. Maintaining knowledge about temporal intervals. *CACM*, 26(11), 1983.
2. S. Amarel. On representations of problems of reasoning about actions. In D. Michie, editor, *Machine Intelligence 3*, pages 131–171. American Elsevier, 1968.
3. A. Barr and E. Feigenbaum. *The Handbook of Artificial Intelligence, Vols. 1 and 2*. William Kaufmann, 1981.
4. R. Brooks. Intelligence without representation. *Artificial Intelligence*, 47(1–3):139–160, 1991.
5. B. Chandrasekaran. Towards a functional architecture for intelligence based on generic information processing tasks. In *Proc. IJCAI-87*, Milan, Italy, 1987.
6. D. Chapman. Planning for conjunctive goals. *Artificial Intelligence*, 32:333–377, 1987.
7. W. Clancey. The epistemology of a rule-based expert system: A framework for explanation. *Artificial Intelligence*, 20(3):215–251, 1983.
8. W. Clancey. Heuristic classification. *Artificial Intelligence*, 27:289–350, 1985.
9. J.-M. David and J.-P. Krivine. Explaining reasoning from knowledge level models. In *Proc. ECAI 90*, 1990.
10. R. Davis. Diagnosis via causal reasoning: Paths of interaction and the locality principle. In *Proc. AAAI '83*, pages 88–94, Aug. 1983.
11. R. Davis, H. Shrobe, W. Hamscher, K. Wieckert, M. Shirley, and S. Polit. Diagnosis based on description of structure and function. In *Proc. AAAI '82*, pages 137–142, Aug. 1982.
12. R. Davis, H. Shrobe, and P. Szolovits. What is a knowledge representation? *AI Magazine*, Spring 1993.
13. T. Dean and D. McDermott. Temporal data base management. *Artificial Intelligence*, 32(1):1–55, 1987.
14. R. Dechter, I. Meiri, and J. Pearl. Temporal constraint networks. *Artificial Intelligence*, 49(1–3):61–96, 1991.
15. J. deKleer. An assumption-based truth maintenance system. *Artificial Intelligence*, 28:127–162, 1986.
16. J. Doyle and R. Patil. Two theses of knowledge representation. *Artificial Intelligence*, 48(3):261–279, 1991.
17. L. Erman, F. Hayes-Roth, V. Lesser, and R. Reddy. The HEARSAY-II speech understanding system: Integrating knowledge to resolve uncertainty. *Computing Surveys*, 12(2):213–253, 1980.
18. B. Faltings. A symbolic approach to qualitative kinematics. *Artificial Intelligence*, 56(2–3):139–170, 1992.
19. K. Forbus. Qualitative process theory. *Artificial Intelligence*, 24:85–168, 1984.

20. K. Forbus, P. Nielson, and B. Faltings. Qualitative spatial reasoning: The CLOCK project. *Artificial Intelligence*, 51(1–3):417–471, 1991.

21. M. Ginsberg and D. Geddis. Is there any need for domain-dependent control information? In *Proc. National Conference on Artificial Intelligence*, pages 452–457, Los Angeles, CA, July 1991.

22. W. Hamscher. Modeling digital circuits for troubleshooting. *Artificial Intelligence*, 51(1–3):223–272, 1991.

23. B. Hayes-Roth, R. Washington, R. Hewett, M. Hewett, and A. Seiver. Intelligent monitoring and control. In *Proc. International Joint Conference on AI*, pages 243–249, Detroit, MI, August 1989.

24. D. Heckerman and E. Horvitz. The myth of modularity in rule-based systems. Technical Report KSL Memo 86-33, Stanford University, 1986.

25. Y. Iwasaki and H. Simon. Causality in device behavior. *Artificial Intelligence*, 29(1):3–32, 1986.

26. L. Joskowicz and E. Sacks. Computational kinematics. *Artificial Intelligence*, 51(1–3):381–416, 1991.

27. W. Kornfeld and C. Hewitt. The scientific community metaphor. *IEEE Transactions on Systems, Man, and Cybernetics*, SMC-11(1), 1981.

28. P. Koton. Combining causal models and case-based reasoning. In J. M. David, J. P. Krivine, and R. Simmons, editors, *Second Generation Expert Systems*. Springer Verlag, 1993.

29. G. Kramer. A geometric constraint engine. *Artificial Intelligence*, 58(1–3):327–360, 1992.

30. B. Kuipers. Qualitative simulation. *Artificial Intelligence*, 24:289–338, 1984.

31. B. Kuipers and D. Berleant. Using incomplete quantitative knowledge in qualitative reasoning. In *Proc. National Conference on Artificial Intelligence*, St. Paul, MN, August 1988.

32. J. Laird, A. Newell, and P. Rosenbloom. Soar: An architecture for general intelligence. *Artificial Intelligence*, 33(3), 1987.

33. V. Lesser, J. Pavlin, and E. Durfee. Approximate processing in real-time problem solving. *AI Magazine*, 9(1):49–61, 1988.

34. H. Levesque and R. Brachman. Expressiveness and tractability in knowledge representation and reasoning. *Computational Intelligence*, 3:78–93, 1987.

35. M. Lowry. The abstraction/implementation model of problem reformulation. In *Proc. IJCAI-87*, pages 1004–1010, Milan, Italy, 1987.

36. D. Marr. *Vision*. W.H. Freeman, 1982.

37. J. McDermott. R1: A rule-based configurer of computer systems. *Artificial Intelligence*, 19(1):39–88, 1982.

38. S. Minton, J. Carbonell, et al. Explanation-based learning: A problem-solving perspective. *Artificial Intelligence*, 40:63–118, 1989.

39. J. Moses. Algebraic simplification, a guide for the perplexed. *CACM*, 14(8):527–537, 1971.

40. A. Newell. The knowledge level. *Artificial Intelligence*, 18:87–127, 1982.

41. R. Patil. Causal representation of patient illness for electrolyte and acid-base diagnosis. Technical Report 267, Laboratory for Computer Science, Massachusetts Institute of Technology, 1981.

42. H. Pople. Heuristic methods for imposing structure on ill-structured problems. In P. Szolovits, editor, *Artificial Intelligence in Medicine*, pages 119–190. Westview Press, 1982.

43. O. Raiman. Order of magnitude reasoning. *Artificial Intelligence*, 51(1–3):11–38, 1991.

44. S. Rowley, H. Shrobe, and R. Cassels. Joshua: Uniform access to heterogeneous knowledge structures. In *Proc. AAAI-87*, Seattle, WA, 1987.

45. Y. Shoham. *Reasoning About Change: Time and Causation from the Standpoint of Artificial Intelligence*. MIT Press, 1988.

46. E. Shortliffe. *Computer Based Medical Consultations: MYCIN*. American Elsevier, 1976.

47. B. Silver et al. A framework for integrating multiple heterogeneous learning agents. In J. M. David, J. P. Krivine, and R. Simmons, editors, *Second Generation Expert Systems*. Springer Verlag, 1993.

48. R. Simmons. Integrating multiple representations for incremental, causal simulation. In *Proc. Conference on AI, Simulation, and Planning*, pages 88–96, Cocoa Beach, FL, April 1991.

49. R. Simmons. The roles of associational and causal reasoning in problem solving. *Artificial Intelligence*, 53(2–3):159–208, February 1992.

50. R. Simmons. Generate, test and debug: A paradigm for combining associational and causal reasoning. In J. M. David, J. P. Krivine, and R. Simmons, editors, *Second Generation Expert Systems*. Springer Verlag, 1993.

51. R. Simmons and R. Davis. Representing and reasoning about change in geologic interpretation. Technical Report AI-TR-749, AI Lab, MIT, December 1983.

52. R. Simmons and J. Mohammed. Causal modeling of semiconductor fabrication. *International Journal for Artificial Intelligence in Engineering*, 4(1):2–21, Jan. 1989.

53. L. Steels. The componential framework and its role in reusability. In J. M. David, J. P. Krivine, and R. Simmons, editors, *Second Generation Expert Systems*. Springer Verlag, 1993.

54. M. Stefik. Planning and meta-planning (MOLGEN: Part 2). *Artificial Intelligence*, 16:141–170, 1981.

55. W. Swartout. Xplain: A system for creating and explaining expert consulting systems. *Artificial Intelligence*, 21(3):285–325, 1983.

56. P. Torasso and L. Console. *Diagnostic Problem Solving: Combining Heuristic, Approximate and Causal Reasoning*. Van Nostrand Reinhold, 1989.

57. J. VanBaalen. Automated design of specialized representations. *Artificial Intelligence*, 54(1–2):121–198, 1992.

58. D. Weld and J. deKleer, editors. *Qualitative Reasoning About Physical Systems*. Morgan Kaufmann, San Mateo, CA, 1990.

59. B. Wielinga, G. Schreiber, and J. Breuker. Kads: A modelling approach to knowledge engineering. *Knowledge Acquisition*, 4(1), 1992.

60. R. Wilensky. *Planning and Understanding*. Addison-Wesley, 1983.

61. D. Wilkins. *Practical Planning: Extending the Classical AI Planning Paradigm*. Morgan Kaufmann, San Mateo, CA, 1988.

62. B. Williams. Qualitative analysis of MOS circuits. Technical Report 767, AI Lab, MIT, 1984.

63. B. Williams. Doing time: Putting qualitative reasoning on firmer ground. In *Proc. AAAI '86*, pages 105–112, Philadelphia, PA, Aug. 1986.

64. P. Winston. *Artificial Intelligence*. Addison-Wesley, Reading, MA, 1984.

Combining Heuristic Reasoning with Causal Reasoning in Diagnostic Problem Solving

Luca Console[1], Luigi Portinale[2], Daniele Theseider Dupré[2] and Pietro Torasso[2]

[1] Dip. Matematica e Informatica, Univ. Udine, Via Zanon 6, 33100 Udine (Italy)
[2] Dip. Informatica, Univ. Torino, Corso Svizzera 185, 10149 Torino (Italy)

Abstract. In this paper we discuss two different approaches for the combination of heuristic and causal reasoning in diagnostic problem solving. In particular, we first present the two-level architecture CHECK which exploits both experiential knowledge and a deeper form of knowledge. While the former is represented by means of a frame-based formalism, the latter is based on a causal network representation. The co-operation of reasoning at the two levels is discussed: the results of the heuristic level are used to focus reasoning at the causal level. Diagnostic problem solving at the causal level has been logically characterized as a form of abductive reasoning. Because of some difficulties of the CHECK approach (mainly regarding the possible lack of consistency of two independently acquired knowledge bases) we investigated an alternative approach, represented by the AID architecture, which mainly relies on a causal representation of knowledge. In AID the abductive formalization of diagnosis plays a major role, and the reasoning process is focused by operational knowledge that is automatically synthesized from the causal model.

1   Introduction

During the seventies several investigations have been devoted to exploit the potential offered by a single uniform representation formalism for problem solving. Production rules [45] showed their suitability for modeling a wide range of problems and, being a simple and powerful tool, they were widely adopted for developing expert systems and became the basic mechanism in the so called "domain independent expert systems". However, some researchers started to question the uniformity principle, since in real-world domains there are different types of knowledge and not all of them can be adequately captured in a single formalism. The integration of formalisms which encourage the structuring of the domain entities in concepts or objects with formalisms which better model actions or inferences has been investigated in the early eighties (see for example [1]). The proposal of using a hybrid approach (usually based on frames plus production rules) became more and more popular in the expert systems community, so that it is currently common practice to develop expert systems by using hybrid tools.

These kinds of hybrid formalisms, however, concern only the representation level and not the conceptual one. They may in fact encourage an accurate analysis of what part of the knowledge can be more usefully represented by means of rules or frames, but by themselves they do not encourage the analysis of different approaches to solve a given problem by taking into account the task to be performed and the types of knowledge available on the domain. In mid eighties [33, 41] it became apparent that the notion of "expert system" as a system which is able to replicate human "expertise" derived from experience is limiting because:

- human experts are able to exploit other kinds of knowledge (for example, knowledge about physical laws) when experiential knowledge fails in solving a case;
- there are significant domains where experiential knowledge is scarce but there are (maybe incomplete) theories which provide a rather formal account of the main phenomena of the domain of interest and there is an actual need for systems supporting the activity of the human agent responsible for solving problems in those domains.

The development of knowledge-based systems based on a "deep" model of the domain was made possible by some progresses in the early eighties in the research area currently called "model-based reasoning" [21]. Proposals for representing the structure and function of a device, for reasoning on such a description, or for providing a causal account of an evolution have been significant steps in extending the capability of a system for dealing with complex phenomena. The main common basis of these different proposals is the search for a description of the domain which does not depend on the human experience in solving problems and which is strongly related to basic laws of the domain to be modeled. Among the tasks that have been investigated, diagnosis received a lot of attention: significant examples of diagnostic systems based on "deep" models have been developed not only in the field of digital circuits (for example DART [24] and HT [19]), but also in the field of medicine (CASNET [46] and ABEL [34]).

The manifesto by Steels on Second Generation Expert Systems [41] pointed out the opportunity of exploiting more than one type of knowledge, integrating some form of heuristic (experience) knowledge with some form of deep knowledge. In this approach the focus of the attention is on the integration and cooperation at a conceptual level of different types of knowledge. The importance of integrating heuristic and causal reasoning has been recognized also in tasks other than diagnosis; for example, in GTD [40] associational and causal reasoning are combined for the solution of interpretation and planning problems (in particular, associational rules generates candidate solutions which are then tested and debugged using causal knowledge).

The second generation approach influenced many research groups and determined a change in the focus of interest of the research activity. Our group active in the Dipartimento di Informatica, University of Torino was not an exception. From 1979 to 1982 most of our efforts were devoted to the development of LITO1, an expert system for supporting the clinical decision (in particular, the assessment of the liver function [29]). The knowledge base, coded by means of production rules, was derived by clinical experience and refined by means of learning algorithms providing as output a set of fuzzy production rules [30]. The need of a more structured approach was apparent when we moved to the development of a diagnostic system in the field of liver diseases. In LITO2 [17] a hybrid representation language (including frames, production rules and advanced mechanisms for approximate reasoning [31]) was designed and developed. The overall diagnostic strategy of LITO2 can be considered as a variant of the "heuristic classification" paradigm [4]. Despite the many nice features of LITO2 (as many other systems following the "heuristic classification" paradigm), two main problems received a very partial solution:

- *Explanation.* The explanation provided by LITO2 was mainly an intelligent trace of the reasoning process rather than a real explanation, because the system has no explicit notion why a given piece of information (for example, a symptom) is related to a given hypothesis. This explanation can be understandable for an expert physician, who already knows the underlying relations between symptoms and diseases, while a less experienced user may encounter more difficulties.
- *Discrimination.* The result of LITO2 is a ranking of diagnoses according to their confidence levels: when we have diagnoses with similar confidence levels and no diagnosis with a higher confidence level, it is difficult to decide which is the solution both because there is no clear criterion for deciding whether a single fault or a diagnosis involving multiple faults actually covers[3] the data and because there is no basis for requesting additional pieces of information which allow to discriminate among potentially competitive diagnostic hypotheses.

This analysis suggested that a general architecture for diagnostic problem solving should include a heuristic component (similar to the one adopted in LITO2), but should also rely on "deep" knowledge. However, the term "deep" denotes a large variety of representation formalisms, rather than a single one. When we started to investigate the problem (second half of 1985), two main paradigms for diagnostic reasoning were known in literature: the structure and function approach (mainly used for diagnosing digital circuits [19, 24]) and the causal approach [34, 41][4].

We decided to investigate the possibility of combining heuristic knowledge with *causal* knowledge mainly because the domains we had analyzed (medicine and mechanical devices) are not easily modeled in a structure and function approach, since this kind of knowledge is not easily available or is very complex even if the domain model is described at a high level of abstraction. Moreover,

---

[3] With an alternative terminology, which is commonly used in the model-based diagnosis community and which we will follow in the paper, it is possible to say that a diagnosis "explains" the data. This notion of explanation is different from the one discussed in the item above but is not independent from it since when explaining the solution to the user, it should be illustrated how such a solution is related to all the relevant data.

[4] At that time, some research efforts had also been devoted to functional models [23, 18].

causal knowledge seems quite adequate for providing real explanations, since the relevance of causality in understanding and explaining phenomena is well known in cognitive psychology. The CHECK (Combining HEuristic and Causal Knowledge) project [44] started in late 1985 with the goal of providing an architecture for diagnostic problem solving where difficult problems such as explanation and discrimination may find an adequate solution. We decided to supplement heuristic knowledge with causal knowledge, rather than just replacing the heuristic knowledge, in order to maintain some degree of cognitive plausibility in our architecture. In fact, at least in the domains more actively investigated by our group, human experts use heuristic knowledge first in order to try to solve (or at least to focus) the diagnostic problem and fall back on other kinds of knowledge (deep knowledge) just when the diagnostic problem is hard to solve, requiring a deeper understanding of the processes occurring in the case under examination.

However, the definition of the co-operation protocol between heuristic and deep reasoning can be problematic. Even if it seems natural that the heuristic level should be able to solve typical cases, the critical point concerns the behavior of the heuristic level when it has to face difficult (not typical) diagnostic cases. In some systems (e.g., [23, 42]), the solution consists in providing the heuristic level with very strong and categorical classification schemes able to solve only "very typical" cases and rejecting as unsolvable all the other ones. We believe that such an approach is too restrictive in many cases, so that it is better to provide the heuristic level with coarser rules: in this way, the heuristic level is able to classify also cases whose descriptions cannot be considered completely typical. As a consequence, the number of cases where the heuristic level completely fails in providing a diagnosis is decreased even if in some cases the system fails in providing an accurate discrimination among potential diagnoses. We believe that it is better to have some solution (even if quite imprecise) from the heuristic level rather than no response at all. In this way the results of the heuristic level can be considered as approximate solutions that can be used to focus deep reasoning, or even to provide the actual solution in cases where no solution can be found at the deep level because the deep model is very incomplete (for example, the pathophysiological evolution of some diseases are still unknown or debated).

At the beginning of the design of CHECK we mainly dealt with the definition of the causal formalism and of the interaction between the heuristic and the causal level in solving a diagnostic problem (see section 2). After some time, it became apparent the need for a precise definition of the solution of diagnostic problems on a causal model. The result, summarized in section 3, was the logical formalization of the causal net formalism adopted in CHECK and the definition of diagnosis as a form of abductive reasoning [12]; particular attention was devoted to the problem of formalizing the reasoning in presence of incomplete causal models [8]. Because of this formalization, we were able to get a deeper understanding of both the limitations and the advantages of the causal formalism, so that we started both to extend the expressive power of the formalism and to reconsider the integration between heuristic and causal knowledge. In particular, we investigated the problem of ensuring that the pruning of the diagnostic space, performed at the heuristic level, is sound (that is no actual solution, possibly involving multiple faults, is excluded). This consideration stimulated a significant revision of the way causal knowledge is supplemented with some form of heuristic knowledge: in particular, we investigated the possibility of automatically synthesizing "operational" knowledge from the causal one and to use this operational knowledge to focus diagnostic reasoning at the causal level. In this way the need of two separate knowledge acquisition phases (one for the heuristic knowledge, the other one for causal knowledge) is avoided and the consistency of the two knowledge sources is guaranteed. Section 4 describes the AID architecture (Abductive and Iterative Diagnosis) where a precise characterization of the diagnostic reasoning in terms of an iterative sequence of abduction, prediction and discrimination steps is provided, and the focusing role of the heuristic level of CHECK is taken by the operational knowledge automatically learned from the causal one. Finally, section 5 compares the two approaches and discusses possible extensions of AID to take into account some of our recent results both in terms of the extension of the representation formalism and in reasoning mechanisms.

2   CHECK

As we noticed in the introduction, CHECK [44] is based on the co-operation between heuristic and causal reasoning. Actually, CHECK includes also a "data" layer, which contains a terminological description of the entities used in the system to represent data. Each datum is represented by an object-like structure and is characterized by a set of attributes specifying features of the datum itself. Data are grouped in classes and subclasses according to their properties and to the role they play in the diagnostic strategy. For example, two different classes can be used for representing symptoms and tests. The taxonomy of data is used in the interaction with the user: in particular data are requested and displayed to the user in clusters which take into account the taxonomy.

2.1   The heuristic level

At the heuristic level diagnostic hypotheses are represented by means of prototypical structures which describe the expected values for the most significant features and symptoms characterizing the hypotheses. Diagnostic hypotheses are organized in taxonomies, so that we have prototypical descriptions of generic faults as well as of specific ones.

The description of a diagnostic hypothesis contains prototypical knowledge, knowledge about the relations of the hypothesis with other ones, and also control knowledge which makes a diagnostic hypotheses an active entity and allows distribution of control along the taxonomy. TRIGGERING rules, which play the role of activation rules, are a particular form of control knowledge. As soon as the user provides some initial data, the TRIGGERING rules of the diagnostic hypotheses at the top of the taxonomy (that is, the most generic ones) are inspected and the diagnostic hypotheses whose TRIGGERING rules succeed are activated. The prototypical description of activated hypotheses is then matched against the data. This match is evaluated by verifying first the NECESSARY conditions (that is, conditions on the value of relevant findings that have to be true if the hypothesis is true); if this match succeeds, some SUPPLEMENTARY conditions are evaluated: they involve findings whose presence can increase the confidence level in the hypotheses, but whose absence does not allow the rejection of the hypothesis.

Because of the intrinsic uncertainty and vagueness in the use of qualitative values for findings and the need of tolerating some variations (or minor distortions) in prototypical knowledge, a fuzzy match is evaluated and a particular form of approximate reasoning is used [43]. When the match can be considered successful for a hypothesis, another type of control knowledge is used: VALIDATION rules, which are associated with diagnostic hypothesis and play the role of confirmation or rejection rules. Moreover, in order to consider all the potential diagnostic hypotheses, in case a hypothesis H has reached a high confidence level, the hypotheses associated with H are in turn activated (note that this kind of link is explicitly represented in the description of H) and their prototypical descriptions are matched against the data. In this way hypotheses can be activated by data as well as by other hypotheses. It is worth noting that during the matching phase further data may be asked by the system (in particular when some NECESSARY findings are unknown and the other ones have matched the condition imposed on their values).

After the VALIDATION step, confirmed hypotheses are considered for "refinement", that is their more specific hypotheses are taken into examination and the same diagnostic process is applied to them. The process is continued until the leaves of the hierarchy of hypotheses are reached. The set of the leaves which are successfully instantiated is passed to the causal level for discrimination and/or confirmation (i.e., is used to focus causal reasoning).

2.2 Representing causal knowledge

Causal knowledge is represented in CHECK by means of causal networks. In the following we shall assume that causal networks are used to model the faulty behavior of a system[5]. A causal network is composed by a set of nodes connected by arcs representing different kinds of relationships. Let us consider the causal network reported in figure 1. Five main types of nodes have been defined in CHECK (a sixth type of node will be discussed later):

- HYPOTHESIS nodes (exhagonal boxes in figure 1) represent the diagnostic hypotheses considered by the system.
- STATE nodes (elliptic boxes) represent non-observable internal states of the modeled system[6];

---

[5] In principle, a causal network can be used to represent also the correct behavior of a system; see the final section and [13].

[6] Actually, as in most approaches to causal modeling [34, 42, 46], each STATE node represents a partial state, that is a situation which describes only partially the state

52

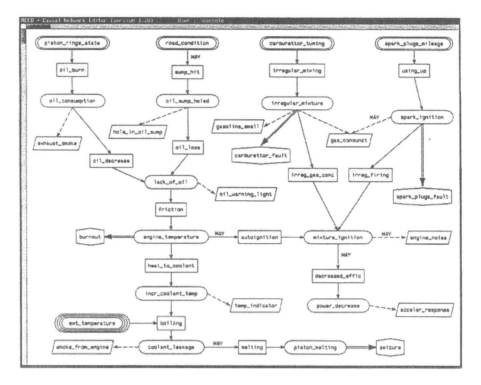

Fig. 1. An example of causal network

- FINDING nodes (rhomboidal boxes) represent observable parameters in the modeled system.
- INITIAL_CAUSE nodes (double-lined elliptic boxes) represent the initial perturbations that may lead the system to a faulty behavior. In the following, we shall assume that INITIAL_CAUSEs are not observable.
- CONTEXT nodes (quadruple-lined elliptic boxes) represent contextual conditions that may influence the behavior of the modeled system.

Each STATE, FINDING, INITIAL_CAUSE and CONTEXT node is characterized by a set of attributes, assuming values in a predefined finite set of admissible linguistic ones[7]. In the case of FINDING nodes, for each attribute we recognize a special value which denotes the "normality" value of the FINDING (i.e., the value associated with a normal behavior of the modeled system); all the other linguistic values denote abnormal (pathological) values of the finding and correspond to external manifestations of the pathological states in the network. Without any loss of expressivity and for the sake of simplicity, we shall impose throughout

---

of the system.

[7] In the case of a pure fault model, the value of attributes of STATE nodes denote only abnormal situations since we are modeling only the faulty behavior of a system.

the paper that each STATE, FINDING, CONTEXT and INITIAL_CAUSE node is characterized by only one attribute.

Three types of arcs have been defined, in the causal network, between nodes: CAUSAL (continuous lines in figure 1), HAM (dashed lines) and DEFINED_AS (double lines).

Each CAUSAL arc connects a conjunction $\{S_1 \ldots S_n, C_1 \ldots C_m\}$ of nodes ($S_i \in$ STATE $\cup$ INITIAL_CAUSE and $C_j \in$ CONTEXT, $n \geq 1, m \geq 0$) to a STATE node T and represents the relationship "S_1 and ... and S_n cause T in the context formed by C_1 and ... and C_m". CAUSAL arcs are compound structures involving a node of a further type: an ACTION node (rectangular box in figure 1) which models the functional transformation describing how the values of the attribute of the caused state depend on the values of the attribute of the causing ones. For example, in figure 1 a causal arc connects the state *incr_coolant_temp* and the context *ext_temperature* to the state *coolant_leakage* by means of the action *boiling*. The state *incr_coolant_temp* has an attribute *intensity* with admissible values *medium* and *severe*; the context *ext_temperature* has an attribute *value* with admissible values *normal* and *high*, and the state *coolant_leakage* has an attribute *intensity* with admissible values *slight* and *severe*. The mapping represented by the ACTION *boiling* is described by the following function:

$f(medium, high) = slight$;
$f(severe, normal) = slight$;
$f(severe, high) = severe$

A condition on the values of the attributes of the causing nodes can be associated with each CAUSAL arc, imposing a restriction on the traversal of the arc; such a condition should coincide with the domain on which the function associated to the arc is defined: notice, for example, that the function "f" above is not defined on the pair (*medium, normal*).

In a causal network we also admit that more than one CAUSAL arc enter a state: such multiple causes are implicitly ORed (for example, *oil_consumption* and *oil_sump_holed* are alternative causes of *lack_of_oil* in figure 1). A major restriction we impose on CAUSAL arcs is that they cannot define cycles; however, this is quite reasonable when the temporal dimension is abstracted from the model.

Each arc labeled HAM (Has As a Manifestation) connects a STATE node S to a FINDING node m and represents the fact that m is an observable manifestation of S. For example, in figure 1 *oil_warning_light* is connected by a HAM arc to the state *lack_of_oil*. As in the case of CAUSAL arcs, a condition and a functional transformation describing the mapping between the attribute of S and the attribute of m is associated with the HAM arc.

Each DEFINED_AS arc connects a STATE S to a HYPOTHESIS node H meaning that the diagnostic hypothesis H is defined as the presence of the STATE S, possibly with some condition on the attributes of S. As an example, in figure 1 we have that the HYPOTHESIS *burnout* is defined in terms of the STATE *engine_temperature* (actually, there is a condition associated with the arc specifying that the *increase* of *engine_temperature* must be *high* or *very_high*).

Diagnostic hypotheses are therefore defined concepts.

Notice that, in most real-world cases, the assumption that complete models can be built is not realistic. For this reason we introduced some mechanisms to represent incomplete knowledge. First of all, the INITIAL_CAUSEs can be abstractions of the actual perturbation processes; moreover, in case they are not observable, the model gives no *direct* way to establish their presence. Another important source of incompleteness is related to the level of detail of the model. When modeling the real world, only processes and conditions at some level of abstraction can be represented, because of the inherent complexity of the system or because of the ignorance of the underlying mechanisms. In particular, at least two different forms of incompleteness can be recognized: given a cause-effect relation, some of its preconditions may be abstracted in the model, or some of the causes of a state may be abstracted. In order to deal with the former case, we introduce the possibility of labeling an arc as a MAY one; such a label expresses ignorance about the actual conditions and processes underlying the relationship itself. The fact that some cause of a state S is missing can be modeled by introducing an extra unknown initial cause and connecting it to S.

2.3 Co-operation of heuristic and causal level

As we noticed, the initial goal of CHECK was to use the heuristic level as a focusing component able to prune the space of hypotheses to be considered by the causal problem solver. In CHECK the heuristic level is invoked first and generates a set of hypotheses to be discriminated (or confirmed) by the causal one. The causal level produces the final (possibly multiple fault) diagnoses, generating causal explanations for them.

The causal reasoner tries to find a portion of the causal network with the following properties:

1. it contains (accounts for) all the findings observed in the specific case under examination;
2. it does not contain any finding which is known to be absent in the specific case under examination.

We say that such a portion of the network *covers* the observations, and the set of diagnostic hypotheses comprised in that portion is a final diagnosis.

Reasoning at the causal level is started from the set of hypotheses generated by the heuristic level. Confirming a hypothesis H consist in confirming its defining state S. This is done in two steps: in the former the system searches for a path connecting some set of INITIAL_CAUSEs to S; in the latter the further consequences are analysed. The systems collects the set of assumptions on INITIAL_CAUSEs and MAY arcs associated with such paths. These assumptions constitute an important part of the explanation produced for the user: they indicate either the "deep causes" of the diagnosed fault(s) or the assumptions made by the system and corresponding to incomplete knowledge. When a FINDING node is reached, the system checks whether the predicted value coincides with the observed one, if any. If they are different, the path is rejected. In case no value is available and the parameter is easy to observe, the user is asked to provide a value.

The same process is repeated for each hypothesis. Some of them can be excluded if no explanatory path can be produced. Moreover, in case no hypothesis covers all the observations, multiple faults are considered (notice that in some cases this may lead to a substantial revision of reasoning at the causal level since the possible interactions among the faults have to be taken into account).

In section 3 we shall analyse more precisely the reasoning process at the causal level, presenting a logical formalization of diagnostic problem solving on causal models.

2.4   Structure of the implemented system

The implementation of CHECK consists of several modules. The kernel of the system, formed by the heuristic and causal reasoners, is implemented in Prolog; in addition, the system has a set of knowledge acquisition and interface modules which are implemented part in Prolog and part in 'C' language on Sun Workstations using the SunView facilities. In particular, causal knowledge can be acquired using a graphical editor, NEED [5], which produces both a graphical description (the one illustrated in figure 1, which is an hard copy of the display of NEED) and a textual representation formed by a set of Prolog clauses. Heuristic knowledge can be acquired using a module implemented in Prolog, using a menu-based interface and directly producing the code constituting the system. The interfaces available in the consultation system are a menu-driven module for data acquisition and EXPL, a module for the display of the solutions which uses the graphical description produced by NEED.

3   Logical formalization of causal reasoning in CHECK

In order to provide a precise definition of diagnostic problem solving on causal models we decided to give a logical characterization of such a process. The basis of such a logical formalization is a logical semantics for causal models which will be outlined in the next subsection. Diagnosis is then defined as form of *abductive* reasoning: given a theory (the logical representation of a causal model) and a set of observations (the findings to be explained), abduction consists in determining a set of assumptions (in our case, assumptions on initial causes and MAY relationships) which, in conjunction with the theory, entails the observations. Abduction is one of the two dominant approaches to the logical formalization of model-based diagnosis (see [8, 36]); the other is the *consistency-based* one [22, 38]. Abduction corresponds to a stronger notion of diagnosis and is a reasonable approach to adopt when one has a fault model of the system to be diagnosed, as in the case we are considering [10].

3.1 Semantics of a causal model

In this section we outline how a causal model can be characterized by means of a set of logical formulae (see [8, 12] for more details). First of all, we define a logical system in which the alphabet of predicate symbols is partitioned into five subsets: "state", "manifestation", "perturbation", "context" (whose correspondence with entities in the model is obvious) and "abstracted condition" symbols corresponding to MAY conditions on arcs. The arity of a predicate symbol equals the number of attributes of the node it represents.

Each CAUSAL relationship is modeled by an implication formula and each ACTION node is modeled as a *function*; for example, the logical model of the causal arc connecting S_1, S_2 to T is:

$$S_1(s_1) \wedge S_2(s_2) \wedge COND(s_1, s_2) \rightarrow T(f(s_1, s_2))$$

where $COND(s_1, s_2)$ is the condition attached to the arc[8].

Also HAM arcs are modeled by implication formulae, while there is no direct logical correspondent for HYPOTHESIS nodes (they are defined concepts); however, we denote with $def(H)$ the formula describing how H is defined in the causal network:

$$def(H) \equiv \exists x[S_H(x) \wedge COND(x)]$$

where S_H is the state symbol corresponding to the state defining the hypothesis H, and $COND(x)$ is the condition possibly on the DEFINED_AS arc.

MAY relationships are modeled through the introduction of "abstracted condition" symbols. The MAY CAUSAL arc between the causing state S and the effect state T is modeled by the formula

$$S(s) \wedge \alpha \rightarrow T(f(s))$$

where α is an abstracted_condition atom and represents an anonymous condition replacing the one abstracted in the model.

The union of the sets of "perturbation" and "abstracted condition" predicates is the set of *abducible* predicates, i.e., those corresponding to the assumptions that have to be made in the process of generating causal explanations.

3.2 Diagnostic problems

For a correct characterization of diagnostic problem solving, we believe that it is quite relevant to take into account the different types of data characterizing a diagnostic problem (see also [37]). The first distinction we introduce is the one between "contextual data" and "observations". Contextual data are a set of parameters characterizing the specific case under examination such as the

---

[8] Notice that, when providing the logical formalization of ORed states, some attention has to be paid to the case where instances of more than one of the causing states are present; however this is outside the scope of the present paper (see [11] for a discussion).

sex and age of a patient in a medical application or the inputs to a device in a technical application. Typically they are known when a case is analyzed (in some sense they are "necessary" to characterize the case itself) but they need not be accounted for (explained) by a diagnosis. Such data correspond to CONTEXT nodes in the causal network.

Data corresponding to observations (findings, results of tests, measurable quantities) play a very different role. These are data that must be accounted for (explained) by a diagnosis. In our opinion, however, there is a further important distinction: the one between normality observations and abnormality observations. When the diagnostic system has just the fault model of the system to be diagnosed, such a distinction should be either provided as external information or the system can assume that abnormality values are those for which a cause is present in the model[9].

Definition 1. A diagnostic problem DP on a causal model is a four-tuple $< NET, HYP, CXT, < \Phi_N, \Phi_A >>$, where:

- NET is the set (conjunction) of logical formulae modeling a causal network $NETWORK$;

- $HYP = \{< H, def(H) > | H$ is a HYPOTHESIS node in the causal network $NETWORK\}$;

- CXT is a set of ground context atoms denoting the set of contextual data;

- Φ_N is a set of ground manifestation atoms denoting the set of "normality observations";

- Φ_A is a set of ground manifestation atoms denoting the set of "abnormality observations".

The findings not occurring either in Φ_A or in Φ_N can be regarded as "unknown" (so we do not assume that everything that is not abnormal is normal). Since we abstract from time, we impose the constraint that $\Phi_A \cup \Phi_N$ can contain at most one instance of each finding; this means that we impose that a finding cannot have more than one (normal or abnormal) value simultaneously. Since we assume that NET is a fault model, solving a diagnostic problem corresponds to determining an explanation for the abnormality observations (whose causes are explicitly modeled) which is consistent with the normality observations. The process of solving a diagnostic problem DP can be therefore reformulated as an *abduction problem with consistency constraints* [13, 15]. From the logical point of view, this amounts to identifying a set of abducibles which, together with the model and contextual data, implies the abnormality observations and is consistent with all the observations.

---

[9] Notice that the possibility of defining a-priori "abnormal" values without running the model during the diagnostic process was a matter of debate in the community of "model-based reasoning" (see [20] for some strong statements and [27] for a reply).

Definition 2. Given a diagnostic problem $DP =< NET, CXT, HYP, < \Phi_N, \Phi_A >>$, the **abduction problem with consistency constraints** corresponding to DP is a four-tuple $AP =< NET, CXT, HYP, < \Psi^+, \Psi^- >>$ where:

- $\Psi^+ = \Phi_A$
- $\Psi^- = \{m(x)|m(y) \in \Phi_A \cup \Phi_N, x$ is an admissible value m different from y$\}$

Ψ^+ characterizes the set of observations that must be covered (explained); Ψ^-, on the other hand, characterizes the set of values which are inconsistent with the observations: if $m(y)$ has been observed, then any value x other than y of the parameter m conflicts with the observations.

Notice that in this definition we assumed that all the abnormality observations must be covered by a diagnosis. This might not always be the case since in many situations some "not very important" abnormality observations are not covered, but are just involved in consistency checking.

We can now formalize the notion of explanation for AP.

Definition 3. Given an abduction problem with consistency constraints $AP =< NET, CXT, HYP, < \Psi^+, \Psi^- >>$, a set E of abducible atoms is an **explanation** for AP if and only if:

1) $\forall m \in \Psi^+ \quad NET \cup CXT \cup E \vdash m$;
2) $\forall m \in \Psi^- \quad NET \cup CXT \cup E \nvdash m$.

The first point represents the fact that the observations in Ψ^+ are "covered" by the explanation, while the second represents the consistency check with respect to the observations. Notice also the peculiar role played by contextual data: they are used to predict the behavior of the system and need not be explained.

In general, there may be more than one explanation for a problem AP. Among the criteria introduced for ranking alternative explanations, a parsimony criterion involving "minimality" (wrt set inclusion) seems adequate. In particular this criterion suggests to limit the attention to those explanations containing minimal sets of abducible atoms. This is reasonable since abducibles (either initial perturbations or abstracted conditions) correspond to abnormal conditions. An in-depth discussion of other parsimony criteria and the relationships among them is reported in [8]. Although the choice of parsimony criteria is important, it should not be over evaluated since in many cases additional tests (or data) can discriminate among competing explanations (see next section).

Finally, given a diagnostic problem DP and the corresponding abduction problem AP, an interesting issue is to define the correspondence between the explanations for AP and the solutions to DP. A solution to DP is a set of diagnostic hypotheses which explains the set of observations. Such a correspondence can be drawn by noticing that each diagnostic hypothesis is defined in the causal network as the presence of a state.

Definition 4. Given a diagnostic problem $DP =< NET, HYP, CXT, < \Phi_N, \Phi_A >>$, the corresponding abduction problem AP and an explanation E for AP, the set

$diagnosis(E) = \{H| < H, def(H) >\in HYP$ and $NET \cup CXT \cup E \vdash def(H)\}$

is a **solution** for DP.

It is worth noting that the solutions associated with minimal (wrt set inclusion) explanations are themselves minimal (i.e., minimal sets of hypotheses covering the observations) (see [8]).

4   From CHECK to AID

The approach proposed in CHECK for the co-operation of a heuristic and a causal level suffers from one important limitation. The idea of not considering at the causal level those diagnostic hypotheses that have been rejected by the heuristic level is correct, in the sense that does not lead to loosing solutions, only in case the heuristic and causal knowledge bases are consistent, i.e., a hypothesis which is rejected by the heuristic level does not belong to any solution at the causal level. The problem regards, in particular, the knowledge acquisition phase. It is certainly unrealistic to assume that consistency is guaranteed if the two knowledge bases are independently acquired from domain experts.

In order to experiment an alternative solution to the integration of different forms of knowledge and to solve the problems mentioned above, we designed a different system, AID (Abductive and Iterative Diagnosis), with the following characteristics:

- *Central position for the logical approach to diagnostic problem solving on causal models.* The idea is to have a system that directly relies (with some modification described in the items below) on a logical representation of causal knowledge and on the abductive definition of diagnosis given in the previous section.
- *Definition of a sequential approach to diagnosis.* In a realistic domain, in fact, diagnosis usually starts from a limited set of observations, from which an initial set of solutions can be formed. Then additional data should be asked to discriminate among such solutions, and the set of current solutions should be updated to take into account the new observations.
  In CHECK, reasoning at the causal level can assume that most of the relevant data have been acquired during reasoning at the heuristic level and therefore there is no attention to minimizing questions to the user. However, if causal reasoning starts immediately after the initial data have been provided by the user, the acquisition of further data should be interleaved in some way with the reasoning process.
- *Use of knowledge compilation as a focusing component.* Reasoning at the causal level can lead to the examination of a very large number of possibilities for the abductive explanation of the observed abnormal manifestations (abductive diagnosis has been shown to be computationally intractable in the worst case [2]).
  These considerations led us to the following choice with respect to the CHECK experience: acquiring only causal knowledge from domain experts and then automatically synthesizing some form of operational knowledge from the deep model; such compiled knowledge should be expressed in a form which

is *homogeneous* with the logical representation available for the deep level and should be synthesized in a way that guarantees a *safe* interaction with deep reasoning, i.e., does not lead to loosing any solution.

These topics will be analysed in more details in the next subsections, where we present the overall organization of the AID diagnostic procedure, analyze its most significant steps and discuss the role of compiled knowledge in it.

4.1 Abductive and Iterative Diagnosis

The diagnostic process of AID can be characterized using the following abstract procedure:

COLLECT DATA: acquire initial data characterizing a specific problem;
EXPLAIN: determine the explanations for the current set of data and the predictions associated with each explanation;
while DISCRIMINATION IS NEEDED AND POSSIBLE: there are different current
    explanations and they do not make the same predictions
do   SELECT TEST: given the predictions of each current explanation,
    suggest which is the observable parameter that provides the "best"
    discrimination among the explanations;
    ACQUIRE NEW DATA;
    REVISE: update the set of explanations by taking into account the new
    observations
endwhile;
DISPLAY SOLUTIONS: output the final set of explanations

The EXPLAIN step

During the solution of a diagnostic problem, it is important to distinguish between *known* and *unknown* findings, that is, findings for which a value has already been acquired or not. Let us say that a set E of abducible atoms *makes a prediction* with respect to a finding m if an atom $m(a)$ is a logical consequence of $NET \cup CXT \cup E$ for some admissible value a of m. It is important to take into account the predictions of E with respect to both known and unknown findings. In fact, predictions with respect to known findings are used to determine whether E is a explanation, given the information acquired so far; predictions with respect to unknown findings can be used to decide further measurements. These considerations lead to the organization of the EXPLAIN step in the following substeps:

– Determination of the "candidate explanations", that is, minimal sets of assumptions that entail the observations to be explained. This can be done by reasoning backwards from such observations and merging sets of assumptions entailing each of them. Since some non-minimal candidate explanation may be generated in this way, it is necessary to filter them out.

- Determination of all the predictions of each candidate explanation on observable parameters. This can be done by reasoning forwards from each candidate explanation.
- Pruning of the candidate explanations that are inconsistent with the observations.

The SELECT TEST step

The predictions of the different explanations can be used to guide the acquisition of further data to discriminate among the different explanations. Our approach, described in detail in [9], derives from de Kleer and Williams' approach to sequential consistency-based diagnosis. In that paper the possibility of determining the optimal sequence of discriminating measurements by adopting classical decision-tree analysis approaches has been discarded for efficiency reasons, in favor of an approach originated in [26] and based on the information-theoretic notion of entropy, which allows to select a single observable parameter that best discriminates (on average) between the competing explanations, rather than the best sequence of observations[10] .

However, some major modifications have to be made to de Kleer and Williams' formalization in order to take into account the difference between consistency-based and abductive diagnosis. In fact, not all of the explanations make a prediction with respect to every unknown finding. Thus, in general, we have to partition the explanations into three sets with respect to a specific possible observation (i.e., observing a specific value a for a finding m):

1. Those which predict $m(a)$ and would therefore remain legal explanations if $m(a)$ were observed.
2. Those which predict $m(b)$ for some $b \neq a$ and should therefore be discarded if $m(a)$ were observed.
3. Those which do not make any prediction with respect to m.

The third class is the most problematic. If all the explanations, including non-minimal ones, were taken into account, then:

I. If a is a normality value, an explanation of the third class would still remain valid after observing $m(a)$.
II. If a is an abnormality value, an explanation of the third class can be discarded after observing $m(a)$ because it does not cover the additional observation.

Since taking into account all the explanations is impractical, one should try to deal only with the minimal ones. In this case, however, when an abnormal value a is observed for m, it would not be correct to discard an explanation E which does not make any prediction about m: in fact, it is possible that a non-minimal

---

[10] This requires some information about a-priori probabilities of the entities represented by assumptions. In the absence of such information, one can assume that they all have the same a-priori probability.

explanation $E' \supset E$ actually predicts $m(a)$. One should then consider if it is possible to add some further assumption to E in order to predict $m(a)$. While this should be checked in the REVISE step after an additional finding has actually been observed, it would be too expensive to make such checks in the SELECT TEST step, since for each current explanation the check should be done with respect to all the possible values of findings for which the explanation does not make any prediction. Some heuristics are then applied, as described in [9].

4.2 Focusing with compiled knowledge

Another feature of AID is the use of a focusing technique based on compiled knowledge. The idea of synthesizing heuristics from deep knowledge have been proposed in the last decade in the model-based reasoning community. On the one hand, in a seminal work [3] Chandrasekaran and Mittal theorized that the part of deep knowledge which is relevant for diagnosis can be compiled into a specialized heuristic problem solver. Such an idea has been followed, with important variations, by some researchers. In particular, in some cases the compilation is performed a-priori and after such a step the deep model is disregarded and only the compiled heuristic one is used for problem solving (see, e.g., [39], which uses model transformation techniques or [32], which uses inductive techniques). In other cases, the heuristic level is compiled and updated dynamically; suppose one has a partial heuristic level, a deep model and a problem to be solved: the heuristic level is applied first and, if it fails, the problem is solved at the deep level and the new heuristic rule learned from such a solution is used to extend the heuristic level. The approach has been suggested in [41] and, since then, many variations have been presented, e.g., in ACES [35] (in which "Explanation Based Learning Techniques" are adopted to learn new rules) or in CASEY [28] (which relies on the use of "Case based Reasoning").

The adoption of knowledge compilation gave rise to an interesting debate in the model-based diagnosis community: Randall Davis [20] argued against its use, pointing out that the content rather than the form of a knowledge base impacts problem solving efficiency and thus knowledge compilation is "either useless or impossible"; other researchers claimed that both the form and the content can be affected by the compilation process which can produce interesting advantages (see [25, 27]).

Our position is the following (see [6, 16] for more comments). We agree with Davis that it is not reasonable to compile an independent heuristic problem solver. It is, in fact, very difficult to compile all possible interactions among faults and, even if this can be done, then the resulting system would result at least as complex as the original one. If only part of the diagnostic competence is compiled into an incomplete but faster problem solver that can deal with some special cases, then such criticisms can be avoided. However, some problems have to be faced (also from a theoretical point of view) when trying to learn a rule by generalizing the solution of a specific problem.

For these reasons we decided to take a different approach in which compiled knowledge is used as a focusing component. In particular, we are interested in compiling "rule-out" conditions that can be easily evaluated on a diagnostic problem (they must be "operational", i.e., they must only involve data which are typically known in the early phases of diagnostic problem solving or that can be easily gathered) and which allow us to safely prune the search space for the abductive problem solver. By safely pruning we mean that we do not want to loose any solution but we only want to avoid useless search.

For this reason we concentrated the attention on the use of operational necessary conditions associated with the entities in the causal model: when such conditions are inconsistent with the data characterizing a diagnostic problem, then the corresponding entities can be safely pruned from the search space. In particular, in order to focus reasoning in AID, it is sufficient to consider the necessary conditions associated with instantiated states which have a common effect or manifestation. For example, consider the problem of explaining a instantiated state S having two alternative causes S_1 and S_2. A priori both causes should be considered; however, if the necessary condition associated with one of them (say S_2) is inconsistent with data, then such a state can be immediately excluded.

In many cases, necessary conditions allow us to discover the inconsistencies at a very early stage. In particular, such conditions allow us to compact many reasoning steps (which may involve a long chain of backward and forward search on the model) in the evaluation of a single formula.

The necessary conditions discussed above can be automatically synthesized from the causal model, by means of constraint propagation techniques and without relying on examples [16].

By taking into account compiled knowledge, the algorithm presented in section 4.1 can be modified as follows:

- In the EXPLAIN step, every time there is more than one choice in backward reasoning for explaining the same entity, the compiled conditions associated to the different choices are evaluated, and some states are possibly discarded. This could involve acquiring some easy-to-get data from the user.
- The selection of the most discriminating test mainly regards data that are more difficult to get. In this way the requests about such data are minimized.

4.3   An example

In this section we briefly illustrate an example of diagnostic problem and how it is dealt with by AID. Let us consider again the network in figure 1. In order to allow to completely follow the reasoning steps with the only aid of the figure, we assume here that the (unique) attribute of each STATE and INI-TIAL_CAUSE node has a unique value, which is an abnormal one. For example, the attributes of *incr_coolant_temp* and *coolant_leakage* have the unique value *severe*; such a value for *coolant_leakage* is associated with the value *severe* for *incr_coolant_temp* and the value *high* for *ext_temperature*. Therefore, the logical model of the network can be simplified without referencing to functions associated to actions, and contains for example the formula:

$$incr\_coolant\_temp(severe) \land ext\_temperature(high) \rightarrow coolant\_leakage(severe)$$

We assume moreover that the FINDING nodes have an attribute which can assume one "abnormality" value, which is the consequence of a state in the fault model, and a "normality" value, for which no cause is provided by the model. We consider as easy-to-get the findings corresponding to gauges and warning lights (*oil_warning_light* and *temp_indicator*) as well as *smoke_from_engine* and *engine_noise*.

Let us consider the diagnostic problem initially characterized by the following observations:

$$\Phi_A = \{acceler\_response(irregular)\}$$
$$\Phi_N = \emptyset$$

There are three alternative direct explanations of *mixture_ignition(irregular)*; suppose that *engine_temperature(high)* is selected first. This instantiated state has associated the necessary condition

$$temp\_indicator(red) \wedge oil\_warning\_light(on)$$

Since no value is known for the findings occurring in this formula, the value of *temp_indicator* is first asked. Suppose that the value *normal* is provided (i.e., *temp_indicator(normal)* is added to Φ_N): then *engine_temperature(high)* can be discarded. In this way, the search for the causes of *engine_temperature(high)*, as well as the determination of the consequences of such causes, can be avoided because all the portion of the network representing the causal evolution from the initial causes *piston_rings_state* and *road_condition* to the state *piston_melting* can be safely pruned. Without the use of compiled knowledge, a straightforward implementation of the logical definition of abductive diagnosis would require several backward and forward inference steps before recognizing that the causal evolutions involving *engine_temperature(high)* are not part of any solution. Therefore, the alternative causes are considered, and two explanations are found:

$$E_1 = \{carburettor\_tuning(irregular), \delta\}$$
$$E_2 = \{spark\_plugs\_mileage(high), \delta\}$$

where δ is the abstracted condition atom associated to the causal arc between *mixture_ignition* and *power_decrease*.

E_1 predicts both *gasoline_smell(intense)* and *gas_consumpt(high)*; E_2 does not predict by itself any *unknown* finding, while *gas_consumpt* is connected to *spark_plugs_mileage*, an instance of which is in E_2. Thus, *gasoline_smell* is selected as the most discriminating parameter to observe: actually, it is perfectly discriminating[11] since in case the abnormal value *intense* is provided, E_1 remains the unique minimal explanation, while if the value *normal* is provided, E_2 is the unique explanation.

4.4 Implementation

There are two Prolog implementations of AID: the one on Sun Workstations includes some of the interfaces developed for CHECK, in particular, NEED and

---

[11] As stated above, the actual choice is done on the basis of the *expected entropy* of the observable parameters; in this case the expected entropy of *gasoline_smell* is 0, while the expected entropy of *gas_consumpt* is greater than 0.

EXPL; a Macintosh implementation of the consultation system, which uses the menu facilities provided by MacProlog, has also been developed.

5 Discussion

AID can be considered as an exploration of an alternative way of combining heuristic and causal knowledge. However, a comparison between CHECK and AID is difficult since the two systems can be analyzed from different points of view. The first remark concerns the fact that in AID the problem of acquiring two knowledge bases and maintaining the consistency between the two is solved by means of the compilation of operational knowledge from the causal one. However, compiled knowledge in AID is different from heuristic knowledge because it does not necessarily capture the expertise of the human problem solver (derived from experience). In this way, operational knowledge does not contain in itself the control knowledge that can be put into the heuristic level of CHECK. In CHECK the heuristic level plays an important role in organizing diagnostic reasoning, in particular in the data acquisition strategy, and in focusing the diagnostic process. The designer of the heuristic knowledge base in CHECK has the possibility of significantly modifying the behavior of the system according to the amount of knowledge he/she puts in TRIGGERING and VALIDATION rules, while the designer of the causal knowledge base is mainly concerned with the domain theory rather than with control issues.

For this reason, we can conclude that the diagnostic strategy in AID is more rigid than the CHECK one. This could suggest that AID is more appropriate in technical domains where there is a reasonable amount of domain knowledge but the experience is scarce. On the other hand, the main advantage of AID (apart from the solution of the consistency problem between the heuristic and causal knowledge bases) is the clear formalization of solutions of diagnostic problems. Such a formalization is very relevant because it allowed us to use the same logical language not only to represent causal models capturing the faulty behaviors of a system, but also to capture behavioral models in which both the correct and the faulty behavior are represented [13]. More importantly, the same logical language that we used to denote causal models can be adopted for denoting component oriented models describing the structure of a device and the possible behavior of its components (i.e., the consequences of the different modes of behavior of the components). Moreover, the logical formalism allowed us to significantly extend the expressive power of the formalism. Some of such extensions are relevant for diagnostic reasoning, since we are able to include knowledge about the taxonomic relations among the faults. In this way we can have models both for very specific faults and very general ones, and the reasoning mechanism is able to determine the *least presumptive* explanations [11]. Other extensions of the logical formalism involving negation as failure are quite useful for capturing complex interactions among faults, blocking processes and similar [11]. Finally, the formalization allowed us to single out a spectrum of logical definitions of diagnosis and to compare such definitions at the knowledge level; in particular, in

[15] we showed that abduction corresponds to a stronger definition of diagnosis, it produces less solutions than a consistency-based definition and corresponds to a stronger notion of explanation. This is related to the fact that the form of abduction used in model-based diagnosis can be regarded as deduction in the completion of the domain theory [10].

A problem which has not yet found a completely satisfactory solution is the problem of diagnosing systems whose behavior evolve in time[12]. In recent years we have considered the problem of extending the causal model to include temporal information as well as the reasoning mechanisms for dealing with data that vary over time. The strict integration of abductive and temporal reasoning for diagnostic problem solving has resulted to be quite complex from a computational point of view [14]; therefore we recently investigated alternative approaches to the problem of diagnosing time-varying systems [7].

Acknowledgements

The authors are grateful to Prof. Gianpaolo Molino (Dipartimento di Biomedicina, Università di Torino) and to Prof. Armando Rocha (Universidad Estadual de Campinas, Brasil) for their useful insights on medical decision making, that have been taken into account in the definition of the CHECK architecture. The CHECK project was supported by Ministry of Public Education of Italy, Regione Piemonte and CNR. Work on the AID system has been mainly supported by "Progetto Finalizzato Sistemi Informatici e Calcolo Parallelo" of CNR under grants 89.00038.PF69, 90.00689.PF69 and 91.00916.PF69.

Several students of the University of Torino contributed to the implementation of CHECK; in recent times, Vincenzo Della Mea and Michela Vinci of the University of Udine developed some modules of AID and the MacProlog interfaces.

References

1. J.S. Aikins. Prototypical knowledge for expert systems. *Artificial Intelligence*, 20(2):163–210, 1983.
2. T. Bylander, D. Allemang, M. Tanner, and J. Josephson. The computational complexity of abduction. *Artificial Intelligence*, 49(1-3):25–60, 1991.
3. B. Chandrasekaran and S. Mittal. Deep versus compiled knowledge approaches to diagnostic problem-solving. *Int. J. of Man-Machine Studies*, 19(3):425–436, 1983.
4. W.J. Clancey. Heuristic classification. *Artificial Intelligence*, 25(3):289–350, 1985.
5. L. Console, M. Fossa, and P. Torasso. Acquisition of causal knowledge in the CHECK system. *Computers and Artificial Intelligence*, 8(4):323–345, 1989.
6. L. Console, L. Portinale, and D. Theseider Dupré. Focusing abductive diagnosis. In *Proc. 11th Int. Conf. on Expert Systems and Their Applications (Conf. on 2nd Generation Expert Systems)*, pages 231–242, Avignon, 1991. Also in *AI Communications* 4(2/3):88–97, 1991.

---

[12] It is worth noting that such a limitation is common to most of the other approaches to model-based diagnosis.

7. L. Console, L. Portinale, D. Theseider Dupré, and P. Torasso. Diagnostic reasoning across different time points. In *Proc. 10th ECAI*, Vienna, 1992.

8. L. Console, D. Theseider Dupré, and P. Torasso. A theory of diagnosis for incomplete causal models. In *Proc. 11th IJCAI*, pages 1311–1317, Detroit, 1989.

9. L. Console, D. Theseider Dupré, and P. Torasso. Introducing test theory into abductive diagnosis. In *Proc. 10th Int. Work. on Expert Systems and Their Applications (Conf. on 2nd Generation Expert Systems)*, pages 111–124, Avignon, 1990.

10. L. Console, D. Theseider Dupré, and P. Torasso. On the relationship between abduction and deduction. *Journal of Logic and Computation*, 1(5):661–690, 1991.

11. L. Console, D. Theseider Dupré, and P. Torasso. Towards the integration of different knowledge sources in model-based diagnosis. In *Lecture Notes in Computer Science 549*, pages 177–186. Springer Verlag, 1991.

12. L. Console and P. Torasso. Hypothetical reasoning in causal models. *International Journal of Intelligent Systems*, 5(1):83–124, 1990.

13. L. Console and P. Torasso. Integrating models of the correct behavior into abductive diagnosis. In *Proc. 9th ECAI*, pages 160–166, Stockholm, 1990.

14. L. Console and P. Torasso. On the co-operation between abductive and temporal reasoning in medical diagnosis. *Artificial Intelligence in Medicine*, 3(6):291–311, 1991.

15. L. Console and P. Torasso. A spectrum of logical definitions of model-based diagnosis. *Computational Intelligence*, 7(3):133–141, 1991.

16. L. Console and P. Torasso. An approach to the compilation of operational knowledge from causal models. *IEEE Trans. on Systems, Man and Cybernetics*, 22(3), 1992.

17. C. Cravetto, L. Lesmo, G. Molino, and P. Torasso. LITO2: a frame based expert system for medical diagnosis in hepatology. In I. De Lotto and M. Stefanelli, editors, *Artificial Intelligence in Medicine*, pages 107–119. North Holland, 1985.

18. J.M. David and J.P. Krivine. Designing KBS within functional architectures: the DIVA experiment. In *Proc. 5th IEEE Conference on Applications of Artificial Intelligence*, Miami, 1989.

19. R. Davis. Diagnostic reasoning based on structure and behavior. *Artificial Intelligence*, 24(1-3):347–410, 1984.

20. R. Davis. Form and content in model-based reasoning. In *Proc. 1989 Workshop on Model Based Reasoning*, pages 11–28, Detroit, 1989.

21. R. Davis and W. Hamscher. Model-based reasoning: Troubleshooting. In H.E. Shrobe, editor, *Exploring Artificial Intelligence*, pages 297–346. Morgan Kaufman, 1988.

22. J. de Kleer, A. Mackworth, and R. Reiter. Characterizing diagnoses. In *Proc. AAAI 90*, pages 318–323, Boston, 1990.

23. P. Fink, J. Lusth, and J. Duran. A general expert system design for diagnostic problem solving. *IEEE Trans. on Pattern Analysis and Machine Intelligence*, 7(5):553–560, 1985.

24. M.R. Genesereth. The use of design descriptions in automated diagnosis. *Artificial Intelligence*, 24(1-3):411–436, 1984.

25. A. Goel (ed.). Knowledge compilation: A symposium. *IEEE Expert*, 6(2):71–93, 1991.

26. G. Gorry and G. Barnett. Experience with a model of sequential diagnosis. *Comput. Biomedical Res.*, 1:490–507, 1968.

27. R. Keller. In defense of compilation. In *Proc. 1990 Workshop on Model-based Reasoning*, pages 22–31, Boston, 1990.

28. P. Koton. Using experience in learning and problem solving. Technical Report MIT/LCS/TR-441, MIT, Cambridge, MA, 1989.

29. L. Lesmo, L. Saitta, and P. Torasso. Computer aided evaluation of liver functional assessment. In *Proc. 4th Annual Symp. on Computer Applications in Medical Care*, pages 181–189, Washington, 1980.

30. L. Lesmo, L. Saitta, and P. Torasso. Learning of fuzzy production rules for medical diagnosis. In M.M. Gupta and E. Sanchez, editors, *Approximate Reasoning in Decision Analysis*, pages 249–260. North Holland, 1982.

31. L. Lesmo, L. Saitta, and P. Torasso. Evidence combination in expert systems. *Int. J. of Man-Machine Studies*, 22:307–326, 1985.

32. I. Mozetic. Diagnostic efficiency of deep and surface knowledge in KARDIO. *Artificial Intelligence in Medicine*, 2(2):67–83, 1990.

33. D. Partridge. The scope and limitation of first generation expert systems. *Future Generation Computer Systems*, 3(1):1–10, 1987.

34. R. Patil. Causal representation of patient illness for electrolyte and acid-base diagnosis. Technical Report LCS-267, MIT, Cambridge, MA, 1981.

35. M. Pazzani. Failure-driven learning of fault diagnosis heuristics. *IEEE Trans. on Systems, Man and Cybernetics*, 17(3):380–394, 1987.

36. D. Poole. Normality and faults in logic-based diagnosis. In *Proc. 11th IJCAI*, pages 1304–1310, Detroit, 1989.

37. J.A. Reggia, D.S. Nau, and P.Y. Wang. Diagnostic expert systems based on a set covering model. *Int. J. of Man-Machine Studies*, 19(5):437–460, 1983.

38. R. Reiter. A theory of diagnosis from first principles. *Artificial Intelligence*, 32(1):57–96, 1987.

39. V. Sembugamoorthy and B. Chandrasekaran. Functional representation of devices and compilation of diagnostic problem-solving systems. In J.L. Kolodner and C.R. Riesbeck, editors, *Experience, Memory and Reasoning*, pages 47–73. Lawrence Erlbaum, 1986.

40. R. Simmons. The roles of associational and causal reasoning in problem solving. *Artificial Intelligence*, 53(2-3):159–207, 1992.

41. L. Steels. Second generation expert systems. *Future Generation Computer Systems*, 1(4):213–221, 1985.

42. L. Steels and W. Van de Velde. Learning in second generation expert systems. In R. Kowalik, editor, *Knowledge-based Problem Solving*. Prentice Hall, 1985.

43. P. Torasso and L. Console. Approximate reasoning and prototypical knowledge. *International Journal of Approximate Reasoning*, 3(2):157–178, 1989.

44. P. Torasso and L. Console. *Diagnostic Problem Solving: Combining Heuristic, Approximate and Causal Reasoning*. Van Nostrand Reinhold, 1989.

45. D. Waterman and F. Hayes-Roth, editors. *Pattern-directed Inference Systems*. Academic Press, 1978.

46. S. Weiss, C. Kulikowski, S. Amarel, and A. Safir. A model based method for computer-aided medical decision making. *Artificial Intelligence*, 11(1-2):145–172, 1978.

Combining Causal Models
and Case-Based Reasoning

Phyllis A. Koton

Intellimation Intelligent Information Systems
7 Grove Street, Wayland, MA 01778, USA

Abstract. Associational reasoning solves common problems quickly. Model-based reasoning can be used to solve unfamiliar, unusual, or difficult problems, but it does so slowly. This paper describes a method for increasing the solution speed of model-based reasoning systems by remembering previous similar problems and making small changes to their solutions. This technique is known as case-based reasoning (CBR). If the CBR system were limited to solving only problems identical to those it had seen before, this technique would be nothing more than caching. However, by integrating a model-based component with CBR, a system can make model-based modifications to previous solutions to fit the details of similar but not identical problems. Only parts of the solution that depend on features which differ in the old and new problem must be modified. Therefore, the computational cost of arriving at the CBR solution is dependent on the magnitude of the difference between the new problem and the retrieved case, and not on the complexity of the problems themselves. For problems that are computationally expensive to solve, then, case-based reasoning has the potential to make a significant improvement in solution speed. The implementation of such a system for the domain of medical diagnosis is presented, and its extension to other domains is described.

1 Introduction

The vast majority of current expert systems rely on *associational* reasoning, associating data with solutions via heuristics, empirical associations, or "rules of thumb." An alternative approach, which solves problems by reasoning about a model of the behavior of objects in the domain, is known as *model-based reasoning* or *causal reasoning*. Human experts are able to use both associational and model-based reasoning. They recognize and quickly solve common problems, but can use more detailed causal knowledge when faced with novel or difficult problems. This section describes a methodology that combines associational reasoning and model-based reasoning to produce a system that is both efficient and robust.

Associational reasoning reduces long chains of inferences in the underlying knowledge to shorter, often uncertain, links between data and solutions. This approach has the advantage of efficiency, because the alternative of following all of the intermediate links and choosing among alternate paths in the problem space can be slow, and is often unnecessary. However, programs using associational reasoning have their limitations. Because such programs solve problems by matching the current situation against a set of predetermined situations, the knowledge base must *anticipate* situations that may arise. If the program is presented with an unanticipated, peripheral, or difficult problem, it may be unable to solve it [1] or worse, appear to solve it but yield a solution that is incorrect [5]. Also, associational knowledge typically must contain many implicit assumptions. For a complicated domain, it might be infeasible or impossible to explicitly enumerate the exact conditions under which the knowledge is applicable. Such systems, therefore, cannot ensure that their knowledge will be applied correctly.

Models provide a different kind of knowledge for reasoning in many domains. Knowledge about the domain that might be excluded from an associational reasoning system is often explicitly represented in the model. Models are typically combined with a general reasoning method, such as simulation or search, affording the model-based system more flexibility than an associational system for the same domain [2, 5, 10]. However, the more explicit knowledge and more general problem solving method creates longer inference chains. For this reason, model-based systems are slower, more complicated, and less widely employed than associational systems. Also, if the relationships in the model are uncertain, long inference chains may generate too much uncertainty to draw conclusions. Associational reasoning allows the relationships to be summarized at a manageable level of uncertainty.

2 Combining CBR and Causal Reasoning

Model-based and associational reasoning can be combined through use of a technique called *case-based reasoning* (CBR) [4]. Case-based reasoning is a problem-solving method that uses existing solutions to solve new problems. The set of existing solutions ("cases") is referred to as the case base. When presented with a new problem, a CBR system (1) recalls a previously-solved similar problem; (2) adapts its solution to fit the specifications of the current problem; and (3) stores the new problem and its solution. Case-based reasoning is clearly associational: features of a problem are associated with a solution to that problem.

Case-based reasoning is increasingly popular as an alternative to other associational reasoning systems (e.g., rule-based expert systems), but it is rarely been applied to domains with a strong causal model. The lack of an explicit causal model gives case-based reasoning programs the same problem seen in other associational reasoning systems: they cannot ensure that their knowledge will be applied correctly. The reason for this is that without an explicit causal model, case-based reasoning programs depend exclusively on coincidence in selecting similar previous problems and in making generalizations. A second problem, also seen in other associational reasoning systems, is that case based reasoners cannot solve problems that have not been anticipated (i.e., have not already been presented to the system).

Integrating model-based and case-based reasoning results in a program which has the strengths of each approach while compensating for their weaknesses. The model-based reasoning component solves complicated and unfamiliar problems, and releases the case-based component from its dependence on coincidence. The case-based reasoning component uses associational knowledge to recognize problems that the system can solve quickly. If no similar previous case is recalled, it serves as a signal that the problem is unfamiliar to the program and that model-based reasoning should be used. This paradigm makes *incremental* use of an explicit causal model of the domain. That is, rather than solving the entire problem using model-based reasoning, the method uses the full power of the causal model only when needed.

3 The Scope of the Method

In order to use the system presented here, a model must be representable as a *causal inference network* (Fig. 1).

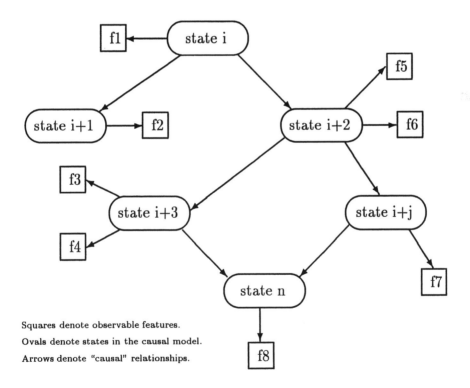

Squares denote observable features.
Ovals denote states in the causal model.
Arrows denote "causal" relationships.

Fig. 1. A causal inference network.

Formally, a model must provide the following information:

$\mathcal{S}$, a finite set of *states*.

$\mathcal{F}$, a finite set of *features* which can be observed, and are associated with states in $\mathcal{S}$.

$C \subseteq (\mathcal{S} \times \mathcal{F}) \cup (\mathcal{S} \times \mathcal{S})$. The relation C is often used to imply causality. In fact, it is not even necessary that the relation be causal. It is sufficient that $(s, f) \in C$ is associational and s temporally precede f (similarly for $(s_1, s_2) \in C$).

The problem presented to the system is then:

$\mathcal{F}^+ \subseteq \mathcal{F}$, some subset of the features which has been observed,

and the solution desired is:

$s \in \mathcal{S}$, a set of states which could have caused the observations.

This form of causal model is consistent with several reasoning tasks, such as diagnosis, interpretation, and monitoring.

There is a certain amount of overhead associated with case-based problem solving that comes from the time necessary to search the case memory for a precedent case. Call this cost C_s. The case-based problem solving paradigm assumes that

1. There is a means by which the similarity between two problems can be determined.
2. The amount of time taken to search the case memory for similar problems is small compared to the solution time of the underlying system. Let us call the average cost of solution in the underlying system C_u.
3. The cost to solve a problem via CBR, C_c, is proportional to the size of the difference between the two problems (see below for conditions for which this assumption holds).

Case-based problem solving can be applied to domains that meet the following criteria:

1. Similar problems recur. Case-based reasoning gains its efficiency from making changes to an existing solution. If the system is presented with a completely new problem (not similar to any it has solved before) it still incurs C_s, the cost of searching the case memory, even though the search will be fruitless. This is in the best case. In the worst case, the CBR system can recall cases that appear to be similar and expend some effort in modifying the precedent only to discover that the solution is incorrect. In this case, we have incurred a cost C_w (for cost of waste). In order for the benefits of case-based problem solving to outweigh the costs,

$$C_w \times P(no\ match) < (C_u - C_c) \times P(match).$$

2. The domain is stable under perturbations. Intuitively, problems that are only slightly different have solutions that are only slightly different. The difference between a new problem p and a precedent p' identifies σ, the subset of the solution to problem p', $S_{p'}$, that we must examine in order to obtain the solution to problem p, S_p. In order for the CBR solution to be efficient, $|\sigma| < |S_p|$. This will be the case when S_p is similar to $S_{p'}$. In unstable domains, usually S_p is not similar to S_p even if p is similar to p'. If the size of the *difference* of the solutions is almost the size of the solution itself, there is little leverage to be gained from making modifications, and the solution might as well be computed *de novo*.

3. Interactions are limited. Let the cost of computing the solution S_p to problem p be denoted as C_{S_p}. C_{S_p} is proportional to $|\sigma|$. In a solution which has no interactions between its elements, $C_{S_p} = \sum_i C_{\sigma_i}$, i.e., the cost of finding the solution to the new problem is the sum of the costs of making each change required by a difference between p, p'.

Whenever there is an interaction between elements of the solution, a small change cannot be treated locally. The elements that interact with the element that was modified must be examined to see if they too must be updated. If the model includes such interactions, the cost $C_{S_p} = \sum_i C_{\sigma_i} + I$, where I is the cost of checking the interactions. If the elements of the system being modeled are highly interdependent, the concept of incremental local changes is impossible, as a change in one place can cause changes in other parts of the solution, which in turn cause other changes, all of which must be tracked down and examined. The interaction term I in the cost function can grow quite large even if the original cost $\sum_i C_{\sigma_i}$ was small. Therefore case-based problem solving is most efficient in domains where interactions between elements of the domain model are limited.

4   Five Steps to Problem Solving

Problem solving in this system is a five-step process.

4.1   Retrieval

Problems that have been previously solved by the CBR system are stored, along with their solutions, in a self-organizing memory system [3]. When presented with a new problem, the CBR system finds a problem similar to the new problem in its case memory. This is called the *retrieved case*. Matching a new case to a previous case is based on features in the problem description that the two problems have in common. However, all features are not equally important in matching a new case to a previous case. Furthermore, the important features for matching may *vary* from case to case. Essentially, the important features are those that played a role in the causal explanation of previous similar cases. The CBR system's similarity metric allows the important features for matching to be determined for each retrieved case individually. It performs this determination using information in the causal model. The CBR system then compares the important features of the retrieved case with the features of the new case to determine similarity.

The retrieval process can use abstractions of features that appear in the problem description, as well as the actual features that occur. For further details, see [7].

4.2 Justification

The match between a new problem and a previously solved problem usually is only partial. There may be differences between the two cases that preclude using even a modified version of a retrieved solution for a new problem. The justification step proves that a retrieved solution can be supported by the features of the new problem. The CBR system evaluates the significance of any differences between the new case and the retrieved case using information in the causal model. If significant differences are found, the match is invalidated.

The justification process uses a set of domain-independent heuristics, termed *evidence principles*, for reasoning about differences between two problem descriptions. Every difference is one of exactly three types.

1. Some feature has a different value in the old and new case,
   A difference of type 1 is said to be insignificant if the two values are members of the same (domain-dependent) equivalence class, that is, whatever is derivable using one value is also derivable from the other. For example, a medical diagnosis system may consider *normal* temperature to be between 98.2 and 98.8, thus temperature(A, 98.6) and temperature(B, 98.3) is an insignificant difference.
2. Some feature in the new case is not present in the retrieved case,
   A difference of type 2 is said to be insignificant if the additional information is not adding anything new to what can be derived from the information already present in the retrieved case. A difference of type 2 is said to be repairable if the retrieved solution can be augmented to account for the additional information (i.e., by adding additional states to the description).
3. Some feature in the retrieved case is not present in the new case.
   A difference of type 3 is said to be insignificant if whatever was derivable from the missing proposition can be alternately derived using propositions in the new case. A difference of type 3 is said to be repairable if the part of the retrieved solution that accounts for the missing information can be removed, without affecting the causal support for the remaining portion of the solution.

If all differences between the new case and the retrieved case are judged insignificant or if the solution can be repaired to account for them, the match is said to be *justified*. The *precedent case* is a retrieved case that has been justified and from which solution transfer will occur. The *precedent solution* is the solution associated with the precedent case.

4.3 Adaptation

If none of the differences invalidate the match, the CBR system adapts a copy of the precedent solution to fit the new case. Associated with each type of repairable difference detected by the evidence principles is an explanation repair strategy which modifies the precedent solution to fit the details of the new case. If all matches are ruled out, or if no similar previous case is found, the system uses model-based reasoning to produce a solution for the case *de novo*. The changes that the system makes to the retrieved solution are limited and local to the difference being considered, and therefore they are computationally inexpensive. However, the CBR system also evaluates each change in the context of the entire solution. This prevents it from being oblivious to unwanted interactions that might be created by its changes.

4.4 Storage

The new case and its solution are stored in the CBR system's memory for use in future problem solving.[1]

4.5 Feature evaluation

Those features that were causally important in the solution of this problem are determined using information in the causal model, and are noted in the memory. Determining which features of the new problem were important to the solution helps the program make better matches in the future, because it allows the program to distinguish between extraneous and important features.

5 Evaluation of the method

The ideas developed for the CBR system were tested in a program, CASEY [7, 6], that solved problems in the domain of diagnosing patients with heart failure. As a complex real-world domain, medical decision making is particularly well-suited as a testbed for combining associational and model-based reasoning. Medical diagnosis involves an associational component as well as reasoning from causal models. Physicians start with a large basic and clinical science knowledge base. Then, the accumulation of cases seen over a physician's career improves his day-to-day problem-solving ability by accumulating associational knowledge. However, when a good physician confronts an unfamiliar problem he refers to his knowledge of pathophysiology – his causal model.

CASEY's performance was evaluated on two counts: *efficiency*, and *quality* of the solution. The program was tested on a set of 45 patients with symptoms of heart failure. Twenty of the cases represented patients with coronary artery disease or aortic stenosis. This set of test cases was specifically designed by a

---

[1] The user has the option of rejecting the system's solution, in which case model-based reasoning is used to produce a solution, which is then stored in memory.

physician for testing CASEY. The remaining 25 cases described patients with various causes of heart failure.

The quality of CASEY's solution was evaluated by comparing its output to the output of a model-based reasoning program (the Heart Failure [8]) for the same patient. CASEY and the Heart Failure program used the identical causal model. A solution was considered *successful* if it was identical to the Heart Failure program's solution. A solution was considered *satisfactory* if it was identical to the Heart Failure program's solution except for the features which CASEY could not explain. In these latter cases, CASEY had already performed most of the task of deriving the causal explanation, and the Heart Failure program could be used to incrementally account for the remaining features.

CASEY produced a solution identical to the Heart Failure program's solution in 14 out of the 45 test cases. It produced a satisfactory explanation for an additional 18 test cases. It gave up on six of the test cases, and produced an incorrect causal explanation for seven test cases. Of the twenty cases specifically chosen for testing CASEY, eleven were solved identically and nine were solved satisfactorily. None of theses were solved incorrectly or were unsolved. An examination of the test cases for which CASEY failed to reproduce even part of the Heart failure program's solution revealed that each one of these cases had a causal explanation that was completely different from any other patient in the memory. Even on these cases, CASEY could often produce part of the causal explanation, but could not account for the combination of features seen in the patient. CASEY failed to produce a solution in precisely those cases for which it had never seen a similar patient.

CASEY's efficiency was evaluated by comparing the number of model states it examined to the number states examined by the Heart Failure program for the same patient. CASEY always examined fewer states than the Heart Failure program by at least an order of magnitude, and often by two or three orders of magnitude.

6   Discussion

Cases that required relatively more effort by the CBR system to solve did not necessarily correspond to cases that the model-based reasoning program required relatively more effort to solve. Problems that can be solved quickly by the model-based reasoning program have features which are specific to only one (or a small number) of states. Problems that require more effort for the model-based reasoning program are those with many symptoms that are evidence for a large number of states, which generate a large number of possible explanations that must be evaluated. By contrast, a simple case for the CBR system is one in which there are few differences between the precedent and the new case. A difficult case for the CBR system is one in which many differences between the precedent and the new case must be analyzed. Therefore the computational cost of arriving at the model-based CBR solution is dependent only on the magnitude of the difference between the new problem and the retrieved case, and not on the complexity of the problems themselves. This results in the tremendous efficiency advantage of case-based reasoning systems. A consequence of this is that as the number of cases solved by the CBR system increases, it requires less effort to solve subsequent cases because it is more likely to find a close match. The model-based reasoning program, conversely, cannot increase its efficiency except by re-implementation.

7 Related Work

There have been a few previous attempts to combine associational reasoning with model-based reasoning. ABEL [9], a program for diagnosing acid-base and electrolyte disturbances, maintained a description of a patient's illness at five levels of detail. The least-detailed level represented associational knowledge and the more-detailed levels were used for model-based reasoning. However, rather than *choosing* when to solve a problem using associational reasoning and when to use model-based reasoning, ABEL always reasoned about the patient at every level of detail. GORDIUS [11] combined associational reasoning and reasoning from a causal model for hypothesis generation in the geology domain. It also was incapable of deciding when to use each type of knowledge. It always used its associational rules to generate hypotheses, and always used its causal model to test proposed hypotheses.

8 Conclusion

We have described a CBR system that integrates associational and model-based reasoning in a program which is efficient in solving commonly-seen problems, while maintaining the ability to reason using a detailed causal model of the domain when necessary. The system overcomes the speed limitation of model-based reasoning by remembering a previous similar case and making incremental small changes to its solution, guided by information in the causal model. The methods used by the system are domain-independent and should be generally applicable in other domains with models of a similar form.

References

1. Davis, R. Expert systems: where are we? and where do we go from here? AI Magazine, **3**:2 (1982) 3–22
2. Davis, R. Diagnostic reasoning based on structure and behavior. Artificial Intelligence, **24** (1984) 347–410
3. Kolodner, J. Maintaining organization in a dynamic long-term memory. Cognitive Science, **7** (1983) 243–280
4. Kolodner, J., Simpson, R., Sycara-Cyranski, K. A process model of case-based reasoning in problem solving. In *Proceedings of the National Conference on Artificial Intelligence*, American Association for Artificial Intelligence (1985) 284–290

5. Koton, P. Empirical and model-based reasoning in expert systems. In *Proceedings of the Ninth International Joint Conference on Artificial Intelligence* (1985) 297–299

6. Koton, P. Reasoning about evidence in causal explanations. In *Proceedings of the National Conference on Artificial Intelligence*, American Association for Artificial Intelligence (1988)

7. Koton, P. *Using Experience in Learning and Problem Solving.* PhD thesis, Massachusetts Institute of Technology (1988)

8. Long, W., Naimi, S., Criscitiello, M, Jayes,R. The development and use of a causal model for reasoning about heart failure. In *Symposium on Computer Applications in Medical Care*, IEEE (1987) 30–36

9. Patil, R. *Causal representation of patient illness for electrolyte and acid-base diagnosis.* TR 267, Massachusetts Institute of Technology, Laboratory for Computer Science, 545 Technology Square, Cambridge, MA, 02139 (1981)

10. Simmons, R., Davis, R. Generate, test, and debug: combining associational rules and causal models. In *Proceedings of the Tenth International Joint Conference on Artificial Intelligence* (1987) 1071–1078

11. Simmons, R. *Generate, Test, and Debug: A Paradigm for Solving Interpretation and Planning Problems.* PhD thesis, Massachusetts Institute of Technology (1988)

Generate, Test and Debug: A Paradigm for Combining Associational and Causal Reasoning

Reid Simmons

School of Computer Science
Carnegie Mellon University
Pittsburgh, PA 15213

Abstract. Efficiency and robustness are two desirable, but often conflicting, goals of problem solvers. This paper examines how a combination of associational and causal reasoning can be used to achieve both goals. We describe the Generate, Test and Debug (GTD) paradigm, which uses associational reasoning to solve most problems efficiently, while relying on causal reasoning to maintain overall robustness. The problem-solving characteristics of associational and causal reasoning are presented, based on an analysis of the types of knowledge and reasoning used in GTD. In particular, we argue that the characteristics depend largely on the extent to which interactions between events are represented and reasoned about — associational reasoning is efficient because it uses rules that (nearly) encapsulate interactions, while causal reasoning is robust because it analyzes the effects of events and their interactions.

1 Introduction

Two desirable characteristics of problem solvers are efficiency and robustness (the ability to solve a wide range of problems). These characteristics are often in conflict, however. In particular, the following claims are often made about systems that use associational reasoning (exemplified by rule-based expert systems) and causal (or model-based) reasoning systems:

1. Associational systems usually perform well within their area of expertise, but they are *brittle* (i.e., their expertise is limited).
2. Causal reasoning systems can handle a wide range of problems, but they are computationally inefficient.

This paper discusses the rationale for these claims in the context of the Generate, Test and Debug problem-solving paradigm. GTD first uses associational reasoning to generate initial hypotheses, which are then tested to see if they are correct; the debugger analyzes detailed causal explanations to determine how to repair faulty hypotheses.

GTD combines the best features of associational and causal reasoning systems: using associational reasoning to solve most problems efficiently, while maintaining robustness by relying on causal reasoning to test and debug incorrect hypotheses. Our work in developing GTD has led to a greater understanding of why associational reasoning is often an efficient problem-solving method, and why causal reasoning tends to be more robust.

Associational reasoning techniques work by associating observable features of the problem with their solution. For example, the observation that one sedimentary formation is on top of another can be associated with the likely interpretation that the upper formation was deposited on top of (and after) the lower one. In contrast, causal reasoning techniques solve problems by reasoning about the relationships between objects and behaviors of events over time. For example, given the same two sedimentary formations as above, plus a model of deposition indicating that deposition always happens from above (adding material along the surface of the earth), causal reasoning can conclude that to end up one on top of the other, the lower formation must already have existed on the surface at the time the upper one was deposited. Hence, the upper formation must have been created later. Simply put, associational reasoning solves problems by recognition, while causal reasoning solves them by analysis.

The central argument of this paper is that the extent to which associational and causal reasoning deal with interactions gives them nearly opposite characteristics — efficient but brittle, versus robust but slow. Associational reasoning is both efficient and brittle since it presumes its rules can be combined (nearly) independently, and so does not perform detailed checks for interactions. Causal reasoning is both robust and slow because it explicitly checks for interactions using detailed models of the structure and behavior of the domain.

These differing characteristics indicate that the reasoning techniques are best suited for different aspects of the problem-solving task. The GTD paradigm first uses associational reasoning, under the presumption that its associational rules are sufficiently independent to produce correct hypotheses most of the time. Causal reasoning is reserved to focus on those problems not handled correctly by the associational reasoner. The presumption here is that the hypotheses are nearly correct, so only a small amount of time-consuming, detailed causal reasoning will be needed to debug them into solutions.

2   The Generate, Test and Debug Paradigm

The GTD paradigm was developed to solve planning and interpretation problems, both of which are of the form: "given an initial state and a final (goal) state, hypothesize a set of events that could achieve the goal state, starting from the initial state." The paradigm, which is described in more detail in [9] and [11], has been implemented in a system called GORDIUS and has been tested for several interpretation and planning tasks. The primary task has been geologic interpretation, where the problem is to come up with a set of events that could explain how a given geologic region was formed. We have also used GORDIUS to do blocks-world planning and to solve Tower of Hanoi problems. In addition, parts of the Test and Debug stages have been used to do mobile-robot planning and to help diagnose manufacturing faults in semiconductor fabrication [13].

The GTD paradigm iteratively refines hypotheses. Hypotheses (e.g., Fig. 2b) are represented by the types of events that occur and constraints on the parameter bindings and temporal orderings of the events. Solutions are hypotheses that correctly account for how the goal state could have arisen, starting from the initial state. Although the problems we have considered may have many possible solutions, the task addressed here is to find just one plausible solution.

The control flow of the GTD paradigm is illustrated in Fig. 1. GTD first uses associational reasoning to generate an initial hypothesis from descriptions of the initial and final states of the problem. The hypothesis is then tested by simulating the hypothesized events. If the test succeeds (i.e., the final state of the simulation matches the goal state), the hypothesis is accepted as a solution. If it fails, a causal explanation is constructed for why the failure was detected, and the hypothesis is debugged to eliminate discrepancies. The repaired hypothesis is then resubmitted for testing, and the debug/test loop continues until the test succeeds. Alternatively, if the debugger appears to be moving far from a solution, the generator may be re-invoked to produce a new hypothesis.

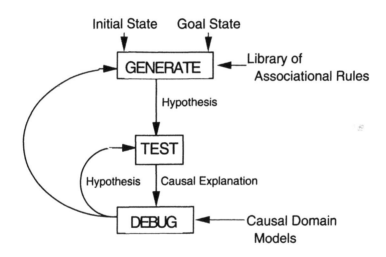

Fig. 1. Control flow of GTD paradigm

The efficacy of this control strategy depends on presumptions that: 1) the generator efficiently produces hypotheses that are correct, or nearly so, for most problems 2) the tester is accurate enough to detect incorrect hypotheses, and 3) the debugger is robust enough to repair any bugs detected by the tester. To help satisfy these presumptions, each stage of GTD uses different types of knowledge and reasoning techniques.

The generation stage uses associational knowledge and a "match and combine" reasoning technique to produce initial hypotheses. A library of domain-specific rules is employed that associate patterns in the initial and final states with events that plausibly explain how the patterns could be achieved. In the geologic domain, for instance, the pattern of an igneous rock surrounded by two rocks of the same composition is associated with the likely interpretation that it arose from the igneous rock intruding (pushing) through an existing rock, splitting it in two (Fig. 3). The rules are matched against the initial and final states of the problem to find applicable interpretations.

Note that each rule explains how only part of the goal state could have arisen. To create a complete hypothesis, the generator combines the interpretations from several rules. In combining interpretations, the generator presumes that the events associated with one rule do not interfere with the achievement of the patterns of other rules. Under this presumption of independence, hypotheses can be constructed in time linearly proportional to the number of goals.

The testing stage uses a combination of simulation techniques to determine if a hypothesis solves the problem. GORDIUS uses detailed qualitative and quantitative simulations to determine whether hypothesized events actually achieve the goal state [7]. A qualitative, causal simulator is used to predict the effects of events. It updates representations of the objects in the domain using models that declaratively represent the preconditions and effects of events. For example, the model of erosion states that it must occur above sea-level, and that it affects formations by removing material from along the surface of the earth. From this, the simulator can infer which formations get affected and how their thicknesses change as a result of an erosion event.

An additional, quantitative diagrammatic simulation is used for the geologic domain to predict the spatial effects of events more accurately. The diagrammatic simulator constructs a sequence of diagrams that reflect geometric and topological changes to the geologic objects. This is needed because the spatial information contained in the causal models is at too abstract a level to enable all the relevant interactions between objects to be detected. For example, while the causal models encode topological relationships between objects, they do not model the shape of objects very well.

To repair bugs found by the tester, the debugging stage uses causal knowledge and reasoning techniques to modify hypotheses. Causal dependency structures are constructed to explain why the test failed — the dependency structures link the effects of events to their manifestations in the simulated state. The debugger uses three different reasoning techniques in conjunction with the dependency structures to repair bugs: 1) it traces through the dependency structures to locate the assumptions that underlie the explanations for why the bugs arose, 2) it regresses values in the goal state back through the dependencies to indicate desired values that need to be achieved, and 3) it uses domain-independent repair strategies that reason about how to replace faulty assumptions with ones that can achieve the desired values.

For example, suppose the desired orientation of some formation S1 is $12°$, while the tester predicts that the hypothesis "first deposit S1 horizontally, tilt all formations by $12°$, then tilt again by $5°$" will produce an orientation of $17°$. The causal dependency structure produced indicates that one of the assumptions underlying the bug is that the parameter of the first tilt event is assumed to be 12°. The general repair strategy for replacing assumptions about faulty parameter values is to change the parameter to a value that fixes the bug. The correct value is determined by regressing the desired orientation of 12° back through the causal explanation for the bug. This process indicates that changing the parameter value from 12° to $(12 - 5)°$ will repair the bug.

The debugger determines how each proposed bug repair interacts with the hypothesis as a whole by estimating the number of bugs remaining in the hypothesis. The estimation technique is similar to the causal simulation used by the tester, but is somewhat less complete and hence less computationally expensive.

3 A Geologic Interpretation Example

An example from geologic interpretation illustrates the various reasoning techniques used in GTD. The task of geologic interpretation is to hypothesize a set of events that can plausibly explain how a geologic region was formed, given a vertical cross-section of the region.

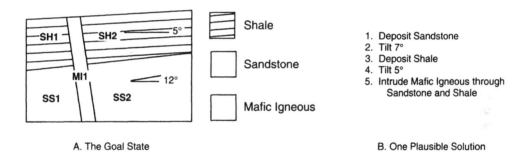

A. The Goal State   B. One Plausible Solution

Fig. 2. Typical geologic interpretation problem

The cross-section (the problem's goal state) describes topological, geometric, and compositional aspects of the region. It is shown schematically as a two-dimensional diagram with a legend identifying the rock types (Fig. 2a). The initial state, which is the same for all geologic interpretation problems we considered, consists simply of bedrock under the sea-level.

GORDIUS begins by matching its library of rules against the goal diagram (the cross-section), combining matching rules to generate an initial hypothesis. The rules, which we call *scenarios*, are heuristics that associate observable patterns in the goal and initial states with sets of events, called *local interpretations*, that could have produced the patterns. For example, the "intrudes-through" scenario (Fig. 3), is used to recognize an igneous formation intruding into an existing rock formation. The scenario pattern (Fig. 3a) matches parts of a diagram where an igneous rock is between two rocks of the same composition, and where the boundaries of the rocks are parallel. One match in Fig. 2 occurs where **MI1** is between **SH1** and **SH2**.

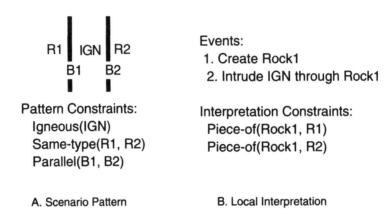

Events:
1. Create Rock1
2. Intrude IGN through Rock1

Pattern Constraints:
Igneous(IGN)
Same-type(R1, R2)
Parallel(B1, B2)

Interpretation Constraints:
Piece-of(Rock1, R1)
Piece-of(Rock1, R2)

A. Scenario Pattern   B. Local Interpretation

Fig. 3. Schematic of "intrudes-through" scenario

The local interpretation of a scenario describes the events that formed the pattern: the types of the events, their parameter bindings, temporal orderings between events (which may include partial orderings), and the objects that are related via a piece-whole hierarchy. The local interpretation of the "intrudes-through" scenario (Fig. 3b) indicates that one event creates formation **Rock1** (where **R1** and **R2** are pieces of **Rock1**), which is followed by an intrusion event that creates the igneous formation **IGN**.

In combining local interpretations, the generator must deal, in an appropriate manner, with events and objects that appear in different interpretations. For example, matching the "intrudes-through" scenario where **MI1** is between **SH1** and **SH2** indicates that a mafic-igneous intrusion occurred, splitting an existing shale formation in two. The scenario also matches where **MI1** is between **SS1** and **SS2**, indicating that a mafic-igneous intrusion split an existing sandstone formation. The generator then *unifies* the intrusion events — it infers that they must be the same event — since they both purport to create **MI1**, and the system knows that each unique object can be created by only a single event.

In this example, applications of the "tilted-sedimentary" scenario (Fig. 6) are used to infer that the sedimentary formations (shale and sandstone) were formed by horizontal deposition followed by a tilt event, where the magnitude of the tilt parameter is assumed to equal the orientation of the formation. Finally, the "sedimentary-over-rock" scenario is used to infer that the shale formation was deposited on top of (and later than) the existing sandstone formation.

This initial hypothesis is then tested. To make testing more efficient, GORDIUS first simplifies the hypothesis by choosing one of the totally ordered sequences consistent with it (Fig. 4). This is a reasonable simplification because our task is to produce one plausible interpretation: if the wrong linearization is chosen, the debugger can be used to repair the choice by reordering events.

1. Deposit1 Sandstone
2. Tilt1 12°
3. Deposit2 Shale
4. Tilt2 5°
5. Intrude1 Mafic Igneous through Sandstone and Shale

Fig. 4. Initial hypothesis produced by the generator (linearized by the tester)

Testing begins with a causal, qualitative simulation. For each hypothesized event, the tester checks whether its preconditions hold in the current (simulated) state of the world. If so, the simulator updates the world state by changing the values of object attributes to reflect the effects of the event. The causal simulator explicitly represents and reasons about time and the existence and persistence of objects. It also records dependencies that represent how the values of attributes depend on one another and on the events that occur. These dependencies are essential for debugging hypotheses (see below).

Since no inconsistencies are detected during the causal simulation of Fig. 4, an additional diagrammatic simulation is run to test the hypothesis in more detail. The diagrammatic simulator works by constructing a series of diagrams that represent the spatial effects of the geologic events. For example, to simulate the effects of erosion, a line is constructed in the diagram at the level of erosion and all pieces of objects that lie above the line are eliminated; the line then represents the new surface of the earth.

The final simulation diagram is then compared with the cross-sectional goal diagram (Fig. 2). In comparing the diagrams, GORDIUS discovers several bugs — one of which is that the orientation of **SS1** is 12° in the goal diagram, but 17° in the simulation diagram.

The debugger uses the dependencies recorded by the simulation to construct a causal dependency structure (outlined in Fig. 5) that explains how the bug arose. The debugger traces back through the dependencies to locate the assumptions that underlie the bug, two of which (the boxed statements in Fig. 5) are: 1) the assumption that the tilt parameter of the **Tilt1** event was 12°, and 2) the closed-world assumption that the orientation of **SS1** persisted from the end of the **Tilt2** event to the current time.

The debugger uses domain-independent repair strategies to replace faulty assumptions [8]. As described in the previous section, the repair strategy for

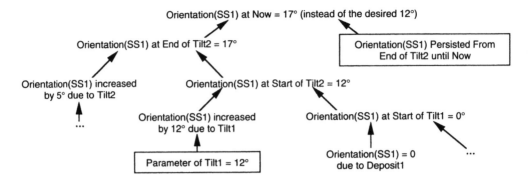

Fig. 5. Causal dependency structure for the bug that the orientation of **SS1** is not $12°$

faulty parameter-value assumptions is to replace the parameter value with one that will fix the bug. By regressing the desired value of $12°$ back through the dependencies, the debugger finds that the value for **Tilt1**'s parameter should be $(12 - 5) = 7°$.

The debugger also considers replacing the persistence assumption that nothing changed the orientation of **SS1** after **Tilt2**. The general strategy for repairing faulty persistence assumptions is to add an event that negates the assumption, in particular, to add an event during the time of the persistence which affects the attribute that is assumed to be persisting. The debugger examines its models of the geologic events and determines that, in this case, adding a new tilt event after **Tilt2** will change the orientation of **SS1**. By regressing values, the debugger determines that the parameter of this tilt event should be $-5°$ (the difference between the desired value of $12°$ and the current value of $17°$).

The debugger then evaluates the suggested repairs (and there are several others for this example) to determine how they affect the hypothesis as a whole. It determines that changing the parameter value of **Tilt1** is a potential solution, but that adding a new tilt event of $-5°$ introduces additional bugs — namely that the orientations of **SH1** and **SH2** are no longer correct. The debugger thus prefers the first repair, producing the modified hypothesis show in Fig. 2b. This hypothesis is then submitted to the tester for verification. In this case, both the causal and diagrammatic simulations succeed, so GORDIUS concludes that Fig. 2b is indeed one plausible interpretation for the problem of Fig. 2a.

4   Achieving Efficiency and Robustness

The problem-solving paradigm described here — using associational reasoning to generate (nearly) correct hypotheses, while using causal reasoning, when necessary, to do debugging — has a rich history in AI (e.g., [3, 4, 5, 15]). Our work has extended this line of research by 1) developing a domain-independent theory of debugging [8], 2) developing multiple specialized representations for reasoning about physical changes [7, 10], and 3) carefully analyzing the problem-solving characteristics of associational and causal reasoning techniques [11]. The latter point is the focus of this section.

Our claim is that associational reasoning tends to be efficient, while causal reasoning tends to be robust. This difference can be explained largely in terms of the extent to which the different techniques reason about *interactions* between events. An interaction occurs when one event influences how, or whether, another event affects the state of the world. Events that do not interact are said to be *independent*. Dealing with interactions has proven to be important not only in planning and interpretation problems, but for various other tasks as well, such as diagnosis [13] and design [17].

Interactions come in several forms, including interactions that interfere with one another, and interactions that cooperate in achieving a goal. For example, in the standard blocks-world domain (e.g., [6, 15]) putting one block on top of another interferes with (prevents) the subsequent movement of the lower block. Examples of cooperative interactions occur in the geologic domain, for instance, where uplift and erosion cooperate to affect sedimentary formations: the uplift raises the formation above sea-level, where the erosion can have an effect.

The efficient behavior of associational reasoning stems from using knowledge (rules/scenarios) that *encapsulate* interactions. A rule that encapsulates interactions is one in which the events within the rule interact cooperatively to achieve a set of goals, and events outside the rule are independent with respect to the achievement of those goals. In the blocks-world domain, for instance, the scenario "to achieve $On(x, y)$ and $On(y, z)$, put y on z, then put x on y" encapsulates the interaction that first putting x on y would interfere with subsequently putting y on z.

An important aspect of using encapsulated scenarios is that they are *composable*, that is, problems can be solved by solving subproblems independently and then conjoining their solutions. Composability has direct bearing on the ability of systems that use associational reasoning to solve problems efficiently, since solving each subproblem independently reduces the need for computationally expensive search [14]. In the best case, where the rules are totally independent, problems can be solved in linear time with respect to the number of goals in the problem.

For example, we can construct a plan for achieving $On(B, C)$, $On(C, D)$ and $On(A, B)$ by twice using the blocks-world scenario above. One application produces the fragment "put C on D, then put B on C" and the second application yields "put B on C, then put A on B." By unifying the two occurrences of "put B on C" (i.e., assuming that they represent the same event), GORDIUS comes up with the solution "put C on D; put B on C; put A on B." Simply combining the fragments produces a correct solution because each instantiation of the blocks-world scenario is independent from one another.

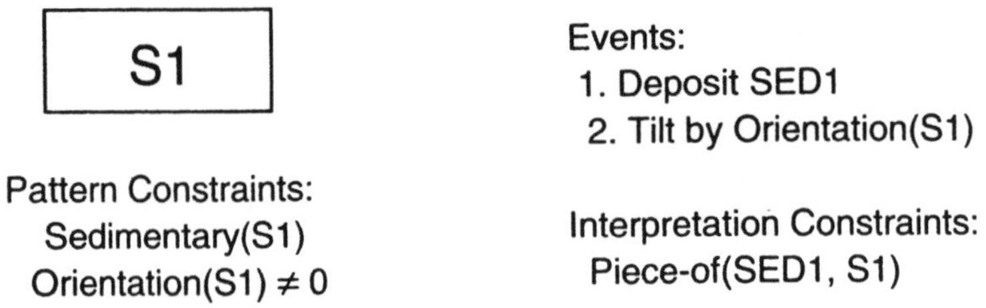

```
┌─────────────────┐
│       S1        │
└─────────────────┘
```

Pattern Constraints:
Sedimentary(S1)
Orientation(S1) ≠ 0

Events:
1. Deposit SED1
2. Tilt by Orientation(S1)

Interpretation Constraints:
Piece-of(SED1, S1)

Fig. 6. The "tilted-sedimentary" scenario

Unfortunately, in complex domains it is often impossible to produce encapsulated rules that are completely independent of one another. Using encapsulated rules that are not independent tends to make a problem solver brittle because 1) the composed solution might not achieve all the goals due to interactions (unintended side-effects), and 2) the rules, being abstractions, might omit details that are crucial to solving a particular problem. For example, as illustrated in Sect. 3, the "tilted-sedimentary" scenario (Fig. 6) is not independent in situations in which there are two sedimentary formations, each tilted at a different angle. Applying the scenario twice results in a faulty interpretation since the tilt event in one local interpretation changes (interferes with) the orientation of the formation that is being created by the other local interpretation.

Thus, associational reasoning is correct to the extent that the encapsulations are, in fact, independent. We believe that part of the difficulty in creating rule-based expert systems, in general, stems from the difficulty in choosing modularizations of knowledge in which interactions are encapsulated to form (nearly) independent sources of knowledge. One way of increasing independence is to create scenarios that have wider scope, for instance, creating a scenario whose pattern matches *two* sedimentary formations each oriented at a different angle. In the end this strategy is futile, however, since in most complex domains there will always be unanticipated interactions.

Given the fact that, in general, scenarios will not be totally independent, it might at first seem desirable to check for unexpected interactions when combining local interpretations (rather than waiting for the test phase), since unprofitable lines of search may be terminated early if it can be shown that they interfere. Unfortunately, checking for interactions is computationally very expensive. Thus, a cost/benefit trade-off exists between the expense of detecting interactions and the desire to prune the search space as early as possible. The response to this trade-off advocated by the GTD paradigm is to supply the generator with scenarios that encapsulate *common patterns of interaction*, that is, encapsulating those interactions that one expects will occur frequently in solving problems in the given domain. The GTD paradigm then relies on the causal reasoning of the debugger to handle any residual interactions.

In contrast to associational reasoning, causal reasoning achieves robustness by explicitly representing and reasoning about interactions in the domain. This is accomplished by using explicit (declarative) models of objects and events in the domain and of how the world works. The GORDIUS system uses models of events that reflect the preconditions and effects of events, models of objects that represent the fact that they exist and change over time, and a model of the world that explicitly represents time, the effects of change, and the persistence of objects over time [10].

These causal models are used in several ways in GORDIUS. The simulator uses them in testing hypotheses to predict the effects of events and to justify causal dependencies between objects and events. The causal models are also used by the debugger, particularly by its repair strategies. The repair strategies determine how to modify hypotheses using a general understanding of how objects change over time, and a specific understanding of how the domain-dependent event models can effect such changes.

Just as the success of associational reasoning depends on the extent to which the encapsulations are independent, the success of causal reasoning depends on the extent to which one can accurately and completely model the domain. By using a detailed, causal understanding of how events interact and by analyzing detailed domain models, causal reasoning can potentially solve a wider range of problems than can associational reasoning, which assumes that subproblems can be solved independently. For example, by reasoning about the cumulative effect of changes, the debugger can hypothesize that a sequence of tilt events, rather than a single event, accounts for the orientation of a formation.

All this added power comes with a high computational cost — in general, the cost of determining how events interact is exponential in the number of events [2]. In addition, because causal reasoning is typically performed at a greater level of detail, techniques that use causal reasoning tend to search larger, more richly connected, search spaces than do techniques that rely on associational reasoning.

In short, the extent to which associational and causal reasoning deal with interactions gives them nearly opposite characteristics — efficient but brittle, versus robust but slow. These differing characteristics indicate that the reasoning techniques are best suited for different roles in solving problems: associational reasoning is used first, under the presumption that the scenarios are sufficiently independent to produce correct hypotheses most of the time; causal reasoning is reserved to focus on those problems not handled correctly by the associational reasoner. The GTD paradigm takes advantage of these different strengths to achieve an overall system that exhibits a high degree of performance (efficiency) and competence (robustness).

As mentioned before, some researchers have used associational and causal reasoning in a similar manner to that of GTD (e.g., [3, 4]). Others have utilized these reasoning techniques in different ways, such as using associational reasoning to prune a causal search space [16], and enabling systems to freely intermingle associational and causal reasoning [1]. The analysis presented here suggests that such efforts may not be taking best advantage of the strengths of the various reasoning techniques.

Although the techniques used in associational and causal reasoning are very different, there is a close relationship between the types of knowledge used. In particular, scenarios represent both an abduction and an abstraction of the domain models used by the causal reasoner.

Abduction transforms valid statements of the form "**A** causes **B**" into heuristics of the form "if **B** is observed, then **A** may have caused it." Abduction is only heuristic because it implicitly presumes that **A** is the sole cause of **B**, which may not be true. In an attempt to handle situations where the abduction is not valid, the GORDIUS generator heuristically prefers scenarios with more specific patterns (i.e., those that explain more of the problem) and interpretations that have fewer events (following Occam's razor).

Besides encoding abductions, scenarios abstract away various types of information present in causal domain models. For one, they abstract away the effects of events that do not interact with one another. As a result, scenario patterns typically contain a small subset of the effects that can be predicted using the causal models. For example, the "intrudes-through" scenario (Fig. 3), which deals with the interactions of an intrusion and a single formation, ignores effects explicitly included in the causal models, such as how the intrusion affects other formations and how it changes the appearance of the surface of the earth. While this abstraction makes scenario patterns easier to match, due to the smaller number of effects encoded, its use might lead to the generation of incorrect hypotheses in situations where the missing effects are important.

Scenarios also abstract away chains of causal reasoning (e.g., prediction or search) used in solving problems. For example, it often involves a fair amount of search to find a set of events that achieves one goal without interfering with the achievement of other goals. By abstracting away this search into a single rule, associational reasoning can avoid the expense in similar situations. One consequence of this abstraction is that debugging becomes more time-consuming, since the reasoning steps must be reconstructed in order to obtain the dependency information needed to modify faulty hypotheses [3, 4]. Another consequence is a lack of flexibility, since scenarios are limited to situations in which the same task and domain models apply. For example, rules useful in performing a diagnostic task are usually not applicable for design or planning tasks.

5 Conclusions

The adage "in the knowledge lies the power" is often used in describing associational, rule-based systems. Our analysis shows that the truth of this adage stems mainly from the fact that associational reasoning is quite weak, so most of the power must come from the knowledge (rules/scenarios) used. In contrast, causal, model-based systems rely to a larger extent on their ability to reason about how the world works, in particular, how objects and events interact over time. The main source of power in such systems derives from the reasoning techniques used. These "equations of power" (associational = knowledge; causal = reasoning) follow directly from our analysis of the extent to which the techniques deal with interactions.

There are a number of crucial presumptions underlying the GTD paradigm and, we contend, most second generation expert systems. Foremost is the presumption that the knowledge needed for solving problems can be modularized into nearly independent pieces. Second, it is presumed that connections exist between the ontologies used by the various reasoning techniques: in our case, hypotheses produced by the generator must be understandable by the debugger. This is handled in GORDIUS by using a common vocabulary of objects, events, parameters, and temporal orderings.

Finally, the efficiency of the overall GTD paradigm depends on the presumption that the hypothesis created by the generator is nearly correct. If this presumption is wrong, the debugger could take a very long time to modify the hypothesis into a correct solution (at worst, it might have to completely replace all the events in the generated hypothesis with a totally new set of events). To avoid this, GORDIUS heuristically estimates how close a hypothesis is to being correct, based on the number of remaining bugs. If it estimates that the debugger is far from a solution, the generator is invoked to produce a new hypothesis.

In summary, we have presented the Generate, Test and Debug paradigm, which was designed to solve interpretation and planning problems. GTD combines the strengths, and compensate for the weaknesses, of associational and causal reasoning. Associational reasoning is used to efficiently generate (nearly) correct hypotheses, which are then tested using a combination of simulation techniques. GTD maintains robustness of the overall system by using causal reasoning to debug incorrect hypotheses by replacing faulty assumptions.

We use the concepts of interactions, independence, and encapsulation of knowledge to explain several observations about the efficiency and robustness of associational and causal reasoning techniques. Associational reasoning uses composable, abstract rules to solve problems efficiently. It produces correct solutions to the extent that the rules are, in fact, independent encapsulations. Causal reasoning, on the other hand, can solve a wider range of problems by explicitly representing and reasoning about the effects of events and how they interact. This combination of reasoning techniques enables the GTD paradigm to overcome much of the brittleness and slow problem-solving behavior inherent in systems that rely on only one type of reasoning technique.

6 Acknowledgements

This paper is an updated version of one entitled "Using associational and causal reasoning to achieve efficiency and robustness in problem solving" that appeared in the IMACS Transactions on Scientific Computing — '88. The research described here was performed while the author was a PhD student at the Artificial Intelligence Laboratory, Massachusetts Institute of Technology, and was sup-

92

ported in part by Schlumberger and the Advanced Research Projects Agency of the Department of Defense under Office of Naval Research contract N00014-85-K-0124. The work benefited from the insights and comments of many people, including my advisor Randy Davis, Walter Hamscher, Drew McDermott, Chuck Rich, Peter Szolovits, Kris Hammond, Marty Tennenbaum, and Reid Smith.

References

1. Chandrasekaran, B.: Towards a functional architecture for intelligence based on generic information processing tasks. Proc. IJCAI-87, Milan, Italy (1987)
2. Chapman, D.: Planning for conjunctive goals. Artificial Intelligence **32** (1987) 333–377
3. Hammond, K.: Case-Based Planning: Viewing Planning as a Memory Task. Academic Press, (1989)
4. Koton, P.: Combining causal models and case-based reasoning. in Second Generation Expert Systems, David, Krivine and Simmons (eds.), Springer Verlag (1993)
5. Rich, C. and Waters, R.: Abstraction, inspection and debugging in programming. MIT AI Memo 634 (1981)
6. Sacerdoti, E.: A Structure for Plans and Behavior. American Elsevier (1977)
7. Simmons, R.: Representing and reasoning about change in geologic interpretation. MIT AI Technical Report 749 (1983)
8. Simmons, R.: A theory of debugging plans and interpretations. Proc. AAAI-88, St. Paul, MN (1988)
9. Simmons, R.: Combining associational and causal reasoning to solve interpretation and planning problems. MIT AI Technical Report 1048 (PhD Thesis) (1988)
10. Simmons, R.: Integrating Multiple Representations for Incremental, Causal Simulation. Proc. Conference on AI, Simulation, and Planning, Cocoa Beach, FL (1991) 88–96
11. Simmons, R.: The roles of associational and causal reasoning in problem solving. Artificial Intelligence **53:2–3** (1992) 159–208
12. Simmons, R. and Davis R.: Generate, test and debug: Combining associational rules and causal models. Proc. IJCAI-87, Milan, Italy (1987)
13. Simmons, R. and Mohammed, J.: Causal modeling of semiconductor fabrication. International Journal for Artificial Intelligence in Engineering **4:1** (1989) 2–21
14. Simon, H.: The Sciences of the Artificial. MIT Press (1969)
15. Sussman, G.: A computer model of skill acquisition. American Elsevier (1977)
16. Torasso, P. and Console, L.: Diagnostic Problem Solving: Combining Heuristic, Approximate and Causal Reasoning. Van Nostrand Reinhold, (1989)
17. Williams, B.: A theory of interactions: Unifying qualitative and quantitative algebraic reasoning. Artificial Intelligence **51:1–3** (1991) 39-94

The Business Analyzer:
A Second Generation Approach to
Financial Decision Support

Walter Hamscher

Price Waterhouse Technology Centre
68 Willow Road
Menlo Park, CA 94025

Abstract. The Business Understander is the architecture of a next generation knowledge-based facility for supporting the understanding of client businesses by Price Waterhouse practitioners. A key component is the Business Analyzer, which finds anomalies in financial results and computes explanations for them. Causal knowledge is represented in the form of constraints among financial variables, while empirical knowledge is represented as probability distributions over alternative assumptions, including modeling assumptions and assumptions about external perturbations. The task of auditing financial statements is used to illustrate the role of these types of reasoning in the Business Analyzer.

1 Motivation

Large accounting firms such as Price Waterhouse provide a rich variety of services to client firms, including auditing, tax consultation, management consultation, and general business advice. A person who provides these services must understand the business of the client in depth. The task of obtaining and maintaining that understanding demands substantial expertise, and its difficulty is compounded by the perpetual change that occurs in the business environment and in the personnel products, and organization of the clients. In addition, practitioners are constantly working with new clients in possibly unfamiliar and highly specialized industries.

Many computerized tools currently exist for managing and analyzing business information. These tools include spreadsheets, document production and retrieval systems, bibliographic and news service databases, financial and statistical analysis packages, and macroeconomic forecasting services. However, these tools fall far short of recording, structuring, interpreting, and filtering the masses of information and raw data that is available about a business.

2 Architectural Overview

The full spectrum of knowledge-based systems technology could provide this assistance in the form of a *Business Understander* system. The Business Understander would provide a common base of expertise about businesses, industries, and particular clients to support a variety of knowledge-based systems through-out the firm. A Business Understander facility would have three main parts:

The Business Modeler for building and maintaining a repository of information about a particular client firm.

The Industry Viewer for accessing information about the industry in which the client operates.

The Business Analyzer for identifying trends, significant changes, and other irregularities in the client business, and finding plausible explanations for those irregularities.

2.1 The Business Modeler

The knowledge obtained by individual service providers about their clients typically has multiple uses at multiple times by multiple people. This knowledge is a valuable asset that is rarely distributed or updated in an organized way. The Business Modeler is intended to make the firm's understanding of its clients available and usable by providing a repository of that understanding including the following types of knowledge:

Financial Models: the traditional notion of a "model of a business" [18]. It includes, for example, the general ledger account balances at regular reporting intervals and the various arithmetic combinations and aggregations of those balances that are found on corporate financial statements. We envision the Modeler as having read-only access to the client data via a network connection.

Operational Models: descriptions of the activities and processes of the client business. Included may be models of production, marketing, accounting procedures, and so forth as well as models of interactions between the client and its suppliers, customers, and competitors [13, 23].

Organizational Models: descriptions of the "chain of command" in a business, information about individual personnel, and general information about each business unit such as location, size, business functions, and legal relationships to other units.

2.2 The Industry Viewer

The industry viewer provides access to descriptions of the industry in which a client operates. The information parallels that in the Business Modeler:

Financial Knowledge: financial statements of competitors, industry norm ratios, and so forth.

Operational Knowledge: items such as descriptions of typical production processes, trade press articles on current issues in the industry, and industry-specific business risks.

Organizational Knowledge: information about the structure and size of industries in terms of geographic, tariff, or other segmentations.

2.3 The Analyzer

Financial analysis provides tools for comparing financial and operational data from a firm with a current model of the firm, the history of the firm, its competitors, and industry norms. The primary function of financial analysis is to identify unexplained discrepancies between expectations and stated performance. The identification of such discrepancies seems to pervasively drive the process of gathering information to understand a business. When things are about as one expects, there is essentially nothing to do: for all practical purposes, the business is understood. Effort centers on finding possible explanations for the discrepancies that have been observed—be they indicators of good news or bad news. A common way of identifying irregularities is to compare the figures of a specific company with the industry norms (cross-sectional analysis); in the terminology used here, industry norms generate expectations about the individual company, which may generate discrepancies.

2.4 Summary

The Business Modeler, the Industry Viewer, and the Business Analyzer each contribute uniquely to the task of understanding a business. The Business Modeler and Industry Viewer would serve as sources of different kinds of information, contributed and browsed by service providers independent of any automated analysis. The Business Analyzer would use the information from these sources to direct service providers in situations where they wish to update their understanding in a more focused fashion. It will also provide a module usable in more specialized knowledge-based practice aids such as tax planning assistants.

In the remainder of this paper we consider the details of the Analyzer. To do this, we first give a brief introduction to auditing, a task domain that we use to illustrate the functionality of the system. Next, we present a small example that illustrates how the Analyzer could be used in planning an audit, and discuss the existing prototype implementation.

3 An Introduction to Auditing

A business participates in transactions with its customers, suppliers, stockholders, creditors, and employees. These transactions have real physical substance, consisting of the delivery of messages, exchanges of goods and legal tender, performance of services, and the like. The accounting process produces a series of successively more abstract images of these activities (Fig. 1). Each of these image layers can be thought of as a summarization of the information in the layer below. The physical events can be viewed as *transactions*—usually changes in the ownership of some object. Every transaction has a monetary value assigned to it and the resulting stream is called a *journal*. These journal entries fall into various categories and are recorded as credits and debits of *accounts* such as "cash sales" and "purchases". At the end of each period the accounts are accumulated into financial statements, consisting of a *balance sheet* (a snapshot of the state of the business at a moment in time) and a *statement of income* (a summary of activity during the period of interest).

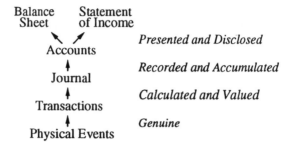

Fig. 1. Accounting Abstractions

Because so much information has been abstracted away to arrive at the financial statements, there are many opportunities for error, theft, and misrepresentation. By law, the financial statements must provide a fair and reasonable picture of the operational and financial status of the business entity. The job of the auditor is to provide reasonable assurance that the transformations performed to produce the images conform to accepted practice. In audit terminology, the issues to be addressed are: *genuine*—did the transaction really occur; *calculated and valued*—was its monetary value correctly assigned; *recorded and accumulated*—do all relevant transactions appear in the accounts and are they legally summarized; *presented and disclosed*—are there facts left out of the financial statements and the footnotes accompanying them that would substantially change the conclusions drawn from the statement. The opinion of the auditor as to the fairness and completeness of the statements is published with the statements.

Auditing can be understood in terms of model-based diagnosis [4, 17]. Model-based diagnosis uses a model and the set of observations made to produce predictions about what actual observations will be made subsequently; comparison of the predicted and actual observations produce discrepancies, which in turn produce candidate explanations. The set of candidate explanations informs the choice of the next observation to make. Further observations ultimately bring the device model into agreement with the real device (Fig. 2).

In auditing, the financial statements of the previous period along with independently verifiable information about the firm—for example, dated bank statements that show its cash balances, third party projections of market growth—produces predictions about what the current period statements should be, while the management of the firm presents the actual statements (Fig. 3). Material discrepancies suggest possible underlying errors, thefts, and misrepresentations. These suggest certain standard audit procedures that gathers new independent observations supporting a modified model of the firm. Ultimately the two views are to be brought into substantial agreement. The resulting causal explanation that links the underlying errors to the observed discrepancies contributes signif-

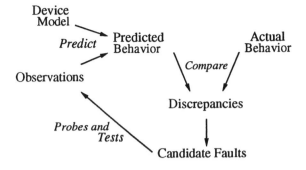

Fig. 2. Model-based Diagnosis

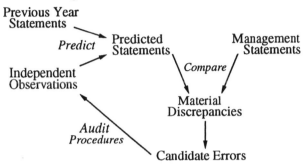

Fig. 3. Auditing as Diagnosis

icantly to the credibility of the audit.

There are certain important differences between standard diagnostic situations, such as troubleshooting circuits, and the task of auditing:

- Auditing has real-time deadlines and is not as sequential as suggested by the diagnosis metaphor. An initial set of candidates results in an audit plan —the set of procedures that members of the audit team will perform—and under ideal circumstances the plan would not change substantially during execution.
- A given audit procedure may yield information about several financial statement items, so the mapping from candidate errors to audit procedures is complex. Examining invoices, for example, yields information about both sales and inventories.
- Many candidate errors could be proposed to explain any given discrepancy. In fact, an important category of error results from the existence of transactions that the journal does *not* record—a situation that is reminiscent of the presence of bridging faults in digital circuits. Generating a more constrained set of candidates depends crucially on background knowledge that here is inappropriately folded into the category of "independent observations": knowledge about how the firm does business—its *operations*.

Because of this and other social factors, the diagnosis metaphor should not be taken too literally: it is simply impossible to automate an entire audit in this way. Yet the metaphor is powerful because it focuses attention on the most important result of the audit, namely, the *explanations* that underly the material discrepancies. For example, if the sales figures appear to be unreasonably high, then it is crucial to construct an explanation that shows that the sales figures are justified by other, independently verifiable figures.

A tool to automate this abductive task and exploit information and techniques not normally available to the auditor at the time of planning the audit would have great value. Protocol analysis has shown that this abductive style of reasoning manifests itself not only in auditing [8, 22] but also in tasks such as financial assessment [2] and going-concern evaluation [23]. Informal study indicates that it also plays a role in variety of other settings, such as tax planning, in which much of the effort is devoted to analyzing differences between prior cases and the case at hand.

The Business Analyzer's job is to construct plausible, parsimonious, and adequate explanations for unexpected financial results. We will also wish to generate questions to help disambiguate among alternative explanations. To clarify these ideas, we now consider an example.

4 Example

Figure 4 shows a simple financial model; the five equations relate eight variables. Of these eight, the variables Unit Cost, Unit Price, and Volume are taken to be exogenous and not directly observable. For the purposes of this discussion, a *diagnosis* is an explanation involving hidden exogenous variables—variables which have not been or cannot be measured directly, but that are related to and influence observed variables. The italicized variables are *operational* in the sense that they describe the operations of a firm—its underlying transactions —rather than being financial statement quantities. The intermediate variables Variable Cost and Indirect Cost relate accounting and operational variables to each other. The intent is that accounting figures such as Gross Profit are to be explained by perturbations in the operational figures such as Volume and so forth.

Suppose we observe that Gross Profit has decreased since last period, but that only accounting numbers are observable. Figure 5 shows three diagnoses. All three of the diagnoses hypothesize disturbances in the exogenous variables Unit Price, Unit Cost, and Volume. Because we assume that these hypotheses cannot be confirmed by direct observation, the consistency, parsimony and likelihood of the diagnoses are important criteria. In this case all three are consistent, and all are parsimonious with only one disturbance to each exogenous variable hypothesized in each. The first two are better explanations than the third (*), because for the first two the hypothesized disturbance entails the observation that we wanted to explain, while the third does not: if both Revenues

$$\text{Gross Profit} = \text{Revenues} - \text{Cost of Goods}$$
$$\text{Revenues} = \textit{Volume} \cdot \textit{Unit Price}$$
$$\text{Variable Cost} = \textit{Volume} \cdot \textit{Unit Cost}$$
$$\text{Cost of Goods} = \text{Variable Cost} + \text{Indirect Cost}$$
$$\text{Indirect Cost} = 15\% \cdot \text{Variable Cost}$$

Fig. 4. Sample financial model, after [20]. Operational variables are italicized.

Unit Price decreased
$\longrightarrow$ Revenues decreased
$\longrightarrow$ Gross Profit decreased

Unit Cost increased
$\longrightarrow$ Variable Cost increased
$\longrightarrow$ Cost of Goods increased
$\longrightarrow$ Gross Profit decreased

* Volume increased
$\longrightarrow$ Revenues increased
$\longrightarrow$ Variable Cost increased
$\longrightarrow$ Indirect Cost increased
$\longrightarrow$ Cost of Goods increased

Fig. 5. Potential diagnoses from Fig. 4

and Cost of Goods increased, then Gross Profit might have either increased, decreased, or stayed the same.

5 Diagnosis with Qualitative Financial Models

The CROSBY system [14, 16], a prototype of the Business Analyzer, addresses the diagnosis problem for financial models consisting of observable accounting variables and hidden operational variables. CROSBY produces explanations like those in Fig. 5 by applying the techniques of model-based diagnosis [4, 17], in particular the heuristic search technology in SHERLOCK[1] [6]. The space of potential diagnoses is defined by the cross product of values that can be taken on by selected exogenous variables. In physical domains these variables would be Boolean-valued and refer to diseases, states of components in designed artifacts, or multiple-valued and refer to behavioral modes of components.

---

[1] Hence the name: Crosby was a banker mentioned in the Sherlock Holmes "Adventure of the Golden Pince-nez".

5.1 Modeling

One version of CROSBY [14] uses a qualitative model with local propagation of constraints. Briefly, quantitative equations like

$$\text{Liabilities} = \text{Debt-to-Equity} \cdot \text{Equity}$$
$$\tfrac{d}{dt}\text{Liabilities} = \tfrac{d}{dt}\text{Debt-to-Equity} \cdot \text{Equity} + \text{Debt-to-Equity} \cdot \tfrac{d}{dt}\text{Equity}$$

are formulated as constraints over the signs $\{-, 0, +\}$ of the variables. Let $[x]$ denote the sign of variable x. Setting a variable to a particular sign constrains the signs of other variables. For example, setting $[\tfrac{d}{dt}\text{Liabilities}] = +$ ("the liabilities increase") forces $[\tfrac{d}{dt}\text{Debt-to-Equity}] = +$, given $[\text{Equity}] = +$ and $[\tfrac{d}{dt}\text{Equity}] = 0$. This allows reasoning to proceed even when quantities are vaguely specified and also when all of the relationships in the system are not completely known. For example, suppose that overhead expenses tend to increase when investment in property, plant and equipment (PP&E) increase; this can be described as $[\tfrac{d}{dt}\text{Overhead}] = [\tfrac{d}{dt}\text{PP\&E}]$. In this version of CROSBY the exogenous variables are the signs of the exogenous parameters of the financial model and their first derivatives.

5.2 Diagnosis

In diagnosis, hypotheses about the values of exogenous variables are not observable, and so a variety of preference criteria come into play, such as consistency (are the hypotheses and their consequences mutually consistent?), adequacy (does each diagnosis account for all observations?), parsimony (do they propose more hypotheses than necessary?), and likelihood (are the hypotheses themselves plausible, and are the observations plausible given the hypotheses?). CROSBY takes the approach of embedding all these criteria into a single quantitative measure: the posterior probability of a diagnosis given the observations.

In essence, CROSBY computes the probability of possible diagnoses by using Bayes' rule in the form

$$p(D|O) = p(O|D)p(D)/p(O)$$

where O is the set of observations and D is the diagnosis—a set of hypotheses about the values of exogenous variables. Although in general a probabilistic formulation of diagnosis with n hypotheses and m observations could require $2^{n+m} - 1$ joint probabilities with intractable computations, CROSBY exploits three key ideas to make this practical.

First, all of the probabilities of the form $p(O|D)$ are computed directly from the financial model, reducing the number of probabilities required dramatically. An important case is $p(O|D) = 1$, which occurs when constraint propagation from the hypotheses actually entail the observations, as in the first two examples of Fig. 5.

Second, many of the intermediate results in computing $p(O|D)$ can be cached for reuse in probability computations for other diagnoses. There is a special case $p(O|D') = 0$ arising from a logical inconsistency between the observations and some set D' of hypotheses, and it is called a *conflict*. Conflicts can prune the search space of diagnoses significantly because all supersets of a conflict are conflicts as well. This caching is implemented by associating an ATMS assumption with each value in the domain of each exogenous variable, and giving each new deduction a label corresponding to the sets of minimal sets of assumptions needed to deduce that value [5, 12].

Third, we need only compute the *relative* likelihoods of different diagnoses. This allows CROSBY to essentially ignore the term $p(O)$ in Bayes' rule since it is a normalization factor affecting all diagnoses equally. Moreover, this supports a heuristic search strategy that terminates after finding the few most likely diagnoses.

The diagnoses that CROSBY finds using the qualitative financial model form the basis of explanations that are comprehensible to human users [14].

5.3 Limitations

The qualitative version of CROSBY exhibits at least two limitations, one at a technical level and one at the knowledge level.

The technical difficulty is that the qualitative values do not permit appropriate levels of ambiguity; for example, in any real company Revenues *always* changes from period to period, but it is important to distinguish relatively large changes from small changes, the latter of which can only be represented as $[\frac{d}{dt}\text{Revenues}] = [0]$. This also interacts with the probability calculations in that generally the larger the change, the less likely it is *a priori*, but its simple sign representation does not provide a way to formulate this.

The knowledge level limitation arises from the fact that equations such as

$$\text{Revenues} = \text{Volume} \cdot \text{Unit Price (from Fig. 4)}$$

implicitly represent causal relationships—in this case, that revenues result from selling goods. Using equations as proxies for causal relationships in this context is a reasonable strategy because there is a clear distinction between unobservable (operational) variables on the one hand and observable (accounting) variables on the other; this ensures that the hypotheses predict the observations and not the reverse. But while CROSBY presumes that experts can estimate the relative likelihoods of perturbations of these operational variables, in fact there is no reason to believe that this is any easier to do than for accounting variables. It may be just as hard if not harder for an expert to make judgements about the relative likelihood of changes in (say) Volume as it is to judge likelihoods of changes in (say) Revenues. A more practical strategy is to represent exogenous variables for which analysts are familiar with and comfortable in making judgements about even if the resulting equations are more remote proxies for causal relations.

Financial ratios [18] can fill this role:

$$\text{Return on Equity} = \frac{\text{Income}}{\text{Equity}}$$

$$\text{Gross Profit Margin} = \frac{\text{Gross Profit}}{\text{Revenues}}$$

$$\text{Inventory Turnover} = \frac{\text{Cost of Goods} \times 2}{\text{Inventory}_{\text{start}} + \text{Inventory}_{\text{end}}}$$

Ratios are used because analysts expect that most things being equal, they remain approximately constant over time for a given company. Cross sectional parameters such as Market Share are technically similar, and provide a basis for comparison between companies of differing sizes. The definitions of these ratios and cross sectional parameters have a basis in causality (for example, the notion that physical goods spend a certain amount of time in inventory supports the *Inventory Turnover* ratio) although the relationship is neither as immediate nor obvious as with operational models.

6   Diagnosis with Quantitative Financial Models

The second version of CROSBY [16] uses a model of companies that incorporates quantitative financial analysis techniques [18]. Figure 6 shows an overview of the data used and makes explicit the categories of hypotheses involved. For example, in financial analysis it is common to use historical data to make projections, with the crucial implicit hypothesis that historical trends will continue. Similarly, reported current period data can be used in analyses only under some hypotheses about the magnitude and direction of errors in the data. CROSBY makes these hypotheses explicit, embodying them as ATMS assumptions, and finds diagnoses essentially as outlined earlier.

As before, the model consists of a set of equational constraints. Each variable has a value that is expressed as an interval over the real numbers—the interval $[0, +\infty)$, for example, denotes all nonnegative numbers. The constraint language ACP [15] propagates intervals through constraints and records justifications and ATMS labels for every interval value predicted. Under a particular set of assumptions, only the most specific interval is visible at any given time.

Each financial number has several attributes: its **reported** value (that is, what the company management says it is), its **actual** value (which is never directly observable) and finally its **error**, which is the percentage difference between the **reported** and **actual**. Errors are modeled explicitly in this way because CROSBY is intended to be used in an audit planning context, in which the auditor is interested in finding anomalies in the accounting numbers that might be best explained by reporting errors. Every reported financial number has five possible error sizes: badly understated $(-1.0, -0.10)$, somewhat understated $[-0.10, -0.01)$, approximately correct $[-0.01, +0.01]$, somewhat overstated $(+0.01, +0.10]$ and badly overstated $(+0.10, +\infty)$.

Suppose, for example, that a company reports its sales in $000s as 555. The **reported** sales is recorded as the interval $[554.5, 555.5)$, since we know that

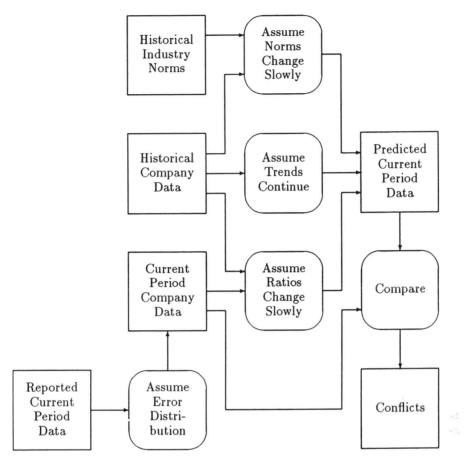

Fig. 6. Information flow in CROSBY. Boxes represent data sets; ovals represent sets of model constraints and the hypotheses that they embody.

the figure 555 has been rounded off. Under the assumption that the error is $[-0.01, +0.01]$, the `actual` sales is the interval $(548.96, 561.05)$. It is this latter interval that participates in constraints that relate, for example, Revenues to Receivables. Under the assumption that the error was $(+0.10, +\infty)$, the `actual` revenues would be $(609.95, +\infty)$. There is a probability distribution for the `error` of any financial number; for example, understatement of Revenues or Assets is typically far less likely than overstatement.

ACP constraints also define the ratios and cross sectional parameters used by financial analysts, as shown earlier. These variables are constrained to meaningful intervals, for example, Gross Profit Margin must fall within $[0, 1]$. These ratios and their movement (or lack of movement) over time are the basis for predictions by the model. Each exogenous variable has *extrapolation methods* for generating predictions of its value based on historical trends. For example, ratios such as Receivables Turnover, or cross sectional parameters such as Market Share, may be predicted as:

- Constant. The `actual` is within an interval around the previous `actual`. The size of the interval depends on the historical regularity of the number.
- Increase (Decrease). The `actual` falls in an interval above (below) the interval predicted by the Constant method.

As with errors, there is a probability distribution over alternative extrapolation methods. Other extrapolation techniques used in CROSBY include linear weighted averaging and univariate regression.

CROSBY has been tested on a variety of examples. One of these examples concerns MiniScribe, a maker of disk drives. During 1986 through 1988 MiniScribe management overstated revenues using such techniques as shipping boxes full of bricks and booking shipments to their own warehouses as sales [19, 21, 25]. The financial data was suggestive of overstatement at least as early as the first quarter of 1988, since MiniScribe appeared to be simultaneously increasing its margins as well as its revenues during a period of industry overcapacity when comparable disk drive manufacturers had poor sales and accumulating inventory. Given data on various combinations of Revenues, Inventory, Receivables, Cost of Goods, and the comparable figures for six close competitors, CROSBY usually concludes with high confidence that MiniScribe Revenues are overstated.

7 Finance is Not Enough

Both versions of CROSBY use an essentially financial model, in which all of the parameters are quantitative and most of them refer to amounts of money. Explanations referring only to dollar quantities may be adequate in a technical sense, but often unsatisfying for the tasks we envision. In the example above, a more satisfying explanation would refer to (say) increased competition to account for decreasing Unit Price. To generate such explanations requires operational models, in which the parameters refer to aspects of business such as the quality of the products, the lead time for new products, the brand loyalty of customers, and so forth.

A substantial amount of operational knowledge can be captured in qualitative constraints. For example, consider the area of Raw Materials (RM) costs and their relationship to overhead. Certain constraints are easily quantifiable, if not necessarily easy to observe:

$$\text{RM Costs} = \text{RM Volume} \cdot \text{RM Unit Cost}$$
$$\text{Total Overhead} = \text{Other Overhead} + \sum_i \text{Dept}_i \text{ Overhead}$$

Other constraints concern parameters that are impossible to quantify, but that clearly play a role in the efforts of experts to construct plausible explanations for observed discrepancies. For example, suppose we observe that raw materials costs have changed significantly. An expert would consider hypotheses involving changes in the quality of the raw materials purchased (higher costs but lower scrap rates), changes in commodity prices or new bulk purchase arrangements, and so forth. If materials costs have decreased, while overhead and capital expenditures have increased, a parsimonious explanation would be that the company has introduced, or increased its use of, Kanban or Just-In-Time techniques. The constraints in Fig. 7 suggest one way of capturing general knowledge of this sort using the "M^+" (monotonically increases) and 'M^-' (monotonically decreases) constraints ubiquitous in qualitative reasoning [11]. Figure 7 shows some of the relationships mentioned in this example.

RM Volume	M^-	RM Quality
RM Unit Cost	M^+	RM Quality
RM Unit Cost	M^-	Use of Bulk Purchases
RM Unit Cost	M^+	Duration of RM Storage
RM Quality	M^+	Use of Kanban
Duration of RM Storage	M^-	Use of JIT
Duration of RM Storage	M^+	Use of Bulk Purchases
Other Overhead	M^+	Use of Kanban and JIT

Fig. 7. Qualitative Constraints

Constraints on qualitative parameters such as these can play the same role in the construction of explanations as do the constraints on financial values. However, they exacerbate the difficulties caused by ambiguous qualitative arithmetic. For the type of constraints contemplated here, the approach described in [3] is a plausible strategy in which competing influences are statically assigned relative strengths. Disambiguation schemes relying on explicit ordinal relationships appear inappropriate because of the impossibility of meaningfully quantifying such parameters.

As the number of qualitative parameters and relationships represented grows larger, organizing the model so as to achieve adequate coverage and fidelity becomes a problem. This suggests organizing the relations around an explicit representation of the structure of the firm, that is, both its relationships between its internal structures and its constrained interactions with the outside world. A proposal for research in this area appears in [13]. The essential features of the abductive reasoning would remain unchanged in spite of the resulting shift in the character of the model.

8   Causal and Empirical Knowledge

The Business Analyzer, as embodied in CROSBY, relies primarily on a constraint-based model of the firm that is implicitly derived from causal relationships. For example, Equity is a quantity derived by subtracting Liabilities from Assets, and not the other way around. Relationships between qualitative parameters such as the quality of the raw materials and their costs are implicitly causal.

Currently the empirical knowledge used by the Analyzer is minimal: the prior probabilities attributed to exogenous disturbances are clearly empirical in nature, for example. Yet the role of that knowledge is crucial, since the probabilities control the search for preferred interpretations, and influence the ordering of discriminating queries. The estimated cost of observing the model parameters is also empirical. There are a number of directions in which the quantity and significance of empirical knowledge as the Analyzer could be extended as it evolved:

- While the use of probabilities to characterize the relative likelihood of different exogenous disturbances is convenient, it is clearly unrealistic to assign a single probability in all models. Heuristic knowledge about the appropriate numbers to use for a given company could be encoded as associational rules.
- Not all companies are affected by the same qualitative parameters, nor are the same quantitative parameters meaningful across all companies. Banks, for example, have no physical inventory to speak of, and hence the model needs to be constructed quite differently. Because auditors and other users cannot be expected to construct entire models by hand, the initial model construction will be another role for empirical knowledge. Work reported by Falkenhainer and Forbus [10] on automating model composition provides encouragement for this idea.
- As noted earlier, there are several potential applications for the Business Analyzer aside from audit planning. Again, because auditors and other users cannot construct whole models by hand, the choice of emphasis and level of detail used in the model and presented to the user will require empirical knowledge about relevant parameters and relationships.

A novel and interesting relationship between causal and empirical knowledge in the Business Analyzer results from the current state of the art in microeconomic modeling. Most current Artificial Intelligence work in model-based reasoning[2] is grounded in classical physics. Reasoning tasks involving business operations are not grounded in physics, but rather in the disciplines of economics, accounting, marketing, human resource management, and so forth. These disciplines are rich in quantitative methods, and appeal to similar types of assumptions (continuity, linearity, closed worlds, and so forth), but do not approach the breadth and predictive power of classical physics.

The thrust of this work is clearly toward model-based reasoning in this domain, but a serious issue arises from the need for comprehensive behavioral models of businesses, and the fact that so many predictive theories in economics are currently based on statistical analysis. Building a statistical model requires one to have some kind of causal theory before one can write the equations down.

---

[2] I am referring to mainstream literature [1, 7, 17, 24]. To paraphrase Justice Potter Stewart's opinion on obscenity in *Jacobelli v. Ohio* (1964): I can't define model-based reasoning, but I know it when I see it.

An important reason for choosing the structure of the equations carefully is to reduce the effects of interdependencies among factors. Hence causal assertions like "the number of potential customers and their ability to purchase was considered an important external determinant of sales" by Elliott and Uphoff [9] justify the inclusion of one or another factors in a given equation, in this case the inclusion of GNP as a contributing factor to the sales of a given firm. Unfortunately, achieving a completely independent set of parameters is impossible in general and in any specific case leaves much room for debate: for example, the equation for prices in [9] is a function of capital expenditures, rather than production costs, even though the latter seem to be much more directly related to the way firms set their prices.

Assuming that the model can be justified, subsequent analysis will assign quantitative values to the parameters, and tell one how well the historical data fit them. But what does one do if the fit is poor—conversely, what does it really mean if the fit is good? The causal story is not at all explicit in the equations, yet that is the background against which one must do all debugging and interpretation. In other words, if one uses the result of statistical analysis to make a prediction, how should one interpret data that either agrees or disagrees with the prediction? These difficulties argue against statistical extrapolation, but it appears that the field of economics currently offers few alternatives.

In short, the experts themselves in this domain rarely embody their models as explicitly causal, nor even axiomatic. Rather, the causal argument is implicit, the models are empirical, and their measure for the fidelity of a theory is purely statistical. Knowledge engineers cannot presume to rewrite the field of economics. Instead they must somehow come to grips with empirical knowledge embodied in a form that is normally taken to be axiomatic: when an economist says that price times demand elasticity equals the incremental quantity of goods sold, it is unwise to treat that knowledge in the same way as when a physicist says that the product of current and resistance equals the incremental change in voltage. This is an important challenge to current work in model-based reasoning, and confronting it must eventually result in a novel synthesis of current techniques for manipulating causal and empirical knowledge.

9 Conclusion

The Business Analyzer is a key component of the Business Understander, a second generation knowledge-based facility for supporting the understanding of client businesses by Price Waterhouse practitioners. The task of auditing illustrates its operation and significance. The CROSBY prototypes demonstrate the representation and use of causal and empirical knowledge for performing this task.

Acknowledgments

The author acknowledges discussions with Richard Fikes, Tom Orsi, Jim Peters, David Scott, Beau Sheil, and Alan Timmins.

References

1. D. Bobrow, editor. *Qualitative Reasoning about Physical Systems*. MIT Press, Cambridge, MA, 1985. Also *Artificial Intelligence 24*.
2. M. J. Bouwman. Human diagnostic reasoning by computer: An illustration from financial analysis. *Management Science*, 29(6):653–672, June 1983.
3. B. D'Ambrosio. Extending the mathematics in qualitative process theory. In *Proc. 6th National Conf. on Artificial Intelligence*, pages 595–599, Seattle, WA, August 1987.
4. R. Davis and W. C. Hamscher. Model-based reasoning: Troubleshooting. In H. E. Shrobe, editor, *Exploring Artificial Intelligence: Survey Talks from the National Conferences on Artificial Intelligence*, pages 297–346. Morgan Kaufmann, San Mateo, Calif., 1988. Also in: P. H. Winston and S. A. Shellard (eds.), *Artificial Intelligence at MIT: Expanding Frontiers* (Cambridge, Mass., MIT Press, 1990), v.1, pp. 380–429, and in W. C. Hamscher, J. de Kleer and L. Console (eds), *Readings in Model-based Diagnosis* (Morgan Kaufmann, San Mateo, Calif., 1992).
5. J. de Kleer. An assumption-based TMS. *Artificial Intelligence*, 28(2):127–162, 1986. Also in: Ginsberg, M. L. (ed) *Readings in Nonmonotonic Reasoning* (Morgan Kaufmann, Los Altos, CA, 1987) 280-297.
6. J. de Kleer and B. C. Williams. Diagnosis with behavioral modes. In *Proc. 11th Int. Joint Conf. on Artificial Intelligence*, pages 1324–1330, Detroit, MI, 1989. Also in: W. C. Hamscher, L. Console, and J. de Kleer (eds), *Readings in Model-based Diagnosis* (Morgan Kaufmann, San Mateo, Calif., 1992).
7. J. de Kleer and B. C. Williams, editors. *Qualitative Reasoning about Physical Systems II*. Elsevier, Amsterdam, October 1991. *Artificial Intelligence 51*.
8. V. Dhar, B. Lewis, and J. Peters. A knowledge-based model of audit risk. *AI Magazine*, 9(3):57–63, Fall 1988.
9. J. W. Elliott and H. L. Uphoff. Predicting the near term profit and loss statement with an econometric model: A feasibility study. *Journal of Accounting Research*, pages 259–274, Autumn 1972.
10. B. Falkenhainer and K. D. Forbus. Compositional modeling: Finding the right model for the job. *Artificial Intelligence*, 51(1-3):95–143, 1991. Also in: J. de Kleer and B. Williams (eds.) *Qualitative Reasoning about Physical Systems II* (North-Holland, Amsterdam, 1991 / MIT Press, Cambridge, Mass., 1992).
11. K. D. Forbus. Qualitative physics: Past, present, and future. In H. E. Shrobe, editor, *Exploring Artificial Intelligence: Survey Talks from the National Conferences on Artificial Intelligence*, pages 239–296. Morgan Kaufmann, San Mateo, Calif., 1988.
12. K. D. Forbus and J. de Kleer. *Building Problem Solvers*. MIT Press, Cambridge, MA, 1992.

13. W. C. Hamscher. Business as a domain for model-based reasoning: A proposal to use explicit representation of the structure and behavior of business entities to assess audit risk. Technical Report 4, Price Waterhouse Technology Centre, Menlo Park, CA 94025, May 1989. Also in *Working Notes of the Workshop on Model-based Reasoning* (International Joint Conferences on Artificial Intelligence, Menlo Park, Calif., 1989).

14. W. C. Hamscher. Explaining unexpected financial results. Technical Report 11, Price Waterhouse Technology Centre, Menlo Park, CA 94025, January 1990. Also in *Working Notes of the Spring Symposium on Automated Abduction*, 96-100 (AAAI Press, Menlo Park, Calif., March 1990).

15. W. C. Hamscher. ACP: Reason maintenance and inference control for constraint propagation over intervals. In *Proc. 9th National Conf. on Artificial Intelligence*, pages 506–511, Anaheim, CA, July 1991. Also in: W. C. Hamscher, L. Console, and J. de Kleer (eds), *Readings in Model-based Diagnosis* (Morgan Kaufmann, San Mateo, Calif., 1992).

16. W. C. Hamscher. Model-based financial data interpretation. In *1st Int. Conf. on AI Applications on Wall Street*, New York, October 1991. IEEE Computer Society Press. Also in *Working Notes of the Model-based Reasoning Workshop* (AAAI Press, Menlo Park, CA, 1991) and *Working Notes of the 2nd International Workshop on Principles of Diagnosis* (Technical Report RT/DI/91-10-7, Dipartimento di Informatica, Universitá di Torino, 1991).

17. W. C. Hamscher, L. Console, and J. de Kleer, editors. *Readings in Model-based Diagnosis*. Morgan Kaufmann, San Mateo, Calif., August 1992.

18. E. A. Helfert. *Techniques of Financial Analysis*. Homewood, 1986.

19. S. Kaufman. Report Finds Massive Fraud at MiniScribe. San Jose Mercury News, page 4D, September 12, 1989.

20. D. W. Kosy and B. P. Wise. Self-explanatory financial models. In *Proc. 4th National Conf. on Artificial Intelligence*, pages 176–181, Austin, TX, August 1984.

21. MiniScribe. Summary of Report of the Independent Evaluation Commmittee of the Board of Directors of MiniScribe Corporation. Exhibit provided in 8-K Disclosure, September 12, 1989.

22. J. M. Peters. A cognitive computational model of risk hypothesis generation. *Journal of Accounting Research*, 28(Supplement):83–103, 1990.

23. M. Selfridge, S. F. Biggs, and G. R. Krupka. GCX: A cognitive expert system for making going-concern judgements. Technical Report 86-20, University of Connecticut Department of Computer Science and Engineering and Computer Applications and Research Center, Storrs, CT 06268, December 1986.

24. D. S. Weld and J. de Kleer. *Readings in Qualitative Reasoning about Physical Systems*. Morgan Kaufmann, San Mateo, Calif., 1990.

25. A. Zipser. How Pressure to Raise Sales Led MiniScribe to Falsify Numbers. Wall Street Journal, page 1, September 11, 1989.

QUAWDS: Diagnosis Using Different Models for Different Subtasks*

Tom Bylander[1], Michael Weintraub[2], and Sheldon R. Simon[3]

[1] Department of Computer and Information Science, The Ohio State University,
Columbus, OH 43210, USA
[2] GTE Laboratories, 40 Sylvan Road, Waltham, MA 02254, USA
[3] Department of Surgery, The Ohio State University, Columbus, OH 43210, USA

Abstract. QUAWDS is a system for interpreting human gait. QUAWDS uses different domain models for different diagnostic subtasks depending on which model can perform the subtask most efficiently and effectively. Associational models are used to identify findings and rate faults. A qualitative model is used to determine causal relationships between faults and findings. Abductive assembly is used to coordinate the different models. By using knowledge from different models, QUAWDS combines their advantages and avoids their limitations.

1 Introduction

Diagnosis is the task of explaining findings (observations of abnormal behavior) in terms of malfunctions and their causes. This task is complex for several reasons. For example, knowledge about a domain might be incomplete so that only partial domain models exist. Multiple faults often occur and interact with each other; thus diagnosis must be performed over a large search space. Furthermore, the system being diagnosed might have mechanisms that attempt to compensate for a fault. As a result, an apparently abnormal behavior might serve to improve the overall functioning of the system. Many domains in medicine have these characteristics.

In this paper, we describe QUAWDS (QUalitative Analysis of Walking DisorderS), a system for interpreting human gait (Weintraub et al., 1990). We begin by describing the domain of human gait analysis. We then discuss the advantages and limitations of traditional diagnostic models, and describe how they have been applied to gait analysis. Next, we present a diagnostic architecture that follows the generic task approach of implementing a reasoning task as a combination of interacting subtasks (Chandrasekaran, 1986). In our architecture, different

* This paper is a considerably updated version of (Weintraub et al., 1990). This work is supported by National Institute on Disability and Rehabilitation Research grants H133C90090 and H133E80017, and National Heart Lung and Blood Institute grant HL-38776. The authors especially thank the OSU Gait Lab staff—notably Jeff Pisciotta, Dr. Inèz Kramers, Sigrun Schaudies, P.T., Lynn Flanagan, Pat Simms, and Cathy Clark—for their time and patience.

domain models are used for different diagnostic subtasks depending on which model can perform the task most efficiently and effectively. Associational models are used to identify findings and rate faults. A qualitative model is used to determine causal relationships between faults and findings. Abductive assembly is used to coordinate the different models. By using knowledge from different models, QUAWDS combines their advantages and avoids their limitations. We illustrate how QUAWDS uses these different models by giving an example of QUAWDS performing an interpretation of patient's gait. We then describe an evaluation of this approach with a clinical evaluation of QUAWDS.

2   The Domain of Human Pathologic Gait

Normal gait is efficient, adaptable, pain-free and requires no ancillary devices. In a normal person, the neurological system controls the muscles through coordinated commands to rotate limbs at several joints, providing body propulsion and stability for walking (Inman et al., 1981, Perry, 1985). A gait cycle consists of the time between a heel strike and the next heel strike of the same foot. The most significant events of the gait cycle are right heel strike (RHS), left toe-off (LTO), left heel strike (LHS), and right toe-off (RTO). These events delimit the major phases of gait: weight acceptance (WA), single limb stance (SLS), weight release (WR), and swing. For example, right WA is from RHS to LTO. Right SLS is from LTO to LHS. Right WR is from LHS to RTO, and right swing is from RTO to the next RHS. These events are illustrated in Figure 1.

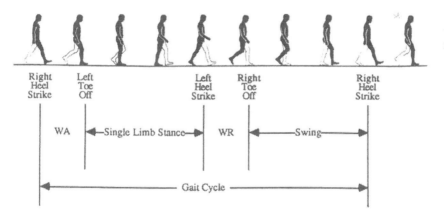

Fig. 1. Gait events and phases during a gait cycle. (Modified from Inman et al., 1981, p. 26; used with permission of the publisher.)

QUAWDS is restricted to pathologies resulting from diseases affecting motor control such as cerebral palsy (CP) or stroke. For example, CP affects the brain, and manifests itself by interfering with the coordination of muscle activity. These effects, and not CP, are the focus in pathologic gait analysis (the fact that the patient has CP is known before gait analysis is performed). The effects include muscle tightness, spasticity, and weakness, all of which affect the patient's gait motions.

The goal of diagnosis in this domain is to identify the improper muscle activity and joint limitations that cause the deviations observed in a patient's gait. The input is the information gathered by the Gait Analysis Laboratory at the Ohio State University. A gait study collects three types of data: clinical, historical, and motion. Clinical data result from the physical examination of the patient, and measures both the range of motion of the different joints and the qualitative strength of different muscle groups. Historical data include information about any past medical procedures or diagnoses. Motion data specify the time/distance parameters of walking (velocity, stride length, stance and swing times, etc.) and the angular position of the patient's leg joints (hips, knees, and ankles) in all three planes during a gait cycle. Motion data also include EMG (electromyograph) data of selected muscle groups, indicating when nervous stimulation occurs during the gait cycle. Typically, the data are gathered before a gait analysis is performed.

This domain is complex for a number of reasons. Patients with neurological disorders such as CP have a wide variation of muscle and joint faults; typically each patient has several faults, usually between 5 and 10. Reasoning about multiple faults is difficult in this domain because gait involves a number of highly interacting components and processes. The domain is further complicated because other muscles might attempt to compensate for faults. Moreover, many gait parameters cannot be directly measured given current technology. For example, EMG data are at best a relative measure of muscle forces (Simon, 1982).

3 Previous Gait Analysis Programs

3.1 Associational Models

Our work on QUAWDS is motivated in part by two earlier gait analysis systems, DR. GAIT-1 and DR. GAIT-2 (Hirsch, 1987, Hirsch et al., 1989). DR. GAIT-1 was intended to diagnose gait disorders resulting from CP, and operated strictly by using knowledge explicitly relating patterns of observations with faults (we call this an *associational model*). DR. GAIT-1 is limited to analyzing the motions of one leg in the sagittal plane (from the side). This program matches the observed leg motions to a set of precompiled motion patterns, and then matches these patterns and EMG information to hypothesize the faults of the patient. Basing the diagnostic problem solving solely on associational models was also the approach taken by other gait analysis systems (Tracy et al., 1979, Dzierzanowski, 1984, Bontrager et al., 1990). These differ from DR. GAIT-1 primarily by their application to different, albeit simpler, subdomains of gait analysis.

The advantage of an associational model is that conclusions can be derived with few or no intermediate steps. The problem with this approach is that a combinatorial number of associational rules is needed to cover all possible situations in a complex domain. For example, in the development of DR. GAIT-1, every new situation required the addition of a new rule. The result was a large and unwieldy rule base. Because of this problem, associational models are often incomplete and make simplifying assumptions, e.g., that faults can be diagnosed independently of each other. Furthermore, the only type of explanation an associational model can give is a run-time trace of the system's execution. Physiological explanations of conclusions cannot be generated because associational models do not explicitly represent relationships between components. Even though associational models are inadequate for complex domains such as gait analysis, they are still useful for certain diagnostic subtasks,e.g., determining the plausibility of faults and discriminating between them.

3.2 Qualitative Models

One way to overcome the problems of associational models is to use a device model that can determine interactions in the device and formulate physiological explanations (Davis and Hamscher, 1988). The key to doing this in gait analysis is to use some understanding about how gait is caused, namely that the joints' motions are caused by a combination of torques resulting from muscles, body weight, and momentum. This idea is implemented in DR. GAIT-2 by qualitatively representing a device model of gait (we call this a *qualitative model*). Like DR. GAIT-1, this system is also limited to considering faults resulting from CP and to analyzing the motions of one leg in the sagittal plane. Also like DR. GAIT-1, DR. GAIT-2 begins by identifying which motions need to be explained, but then uses its qualitative model of gait to generate and select faults. The qualitative model represents a joint's motion during a phase as a qualitative sum of all the torques acting on it. For each finding, DR. GAIT-2 hypothesizes all faults that are physically reasonable, and uses heuristic knowledge about CP to choose the best fault (or combination of faults) that explains the findings.

Unfortunately, there are several difficulties in doing diagnosis based on qualitative models. First, quantitative models with sufficient predictive and explanatory power must be available before an accurate qualitative model can be constructed. In gait analysis, developing quantitative models of gait is an open research problem (Hemami, 1985). Second, qualitative models introduce several sources of ambiguity (Kuipers, 1986, Struss, 1990). As a rule, qualitative simulation does not predict a single sequence of states; but produces several alternative state sequences. Additional information is required to disambiguate between them (de Kleer and Brown, 1983). Lastly, the computational complexity of such a model is a concern (Bylander et al., 1991a). Even if a powerful qualitative model can be constructed, there is still the problem of searching a large hypothesis space. If n different malfunctions can occur, there are 2^n possible sets of malfunctions. This large hypothesis space is not just an abstract possibility; as previously mentioned, multiple faults are usually the case in pathologic gait.

3.3 Combining Models

Clearly, there is a need to modify the assumptions that qualitative models can always be constructed from quantitative models and that such qualitative models can perform diagnosis efficiently and effectively. In gait analysis, there is no direct path from a quantitative model to an efficient and effective qualitative model; instead, such a model must be knowledge engineered and restricted to specific subtasks. Diagnostic associations acquired from human experts (or other sources) are still needed to help guide the search through the hypothesis space. We have used a generic task approach (Chandrasekaran, 1986) to develop a diagnostic architecture that takes advantage of the information available from each type of model. Figure 2 illustrates the high-level functions and components of the architecture. One associational model identifies the findings; another associational model determines the relative plausibilities of potential faults; and the qualitative model generates the set of faults offering to account for a finding and determines the explanatory coverage of single or multiple fault hypotheses, taking fault interaction into account. Another component, a hypothesis assembler, coordinates these subtasks and constructs a composite diagnosis.

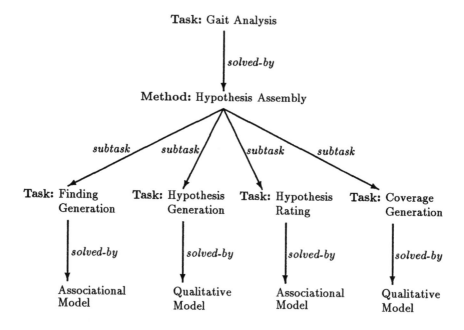

Fig. 2. The Composite Architecture of QUAWDS

4 The Composite Architecture of QUAWDS

Our goal is to design and implement a knowledge-based system that performs diagnosis using the strengths of associational and qualitative models while avoiding their potential pitfalls. One mechanism for solving this problem is hypothesis assembly (Josephson et al., 1987), which constructs an explanation of the findings from the set of faults based on the plausibility of the faults and what findings they explain.

4.1 Hypothesis Assembly

Diagnosis by hypothesis assembly uses the findings (the observations that need to be explained) to drive the processing. There are several criteria that an assembly strategy should consider in building a composite fault hypothesis (Josephson et al., 1987): (1) The assembler should work towards explanatory completeness (explaining all of the findings), but (2) should also maintain parsimony by avoiding faults that add little to the explanatory power. (3) The assembler should prefer more plausible faults and avoid selecting faults that have low plausibility.

The process of abductive assembly can be viewed as a form of hill climbing: given the current working set of faults, the assembler must decide what fault to add or remove from the working set in order to form a better explanation of the findings. Various examples of abductive assembly have been presented in the literature (Josephson et al., 1987, Goel et al., 1988, Peng and Reggia, 1987). Most formulate the problem as a set covering problem. In complex domains such as gait analysis, the problem is complicated because the addition of another fault will not always add to the explanatory power of the working set. Our version of abductive assembly is almost identical to that presented in (Bylander, 1991).

The two basic phases in assembly are construction and parsimony. The goal of the construction phase is to include the most plausible faults that add explanatory coverage. For each finding to be explained, the most plausible fault that explains the finding is added to the working set. In case of a tie, all the faults in the tie are added.

The goal of the parsimony phase is to remove superfluous faults from the working set. A fault in the working set is considered superfluous if all of the findings that it explains are explained by the other faults in the working set. After all superfluous faults are identified, they are removed. This phase also checks for the consistency of the faults in the working set. Faults that are inconsistent are removed from the working set. The remaining faults in the working set are now permanent members, and findings that they explain are removed from further consideration.

The construction and parsimony phases are repeated until no more faults are selected. The final answer consists of two parts: the faults in the working set, which correspond to faults which are considered true, and the faults that were superfluous in the last parsimony phase, which correspond to decisions that abductive assembly was unable to resolve.

Abductive assembly requires other subtasks that perform the following functions: identify a finding to be explained, find the set of faults that can account for a finding, determine the rating of a fault, and determining the set of findings a fault or set of faults accounts for. In our architecture, these functions are determined by either a qualitative or associational model as illustrated in Figure 2.

4.2 The Subtasks of Hypothesis Assembly

The first subtask of hypothesis assembly is to identify the findings. Given the set of observations about a case, this subtask determines which ones need to be explained. The relevant observations for QUAWDS are the patient's joint motions. A simple associational model is used. The primary association is: rotational motions differing by more than 10° from normal for a sufficient duration of the gait cycle need to be explained.[4]

The second subtask of hypothesis assembly is to find the set of faults that can account for a finding. This set is determined by the qualitative model. In the diagnosis of complex, interacting systems such as human gait a large number of faults can contribute, either directly or indirectly, to a finding. For example, the calf muscle (gastroc/soleus) can directly affect the ankle, which in turn can affect the knee. In order to maintain efficiency, only a small number of faults accounting for a finding should be considered. In QUAWDS, we assume that each fault will directly result in some findings. Thus, for each finding, only those faults that can directly contribute to the finding are identified by this subtask. The qualitative model of QUAWDS, simply by its knowledge of which muscles affect which joints, can determine what components or processes are involved in an finding. For example, the qualitative model identifies the anterior tibialis (the muscle along the shin), gastroc/soleus (the calf muscle) and other factors (e.g., knee position) as possible causes of *excessive plantarflexion* of the ankle (pointing the foot down). Both the anterior tibialis and the gastroc/soleus are considered "direct" causes of ankle motion while other muscles affecting knee motions are considered "indirect" causes.

The third subtask is the evaluation of the plausibility of a fault. In QUAWDS, structured matchers (Bylander et al., 1991b) rate faults. For each fault, there is knowledge to evaluate its presence or absence in particular cases. As is typical in systems using associations, domain experts can provide rules associating findings with faults typically causing them. Thus, associational knowledge can give valuable insights into which faults should be considered. For instance, the fault *underactive anterior tibialis* would be considered plausible if *excessive plantarflexion* is observed during SWING.

The fourth subtask is determining which findings a single or multiple fault can account for. This is determined by the qualitative model. The set of findings

---

[4] The motion data that are collected are susceptible to error. The data often has small periods of error that will exceed this threshold, and these should not be considered in the analysis. How QUAWDS determines an abnormal motion is described more fully in (Simon et al., 1992).

accounted for by a single or multiple fault hypothesis is called its explanatory coverage. The qualitative model in QUAWDS is similar to the one in DR. GAIT-2; each rotation results from a combination of the torque producing forces—muscles, joints, and other forces—acting upon it. What is new in QUAWDS is that a period of abnormal angular joint position are traced to to a period of abnormal angular acceleration that preceded it, which can be accounted for by some muscle or joint producing an abnormal torque. For example, the fault *overactive gastroc/soleus* during WA would account for *excessive plantarflexion* during the first half of SLS provided the muscle is not *weak*.

The construction phase of QUAWDS's hypothesis assembler uses these four subtasks until all of the findings are explained by a set of faults. The parsimony phase uses the fourth subtask (coverage generation) to determine which faults are superfluous.[5] Any remaining faults that are inconsistent are also removed. QUAWDS then reiterates over the construction phase and parsimony phase considering only those findings not explained by its working answer. This process continues until QUAWDS cannot identify any more faults to include in its working answer. QUAWDS then reports its working answer, and for the findings not explained by this answer, QUAWDS presents the alternative faults it considered.

The design of QUAWDS took place through interviews with the expert and observations of the expert solving actual cases. In the course of QUAWDS' development, the designers considered about 100 cases. QUAWDS is implemented in Interlisp and Loops on a Xerox 1109. Currently, we are reimplementing QUAWDS in Common Lisp. The motion data are electronically transferred to QUAWDS from by the gait laboratory equipment that gathers and processes the gait motion sensory data. The clinical examination, patient medical history, and EMG data are entered using a menu-driven user interface designed for novice computer users. It takes about 5 minutes to enter this data. It takes QUAWDS about 10 minutes to process a case and determine an interpretation of the patient's gait.

5 An Example of QUAWDS Performing a Gait Analysis

To illustrate how QUAWDS works, consider the following example taken from QUAWDS' interpretation of a gait study of a 5 year old diplegic (both legs affected) CP patient. This patient has had lengthenings of the hamstring muscles on both legs because of a severely crouched gait. The clinical exam reveals a limitation in the range of motion at the hip on both sides and a limitation in the range of ankle dorsiflexion (pointing the foot up). The observed motions are given in Figure 3. To maintain the simplicity of this example, only the sagittal plane motions are given.[6]

The first step in the processing is to identify the set of observations that need to be explained. Each observation in this set is called a finding. This step

---

[5] A fault is considered superfluous if the other faults in the set are sufficient to explain all the findings. This is a realization of Occam's Razor.

[6] In this case, there are 6 non-sagittal plane motions that are identified as needing explanation.

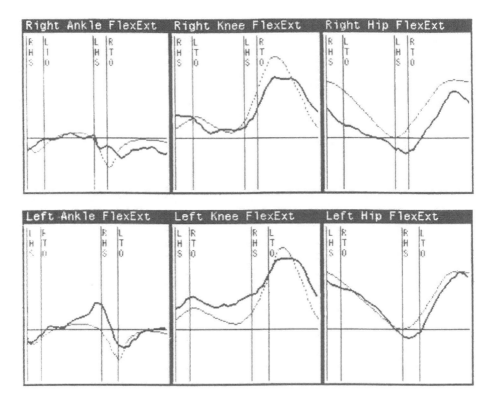

Fig. 3. Motion data in the sagittal plane. Normal is the thin line.

is determined by the observation identification component in the architecture. In pathologic gait analysis, findings are segments of the gait cycle in which the motion of a particular joint deviates from normal. As previously mentioned, this function is accomplished by an associational model. For example, motion findings differing by more than 10° from normal are important to explain. During an interpretation, QUAWDS identifies how the observed position of the joint has deviated from normal—either being more flexed (increased) or more extended (decreased) in the sagittal plane—during any part of the gait cycle. These periods are reported as a percent of the phase in which these deviations begin and end. Motion deviations that begin at the start of a phase are reported as beginning from 0% of the phase, and motion deviations that end at the end of a phase are reported as ending at 100% of the phase. QUAWDS also reports the periods of abnormal angular acceleration that to which it traces each motion deviation. These periods are identified in the same way as the motion deviations. In this example, QUAWDS identifies the following set of findings (typewriter font indicates actual output from QUAWDS):

```
Decreased angular position of Left Hip FlexExt from 50 WR
to 25 SWING is caused by decreased angular acceleration
```

```
from 75 SLS to 50 WR
```

This finding identifies that the patient's left hip position in the sagittal plane (FlexExt) is decreased (extended) from normal from mid-WR (50%) until the first quarter of swing (25%). The left hip's decreased position is traced to decreased angular acceleration from the last quarter of SLS (75%) until mid-WR (50%).

```
Increased angular position of Left Knee FlexExt from 75
SWING to 100 SWING is caused by increased angular
acceleration from 50 SWING to 75 SWING

Increased angular position of Left Knee FlexExt from 50 SLS
to 100 SLS is caused by increased angular acceleration from
25 SLS to 50 SLS

Increased angular position of Left Ankle FlexExt from 75
SLS to 100 WR is caused by increased angular acceleration
from 50 SLS to 75 SLS

Decreased angular position of Right Hip FlexExt from 0 WR
to 75 SLS is caused by decreased angular acceleration from
75 SLS to 100 SLS and from 50 SWING to 100 SWING

Decreased angular position of Right Knee FlexExt from 25
SWING to 50 SWING is caused by decreased angular
acceleration from 0 SWING to 25 SWING

Decreased angular position of Right Ankle FlexExt from 75
SWING to 100 SWING is caused by decreased angular
acceleration from 50 SWING to 75 SWING
```

As previously mentioned, a gait study collects data on the patient's range of motions—both those measured during the clinical exam and those measured dynamically—and EMG data. Dynamic range of motion measurements indicate a joint's observed range of motion during a gait cycle; this can be different than the clinical exam data because the forces exerted on a joint during gait are greater than those applied in a clinical exam. EMG data identify disphasic muscle activity over the tested muscle groups. In this example, both knees' range of motion is significantly decreased. The clinical exam also indicates some tightness of the hamstrings.

Given the set of findings, the assembler processes each finding one at a time and selects the highest rated fault(s) to explain the finding. For example, consider the finding that the right hip is decreased nearly all of the gait cycle is selected.

```
Considering the finding:
(Right Hip FlexExt 0 WR 75 SLS decreased)
```

Given this finding, the assembler now needs to know the set of faults that could cause this finding. In gait, there are several types of muscle faults. Muscles can be weak (the muscle is active with abnormally low force), underactive (the muscle is not active when it should be), tight (the muscle passively produces force because it is abnormally short), or overactive (the muscle is active with abnormal timing or abnormally high force). This set is determined by the qualitative model by tracing the finding to abnormal angular acceleration and enumerating the possible muscle faults that could cause it.

In this example, the finding is abnormal hip extension during most the gait cycle, i.e., hip flexion/extension is abnormally decreased. QUAWDS first determines the abnormally decreased angular accelerations that preceded the abnormal position or occurred during the decreased position. In this case, QUAWDS identifies decreased angular accelerations during two intervals: late SLS and the second half of SWING. Consider the decreased angular acceleration which occurs in the second half of SWING. This acceleration could be caused by increased torque from a hip extensor (the hamstrings or gluteus maximus) or by decreased torque from a hip flexor (the iliopsoas or rectus femoris). Increased torque can be caused by an overactive or tight muscle. Passive range of motion within the clinical exam data indicates that the hamstrings and gluteus maximus are not tight enough to cause this finding. EMG data reveal that the hamstrings are on during the second half of SWING, and EMG data were not collected for the gluteus maximus. Thus, *overactive right hamstrings* and *overactive right gluteus maximus* are possible faults. The iliopsoas is not normally on during late SWING, so it cannot produce less torque than normal. However, the rectus femoris is normally active during late SWING. No EMG data are available for this muscle, so the faults *weak right rectus femoris* and *underactive right rectus femoris* are possible. Although the equation used by the model include the motions of other joints as forces affecting hip motion (e.g., knee motions), QUAWDS does not generate hypotheses directly producing these motions because they will be generated when abnormal motions of that joint, if any, are considered.

```
The decreased flexext of the right hip from 75 SLS until
100 SLS can be directly explained by overactive right
gluteusmaximus, underactive right rectusfemoris, or weak
right rectusfemoris.

The decreased flexext of the right hip from 50 SWING until
100 SWING can be directly explained by overactive right
gluteusmaximus, overactive right hamstrings, underactive
right rectusfemoris, or weak right rectusfemoris.
```

The next step in hypothesis assembly is to rate the plausibility of the faults. In QUAWDS, faults are rated using an associational model. This function is done by using structured matchers implemented in CSRL (Bylander and Mittal, 1986). The rating of each fault results from rules that match against the set of observations. These rules are hierarchically organized into "knowledge groups," where each knowledge group represents an abstraction from various features of the data. The results of "lower-level" knowledge groups can be combined by "higher-level" knowledge groups that represent more abstract features of the data. Figure 4 gives an example of the knowledge groups used for the fault *overactive right hamstrings*. The rotation knowledge group is highest if there is any abnormal hip extension or abnormal knee flexion. The EMG knowledge group is highest if EMG data indicates that the hamstring is active when it should not be. The motion knowledge group combines the rotation and EMG factors. The nonmotion knowledge group is highest if the right hamstrings have reduced range of motion (over time, an overactive hamstrings will tighten the hamstrings), the patient has cerebral palsy (CP tends to result in spastic muscles), and there has been no prior surgery on the muscle. The summary knowledge group combines the motion and nonmotion factors.

In our example, the faults *overactive right hamstrings, overactive right gluteus maximus*, and *weak right rectus femoris* are considered the most plausible. For *overactive right hamstrings*, motion factors are favorable, but a previous surgery to lengthen the hamstrings would tend to weaken this muscle. For *overactive gluteus maximus*, rotation and nonmotion factors are favorable; however, no EMG data were gathered on this muscle. For *weak right rectus femoris*, the rotation factor is favorable, but there is no nonmotion evidence for this fault. Lacking any EMG data for the right rectus, QUAWDS prefers *weak* over *underactive right rectus femoris*. This amount to a default assumption that muscles are active when they should be unless there is information to the contrary.

```
Focusing on acceleration:
(Right Hip FlexExt 75 SLS 100 SLS decreased)
     Faults being considered are:
     +2: Overactive Right GluteusMaximus
     +2: Weak Right RectusFemoris
     +1: Underactive Right RectusFemoris

Focusing on acceleration:
(Right Hip FlexExt 50 SWING 100 SWING decreased)
     Faults being considered are:
     +2: Overactive Right Hamstrings
     +2: Overactive Right GluteusMaximus
     +2: Weak Right RectusFemoris
     +1: Underactive Right RectusFemoris
```

The assembler now calls upon the qualitative model to determine the explanatory coverage of *overactive right hamstrings, overactive right gluteus maximus, weak right rectus femoris*, and other faults. The model uses a set of qualitative differential equations (de Kleer and Brown, 1984) that describe the main torque-producing forces in gait. An equation is specified for each rotational motion of interest during each segment of the gait cycle. Each equation specifies the muscles and indirect forces that produce torques affecting the rotation

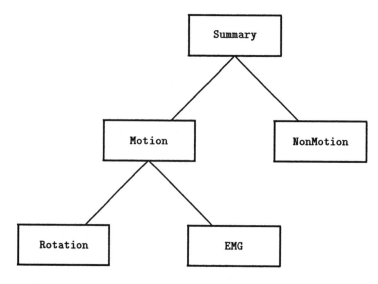

Knowledge group organization for *overactive right hamstrings*

predicates		confidence
Increased?(Right Hip Extension)	Increased?(Right Knee Flexion)	value
T	?	1
?	T	1
?	?	−3

The rotation knowledge group for *overactive right hamstrings.*
"?" means any value is acceptable.

Fig. 4. Knowledge groups used for *overactive right hamstrings*

(Hirsch et al., 1989). For example, the sagittal plane motion of the hip during SWING is described by:

$$
\begin{aligned}
\text{hip flexion/extension} = & + \text{iliopsoas} + \text{rectus femoris} \\
& - \text{hamstrings} - \text{gluteus maximus} \\
& + \text{knee flexion/extension}
\end{aligned}
\tag{1}
$$

That is, the iliopsoas and rectus femoris muscles flex the hip, the hamstrings and gluteus maximus muscles extend the hip, and knee flexion tends to cause hip flexion. In addition, each term on the right-hand side of these equations is augmented with information describing its relative strength to the other terms. For example, the hamstrings and gluteus maximus are much more powerful than rectus.

Also, if the knee is less flexed during SWING, and if some fault explains the decreased knee flexion, then this fault would, in the right circumstances, also explain the abnormal hip extension. For example, if *overactive quadriceps* explain a lack of knee flexion during SWING, it would also explain the hip extension, provided that the "amount" of hip extension does not exceed the "amount" of decreased knee flexion during SWING.

The qualitative model determines that both *overactive right hamstrings* and *overactive right gluteus maximus* can explain all of the decreased hip motion, and that *weak right rectus femoris* can explain the acceleration in late SLS, but not one in the second half of SWING. The effect of normal hamstring action during the second half of SWING is judged to overwhelm any effect of the rectus.

```
Faults selected for explaining:
(Right Hip FlexExt 0 WR 75 SLS decreased)
are: Overactive Right Hamstrings
     Weak Right RectusFemoris
     Overactive Right GluteusMaximus
```

This processing continues until all of the findings are explained. To maintain the brevity of this example, we will only report the results of the investigation over the remaining findings. The decreased right knee finding is explained by *overactive right quadriceps*. The decreased right ankle finding is explained by *overactive right gastroc/soleus*. The decreased left hip finding is explained by *overactive left gluteus maximus* and *weak left rectus femoris*. The increased left knee finding is fully explained by *overactive left hamstrings* and partly explained by *weak left quadriceps*. The increased left ankle finding is explained by *weak left gastroc/soleus*.

```
Faults selected for explaining the findings are:
Overactive Right GastrocSoleus
Overactive Right Quadriceps
Weak Left RectusFemoris
Overactive Left GluteusMaximus
Weak Left GastrocSoleus
Weak Left Quadriceps
Overactive Left Hamstrings
Overactive Right Hamstrings
Weak Right RectusFemoris
```

Next, QUAWDS enters its parsimony phase. Here, four of the above faults are not superfluous: *overactive right quadriceps*, *overactive right gastroc/soleus*, *overactive left hamstrings*, and *weak left gastroc/soleus*. In the context of the above faults, each of these four is needed to explain some finding.

```
Looking for superfluous faults:
    Weak Left RectusFemoris is superfluous.
    Overactive Left GluteusMaximus is superfluous.
    Overactive Right Hamstrings is superfluous.
    Weak Right RectusFemoris is superfluous.
    Overactive Right GluteusMaximus is superfluous.
    Overactive Right GastrocSoleus is not superfluous.
    Overactive Right Quadriceps is not superfluous.
    Weak Left GastrocSoleus is not superfluous.
    Overactive Left Hamstrings is not superfluous.


Set of faults after parsimony are:
    Overactive Right GastrocSoleus
    Overactive Right Quadriceps
    Weak Left GastrocSoleus
    Overactive Left Hamstrings

Considering findings assuming the following faults:
    Overactive Right GastrocSoleus
    Overactive Right Quadriceps
    Weak Left GastrocSoleus
    Overactive Left Hamstrings
```

Now QUAWDS reconsiders those findings not explained by these four faults. The following faults are reselected: *overactive right hamstrings, overactive right gluteus maximus,* and *weak right rectus femoris* are again selected to explain the decreased right hip finding; and *weak left rectus femoris* and *overactive left gluteus maximus* are selected to explain the decreased left hip finding.

```
Faults selected for explaining the findings are:
Weak Left RectusFemoris
Overactive Left GluteusMaximus
Overactive Right Hamstrings
Weak Right RectusFemoris
Overactive Right GluteusMaximus
Overactive Right GastrocSoleus
Overactive Right Quadriceps
Weak Left GastrocSoleus
Overactive Left Hamstrings
```

After a second parsimony phase, no additional progress is made, i.e., the same set of faults remain after superfluous faults are removed. As a result, the four faults *overactive right quadriceps, overactive right gastroc/soleus, overactive left hamstrings*, and *weak left gastroc/soleus* are considered true, and QUAWDS is unable to resolve the two hip findings.

```
    Looking for superfluous faults:
        Weak Left RectusFemoris is superfluous.
        Overactive Left GluteusMaximus is superfluous.
        Overactive Right Hamstrings is superfluous.
        Weak Right RectusFemoris is superfluous.
        Overactive Right GluteusMaximus is superfluous.
        Overactive Right GastrocSoleus is not superfluous.
        Overactive Right Quadriceps is not superfluous.
        Weak Left GastrocSoleus is not superfluous.
        Overactive Left Hamstrings is not superfluous.
    Set of faults after parsimony are:
        Overactive Right GastrocSoleus
        Overactive Right Quadriceps
        Weak Left GastrocSoleus
        Overactive Left Hamstrings
```

Our domain expert (the third author of this paper) judges that *overactive right hamstrings* is the cause of the right hip finding. In this case, QUAWDS gives too much weight to the previous hamstring lengthening operation and does not give enough weight to the restrictive passive range of hip motion.

6 Results of a Clinical Evaluation of QUAWDS

QUAWDS was tested on 32 gait studies of ambulatory patients with different types of CP. These cases had never been analyzed by QUAWDS nor had been part of its development. The cases were mainly patients with are diplegic CP (both sides affected), but some cases are hemiplegic. The patient reports produced by The Ohio State Gait Analysis Laboratory were used as the performance standard.

The discrepancies between QUAWDS and the patient reports were then evaluated by Dr. Sheldon Simon (the third author of this paper) to determine the significance of the differences. This evaluation was done as a blind study to minimize his bias toward QUAWDS or the gait study reports. It should be mentioned that Dr. Simon participated in writing these reports albeit several months before the evaluation. The results of this evaluation are presented in this section; QUAWDS' performance over the cases is very encouraging.[7]

6.1 Identifying Findings

To normalize the motions of each case, we define a period to be 10% of a gait cycle. For these cases, the reports identified 1070 periods of abnormal sagittal

---

[7] For a better description of the evaluation methodology and evaluation results, the reader is referred to (Simon et al., 1992).

plane motion. QUAWDS identified most of the findings mentioned in the reports (914 periods or 85%). Of those periods not identified by QUAWDS, the majority (98 periods or 9%) were judged by the domain expert to be insignificant and not in need of explanation. The remainder (58 periods or 5%) were judged to be an error of omission. Most of these errors resulted from the patient's motions being very close to but not exceeding the 10° threshold.

In addition to the findings mentioned in the reports, QUAWDS identified 65 periods that are not mentioned. 19 (29%) of these periods were judged insignificant. QUAWDS did identify 46 (71%) periods not mentioned in the reports that were judged by the domain expert to be significant and should have been included in the gait report.

With nonsagittal plane motions, the reports identified 481 periods of findings. QUAWDS identified 313 of these periods (65%). 111 of the periods not identified (23%) are judged by the domain expert to be significant. The remaining 56 periods (12%) were judged to be insignificant. Most of these mistakes occurred because the criteria QUAWDS uses to identify abnormal nonsagittal plane motions are too liberal for these planes.

In addition to the findings identified in the reports, QUAWDS also identified 41 periods not mentioned in the reports. 24 of these periods (59%) are judged by the domain expert as important to explain, and the remainder are judged insignificant.

Out of a total of 1656 periods either mentioned by the reports or QUAWDS, 1466 were judged to be significant (or identified by both the reports and the program), 88% of which are identified by QUAWDS, and 95% of which are identified by the patient reports. Of the 190 insignificant periods, 81% are mentioned by the patient reports and 19% are mentioned by QUAWDS. Thus, for identifying findings, QUAWDS is quite comparable to the patient reports.

6.2 Diagnosing Faults

For the findings that QUAWDS identified, it proposed 226 faults to explain the motions (an average of 7 faults per case). Of these faults, QUAWDS selected the same muscle fault as the report 45% of the time. QUAWDS selected an alternative acceptable fault 23% of the time. In fact, the domain expert considered nearly all of these diagnoses to be better than those given in the report. Thus, 68% of QUAWDS' proposed faults are considered equal or better than the reports.

Sometimes, QUAWDS does not propose a specific fault, but a set of alternatives, i.e., QUAWDS proposes that one out of a set of alternatives is the fault, but is unable to specify which one. 12% of the time, QUAWDS includes the fault preferred by the domain expert in a set of alternatives. In these situation, no EMG data are available to discriminate between alternatives. Also, QUAWDS does not represent the expert's preferences, which are related to the particular phase in which the finding occurred, and the expert's assumptions about muscle activities and body weight.

QUAWDS got an answer judged by the domain expert to be incorrect 15% of the time. The most frequent error QUAWDS made is because QUAWDS inappropriately attributed a knee motion during swing phase to the rectus femoris when it was attributable to the patient's momentum. Modifying QUAWDS' qualitative model to include the effects of velocity during swing would alleviate this problem.

QUAWDS did identify 11 faults not mentioned in the reports (5%). Of these, 8 are considered to be correct and 3 in error. Most of these involved non-sagittal plane motions that the gait study did not explain.

Thus, about 80–85% of the time, QUAWDS proposes faults that agree the reports, specify an acceptable alternative, or does not exclude the preferred fault. Most of the outright errors appear to be correctable with modest modifications. While much progress remains to be made, these results suggest that QUAWDS is well on its way to becoming a significant tool for performing gait analysis.

7   Other Approaches

There have been several other efforts to integrate associational and qualitative models, which can be broadly divided into three classes. The first approach compiles qualitative models into associational models (Chandrasekaran and Mittal, 1983, Swartout, 1983). Because run-time problem solving relies solely on an associational model, it has the problem of compiling associations for a combinatorial number of situations.

The second approach uses an associational model to index into qualitative models, but does not use the associational model for further guidance (Chandrasekaran et al., 1989, Fink and Lusth, 1987, Patil et al., 1981). A somewhat different approach to this problem uses a qualitative model to index an associational model (Hunt, 1989).

The third approach, taken (Simmons, 1992) and this paper, uses associational and qualitative models cooperatively. The primary difference is that Simmons' approach assumes that the qualitative model can test the correctness of faults generated by the associational model. This type of knowledge does not exist for gait analysis, medicine in general, or, we suspect, any complex physical system for which complete simulation is infeasible. Instead, our qualitative model permits differentiation of faults based on detecting superfluous faults. Admittedly, this is much weaker knowledge, but it is the strongest available knowledge in many domains.

An alternative representation to either associational models or qualitative models is belief networks (Pearl, 1986). The construction of a belief network for gait analysis will be complex because of the interaction among joints and limb segments and the large hypothesis space.

The interaction among joints and limb segments is such that an effect on one rotation can affect several other rotations. As a result, each single and composite fault hypothesis affects most of the 12 rotations that QUAWDS currently represents. Although techniques exist for removing these causal cycles (Lauritzen and Spiegelhalter, 1988), undoing the cycles is computationally complex.

The large hypothesis space in gait interpretation arises because CP patients typically have several faults; (in our experience is it is typical for a patient to have 5 to 10 faults). Either the belief network must be run for each composite fault hypothesis that is considered (Pearl, 1987), in which case something like QUAWDS ' hypothesis assembly process is needed anyway, or each possible composite fault hypothesis must be represented in the network (Lauritzen and Spiegelhalter, 1988). QUAWDS represents 72 different individual fault hypotheses, so the number of all possible 10-part composite hypotheses is $\binom{72}{10} \approx 5 \times 10^{11}$, meaning the hypothesis space is far too large to explicitly represent.

Thus, to maintain efficiency both in the size of the representation as well as the amount of computation necessary to infer a solution, we prefer to cast the problem of gait analysis as a generative problem where solutions are constructed out of a small set of preenumerated categories.

8 Conclusion

As the evaluation indicates, QUAWDS is able to identify and analyze the abnormal gait motions of patients with CP. QUAWDS is successful because gait analysis knowledge is distributed among four diagnostic subtasks and because each subtask uses the appropriate kind of model.

QUAWDS' architecture incorporates associational models, which are appropriate for selecting which findings need to be explained and evaluating the plausibility of faults, and a qualitative model, which is appropriate for generating faults to explain a finding and determining the explanatory coverage of a single or composite fault hypothesis. Hypothesis assembly is an suitable control strategy for integrating these different types of knowledge.

References

Bontrager, E., Perry, J., Bogey, R., Gronley, J., Barnes, L., Bekey, G., Kim, J.: GAIT-ER-AID: An expert system for analysis of gait with automatic intelligent preprocessing of data. In *Fourteenth Annual Symposium on Computer Applications in Medical Care*, Washington, D.C. (1990) 625–629

Bylander, T.: The monotonic abduction problem: A functional characterization on the edge of tractability. In *Proc. Second Int. Conf. on Principles of Knowledge Representation and Reasoning*, Cambridge, Massachusetts (1991) 70–77

Bylander, T., Allemang, D., Tanner, M. C., Josephson, J. R.: The computational complexity of abduction. Artificial Intelligence **49** (1991) 25–60

Bylander, T., Johnson, T. R., Goel, A.: Structured matching: A task-specific technique for making decisions. Knowledge Acquisition **3** (1991) 1–20

Bylander, T., Mittal, S.: CSRL: A language for classificatory problem solving and uncertainty handling. AI Magazine **7**:3 (1986) 66–77

Chandrasekaran, B.: Generic tasks in knowledge-based reasoning: High-level building blocks for expert system design. IEEE Expert **1**:3 (1986) 23–30

Chandrasekaran, B., Mittal, S.: Deep versus compiled knowledge approaches to diagnostic problem-solving. Int. J. Man-Machine Studies **19** (1983) 425–436

Chandrasekaran, B., Smith, J. W., Sticklen, J.: Deep models and their relation to diagnosis. Artificial Intelligence in Medicine, **1** (1989) 29–40

Davis, R., Hamscher, W.: Model-based reasoning: Troubleshooting. In Shrobe, H. E., editor, *Exploring Artificial Intelligence*, Morgan Kaufmann, San Mateo, California (1988) 297–346

de Kleer, J., Brown, J. S.: Assumptions and ambiguities in mechanistic mental models. In Gentner, D. and Stevens, A., editors, *Mental Models*, Lawrence Erlbaum, Hillsdale, New Jersey (1983) 155–190

de Kleer, J., Brown, J. S.: A qualitative physics based on confluences. Artificial Intelligence **24** (1984) 7–83

Dzierzanowski, J.: *Artificial Intelligence Methods in Human Locomotor Electromyography.* PhD thesis, Vanderbilt University (1984)

Fink, P. K.,Lusth, J. C.: Expert systems and diagnostic expertise in the mechanical and electrical domains. IEEE Transactions on Systems, Man, and Cybernetics **17** (1987) 340–349

Goel, A., Sadayappan, P., Josephson, J.: Concurrent synthesis of composite explanatory hypotheses. In *Proceedings of the Seventeenth International Conference on Parallel Processing*, St. Charles, Illinois (1988) 156–160

Hemami, H.: Modeling, control, and simulation of human movement. Critical Reviews in Biomedical Engineering **13** (1985) 1–34

Hirsch, D., Simon, S. R., Bylander, T., Weintraub, M., Szolovits, P.: Using causal reasoning in gait analysis. Applied Artificial Intelligence **3** (1989) 253–272

Hirsch, D. E.: An expert system for diagnosing gait for cerebral palsy patients. Technical Report MIT/LCS/TR-388, Lab. for Computer Science, MIT, Cambridge, Massachusetts (1987)

Hunt, J.: Towards a generic, qualitative-based, diagnostic architecture. Technical Report RRG-TR-145-89, Dept. of Computer Science, University College of Wales, Aberystwyth, Dyfed, U. K. (1989)

Inman, V. T., Ralston, H. J., Todd, F.: *Human Walking.* Williams & Wilkins, Baltimore (1981)

Josephson, J. R., Chandrasekaran, B., Smith, J. W., Tanner, M. C.: A mechanism for forming composite explanatory hypotheses. IEEE Trans. Systems, Man and Cybernetics **17** (1987) 445–454

Kuipers, B. J.: Qualitative simulation. Artificial Intelligence **29** (1986) 289–338

Lauritzen, S. L., Spiegelhalter, D. J.: Local computations with probabilities on graphical structures and their application to expert systems. J. Royal Statistical Society **B50** (1988) 157–224

Patil, R. S., Szolovits, P., Schwartz, W. B.: Causal understanding of patient illness in medical diagnosis. In *Seventh International Joint Conference on Artificial Intelligence*, Vancouver, British Columbia (1981) 893–899

Pearl, J.: Fusion, propagation, and structuring in belief networks. Artificial Intelligence **29** (1986) 241–288

Pearl, J.: Distributed revision of composite beliefs. Artificial Intelligence **33** (1987) 173–215

Peng, Y., Reggia, J. A.: A probabilistic causal model for diagnostic problem solving. IEEE Transactions on Systems, Man, and Cybernetics **17** (1987) 146–162

Perry, J.: Normal and pathologic gait. In *Atlas of Orthotics*, C. V. Mosby, St. Louis (1985) 76–111

130

Simmons, R. G.: The roles of associational and causal reasoning in problem solving. Artificial Intelligence **53** (1992) 159–207

Simon, S., Weintraub, M., Bylander, T.: A study in automated pathologic human gait interpretation. Technical report, Lab. for AI Research, CIS Dept., Ohio State U., Columbus, Ohio (1992)

Simon, S. R.: Kinesiology—Its measurement and importance to rehabilitation. In Nickel, V. L., editor, *Orthopedic Rehabilitation*, Churchill Livingstone, New York (1982) 45–65

Struss, P.: Problems of interval-based qualitative reasoning. In Weld, D. and deKleer, J., editors, *Qualitative Reasoning About Physical Systems.* Morgan Kaufmann, San Mateo, California (1990) 288–305

Swartout, W. R.: XPLAIN: A system for creating and explaining expert consulting programs. Artificial Intelligence **21** (1983) 285–325

Tracy, K., Montague, E., Gabriel, R., Kent, B.: Computer-assisted diagnosis of orthopedic gait disorders. Physical Therapy **59** (1979) 268–277

Weintraub, M., Bylander, T., Simon, S. R.: QUAWDS: A composite diagnostic system for gait analysis. Computer Methods and Programs in Biomedicine **32** (1990) 91–106

Integrating Functional Models and Structural Domain Models for Diagnostic Applications

John E. Hunt and Christopher J. Price

Artificial Intelligence and Robotics Research Group, Department of Computer Science, University of Wales, Aberystwyth, Dyfed, SY23 3BZ, United Kingdom.

Abstract. In diagnostic applications knowledge of the function of a device, or what the device is intended to do, can be very important. However, many model-based diagnostic systems rely solely on knowledge about the structure of a device and how the components of that device behave. The operation of the whole device is then synthesised from this information. This type of system only represents knowledge of the *how the system works* type, not of the *what it is for* type. However, diagnostic engineers do not just use structural knowledge — they also use knowledge about the *function* of a device — something which is beyond the scope of a purely structural model-based system. If second generation expert systems are to emulate the capabilities of human experts; they too must be able to reason about the structure of the device and the function of the device. In this chapter we consider why knowledge of the function of a device is important for diagnosis. We then present some of the issues involved in any system which integrates multiple domain models. The Integrated Functional and Structural Modelling system we have developed is then introduced and a diagnostic system built around this approach is presented.

1   Introduction

A great deal of research has been done into what is often called model-based reasoning [23]. In man-made devices much of this work has concentrated on systems which represent the structure of a device and the way in which the components behave. The operation of the whole system is synthesised from such descriptions. Such systems have been used successfully to perform a variety of expert system tasks including diagnosis.

Although a sufficiently detailed structural model could, at least in theory, be used to deduce all possible behaviours, it could not deduce the purpose or goals of a particular device. Recently there has been a growing interest in the representation of the function(s) of a system (for example see [20]). This has led to the development of systems which only represent knowledge about the functionality of a device [11, 19, 21]. Reasoning in these systems relies solely on knowledge of what the device is for.

One assumption which has predominated during much of this work is that when developing the model-based system, an attempt is made to pick the "best" level of model for a particular application or domain. The only type of model switching that occurs is hierarchical or based on abstractions and resolutions.

Much of our recent work has been applied to the automotive engineering domain. In this domain it has become clear that in order to be able to predict the full effects of possible candidate faults, it is necessary to reason at more then one level of model. It is therefore necessary to construct a system within which knowledge about the function of a device (or what the device is intended to do) is integrated with knowledge about the structure of the device. This chapter describes a system which attempts to do just that for devices taken from the automotive engineering domain.

The structure of the rest of this chapter is as follows: *Section two* considers why knowledge of the function of a device is important for diagnosis. *Section three* considers some of the issues which must be addressed in any system which integrates multiple domain models. *Section four* presents the Integrated Functional and Structural Modelling system we have developed. *Section five* considers how this system can be used as part of a diagnostic expert systems. Finally *section six* considers some related work.

2 Why is knowledge of function important?

In this section we consider the limitations of a purely structural analysis of a very simple circuit — the windscreen wash circuit — and consider why the use of functional knowledge can help to overcome some of these limitations. We then present some of the additional benefits which a system incorporating functional knowledge can obtain. These include the ability to focus the analysis, aid in mapping effects to symptoms (important for diagnostic systems) and help in selecting appropriate type of models.

2.1 The windscreen wash system

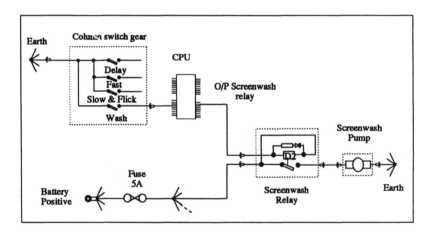

Fig. 1. Main details of the windscreen wash system

Many model-based reasoning systems generate a description of the possible behaviour of a physical artifact by reasoning about the structure of a system (what components constitute that device and the relationships between them) and the operation of each of its components. The operation of the whole device is then synthesised from the operation of its component parts. For example, consider the simple circuit illustrated in figure 1. This figure illustrates the main structural details of a windscreen wash control circuit. The nodes with extra wires emerging show where the windscreen wash system intersects with systems that are providing other functions. The CPU in the system is a complex component with a functional description which extends to many pages. Only a small part of that description concerns the windscreen wash system.

The operation of the windscreen wash system is considered briefly below:

The operation of the electrical circuit The electrical circuit consists of a fused line from battery positive which powers a device (the windscreen wash pump in this case) when a relay is closed. The relay is negatively switched — it is activated when it receives a grounded input from the CPU. The output from the CPU to the relay is normally open, and is pulled low when the screenwash switch is closed (which pulls the input to the CPU low).

The operation of the windscreen wash hydraulic system The aim of this system is to pump water at the screen. It does this by drawing water from the water bottle via the water pump. This then pumps the water through the flexible tubes and the junction pipes to a nozzle on the car bonnet. Water is then squirted from the nozzle. If the nozzle is appropriately set, then the water will be squirted at the windscreen.

2.2 Modelling the windscreen wash system

Using an appropriate structural model-based reasoning system, the operation of the windscreen wash electrical circuit can be obtained. In some simple devices such an analysis will generate enough information to fully understand that device, for example [2, 18]. However, in general the function of a device, or what that device is actually for, involves an account of the intention or design purpose of the device. In the case of the windscreen wash system a purely electrical structure based analysis could state that there was current flowing through the pump and possibly that the pump was active, it cannot tell you what the pump was actually doing. For example, was it pumping hot air, cold air or water, petrol or oil? In order to determine this either additional knowledge about windscreen wash systems in general is required, or information beyond the scope of the electrical model is required. For example, what the pump is connected to, which might be a rubber pipe, and a fluid reservoir.

In order to understand the significance of the decision about what level to model the windscreen wash system, consider the following diagnoses for a windscreen wash system which is not squirting water at the windscreen.

The screenwash bottle is empty. In order for the screenwash system to squirt water at the screen, the screenwash bottle must contain some water. If the bottle is empty then no water will be squirted at the screen.

The output pipe from the water pump has a large hole. If there is a hole in this pipe, then as water is pumped from the water pump it may get squirted over the underside of the bonnet and the engine rather than the windscreen

Input to relay from positive feed has gone open circuit. When the screenwash button is pressed, the relay closes as normal, but no power goes to the screenwash pump. Therefore the screenwash pump does not squirt water at the screen.

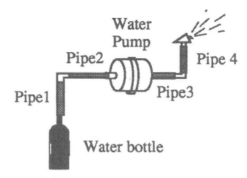

Fig. 2. The hydraulic part of the windscreen wash system

The screenwash pump has stalled. If the pump stalls, no water will be pumped by it, there will therefore not be any water pumped at the screen. In addition, as the relay manufacturers demand that the wires in the circuit are large enough that the fuse will blow before the relay does, and the pump has a stall current of 10 amps whereas the fuse is rated at 5 amps, the fuse will blow. The relay is designed in such a way as to ensure that it will not feed that current back to the CPU.

As the empty wash bottle is the simplest fault to correct, the human expert would check the wash bottle first. If this was not empty then other possible faults would be considered. The expert might then check all the pipes to make sure none of them had split. In the case of the stalled screenwash pump the human expert could check to see if the fuse fail light on the dashboard was on. If it was then he would check for a stalled pump and a blown fuse before considering any other candidate faults.

As the above examples show, the human expert reasons about the windscreen wash system from different viewpoints. For example, the analysis of the effects of an open circuit is at the level of the electrical circuit itself, the analysis of the pipes might be at the level of fluid flows, while the analysis of the effects of an empty screenwash bottle is only at a functional level.

In the case of the stalled pump, this analysis involves all levels. That is, in order to find all of the electrical changes which occur because of the stalled pump, it is necessary to analyse the structure of the system — propagating currents and voltages through pieces of circuit where necessary. However, the effects of the stalled pump are not at the electrical level. First it is necessary to determine how a non working pump will affect the hydraulic part of the system. In this case, it will mean that no water is drawn from the water bottle and pumped through the pipes to the nozzle. This, however, is not the end of the story, because we must now decide what the effect of not having water being pumped from the nozzle has on the intended function of the system. This effect is at the functional level — no water is squirted at the screen (such information cannot be decided from the circuit diagram alone).

2.3 Focussing the analysis

It has been argued that hierarchical modelling is a powerful tool in overcoming the complexity encountered in representing real world systems. However, in many real world systems, there is no clear cut, clean hierarchy to exploit. This is particularly true when you start to consider how to represent a system using multiple models.

However, by explicitly representing the functions of the system, it can be possible to focus in on a particular part of a system. This part can then be analysed in more detail. This fact has already been acknowledged by a number of researchers [7, 22].

2.4 Mapping effects to symptoms

If we now consider the diagnostic process within the domain of electromechanical automobile subsystems, we see that often the symptoms that are available are at the level of "there is no water being squirted at the screen" and "there is no hot air being blown at the driver". The aim is then to find the modification to the subsystem which has resulted in this functional deviation. This modification will be some change in the structure of the subsystem or the operation of one of its constituent parts. A purely electrical structural analysis does not possess enough information to be able to generate an appropriate description which would match the symptoms. It could state that the pump was not working, but what is the effect of a non working pump? In order to match this behaviour with the symptoms, additional knowledge is required, which is not part of the electrical system.

2.5 Focusing on the type of model

Knowledge of the intended functions of a device is also important because a structural analysis based on the first principles of the domain could generate many effects. In the case of the electrical domain it could produce such effects as the generation of heat or magnetic fields etc. However, many of these "side-effects" may not be interesting or significant in the current device. Without some knowledge of the intended function(s) of the device it is not possible to determine which of these are irrelevant and which of these are significant[1] (similar points have also been made by Iwasaki and Simon in [10]). An associated point is that knowledge of the device's intended function can also help in the identification of appropriate component models. For example, a wire can be modelled as an electrical conductor, however if it is being used to tie up a bail of hay, such a model might not be appropriate.

3 Integrating multiple models

If we consider the major elements of the windscreen wash system we realise that we are in fact dealing with at least two domains namely; the electrical domain and the pneumatic domain. These domains have very different terminology, for example one

---

[1] This is important for tasks such as diagnosis in which an insignificant side-effect under normal conditions may become significant when the device is behaving abnormally.

deals with voltage and current and uses Kirchoff's and Ohm's laws, while the other deals with pressure and flow and is based on fluid dynamics theory. However, in order to be able to reason fully about this system, we must be able to model both the electrical elements of the system and the pneumatic elements of the system and to integrate the results of analysing these models. We must then be able to interpret these results at a functional level. Multiple models of the system being analysed are therefore required in order to generate a diagnosis which would be impossible using either type of model alone.

However, there are a number of major issues associated with reasoning using multiple models. These include deciding when to switch between the available models, how to execute that shift and how to translate the available information between the different models. We have already developed a system which integrated a functional modelling system with an electrical structural analysis system using a separate controller [7]. However, as discussed in [6], this is a relatively inflexible system. For example, it would require some reimplementation in order to use another analysis method.

In the remainder of this section we consider how to decide when to shift between models and which model to shift to. We also address the issues of translating and integrating information between diverse models. We conclude by suggesting that functional knowledge can be used as framework within which to integrate multiple models.

3.1 Deciding when to shift between models

Much of the research that has been done into multiple models has concentrated on models which are abstractions of each other. The graph of models work, for example, seems to assume that models can be arranged in a hierarchy, with simpler models partitioned, and links going across the hierarchy as well as up it. Where that is the case, then switching between models is simplified — you use the results of reasoning to move either across the graph or up the hierarchy[2].

However, we are considering functional models, and structural models from different domains. These models are not partitioned nearly so tidily. However, each provides valuable information for tasks such as diagnosis. Deciding to switch between models is sometimes done because reasoning with a simpler model failed (as for the graph of models work). Sometimes a move is made from one model to another because the required information is not available in the current model, or because the information that is available can only be analysed by a particular type of model. At other times, it is done because the system is trying to accomplish a different part of the diagnostic task.

3.2 Identifying where to shift to

Having decide that it is necessary to switch from the current model, it can be difficult to select which model should be chosen next? One approach might be to use the type of the components returned by the original model to decide which analysis method is now appropriate. This, however, assumes that there is some way of associating a particular component with a particular type of analysis. For example, a wire might well

---

[2] Translation between models is also much easier because of the partitioned nature of the graph.

be analysed by an electrical circuit analyser. However, in the case of the windscreen wash system, both an electrical and a hydraulic analysis might be appropriate for the water pump component.

Access to the operations which were being considered when the decision to switch between models was made might allow an appropriate analysis method to be selected. However, this relies on the module which handles model switching having are great deal of knowledge about why model switching is taking place.

3.3 Translating between models

A significant aspect of any multiple model system is the translation from one model to another. One of the problems that such a shift of perspective causes is that the terms used to describe system behaviour in one model are unlikely to be the same as the terms used to describe the same system behaviour in another type of model. Facilities must therefore be provided for the necessary translation to take place. In the system mentioned above, the controller used a model state translator to translate the state of the system between the two models[3]. This state translator used dictionaries of generic mappings to perform the translations. For example, a generic mapping of how to translate a switch is used to translate all switches. However, these translations are performed without reference to the actual models. This means that the translator, by default, only deals with the general cases. Such a translator was necessary due to the loosely coupled nature of the system. However, if a particular partial state description in one model must be translated into a non-standard description in the other model, exception handlers must be written.

3.4 Integrating information from different domains

Translation is not the end of the story; it is still necessary to integrate the translated information. That is, what effect does an operating pump have on the fluid flow model of the screen wash system. It is necessary to understand how active pumps operate, and what effect they might have on fluid flows. In order to determine this, it is necessary to understand the purpose of the pump and how that purpose relates to the fluid flow model.

3.5 Using functional knowledge as an integration framework

One way in which the integration of diverse domains can be achieved is through the use of known functionality. This is because each of the subsystems in this system performs a particular function. For example, the function of the electrical circuit is to activate or deactivate the water pump. The function of the hydraulic subsystem is to take water from the water bottle and squirt it at the windscreen. If we consider how a functional model of the windscreen wash system might be built we can see that from the functional point of view, it does not matter which domain (or domains) the associated subsystem might be in, the functions are all associated with the windscreen wash system.

---

[3] Note that the problem of translating the state of devices is simplified in this situation because both models are representing information from the same domain; that of electrical circuits.

If each subsystem has an associated function, and each function interacts with other functions at a functional level, we have already integrated subsystems from different domains. We suggest that, if each of these functions is associated with an appropriate structural representation and if this structural level is analysed using an appropriate domain model, it is possible to integrate models from multiple domains in a principled and engineered manner[4].

The decision to move to another model is taken when it is necessary to obtain information which is beyond the scope of the functional model. For example, determining the state of the water pump within the electrical circuit. It is also possible to identify which of the structural models to switch to by examining the function which is being executed at the time. Although the designer does not need to know what the actual structure of the system is, they should be able to associate a given (low level) function with either the hydraulic, or electrical domain. If they can do this, then when the system is analysing the model, it should be possible to switch to a given function's associated domain.

Translating and integrating information should also be simplified as we now have the context in which the domain models are being used. That is, if we know that the water pump is active (in the terms of the electrical domain) then at the functional level it is *pumping*. As we also know what the relationship is between a *pumping* water pump and the hydraulic domain we can determine what the effects are of the water pump's behaviour on the flow of water through the windscreen wash system. The result of this can then be translated back into the terms used in the functional model.

4   An Integrated Function and Structure Model

We aim to provide a framework within which multiple domain models can be integrated. This framework relies on the use of a functional representation to perform this integration. Figure 3 illustrates how the use of functional knowledge can be used to integrate the results of performing an electrical circuit analysis and a pneumatic system analysis. This section considers the facilities provided by the integrated function and structure modelling (IFSM) system, it then describes the IFSM language with reference to the windscreen wash system and it concludes with a description of how such a model can be analysed. We have also used the IFSM system to model more complex electromechanical devices such as the cruise control system discussed in [6].

4.1   The facilities provided by the IFSM

At the heart of an integrated function and structure model (an IFSM) is a "core" representation. This enables core device objects to be defined which represent whole systems, subsystems or components. The core representation itself provides a *skeleton* to which other representations can be linked. The intuition behind this is that for any given system or subsystem there are a variety of ways of viewing that system. It might be appropriate to view it structurally, functionally or as a set of processes.

---

[4] Indeed from observations of automotive engineers, it appears that this is the way in which many engineers appear to approach the problem of interfacing multiple domains.

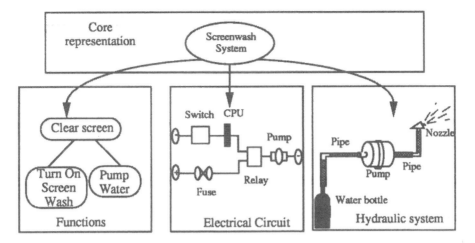

Fig. 3. Integrating multiple domain models

The core device node itself assumes nothing about how the system associated with it should be represented. Nor does the core representation impose any structure on its associated representations. Figure 3 illustrates how this might work for the pneumatic subsystem. A developer can define a core device object, such as the windscreen wash system. He can then define a set of functions which describe what that device does. The developer can also define the structure of the electronic circuit and the hydraulic circuit of the device (a set of events can also be defined such as a switch being turn on). Each of these representations is independent of the other and each can refer to "items" defined in other core device objects. The links between the "items" in these representations can be hierarchical, however these hierarchies need not necessarily reflect the hierarchy of the core device nodes nor the hierarchies in any other representation.

Hierarchical modelling is a major weapon in the battle to overcome the complexity encountered in representing real world systems. However, the core representation is a collection of abstract nodes rather than a specific hierarchical structure. Indeed no explicit representation of the relationship between different core device nodes exists[5]. This is because different hierarchies are defined via the functions and structures. The core device nodes are abstract entities representing some significant system concept which might be a particular device or sub-assembly, but which might also be a virtual feature of the real world.

4.2 Modelling the windscreen wash system as an IFSM

Figure 4 and appendix A illustrate some of the features which the IFSM language possesses. These features enable the developer to describe the function(s) of the system and the events which can occur. It also provides facilities which allow the developer to

---

[5] Although a set of implicit relationships do exist through the association of functions and/or structures.

define appropriate structural models. The IFSM language has already been described in some detail in [6]. We shall therefore present a description of the windscreen wash model rather than a comprehensive description of the language. The *define_device_node* and *enddefine_device_node* statements determine the scope of the core device node being defined. Within the scope of the core device node the events, functions and structures can be defined. These are discussed below.

Events Events are external influences on a device. For example the windscreen wash system has a *switch the screen wash system on / off* event. It is through these events that the outside world can cause the behaviour of the system to alter — where "outside world" refers to something outside the world of the device. It may therefore refer to a human or another device interacting with the device.

Functions Functions define what the device is for, and that is all that they define — they do not state how the function is achieved. When a function becomes executable it can cause the "functional description" of the device's behaviour to alter.

Appendix A illustrates the *clear_screen* function of the windscreen wash system. All function definitions are defined between the **functions** and **endfunctions** keywords[6]. The clear screen function states that in order for the function to be executed, the screen wash switch must be switched on. When this occurs, the activate water pump function of the windscreen wash circuit is analysed. The result of this function is saved in the *water_pump_state* variable. Then if the water pump has been activated, then the pump water function of the hydraulic system is analysed. The result of this analysis is saved in the *water_pumped* variable. If water is being pumped, then the result of this function is that the *water_squirted_at_screen* variable is set to true.

The **of** statement is used to indicate the device object associated with the function which precedes it. If the function is defined within the current object the **of** is not required.

Structures The *structure* and *endstructure* keywords are used to define the scope of the structure definitions. Appendix A illustrates an example of an electrical and a hydraulic structural definition. The structure definition facilities provided by the IFSM language are easily extendible. This achieved through the use of a **define_structure** *<type>* statement. This allows the model developer to add new structure types as required without the need to directly modify the IFSM language. For example, the *define_structure electrical* and *enddefine_structure* statements are used to define the electrical structure of the system. The *define_structure hydraulic* and *enddefine_structure* statements are used to define the hydraulic system structure. The syntax of the definitions is dependent upon the type of circuit analysis method being used and so is beyond the scope of the IFSM to define or verify. In appendix A the syntax used is that required by the qualitative circuit analyser of Lee and Ormsby [12, 13].

---

[6] Within these keywords there is also a set of functional state variable declarations. These are used to define the variables which represent the functional state of the device and the range of values they can take.

This approach relies on the developer correctly specifying the structure definition, as no syntax checking etc. of these descriptions is performed by the IFSM compiler. Instead it is performed dynamically at runtime by the associated analysis system. This represents a least commitment approach. It is however, appropriate to take this approach as it assumes nothing about which analysis methods should be integrated into the IFSM.

This means that another analysis method can be integrated into the IFSM with the minimum of effort. For example, it might be useful to be able to reason about the mechanical features of a system using a mechanical simulator similar to that described by Price, Hunt and Lee in [16]. In that case the syntax used to describe the mechanical structure would reflect the syntax of the RIDDL language used to represent mechanical devices. The analysis system could be integrated without the need to extend the IFSM language. All that would be required would be that a function was made available to the IFSM analysis system through which it could initiate the RIDDL system.

Within the structure definitions statements can also be made about how to translate particular functional states. For example, appendix A illustrates how the state of the windscreen wash switch should be translated into the electrical domain language. Appendix A also illustrates how the functional state of the water pump should be translated into the language of the hydraulic domain. Most of the functional state of the system does not need to be translated into the electrical or hydraulic domain languages. Instead only specific functional variables which reflect the state of particular components need to be translated. The translation of these variables is often dependent on the function of the system within which that variable exists. For these reasons it is appropriate to define the translations within the device object.

4.3   Analysing an IFSM

In order to gain an understanding of how a integrated function and structure model would be analysed, it is necessary to consider how the associated reasoning system would operate. This section presents an overview of the current approach. It describes three analysis modules which process a model given a set of inputs.

The analysis algorithm   A model analyser has been constructed which can predict the behaviour of the system given an initial set of inputs. These inputs can specify particular events, initial states for both components and functional state variables (these are used to override the default values) and the absence of specified functions. The analysis algorithm has the following structure:

Initialise model state using inputs.

This is done using the default state information provided by the model and the initial input set. One of the inputs must be the name of the device node where the analysis must start.

Determine effects of inputs.

The system then searches the specified device node for all those events and functions whose preconditions are met. Once it has found all the executable events and functions, the system the processes each in turn. These steps are considered in greater detail below:

Identify executables. For each *event* or *function* whose preconditions are met, add those events or functions to the *executables* list. Events are added in front of all the functions.

Process model. While the *executables* list is not empty, process each member of the list in turn. Depending upon the type of the member, take one of two actions;

- If the member is an *event* then execute the action defined by it. If this action causes any change in the functional state of the system, then add any newly executable functions to the *executables* list and remove any functions from the *executables* list whose preconditions are no longer met.
- If the member is a *function* then for each statement in the function body;

  1. If the statement is an assignment statement then evaluate it.
  2. If the statement is a control statement then determine the flow of control and call evaluate body on the statements identified by the if statement.
  3. If the statement refers to a function associated with another abstract device node, then call *evaluate function body* on that abstract device node function.
  4. If the statement refers to the state of an electrical component then call *determine state from electrical domain* module on that statement. Once a result has been returned by this module, replace the *ElectricalStateof* reference with the result and re-apply the *evaluate function body* module.
  5. If the statement refers to the behaviour of a hydraulic circuit then call *determine state from hydraulic domain* module on that statement. Once a result has been returned by this module, replace the *FluidStateof* reference with the result and re-apply the *evaluate function body* module[7].

As it stands this algorithm performs a depth first search of the available set of executables. This is not ideal as it takes no account of functions which might actually want to be executed in parallel. This is an area for further work. The modules referenced above are described below.

The *determine state from electrical domain* module In order to determine the state of a component, for example, the water pump in figure 4, it is necessary to consider the circuit within which the water pump is used. This is because, the water pump itself has no circuit — it is used within a larger device/circuit — the system must therefore find the device object associated with that circuit. It is therefore necessary to retrace the device objects which have been processed. These device objects can be found by tracing the functions whose execution led to the state of the component being requested. The actual process takes the following steps:

1. Find the function which called the current function.
   If a function can be found then
   - Find the core device object associated with this function.
   - Find the electrical circuit structure definition.

---

[7] These actions are not complete and would need to be extended as new types of information were added, for example, the addition of a process representation might necessitate a new action to be defined.

- If the electrical circuit structure is empty, then go to step 1.
- If the circuit does not possess the component then go to step 1.
- If the electrical circuit possess the component, then return the circuit definition.

2. If the search has reached a terminal node, generate an appropriate warning message and stop the search.

In the case of the example illustrated in figure 4, the *activate_water_pump* function is called by the *turn_on_screen_wash* function. The device object associated with this function (the *windscreen_wash_circuit* object) does not possess a electrical circuit definition. The search procedure therefore continues. The *turn_on_screen_wash* function is called by the *clear_screen* function. The device object associated with this function is the *windscreen_wash_system*. This object does possess a description the structure of the electrical circuit, and this circuit refers to the water pump. It is therefore only at this higher level that is possible to analyse the circuit associated with the water pump, enabling the state of the water pump to be determined (e.g. whether it is active or inactive).

```
    define_function activate_water_pump;
        preconditions [[screen_wash_switch_state of screen_wash_switch] = on];
        if (ElectricalStateOf(water_pump) = active) then
            active → w_p_state;
        else
            inactive → w_p_state;
        endif;
        postcondition [w_p_state];
    enddefine_function;
```

Fig. 4. The *activate_water_pump* function of the water pump

Once an appropriate circuit description has been found, it is necessary to obtain the functional state of the device object and then translate the state using the translation information provided by the electrical_state definitions provided within the object. Once this is done, the circuit description can initialised with the translated state information and the circuit analysis performed.

The actual circuit analysis is performed by a separate qualitative circuit analyser (the QCA) [12, 13]. This can analyse the behaviour of circuits such as hydraulic circuits and electrical circuits (depending upon the domain model specified). QCA works by constructing a network which represents the circuit; each component is a node in the network, while each connection between nodes is represented as an arc. QCA finds a path through the network between the *source* and *sink* in the circuit. It then determines the direction of flow through the circuit. When instantiated with an electrical domain model, it can identify whether a component is active or not.

Once the state of the water pump has been determined, that state can be returned to the *activate_water_pump* function.

The *determine state from hydraulic domain* module This module is basically the same as the determine state from electrical domain module, except that it searches for a hydraulic system definition and a hydraulic state definition. It then initiates the qualitative circuit analyser with a fluid dynamics domain model.

Handling potential faults The IFSM system can be used to generate a description of the effects of a potential fault. For example, it could be used to identify what the effect of the positive input to the water pump shorting to ground would be (see appendix B). In order to obtain such an analysis, potential faults can be described in structural terms. For example, the above fault would be represented as an *arc* from *wire6* (the positive input to the water pump) to *ground*. Notice that faults are **not** described functionally, indeed no change is made or required to the functional representation. This is appropriate as it is not possible to predict what effects a structural fault will have on the functionality of the system until a full structural analysis has been performed (see section 6.1 for a more detailed discussion of this issue). In the IFSM system, the functional effects of a fault are generated (dynamically) through the low level functions reliance on structural analysis for their result. For example, if the result of structurally analysing the windscreen wash circuit is that the water pump is inactive, then the functional representation will state there is no water being squirted at the screen (even though the windscreen wash switch is on).

4.4   Implementation of the IFSM environment

The model analyser has been implemented in POP11 [1] using the Flavours object oriented language extension and consists of 1800 lines of code (including the IFSM Langauge definitions). The QCA has been implemented within Common Lisp using CLOS. The facilities available within the POPLOG environment for multi-language programming have been extensively used to integrate the two analysis systems. An example of an interactive session with this system is presented in appendix B.

POP11 possesses a Pascal like syntax but Lisp like list processing facilities and a simple pattern matcher. These combined with the facilities provided by the Flavours library make it a very good language within which to construct analysis systems. The ability to extend the basic syntax of the language makes it very easy to define new languages. This facility has been extensively used to define the IFSM language. This greatly simplified (and speeded up) the process of constructing the language.

The effect of compiling an IFSM definition of a device is that an object oriented internal representation of that device is generated. The basis of this representation is a device flavour definition. This defines facilities for evaluating preconditions, deter-mining postconditions, identifying which functions associated with a device object are executable at any time, generating a description of the functional state of the system, evaluating function definitions and initiating the qualitative circuit analysis.

Within the IFSM system, each device object definition is represented as an instance of the *device* flavour. Instance variables are used to hold information about the functional state variables, the events which can occur, the preconditions on functions, the electrical structure, electrical states, hydraulic structure and hydraulic states. Methods are used to represent the actual definitions of what happens when an event occurs or a function is performed.

An analysis is initiated by sending a *return_executable_functions* message and a *return_events* message to the chosen device object. The object responds to these message by executing the methods associated with these messages. When an event or function is to be evaluated, a message is sent to the device object. This message causes a method associated with the function or event to be executed. This can lead to messages being sent to other device objects requesting them to perform some event or function.

5 Using the IFSM within a diagnostic system

In previous work we have shown the need to augment a model-based system with knowledge which is not naturally part of any model, but which is essential for the generation of an actual diagnosis [17]. We have developed an architecture which allows the integration of a model-based system with appropriate additional information, in a principled well engineered manner [9]. We have constructed a variety of diagnostic systems within this architecture using a number of different analysis methods [7, 8, 9]. This has proved to be a straight forward task requiring no modification of the model analysers (each of the analysers was implemented without prior knowledge of the architecture).

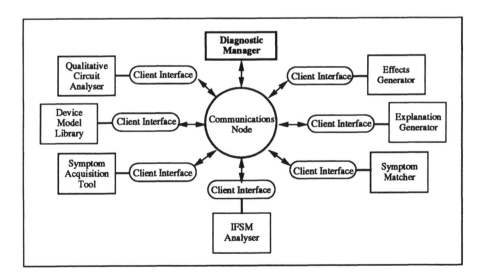

Fig. 5. The structure of the diagnostic system

We have integrated the IFSM system into our diagnostic system[8]. Some of the modules of this system are illustrated in figure 5. The diagnostic manager directs the other modules during the overall generation of the diagnosis. It does this using information provided by the other modules during an initial configuration phase. Each of the other modules can communicate with any other module at any time. This communication is achieved via the central communications node. All modules and the manager are connected to this node by client interfaces. The communications node is the mechanism used by the effects generator, the explanation generator and the symptom matcher to access the IFSM analyser. It is also the mechanism through which the IFSM analyser initiates the QCA module. Modules not illustrated in figure 5 include a data library which contains information on component reliabilities, and another which reasons about useful diagnostic strategies (such as candidate ordering and the single fault assumption). The diagnostic system is considered in more detail below.

5.1 The diagnostic manager

The manager provides facilities for achieving the high level control of the diagnostic system. That is it provides facilities for representing:

- knowledge of the goals that a diagnostic system must satisfy in order to generate a diagnosis. These goals include the acquisition of a set of initial symptoms, the generate of a set of candidates, discrimination between candidates, test generation and candidate verification.
- knowledge about the sub-tasks used to achieve these goals.
- useful diagnostic strategies, such as the single fault assumption.
  The actual diagnostic strategies are not permanently maintained within the manager. Instead they are maintained within a separate client. This promotes the domain independent nature of the manager.

It also possesses inferencing mechanisms for processing this knowledge. That is, it possesses reasoning strategies for:

- selecting which goal to satisfy next, based on the current state of the diagnosis.
- determining which sub-task, or sub-tasks, should be processed to achieve the current goal.
- allocating these sub-tasks to appropriate clients dynamically during problem solving, using information about the clients and the current state of the diagnosis.
  In order to reduce the potential complexity of the sub-task allocation process, each client is required to supply the manager with information about its problem solving role. This information is supplied to the manager either during an initial configuration phase or dynamically during problem solving when the client becomes available. This information is then used by the manager to assign sub-tasks.
  It also possesses facilities for selecting between clients when more than one client can process a sub-task. The diagnostic manager can auction the sub-task among the

---

[8] We have also integrated the IFSM system into a model-based failure mode and effects analysis system.

clients. Based on the reply, the client with the "highest" bid is selected. If there is more than one client with the top bid, then the task is allocated to both clients.

- processing diagnostic strategies. For example, it can retract the single fault assumption if necessary.
- mediating between contradictory results.

5.2 The client specification

A client is the combination of the client interface with some resource, such as a problem solver, user interface, database or simulator. This allows a model-based system, a heuristic-based classifier, a user interface written in Pascal, or an Oracle database to be easily and simply combined within a single system.

The client interface provides facilities for:

- connecting the resource's existing interface to the communications system.
- exchanging information with the manager and any other clients connected to the communications system. The definition of the communications language is made available to the client interface when it is instantiated.
- explicitly representing the problem solving role of the client and any other relevant information which is to be made available to the manager.
- accepting a sub-task directly allocated to the client via a communications message.
- determining whether a general request for information or some sub-task can be accepted, based on the role of the client.
- handling registration details. The interface provides facilities for processing registration requests from the manager, or for generating registration broadcasts when the system comes "on-line".
- generation of "bids" for sub-tasks. When a manager initiates an auction in which the clients bid for a sub-task, the client interface uses available information about the resource to determine whether the sub-task is within the scope of expertise of the resource and to what extent the current case may be within this scope.

  The value of any particular bid is generated heuristically, based on the sub-task to process and on the features of the current case. A bid is a *local* estimate of the ability of the client to process the sub-task. It is made without reference to any other client.

The client interface also builds up profiles of the clients with which its resource has successfully cooperated. It can then use this information to decide whether to direct subsequent requests for cooperation to a particular client (or clients) or whether to broadcast a general request to all clients. If a request to a particular client fails to generate a result, then a request to all clients for the same information is broadcast instead.

The clients within the system are described briefly below:

The IFSM analyser This client determines the effects of specified situations on a given model using the algorithm described in section 4.3.

The qualitative circuit analyser This client performs the circuit analysis described in section 4.3 when instantiated with an appropriate domain model.

The symptom matcher This module is a domain specific matcher which takes a set of symptoms and compares them to the description generated by an IFSM analysis.

The explanation generator This is a domain specific module which uses the IFSM analyser and the qualitative circuit analyser to generate user explanations.

The effects generator This client uses the IFSM analyser to generate a description of the behaviour of a system given a specified candidate fault. It then uses the symptom matcher to determine whether that candidate fault is a possible explanation of the observed symptoms.

Symptom acquisition tool This client is used by the diagnostic manager to obtain information about the behaviour of the actual device. The current tool uses a description of the system and the explanations generator in order to acquire the symptoms from the user.

Device model library This database client contains libraries of model descriptions of real systems and their constituent parts. It is a very simple retrieval system which looks in specified directories for a file containing the description of the device or component specified.

Data library The data library is a database client which maintains information on component reliabilities, component histories etc.

Diagnostic strategy client This client makes a set of diagnostic strategies available to the diagnostic manager. In order to identify which strategies are appropriate it uses information on the current domain and the current device.

5.3 The communications system

All modules in the system are connected together via the central communications node. This node provides facilities for broadcasting general messages to all modules connected to it, or for targeting messages for specific modules. It also maintains a database of previous communications which a client interface can access. As described above, the client interface builds up profiles of the clients with which its resource has successfully cooperated. It can then use this information to decide whether to direct subsequent requests for cooperation to a particular client (or clients) or whether to broadcast a general request to all clients. Although, one particular client may never have made a particular request before (and therefore does not possess any client profile information about that request) other clients in the system may well have. The communications database maintains information on the types of broadcast requests issued and which clients answered that request. This enables the clients to take advantage of this information and augment their own client profile databases. This improves the performance of the system.

5.4 An example session

We assume below that a set of symptoms have already been obtained from the user.

When the diagnostic manager selects the *generate_candidate_faults* goal, it must identify which clients to use to satisfy this goal. In the system described above there are two clients whose problem solving roles are consistent with the candidate generation sub-task; these are the heuristic candidate fault generator and the model-based candidate fault generator. This results in the manager invoking the sub-task auction process. This process auctions the sub-task between the eligible clients. The client with the highest "bid" is allocated the sub-task. In this case, the model-based candidate fault generator has the highest bid and is therefore allocated the sub-task along with the *occams razor* diagnostic strategy.

The model-based candidate fault generator receives the allocated sub-task. It is the responsibility of each client to decide how to (and indeed whether to) handle the strategies. In the case of the model-based candidate fault generator, it chooses to modify the steps it uses to generate a list of candidate faults such that it first considers single faults. In order to determine if a candidate fault can explain the available symptoms this client must obtain an analysis of a model of the device containing the faults. To do this it initiates the IFSM analyser client. This client processes the functional part of the model, using the qualitative circuit analyser (initialised with the appropriate domain model) whenever it needs to perform a structural analysis. Once this process is completed, the IFSM analyser returns a description of the behaviour of the model.

The effects generator must then use the symptom matcher to compare the generated effects with the available symptoms. This client returns a result which the effects generator uses to specify the status of the candidate fault. Once the model-based candidate fault generator has considered all of the candidate faults, it returns the results of its analysis to the diagnostic manager. The manager incorporates the results into its internal databases. It then continues with the diagnostic task. This may involve further interaction with the user via the symptom acquisition tool, explanation generation by the explanation client (which may also involve the IFSM client) and candidate ordering using the fault reliability database.

6 Related work

6.1 Functional modelling

Some research has already examined how knowledge of the function of devices can be represented (for example, [11, 19, 20]). For example, in the case of Sticklen's approach [21] (termed the FM approach) the top-level functionality of the windscreen wash system can be represented by associating a device with a function or functions, and those functions with a behaviour or behaviours. A behaviour description defines how a function of a particular device is accomplished[9]. A behaviour consists of a set of condition statements which indicate under what device state the behaviour is applicable, along with references to methods used to achieve some change in the state of the device, and statements about the effects of these methods on the device state. This system is discussed briefly below.

The FM approach The FM model of the windscreen wash system specifies that the screenwash subsystem has only one function; that of washing the windscreen and

---

[9] This is in contrast to the IFSM, in which there is no explicit explanation of how a function is achieved.

that this function is achieved by the squirt water at screen behaviour. This behaviour is illustrated in figure 6, and describes how the action of washing the screen is implemented by the subsystems. For example, if the *screen_wash_switch_on* condition is true (*present*), then the behaviour will be executed. Then using the *switch_circuit_on* function of the windscreen wash switch circuit, the *pump* will be activated. If the pump is activated then water will be pumped and by some knowledge about how the windscreen wash system works, water will be squirted at the windscreen.

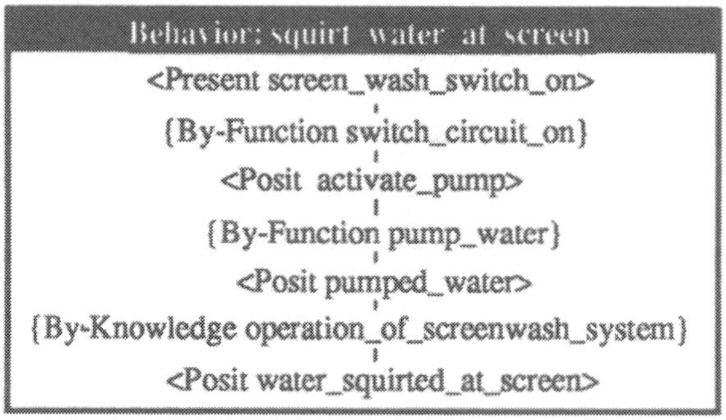

Behavior: squirt water at screen

      \<Present screen_wash_switch_on\>
      {By-Function switch_circuit_on}
      \<Posit activate_pump\>
      {By-Function pump_water}
      \<Posit pumped_water\>
      {By-Knowledge operation_of_screenwash_system}
      \<Posit water_squirted_at_screen\>

Fig. 6. The squirt water at screen behaviour

The functions referenced in the behaviour can also be expanded and the behaviours associated with each function evaluated in the same way as the *squirt_water_at_screen* behaviour. The *By-Knowledge* reference is a pointer to a piece of world knowledge that cannot be analysed further. In this example, it points to some knowledge about the operation of the windscreen wash system. Note that this is a functional description of the behaviour of the windscreen wash system, it does not have any concept of electrical connectivity nor of the fluid flow dynamics of the hydraulic system.

The FM approach also includes an algorithm for determining the effects of some situation on the operation of the functional model. This algorithm is called the consequence finding algorithm. This process essentially takes a set of initial (exceptional) conditions, including any functionality of the device which is assumed to be unavailable or altered, and analyses the effects of the initial situation on the functional model. For example, the effect of stating that the *screen_wash_switch_on* is ABSENT is that the precondition on the execution of the *squirt_water_at_screen* behaviour will not be met. The result of this is that the function *switch_circuit_on* will not be executed resulting in the *activate_pump* state not being asserted. If this process is followed for the whole of the graph the final result will be that the assertion *\<POSIT water_squirted_at_screen\>* will not be executed. Thus the deduced consequence of the screen wash switch not being on is that the windscreen wash system will not squirt water at the windscreen.

Limitations of a purely functional model There are a number of limitations associated with the use of a purely functional approach in the domain of electromechanical devices. These limitations include the fact that functional models terminate at a functional level, that the operation of a device is described in pseudo functional terms, and that the analysis performed is based purely on the use of functional knowledge. Each of these limitations is considered in greater detail below.

Terminates at a functional level In the FM approach, reasoning never goes beyond knowledge of the device's functionality. Understanding of the system is based around the functions of a device and the functions of a device's functional subsystems. Thus it can handle situations in which known functionality is present and situations in which it is absent. However, it cannot handle situations in which unknown functionality is present. This has significant implications for tasks such as diagnosis. A purely functional approach cannot (easily) deal with situations in which:

- the function of one of the constituent parts has altered. For example, the spring on an engine throttle mechanism could become slack or in the case of the windscreen wash system the pump could stall.
- the structure of the device has altered. For example, two components with relative motions can become fixed together, such as a metal block on a metal runner.
- some of the structure has been removed. For example, a component might fall out of the device of which it is a constituent part. This is illustrated by the removal of a spring that returns a component to its home position.
- some new structure has been added to the system. For example, a piece of metal could fall into a clock escapement mechanism or a short could occur between two wires.

In diagnosis these situations occur frequently. However, a purely functional model hinges on the use of known functionality and not on deriving large scale behaviour from small scale behaviour. As the above failures may alter the functionality of the system, a purely functional model may not be able to generate a complete description of their affects.

Describes a device's operation functionally A functional representation of a device, defined using the FM approach, is a conceptual abstraction of what a device is for and how it was intended to work. That is, both knowledge of the function of a device and knowledge of how those functions are achieved is represented (i.e. in behaviours). Such behaviours attempt to explain functionally how a function is achieved. In the domain of man-made devices this is inappropriate. For example, in the case of the *squirt_water_at_screen* behaviour (figure 6) the description provided has little to do with the the operation of the circuit and its components. Instead it is a causal description of what happens when the switch is closed and a circuit is formed. In this case an attempt has been made to capture the result of a structural analysis. Such knowledge is not at the functional level, and by its nature is prone to many of the problems associated with shallow expert systems.

Lack of deeper understanding The FM system actually provides an organised view of the "causality" associated with a physical system. This causality is represented in small "chunks" called behaviours. However, in common with any purely causal model (see Rieger [14] for examples of causal models) the causal links being represented rely on the model builder correctly describing the operations taking place. For example, in the *squirt_water_at_screen* behaviour, the *By-Knowledge* link could have stated that it was because the *sky_is_pink* that water is squirted at the screen! Similarly, because the causal descriptions are precompiled, if the windscreen wash system was redesigned with a different structure, even though the function remained the same, the *squirt_water_at_screen* behaviour would need to be reappraised, and possibly a new behaviour defined.

In order to understand the implications of these limitations for the diagnosis of man-made electromechanical devices, consider the effect of the stalled pump. The full effects of this situation are described below:

> If the pump stalls, no water will be pumped by it, there will therefore not be any water pumped at the screen. In addition, as the relay manufacturers demand that the wires in the circuit are large enough that the fuse will blow before the relay does, and the pump has a stall current of 10 amps whereas the fuse is rated at 5 amps, the fuse will blow. The relay is design such that it will not feed that current back to the CPU.

If this fault condition was analysed using a purely functional model (such as Sticklen's approach) then the result obtained would be that the *water_squirted_at_screen* state variable would be *absent*.

The functional model can determine what the effect of the fuse blowing would be (at a functional level), but it cannot detect that the fuse will blow unless this outcome is added to an altered *switch_circuit_on* function. This could certainly be done, but such an addition raises issues of reusability and generality:

1. Such an extended model might be less reusable than the original model. That is, if the modified functional model of the control valve was re-used in a different design then the addition might not be appropriate as it was not part of the device's specified operation. In the case of the negative output line from the master on/off switch shorting to battery positive a fault model would certainly need to take into account the structure of this particular windscreen wash system. If the modified functional model was re-used in the design for a new windscreen wash system which had a different circuit structure for major switches, then the model would have to be changed again to reflect the new outcome.
2. In order to be able to reason functionally about the effects of all possible failures of this kind, it would be necessary to have *a priori* knowledge of those very effects. Such knowledge can only be obtained by manually performing a complete analysis of all possible faults in that subsystem — an operation which may not be feasible. In fact it may be that we should never attempt to determine what the effects of some condition are based solely on functional information. For example, unless an analysis of the *negative output line from the master on/off switch shorting to battery positive* failure condition had already been performed manually, we might have been tempted to accept the functional models result as complete!

That is not to say that knowledge of the intended function is unimportant in model-based reasoning, merely that a complete understanding of a device can not be achieved through such a representation. Just as knowledge about the structural aspects of a circuit is incomplete without non-structural knowledge such as the function of a circuit, functional knowledge is incomplete without structural knowledge. In fact both structural and non-structural knowledge are required in order to gain a full understanding of the operation of a man-made device.

6.2 Integrating functional models with lower analysis

Sticklen has experimented with integrating the functional modelling system with the QSIM algorithm [22]. However, his primary aim in this work is to use the functional model's ability to focus in on a subset of the whole system, in order to constrain the envisonment performed by QSIM. He does not attempt to use the QSIM system to provide information on situations which are beyond the scope of the functional model. While the approach he has taken illustrates one of the major benefits of integrating a functional representation with a lower level analysis method, it does not address the limitation of the functional approach which concerns us here.

Work on the EDISON project [5] has also considered how functional knowledge can be integrated with lower level analysis. EDISON is a project which aims to construct an engineering design invention system which exploits "naive mechanics". This involves two issues: the breadth of and interactions between knowledge needed for creative reasoning and the amount of knowledge needed to describe mechanical devices, their behaviour, function and use. This second issue has led to the development of a functional representation which is similar to that developed by Sembugamoorthy and Chandrasekaran [19] but tuned for the purely mechanical devices. This representation is integrated with a qualitative reasoning system based on processes called behavioural process primitives (BPP). In EDISON the functions organise BPP's into a set sequence which explains how the functions are achieved. In this respect they perform the same operation as the behaviours in the FM approach. However, unlike behaviours they are analysed at the process level rather than the functional level.

7 Further work

There are a number of areas associated with the IFSM system which require further work, these include:

Greater interaction. The qualitative circuit analyser described in this chapter can not explicitly analyse a component such as the CPU in the windscreen wash system. Earlier we said that it might be possible to overcome this problem by allowing the simulator to use a functional model. This could analyse the CPU and inform the circuit simulator of the outputs of the CPU given a specific set of inputs. Such a process is still beyond the scope of the IFSM system. This would require extensions to the circuit analyser (something we have avoided so far) and significant changes in the IFSM reasoner.

Integrating other non-structural models. We believe that a number of other classes of models, other than functional and structural, could prove useful for diagnosis.

However, the integration of such models is outside the scope of the IFSM. For example, if we wished to incorporate simpler models of causality, or a system such as IQE [3] for modelling processes[10], we would find the IFSM system rather limiting. It could probably be done, but would require extensions to the IFSM language and the IFSM analyser.

In part this is because the IFSM system was designed with the express intention of integrating functional models with structural domain models for representing devices taken from the automotive engineering domain. It is also due to our belief that in order to obtain a clearer picture of why model switching takes place between this larger set of models, we need a better analysis of the diagnostic process for particular diagnostic tasks. If we are able to obtain such an analysis, then it might be possible to construct a reasoning manager which will be able to reason about the required model-switching.

The core representation. For electromechanical systems drawn from the automotive engineering domain, our core device representation has been successful. However, in some domains it is more difficult to identify an appropriate set of abstract systems and subsystems. In these domains it may not be possible to use the IFSM system. We are currently re-examining the notion of a core representation and the limits of its applicability.

8 Conclusions

Integrating multiple models promises to enable a level of analysis beyond that possible using only a single model. In this chapter we have described a framework which exploits a knowledge about the functionality of a device, in order to integrate two structural domain models. We have successfully used this framework to model a number of electromechanical devices such as the windscreen wash system and the cruise control system.

It is important to note that the IFSM framework is not general enough for many systems in other domains — it was designed specifically for integrating functional models with structural models. We have made a preliminary examination of some of the issues involved in constructing flexible multiple modelling systems; from this it is clear that such systems are still a long way off. However, the IFSM framework has proved to be very useful as an experimental platform in the domain of automotive engineering systems and to be a practical system upon which advanced expert systems can be constructed.

Acknowledgements

We would like to thank Prof. Mark Lee and Andrew Ormsby who provided the qualitative circuit analyser.

---

[10] IQE would be preferable to QPE [4] as it has been specifically designed to provided answers such as "is *some proposition* true in this state?". This is exactly what we require. QPE on the other hand has been designed to generate a complete envisonment.

Appendix A: The windscreen wash core object definition

In this appendix we only present the windscreen_wash device object definition. The complete windscreen wash model runs to 362 lines.

```
define_state_spaces
    system_states = [active inactive];
    switch_states = [on off];
enddefine_state_spaces;
define_device_object windscreen_wash;
    events
        define_event switch_on_windscreen_wash;
            "on" → screen_wash_switch_state;
        enddefine_event;
        define_event switch_off_windscreen_wash;
            "off" → screen_wash_switch_state;
        enddefine_event;
    endevents;
    functions
        define_functional_state_variables
            water_pump_state range system_states default inactive;
            water_pumped range Boolean default false;
            water_squirted_at_screen range Boolean default false;
            screen_wash_switch_state range switch_states default off;
        enddefine_functional_state_variables;
        define_function clear_screen;
            preconditions [[screen_wash_switch_state of windscreen_wash] = on];
            turn_on_screen_wash of windscreen_wash_circuit → water_pump_state;
                if (water_pump_state = active) then
                    squirt_water of hydraulic_system → water_pumped;
                    if (water_pumped = true) then
                        true → water_squirted_at_screen;
                    endif;
                endif;
                postcondition water_squirted_at_screen;
        enddefine;
        define_function deactivate_windscreen_wash;
            preconditions [[screen_wash_switch_state of windscreen_wash] = off];
            turn_off_screen_wash of windscreen_wash_circuit → water_pump_state;
                if (water_pump_state = inactive) then
                    stop_water of hydraulic_system → water_pumped;
                    if (water_pumped = false) then
                        false → water_squirted_at_screen;
                    endif;
                endif;
                postcondition water_squirted_at_screen;
        enddefine;
    endfunctions;
    structures
        define_structure electrical
```

```
components [
    [chassis :name ground]              [battery :name positive_terminal]
    [wire :name wire1]                  [wire :name wire2]
    [fuse :name fuse]                   [switch :name switch :state closed]
    [wire :name wire3]                  [wire :name wire4]
    [resistor :name cpu :resistance load]   [wire :name wire5]
    [connector :name relay]             [wire :name wire6]
    [resistor :name pump :resistance load]  [wire :name wire7]]
connections [
    [arc wire1 ground]  [arc positive_terminal wire2]  [arc wire1 switch]
    [arc wire2 fuse]  [arc cpu wire5]  [arc switch wire3]  [arc fuse wire4]
    [arc wire3 cpu]  [arc wire4 relay]  [arc wire5 relay]  [arc relay wire6]
    [arc wire6 pump]  [arc pump wire7]  [arc wire7 ground]]
states [
    [screen_wash_switch_state switch [[on closed] [off open]]]]]
```
enddefine_structure; /* electrical */
define_structure *hydraulic*
```
    components [
        [source :name water_bottle]     [sink :name 'nozzle]
        [pipe :name pipe1]              [pipe :name pipe2]    [pipe :name pipe3]
        [connector :name connector1]   [connector :name connector2]
        [pipe :name pipe4]              [pump :name water_pump]]
    connections [
        [connection pipe1 water_bottle]   [connection pipe2 water_pump]
        [connection pipe3 water_pump]     [connection pipe1 connector1]
        [connection pipe2 connector1]     [connection pipe3 connector2]
        [connection connector2 pipe4]     [connection pipe4 nozzle]]]
    states [
        [water_pump_state water_pump [[active load] [inactive open]]]]]
```
enddefine_structure; /* hydraulic */
endstructures;
enddefine_device_object; /* windscreen wash system */

Appendix B: Example output from the IFSM System

Below we present a trace of an interactive session with the IFSM system. It illustrates the effects of switching the system on and then off in terms of the the functions executed and the circuit analyses performed. It also illustrates how a structural fault (such as wire6 shorting to ground) can effect the function of the system.

```
: start(windscreen_wash);

Please select the event to perform:
 1. switch_on_windscreen_wash
 2. switch_off_windscreen_wash
 3. Exit event selection
Please make a selection: 1
```

```
    The functional state of the system is currently :
        The value of water_pump_state is INACTIVE
        The value of water_pumped is <false>
        The value of water_squirted_at_screen is <false>
        The value of screen_wash_switch_state is off

        *******    Starting the simulation   *******
Evaluating function clear_screen of windscreen_wash
Evaluating function turn_on_screen_wash of windscreen_wash_circuit
Evaluating function activate_water_pump of water_pump
Evaluating the electrical state of water_pump within the context
                    of the windscreen_wash
QCA > Analysing circuit using the QCA
QCA > Circuit analysis complete
Evaluating function squirt_water of hydraulic_system
Evaluating function pump_water of water_pump
Evaluating the fluid flow state of water_pump within the context
                    of the windscreen_wash
QCA > Analysing circuit using the QCA
QCA > Circuit analysis complete
        *******        Simulation complete    *******

    The new functional state of the system is presented below:
        The value of water_pump_state is now ACTIVE
        The value of water_pumped is now <true>
        The value of water_squirted_at_screen is now <true>
        The value of screen_wash_switch_state is now on

Do you wish to specify a fault? n

Please select the event to perform:
 1. switch_on_windscreen_wash
 2. switch_off_windscreen_wash
 3. Exit event selection
Please make a selection: 2

    The functional state of the system is currently :
        The value of water_pump_state is ACTIVE
        The value of water_pumped is <true>
        The value of water_squirted_at_screen is <true>
        The value of screen_wash_switch_state is on

        *******    Starting the simulation   *******
Evaluating function deactivate_windscreen_wash of windscreen_wash
Evaluating function turn_on_screen_wash of windscreen_wash_circuit
Evaluating function deactivate_water_pump of water_pump
Evaluating the electrical state of water_pump within the context
                    of the windscreen_wash
QCA > Analysing circuit using the QCA
QCA > Circuit analysis complete
```

```
Evaluating function stop_water of hydraulic_system
Evaluating function stop_pumping of water_pump
Evaluating the fluid flow state of water_pump within the context
                        of the windscreen_wash
QCA > Analysing circuit using the QCA
QCA > Circuit analysis complete
                *******        Simulation complete      *******
```

     The new functional state of the system is presented below:
          The value of **water_pump_state** is now INACTIVE
          The value of **water_pumped** is now <false>
          The value of **water_squirted_at_screen** is now <false>
          The value of **screen_wash_switch_state** is now off

Do you wish to specify a fault? y

Please select the fault domain:
 1. electrical
 2. hydraulic
 3. Exit fault selection
Please make a selection: 1

Do you wish to specify a component fault? n
Do you wish to specify a faulty connection? y

Please select a connection to modify
 1. [arc wire1 ground]
 2. [arc positive_terminal wire2]
          . . . .
 12. [arc wire6 water_pump]
 13. [arc water_pump wire7]
 14. [arc wire7 ground]
 15. Exit connection selection
Please make a selection: 12

The current description of the connection is
        [arc wire6 water_pump]
Please input new connection description: arc wire6 ground
 The new connection description is [arc wire6 ground]
Is this correct? y

Please select a connection to modify
 1. [arc wire1 ground]
          . . . .
 14. [arc wire7 ground]
 15. Exit connection selection
Please make a selection: 15

Please select the event to perform:
 1. switch_on_windscreen_wash

```
2. switch_off_windscreen_wash
3. Exit event selection
Please make a selection: 1

        The functional state of the system is currently :
            The value of water_pump_state is INACTIVE
            The value of water_pumped is <false>
            The value of water_squirted_at_screen is <false>
            The value of screen_wash_switch_state is off


            *******   Starting the simulation   *******
Evaluating function clear_screen of windscreen_wash
Evaluating function turn_on_screen_wash of windscreen_wash_circuit
Evaluating function activate_water_pump of water_pump
Evaluating the electrical state of water_pump within the context
                    of the windscreen_wash
QCA > Analysing circuit using the QCA
QCA > Circuit analysis complete
            *******      Simulation complete    *******

        The new functional state of the system is presented below:
            The value of water_pump_state is now INACTIVE
            The value of water_pumped is now <false>
            The value of water_squirted_at_screen is now <false>
            The value of screen_wash_switch_state is now on
```

References

1. R. Barrett, A. Ramsey and A. Sloman, 'POP11 A Practical Language for Artificial Intelligence', Pub.Ellis Horwood Ltd., (1985)
2. R. Davis, 'Diagnostic Reasoning based on Structure and Behaviour', *Artificial Intelligence* Vol. **24**, (1984).
3. D. De Coste and J. W. Collins, 'IQE: An Incremental Qualitative Envisioner', Proc. QR-91, Fifth *International Workshop on Qualitative Reasoning about Physical Systems*, pp 58–70, (May 1991).
4. K. D. Forbus, 'Qualitative Process Engine', in *Readings in Qualitative Reasoning About Physical Systems*, D. S. Weld and J. de Kleer (eds.), pp 220-235, (1990).
5. J. Hodges, 'Naive Mechanics: A Computational Model of Device Use and Function in Design Improvisation', *IEEE Expert* Vol. 7(1), pp 14-27, (1992).
6. J. E. Hunt 'Integrating Multiple Domain Models Using A Functional Representation', in *Applications of Artificial Intelligence in Engineering VII, Proc. of the 7th International conference in Engineering*, pp 1185-1208, (1992).
7. J. E. Hunt and C. J. Price, Multiple-Model Diagnosis of Electro-mechanical Subsystems', in Systems Engineering Journal, Vol. 2, No. 2, pp 74-89, (1992).
8. J. E. Hunt and C. J. Price, 'An Augmented Model-Based Diagnostic System Exploiting Diagnostic and Domain Knowledge', in in *Research and Development in Expert Systems VIII*, I. M. Graham and R. W. Milne (eds.), Proc. of Expert Systems 91, Pub. Cambridge University Press, pp 3–17, (1991).

9. J. E. Hunt, *A Task Specific Integration Architecture for Multiple Problem Solver, Model-Based, Diagnostic Expert Systems*, Ph.D. , UCW Aberystwyth, Dyfed, Wales, U.K. (1991).

10. Y. Iwasaki and H. A. Simon, 'Causality in Device Behavior', *Artificial Intelligence* Vol. **29**, No. 1, pp 3-32, (1986).

11. A. Keuneke, *Machine Understanding of Devices: Causal Explanation of Diagnostic Conclusions*, Ph.D. The Ohio State University, (1989).

12. M. H. Lee and A. R. T. Ormsby, 'A Qualitative Circuit Simulator', in Proc. *Second Annual Conference on AI Simulation and Planning in High Autonomy Systems; "Integrating Qualitative and Quantitative Knowledge for Complex System and Simulation Models"*, pp 248–252, Pub. IEEE Computer Society Press, (1991).

13. A. R. T. Ormsby and M. H. Lee, *A Qualitative Circuit Analyser*, UCW, Aberystwyth Internal Report Number UCW-RRG-92-010, 1992.

14. C Rieger and M. Grinberg, 'A system of cause-effect representation and simulation for computer-aided design', *Artificial Intelligence and Pattern Recognition in Computer-aided Design*, ed. Latombe, North-Holland. pp 299–333, (1978).

15. C. J. Price, J. E. Hunt, M. H. Lee and A. R. T. Ormsby, 'A Model-based Approach to the Automation of Failure Mode Effects Analysis', to appear in the Proc. of the *Institution of Mechanical Engineers, PartD: Journal of Automobile Engineering*, (1992)

16. C. J. Price, J. E. Hunt, and M. H. Lee, 'Diagnosing Mechanical Devices Using Qualitative Modelling', in *Intelligent Diagnostic Systems* (Ed. K.F. Martin, J. H. Williams and D. T. Pham), to be published by Springer Verlag, (1992).

17. C. J. Price and J. E. Hunt 'Using Qualitative Reasoning to Build Diagnostic Expert Systems', in *Research and Development in Expert Systems VI*, N. Shadbolt (ed.), pp12-23, Cambridge University Press, (1989).

18. C. J. Price and J. E. Hunt 'Simulating Mechanical Devices', in *POP11 COMES OF AGE: the advancement of an AI programming language*, J. Anderson (ed.) Pub. Ellis Horwood, (1989).

19. V. Sembugamoorthy and B. Chandrasekaran, 'Functional Representation of Devices and Compilation of Diagnostic Problem-Solving Systems', in *Experience, Memory and Learning*, J. Kolodner and C. Riesbeck (eds.), Pub. Lawrence Erlbaum, (1986).

20. J. Sticklen (ed.), 'Functional Reasoning: Organizing Complexity', *Special Issue IEEE Expert*, Vol. **6**, no 2, April 1991.

21. J. Sticklen, and B. Chandrasekaran, 'Integrating classification-based compiled level reasoning with function-based deep level reasoning', in *Causal AI Models, Steps Toward Applications*, Werner Horn (ed.), pp 191–220, Pub. Hemisphere Publishing Corp., (1989).

22. J. Sun and J. Sticklen 'Steps toward Tractable Envisonment via a Functional Approach', Proc. *1990 Workshop on Model-Based Reasoning, held at AAAI-90*, pp 50–55, (1990).

23. D. S. Weld and J. de Kleer (eds.), *Readings in Qualitative Reasoning About Physical Systems*, Pub. Morgan Kaufmann, (1990).

Multiple Models for Emergency Planning

Olivier Paillet

Alcatel Alsthom Recherche
Route de Nozay - 91460 Marcoussis - France
paillet@aar.alcatel-alsthom.fr

Abstract. The Second Generation Expert Systems approach begins to be widely used in areas such as diagnosis. In this paper, we will demonstrate its potential use to solve real-world problems in planning. This approach is illustrated by an expert system that builds restoration plans after a failure on a power transmission network. Organized around a blackboard, it integrates planning knowledge sources containing restoration expertise, a qualitative model used to predict the results of the plan, and a quantitative model used to verify the correctness of the plans towards numerical constraints. We will describe the benefits of this architecture for emergency planning systems, and the possibilities offered by the coupling of models and heuristics, for instance to reason with incomplete information.

1 Introduction

Large industrial processes become more and more present in our daily life, providing us with services like electrical power or communication. As we get more used to them, we demand more of their quality. At the same time, their complexity increases, and they are prone to failures like any physical system. In such a context, an efficient control is a critical issue. Control is already highly computerized, but operators are still needed to cope with complex problems that cannot be treated by automatic reactions. Their role is to interpret events, to diagnose problems and to define and execute corrective actions.

Many A.I. solutions have been proposed to support on-line interpretation and diagnosis [11] [15] [16] [17] [19], but the definition of corrective actions is sometimes also a very complex task. It is a planning problem, but with real-time constraints: it is better to produce a "correct" plan in a certain time limit than the "best" plan too late. A partial plan solving the most important problems is useful even if less important ones are still pending. We call *emergency planning* this kind of situation.

Planning has long been a major application area for Artificial Intelligence, and a large amount of work has been undertaken to define general planning frameworks [18]. However, in spite of promising early stages, complexity limitations have appeared [4] and the interest of universal planning systems has decreased. Besides, the frame problem remains a major issue, and severely limits the representation of actions in the conventional formalisms. For many real-world problems, simple formalisms such as the common Add-Delete lists of STRIPS [10] reveal themselves insufficient. However, some planning problems can be practically solved by an expert system approach. One must relax the optimality and the completeness requirements, and try more pragmatically to "quickly" build "correct" plans, with an extensive use of expert knowledge. This approach is consistent with the needs of emergency planning.

The expert systems area evolves too. Model-based reasoning techniques [6] are now widely used in diagnostic systems. To overcome the limitations of purely model-based approaches, the current trend is to develop so-called second generation expert systems, characterized by two keywords: specialization and cooperation. Specialization is the process of decomposing systems in tasks close to human problem solving practices, using a specific kind of knowledge (heuristics, qualitative models, ...) and a specific control mechanism. Cooperation is the definition of integration principles between these tasks to solve a complete problem [3] [12] [2].

The second generation approach is not necessarily limited to diagnosis. In this paper, we will present the potential use and benefits of the second generation expert systems approach for emergency planning, and attempt to define an appropriate framework. The approach is illustrated by an application, called MARS, that builds restoration plans on-line after a failure on a power transmission network. Organized around a blackboard, it integrates a knowledge-based planner, a qualitative model to predict the results of the plan and a quantitative model to verify the correctness of the plans towards numerical constraints. Particular cooperation mechanisms are defined to handle the constraints of emergency planning, and particularly incremental ("anytime") reasoning and reasoning with incomplete information.

Section 2 describes the principles of emergency planning. Section 3 presents the MARS application. Section 4 discusses the second generation expert systems approach for emergency planning.

2 Emergency planning

Emergency planning is defined as the process of building plans correcting an abnormal situation or behaviour of a physical process. In practice, most complex and potentially dangerous processes are equipped with automatic devices that are expected to prevent major risks and to handle a set of predefined potential malfunctions. Following these automatic reactions and controls, emergency planning occurs at a second stage, when human operators must cope with unexpected events and optimize the system behaviour. We will only consider the case of discrete and instantaneous actions, executed sequentially by the operator.

As a planning problem, emergency planning has some important characteristics:

- Emergency planning is subject to real-time constraints. Unlike conventional planning, the time spent before actions are executed is a major efficiency criterion. Corrective actions must be executed very quickly for many obvious reasons, including security risks and economical losses that can follow abnormal behaviours. Some hard real-time constraints also exist, for instance when the operator has a fixed time to react before the execution of an automatic safety procedure, like an emergency stop.
- Planning must deal with context-dependent and secondary effects of actions. Complex physical systems are often highly coupled, and the modification of a parameter generally has an influence on many others. These effects can result from the physics of the process, because of the causal links relating its different

parameters. For instance, opening a damper on a process does not only chage its state to "open", but could start an evolution of the whole process in order to reach a new equilibrium. Secondary effects are also due to the automatic control devices.

- Planning must deal with incomplete information, and with errors in the execution phase. The supervision system can never provide a complete information on the process, particularly when failures occur, and is itself subject to failures.
- For the two previous reasons, the operators' behaviour is partly opportunistic: the choice of the best action depends on the result of the previous ones. In particular, the result of previous actions can confirm or infirm some hypotheses concerning unknown state variables.

All these characteristics are weel-known limitations of universal planning methods and call for appropriate solutions.

3 An application example: the MARS system

3.1 The problem: power network restoration

Power transmission networks are large and complex systems, and are prone to local failures. They are protected by automatic devices that disconnect faulted areas after a failure to suppress short circuits or overloads. The objectives of the operators are to restore the power supply of loads in the disconnected areas and to consolidate the network by a restoration of non-faulted elements. The restoration is a reconfiguration process: the fauted components must be isolated and a new network topology has to be found in order to supply the disconnected customers with power. A restoration plan is a sequence of discrete actions on the network (open or close switches, disconnect automatons, ...). In order to build these plans, the operators must take into account general restoration guidelines as well as local constraints, but most of the procedure depends on their experience. The restoration is also difficult because the network state is often incompletely or incorrectly known. Network restoration is a typical example of emergency planning problem.

The MARS project[1] was launched with the objective of designing an automated decision support system for network restoration. The goal of MARS is to help operators in electrical dispatching centers to restore the network after local failures. The dispatching system will provide diagnosis and remote operation facilities. After a failure, the diagnosis subsystem will locate the failure and identify the network topology. Then, MARS will have to generate restoration plans, together with the dispatchers, and to design the appropriate remote operations to perform (Figure 1).

3.2 Knowledge representation

No network restoration algorithm can be defined, and universal planning methods are insufficient to cope with the difficulties of emergency planning. As skilled operators already perform network restoration, a knowledge-based approach appears as a possible way to automate or assist this task. Several kinds of knowledge exist and could be used to perform supervision and control tasks.

---

[1] MARS is a joint project between Electricité de France and Alcatel Alsthom Recherche

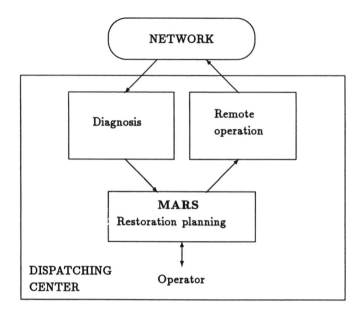

Fig. 1. Position of MARS in a dispatching center

Qualitative and quantitative models. Industrial processes like power networks being manufactured systems, knowledge about their physical structure generally exists. This knowledge can be expressed in terms of interconnected components, as well as knowledge about the behaviour of these components in response to external events.

The behavioural knowledge can be used to predict the results of planning actions, and particularly to compute all their secondary effects, at an appropriate abstraction level for planning. The structural knowledge can be used to find paths to supply a component with power.

A qualitative description of the network is sufficient to take most of the planning decisions. For instance, it is sufficient to know if a transformer is powered or not to decide to restore it. For this purpose, the electrical network can be described by a qualitative model, containing components characterized by a set of discrete variables (like "powered" or "not powered" for an electrical device, "open" or "closed" for a switch, "awake" or "asleep" for an automaton). Components are interconnected by several natures of links: electrical links or functional links (like a "monitoring" link between an automaton and an electrical device, or an "action" link between an automaton and a switch). The behaviour of an element is determined by behaviour rules that associate state changes of connected elements with other events occurring a certain time later. Behaviour rules can differ according to the operating modes of components. The size of the model is typically limited to several hundreds variables, since only a part of the network surrounding the failure has to be considered in the restoration process (Figure 2).

The qualitative model can determine which parts of the network are powered after a restoration procedure, but cannot verify if the restoration plan is operationally acceptable and does not violate constraints such as voltage or current limits. For this purpose, a quantitative model is added in order to compute the voltages and load flow in the network.

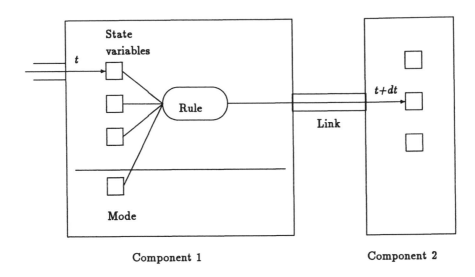

Fig. 2. The qualitative model

Plans. The solution -a restoration plan- can be defined as a sequence of *operations*, possibly recursively decomposed into sub-operations or elementary actions. The state resulting from the execution of a partial plan is called a *situation*, characterized by the value of the state variables at that point.

As mentioned earlier, the state of some elements is sometimes unknown. In practice, when operators have a doubt on the state of an element that would be useful in the restoration process, they perform special trial operations to determine its actual state. Similarly, the plans elaborated by MARS contain test operations. These are somewhat different from others operations: they have two or more resulting situations, associated with the various hypotheses on the actual value of the variable. Then plans in MARS are conditional. Of course, conditional planning introduces more combinatorial complexity and must be severely controlled. Here, uncertainty only concerns a limited part of the components, and components are tested only if they are useful to a particular operation.

Incomplete information and alarms. The models can be used to predict network states, but only if the values of all variables are precisely known. But, particularly in the case of failures, the information is often incomplete. For instance, if the diagnosis could not conclude precisely which components are faulty, some components remain doubtful. It is possible to simulate the behaviour of working or broken components, but not of doubtful components.

We handle this problem with the notion of *alarm*. When the simulator faces a situation where it is unable to predict the behaviour of a component, a special object called a simulation alarm is generated, and the simulation is interrupted. The planning process can then decide how to solve the problem: the component can be isolated, so that it is not involved in the simulation anymore, or a test operation can be planned to suppress the uncertainty.

This mechanism is extended to the detection during a simulation of all events that would reveal dangerous on the actual network. For instance, the qualitative simulation could predict that a component in short circuit will be energized; the numerical load flow could predict that a line will be overloaded. In these cases, the simulation is also interrupted, a specific alarm is generated and handled at the planning level. Again, several remedial actions can be undertaken, or the planning system can backtrack and try to find another plan.

Restoration knowledge. Skilled operators have learned, by instruction and practice, appropriate procedures to apply when facing abnormal situations. Several kinds of planning knowledge can be identified.

- *Orientation knowledge* is used to determine overall priorities between problems to tackle, like ranking of emergencies, taking into account general operation policies, or to choose between several alternative operations, taking into account the result of previous ones. In MARS, orientation knowledge is represented by three kinds of structures: *triggering rules* identify remaining problems to solve in the partial plans, and determine which high-level procedures can solve them. Symbolic or numerical *criteria* evaluate candidates with an appropriate evaluation function and select the "best" candidates. *Propagation rules* trigger criteria evaluation when some events occur, such as the evaluation of other criteria or a modification of some solution components.
- *Procedural knowledge* defines how to perform an operation. Typically, this knowledge decomposes high-level goals into more simple subgoals, for instance: "To restore a bus-bar, isolate this bus-bar from connected faulty or doubtful components, identify a powering source, and close the path between this source and the bus-bar". In MARS, procedural knowledge is represented by Prolog-like first order rules, exploited by a backward chaining algorithm.

Multiple models. In summary, various forms of knowledge can be identified and used for network restoration (Figure 3). The following section will illustrate how they can be integrated into an operational decision support system for emergency planning.

3.3 Architecture

The blackboard architecture. Taking advantage of the natural decomposition of knowledge, the planning system can be decomposed into several subtasks, having

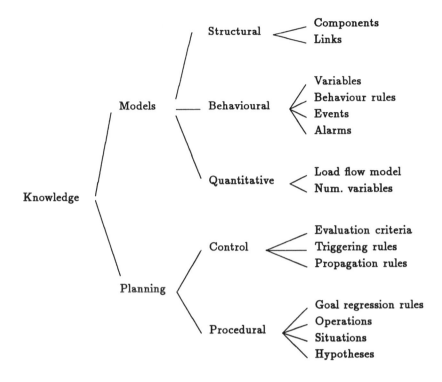

Fig. 3. Multiple types of knowledge

their particular knowledge representation and control structure. A blackboard architecture [8] is used to integrate these subtasks. MARS is divided into three levels (Figure 4): a planning level, a qualitative level and a quantitative level.

The *planning level* contains a blackboard, the planning knowledge sources and the control tasks of the planning process. The blackboard is a common memory, shared by the planning knowledge sources, storing the state of the resolution process. It is divided in two areas: domain and control. The *domain area* describes the restoration plan at two levels of abstraction: a strategy level defines a general guide-line to the restoration process in terms of restoration areas and priorities. A procedure level defines the plan in terms of situations, operations and hypotheses. The *control area* memorizes all control information, such as the Knowledge Source Activation Records (KSARs) and their evaluation.

The *qualitative level* consists of the qualitative model of the network and a discrete events simulator. The model contains components with particular attributes describing their qualitative state, their connections to other components and their behaviour rules.

The *quantitative level* is defined by a standard load-flow model which computes voltages and currents in the network.

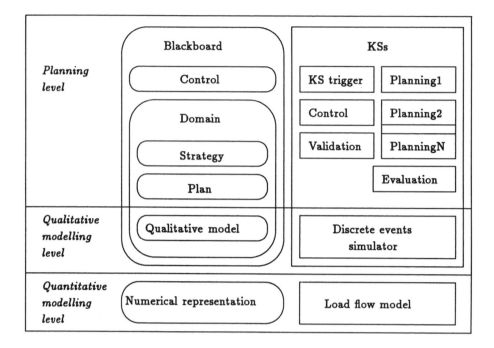

Fig. 4. Architecture of MARS

Knowledge Sources (KS). Procedural knowledge is encoded in *Planning KSs*. Various kinds of planning KSs exist in MARS: some try to expand a partial plan, others correct plans which execution can raise problems (determined by alarms generated in the qualitative simulation). Planning KSs consist of goal decomposition rules, and their internal control strategy is a Prolog-like resolution procedure. The granularity of KSs is particularly important: each KS execution has to result in a partial information that is useful for the operator, such as a partial plan restoring the power for one customer. With this approach, after each blackboard cycle, a useful partial solution that can be presented to the operator, while it is expanded by subsequent KSs. This is a form of anytime reasoning [7] with discrete and coarse grain improvements of the solution.

Orientation knowledge is encoded in two tasks: a triggering task and a control task. The *KS trigger* task is a rule base that computes the Knowledge Sources Activation Records (KSARs). One triggering rule is defined for each KS. The conditions of these rules are tests on the characteristics of a situation, on the value of state variables in the qualitative model, or on alarms generated by the simulation. The *control task*, characterizes, compares and selects KSARs. The comparison is performed using evaluation functions, triggered by rules and computing criteria. The selection is done according to the nature of each criterion: some criteria select only a "best" candidate, or choose all candidates that receive a particluar evaluation. The result of the control task is a permanent and opportunistic updating of a "best KSAR", that should be activated next.

A particular *evaluation* KS is defined to call the discrete events simulation, when a new partial plan has been created, in order to predict its results. When needed, it also calls the numerical simulator to check numerical constraints. The principle of the discrete events simulation is the following: an event (state change of a component) triggers behaviour rules, creating other events occurring a certain time later. All events are collected in a central agenda and sorted by priority. The simulation performs a loop on the agenda, activating each time the event with the highest priority. The possible risks (such as energizing a short circuit) are detected as side effects of behaviour rules, and associated alarms are generated and recorded in the plan.

A *validation* KS monitors the progress of the problem-solving and interacts with the user to validate or reject partial solutions or dead ends.

Link between the plan and the model. Situations in the plan are linked to the qualitative model by *viewpoints*. A viewpoint memorize the network state in a situation, ie the network state that will result from the execution of the partial plan until this situation. A viewpoint only stores the variable values that differ from the previous situation, taking advantage of the fact that typically few variables are modified by a planning action. This approach prevents an explosion in memory requirements that would happen if all the model states of all situations were explicitly stored.

Situations do not contain only state variables, but also an abstraction describing the qualities or troubles of the current partial plan as far as the restoration process is concerned. In particular, when simulation alarms are generated, they are recorded in the corresponding situation.

Cooperation principles and resolution method. The overall problem-solving strategy is simply represented by the standard loop of the blackboard architecture, until a solution is found and accepted:

1. Detect candidate KSARs
   The *KS triggering* task updates the set of candidate KSARS according to the modifications of the plan that occured during the last cycle.
2. Select best KSAR
   The *Control* task selects the most urgent KSAR to activate.
3. Trigger the KSAR
   The KS associated to the KSAR is called with the attribute values of the KSAR as arguments. Depending on the nature of the selected KS, the action performed in this step can extend a partial plan, correct a potentially dangerous partial plan or predict the consequences of a new partial plan.
4. Validate the current partial solution. Go to 1.
   The *Validation* task is activated. If necessary, it interrupts the resolution process to present the partial solutions to the user. The validation of a partial solution by the user avoids possible subsequent backtracks.

So, the first integration of heterogeneous tasks occurs at this overall resolution level. Some more specific cooperation mechanisms are defined using the simulation alarms. The principle of simulation alarms has already been defined: they are generated when potentially dangerous consequences of plans are detected by the simulators. Specialized planning KSs are triggered by alarms in order to try to correct this abnormal behaviour, otherwise the partial plan is rejected. These mechanisms are examples of the possibilities offered by a close cooperation between a qualitative simulation and a planning system.

3.4 Implementation and results

A prototype of MARS runs on Unix workstations. The planning and the qualitative level are implemented in SPOKE [2], an object oriented programming environment written in C [1]. The load flow model is implemented in FORTRAN. The blackboard is implemented using BBOP [9], a blackboard shell implemented on top of SPOKE ENGINE, the production system of SPOKE. The planning KS use PROLORE, a deductive system for SPOKE. PROLORE adds predicates and Horn clauses to SPOKE. Its control structure is a PROLOG-like backward-chaining resolution procedure. The link between the plan and the qualitative model uses a general viewpoint mechanism for SPOKE.

MARS has been experimented on a set of actual complex failures that occured on french regional power networks. The plans produced by MARS were correct. The complete resolution takes typically several minutes, but the problem being solved incrementally, first suggestions of actions solving the more urgent problems are proposed within less than a minute. Also very important, the plans are detailed up to the level of actual remote operations to be performed by the operator, thus reducing the risk of human errors when the solution is applied.

4 A framework for emergency planning

The architecture chosen for MARS had many advantages towards the objectives of a emergency planning system. We go back to these points and discuss our approach for this application area on a more conceptual basis, concerning the application of the "second generation" approach to emergency planning.

4.1 Functional decomposition

The decomposition of a system in tasks having their own knowledge representation and control structure has many advantages: the problem-solving process becomes explicit and possibly closer to the actual cognitive processes of human experts, knowledge acquisition and maintainability is facilitated [3] [5]. These advantages apply to a planning system of our kind: restoration knowledge is located in small tasks or knowledge sources that have a well defined role in the planning process and clear semantics for the experts. This architecture offers possibilities to represent different reasoning behaviours, like a "goal regression" at a low level to perform a simple action, or an opportunistic task selection at a higher level.

---

[2] SPOKE has been developed by Alcatel Alsthom Recherche and is commercialized by Alcatel ISR

4.2 "Heuristic commitment"

In general planning systems, the completeness requirement leads to exponential searches: in linear planning, all possible orders of goals must be explored when the system fails; in non-linear planning, the conflict resolution between parallel branches of the plan causes exponential searches to assure the existence of a correct order [4]. In practice, the use of expert knowledge avoids exploring unuseful orders or permutations. Very often, the experts can determine a correct order of actions, and the study of permutations would not help.

4.3 The use of models in planning

In diagnosis, model-based reasoning is supported by a set of procedures exploring the model to generate failure hypotheses or to test if the behaviour of the model under some hypotheses corresponds to observations. Here, similar procedures support the planning process. Various "candidate generation" procedures explore the model to propose candidates in certain planning tasks, for example power sources that are candidate to supply power to a disconnected area. "Test" procedures are defined by simulations of partial plans to predict their effects on the network. In addition, these procedures can be dedicated to a problem-solving process (here, the planning process) to provide additional information: for example, the alarm generation mechanism of the qualitative simulation in MARS informs the planning process about the possible dangers or difficulties in the execution of a plan.

Qualitative models are good candidates to be used for planning. Planning has to take decisions on the basis of an abstract and discrete description of the world; a set of qualitative state variables represents such a description. The role of qualitative models is double: they are used to predict the results of the plan, and they provide an abstract description of the world for planning. These two roles might well be decoupled: one could think of using a quantitative model for simulation, and only use the qualitative representation as an abstract description of the results. On the opposite, a simple qualitative simulation can be quicker and sufficiently precise to predict the necessary results for the planning task; numerical simulations could be used only to validate the potential solutions, as it is done in MARS.

4.4 Planning as search through a qualitative space

Our planning process can be described at a high level as a heuristic search, in a space represented by the qualitative model. Each situation in the plan represents a particular state of the model, and the planning KSs suggest possible developments of the restoration plan from a particular situation. The plan can be viewed as a search tree where nodes are situations and arcs are partial restoration plans. The development of the tree is controlled by meta-knowledge choosing at each step the best development of the plan, in accordance with the restoration strategy and to characteristics of the state resulting from the current plan. With this approach, we can easily develop the most promising branches of the plan, backtrack when the development of a branch reveals itself uninteresting, and we can compare several alternative plans developed in parallel.

4.5 Real-time

If we go back to the requirements of emergency planning systems, we can characterize the needs in some words: we need to quickly find correct plans rather than guarantee completeness; we would like to guarantee a solution (even partial) after some time limit. The framework presented here, "planning as search through models", has major advantages towards these goals because:

- it is constructive: it starts from the situation following the failure and progressively adds actions to a partial restoration plan. Partial plans are permanently executable and treat the major problems first.
- it is thus interruptible: at any time, it is possible to stop the search process and use the partial results constructed so far.

5   Acknowledgements

MARS is a common research project between Alcatel Alsthom Recherche (AAR) and Electricité de France (EDF). Many thanks to MM Harmand, Heilbronn, Mondon and Vu of EDF for their collaboration. Hélène Fargier of AAR had a major role in the design and implementation of MARS, as well as Chantal Benoit. Special thanks to Véronique Triaire who corrected a lot of mistakes in this paper.

References

1. C. Benoit, M. Bidoit, L. Henninger, R. Velly: *LORE: an Object-based Programming Environment*, TOOLS 89, Paris, november 1989
2. J.C. Bonnet, M. Uszynski: *RAMSES: a Second Generation Expert System for Train Maintenance*, Avignon 89, specialized conference on Second Generation Expert Systems
3. B. Chandrasekaran: *Towards a functional architecture for intelligence based on generic information processing tasks*, IJCAI87, Milan 1987
4. D. Chapman: *Planning for Conjunctive Goals*, AI Journal, Vol. 32, 1987
5. J.M. David, J.P. Krivine: *Designing Knowledge-based Systems within Functional Architecture: the DIVA Experiment*, CAIA89, Miami 1989
6. R. Davis: *Diagnostic Reasoning based on Structure and Behaviour*, Artificial Intelligence 24, 1984
7. T. Dean, M. Boddy: *An Analysis of Time-Dependant Reasoning*, AAAI 88, Saint Paul, Minnesota, 1988
8. R. Engelmore, T. Morgan: *Blackboard Systems* - Addison Wesley 1988
9. H. Fargier, O. Paillet: *A Framework for Blackboard Applications*, AAAI Workshop on Blackboard Systems, AAAI 91, Anaheim, 1991
10. R. Fikes, N. Nillson: *STRIPS, a New Approach to the Application of Theorem Proving to Problem-Solving*, Artificial Intelligence n.2, 1974
11. S. Feray-Beaumont, S. Gentil, L. Leyval: *Declarative modelling for process supervision*, Revue d'Intelligence Artificielle, Vol.3, n.4, 1989
12. P. Fink: *Control and integration of Diverse Knowledge in a Diagnostic Expert System*, IJCAI 85
13. B. Hayes-Roth, F. Hayes-Roth, S. Rosenschein, S. Cammarata: *Modeling Planning as an Incremental, Opportunistic Process* - IJCAI 79

14. B. Hayes-Roth: *A Blackboard Architecture for Control* - Artificial Intelligence, Vol. 26, No3, 1985

15. M.R. Herbert, G.H. Williams: *An Initial Evaluation of the Detection and Diagnosis of Power Plant Faults using a Deep Knowledge Representation of Physical Behaviour*, Expert Systems, Vol.4, n.2, May 1987

16. F. Jakob, P. Suslenschi: *Situation Assessment for Process Control*, Robotics and Computer-Integrated Manufacturing, Vol.3, n.2, 1987

17. A. Paterson, P. Sachs, M. Turner: *ESCORT: the Application of Causal Knowledge to Real-time Process Control*, Expert Systems 85, Cambridge University Press, 1985

18. W. Swartout ed.: *DARPA Santa Cruz Workshop on Planning*, AI Magazine, Summer 1988

19. Hwee Tou Ng: *Model-based, Multiple-Fault Diagnosis of Dynamic, Continuous Physical Devices*, IEEE Expert, December 1991

20. D. Wilkins: *Domain Independant Planning: Representation and Plan Generation*, Artificial Intelligence n.22, 1984

Knowledge-Based Design Using the Multi-Modeling Approach

Giovanni Guida and Marina Zanella

Dipartimento di Elettronica per l'Automazione,
Università di Brescia, Brescia, Italy

Abstract. This paper deals with the use of multiple models for design tasks. In particular, it shows that the multi-modeling approach can offer a valid background for facing some of the fundamental problems involved in the development of knowledge-based systems for design. After an introduction to the design task and an analysis of the main open problems, the issue of using multiple models for design is discussed. Later, a survey of the multi-modeling approach to the representation and reasoning about physical systems is presented. The standpoints of the proposed approach to design are then illustrated, and the specifications of an experimental prototype, called CDM, are discussed. The architecture and the general mode of operation of CDM are presented, and the techniques used for organizing and representing domain knowledge are illustrated. A sample design session with CDM is discussed in detail.

1   Introduction

1.1   The design process

Engineering design is a process which takes in input a set of specifications of the artifact to be built and produces in output a final design description, containing sufficient information to manufacture, fabricate or construct the desired system. The design process generally involves several conceptual steps and features a typical iterative nature. A commonly accepted view of the design process (Maher, 1990) includes three main phases, namely design formulation, design synthesis and design evaluation, as illustrated below.

Design formulation involves identifying the requirements and constraints of the artifact to be built. These are globally referred to as the artifact *specifications*, and include, either implicitly or explicitly:
- the definition of the intended behavior;
- the identification of the desired operational conditions and of the intended interaction with the environment;
- the statement of specific requirements or constraints concerning technical or technological aspects, reliability and safety conditions, costs, manufacturing, etc.

Design formulation is the first phase of the design process, but this does not imply that specifications are complete and correct from the beginning. On the contrary, they may be refined several times during the design process: *reformulation* steps are an integral part of design.

Design synthesis concerns transforming the artifact specifications into one or more alternative *design structures* which allow the fulfillment of requirements and, at the same time, the respect of constraints. Design synthesis is a typical problem-solving activity which involves a variety of knowledge sources, including - among others - physical and engineering principles, domain knowledge, design methods and heuristics, technological knowledge about available components and manufacturing techniques, etc. Design synthesis can generally be split into two steps, namely draft synthesis and detailed synthesis. *Draft synthesis* results into the topology of the artifact, which specifies its architecture, its components and the connections between them, without stating however any definite value for constructive parameters (geometrical, physical, etc.). *Detailed synthesis* specifies the precise numeric setting of all relevant design variables through appropriate calculation and, if needed, optimization procedures. The distinction between draft and detailed design is very helpful for tackling projects where, given the topology of the design, proven numeric (or symbolic) optimization techniques are available to compute parameter values (Chandrasekaran, 1990).

Design evaluation concerns proving whether the designed structure of the artifact fully complies with the set of formulated specifications, particularly whether the expected behavior and the actual behavior of the designed artifact coincide. The result of evaluation is a *validated design structure*. If any inconsistency is detected during evaluation, the parts of the designed artifact responsible for failures must first be identified (*diagnosis*), and then the design structure has to be revised or changed (*modification*), or a design reformulation has to be performed. Evaluation is usually done separately for draft and detailed design: only after a validated result of draft design has been produced, detailed design is performed and, eventually, its result is evaluated.

Usually the final, detailed description of the artifact which is appropriate for manufacturing, fabricating or constructing the desired system is something different from the validated detailed design, since manufacturing, fabrication or construction standards have to be taken into account. Therefore, the validated detailed design structure has finally to be converted into a proper *design description*. This last phase concerning the *production of the design description* can generally be performed through available computer-aided systems.

1.2 Routine, innovative, and creative design

At an abstract level, the design process, as well as each one of the phases previously described, can be thought of as a search in the space of eligible solutions (Maher, 1990), usually called the *design space*. The size of the design space depends both on the content and amount of the knowledge at hand and on the nature of the operators used to generate alternative solutions. In any case, the design space is generally very large, and the design process usually explores only a portion of it. On one hand, if no constraints at all are imposed to the design process except the respect of first physical principles, a very wide search space is explored, while, on the other hand, if only limited parameter adjusting is allowed, a much narrower design space is generated. Moreover, the portion of the design space which is actually explored also depends on the objective function, which guides the search, such as, for example, maximum function sharing, minimal component set, minimum cost, etc. Clearly, an extensive search in a large design space, guided by meaningful goals, makes the discovery of a final solution of high quality and originality more likely. But the size of the search space is not the only element which can affect the quality and originality of the solution: also the intrinsic power of the design operators used is very important. In fact, creating new candidate solutions primarily depends on the operators available and on the quantity and quality of the knowledge to which they can be applied.

From the point of view of the originality of the generated design, the design process can be classified into routine, innovative, and creative (Brown and Chandrasekaran, 1985; Coyne et al., 1987; Gero, 1990).

Routine design produces a final result from a restricted design space defined by a set of chosen design variables together with their acceptable ranges. These are derived from existing designs and design practice. Routine design generally does not produce highly original designs, while being appropriate to tailor existing designs to new, slightly different, but not exceptional, situations.
Innovative design differs from routine design since it is allowed to assign unusual values to a set of chosen variables, i.e. values that are outside the predefined ranges of routine design. The set of design variables relevant to innovative design is generally the same of routine design. Therefore, also innovative design operates in a restricted design space and cannot produce highly original solutions; however, it can adapt existing designs also to a new, exceptional situations.
Creative design does not confine the design space to the exploration of a fixed set of design variables, but it allows the design process to generate entirely new designs, possibly without even starting from already available design prototypes.

Note that the distinction between routine, innovative and creative design does not necessarily imply an increasing complexity of the search process and an increasing size of the search space. The nature of the design process is determined, first of all, by the objectives of the design activity, and, second, by the type and quality of available knowledge and design operators. For example, the repertoire of available elementary components and the capabilities of constructive operators that assemble candidate structures heavily affect the appearance of the artifacts that can be assembled. The search for an innovative or creative solution is, of course, complex and long - if not even impossible - within a design space intrinsically oriented towards routine design, but may be easy and short within a more appropriate design space.

1.3   Scope and purpose

Several approaches to automating the various phases of the design process have been proposed in the literature.
Focusing on the synthesis phase, we mention four generic problem-solving methods which have been successfully applied to the design task.

Problem decomposition - solution composition (Maher, 1990; Chandrasekaran, 1990) is based on the well established idea of dividing a large complex problem into a set of smaller simpler problems and then gluing the subproblem solutions into one solution. Alternative decompositions and recompositions may be taken into account for the same problem. *Case-based reasoning* (Maher, 1990; Chandrasekaran, 1990; Slade, 1991) uses task and domain knowledge in the form of successfully solved past cases. Given a new problem, analogy is exploited in order to select previous similar cases out of the episodic memory and then to transform their specific solutions into an appropriate solution for the current problem. *Transformation* (Maher, 1990) generalizes design experience into transformational rules, thus creating generalized design grammars or plans (Carbonell, 1983). When a new problem is encountered a set of applicable rules is selected and then the rules are used to solve the problem at hand. *Constraint satisfaction* (Chandrasekaran, 1990) is used to solve well-structured problems whose solutions may be obtained by exploiting the search space determined by a set of simultaneous constraints. Several computational algorithms can be applied in order to explore this search space, such as optimization techniques, constraint propagation or equation solving procedures.

The design evaluation phase may exploit several evaluation methods, such as simulation or specific engineering analysis. *Simulation*, either quantitative or qualitative, takes in input the system structure and generates in output the system behavior. Then, the evaluation of the designed artifact can be performed by comparing the expected behavior with the simulation results. *Engineering analysis* employs special-purpose techniques, such as, for example, finite elements analysis, in order to test the properties of interest of a given system thus proving whether artifact specifications are fulfilled. The diagnostic step of the design evaluation phase may be accomplished by resorting to typical diagnostic methods, including both *associative diagnosis* which finds out possible faults by consulting a compiled knowledge base which directly relates faults to their potential causes, and *model-*

based diagnosis which can discover the first cause of a fault in a system by handling a proper model of the system itself.

Although several approaches to engineering design have been proposed in the literature, several open problems still exist. In particular, past work in the field of knowledge-based design has proved that the use of multiple models is quite useful both in the synthesis (Gero, 1990) and in the evaluation phase (Bradshaw and Young, 1991). However, no clear and organic framework has been devised so far to support a disciplined, effective and coherent representation and exploitation of multiple models of the same device in the design task. Some progress in this direction has been made, for example, in (Gero, 1990; Chandrasekaran, 1990; Bradshaw and Young, 1991; Franke, 1991), yet the proposed solutions are weak from a methodological point of view. None of the above mentioned approaches takes the issue of the cooperation of many diverse models as the epistemological foundation for the development of general and powerful reasoning mechanisms, nor exploits the consequences of multiple modeling with full generality. More specifically, the question of how partial results obtained through reasoning within a model can be exported to other models in order to progress in the problem-solving activity has been tackled only in partial ways applicable to very specific situations.

The research described in this paper has the long-term objective of developing an integrated, knowledge-based support system, to help designers throughout the entire design process, focusing on creative design at the draft level. Detailed design is not considered, at least for the moment, since for this task several traditional tools are available, which could be appropriately integrated with the present project in a later phase. The class of engineering designs that is considered in this work is made of the possible assemblies of a number of different elementary components belonging to a given technological domain.

The main assumption of our research is that an essential contribution to creative design can be obtained by exploiting many, diverse knowledge sources on the application domain at hand, used in a highly cooperative way. In particular, the fundamental claim of this work is that the multi-modeling approach to physical system representation (Brajnik et al., 1989, 1990, 1991; Chittaro et al. 1989, 1992, 1993) can offer an appropriate background for tackling most of the problems involved in the design process.

2   Using Multiple Models for Design Tasks: Issues and objectives

In recent years, several projects have been developed which are aimed at integrating and using different models of the same system in order to take advantage of their cooperation in the accomplishment of some specific tasks. Proposals span a wide range of possibilities and perspectives: relaxing real-valued variables and using qualitative models (Murthy, 1988); resorting to different ontologies (Collins and Forbus, 1987; Rajamoney and Koo, 1990; Liu and Farley, 1990); using different aggregation levels (Davis, 1984; Genesereth, 1984; Liu and Farley, 1990; Rajamoney and Koo, 1991), exploiting models featuring different approximations (Weld, 1990; Addanki et al., 1989) and, finally, using models based on different time-scale abstractions (Kuipers, 1987).

In fact, it is widely recognized that no single type of knowledge can be adequate for a wide range of problem-solving tasks. For instance, design optimization problems may be very hard using structural or behavioral knowledge, but can be greatly simplified resorting to functional knowledge, which can support reasoning about alternative system structures (Franke, 1991). On the other hand, however, behavioral and structural models are necessary for all types of analytic tasks, such as simulation or diagnosis (Davis, 1984; De Kleer and Brown, 1984; Bradshaw and Young, 1991). Besides, it is rather intuitive to realize that the use of only one kind of knowledge casts a heavy limit on the creative power of any synthesis activity.

Moreover, it is known (Rasmussen, 1986) that adopting a single kind of knowledge generally conflicts with an economic use of knowledge and a high cognitive coupling. The claim that the cooperation of multiple models of the same system improve the effectiveness and efficiency of reasoning processes is strongly supported by cognitive motivations. In fact, experimental activity in the cognitive field has provided enough evidence that human experts typically use multiple representations in complex problem-solving tasks (Larkin et al., 1980; Chi et. al., 1982; Larkin et al., 1988; Bauer and Raiser, 1990). These experiments have also suggested that experts are able to flexibly switch from one representation to another and are very skilled in reformulating problems and partial results in different models.

In addition, resorting to a single kind of knowledge in the accomplishment of complex engineering tasks makes the reasoning activity opaque and difficult to explain. In fact, the knowledge employed to justify and explain the system behavior is generally not the same used for the basic reasoning tasks.

Finally, experience has shown that the computational effort needed to achieve a specific goal grows very fast with the number of variables of the model. So, efficiency cannot in general be achieved using only a single knowledge type: a proper problem decomposition and the cooperation of a variety of knowledge sources, organized at different levels of aggregation and accessible under appropriate views, is possibly the only way of adequately coping with complexity issues (Davis, 1984; Genesereth, 1984; Struss, 1988; Falkenhainer and Forbus, 1988).

Past work in the field of model-based reasoning about physical systems using multiple models has mostly focused on the use of structural and behavioral knowledge in order to support a variety of tasks, such as design, simulation, prediction, diagnosis, explanation, etc. (Williams, 1990; Bobrow, 1984; Iwasaki and Simon, 1986). Milestones of this research field are the component-based approach of ENVISION (De Kleer and Brown, 1984), the process-based approach of Qualitative Process Theory (Forbus, 1984), and the constraint-based approach of QSIM (Kuipers, 1986; Kuipers and Chiu, 1987; Lee and Kuipers, 1988). Some researchers have also investigated the use of functional and teleological knowledge. Teleological analysis (De Kleer, 1984) and functional representation (Sembugamoorthy and Chandrasekaran, 1986) have been two pioneering approaches in this field. More recently, the role of teleological knowledge for the evaluation and explanation of physiological systems has been investigated (Downing, 1990). The exploitation of teleological knowledge has also been proposed in design tasks for capturing design rules and for facilitating the reuse of components, as well as in diagnosis tasks for focusing the candidate generation process (Franke, 1991). Moreover, representing the purpose of a device and of its constituent parts has been advocated as a way to cope with the computational complexity of using structural and behavioral models (Sticklen and Bond, 1991).

3   The Multi-Modeling Approach: Basic concepts

3.1   Basic concepts

In recent years, a novel approach to the representation and reasoning about physical systems, called *multi-modeling*, has been proposed (Brajnik et al., 1989, 1990, 1991; Chittaro et al., 1989, 1992, 1993). The main concepts of this approach, which constitutes the background of the present work, are briefly surveyed below. For technical details the reader may refer to (Chittaro et al., 1993).

The key point of the multi-modeling approach is to opportunistically exploit many diverse models of a system for the execution of complex problem-solving tasks such as diagnosis, design, control, planning, etc. The models considered are based on different ontologies, representational assumptions, epistemological types, and aggregation levels. More specifically, in the multi-modeling approach five types of models are considered: structural, behavioral, functional, teleological and empirical. The main claim underlying this approach is that each knowledge type has a different role in reasoning about an artifact, and the cooperation of several different knowledge types is generally necessary to face complex tasks.

3.2   Knowledge modeling and organization

The concept of *model* we assume in the multi-modeling approach is that of a symbolic representation of a physical system appropriate for a given purpose. So, a model is only a partial representation of reality, and depends on subjective decisions of the model designer. In particular, modeling requires going through four fundamental choices concerning ontologies, representational assumptions, epistemological types, and aggregation levels. We illustrate these concepts in detail below.

Ontologies

Building a model requires, first of all, making some assumption about which entities constitute the real system and must be represented in the model. This decision defines the *ontology* of the model. We distinguish between two ontologies:
- *Object-centered ontology*, which assumes that reality is made of individual objects, whose properties can be stated independently from any observer and from any environment (i.e., in an objective, context-independent, and universal way). This ontological perspective enforces modularity and reusability of the representation of objects. According to the granularity of the individual objects, we further distinguish between i) *macroscopic ontologies*, which assume that reality is made of individual macroscopic objects, and ii) *microscopic ontologies*, which assume that reality is made of elementary individuals at an atomic or molecular level.
- *System-centered ontology*, which assumes that reality is made of systems. A system is intended as an organized unit, composed by elements which cannot be defined in isolation but solely with reference to the totality in which they appear. This ontological perspective enforces the representation of a system in terms of specific and context-dependent properties.

The component-centered approach (De Kleer and Brown, 1984) to qualitative modeling of physical systems is a good example of a theory based on a macroscopic object-centered ontology. The charge-carrier ontology (Liu and Farley, 1990) and the microscopic theories used by (Rajamoney and Koo, 1990) for reasoning about physical systems at the molecular level are examples of microscopic object-centered ontologies. Examples of the use of a system centered ontology can be found in the functional modeling approaches (Rasmussen, 1986; Keuneke and Allemang, 1989; Sembugamoorthy and Chandrasekaran, 1986)

Moreover, in some cases, both ontologies are present, such as, for example, in the process-centered approach (Forbus, 1984), developed on top of the component-centered approach (De Kleer and Brown, 1984) by modeling explicitly not only individual components but also the processes which act on them. Note that the representation of processes derives from looking at a physical system from a system-centered perspective. We call *hybrid ontology* an ontological perspective that mixes aspects of both the object-centered and the system-centered ontologies.

Models of the same system based on different ontologies can be related to each other through specific *ontological links*, which explicitly connect corresponding knowledge elements in different ontologies.

Representational assumptions

Another very preliminary decision to be made in the modeling activity concerns what to represent of the real system in the model. This decision concerns two basic issues:
- the *scope* of the model, i.e. those aspects of the real world which are considered relevant to the purpose of the model and therefore must be included in the model, and those which, on the other hand, are considered immaterial and thus can be disregarded;
- the *precision* of the model, i.e. the degree of accuracy of the representation.

These choices are referred to as *representational assumptions*. Different representational assumptions lead to different models of the same system: we call such models *approximations*. Note that scope and precision are independent: we may have models with the same scope but featuring different precisions (such as, for example, a behavioral quantitative model of a system and its qualitative version), and models having the same precision but different scopes (such as, for example, models which consider or do not consider friction, or models which assume or do not assume the hypothesis of rigid body). Models of the same system based on different representational assumptions can be related to each other through specific *representational links*, which explicitly specify i) the representational assumptions that must be added or retracted in order to switch from one approximation to another (Addanki et al., 1989), and ii) the relationships connecting corresponding knowledge elements in different approximations.

In our approach, the scope of a model is organized according to physical views. The concept of *physical view* (Struss, 1988) represents a feature of knowledge organization that allows the indexing of the relevant aspects included in a model according to given physical perspectives (for example, the thermal perspective, the electric perspective, the mechanical perspective, etc.). The availability of physical views allows the reasoning process to consider only those parts of the scope of a model which are relevant to the current problem-solving step, discarding other details which turn out to be useless or immaterial for the progress of problem-solving.

Epistemological types

By *epistemological type* we mean the class of epistemological features a model can represent about the system at hand. In our approach we identify five epistemological types:

- *Structural knowledge*, i.e. knowledge about system topology. This type of knowledge describes which components constitute the system and how they are connected to each other (their adjacency).
- *Behavioral knowledge*, i.e. knowledge about potential behaviors of components. This type of knowledge describes how components can work and interact in terms of the physical quantities that characterize their state (variables and parameters) and the laws that rule their operation.
- *Functional knowledge*, i.e. knowledge about the roles components may play in the physical processes in which they take part. This type of knowledge relates the behavior of the system to its goals, through functional roles, processes, and phenomena.
- *Teleological knowledge*, i.e. knowledge about the goals assigned to the system by its designer and about the operational conditions which allow their achievement through a correct operation. This type of knowledge concerns the high-level reasons which are behind the system concept and which, possibly, have determined its actual structure.
- *Empirical knowledge*, i.e. knowledge concerning the explicit representation of system properties through direct empirical associations. This type of knowledge may be derived from observation, experimentation, and experience, and may include, in particular, the subjective competence that usually human experts acquire through direct interaction with a system.

Let us note that the five epistemological types defined above can be appropriately grouped into three categories. Structural and behavioral knowledge are *fundamental knowledge*, i.e. basic knowledge exploited to reason about a system using the objective and neutral language of natural sciences. On the other hand, functional and teleological knowledge are *interpretative knowledge*, i.e. knowledge derived from an interpretation of fundamental knowledge in terms of functions and goals of system components. This knowledge does not have the same generality and objectivity of fundamental knowledge; for example, when we say "component X is devoted to ..." we express a relationship between a system component (its structure and behavior) and a goal, which is generally not valid for other components of the same type in the same or in other systems. Finally, *empirical knowledge*, is a separate category, which concerns explicit statement of system properties and can refer to both fundamental and interpretative knowledge.

Models of the same system based on different epistemological types can be related to each other through specific *epistemological links*, which explicitly connect corresponding knowledge elements in different models.

Aggregation levels

By *aggregation level* of a model we mean the degree of granularity of the represented knowledge. For example, a structural model of a plant may be represented at the level of major subsystems or may be further refined at that of elementary components. Of course, for a physical system (once representational assumptions have been defined and the specific ontology and epistemological type have been chosen) several models featuring different aggregation levels may generally be identified.

Models of the same system based on different aggregation levels can be related to each other through specific *aggregation links*, which explicitly connect corresponding knowledge elements in different models.

In the multi-modeling approach any choice about ontology is allowed, as well as any kind of representational assumptions, epistemological types, and aggregation levels. The only restrictions that are imposed to the organization of the various models of a system are the following:

- Models are separate, i.e. any individual model is allowed to encompass only one specific choice about ontology (possibly an hybrid ontology), representational assumptions, epistemological types, and aggregation levels.
- Models are not independent, i.e. any individual model is based on the existence and on the characteristics of other models. As a consequence models must be explicitly and appropriately connected to each other.

As far as the former point is concerned, note that its primary motivation - in addition to the generic issue of modularity - is the requirement of a multiple use of knowledge. In fact, according to the specific problem-solving task considered, different types of knowledge may be useful in different moments and with different roles, and, therefore, their representations must be as far as possible separate.

As far as the latter point is concerned, let us note that not all possible links between models are meaningful or necessary. For epistemological links, for example, we assume, in our approach, the following set of (bi-directional) direct links: structural-behavioral, behavioral-functional, functional-teleological, empirical-teleological, empirical-functional, empirical-behavioral, empirical-structural. These links can be combined transitively to give other links, such as structural-functional, or teleological-structural.

Finally, let us stress that models are not required to be complete. In other words, models can represent only parts of a system. This may happen, for example, in analytic tasks when knowledge about the system is not available, or, in synthetic tasks when the system is unknown since it has still to be designed and built. However, in order to effectively use the available knowledge in a cooperative way even in the case of incomplete models, representations have to be connected to each other with appropriate ontological, representational, epistemological, and aggregation links.

3.3 Reasoning

The execution of a problem-solving task within the multi-modeling approach is based on two fundamental mechanisms:
- *reasoning inside a model*, which exploits knowledge available within a single model by using *model-specific problem-solving methods*, implemented through *basic reasoning utilities*;
- *reasoning through models*, which supports opportunistic navigation among models in order to allow each individual step of the problem-solving activity to exploit the most appropriate knowledge source.

The overall reasoning process is constituted at domain level by a sequence of "reasoning inside a model" steps which are guided at control level by a "reasoning through models" activity, which continuously monitors and directs the exploitation of available knowledge sources. This clearly implies that appropriate mechanisms for translating partial results from one model to another are available.

The control regime of the "reasoning through models" mechanism is determined by two main types of knowledge:

- Knowledge about the tasks the system is requested to solve.
  The multi-modeling approach is in principle suitable to reason about a large variety of *tasks*, such as interpretation, diagnosis, design, simulation, etc. When the reasoning mechanism is tailored to a specific application, the relevant *task-specific problem-solving methods* are provided (Chandrasekaran, 1986; Steels, 1990). These are used to decompose the tasks at hand into sub-tasks until elementary tasks are obtained which can be solved using a single knowledge source through appropriate model-specific problem-solving methods.

- Knowledge about effective exploitation of available domain knowledge.
  During system operation several control problems must be solved concerning the most appropriate use of available knowledge sources. These include:
  - choosing the most suitable model to be used for solving an elementary task, when several alternative models are available (*initial model selection*);
  - selecting a new model where the reasoning activity can continue after a failure has occurred during the execution of a model-specific problem-solving method (*failure-driven model selection*);
  - monitoring the execution of a model-specific problem-solving method and detecting when it might be appropriate to switch from the currently used model to another one which is supposed to be more suitable to continue the reasoning activity (*opportunity-driven model selection*);

- determining the appropriate focus of attention for the execution of a basic reasoning utility by activating the relevant physical views (*focus control*).

4   The CDM Prototype: Standpoints and specifications

4.1   Standpoints

The standpoint of the research reported in this paper is the adoption of the multi-modeling approach as an appropriate background to tackle design tasks, in particular creative draft design. The reasons underlying this choice are manifold, and various advantages are expected from the cooperation of multiple models in performing such a complex task as engineering design. The most important points are briefly illustrated below.

Design as mapping between abstractions

Generally, the potential users of a system can provide initial specifications at the teleological level, i.e. they can state the purpose for which the artifact has to be designed. Then, the designer - or the design support system - has to gradually proceed from teleology to function, and from function to structure and behavior in order to identify the appropriate topology of the desired artifact. Thus, from a very basic point of view, design can be interpreted as a mapping between abstractions. The multi-modeling approach offers many of the fundamental features which are needed to implement a reasoning process which can easily and naturally walk through several abstraction levels, not only top-down - from teleology to structure - but also freely jumping from one abstraction to another, as it is often necessary in complex design tasks.

Cognitive plausibility

The ability to endow a design support system with a reasonable degree of cognitive plausibility is recognized as an important issue both for improving user acceptance and for making system development more effective, controlled, and easy. Moreover, cognitive plausibility is a fundamental prerequisite to support both transparency of system behavior and justification and explanation capabilities. The choices or suggestions made by the system are much easier to explain if they are the consequences of comprehensible processing steps, documented by understandable progressive representations of the artifact being designed. These features are all within the scope of the multi-modeling approach.

Creative power

The performance of a support system for creative design should feature strong creative power in assembling components available in the domain of interest. Considering the design process as a search in the design space, this should be creative in nature, so that the system can produce creative designs within reasonable computation time and effort. Hence, fundamental knowledge about available components and their possible connections has to be wide, detailed and multi-faceted, describing different abstractions, views, aggregation levels, and operational modes. The multi-modeling approach supplies mechanisms capable to create a structured and rich description of components, as well as of any partial assembly of the artifact being designed.

Effectiveness and efficiency

The issue of effectiveness and efficiency includes several aspects which are shortly discussed below.

Incrementalism. The progressive generation of multiple models of the artifact being designed, which is typical of the multi-modeling approach, perfectly reflects the incremental nature of the design process, that is the step-wise production of descriptions of lower and lower abstraction level, starting from the initial specifications. This, not only contributes to improve cognitive plausibility, but also enables the design support system to exploit a step-by-step methodology, thus reducing the computational complexity of the overall design process. Each step can be accomplished by reasoning inside models of one epistemological type, namely that which is the most appropriate for the processing performed during the step itself, thus improving both the efficiency and the effectiveness of the reasoning activity.

Focusing. Reasoning about physical systems becomes more effective and efficient if only those pieces of knowledge which are relevant to the particular physical aspect of interest are taken into account in each specific step, such as, for example, mechanical, thermal, electric, etc. The view mechanism provided by the multi-modeling approach is appropriate to implement a dynamic control of the focus of attention.

Opportunistic navigation through models. The exploitation of many, diverse models of the device being designed, such as those available in the multi-modeling approach, besides enforcing a better cognitive plausibility, makes it possible to opportunistically switch from one model to another. This can ensure that the most appropriate model is used in each specific reasoning step and that, at the same time, the results of previous processing steps are effectively exploited, being sharable among all relevant model-specific problem-solving methods.

Decomposition knowledge. A rich representation of decomposition knowledge is needed in order to enhance the performance of problem decomposition operators. In fact, the availability of both good knowledge and powerful operators relieves to a great extent the design support system from the use of more computation-intensive kinds of reasoning, such as resorting to first physical principles, nevertheless obtaining valid and highly original results. Teleological knowledge, which is quite supported by the multi-modeling approach, may effectively play the role of decomposition knowledge when it is applied to design tasks, since it allows the global goal of the artifact, described by its specifications, to be progressively decomposed into simpler subgoals.

Empirical knowledge. A separate source of empirical knowledge is provided by the multi-modeling approach, which can store both associations and cases representing specific features of the task and of the domain at hand. In design applications this knowledge source is the repository of the actual design expertise valid in the particular domain of interest, such as, for example, rules of thumb or prototypical cases derived from experience which can speed up the accomplishment of specific reasoning steps.

4.2   Aim, scope and specifications of the CDM prototype

The long-term objective of our work is to develop a generalized, cooperative, interactive environment for supporting a designer in the high-level stages of the design task, possibly resorting to traditional CAD packages for the lower-level stages, such as the production of the final design description. In order to pursue this goal, an explorative approach has been adopted. After a first phase dedicated to conceptual investigation and working out of simple design examples, the development of a running prototype has been undertaken. This is considered a crucial step in focusing problems and experimenting with possible solutions. In particular, the development of the prototype has the following major goals:
- showing the appropriateness the multi-modeling approach, which has already been successfully employed for diagnosis, for design tasks;
- investigating in particular the role and use of teleological and functional knowledge in creative design;
- investigating the nature of design knowledge, its representation and use in the frame of the multi-modeling approach, focusing in particular on domain-independent strategies for design.

The prototype presently being developed is called *CDM* (*Creative Design through Multi-modeling*) and is implemented in LPA Prolog in a MS-DOS/Windows environment. The class of problems that can be solved by CDM includes the design of lumped-parameter devices whose desired behavior, which may be described by transitions in a state diagram, is governed by the laws of physical system dynamics.

In the implementation of CDM the three design phases introduced in section 1.1 have been interpreted as follows.

Design formulation is viewed as a teleological specification, i.e. the user initially states the specific purpose of the artifact to be designed using teleological primitives. The user is also allowed to add particular requirements and constraints, as well as to specify requested or forbidden components or design solutions. Requirements and constraints may concern, for example, properties of the artifact (such as, its size, or its weight), operational conditions (such as, external pressure or temperature), or characteristics of the design process itself (such as, time and cost). CDM analyzes the initial specifications for consistency and, if needed, interacts with the user asking for corrections and refinements.

Later CDM performs a draft synthesis, following a kind of "problem decomposition - solution composition" methodology (Chandrasekaran, 1990; Maher, 1990) and exploiting qualitative reasoning. Function sharing (Ulrich and Seering, 1988), that is the simultaneous implementation of several functions by means of a single structural element, is pursued throughout the synthesis. In the synthesis phase the initial system-centered abstract description (at teleological level) proper of system specification, is progressively transformed into more and more concrete and detailed descriptions (at functional and behavioral levels), and finally into a component-centered domain-specific description (at structural level). CDM can generate and explore several design hypotheses which are shown to the user, who is allowed to ask explanations about the design strategies and principles utilized, query about the expected behavior of the proposed design hypotheses and the underlying physical principles, and browse the assumptions made during the design process. The user can incrementally correct and complete the initial specifications and let CDM generate further design hypotheses. The designer can also directly manipulate the design hypotheses or the intermediate design structures generated by CDM or propose his/her own solution and ask CDM for comments and critiques. This kind of cooperative work continues until a satisfactory solution is found.

The evaluation phase can verify both automatically created and user made design structures. It involves the transformation of the structural description of the artifact into a behavioral description and, finally, into a teleological description which is compared against the last validated specifications. Besides checking the structure against specifications, an expert-critiquing functionality (Silverman and Mezher, 1992) can be invoked to check the global quality of the obtained result. Interactive expert-critiquing is specially useful to correct possible bad or inappropriate design choices made either by the system or by the designer who may be affected by various types of knowledge lacks, competence flaws, and bias.

5 The CDM Prototype: Architecture, knowledge representation and reasoning mechanisms

5.1 CDM architecture

Basic structure

CDM is based on the concept of blackboard architecture (Hayes-Roth, 1985; Nii, 1986a; Nii, 1986b). It supports the decomposition of the design problem into a limited number of interacting subproblems, and hosts a collection of individual problem solvers, called *specialists*, each one devoted to face a specific class of subproblems. Each specialist is to a large extent independent from the others, exploiting as much as possible different reasoning techniques and different knowledge sources. While no problem solver is supposed to have enough competence to solve the entire design problem at hand, it is assumed that the cooperative interaction of all available specialists can produce the desired solution. No constraint is put on the number of specialists which might be devoted to a specific single subproblem: a subproblem can be tackled from several different viewpoints, thus extending the overall problem-solving power and flexibility of the system. Specialists at problem level can operate concurrently and have no mutual awareness. In the present version of CDM, five specialists are available to implement the "reasoning inside a model" capability through appropriate model-specific problem-solving methods, namely: a *teleological specialist*, a *functional specialist*, a *behavioral specialist*, a *structural specialist*, and an *empirical specialist*. Each specialist has access to its own *specialist knowledge base*, and can operate in a dedicated *specialist area* of the *common blackboard*.

CDM architecture includes a dedicated mechanism, called *control manager*, for controlling the activity of the various specialists, in order to obtain a globally cooperative behavior, aimed at the complete solution of the design problem at hand. Therefore, the architecture is split into two levels, namely:
- a control level, where cooperation and interaction between specialists is dealt with in a centralized way under the responsibility of the control manager;
- a problem level, where problem solving in the specific competence area of each individual specialist takes place.

Control level activities are centralized and supervised by the control manager, which coordinates the activities of problem level specialists towards the achievement of a global purpose. The control manager uses a dedicated *control knowledge base* which contains knowledge about both general and task-specific problem-solving methods, and operates on a *control blackboard*. Moreover, it has full visibility on the common blackboard at problem level.

Mode of operation

The operation mode of the proposed architecture is based on the assumption that tentative partial results produced by individual specialists are progressively accumulated in the *solution area* of the common blackboard and iteratively revised under the supervision of the control manager, until the desired final result is obtained. Note that the common blackboard also includes a *specification area*, containing the current specifications of the artifact to be designed. At problem level, specialist operation is organized in an assign-execute fashion, where each specialist contributes to the global solution focusing on a specific subproblem chosen by the control manager, which activates the relevant specialist to work on that task. Whenever a specialist obtains some (positive or negative) result on the assigned task, it reports to the control manager, which initiates all the proper actions to proceed further with the global solution process.

Communication among specialists is achieved only through the common blackboard; direct specialist-to-specialist communication is not allowed. Communication between the specialists and the control manager is realized by means of a message-passing mechanism which carries control and coordination information and is implemented through a shared-memory technique. Messages from the control manager to a specialist and, vice versa, from a specialist to the control manager are written in a specific *communication blackboard* which is organized in such a way that all the messages originating from the specialists are directed to the control manager, while the messages of the control manager are addressed only to the relevant specialists.

The control manager

The main purpose of the control manager is the implementation of the "reasoning through models" capability. It initially selects the overall design strategy (i.e. the task-specific problem-solving method to adopt), decomposes the design problem at hand, determines the focus of attention, assigns the solution of specific subproblems to the relevant specialists, dynamically monitors their activity and (partial) results, revises the choices taken in front of a failure or of a new opportunity. Moreover, the control manager is able to properly react to events occurring at problem level, i.e. to messages coming from the specialists or to changes in the common blackboard.

Note that, from the viewpoint of reasoning strategies, CDM is an open system, since it can support a large variety of possible design strategies. In fact, on one hand, the system can resort to an a-priory unlimited control knowledge base, and, on the other hand, the architecture can host an high number of specialists capable of implementing different model-specific problem-solving methods.

Presently, two design strategies have been considered, namely top-down and bottom-up. The *top-down strategy* addresses the class of design problems where only highly abstract and loosely constrained specifications are available. It progressively transforms specifications into more concrete descriptions, following a waterfall process. The *bottom-up strategy* is able to face design problems where partial solutions have been proposed or are already known (they were either provided by the user or automatically produced by the system in preceding sessions). First, the assigned partial solutions are analyzed in order to check whether they are actually useful for the problem at hand and to identify what is lacking in order to fulfill the specifications. Then, the necessary parts of the artifact are synthesized, and its final structure is produced.

In the present implementation of CDM, the control knowledge base is partitioned in such a way that there is a clear distinction between general design knowledge, and design knowledge relevant to each one of the specific specialists.

5.2   Modeling and representation of domain knowledge

Domain knowledge is represented in CDM within the specialist knowledge bases and a common knowledge base, called *component library*, which can be accessed by all problem level specialists and contains the representation of the components available in the domain at hand. These knowledge sources are shortly described in the next pages.

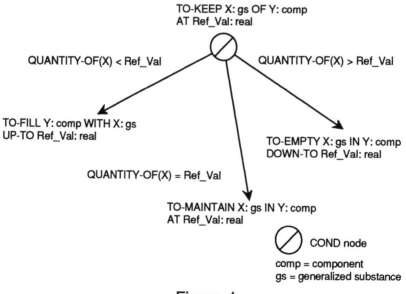

Figure 1

The *teleological knowledge base* contains all available one-level decompositions of every non-elementary goal considered by the system. Each decomposition is represented through an extended AND/OR tree of depth one, which includes, in addition to the common AND and OR operators, also a conditioned AND (COND) operator that describes alternative decompositions which are valid under stated (mutually exclusive) conditions. The COND operator makes it possible to describe the different goals attained by the artifact in distinct global operational conditions, called *states* of the artifact. Figure 1 shows an example concerning the decomposition of the goal "TO-KEEP X: generalized substance OF Y: component AT Ref_Val: real", whose meaning is keeping the quantity of a substance at a fixed reference value in a component. Three operational conditions are taken into account by means of a COND operator, that is (i) when the substance is below the reference value and then the goal becomes filling the component with the substance, (ii) when the substance is exactly at the reference value and therefore the goal is to maintain it unaltered, and (iii) when the substance is above the reference value and then the goal is emptying the component.

The *functional knowledge base* contains a representation all possible valid links between goals at teleological level and phenomena at functional level. The same phenomenon may be associated to several goals. Moreover, each phenomenon considered is defined through an appropriate process network, and each process through the relevant functional role network.

primitive goal	TO-ACCUMULATE X: generalized substance INTO Y: component
elementary phenomenon	RESERVOIR-CHARGING (Physical_View = VIEW(X), Reservoir_Component = Y)
process network	RESERVOIR-CHARGING (Physical_View = VIEW(X), Reservoir_Component = Y)
process	RESERVOIR-CHARGING (Physical_View = VIEW(X), Reservoir_Component = Y)
functional role network:	GENERATOR--CONDUIT--RESERVOIR (Physical_View = VIEW(X), Reservoir_Component = Y)

Figure 2

Thus, a complete link between teleology and function, including the three levels of phenomena, processes, and functional roles, is established, as it is displayed in the example in Figure 2 for the primitive goal "TO-ACCUMULATE X: generalized substance INTO Y: component". In this example, where the involved constraints are not shown, the RESERVOIR-CHARGING phenomenon is associated to a process network, that, since the phenomenon is elementary, includes just one process, namely RESERVOIR-CHARGING which, in turn, is defined through the functional role network (GENERATOR--CONDUIT--RESERVOIR). This means that the goal of accumulating a generalized substance X inside a component Y requires that a phenomenon occurs within the physical domain defined by the view of the generalized substance itself (that is, VIEW(X)). The phenomenon is realized by a process which can be implemented by means of three components playing, within VIEW(X), the roles of a generator, a conduit and a reservoir respectively. The reservoir is, of course, Y (Reservoir_Component = Y).

The *behavioral knowledge base* contains rules stating how to use the physical laws to deduce the behavior of a complex artifact from its topology.

The *structural knowledge base* contains rules capable of selecting the components of the artifact to be designed, on the basis of the functional roles they are expected to play in given physical views. Another set of structural rules support the correct connection of system components through appropriate nodes, in such a way as to generate a coherent topology of the artifact. Finally, additional rules support topological choices concerning possible geometrical and spatial constraints.

In the present CDM version the *empirical knowledge base* contains heuristic rules which support the correct and effective use of knowledge of all other epistemological types, namely, teleological, functional, behavioral, and structural. For example, empirical knowledge may concern usual topological choices, border conditions, environmental constraints, etc.

As already mentioned above, the *component library* is dedicated to store the representation of all available components in the considered domain, such as tanks, pumps, pipes, valves, sensors, switches, etc. It contains knowledge of all the involved epistemological types (with the exception of the empirical one) and can be used by all relevant specialists. An appropriate interface allows the user to effectively manage the component library, through define, update, delete, edit, and browse facilities. Components in the library may be primitive or aggregate. *Primitive components* are provided only by the user, while *aggregate components* may be defined either by the user or by the system itself as a result of past experience.

The example shown in Figure 3 illustrates the (slightly simplified) definition of a component, namely a hydraulic pump.

terminal: hydraulic
Q: real; {flow, a positive value identifies an input flow, a negative value an output flow}
P: non-negative real; {pressure}
terminal: electric
V: real; {voltage}
I: real; {current}
component: pump
    STRUCTURAL MODEL
        terminals: TH_1, TH_2: hydraulic;
                TE_1, TE_2: electric;
    BEHAVIORAL MODEL
        operational modes:
        ON [condition: $TE\_1.V - TE\_2.V = VCONST$]
        OFF [condition: $TE\_1.V - TE\_2.V = 0$]
        view hydraulic
        parameters:
        E: positive real; {efficiency}
        R_i: positive real; {hydraulic resistance}
        W: positive real; {power}
            operational mode ON
            physical laws: $TH\_1.Q > 0$
                        $TH\_1.Q + TH\_2.Q = 0$
                        $TH\_1.P - TH\_2.P = R_i * TH\_1.Q$
                        $TH\_1.P - TH\_2.P = W * E / TH\_1.Q$
            operational mode OFF
            physical laws: $TH\_1.Q + TH\_2.Q = 0$
        view electric
        parameters:
        R: positive real; {electric equivalent resistance}
            operational mode ON, operational mode OFF
            physical laws: $TE\_1.I + TE\_2.I = 0$
                        $TE\_1.V - TE\_2.V = R * TE\_1.I$
    FUNCTIONAL MODEL
        view hydraulic
            operational mode ON
            functional role: generator
            operational mode OFF
            functional role: conduit
        view electric
            operational mode ON, operational mode OFF
            functional role: conduit

Figure 3

196

6   Creative Design Through Multi-Modeling: A case study

6.1   The sample problem

The performance of CDM has been tested by means of a few mechanical and hydraulic problems, such as the sample problem, partially inspired by (Williams, 1990), which is dealt with below. It concerns the system shown in Figure 4, which is the result of the design activity. The intended purpose of the artifact is to maintain a constant level in a tank from which unpredictable quantities of fluid are taken at unpredictable times. In the proposed solution the tank whose level is expected to be kept constant, i.e. tank TA, is supplied by the pump PU connected with another tank, namely FEED-TA. The two tanks are connected through the pipe PP. The level sensor LS in tank TA is a floating switch that closes the electric circuit involving the pump in case the level falls below the threshold value. In case the fluid level is exactly equal to the reference value, the sensor opens the electric circuit, and the valve VA is activated to interrupt the flow between the two tanks. An electric generator, namely GE, is included in the electric circuit.

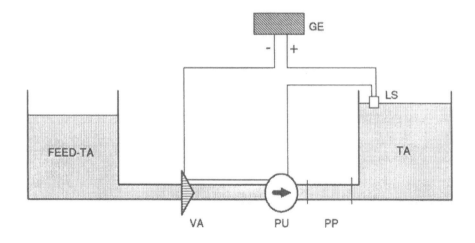

Figure 4

6.2   A sample design session

When CDM is started, the control manager engages the user in the following dialogue:

CDM: Choose the goal of the artifact you want to design
in the list shown below.

Ask for explanations, if needed

TO-KEEP X: generalized substance
OF Y: component AT Ref_Val: real

TO-FEED X: component WITH Y: generalized substance
FROM Z: component

TO-TRANSDUCE X: generalized substance
INTO Y: generalized current

... ...

The user selects the goal "TO-KEEP X: generalized substance OF Y: component AT Ref_Val: real". Here, "generalized substance" and "component" represent the type of the two variables "X" and "Y" respectively. Therefore CDM asks:

CDM: Please provide values for variables X and Y

USER: X = Mass
                 Y = Tank

Now the system checks whether the generalized substance Mass and the component Tank are known, i.e. whether they belong to the available domain knowledge. Since they are known, the following initial specification is put in the specification area of the common blackboard:

primary-goal:
TO-KEEP Mass: generalized substance OF Tank: component
AT Ref_Val: real

The dialogue continues then as follows:

CDM: Are there any specific requirements or constraints
                 to be considered in the design activity?

USER: No

At this point, the control manager chooses the most appropriate design strategy to apply in order to solve the problem at hand. In this case, since there are only teleological specifications in the specification area of the common blackboard and the solution area is empty, the top-down solution strategy is selected and the teleological specialist is invoked.

The first task of the teleological specialist is to translate the stated goal of the artifact, called *primary goal*, into the specific goals characteristic of the different operational states of the artifact to be designed. In order to identify the expected operational states, some further questions are put to the user:

CDM: How is the Mass of the Tank expected to vary as a
            consequence of external causes?
            Choose one of the following answers:

            Increase
            Decrease
            Both increase and decrease

USER: Decrease

CDM: What are the initial conditions of the Mass
            of the Tank? Choose one of the following answers:

            Equal to Ref_Val
            Above Ref_Val
            Below Ref_Val
            Either above or below Ref_Val
            Either above or equal to Ref_Val
            Either below or equal to Ref_Val
            Either above or below or equal to Ref_Val

USER: Either below or equal to Ref_Val

The teleological specialist then updates the initial specifications by adding the newly acquired information. By processing them, it establishes that two operational states, namely S1 and S2, are possible: the former occurs when Mass is below the reference value and, therefore, Tank has to be fed, the latter occurs when Mass is exactly at the reference value and, then, it has not to be altered. Note that the two goals implied by these states coincide with the two left-most subgoals shown in Figure 1 (the third subgoal is not considered because Mass cannot exceed the reference value in this example). Since two states have been identified, two *specific goals* are generated, namely:

specific-goal-1:
TO-FILL Tank: component WITH Mass: generalized substance
UP-TO Ref_Val: real

specific-goal-2:
TO-MAINTAIN Mass: generalized substance IN Tank: component
AT Ref_Val: real

Now the task of the teleological specialist is to decompose the specific goals into subgoals, until primitive goals are obtained. Figure 5 shows the decomposition of specific-goal-1 created by the teleological specialist.

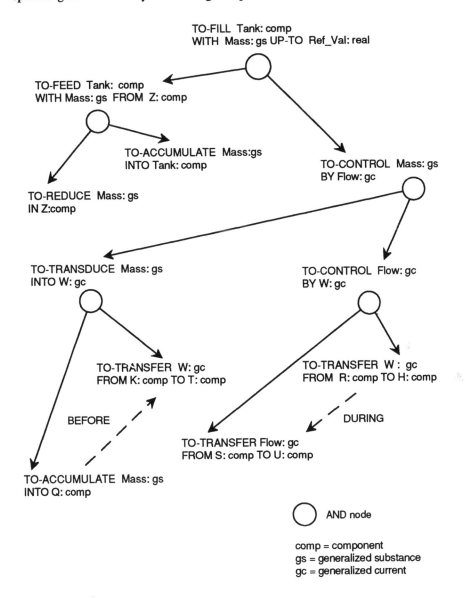

Figure 5

Decomposition is performed top-down by applying the one-level decompositions stored in the teleological knowledge base. While creating a new level, the teleological specialist tries to assign a value to each involved variable. In the decomposition tree of Figure 5, the initially known values, namely Mass and Tank are propagated, and one new assignment is made: namely the value Flow has been assigned to the generalized current used to control Mass. In fact, while decomposing the goal "TO-FILL Tank: component WITH Mass: generalized substance UP-TO Ref_Val: real" into the two subgoals "TO-FEED Tank: component WITH Mass: generalized substance FROM Z: component" and "TO-CONTROL Mass: generalized substance BY F: generalized current", the teleological specialist tries to instantiate the unknown variables Z and F. In order to instantiate F it sends a message to the control manager, asking for the appropriate value for a generalized current capable of controlling Mass within component Tank. The control manager invokes then the behavioral specialist which can answer the question by resorting to the behavioral model of component Tank and applying the rule that a variable X can be controlled by a variable Y if the equation $Y = dX/dt$ holds. Since the equation $Flow = dMass/dt$ can be found in the behavioral model of component Tank, it can be concluded that Flow can control Mass. Later the value Flow is properly propagated by the teleological specialist to the following levels of the decomposition tree.

Note that in the decomposition tree of a specific goal, the subgoals having the same parent are not independent, but are either connected by temporal relations (such as, BEFORE, DURING, etc.) or by simple correlation, in case they share some variables.

Once a decomposition tree has been constructed for each specific goal, it is written in the solution area of the common blackboard, and then the teleological specialist terminates its task.

At this point the control manager invokes the functional specialist whose first task is to translate the primitive goals of each decomposition tree into elementary phenomena, then to transform phenomena into processes and, finally, processes into functional role networks. So, for example, the primitive goal "TO-ACCUMULATE Mass: generalized substance INTO Tank: component" is progressively transformed according to the pattern already shown in Section 5.2, until the following functional role network is obtained:
GENERATOR--CONDUIT--RESERVOIR (Physical_View = hydraulic,
Reservoir_Component = Tank).
Now the functional specialist verifies that Tank may actually act as a RESERVOIR in the hydraulic view.

Note that the value of the physical view may remain unknown for some functional role networks, since the value of the involved generalized variable is not given. So, for example, the primitive goal "TO-TRANSFER W: generalized current FROM K:

component TO T: component" is transformed into the following functional role network:
GENERATOR--CONDUIT (Physical_View = ..., Generator_Component = K, Conduit_Component = T).

Thus, each primitive goal in every decomposition tree is replaced by the corresponding functional role network. At this point, the decomposition trees are processed by the functional specialist in order to properly combine functional roles. A number of rules residing in the functional knowledge base can be used to this purpose, such as rules aimed at avoiding component duplication, enforcing function sharing, recognizing the need for a transducer, etc. By iteratively applying these rules, the functional specialist tries to unify as many variables as possible. Two variables of the same type are if they can be assumed to represent the same entity. When an instanced variable is unified with an uninstanced one, the latter inherits the value of the former. Variable unification is a crucial mechanism in the design process and is primarily aimed at supporting function sharing. Two kinds of function sharing are considered:
-   *inter-view function sharing*, that occurs when a single component plays two (or more) functional roles in two (or more) views, within the same operational state of an artifact;
-   *inter-state function sharing*, that occurs when a single component plays two (or more) functional roles in two (or more) operational states of an artifact.

The next step for the functional specialist is to reorganize the decomposition trees in such a way as to aggregate all functional roles showing the same physical view. Each one of these aggregates represents a physical circuit. In fact, according to the multi-modeling formalism, every complex artifact can be considered as composed by a number of physical circuits, which generally intersect one another through components playing different roles in different circuits. In our example, two hydraulic circuits and a third circuit having an uninstanced view are identified:

Circuit = C1
Physical_View = hydraulic
Components:

Z:	RESERVOIR I State = TO-FILL, TO-MAINTAIN
O:	CONDUIT I State = TO-FILL
	BARRIER I State = TO-MAINTAIN
T:	GENERATOR I State = TO-FILL
	CONDUIT I State = TO-MAINTAIN
U:	CONDUIT I State = TO-FILL, TO-MAINTAIN
Tank:	RESERVOIR I State = TO-FILL, TO-MAINTAIN

Circuit = C2
Physical_View = hydraulic
Components:

Q: RESERVOIR | State = TO-FILL, TO-MAINTAIN

Circuit = C3
Physical_View = ...
Components:
    Q: CONDUIT | State = TO-FILL
             BARRIER | State = TO-MAINTAIN
    K: GENERATOR | State = TO-FILL, TO-MAINTAIN
    T: CONDUIT | State = TO-FILL, TO-MAINTAIN
    O: CONDUIT | State = TO-FILL, TO-MAINTAIN

Here, TO-FILL and TO-MAINTAIN identify the two operational states of the artifact. Circuit C1 intersects C3 through components T and O, whereas C3 intersects C2 through component Q. These intersections implement inter-view function sharing. Moreover, each one of components O, T and Q plays a double role within one physical circuit it belongs to. These mutually exclusive roles implement inter-state function sharing.

After the above set of interconnected circuits is written in the solution area of the common blackboard, control passes to the structural specialist, whose first task is to find out an appropriate value for all variables of type component. In order to accomplish its tasks, the structural specialist consults the structural knowledge base and the component descriptions in the component library. In our example, the structural specialist is unable to find a component with all the characteristics required by Q, whatever is the value to assign to variable Physical_View of circuit C2. Therefore, the system asks the user whether a component complying with the stated requirements exists and can be used in the design:

CDM: Do you know any component that can implement the
             functional role RESERVOIR in the hydraulic view and
             can be alternatively a CONDUIT or a BARRIER in a   different
view?
             Ask for explanations, if needed

USER: No

Since the user cannot provide any help, the structural specialist is definitely unable to perform its tasks given the current content of the solution area of the common blackboard; therefore, it writes a message in the communication blackboard, stating the type of failure occurred (unable to assign a proper value to component Q). The control manager, in turn, writes a message in the communication blackboard in order to activate the teleological specialist to recover the failure occurred (changing some part of the decomposition trees which involves Q). There are several alternative actions that the teleological specialist can undertake in order to execute the assigned task. For example, it might produce a different decomposition through chronological backtracking, starting from the parent of a node containing variable Q. In our case, however, another method is followed: the decomposition tree is left unaltered, while it is tried to change the variables that determine the views under which Q is considered. Q appears only once in the decomposition tree of Figure 5, namely in the subgoal "TO ACCUMULATE Mass: generalized substance INTO Q: component". Since within this goal Q comes together with the generalized substance Mass, it is realized that it is Mass to enforce the hydraulic view of Q. In order to change the view, Mass has to be replaced by a variable which can carry the same information, but has an associated view different from hydraulic. To this purpose the behavioral and functional specialists are invoked and, finally, the variable Level is chosen, which is associated to the geometrical view. Such a substitution is legal since the two variables Mass and Level are linked by a non-differential equation and therefore they are regarded as equivalent.

After the teleological specialist has changed the decomposition tree, the functional specialist is invoked and, finally, the following new circuit C2' is obtained, which replaces C2:

Circuit = C2'
Physical_View = geometrical
Components:
    Q: RESERVOIR I State = TO-FILL, TO-MAINTAIN

The structural specialist chooses the actual components appropriate to implement the above set of interconnected circuits C1, C2' and C3. Physical_View of circuit C3 is instanced to electric, and the component variables of C1, C2' and C3 are replaced by the following components (the names of the physical components shown in Figure 4 are is square brackets):

Tank [TA]
Z = tank [FEED-TA]
O = Valve [VA]
T = Pump [PU]
U = Pipe [PP]
Q = Geometrical-Electric Transducer [LS]
K = Electric Generator [GE]

At this point the structural specialist has to add the appropriate boundary conditions to the above mentioned physical circuits. The choice about whether and how to connect the physical circuits involved in the design of the artifact to the external environment is made either automatically by the system, by exploiting known heuristics, or by the human user. In our example, the user chooses not to connect the artifact to any external agent or device.

Finally, the structural specialist connects the terminals of the above listed components through appropriate nodes in such a way as to correctly realize the three physical circuits C1, C2' and C3. The final topology of the artifact (graphically shown in Figure 4) is then obtained and written in the solution area of the common blackboard.

In the example described above, since the user has made no proposal or direct intervention during the synthesis phase, the obtained designed structure is correct by construction, i.e. the designed artifact can attain the primary goal initially stated by the user. Therefore, as it is not necessary to verify whether the designed artifact complies with its specifications, the design process is concluded.

7   Conclusions

The experimental activity with the CDM prototype is ongoing. A first implementation will be concluded shortly and will be used for extensive experiments with the sample problem discussed in the previous section. The results so far available provide full support for the main claim of our work concerning the suitability of the multi-modeling approach as a valid background for design tasks, and are positive enough to encourage the continuation of the project.

Future research, after the first CDM prototype will be completely developed and experimented, will focus on the following points:
- development of a powerful man-machine interface capable of supporting a flexible and effective dialogue about system specifications and performance;
- design of a robust explanation and justification module, capable of making the user fully aware of the design decisions taken by the system and of reasons behind them;
- design of a powerful expert critiquing module (Miller, 1986; Silverman and Mezher, 1992), devoted to enable the system to actively react to the requests, suggestions and proposals made by the user.

Acknowledgments

The research reported in this paper has been supported by the Ministry for University and Scientific and Technological Research of Italy.
The multi-modeling approach presented in section 3 is the result of a project carried out at the Artificial Intelligence Laboratory of the University of Udine (Udine, Italy) by G. Brajnik, L. Chittaro, G. Guida, C. Tasso, and E. Toppano. The authors are indebted to all the researchers who have contributed to this project in past years.
The authors also wish to express their thanks to A. Gallo and M. Moruzzi who are currently working at the implementation of the CDM prototype.

References

Addanki S., Cremonini R., and Penberthy J. 1989. Reasoning about assumptions in graphs of models. Proc. 11th International Joint Conference on Artificial Intelligence, Detroit, MI, 1432-1438.

Bauer M.I. and Reiser B. 1990. Incremental envisioning: the flexible use of multiple representations in complex problem solving. Proc. 12th Conference of the Cognitive Science Society, Cambridge, MA, 317-324.

Bobrow D.G. (Ed.) 1984. Special Volume on Qualitative Reasoning about Physical Systems. Artificial Intelligence 24.

Bradshaw J.A. and Young R. 1991. Evaluating design using knowledge of purpose and knowledge of structure. IEEE Expert 6(2), 33-39.

Brajnik G., Chittaro L., Guida G., Tasso C., and Toppano E. 1989. The use of many diverse models of an artifact in the design of cognitive aids. Proc. 2nd European Meeting on Cognitive Science Approaches to Process Control, Siena, I, 69-79.

Brajnik G., Chittaro L., Tasso C., and Toppano E. 1990. Epistemology, organization and use of functional knowledge for reasoning about physical systems. Proc. AVIGNON '90: 10th International Workshop on Expert Systems and Their Application: General Conference Second Generation Expert Systems, Avignon, F, 53-66.

Brajnik G., Chittaro L., Guida G., Tasso C., and Toppano E. 1991. Representation and use of teleological knowledge in the multi-modeling approach. In Ardizzone E., Gaglio S., and Sorbello F. (Eds.), Trends in Artificial Intelligence, Springer Verlag, Berlin, FRG, 167-176.

Brown D.C. and Chandrasekaran B. 1985. Expert systems for a class of mechanical design activity. In Gero J.S. (Ed.), Knowledge Engineering in Computer-Aided Design, North-Holland, Amsterdam, NL, 259-282.

Carbonell J.G. 1983. Learning by analogy: Formulating and generalizing plans from past experience. In Michalski R.S., Carbonell J.G., and Mitchell T.M. (Eds.), Machine Learning, An Artificial Intelligence Approach, Tioga, Palo Alto, CA, 137-162.

Chandrasekaran B. 1986. Generic tasks in knowledge-based reasoning: High-level building blocks for expert system design. IEEE Expert 1(3), 23-30.

Chandrasekaran B. 1990. Design problem solving: A task analysis. AI Magazine 11(4), 59-71.

Chi M.T.H., Feltovitch P.J., and Glaser R. 1982. Categorization and representation of physics problems by experts and novices. Cognitive Science 5, 121-152.

Chittaro L., Costantini C., Guida G., Tasso C., and Toppano E. 1989. Diagnosis based on cooperation of multiple knowledge sources. Proc. AVIGNON '89: 9th International Workshop on Expert Systems and Their Application, Avignon, F, 19-33.

Chittaro L., Guida G., Tasso C., and Toppano E. 1992. Developing diagnostic applications using multiple models: The role of interpretative knowledge. In Guida G. and Stefanini A. (Eds.), Industrial Applications of Knowledge-Based Diagnosis, Elsevier, Amsterdam, NL.

Chittaro L., Guida G., Tasso C., and Toppano E. 1993. Functional and teleological knowledge in the multi-modeling approach for reasoning about physical systems: A case study in diagnosis. IEEE Trans. on Systems, Man, and Cybernetics, to appear.

Collins J. and Forbus K. 1987. Reasoning about fluids via molecular collections. Proc. 6th National Conference on Artificial Intelligence, Seattle, WA, 590-594.

Coyne R.D., Rosenman M.A., Radford A.D., Balchandran M. and Gero J.S. 1987. Innovation and creativity in knowledge-based CAD. In Gero J.S. (Ed.), Expert Systems in Computer-Aided Design, North-Holland, Amsterdam, NL, 435-465.

Davis R. 1984. Diagnostic reasoning based on structure and behavior. Artificial Intelligence 24, 347-410.

De Kleer J. 1984. How circuits work. Artificial Intelligence 24, 205-280.

De Kleer J. and Brown J.S. 1984. A qualitative physics based on confluences. Artificial Intelligence 24, 7-83.

Downing K. 1990. The qualitative criticism of circulatory models via bipartite teleological analysis. Artificial Intelligence in Medicine 2(3), 149-171.

Falkenhainer B. and Forbus K.D. 1988. Setting up large scale qualitative models. Proc. 7th National Conference on Artificial Intelligence, St. Paul, MN, 301-306.

Forbus K.D. 1984. Qualitative process theory. Artificial Intelligence 24, 85-168.

Franke D.W. 1991. Deriving and using descriptions of purpose. IEEE Expert 6(2), 41-47.

Genesereth M.R. 1984. The use of design descriptions in automated diagnosis. Artificial Intelligence 24, 411-436.

Gero J. S. 1990. Design prototypes: A knowledge representation schema for design. AI Magazine 11(4), 26-36.

Hayes-Roth B. 1985. A blackboard architecture for control. Artificial Intelligence 26, 251-321.

Iwasaki Y and Simon H.A. 1986. Causality in device behavior. Artificial Intelligence 29, 3-32.

Keuneke A. and Allemang D. 1989. Exploring the No-Function-In-Structure principle. Journal of Experimental and Theoretical Artificial Intelligence 1, 79-89.

Kuipers B. 1986. Qualitative simulation. Artificial Intelligence 29, 289-338.

Kuipers B. 1987. Abstraction by time-scale in qualitative simulation. Proc. 6th National Conference on Artificial Intelligence, Seattle, WA, 621-625.

Kuipers B. and Chiu C. 1987. Taming intractable branching in qualitative simulation. Proc. 10th International Joint Conference on Artificial Intelligence, Milano, I, 1078-1085.

Larkin J.H., McDermott J., Simon D.P., and Simon H.A. 1980. Expert and novice performance in solving physics problems, Science 208, 1335-1342.

Larkin J.H., Reif F., Carbonell J., and Gugliotta A. 1988. FERMI: A flexible expert reasoner with multi-domain inferencing. Cognitive Science 12, 101-138.

Lee W. and Kuipers B. 1988. Non intersection of trajectories in qualitative phase space: A global constraint for qualitative simulation. Proc. 7th National Conference on Artificial Intelligence, Saint-Paul, MN, 268-291.

Liu Z. and Farley A.M. 1990. Shifting ontological perspectives in reasoning about physical systems. Proc. 8th National Conference on Artificial Intelligence, Boston, MA, 395-400.

Maher M.L. 1990. Process models for design synthesis. AI Magazine 11(4), 49-58.

Miller P. 1986. Expert Critiquing Systems, Springer Verlag, Heidelberg, FRG.

Murthy S. 1988. Qualitative reasoning at multiple resolutions. Proc. 7th National Conference on Artificial Intelligence, Saint-Paul, MN, 296-300.

Nii H.P. 1986a. Blackboard systems: The blackboard model of problem solving and the evolution of blackboard architectures. AI Magazine 7(2), 38-53.

Nii H.P. 1986b. Blackboard systems: Blackboard application systems, blackboard systems from a knowledge engineering perspective. AI Magazine 7(3), 82-106.

Rajamoney S. and Koo S. 1990. Qualitative reasoning with microscopic theories. Proc. 8th National Conference on Artificial Intelligence, Boston, MA, 401-406.

Rasmussen J. 1986. Information Processing and Human-Machine Interaction. An Approach to Cognitive Engineering. North-Holland, Amsterdam, NL.

Sembugamoorthy V. and Chandrasekaran B. 1986. Functional representation of devices and compilation of diagnostic problem solving systems. In Kolodner J.L.

and Riesbeck C.K. (Eds.), Experience, Memory and Reasoning, Lawrence Erlbaum , Hillsdale, NJ, 47-73.

Silverman B. G. and Mezher T. M. 1992. Expert critics in engineering design: Lessons learned and research needs. AI Magazine 13(1), 45-62.

Slade S. 1991. Case-based reasoning: A research paradigm. AI Magazine 12(1), 42-55.

Steels L. 1990. Components of expertise. AI Magazine 11(2), 29-49.

Sticklen J. and Bond E. 1991. Functional reasoning and functional modeling. IEEE Expert 6(2), 20-21.

Struss P. 1988. Extensions to ATMS based diagnosis. Proc. 3rd International Conference on Applications of Artificial Intelligence in Engineering, Palo Alto, CA, 878-882.

Ulrich K.T. and Seering W.P. 1988. Function sharing in mechanical design. Proc. 7th National Conference on Artificial Intelligence, Saint-Paul, MN, 342-346.

Weld D. 1990. Approximation reformulations. Proc. 8th National Conference on Artificial Intelligence, Boston, MA, 407-412.

Williams B.C. 1990. Interaction-based invention: Designing novel devices from first principles. In Gottlob G. and Nejdl W. (Eds.), Expert Systems in Engineering, Principles and Applications, Springer-Verlag, Vienna, A, 118-134.

Part III

Knowledge Level Approaches

Issues in Knowledge Level Modelling

Walter Van de Velde

Vrije Universiteit Brussel, AI-Lab
Pleinlaan 2, B-1050 Brussels, Belgium

Abstract. Since its introduction in the early 80s the notion of knowledge level has been an important catalizer of research in knowledge systems. This chapter discusses how it is being turned into a useful tool for the development of knowledge systems and how the original and present interpretations can be tied together again. It shows how the knowledge level changed our views on what knowledge systems are and how the problems with first generation expert systems might be overcome. Two other issues are discussed in some more detail. The first one is the precise methodological role of the knowledge level. The second issue concerns the nature of knowledge level theories of problem solving and its implications for next generation architectures. *

1 Introduction

The notion of 'knowledge level' was introduced by Allen Newell more than a decade ago [28]. Ever since it has provided a common perspective for researchers in Artificial Intelligence (AI) and in knowledge systems in particular. Its impact has been tremendous. Newell managed to make explicit what had become common practice in AI, namely talking about intelligent systems in a language of 'knowing' and 'wanting'. Moreover, he gave this language a role in systems engineering by postulating the knowledge level as a computer systems level to be studied in line with other levels such as the register-transfer level or the symbol level. It is no surprise then that Newell's treatment of knowledge was particularly attractive to the system oriented mind of computer scientists who are, after all, still the majority of AI researchers.

The notion of knowledge level has been used most visibly within the so called modelling approaches toward knowledge systems. In these approaches developing a knowledge based system is viewed as the construction of a series

* This research is partially funded by the ESPRIT Programme of the Commission of the European Communities under projects number 5248 (KADS-II) and 5477 (CONSTRUCT). The partners in KADS-II are Cap Gemini Innovation (F), Cap Gemini Programator (S), Netherlands Energy Research Foundation ECN (NL), Eritel SA (ESP), IBM France (F), Lloyd's Register (UK), Swedisch Institute of Computer Science (S), Siemens AG (D), Touche Ross MC (UK), University of Amsterdam (NL) and Vrije Universiteit Brussel (B). The partners in CONSTRUCT were Siscog (P), Renault (F) and Vrije Universiteit Brussel (B). This research is also financed by a "Inter-Universitaire Attractie Pool" on knowledge system and the IMPULS project ADIOS, both from the Belgian government.

of models related to some (problem solving) behaviour. In particular the knowledge level model is a model in terms of the knowledge that rationalises that behaviour. It has become 'en vogue' to assimilate the knowledge level idea in any encompassing treatment of knowledge systems. It ties together and to some extend unifies different approaches toward the theory and practice of knowledge systems [7, 11, 20, 26, 27, 35, 46, 48].

No doubt taking a knowledge level perspective has greatly improved our understanding of what knowledge systems are and how we can build them. For example, it has provoked a profound shift in knowledge acquisition: rather than extracting knowledge from an expert the aim of knowledge acquisition is to build a consolidated model of an expert's problem solving behaviour in terms of knowledge. Nevertheless the knowledge level is not beyond critique and several authors have pointed out problems with it. Some of these problems required further clarification [13] or minor repairs [33, 37]. Others have been claimed to be unrepairable, which would render the knowledge level useless [45].

When one looks at knowledge level descriptions as they are presently used in knowledge systems then one finds striking differences with Newell's original notions.[1] For example, at the knowledge level according to Newell there is no structure, whereas most models as we now see them are highly structured. How and why are these models different? The aim of this paper is to clarify this and other issues. It is not an introduction to knowledge level modeling but brings together ideas and interpretations to provide a (subjective) bird's eye view on the state of the art and the field's present research directions.

This paper starts with a brief recapitulation of Newell's notion of knowledge level (Sect. 2). Then Sect. 3 highlights the differences with the knowledge level models as they are practiced in contemporary knowledge engineering. An approach to relating the two notions, called two step rationality, is put forward in Sect. 4. Section 5 takes a closer look on the structures that one finds in knowledge level modelling. Then Sect. 6 digs deeper into the nature of problem solving itself from a knowledge level perspective while Sect. 7 discusses implications for future generation architectures. In Sect. 8 the methodological role of knowledge level modelling is discussed. Finally, Sect. 9 is a brief conclusion.

2   The Knowledge Level According to Newell

The knowledge level [28] provides the means to 'rationalise' the behaviour of a system from the standpoint of an external observer. This observer treats the system as a 'black box' but maintains that it acts 'as if' it possesses certain knowledge about the world and uses this knowledge in a perfectly rational way

---

[1] The knowledge level has broader scope than knowledge systems alone. It can be used for characterising the behaviour of any complex system, for example of an autonomous agent, even if it is behaviour- rather than knowledge based. In addition the knowledge level can be used to describe different aspects of intelligent behaviour, like learning [17, 41]. In this paper I only consider the problem solving or performance aspects.

toward reaching its goals. The behaviour of the agent is explained and predicted in terms of the reasons that the agent is assumed to have to take certain actions in order to reach ascribed goals.

In more detail a knowledge level description is based on the following model of the behaviour of an agent [17]:

> The agent possesses *knowledge*
> Some of this knowledge constitutes the *goals* of the agent
> The agent has the ability to perform a set of *actions*
> The agent chooses actions according to the *principle of rationality*:
> > The agent will select an action to perform next which according to its knowledge leads to the achievement of one of its goals.

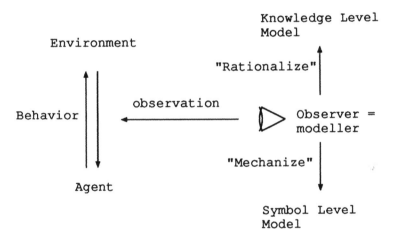

Fig. 1. Knowledge level and symbol level model are models of observed behaviour, i.e., of observed interaction between an agent and the environment.

The knowledge level, according to Newell, is a level of description above the symbol level. The symbol level provides a means to 'mechanise' a behaviour. At the symbol level a system is described as a mechanism over symbols and representations (structures of symbols). Neither type of description makes a claim about the real nature of the agent. The observer only assumes that the agent acts 'as if' it has such knowledge or mechanisms. The crucial difference is that the symbol level is system oriented, whereas the knowledge level is world oriented. A knowledge level model is in terms of knowledge about the world and the environment in which the agent's problems and actions occur (see Fig. 1).

To summarise:

- Observation creates a 'what' model of agent behaviour, e.g., a series of episodes of the agent's activities.

- Mechanisation creates a 'how' model of agent behaviour, e.g., in terms of agent structure and local laws of interaction.
- Rationalisation creates a 'why' model of agent behaviour, e.g., in terms of world knowledge and a principle of rationality.

Note that the object of modelling at the knowledge level is not knowledge but behaviour, i.e., observed interaction between an agent and its environment [13]. A knowledge level model is a model of behaviour in terms of knowledge, just like a symbol level model is a model of interaction in terms of symbols and representations. What ties all these models together is the fact that they all model one and the same thing, namely observed interaction. The different models are coherent and consistent to the extend that they model, and to a certain degree predict, the same class of behaviours.

The emphasis on knowledge instead of on representation and implementation issues is the major source of power of the knowledge level idea. It allows one to make meaningful statements about system behaviour without reference to the structures and mechanisms within the agent that realise that behaviour. But consequently it is natural to ask whether a knowledge level model is at all useful to construct systems that behave accordingly. When one writes down (or encodes, for example as a rule) knowledge then it becomes symbol level. The question is, however, whether that encoding can be used to implement the agent. According to the theory it is the observer who creates the knowledge as an annotation of observed behaviour and who uses it at all times to best explain observed and subsequent behaviour. Knowledge should be viewed as an element in the model of behaviour that is constructed by the observer [14]. If it is created through the process of observing interaction then it is not even obvious that knowledge ascribed at some point is also useful for the explanation of subsequent behaviour.

3 The Knowledge Level in Practice

The original aim of the knowledge level was to clear up confusion concerning the usage of the terms 'knowledge' and 'representation'. The idea immediately resonated with ongoing research toward understanding and building knowledge systems from a knowledge content (epistemological) perspective [10, 38, 7]. Clancey's model of heuristic classification [11] illustrated the power and scope of competence models that make explicit the kinds of knowledge embodied in a system and their roles in an overall pattern of reasoning. Here are only some of the most representative approaches in knowledge engineering that in one form or another use the knowledge level notion:

- Generic Task Approach [7, 3]
- KADS [46] and CommonKADS [48]
- Role-Limiting Methods [26, 24]
- Components of Expertise [35] and the Componential Methodology [36]

- Method instantiation and configuration approaches (Protege [27] and Protege-II [30])
- KIF [19] and OntoLingua [20]

They take the knowledge level as a source of inspiration or as a way to explain what they are doing. If one looks more closely then one finds striking differences with the original knowledge level descriptions. To distinguish these models from the knowledge level descriptions a la Newell I use the capitalised "Knowledge Level model", or KL-model. The most obvious difference between a knowledge level model and a KL-model is that the latter has lots of structure. As a consequence a KL-model implies other than 'why' aspects of a system's behaviour. For example one finds notions of 'task' and 'method' that seem to relate more to 'what' and 'how' models of behaviour.

So knowledge level models and KL-models are different but related things (Fig. 2):

A KL-model is a structure that is imposed on knowledge when it is being put to use in a class of problem situations.

A KL-model describes a structure on knowledge. Like the knowledge itself, this structure is ascribed by an observer. It is a use-specific window on the knowledge level, which in turn is a model of behaviour. For example, the model of heuristic classification is visible in a pattern of inferences that contribute to abstract, heuristic match and refinement steps in reasoning [11]. This well known example also illustrates what is meant by structure, namely role-limitation [26]: the role in reasoning of parts of the knowledge is being specialised. In addition, these parts of the knowledge are being organised, for example into hierarchies or causal networks. What counts in a KL-model, however, is not only the knowledge that the agent seems to be using but, more importantly, the structure *within* which this knowledge is being used for achieving goals. This structure becomes visible through the process of reasoning.

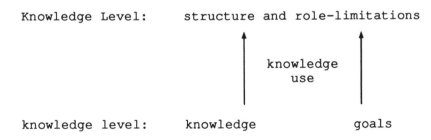

Fig. 2. A KL-model is a structure that is imposed on knowledge when it is being put to use in a class of situations.

KL-models are models of specialised intelligence. Newell banned all structure from the knowledge level to account for the fully rational exploitation of an agent's knowledge in a model of general intelligence. The KL-model, on the other hand, is characterised by a deliberate restriction of flexibility. This restriction allows the agent to reach a limited range of goals in a limited range of situations, but to do so in a highly adapted (expert) way. They are expert in a specialised task. Intelligence in this context is not so much related to the capability of producing isolated episodes of rationalisable behaviour but rather to the re-occurrence of a structure of such a rationalisation over a range of behaviours.

4 Two Step Rationality

How can the above be reconciled with Newell's notion of knowledge level? The principle of rationality (Sect. 2) relates knowledge to behaviour in a single step [28]. It serves as a global interpreter for the knowledge of the agent in order to understand observed behaviour or to predict future behaviour. Two step rationality [42] views this process as consisting of two steps: configuration and application (Fig. 3):

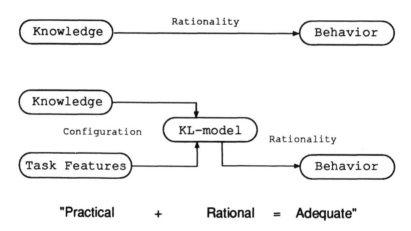

Fig. 3. Two step rationality decomposes the principle of rationality. It reflects the fact that adequate behaviour is both practical and rational.

In the first step, called 'configuration', knowledge is configured into a model of the problem-situation that the agent is faced with (called the 'task instance'). In this step the agent is thought of as imposing a structure on selected pieces of its knowledge, and assigning roles to these in its reasoning. This structure is what we have referred to as the KL-model. It captures the way in which the agent frames a task instance. The ability to appropriately configure a KL-model is probably at the heart of excellence in problem solving and rational behaviour. The goal of configuration is to enable the practical application of the principle of rationality within the boundaries of the KL-model. This 'application' is the second step in two step rationality. To the extent that the task model is adequately configured knowledge can be practically applied and leads to satisfactory goal directed behaviour.[2]

What makes every task instance different from the other one are the specific circumstances in which it is to be solved. These circumstances may be related to the characteristics of the environment (critical, static or highly dynamic, size and complexity) and the agent's interaction with it (accessibility and reliability), or may impose additional restrictions on the task (quality or specificity of solution, limited resources). These aspects of a task instance are called the 'task features'. An important class of task features follow from the epistemological problems (i.e. problems with the knowledge) and the pragmatic problems (i.e. problems with the pragmatics of using the knowledge) that an agent is faced with [35]. Epistemological problems arise because we are dealing with models of a real and open-ended world. Every model is an approximation, not only because it is unprecise but, more fundamentally, because it introduces assumptions about the world. Problems of pragmatics are forced upon us by the reality of the task environment. They follow from the practical limitations of the complete system of the agent and its environment, for example the impossibility to make sufficiently precise measurements or to exhaustively explore a range of possible malfunctions. Steels argues that real expert knowledge (for example a situation specific way of dealing with an unknown factor) is aimed exactly at satisficing performance in spite of these problems.

Task features play a fundamental role in configuring the KL-model. The KL-model must be such that the behaviour resulting from the application of the principle of rationality within the boundaries of that model is also practical, i.e., complies with the task features of the task instance. The decomposition of the principle of rationality reflects the fact that there is more to rationality than just being logical. The task features of a task instance determine what behaviour is practical, i.e., feasible and appropriate within the actual agent-task-environment combination. Once a KL-model has been configured to comply with these practical constraints the principle of rationality can freely explore possibilities. The pragmatic concerns are thus taken care of in configuration, the rational concerns by the application of the principle of rationality within the KL-model [42].[3]

---

[2] An alternative to two step rationality is to model an agent as consisting of a structure of smaller agents, each one being specialised and perfectly rational in its specialisation [37]. I prefer to reserve the notion of agent for an embodied and observable being. Its application as a structuring device makes it counterintuitive to account for the dynamic configuration of knowledge in different models.

[3] One could consider the rationalisation of configuration. Such a rationalisation would need to refer to detailed knowledge of the agent's constitution, evolution and adaptation over time, and details of the embedding and the interaction with the environment. This may be possible but would need to refer to details of the agent's physical embedding and adaptation to the world. This does not seem very practical and uncompatible with a black-box treatment of the agent. Much of this knowledge should therefore be considered tacit, i.e., implicit in the structure and interaction of the agent-environment system.

5 Varieties of KL-Models

Newell proposed to model in terms of knowledge, goals and actions. That is all of structure that there is at the knowledge level. The various approaches toward Knowledge Level modelling use different but related notions. Task, generic task, problem solving method, inference, domain model, case model, role-limiting method and knowledge role are only some of the terms one encounters in the literature. The reader is referred to some of the other chapters in this volume for detailed explanations on these.

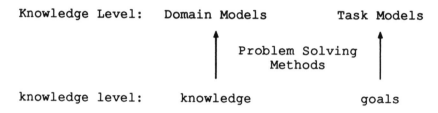

Fig. 4. The domain models and task models are KL-structures that organise (world) knowledge and goals at the knowledge level. The organising principles are captured in problem solving methods.

Three terms - or at least the concepts they indicate - seem to gain wide acceptance in the knowledge systems community: *domain model, task model* and *problem solving method*. They represent three different perspectives on the knowledge level and correspond to three paradigmatic approaches to KL-modelling (Fig. 4):

Domain model: A domain model is a means to talk about domain knowledge in a precise and systematic way. It expresses what one assumes collections of statements about the world to mean. For example it may describe what one knows about the functioning of the human heart, or it may capture a heuristic mapping between symptoms and malfunctions of cars. A domain model is more than a collection of pieces of knowledge. Its 'coherence' is reflected in the terminology and structure used to describe these pieces (for example, 'cause' and 'effect' related by some 'causal relation') and in the implied meaning of these terms (in this example, the meaning of causal relationship and the conclusions one can draw therefrom, for example based on transitivity). These elements constitute the model ontologies and account for predictive power, an essential feature of any model.

Model oriented approaches in knowledge engineering are quite old [15, 16] and reasoning from first principles has become an active line of research. Here the idea is that the kind of knowledge that is available about a domain gives a clue for the kind of reasoning that is being done for a certain task. Terms such as 'causal' or 'qualitative' refer to the kinds of domain models that are being used. Such a domain model provides a reasoner with a repertoire of reasoning steps that are not specific for a task but can be usefully combined for a variety of tasks, like for prediction and diagnosis. Domain and model ontologies are studied for example in OntoLingua [20] and in CommonKADS [47]. It is becoming increasingly clear that domain knowledge is an important indicator for the kind of KL-model that is appropriate [29, 49].

Task model: A task model is a means to talk about goals in a precise and systematic way. It expresses what it means to achieve a goal and how the goals are interrelated. For example, the goal of diagnosing a car is to find an acceptable explanation of a malfunction. This may be achieved by the task of finding a faulty component who's normal functioning contributes to the disabled function of the car. Alternatively, the same goal may also be achieved by finding a faulty component who's faulty behaviour explains the malfunction and is consistent with observed symptoms. A task model also captures the way in which goals contribute to other goals. For example, the goals of identifying relevant components, and of testing for their proper functioning may both contribute to the higher level goal of diagnosing the car. This leads to a task decomposition or task structure. The well-known task decomposition of Mycin is another example of such a task decomposition.

The original KADS methodology is prototypical of the task oriented approach [46]. An application task (or real-life task) is decomposed into a series of so called generic tasks. A generic task is basically no more than an index to an interpretation model, an inference structure for the generic task. Such an interpretation model is independent of domain knowledge. It only requires certain inferences to be possible in the domain but does not say what models these have to be based on. So KADS advocates an analysis of the task, prior to making decisions on domain knowledge. The early work on Generic Tasks [6] was also task oriented.

Problem solving method: A problem solving method is a means to relate task and domain models in order to accomplish goals. It describes roles that task and domain models have to play in order to achieve goals. For example a method of generate and test may be applied for the goal of diagnosis. The role of 'generate' may be played by the task that finds candidate components using, for example, a structural domain model. The role of 'test' may be played by a task that checks whether the component is malfunctioning or not using, for example, a model of the components proper functioning. A problem solving method is different from a task model because it can be non-specified for a task and it may give rise to multiple task models. For example the method of heuristic classification or constructive problem solving can be applied for many different types of applications [39]. A problem solving method is not a fully specified way to accomplish a task, but its application generates a way of accomplishing a task.

The research by John McDermott and his team at Digital [24] is prototypical for the method oriented approach. They have embarked on an encompassing effort to catalogue problem solving methods and to systematically probe for their scope of applicability by doing a series of applications and variations on them. The idea that the notion of problem solving method makes sense independent of the notion of task was convincingly argued for by Clancey [11] but in practice methods seem to remain closely linked to tasks. The Generic Tasks of Chandrasekaran [7] are closer to methods than they are to tasks. For example, CSRL embodies a classification method that can be used for other tasks than diagnosis alone (compare [5] and [4]). Method instantiation and configuration is also an important element in the work on Protege [27] and Protege-II [30].

The domain, task and method perspective are related views on problem solving. Each of them describes knowledge in its own language: model specific, task specific, method specific. A KL-model brings together these three perspectives in a coherent model. More and more the importance of all three aspects is being recognized and taken into account [8, 36, 48]. These KL-models, however, focus on describing the process of problem solving and have little to say about what problem solving is. For example a role-limiting method makes explicit control over actions that, when it is followed leads to the completion of some goal. However, the aim of a genuine knowledge level theory of problem solving must focus on 'why' questions. Why is an action taken? A knowledge level answer to this should refer to the world, rather than to a control regime imposed by a method. This leads us to considering more seriously what problem solving is all about.

6 The Nature of Problem Solving

In Newell's approach the knowledge level rationalises behaviour in terms of the reasons that an agent has to believe that certain actions will lead to achieving certain goals. In this sense knowledge is a means to an end, a resource for behaviour [28]. The goal of problem solving is to select one of the possible actions. More recently a different view is being explored, namely the view of problem solving as modelling. The idea is that problem solving is the construction of a situation specific model [12] or case model [35, 47].

From a knowledge level perspective the agent's perception of the world is through knowledge alone. A goal therefore must correspond to a desired state of ones knowledge about the world. Consequently this knowledge must refer to the specific systems that the goal is about. This model - let us call it the case model - at every moment during problem solving summarises the agent's understanding of the problem, and allows it to eventually conclude that the goal has been reached.

The actions are the means that the agent has for interacting with the world [28]. Again, since at the knowledge level the agent's perception is through knowledge an action must be viewed as a way of obtaining knowledge about the reality. Actions of perception naturally fit in this scheme but also genuine acts of interaction do [41]. For example when a spray-painting robot paints some part then it will probably assume that the part has paint on it afterwards.[4] In the problem solving as modelling view, then, the actions are not the goal of problem solving but are themselves a means to an end. That end is the construction of a model of part of the world that allows the agent to conclude eventually that its goals have been achieved.

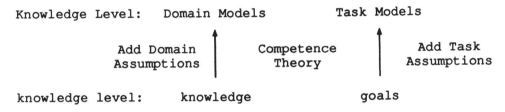

Fig. 5. The domain and task models embody assumptions that are linked by the method's competence theory form a theory about the problem to be solved.

The view of problem solving as modelling can be linked to the Knowledge Level approach outlined so far. Modelling a system in the world is to make assumptions about that world (Sect. 3). For example assuming a causal model of a car's functioning implies an assumption that this causal view leads to a sufficient approximation of what the car's functioning is all about. Thus, making a domain model is not just packaging statements about the domain, but it entails augmenting these statements with a series of assumptions about how the information about the systems is connected. To decide to model a system in a certain way means to *assume* that these assumptions hold as well as all the conclusions that follow from them.

Similarly a task model embodies assumptions about the meaning of goals. For example, if one models a diagnostic task as a process of generate and test over components of a system, then one implicitly assumes that the fault one is looking for can be localised in a component, and for instance not in the external working conditions of the system or in the connections between the components. Thus, modelling a task corresponding to a goal is to make more precise what one *assumes* that goal to mean.

The role of the problem solving method is to tie domain and task models together in an argument on what accomplishing the task means in terms of the available models. I have called this the *competence theory* of the method [39]. For example, a heuristic classification problem solver assumes that the solution to its problem is within the differential. This is no more than an assumption, but it is what the problem solver believes that it can say about the problem. It defines

---

[4] The action of hitting a nail with a hammer can be assumed to entail that the nail is deeper in the wood, that the nail is deeper in the wood with some probability, or that a loud sound has been produced. The 'effect' of the action simply depends on what assumption the agent makes about it.

222

its competence. In addition the competence theory also allows one to make more precise what rationality means. For example, a heuristic classification problem solver will use its knowledge and actions to reduce the size of the differential. I called this a (method specific) *specialized principle of rationality*. It contains the basis for all "why" questions about the system's behavior: actions are taken to get the model into the state dictated by the principle of rationality. This model is the case model and it is obtained from the partial instantiation of the competence theory through actions. Specific control regimes (e.g., data-driven or hypothesis-driven heuristic classification) correspond to different ways of operationalising the specialized principle of rationality [42]

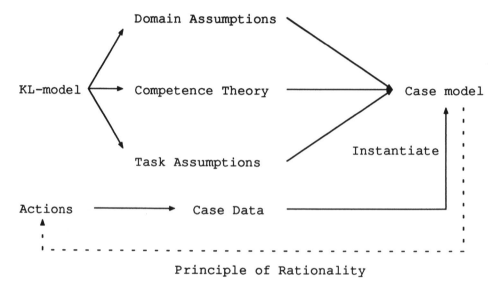

Fig. 6. Problem solving as modelling is a process of instantiating assumptions linked by the method's competence theory and using the case data assumed from interacting with the world. The method's principle of rationality drives the interaction process toward instantiating the case model.

The configuration of models, tasks and methods entails a set of assumptions that together can be interpreted as a model of the problem. The goal of problem solving is to instantiate this model by grounding it in reality by making derivations from the case-specific knowledge obtained by the agent's actions and the assumptions embodied in the domain and task models. The form of the case model is determined by the selection of problem solving method.

In this view problem solving is no longer an input-output process (as in KADS-I [46]), neither a means to select actions (as in Newell's knowledge level theory [28]), nor is it a model transformation process (as in Components of Expertise [35]). Rather it is a process of organising knowledge (obtained through actions) by making assumptions (i.e., constructing a model) that allow one to conclude (in effect, only assume) that the task is accomplished. Successful problem solving is a matter of making the right assumptions and exploring their consequences. Problem solving is thus viewed as the 'creation' of a suitable case model and the interaction with the world is only a resource for this, almost a side-effect in the process of maintaining an internal organisation and identity [42]. We are now in a peculiar position by claiming that knowledge is a resource for action and action is a resource for knowledge. This circular view on knowledge and behavior is reminiscent of Maturana's view of autonomous systems [25]. We use it here as a view from the observer's perspective without making claims, as Maturana does, about implications for a biological theory of cognition. However, I will argue that it does have some implications for the design of future generation AI architectures.

7   Next Generation Architectures

Second generation expert systems [34] were developed in the early 80s to overcome a number of problems of the first generation, rule based systems. These problems were, in a nutshell brittleness, poor explanation capabilities and maintainability. The basic idea at that time was to 'deepen' the analysis of the knowledge that these systems embody. This has been interpreted sometimes as deepening of the knowledge, for example by making explicit first principles of a domain. However, second generation expert systems do not necessarily embody deep knowledge in this narrow sense. More generally, the idea is that the knowledge which they embody is analysed and represented up to its constituent role-specific pieces [15, 16, 38, 10]. In retrospect we now view much of the work on second generation expert systems as contributions to a knowledge level theory of specialised intelligence.

> *Second generation expert systems reflect in their structure the use-specific structure within which specialised knowledge leads to adequate behaviour for a limited number of problem situations.*

This structure is what we have called the KL-model. The Generic Task approach was the first to illustrate the idea of linking re-usable models to re-usable pieces of code [7]. Ever since methodological approaches to second generation expert systems almost invariably rely on mapping the structure of a KL-model to the architecture of the application [24, 37, 43]. This KL-model or parts of it are used to "stuff in" the specialized knowledge [27].

It is remarkable that architectures are focused on making control decisions explicit, either in method or in task specific ways. Task specific shells, for example, hard-wire the structure of knowledge and the control of using it, and are therefore limited in scope. Method specific shells are slightly broader since they use a method specific rather than a task specific terminology [24, 22]. They therefore require an additional mapping from task to method. In a more sophisticated approach the methods are configured from smaller building blocks [30] or re-usable chunks of models and executables can be put together, inspected and modified at all levels of descriptions [36]. These approaches acknowledge the fact that similar tasks can be solved in different and sometimes highly specific ways but, once instantiated, the task-method-knowledge combination remains fixed.

Architectures like this exhibit a form of brittleness that arises not from a lack of knowledge, but from a lack of flexibility in using the knowledge. They make more explicit what the boundaries of their competence are, they certainly do not account for a graceful degradation of performance. Steps have been taken toward greater flexibility. A first one is to provide for dynamic method selection [31]. Based on problem characteristics, a system will choose the most adequate problem solving method. A complementary approach is to enable preferred problem solving methods by sustained learning of the knowledge that they require [40, 1].

But from a fundamental perspective all these are ad hoc solutions. Problem solving methods are still a "what" perspective and thus occupy a strange position at the knowledge level which is concerned with "why". In the problem solving as modelling view, however, the control follows from the need to evolve the case model into a certain state. For example a heuristic classification problem solver will use its knowledge to minimise the size of the differential. Actions will be executed that can lead to new knowledge that enables this minimisation. So, control is genuinely a result of the present state of knowledge about the problem, reflected in the case model [42]. Such architectures have not been extensively explored but they would reflect much more the real nature of problem solving from a knowledge level perspective.

Next generation expert systems support the process of problem solving as modelling by making explicit the case models that they are creating, grounding all interaction in the need to evolve this case model into a state with specified characteristics.

The idea of problem solving as modelling also provides for a powerful framework to model interaction. A knowledge system is useful to the extend that it contributes to the construction of a useful case model, as the result of an interaction between the agents, the systems and the world. Problem solving is realised by a process that involves agents and systems that work toward an understanding of the problem, i.e., the case model. This case model should be the primary vehicle of communication among the different agents. Clancey pointed out that the metaphor of blackboard systems is useful for this: all systems involved in the problem solving process work on and communicate through a common blackboard which at all times reflect the state of understanding of the problem [12]. Again we are far from the view that problem solvers are input-output devices. They are triggers of interaction that leads to the construction of a case model that is acceptable to all the agents involved in the process.

8 Roles of Knowledge Level Modelling

Knowledge level analysis is not a goal in itself but has a role to play in a broader methodological approach toward knowledge system development. Three roles are the basis for common methodological usage of Knowledge Level models:

1. Guidance in knowledge acquisition
2. Functional specification of system
3. High-level design of system

A fourth role, support for sharing and re-use, is a natural complement to these roles.

Guidance in Knowledge Acquisition. If a knowledge level model is a model in terms of knowledge, then its creation is equivalent to knowledge acquisition. A KL-model (in the sense of Sec. 3), by proposing an adequate structure on knowledge, can serve as a frame for knowledge acquisition. It helps in interpreting observed behaviour or in understanding protocols. This is the original role intended for the KADS interpretation models [2]. It is also the role explicit supported by the MOLE [18] and Protege work [27, 30] where dedicated knowledge acquisition tools take care of "stuffing" the knowledge in the right slots of a pre-selected or constructed KL-model.

Functional Specification of System. A knowledge level model predicts behaviour. It can therefore be naturally interpreted as a functional specification of a system's behaviour. It could be argued that it becomes necessary to use a knowledge level model as soon as goal-directed behaviour is too complex to capture it in an enumerative or algorithmic way. But the effect is the same: a knowledge level model, together with the principle of rationality serves to predict or specify what a system will do in a given situation. As such it plays the role of a functional specification. It is functional in the sense that it has no necessary implications for how the behaviour should be realised, but restricts system behaviour to a number of possibilities.

High-Level Design of System. It was already pointed out that a Knowledge Level model has more structure to it than originally intended. Basically, this is clear from the more elaborate ontology that one uses in Knowledge Level modelling. Instead of goals and knowledge, a much richer terminology is being practiced. Notions like domain model, task, problem solving method, mechanism, inference or knowledge role allow additional structure in the knowledge level model. It is tempting to view this structure as a high-level design of a system.

Sharing and Re-Use. Most modelling approaches to knowledge engineering assume that models associated with applications that have similar requirements will be similar. Generic or re-usable models capture these similarities and are a cornerstone in the support that such methodologies provide. For example, a KADS interpretation model [2] contains a re-usable inference structure and task decomposition, appropriate for a class of tasks. Similarly, a Generic Task [7] is a packet of a task and domain model that is re-usable for a series of similar tasks.

With respect to the last role it is assumed that an analysis of the requirements of the application provides an index to a re-usable model. This is what we have called the task features previously. The earliest attempts to come up with a categorisation of application types followed a task oriented approach [9, 21, 2]. More recently other than the task perspective have been explored. McDermott's taxonomy of problem solving methods [26] takes a method orientation. Work on re-usable ontologies [20] researches into generic terminology and structures within certain domains. Work on KIF - the knowledge interchange format - is prototypical for this research [19]. KIF is a logic based language that can be used as an implementation independent format for exchanging knowledge bases. A specialisation of KIF, called OntoLingua [20], can capture in a general and standardised way ontologies that are useful in domains such as medical diagnosis or design. Steels' Componential Methodology [36] supports the usage of chunks that contain any combination of task, domain, problem solving method with or without associated pieces of code. Although the idea of re-usable models is shared by many approaches, the foundations of generic models and the selection and modelling mechanisms that are needed to work with them are not well researched [44].

A major weakness in the combination of these roles is that it hides a subtle shift from observed behaviour (for example from an expert) to system behaviour. As Linster put it, there is modelling for making sense and modelling for system design [23]. It is tacitly assumed that a smooth transition from the one to the other is possible and useful. The assumption behind this role is that a KL-model can be found that is adequate for the range of situations one wants to deal with. Moreover this can be done *before* the detailed knowledge has been acquired (see also the tools described in [22] and [30]). Consider the situation of a human expert behaving in an environment, and then replace that expert by a system, or by an agent-system combination (Fig. 7). What is the relation between the knowledge level models for these three behaviours? Can we assume that they are the same, that they are related or are they really different?

Various authors, implicitly or explicitly motivated by these issues, are exploring ways to deal with them. A first approach is to explicitly distinguish between models for analysis and models for design. This is, for example, done in CommonKADS [48] but the relation and transition between the 'present' and 'target' models is largely an open issue. A second approach is to support knowledge level modelling for end-users themselves, as it is done in the Componential Methodology [36]. Here modelling is always done in the context of designing an application, and it is grounded in the needs and understanding of the users. A third approach is to restrict knowledge level modelling only as a tool for analysis. Here the aim is to find out about those features that make up interesting knowledge-based and goal-directed behavior, in particular the epistemological and pragmatic problems (Sect. 4). The knowledge that is used to

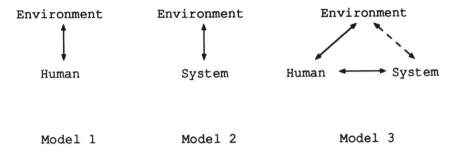

Fig. 7. A human expert, an artificial system and a human-system combination in a similar problem-situation. How are the knowledge models related to eachother?

overcome these problems may be ephemeral, but the problems themselves are not. How to deal with these problems is treated as an entirely separate problem and the knowledge level analysis may or may not be useful here. This is my understanding of some of the suggestions in [32].

9 Conclusion

The purpose of this paper was to bring together views and ideas on knowledge level modelling for knowledge systems. The main points it has been making are:

- The knowledge level is a model of behaviour in terms of knowledge that rationalises the observed behaviour.
- The knowledge level models as they are used in knowledge systems research are use-specific views on the knowledge level. They describe a structure on knowledge and goals.
- The notion of two-step rationality links Newell's knowledge level to current modelling approaches.
- Configuring a knowledge model is to augment knowledge and goals with assumptions about the world. These assumptions are linked by the competence theory of a problem solving method.
- The goal of problem solving as modelling is the instantiation of this theory into a case model.
- Actions are the means that the agent has to obtain knowledge about the world.

The implications of the above points for computational architectures of knowledge based behaviour were briefly explored. It is argued that explicit problem solving methods aim at making explicit the control in problem solving and that this leads to a form of brittleness because of lack of flexibility. On the other hand the notion of case model is not fully exploited. It is suggested that newer architectures will make explicit the goal of problem solving as modelling, making control emergent from the operationalisation of the method's principle of rationality.

With respect to the role of knowledge level modelling in knowledge systems development three possibilities have been listed that typically go together in methodologies. However, the combination of these roles hides an implicit assumption which is not necessarily valid. As an alternative I have suggested the use of knowledge level modelling as a way to find out relevant characteristics (task features) of a problem situation, as a pre-requisite for the construction of a solution for that (organizational) problem situation. This can be done in a variety of ways, including the introduction of a knowledge system.

Viewing knowledge as a means of modelling behaviour (not necessarily of generating it) calls for a re-orientation of knowledge engineering. Knowledge systems are rarely problem solvers themselves. They support a process of a-gents interacting with the environment and building their case model of the problems and situations that they are faced with. Understanding how to support this process requires more than knowledge acquisition alone. Moreover it can be supported in other and maybe better ways than by building a knowledge system. Knowledge engineering must be concerned with analysing and shaping knowledge based processes. As this paper has tried to show, the knowledge perspective remains an important tool to do this, but it seems that some of the issues that it raises (e.g. the role and nature of the 'grounding' relation in Fig. 7) must be taken more seriously.

References

1. A. Aamodt. *A knowledge-intensive approach to problem solving and sustained learning.* PhD thesis, University of Trondheim, Norwegian Institue of Technology, Trondheim, Norway, May 1991.

2. J. A. Breuker, B. J. Wielinga, M. van Someren, R. de Hoog, A. Th. Schreiber, P. de Greef, B. Bredeweg, J. Wielemaker, J. P. Billault, M. Davoodi, and S. A. Hayward. Model Driven Knowledge Acquisition: Interpretation Models. ESPRIT Project P1098 Deliverable D1 (task A1), University of Amsterdam and STL Ltd, 1987.

3. D. C. Brown and B. Chandrasekaran. *Design Problem Solving: Knowledge Structures and Control Strategies.* Research Notes in Artificial Intelligence. Pitman, London, 1989.

4. T. Bylander and S. Mittal. CSRL: A language for classificatory problem solving and uncertainty handling. *AI Magazine*, 7, 1986.

5. T. Bylander, S. Mittal, and B. Chandrasekaran. CSRL: A language for expert systems for diagnosis. In *IJCAI-83*, pages 218–221, 1983.

6. B. Chandrasekaran. Toward a taxonomy of problem-solving types. *AI Magazine*, 4(4):9–17g, 1983.

7. B. Chandrasekaran. Generic tasks in knowledge-based reasoning: High level building blocks for expert system design. *IEEE Expert*, 1(3):23–30, 1986.

8. B. Chandrasekaran. Generic tasks: The evolution of an idea. Technical report, Ohio State University, 1992.

9. B. Chandrasekaran and S. Mittal. Deep versus compiled knowledge approaches to diagnostic problem solving. *Int. J. Man-Machine Studies*, 19:425–436, 1983.

10. W. J. Clancey. The epistemology of rule-based expert systems – a framework for explanation. *Artificial Intelligence*, 20:215–251, 1983.

11. W. J. Clancey. Heuristic classification. *Artificial Intelligence*, 27:289–350, 1985.

12. W. J. Clancey. Model construction operators. *Artificial Intelligence*, 53(1):1–115, 1992.

13. William J. Clancey. The knowledge level reinterpreted: Modeling how systems interact. *Machine Learning, Special Issue on Knowledge Acquisition*, 4(3, 4):285 – 292, 1989.

14. William J. Clancey. The frame of reference problem in the design of intelligent machines. In K. vanLehn and A. Newell, editors, *Architectures for Intelligence: The Twenty Second Carnegie Symposium on Artificial Intelligence.* Erlbaum, Hillsdale, NJ, 1990.

15. R. Davis. Expert systems: where are we? and where do we go from here? AI Memo 665, MIT AI-Lab, 1982.

16. R. Davis. Reasoning from first principles in electronic trouble shooting. *International Journal of Man-Machine Studies*, 19:403–423, 1983.

17. T. G. Dietterich. Learning at the knowledge level. *Machine Learning*, 1:287–316, 1986.

18. L. Eshelman. MOLE: A knowledge-acquisition tool for cover-and-differentiate systems. In S. Marcus, editor, *Automating Knowledge Acquisition for Expert Systems*, pages 37–80. Kluwer Academic Publishers, The Netherlands, 1988.

19. M. Genesereth and R. E. Fikes. Knowledge interchange format version 3.0 reference manual. Report Logic 92-1, Logic Group, Stanford University, CA., 1992.

20. T. Gruber. Ontolingua: A mechanism to support portable ontologies. version 3.0. Technical report, Knowledge Systems Laboratory, Stanford University, CA, 1992.

21. F. Hayes-Roth, D. A. Waterman, and D. B. Lenat. *Building Expert Systems*. Addison-Wesley, New York, 1983.

22. G. Klinker, C. Bhola, G. Dallemagne, D. Marques, and J. McDermott. Usable and reusable programming constructs. *Knowledge Acquisition*, 3:117–136, 1991.

23. Marc Linster. *Knowledge acquisition based on explicit methods of problem–solving.* PhD thesis, University of Kaiserslautern, 1992.

24. S. Marcus, editor. *Automatic knowledge acquisition for expert systems.* Kluwer, 1988.

25. H. Maturana. Biology of cognition. In F. Varela and H. Maturana, editors, *Autopoiesis and Cognition.* Reidel, London, 1980.

26. J. McDermott. Preliminary steps towards a taxonomy of problem-solving methods. In S. Marcus, editor, *Automating Knowledge Acquisition for Expert Systems*, pages 225–255. Kluwer Academic Publishers, The Netherlands, 1988.

27. M. A. Musen. *Automated Generation of Model-Based Knowledge-Acquisition Tools.* Pitman, London, 1989. Research Notes in Artificial Intelligence.

28. A. Newell. The knowledge level. *Artificial Intelligence*, 18:87–127, 1982.

29. R.C Paton, H.S Nwana, M.J.R. Shave, T.J.M. Bench-Capon, and S. Hughes. Foundations of a structured approach to characterising domain knowledge. *Cognitive Systems*, 3(2):139–161, November 1991.

30. A. Puerta, J. Egar, S. W. Tu, and M. A. Musen. A multiple-method knowledge-acquisition shell for the automatic generation of knowledge-acquisition tools. In

Proceedings of the 6th Knowledge Acquisition for Knowledge-Based Systems Workshop, Banff, Canada, pages 20.1–19. SRDG Publications, University of Calgary, October 1991.

31. William F. Punch and B. Chandrasekaran. An investigation of the roles of problem-solving methods in diagnosis. In *Proceedings of the Tenth International Workshop: Expert Systems and their Applications*, pages 25–36, Avignon, France, 1990. EC2.

32. P. Rademakers and R. Pfeifer. The role of knowledge level models in situated adaptive design. In B. Neumann, editor, *Proceedings of the Tenth European Conference on Artificial Intelligence*, pages 601–602. John Wiley and Sons, Ltd., 1992.

33. A. Th. Schreiber, J. M. Akkermans, and B. J. Wielinga. On problems with the knowledge level perspective. In L. Steels and B. Smith, editors, *AISB-91: Artificial Intelligence and Simulation of behaviour*, pages 208–221, London, 1991. Springer Verlag. Also in: *Proceedings Banff-90 Knowledge Acquisition Workshop*, J. H. Boose and B. R. Gaines (editors), SRDG Publications, University of Calgary, pages 30-1 – 30-14.

34. L. Steels. Second generation expert systems. *Future Generation Computer Systems*, 1(4):213–221, 1985.

35. L. Steels. Components of expertise. *AI Magazine*, Summer 1990. Also as: AI Memo 88-16, AI Lab, Free University of Brussels.

36. L. Steels. Reusability and configuration of applications by non-programmers. Technical Report AI Memo 92-4, AI-Lab, Vrije Universiteit Brussel, Brussels, 1992.

37. J. Sticklen. Problem solving architecture at the knowledge level. *Journal of Experimental and Theoretical Artificial Intelligence*, 1989.

38. W. R. Swartout. XPLAIN: A system for creating and explaining expert consulting systems. *Artificial Intelligence*, 20:285–325, 1983.

39. W. Van de Velde. Inference stucture as a basis for problem solving. In Y. Kodratoff, editor, *Proceedings of the 8th European Conference on Artificial Intelligence*, pages 202–207, London, 1988. Pitman.

40. W. Van de Velde. *Learning from Experience*. PhD thesis, Vrije Universiteit Brussel, Brussels, 1988. also as VUB AI-Lab TR–88-1.

41. W. Van de Velde. Reasoning, behavior and learning: a knowledge level perspective. In *Proceedings of Cognitiva 90*, pages 451–463, November 1990.

42. W. Van de Velde. Tractable rationality at the knowledge-level. In L. Steels and B. Smith, editors, *Proceedings AISB'91: Artificial Intelligence and Simulation of Behaviour*, pages 196–207, London, 1991. Springer Verlag.

43. J. Vanwelkenhuysen and P. Rademakers. Mapping knowledge-level analysis onto a computational framework. In L. Aiello, editor, *Proceedings ECAI-90, Stockholm*, pages 681–686, London, 1990. Pitman.

44. J. Vanwelkenhuysen and W. Van de Velde. What's the problem when working with generic models. Technical Report AI-Memo 92-07, Vrije Universiteit Brussel, AI-Lab, Brussels, 1992.

45. R. E. Vinkhuysen. On the non-existence of knowledge level models. In B. Neumann, editor, *Proceedings of the 10th European Conference on Artificial Intelligence*, pages 620–622, Chichester, 1992. John Wiley and Sons, Ltd.

46. B. J. Wielinga and J. A. Breuker. Models of expertise. In *Proceedings ECAI-86*, pages 306–318, 1986.

47. B. J. Wielinga, A. Th. Schreiber, and J. A. Breuker. KADS: A modelling approach to knowledge engineering. *Knowledge Acquisition*, 4(1), 1992. Special issue 'The KADS approach to knowledge engineering'.

48. B. J. Wielinga, W. van de Velde, A. Th. Schreiber, and J. M. Akkermans. Towards a unification of knowledge modelling approaches. In Jean-Marc David, Jean-Paul Krivine, and Reid Simmons, editors, *Second Generation Expert Systems*. Springer-Verlag, 1992. To appear. Also as: Technical Report ESPRIT Project P5248, KADS-II/T1.1/TR/UvA/004/3.0.

49. B. Woodward. Knowledge acquisition at the front end: Defining the domain. *Knowledge Acquisition*, 2(2):73–94, 1990.

Generic Tasks and Task Structures: History, Critique and New Directions*

B. Chandrasekaran[1] and Todd R. Johnson[2]

[1]Department of Computer and Information Science, Laboratory for Artificial Intelligence Research, The Ohio State University, Columbus, OH 43210, USA
[2]Department of Pathology, Laboratory for Knowledge-Based Medical Systems, The Ohio State University, Columbus OH, 43210, USA

Abstract. We have for several years been working on an approach to knowledge system building that argues for the existence of a close connection between the tasks which the knowledge system is intended to solve, the methods chosen for them and the vocabulary in which knowledge is to be modeled and represented. We trace the historical origins of the idea that we have called *Generic Tasks*, and outline their evolution and accomplishments based on them. We then critique their original implementations from the perspective of flexible integration. We follow this with an outline of our current generalization of the view in the form of a theory of *task structures*. We describe the architectural implications of this view and outline some research directions.

1   Introduction

We and our colleagues have been working for about a decade on an approach to the construction of knowledge systems that can be best characterized as *task-oriented*. In this approach, the nature of the task that is set for the knowledge-based system (KBS) takes primacy in analysis. The properties of the underlying general architecture on which the knowledge system is implemented are considered relatively unimportant. Our work has gone through much evolution, and in fact, recently, the evolution has been many-branched, i.e., different researchers are taking somewhat different paths.

Our work has had three phases: initial work on MDX and associated systems during which we developed our understanding of the importance of a task-oriented perspective; a second phase in which the task-level emphasis was made explicit and a specific version of it, the Generic Task (GT) approach, was developed in some detail; and the third, current, phase, in which the GT approach is evolving into the broader view that we call *Task Structures* which places greater emphasis on multiplicity of methods for tasks and flexibility in invoking them. The current phase has also introduced new points of view regarding the relationship of the task-oriented view to general architectures.

---

* Portions of this paper appear as part of Chandrasekaran, B., Johnson, T.R., Smith, J.W.: Task-structure analysis for knowledge modeling. Communications of the ACM, (September) 1992.

In writing this paper, we have assumed a general familiarity on the part of the readers with our work on the first two phases, which is well-documented in the literature. What we plan to do is to quickly review the history of the first two phases, then spend more time on our recent concerns and ideas.

2   Generic Tasks: A Historical Overview

2.1   Diagnosis as Classification

In the late 70's, inspired by the work of the Stanford group on Mycin and related diagnostic systems, we began to investigate medical diagnostic problem solving. Specifically, at a seminar during 1977, at the suggestion of Jack Smith, our medical collaborator, we examined some solution protocols from Harvey and Bordley [35], a book of medical case analyses. Fernando Gomez, a member of our group, proposed that the reasoning involved in the cases that we looked at could be viewed as a form of classification reasoning, i.e., one in which a set of data describing the case (symptoms or observations) was classified into one or more disease classes. (This was some time before Clancey published his analysis of Mycin [23] as a heuristic classification problem solver.) Gomez and Chandrasekaran [32] also proposed that the diagnostic knowledge could be organized as a classification hierarchy of disease concepts, and implemented as a community of specialists, with one specialist for each diagnostic concept. The specialist would have procedural knowledge about how to establish the concept, and if the concept is established, control would be transferred to the child concept. The idea of concepts as specialists has many reverberations from the past and the present: Wittgenstein's ideas [74] on the active nature of concepts, Minsky's view of a Society of Mind [51], and object-oriented programming are some examples that come to mind.

2.2   Diagnosis as Classification + Intelligent Database

Our medical diagnostic system, MDX [19] [18], was based on the classification perspective. Sanjay Mittal, who took on the task of implementing MDX soon saw the need for another type of reasoning to augment classification. Classification specialists had knowledge that helped map from the case data to confidence values in various hypotheses, but the types of case data that the classification specialists could handle were often different from the observations that described the case. The observations had to be normalized or otherwise converted to a form that the classification specialists could handle. Otherwise the procedures in each of the classification specialists would have to contain many combinations to account explicitly for each form in which the data could appear as observations. To give a simple example, a classification specialist in the medical domain might need information about exposure to anesthetics, while the case data might not have any information about this, but instead might record that the patient recently underwent major surgery. The latter information can be used to infer exposure to anesthetics.

Mittal [18] decided to create an "intelligent database" that would use domain knowledge to make inferences from available observations about the presence or absence of information that the classificatory specialists could use. Separating the database in this way enabled us to keep the classificatory activity perspicuous. Mittal implemented the database in the same specialist-community style as the classification module. The database had specialists that specialized in different types of medical data. These specialists were organized in a way that reflected the hierarchical and other relations between the types of data. Inferential knowledge about data was represented at different levels of abstraction in the various data specialists. Once we modularized the database this way, we could identify more examples of reasoning that could be supported by the database, e.g., spatial and temporal reasoning about data [18, 20, 52, 53]. Spatial reasoning was needed for reasoning about radiographic information., e.g., to infer obstructions in the bile duct from descriptions of shapes and location of masses in x-rays. Temporal reasoning was needed to answer questions about temporal relations between data; for example, to decide if some quantity was rapidly rising or not based on a sequence of its values.

About the time we were developing this view of diagnosis as classification, Clancey was making his own analysis of Mycin as a *heuristic classification* system. He decomposed heuristic classification into three subtasks: data abstraction, heuristic match (of data to categories), and (category) refinement. While our classification problem solver was explicitly performing both concept-establishment and concept-refinement, and our data retrieval module was performing several other types of inferences in addition to data abstraction, MDX and Clancey's Neomycin system were talking about the same kinds of subtasks and at approximately the same level of abstraction. (However, the order in which subtasks were invoked was quite different in the Neomycin and MDX implementations. The similarities are at a fairly abstract level of the types of subtasks.)

2.3 Diagnosis as Abduction

As the range of diagnostic problems we considered widened, we started to look at diagnostic problems for which classification was not enough. MDX could handle multiple malfunctions as long as the malfunctions were more or less independent. The kind of diagnosis that, for example, Internist [50] and Abel [57] could perform, where the diagnoses involved selecting subsets of hypotheses from among relevant hypotheses, was beyond MDX's capability. In [32], we recognized the need for an Overview problem solver which could perform an evaluation of how well the hypotheses were explaining the data, but we made no suggestion about how the problem solving would proceed.

At about this time, John Josephson joined our group. His philosophical interest was in using abductive reasoning, i.e., reasoning to the "best explanation," as the central strategy in arriving at increasingly reliable knowledge in spite of uncertainty. Pople [60] had earlier shown that the diagnostic problem had a strong abductive character. Our diagnostic approach was ready for the addition of the abductive view. It turned out that we could view the classification problem solver as a module that generated a number of highly plausible hypotheses along with an account of what each hypothesis could explain. We added a new problem solver, an *abductive assembler*, that would select the best subset of these hypotheses by reasoning about which subset explained the data most satisfactorily. Again, following the paradigm already set, we looked at abductive assembly as a distinct type of problem solving, and started identifying the types of knowledge needed and the kinds of strategies that were available to perform the task. Abduction evolved, over the next few years, into one of the most active areas of research within our Laboratory. It was during this time that Josephson, Smith, and a number of graduate students developed a complex abductive system called RED. (The results of almost a decade of our Lab's research on abduction are summarized in [45].)

2.4 Hypothesis Assessment by Hierarchical Matching

Diagnosis as classification requires as a subtask assessing the concepts in the classification hierarchy, or, more precisely, requires determining how likely a given classificatory concept is, given the case data. Mycin had popularized a form of certainty factor calculus for performing this task, and a number of probabilistic techniques had been used in traditional pattern recognition for this subtask. In MDX this was accomplished by a form of template matching against the concept description. The technique [9, 21] combined qualitative measures of the presence of data ("high," "medium," etc.) to reach conclusions about hypotheses with a qualitative measure of certainty attached to the conclusions ("likely," "unlikely," etc.). The essence of the matching was hierarchical, feature-based pattern matching. This technique side-stepped the need for assigning numerical values and combining them when the data didn't have such numerical precision and when the task only called for qualitative evaluation. We saw that this type of problem solving had the potential for wide use, not only as part of diagnosis, but wherever hypotheses or concepts of any sort had to be matched against a situation description. Later this technique was generalized to *structured matching*, in which one choice out of a small number of choices is made by hierarchically matching features.

2.5 Routine Design: Plan Selection, Instantiation and Refinement

Around 1981, David Brown took on as his thesis topic design as a possible application area for KBS's. Brown and Chandrasekaran analyzed the problem solving activity of an expert designer of a mechanical device called an air-cylinder and identified the design activity as a form of routine design [5]. We saw that, similar to our analysis of classification, the designer's knowledge could be decomposed into a number of design concepts that were hierarchically organized, reflecting the hierarchical structure of the object that was being designed. Again, this form of problem-solving activity had characteristic types of knowledge (for example, *plans*), problem-solving subtasks (*plan selection, plan refinement*), and problem-solving strategies (*top-down design*).

2.6 Generic Tasks: The Initial Formulation

By 1983, we had gained experience with several tasks. In particular we were beginning to learn how to decompose a complex task into component tasks. Chandrasekaran had started formulating the notion of a *Generic Task* [11, 13]. The main intuition was that classification, data retrieval, plan selection and refinement, state abstraction and abductive assembly all were in some sense re-usable subtasks. These subtasks were proposed as especially useful as components in other more complex problem-solving tasks. In our work on diagnosis we had shown how classification, data retrieval and abductive assembly came together. The work on design also used a form of intelligent data manager in conjunction with the planner. We viewed these generically useful components as building blocks and called them Generic Tasks (GT's). We knew that we did not have an exhaustive list of GT's yet, but we were confident that we had identified some important ones and that they were illustrative of the kind of generic components that we should be looking for.

Note the distinction between tasks, such as diagnosis and design that are in some sense generic, and Generic Tasks. Diagnosis and design were not in our list of GT's. We viewed them as compositions of GT's of the type that we had identified. One of the criticisms often made about the GT approach [37] is that it would lead to multiple representation of the same knowledge. The example often used involved the use of structural knowledge of a device in both diagnosis and design. If one built task-specific knowledge representations for each of these tasks, the argument went, one would need to replicate the structural knowledge in the two modules. However, as we have shown elsewhere in detail [17], both diagnosis and design use structure-to-behavior simulation as a subtask, and structural information is the knowledge that is needed to carry out this subtask. If we create a module for this type of simulation that can be invoked during design or diagnosis as needed, structural knowledge need only be represented once in this module.

The specialist architecture that we had adopted was particularly helpful in composing the GT's. Message passing between specialists was the glue with which to compose the specialists of different types. However, we soon started to recognize that, in identifying the task-level view so closely with the specialist-style implementational approach, we were mixing implementation-level talk with task-level talk. We began to describe [12] each GT in terms of the input-output description of the task, the method/strategy that was appropriate for it and the knowledge that the method needs.

Generic Task Shells. Since each GT had a clear characterization in terms of types of knowledge needed and some family of parameterizable methods, it was a natural step to propose a shell for each of the GT's that we had identified. Bylander, with the design assistance of Mittal, built the first such language, CSRL [10]. It enabled a knowledge engineer to encode classification hierarchies in the domain of interest and either accept the *Establish-Refine* strategy that was the applicable default strategy for hierarchical classification, or specify local variations on the strategy. When the domain-specific knowledge was encoded and the method was specified using CSRL, the compiler produced a classification problem solver. Brown [4] similarly built DSPL, a language in which to specify domain knowledge and control for building routine design problem solvers. In later versions of CSRL and DSPL, graphical user interfaces of considerable sophistication were added which relieved the system builders of much of the need to do "programming." A separate shell called HYPER [41] was built for the hypothesis assessment task.

We designed PEIRCE as a shell for constructing abductive assembly systems [61]. Sticklen built a data-base shell called IDABLE [38] for constructing intelligent data base modules as data servers for knowledge systems.

This general style of paying attention to the knowledge needs of the task and characteristic strategies was a hallmark of our approach to a number of other problems in knowledge systems. For example, Sembugamoorthy and Chandrasekaran identified a form of functional reasoning as a generic activity that was useful in simulation of devices [65], and we identified the types of knowledge needed to represent knowledge about how devices worked. Allemang built a generic shell to support the acquisition and use of functional representations.

The GT shells found wide use in chemical engineering, nuclear engineering, medical applications, speech recognition, planning and design. Josephson led an effort to build an integrated toolset which was based on a uniform agent-oriented formalism to implement a specialist architecture [46], while Sticklen and Punch at Michigan State moved to build a Smalltalk-based GT toolset. In addition, a number of organizations over time also implemented their own versions of the shells.

Advantages of GT's. It seemed to us that we were engaged in a new approach to knowledge representation (KR). In traditional KR, knowledge was represented independently of the task. Since there was no theory of tasks to help in identifying types of knowledge, the only terms that were available were very general and task-independent, such as predicates, sets and set membership and subset relations. On the other hand, because of the emphasis on tasks and the role different types of knowledge played in their achievement, our approach to knowledge representation provided a larger vocabulary of task-related terms, and additionally, related the knowledge to how it was going to be used. As we develop an understanding of more such tasks, more knowledge-level terms will be identified for the representation of knowledge.

Bylander and Chandrasekaran outlined [8] how the GT view facilitated knowledge acquisition by providing the vocabulary in terms of which to seek knowledge for the task, and by guiding in the organization and use of the knowledge thus acquired. Chandrasekaran, Tanner, and Josephson [22] similarly showed how the task-view also provided important points of leverage in the generation of explanations of problem solving.

The GT's also appeared to have computational advantages. Goel *et al.* [30] showed how, if the right kind of knowledge was available, hypothesis generation by classification had a computational complexity that was linear in the number of hypotheses. Goel and Bylander similarly analyzed the computational properties of structured matching [28] (see Section 2.4). Bylander *et al.*, showed in a series of papers which culminated in [7] that many of the strategies used in the construction of our abductive assembler (see Section 2.3) had attractive computational properties, explaining how knowledge of the right type can help solve problems in acceptable time even though the general abductive problem was NP-complete.

We now had a system-building style in which we had a general architecture of message-passing modular specialists. Each GT language was built by specializing this architecture for the GT at hand into a task-specific architecture (TSA). This architecture, when instantiated with domain knowledge, produced a problem solver for the corresponding task in that domain. Our attitude to general purpose architectures at this point in time was two-fold. One, they strictly served the role of universal machines in enabling the construction of TSA's. It didn't matter whether the underlying architecture was LISP, Prolog, a rule-interpreter, or whatever. Two, emphasis on general purpose architectures often made people view what were essentially content[1] issues at the task

---

[1]The term "content" is often used in AI discussions to contrast it with "form." The content of a representation is roughly what types of information is carried by the representation, while the form is the syntactic aspects of how the representation is encoded. "Form" also corresponds to a computational architecture in that there is a correspondence between architectures and programming languages. Newell's Knowledge vs. Symbol-level

level as syntactic issues in the programming language corresponding to the underlying architecture.

2.7 GT's as Functional Building Blocks: The Platonic View

In [14], Chandrasekaran outlined a view of GT's as "building blocks" of intelligent systems. We can call it the Platonic View since it proposed that a set of abstract GT's existed which together functionally captured the capability of intelligence in solving problems. The proposal was explicitly *not* claiming that the GT's we had identified were all that were there, but we hoped that with further work we would be able to identify a number of such strategies that were sufficient to cover a large part of problem solving. GT's such as classification, plan instantiation and refinement, and abductive assembly seemed ubiquitous as components in many different problem solving tasks. They all could be defined functionally, thus avoiding the vexing problem of the right general architecture. They all had attractive computational properties. The GT's that we were working with seemed more than accidental, *ad hoc* entities.

2.8 Other Work in the Same Spirit

By 1987, Newell's paper on the Knowledge Level [56] had become more widely known and read in AI. In our group, we realized that we had in fact been working at and arguing for precisely the knowledge-level view of knowledge systems. Our arguments against general purpose architectures, which were the bones of contention in the field, could now be seen as arguments against a premature commitment to symbol-level issues.

From 1987-89, we became aware of a number of efforts outside our Laboratory to investigate knowledge-based problem solving at the Knowledge Level. We have already mentioned Clancey's work on Heuristic Classification and the Heracles shell based on it. KADS work in Europe [3] proposed a number of primitive inference terms to use in describing the problem solving behavior of agents. (Hadzikadic [34] in the US had also made a similar proposal, but it was not widely known.) The KADS work at that time seemed to have somewhat different goals from those of the GT work. For one thing, it offered to provide support for analyzing and describing problem-solving behavior in terms of generic inferences, whereas the GT approach offered direct support for implementation in the form of building blocks that could be used to instantiate problem solvers. There were no proposals in KADS of that period about strategies or methods by which problems were solved. The KADS inference primitives seemed much more fine-grained than GT terms such as classification and plan refinement, i.e., they seemed to be at the level of internal operators that our GT's were using. However, there was

---

distinction is one attempt to capture this distinction more formally. What is content at one level may be form at another level. Consider an assembly language, LISP that compiles into the assembly language, and a knowledge representation language such as KL-ONE written in LISP. LISP has a content theory of some computational objects, but KL-ONE is a further content theory for which LISP provides the formal substrate. KL-ONE is in turn a formal substrate for a representation of knowledge in some domain in KL-ONE.

no obvious direct mapping from the operators that GT's were using and the inference primitives in KADS. Over time, the KADS view has evolved into a more comprehensive framework, called KADS-2 [72], which has many layers spanning from analysis through strategies to implementation. KADS-2 has a clear role for methods in the spirit of GT's in what they have called "the blue book," a compendium of abstract methods of general usefulness. But there is still an unresolved issue of the status of the inference primitives from KADS-1 which now reside in one of the layers of KADS-2. Their status as a closed and orthogonal set of ontological primitives, how they arise and how they relate to other such sets of primitives are all unclear and need further research. We come back to this issue again in the last section of the paper (Section 5.1).

The role of the structure of tasks in guiding the construction of knowledge systems began to be investigated by many other researchers. McDermott and Marcus [48, 49] wanted to know what role different types of knowledge played in different types of methods. They identified very general methods such as "Propose-and-Refine" for configuration problems, and identified the role knowledge played in the achievement of such methods. In France, David and Krivine [26] worked on TSA's for diagnosis. They made a useful distinction [25] between functional architectures at the knowledge level for a task, and GT's as particular components of functional architectures that have proved to be recurrent and ubiquitous in various knowledge systems performing the task. Gruber and Cohen [33] identified uncertain reasoning as a generic activity and proposed generic methods and representations to handle this problem. Musen's work on Protege [54] was quite close in spirit to DSPL. Steels' work on componential frameworks [66] was to come later, but it also shared the spirit of the GT work (we discuss this approach later in the paper as well). Thus a community was emerging with similar goals, with approaches that shared some ideas and differed on others. Specifically, they shared two features. First, they identified tasks at various levels of abstraction above the implementation language level. Second, they identified types of knowledge and reasoning strategies needed to accomplish such tasks.

Later in the paper, we discuss in some detail the relation of our approach to KADS, the componential framework and role-limiting methods.

2.9 Critiques of the GT Approach

As experience accumulated in our Lab in using the GT approach for a variety of complex problems, a period of assessment began from 1988 onwards. While there was widespread acknowledgment of the utility of the GT approach, there were critiques of aspects of the approach from researchers outside our Laboratory as well. We have already dealt with a recurrent criticism that the GT view might lead to redundancy of knowledge representation. What we now want to discuss is the series of critiques of GT from those participating in its development.

The first set of questions concerned the criteria for a GT: How many GT's are there? What kinds of tasks count as GT's? (See Sections 3.7–3.9 for the answers that we ended up with to these questions.) In one sense, there are just two generic tasks: abduction and planning. All agents have to make sense of the world and build more or less veridical internal models of the environment (the problem of abduction), and using such models plan actions on the world to achieve goals (the task of planning). In this view, GT's such as classification are a means to an end, subtasks of the two major tasks. This sense of generic tasks, which emphasizes goals, is different from the building block view of GT's that we were promulgating and that emphasized generic capabilities useful for a number of goals.

We also became increasingly aware of a terminological problem: the conflation between a task and a method in the GT way of speaking. Each GT such as classification was both a task (classification had the goal of identifying a class that best characterized a set of observations) and a method (in CSRL, the classification task was performed by the hierarchical classification method). Of course the methods could set up subtasks (CSRL set up the subtask of data abstraction/retrieval). Classification used as a building block for the task of diagnosis was a method for the subtask of hypothesis generation, but it also came with the method of hierarchical classification. In fact one of the proposed strengths of the GT view was that each such task came with a preferred default method. Nevertheless it was becoming clear that we needed to make a clear distinction in our discussions between tasks and methods.

Once we started looking at the methods inside GT's separately, it was clear that the rigidity of the methods for GT's was becoming a problem. It is true that the top-down method of *Establish-Refine* is a good general strategy for hierarchical classification, but there are instances in which a different control strategy is needed. For example, at times a disease at a higher level can only be established if any of its subtypes can be established. A knowledge engineer should be able to specify different strategies.

As a result, we gave CSRL increased flexibility in method specification, ways in which the default strategy can be modified. The theoretical issue was how far flexibility could be pushed within the framework of the GT and the corresponding notion of a task-specific architecture.

There was another aspect to the flexibility issue: flexibility in the way different GT problem solvers were hooked up to solve a complex problem. In building our diagnostic systems, we would typically know at system-building time how these components would be put together: for example, for diagnosis, the abductive assembly system would invoke the classifier for hypothesis generation, the classifier would invoke the appropriate hypothesis assessors for evaluating the various hypotheses, and so on. Later in MDX-2 [67], when knowledge was missing in any of the components, the functional model of the device under diagnosis would be invoked to derive the missing knowledge. However, it was becoming increasingly clear that a more opportunistic, run-time choice of methods could be beneficial in several applications.

"Chunkiness" of some of our GT's was also becoming a problem. We noted that our classification tool, CSRL, was actually two GT's in one: one for the problem of navigating classification hierarchies and the other for the problem of assessing each of the hypotheses selected during navigation. It seemed wise to separate out the assessment GT from CSRL. This was in fact done quite early in our work, during about 83-84. The hypothesis assessment GT, along with its symbolic abstraction method, became knows as HYPER [41]. It found extensive use wherever we found the task of symbolic assessment of how well a set of data fits a hypothesis, concept or a plan.

The chunkiness problem was actually quite severe in DSPL. DSPL solved a number of subproblems: plan assessment, plan selection, plan refinement, and failure handling. For each of the subtasks it had a method. When users wanted to adopt a different method for a subtask, DSPL provided escape into LISP for coding the new method. This was of course a good thing, since it avoided the tools becoming representational prisons from which escape was impossible, but the problem is that LISP is not a language that has any theory of problem solving implicit in it. The language into which one escapes should preferably be one which is built on a uniform framework for problem solving. Thus, it seemed that either we had to provide a larger repertoire of methods, or provide a task-independent problem-solving framework to solve the local problem and get back into the GT tool.

Another problem concerned the multiplicity of ways in which people used the GT's in solving a new problem. In a recent experiment to study how users of GT were using the tools to model real-world problems, a number of GT researchers were asked to design a system to assign employees to various rooms so that a set of constraints are satisfied [1]. Most subjects viewed the problem as an instance of routine design in which plans are selected and instantiated so as to satisfy the constraints. But one GT analyst chose to view the problem as an instance of the assembly problem, i.e., a problem where objects (rooms) are assembled such that a set of constraints are satisfied, and proposed the use of the abductive assembly tool, with the understanding that the intended criterion for assembly was not explanation but coverage of design constraints. We are confronting the issue of what it means for a problem to be a certain type. Is abductive assembly a special type of configuration problem? Is design a particular type of assembly problem? (These issues, by the way, are not unique to the GT approach; they are problems for any general theory of tasks and methods.)

The above considerations were taking their toll on two aspects of our stance. One of them concerned the Platonic View, that GT's were abstract functional building blocks of intelligence, and the other was the associated architectural view that intelligence was a collection of task-specific architectures, each devoted to one of the GT's. Skepticism about this position led to re-examination of our belief that general purpose architectures were just Turing-Universal machines for implementing GT-level TSA's.

It was beginning to seem unlikely that a GT such as routine design (as captured in the tool DSPL) could be a building block: there were too many subtasks and methods rolled into one. What are the elementary tasks and how to tell?

Multiplicity of methods for a given task and emergence of complex methods from more elementary pieces reintroduced the issue of an appropriate general architecture. For handling the multiplicity of methods, we needed an architecture in which methods could be invoked, evaluated and chosen at run-time. If that architecture could also explain how methods that we recognized as GT-like could emerge, and could support writing of new methods in a uniform framework, so much the better.

In response to these questions, the GT approach evolved into a framework that we have called the Task Structure view. In the next section of the paper, we describe this view and its architectural implications.

3   The Task Structure Perspective

In [15] and more elaborately in [16], Chandrasekaran described this form of analysis. Let us first clarify some terminology before describing the task structure approach.

3.1   Tasks

The term "task" has been used in many senses in the field, contributing to some confusion. The term has been used to denote an instance of a problem, a problem class, and both a problem class and an abstract description of a method of solving the problem. Newell and Simon use the term to refer either to a problem instance or a class of problems of the same type. In Clancey [24], the term task refers to the basic subgoals that can be set by an expert system (e.g., APPLYRULE!, GROUP-AND-DIFFERENTIATE, etc.), i.e., it includes a high level description of the method. In our work on GT's, we also included a method description as part of a Generic Task. Similarly, Wielinga et al., [72] use the term "task" to refer to the sequence of operations (at an appropriate level of abstraction) that a particular system performs. We think it is useful to separate the intended set of problem instances for a knowledge system from the methods used by it to solve them, i.e., separate the task from the method.

In the rest of the paper, we will use the term "task" to refer to a *type* of problem, or equivalently, a set of problem instances with something in common. Thus diagnosis is a task, i.e., a type of problem in which the goal is to identify the causes of a given set of abnormal behaviors of some system. The task can be at different levels of generality. For example, we can have diagnosis, and medical diagnosis, which is a type of diagnosis and so on. How a set of problem instances gets grouped into a type of problem is determined purely on pragmatic grounds of the usefulness of such a grouping. For example, treating diagnosis as a type of problem enables us to study general strategies for that class of problems. Note that we explicitly do not include, as part of the task description, any specification of *how* the task will be accomplished.

3.2 Methods, Operators, Subtasks and Inferences

Methods are ways of accomplishing tasks and may be of many types: they may be computational, or "situated," i.e., involve extracting information from the surrounding physical world. For example, the task of predicting behavior of a device may be solved by a computational method that performs a simulation, or it may be solved by manipulating a physical model of the device and seeing what happens. Within the class of computational methods, a method may be couched as executing a precompiled algorithm, search in a state space, as a connectionist network and so on.

Let us focus on computational methods. Abstractly, such a method can be described in terms of the *operators* it employs, the *objects* that it operates on, and any additional knowledge about how to organize operator application to satisfy the goal. Note that any algorithm can be abstractly characterized in these terms. The problem-space formalism is a general way of formulating such methods. In this model, the goal is described as the desired knowledge state of the problem-solving agent. The initial state is the knowledge state corresponding to what is known at the start of problem solving. Thus the initial state in diagnosis contains knowledge of the symptoms, while the goal state description includes the causes of the symptoms. The operators transform one state into another state. Whenever two or more operators are applicable to a state knowledge that indicates which operator to select is needed. This is called *search-control knowledge* [47] because it indicates how the problem space is searched.

Operators are the *subtasks* of a method. The only difference between the definition of an operator and our definition of a task is that operators also come with preconditions. Nonetheless an operator is a task. It specifies a class of problems to be solved. Thus, we use the terms *operator* and *subtask* interchangeably.

Subtasks can be accomplished either directly or through additional problem solving using a method. A subtask can be accomplished directly if all its preconditions are satisfied and the knowledge to accomplish the subtask is in a form that can be applied without further problem solving. More commonly, however, subtasks require additional problem solving using a method. A subtask, of course, can have alternative methods associated with it.

It might seem that the problem-space formalism is only appropriate for describing search methods. However, algorithms that do not perform search can still be viewed as special cases where the choice of which operator to apply to which state is completely specified, and all preconditions for operator application are satisfied. Thus the problem-space formalism is sufficiently general to include all algorithms whether they perform search or not.

Often the term "inference step" is used as part of method descriptions, and researchers speak of "inference structures". This terminology arises from the "reasoning metaphor," in which agents solve problems by making inferences from available knowledge to generate new knowledge. The agent's goal is to make a series of inferences such that a clause or proposition which meets the informational requirements of the goal is generated as one of the new pieces of knowledge. We can map the reasoning metaphor to the problem-space metaphor as follows. Each state in the problem space corresponds to a certain knowledge state for the agent. Each operator if applicable and applied enables the agent to be in a new knowledge state which typically adds knowledge to previous states. Thus there is a correspondence between "inference rule" in the reasoning view and "operators" in the problem solving view. Corresponding to "operator schemas," wherein the agent instantiates an operator schema before applying it, we might also have inference rule schemas.

3.3 Example: The Method of Hierarchical Classification

Let us consider how to represent the *Establish-Refine* method for hierarchical classification [32] using the framework described above. Hierarchical classification is used in many diagnosis systems as a way of quickly focusing on possible malfunctions. The initial state of the classification task is a set of data (e.g., manifestations in a diagnosis task) and an initial high level hypothesis (e.g., *liver disease*). The goal state is one containing plausible malfunction hypotheses, i.e., the most detailed hypotheses consistent with the data. The method works by first considering a high-level malfunction category, such as *liver disease*, to determine if the malfunction appears likely given the data at hand. If it appears likely then the malfunction is refined to more specific diseases, *hepatitis* and *cancer*, for example. The more specific malfunctions are then evaluated against the data and any that appear likely are refined. This process continues until no more malfunctions can be refined.

We can specify this method using two subtasks:

> *evaluate* hypothesis
> *refine* hypothesis

The first, evaluate, takes some hypothesis (such as a malfunction hypothesis) and assigns a likelihood based on the current case data. A precondition for applying *evaluate* to a hypothesis is that the hypothesis must not have already been evaluated. The second subtask, *refine*, takes a hypothesis as input and produces the refinements for that hypothesis. *Refine* has two preconditions: the hypothesis must be likely and must not have already been refined.

We must also specify the operator proposal knowledge, that is knowledge that determines when an operator should be considered for application to a state. For the hierarchical classification method we are describing, the operators *evaluate* and *refine* should be proposed whenever their preconditions are met.

The initial and goal states and the subtasks define a search space or problem space. Figure 1 illustrates the search space that results when the hierarchical classification method described above is applied to a liver diagnosis problem. The search space is the set of states reachable from the initial state by applying the operators for the method. The figure shows part of the search space of the task, beginning with the initial state, *S1*, containing manifestations indicative of a viral infection (labeled *Data*) and the high level hypothesis *liver disease*. The only operator applicable to this state is *evaluate liver disease*. Application of this operation results in a new state, *S2*, in which *liver disease* is rated likely (in the figure this is noted by setting the hypothesis in bold face). Only one operator is applicable to *S2*, *refine liver disease*, resulting in *S3* which contains the refinements of *liver disease*: *cancer* and *infection*. At *S3* two operators are applicable: *evaluate cancer* and *evaluate infection*; hence the tree branches to show both possibilities: *evaluate cancer* results in *S4'* in which *cancer* is determined to be unlikely and *evaluate infection* results in *S4"* in which *infection* is rated likely.

In the problem-space framework, problems are solved by searching through a problem space for a path from the initial state to the goal state. Problem-space search is done by enumerating operators applicable to the current state (which at the start of problem solving is the initial state of the task instance), selecting from these a single operator and then applying that operator to the current state. The resulting state then becomes the new current state and the whole process of operation selection and application is repeated until the goal state is reached.

Search-control knowledge guides the search through the problem space. For example, in hierarchical classification the agent might apply a heuristic that it is better to evaluate hypotheses with higher likelihoods than those with low likelihoods, or it might decide that the decision about which *evaluate* operator to apply is not important, hence either operator can be selected. In the task structure, to insure that the method is as general as possible, we specify the minimum amount of domain independent search-control knowledge needed for each method. In the *Establish-Refine* method described above, no search-control knowledge is specified because any such knowledge would unduly constrain the method. For example, if either of the heuristics mentioned above were included in the search-control knowledge for the classification method, it would limit the application of the method to those domains and task instances in which the heuristics apply.

The independent specification of search-control knowledge and subtasks lead to two of the primary advantages of the problem-space approach to specifying methods:

1. We are not forced to specify a particular operator sequence. We can specify the search-control knowledge that is general to all task instances for a method and defer other decisions about operator sequencing to system designers or run-time computation. By doing this, we insure that the method can be applied to as wide a range of task instances as possible. In contrast, early GT work often overconstrained the sequencing of operators, limiting the use of each method to a narrow range of problems.

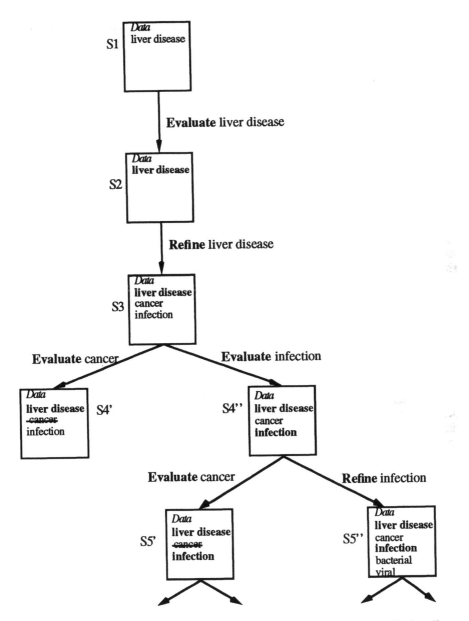

Fig. 1. Part of the search space for the Establish-Refine method as applied to liver disease. The data for this example is indicative of a viral infection. Hypotheses in plain text are unevaluated; those in bold are likely; and those shown with a line through them are unlikely.

2. Search-control knowledge ensures a dynamic or situated system. Each bit of search control knowledge is sensitive to the operators and the current state, hence the precise sequence of operators is determined dynamically at run-time.

3.4 The Task Structure

With the clarification of the terminology of tasks, methods, operators and subtasks behind us, we are now ready to formulate our notion of a Task Structure. The Task Structure is the tree of tasks, methods and subtasks applied recursively until tasks are reached that are in some sense performed directly using available knowledge. Figure 2 graphically represents part of the task structure for diagnosis. A task (as we defined earlier) is a problem type, such as diagnosis. Tasks are represented graphically using circles. A method is a way of accomplishing a task. These are represented graphically using rectangles. In the figure, *Bayesian Explanation, Abductive Assembly* and *Cover-and-Differentiate* are identified as methods for doing diagnosis. All of these methods can be classified as abductive methods, hence they appear as a subtype of *Abduction Methods*. In general, a task can be accomplished using any one of several alternative methods, so in the task structure we explicitly identify alternative methods for each task. A method can set up subtasks, which themselves can be accomplished by various methods. For example in the *Diagnosis* task structure *Abductive Assembly* has been decomposed into two subtasks: *Generate Plausible Hypotheses* and *Select Hypotheses*.

In addition to knowledge of the tasks, methods and subtasks, four other kinds of knowledge play important roles in the task structure: 1) subtask preconditions; 2) subtask proposal knowledge, i.e., knowledge about when to attempt a subtask (which can differ from the preconditions); 3) search-control knowledge for sequencing subtasks; and 4) method-selection knowledge for selecting between multiple methods for a task. Method-selection knowledge is associated with a task or task/method combination.

3.5 Examples of Task Structures for Design and Diagnosis

The following descriptions of design and diagnosis illustrate the main points about specifying task structures.

Design. Part of the task structure for design is shown in Figure 3 (this is abstracted from the task structure description in [16]). The top task for the design task structure is, of course, *Design*. The design task can be solved using a family of methods called *Propose-Critique-Modify* (PCM). These methods have the subtasks of proposing partial or complete design solutions, critiquing the proposals by identifying causes of failure if any and modifying proposals to satisfy design goals. Hence the three subtasks shown for PCM: *Propose, Critique* and *Modify*. These subtasks can be combined in fairly complex ways, but the following is one straight-forward way in which a PCM method can organize and combine the subtasks.

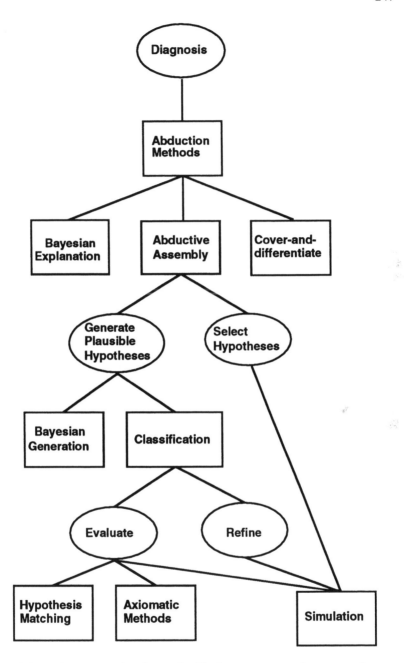

Fig. 2. Part of the task structure for diagnosis. Circles represent tasks; rectangles represent methods. See Section 3.5 for a discussion of the role of simulation.

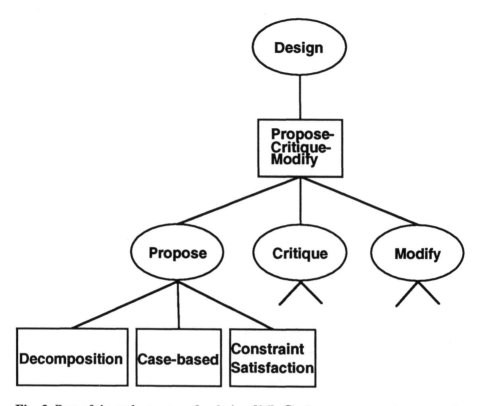

Fig. 3. Part of the task structure for design [16]. Circles represent tasks; rectangles represent methods.

Step 1. Given design goal, propose solution. If no proposal, exit with failure.
Step 2. Verify proposal. If verified, exit with success.
Step 3. If unsuccessful, critique proposal to identify sources of failure. If no useful criticism available, exit with failure.
Step 4. Modify proposal; return to 2.

There can be numerous variants on the way the methods in this class work. For example, a solution can be proposed for only a part of the design problem, a part deemed to be crucial. This solution can then be critiqued and modified. This partial solution can generate additional constraints, leading to further design commitments. Thus, subtasks can be scheduled in a fairly complex way, with subgoals from different methods alternating. One could generate all such variations and identify them all as distinct methods, but both the need for descriptive parsimony and the sheer numerousness of the methods argue against doing that.

Each of the PCM subtasks can be achieved using various methods. Three such families of methods are shown for the *Propose* task (see Figure 3): *decomposition, case-*

based and *constraint satisfaction*. In decomposition methods, domain knowledge is used to map subsets of design specifications into a set of smaller design problems. The use of design plans is a special case of the decomposition method. Case-based methods are those retrieving from memory cases with solutions to design problems similar or close to the current problem. Constraint-satisfaction methods use a variety of quantitative and qualitative optimization or constraint-satisfaction techniques.

Diagnosis. Part of the task structure for diagnosis is shown in Figure 2. The diagnosis task can be viewed as an abductive task, the construction of a best explanation (one or more disorders) to explain a set of data (manifestations). The task structure shows three typical subclasses of abductive methods: *Bayesian, abductive assembly* [44] and *parsimonious covering* [59]. Bayesian methods require knowledge of prior probabilities of disorders and conditional probabilities between disorders and manifestations. They use this knowledge to estimate posterior probabilities of disorders. Abductive assembly requires knowledge of disorders and the manifestations that they explain. This method works by first generating plausible hypotheses to explain parts of the data and then using these hypotheses to assemble a complete explanation of the data. Parsimonious covering works by stepping through each manifestation, updating the current set of parsimonious explanations as each manifestation is considered. Two subtasks for abductive assembly are shown in the diagram, generate-plausible-hypotheses and select-hypotheses. These tasks can be done using many kinds of methods. Bayesian and classification methods have typically been used to generate plausible hypotheses, so these are shown in the task structure.

Role of Simulation. The task structure for diagnosis also shows that simulation can be used to implement many subtasks. By simulation we mean structure-to-behavior simulation, i.e., determining how some device will behave under changes to its structure by simulating its behavior under those conditions.

Simulation can be used to evaluate a hypothesis because the simulation can reveal whether the hypothesis is possible given the data about the device. Causal refinements of a category can be determined by simulating to determine the possible outcomes of a set of inputs to a device. Simulation plays an important role in many task structures because it is a fairly general method for generating knowledge based on the structure of a device. We did not show the simulation method in the design task structure, but there too it can play an important role, especially for critiquing designs, by generating some of the knowledge needed for the subtask of design verification.

These task structures are based on the methods and subtasks implicit in many expert systems that perform the tasks. Neither of the task structures is meant to be complete; however, both capture a wide range of the methods useful for achieving the respective tasks. As we discover additional methods, these can be added to the structure. Some methods, such as depth-first search, are so general they can be used to solve any problem (see Section 3.7). These methods are not listed in the task structure since they would appear everywhere, cluttering the diagram.

The task structure is meant to be an analytical tool. We do not mean to imply that the implementation of a system must have a one-to-one correspondence to the task structure, but that a system that performs diagnosis or design can be viewed as using some of the methods and subtasks. In particular, the task structure does not fix the order of subtasks or dictate that a single method must be used to achieve each task. It is also not meant to correspond to a procedure-call hierarchy, although that is one way to directly implement a task structure. The task structure simply provides the vocabulary to use in describing how systems performing the task work. The systems being described might be based on neural networks, production rules, frames, or a task-specific language; this is unimportant for the use and construction of the task structure.

3.6 Direct Versus Derived Knowledge.

The knowledge in a task structure can be available in two forms: it can be directly available or it can be computed by another method. Directly available knowledge is that which is in a form that maps the input of the task to the output. For example, directly available knowledge for *refine* is of the form:

   If task is *refine h1* then refinements are *r1, r2, r3...*

For instance:

   If task is *refine* *liver disease* then refinements are *infection* and *cancer*.

No complex computation (i.e., other subtasks) is required to use this knowledge to accomplish the *refine* task; the knowledge is in a form directly applicable to the task. If knowledge is not directly available, it must be derived from existing knowledge or acquired anew from the external environment. In either case, a method must be used to acquire knowledge of the desired form. In the example in Figure 1, *refine* can be accomplished using a method that knows about different refinement dimensions, such as refinements along etiologic and subpart relations. This method can evaluate various dimensions and then select the dimension appropriate for the task instance. For example, using etiology *liver disease* could be refined to *infection* and *cancer*; using anatomic structure *liver disease* could be refined to *central area* and *portal area*. The most appropriate dimension to use depends on the task instance, i.e., the kinds of manifestations available.

   Whenever knowledge needed to carry out a method is not directly available, subtasks to acquire the knowledge can be created and set up as new problems. These subtasks are viewed like any other task: they have an initial state and a goal state and can be accomplished by the application of a method consisting of a set of operations. Hence, although a method requires certain kinds of knowledge to be applied to a task, this knowledge does not have to be known before problem solving can begin, but can be dynamically acquired or derived at runtime.

   This idea is also closely related to the distinction between "deep" and "shallow" knowledge, sometimes called "deep" and "compiled" knowledge. There is also often another distinction between model-based and rule-based reasoning, where models are supposed to be more general knowledge that describes the principles of the domain, while rules are supposed to refer to relatively *ad hoc* associations between evidence and hypotheses. In [17], we provide an analysis of these terms and develop a notion of "depth" of knowledge that is important for knowledge modeling. We give a brief description of this idea.

Let $K(T,M)$ denote the knowledge needed by method M in performing the task T. If a knowledge system performing T using M has the knowledge $K(T,M)$ directly available in its knowledge base, let us say that the knowledge system has the knowledge in a compiled form. However, suppose some knowledge element k in $K(T,M)$ is missing in the knowledge base, and the task of generating this knowledge is set up as a subtask. If there exists some other body of knowledge in the knowledge base, say K', such that by additional problem solving using K' we can generate the knowledge element k, we can say that K' is deep relative to k.

In the *refine* example above we saw that anatomic structure is one of the dimensions along which refinement could be done. In the model-based reasoning approach, structural descriptions of the device under diagnosis are used to generate refinement hypotheses. From the device model, we can generate a list of malfunctions (e.g., one malfunction category can be assigned to the failure of each of the functions of each component; moreover, malfunction categories can correspond to errors in connections between components). The same structural model can be used to generate knowledge needed for the *Evaluate* subtask in Figure 2. The structural model can be simulated for each malfunction, and information about the relation between malfunctions and observations, which is the type of knowledge needed for the methods of the *Evaluate* subtask, can be generated (See 3.5 for information on simulation). Thus the structural model is a deep model for the methods of classification and hypothesis evaluation that are used in the diagnostic task.

The approach to defining the notion of depth of knowledge in the framework of tasks, methods and knowledge generalizes previous work in the field that has equated structural models with deep models. Under our definition depth is a relative notion, i.e., it is relative to a method for a task, and there is no notion of characterizing knowledge as deep or shallow in some absolute way.

3.7 What Kinds of Methods Belong in the Task Structure?

In the task-structure framework, methods are attached to tasks, rather than identified as independent objects. A criticism is that some methods are applicable to all or many tasks and as such they need not be indexed by tasks at all. The problem here is a shifting sense of the word "task." The technical definition of "task" that we are using in the Task-Structure framework is that of class of problem instances. It is certainly true that there are very general methods such as *generate and test* that can be used for, say, diagnosis and design. This doesn't make the notion of a method exist independent of tasks. Tasks as classes of problem instances can be partially ordered in a generalization hierarchy. For example, the task of "problem solving" includes all instances of all problems, while diagnosis and design are subtypes of problem solving. Thus both *generate and test* and *classify* are in fact methods associated with tasks. *Generate and test* is associated with the most general class of tasks, while *classify* is associated with a subclass. Of course, all subtypes can inherit the methods associated with the parent. Thus diagnosis can be solved by *generate and test* as well. (The task structure doesn't usually indicate such general methods due to reasons of descriptive economy.) The particular instantiation of *generate and test* for diagnosis would be somewhat more specific, since only diagnostic hypotheses will be generated, and only task-specific tests will be used.

There is another sense in which it is often said that methods are independent of tasks. Thus one might say that *qualitative simulation* as a method is task-independent, since it can occur as part of say both diagnosis and design. But this is again based on a highly restricted use of the word "task." We saw earlier that *qualitative simulation* is a method that can be used for many subtasks in the task structures for both diagnosis and design. That is, ultimately, methods are always in the service of goals. Methods that appear to be independent of goals are in fact either methods for very general problems or for tasks that are very specific but that appear as subtasks for a number of tasks.

3.8 Task Structure and Domain Knowledge

The Task-Structure approach helps in understanding how domain knowledge comes about to be in certain forms, and in modeling this knowledge.

Methods require characteristic types of knowledge. The Task Structure view associates tasks with methods that accomplish them and the knowledge required to use the methods. The multiple levels of the task structure show how knowledge can be decomposed into bodies of knowledge that are associated with specific tasks. The task structure also highlights the generality and specificity of the knowledge needed for a problem-solving method. That is, it allows methods to be compared based on the required knowledge; hence, we can see how some methods require little domain knowledge (such as depth-first search, which only requires knowledge to recognize a goal state) while others require considerable domain knowledge (such as hierarchical classification, which needs a domain-specific hierarchy of categories).

Normative algorithms for complex problems are less useful than they seem. The Task Structure view should be contrasted with what one might call a "uniform normative algorithm" view of how to solve complex problems such as diagnosis or design. For example, there have been proposals for a general algorithm for diagnosis: "diagnosis from first principles" [63] and Bayesian networks [58] are two examples. The general algorithms, while they guarantee an optimal solution within their respective frameworks, are typically intractable. Engineering of systems to solve the tasks is done by one of two approaches. In one, additional knowledge which constrains the choices and produces tractable behavior is brought to play; however, this knowledge is just thought of as domain-specific knowledge. One way of viewing the methods in the task structure is that they identify types of such constraining knowledge for classes of problems. In the other approach, various forms of heuristic approximations of the general algorithm are used, which of course no longer have the normative properties that are associated with the original algorithm. The general algorithms also do not always make contact with the form in which knowledge is actually available in various real world domains. Thus, the Bayesian framework may be fine for a domain where the needed prior and conditional probabilities (or good approximations to them) are available, but in other domains where the domain knowledge takes other forms, there is often a need for translating from these forms to the probabilistic forms in which knowledge is needed.

The Task-Structure approach on the other hand views the solution of complex problems as arising out of the interaction of many local methods for local tasks. In any domain where there is a record of successful human problem solving, the knowledge in the domain helps to decompose the task into manageable subtasks such that each of the problems can be solved to the degree of precision and accuracy needed for the domain. It then becomes the task of the AI theorist to develop vocabularies of generic tasks, methods and knowledge. Thus the attention is shifted from the search for uniform algorithms to modeling knowledge and methods by which tasks are decomposed and subtasks are accomplished.

The fact that we do not start with a uniform normative algorithm does not mean that we cannot be precise about the behavior of systems built in the Task-Structure framework. Bylander *et al.* [7] and Goel *et al.* [30] are examples of analyses in which the role of specific types of knowledge in producing good computational properties is studied within the general framework of the task structure view. For example, Goel shows why classification is an attractive method, if knowledge in the form of classification hierarchies is available, and Bylander *et al.* show how knowledge about the existence of certain types of causal links (and non-existence of other types) makes the abductive assembly method tractable.

Domain knowledge evolves in order to match the needs for attractive methods. We can also see how such task structures evolve in real world domains. If classification is a generally effective method for the generate-hypotheses subtask of diagnosis, then over time, the problem solving community develops the knowledge needed to apply it. Thus the medical community has devoted hundreds of years to the development of disease taxonomies, which is the form in which the classification method needs knowledge. Knowledge compilation techniques (see Section 3.6) are also a means by which knowledge in a less direct form is converted into knowledge in a form that is more directly usable by a computationally attractive method. In domains and tasks of importance, domain knowledge tends to evolve over time so that methods with good computational properties can be supported.

Task-structures capture regularities in a body of knowledge. Often AI approaches are categorized as either a good way of solving a problem (ideally a way that is justified as rigorous in some way and hence offered as prescriptive) or a model of how a human agent solves it. We have already described the problems in using such prescriptive methods for building knowledge systems. If the human agent whose problem solving is modeled is a certified expert, then perhaps the model may be expected to perform well in the same task domain. Additionally, the issue of knowledge availability does not arise since the model only uses the knowledge acquired from the expert. However, cognitive modeling in this sense restricts knowledge systems to be models of individual human problem solvers.

The Task-Structure analysis represents a third way between prescriptive techniques for solving a problem and cognitive models of individual agents. The methods in the structure need not model the knowledge of any individual agent but could model the structure of the corpus of human knowledge in the domain. The collective knowledge of a community of problem solvers can transcend the errors and limitations of individual agents and be a stable, robust and convergent body of knowledge. We just discussed how domain knowledge evolves to satisfy the needs of computationally attractive methods.

Since much of this community knowledge is meant to be used by individual agents most of the time, this knowledge has certain interesting properties. Individual agents should be able to use, learn and generate it. Certainly parts of it could be in the form of specialized computational models, but in general the knowledge is qualitative and robust (i.e., insensitive to small errors in data or reasoning). Methods of this type have manageable computational complexity. Complex methods are decomposed into subtasks and methods for them.

The means-ends (or goal-subgoaling) character implicit in the task structure (i.e., the methods are the means which in turn set up subgoals) and the relatively low complexity of the methods are properties that reflect the fact that the intended users of the community knowledge are human agents. Of course, when we wish to mechanize problem solving, we don't have to be restricted to these methods, but use of these methods helps to ensure that the domain knowledge needed to execute them is likely to be available.

Task structures retain the knowledge-modeling advantages of the earlier task-specific tools. Since methods are characterized by the knowledge they require, domains can be modeled by tools appropriate for the knowledge that is available in the domain. High-level tools based on this concept, such as CSRL [10], DSPL [6], MUM [33], and MOLE [27], can be viewed as method-specific shells. Much has been written about how they facilitate knowledge modeling, knowledge acquisition, explanation and learning.

Task structures suggest how generation of new knowledge can itself be viewed as a reasoning task. During knowledge modeling appropriate questions can identify sources of deep knowledge for various methods in the task structure.

Task structures suggest how methods of different types can be combined. Quantitative and qualitative knowledge, heuristic and algorithmic knowledge can be appropriately combined for the accomplishment of a task. For example, if a subtask can be accomplished using a known technique, for instance by solving a set of differential equations, that method can be used instead of more traditional AI methods. The method that set up this subtask is concerned with the solution, not how it was arrived at, so the original task can be implemented using a different kind of method or even a different computational architecture. The only requirement is that there is an underlying architecture which can set up goal stacks, invoke methods and unwind the goal stack as methods return solutions.

Task structures have a number of architectural implications. Overdetermination and rigidity in methods are avoided by using the task structure because a complete method does not need to be specified (only the subtasks need to be given and not all of these have to be used to accomplish a task). Furthermore, multiple methods can be used to model domains that do not warrant the selection of a single method for accomplishing a task. Overdetermination and rigidity of implementation can be avoided by dynamically determining methods and subtask sequencing at runtime. We will next discuss some architectural alternatives to achieve this kind of dynamic selection of methods.

3.9 Architectures for Supporting Task Structures

So far we have presented the task structure as an analysis technique. We can, however, also ask about the architectural implications of such an analysis. An obvious possibility is to support each of the methods by a method-specific shell. In fact the earlier generation of GT's can be viewed as method-specific shells (except that the method that a GT supported was the only one for the task). If we want the system to have the flexibility to select methods at run-time, we also need, in addition to method-specific architectures, a capability to invoke methods, assess them and select one to achieve a goal. We will now discuss the TIPS architecture of Punch [62] and the Soar/GT work of Johnson and Smith [43], both of which were attempts at LAIR to achieve flexibility in problem solving behavior.

The germs of the task structure view were contained in the work that William Punch began in 1988 towards building diagnostic systems. MDX2 [67] had shown how causal models could be used to generate missing diagnostic knowledge, but which model to use had been hard-wired at design time. Punch wanted the diagnostic system to invoke different types of models selectively as run-time problem solving needs dictated. He developed the TIPS architecture as a solution to this problem. TIPS had the ability to invoke different methods for a problem-solving goal (the methods had to be appropriately indexed as being relevant to a goal), evaluate them, order them, and select the most appropriate one. (See [16] for the criteria for method selection.) The selected method may set up a subgoal for which the architecture would again invoke and select methods. Thus, during diagnosis, the system might invoke a method that used simulation of a physiological model for a local subgoal in one problem instance, while for another problem instance the heuristic match method might be chosen. TIPS used a simple *sponsor-selector* scheme for partial ordering of the appropriateness of the methods. This scheme called for the knowledge engineer to represent in advance the conditions on the state of problem solving under which a method was appropriate. Punch independently invented several features of the Soar architecture that we will discuss shortly. More recently Herman has built DSPL++ [36] as a flexible architecture for design problem solving in a framework that explicitly follows the design task structure as developed in [16]. DSPL++ supports a number of different methods for the Propose subtask of design, and is extensible, i.e., methods can be added. DSPL++'s techniques for invoking, evaluating and selecting methods were similar to those of TIPS. (Dynamic method selection has also been investigated by [2], [70], and [69].)

This brings us to the Soar phase of our work. Around 1988-89, Jack Smith had become excited by Soar as a general architecture [47]. In an earlier era, we would have reacted to it as just another general purpose architecture, but with the recent awareness of the need for an architecture that can support flexibility, we saw that Soar offered us three capabilities:

1. Unlike earlier general purpose architectures, Soar's problem-space construct was consistent with a key insight of the GT view: the close connection between the task, the method and the knowledge needed to support the method. Each problem space was in fact the agent's way of bringing the task and the knowledge together in one organized entity.

2. Universal subgoaling was a way of achieving great run-time flexibility in the invocation and choice of methods. Soar's preference scheme for ordering choices had many similarities to Punch's sponsor-selector mechanism for doing the same, but was more general.

3. Soar's chunking mechanism could explain how higher level GT's such as DSPL's could come about and be put to general use without their being initially available in that chunked form. That is, the TSA's that we have been proposing could be seen as emergent virtual architectures for classes of problems.

But we also saw that Soar had no content theory of tasks or of methods (except for a collection of weak methods). The GT's and later the methods in the task structures that we identified for diagnosis and design are a content theory of those tasks. Thus it appeared that it would be an interesting and important research direction to see how the GT idea could be worked out in the context of Soar as the underlying architecture.

This is what Todd Johnson did for his thesis [40, 42]. There are several ways of implementing GT's (or generic methods in the task structure) in the Soar framework. First, each of the methods can be implemented directly as a problem space. We can go all the way from a fully procedurally specified method (one all of whose control choices are specified ahead of time) to one whose control behavior is all determined at run-time. For example, in classification, depending upon the search-control knowledge that is made available, a hierarchical control structure can emerge, or an exhaustive search of the hypothesis space can take place.

If the methods are complex, that is, if they can be decomposed into many subtasks, then a finer-grained control behavior can be obtained if the sub-methods are treated as the units for invocation and selection. Extremely flexible interlacing of subtasks from different methods can be achieved. For example, during diagnosis a subgoal in the abductive assembly method can be followed by a subtask in the classification method. Because problem spaces permit implementing methods whose control is not specified in advance but can emerge at run time as a function of available knowledge, a full range of control can be implemented. The complex methods that characterized earlier GT implementations can be obtained as special cases in this framework. In particular, the chunking mechanism of Soar can be used to demonstrate the emergence of the somewhat more compiled virtual architectures such as DSPL.

The role of the chunking mechanism in Soar in producing GT-like architectures as a result of experience is relevant for an issue that we noted in our discussion of the early history of GT's. We said that our attitude to lower-level architectures (rules, frames, logic, etc.) was that they were just implementation alternatives without any intrinsic theoretical interest. Functionally, we argued, once we extracted the knowledge and strategies by an analysis at the task-level, the problem solver can be implemented in any of a numerous array of lower-level architectures. However, the fact that GT-level architectures can emerge from the appropriate lower-level architecture as a result of suitable learning mechanisms means that not all lower-level architectures are equivalent.

If the methods themselves can be written in the same architecture which is used for dynamically selecting methods, and if the learning mechanisms of this architecture can chunk or compile method-specific virtual architectures as a result of problem solving experience over a number of problems of a certain type, then significant unification would have been achieved. The problem-space perspective and the associated computational architecture provides a framework in which this unification is possible. The computational architecture comes with a learning mechanism of the appropriate type for chunking the GT's. This suggests that not all implementational alternatives are equally desirable. The alternatives can be evaluated with respect to how they support problem solving, learning, and dynamic invocation, all in a unified framework.

In the Soar implementation of GT's, we get the best of both the worlds: the task-level leverage of the GT perspective and the flexibility and opportunism of the Soar architecture. But the range of architectures that are useful in practice as technology for knowledge systems still occupies a large space, and there is room for a number of architectures with different degrees of flexibility. The Soar implementation of GT's occupies one niche, where the subgoals in different methods can be combined very flexibly at run time. TIPS and DSPL++ occupy another niche, where methods, with all their subgoals, can be invoked and combined at run time as units. The earlier CSRL/DSPL systems occupy yet a third niche where the designer has enough information to hard-wire what method will be used for which subtask at design time. Unifying them all is the Task-Structure view that identifies the goals, methods for them and the knowledge needed to implement the methods.

3.10 RedSoar: An Abductive System in Soar

To emphasize the importance and role of the Task Structure for describing systems, as well as to give a sense of how the Soar architecture can support the realization of task structures, let us consider three descriptions of RedSoar, an abductive system that interprets immunohematologic tests in order to identify antibodies present in a patient's blood [39]. In describing a complex knowledge system such as RedSoar, we can use three levels: 1) the Task Structure; 2) a computational level (such as problem spaces); and 3) a symbol level. Figure 4 shows each of these levels for RedSoar. RedSoar uses abductive assembly of antibody hypotheses to construct a best explanation of the test data. In the task, the test data are the manifestations; antibodies are the "disorders" or explanations. RedSoar is directly implemented in Soar's production-rule language and can be described by listing all the rules in the knowledge base, such as those in Figure 4c. About 1000 of these rules constitutes the symbol-level view of RedSoar. However, this description fails to capture the task-level control and knowledge in the system. To do this, RedSoar can be described at a computational level by listing the problem spaces defined by the Soar production rules, as in Figure 4b. That is, we can abstract away from the symbol level production rules to focus on the problem spaces, their initial and desired states and their operators. This level of description is much closer to the task level but would still contain too many details present as artifacts of the implementation (e.g., extra operators that must be used for low-level manipulation of representations). At the Task-Structure level (see Figure 4a), we can simply describe the system as using abductive assembly and then point out how it generates and selects hypotheses: i.e., the methods and knowledge that it uses. RedSoar uses conditional and *a priori* probabilities to generate plausible hypotheses and a scoring function based on explanatory coverage and plausibility ratings to select a hypothesis. As shown in the figure RedSoar also uses two additional subtasks, *Rule-out* and *Confirm* hypotheses. These are domain-specific subtasks. The first allows the system to quickly rule-out clearly absent antibodies. The second lets the system focus on antibodies that are likely present. By describing RedSoar at this level, a comparison can be made between it and other abductive assembly systems by comparing the methods and knowledge used to generate and select hypotheses.

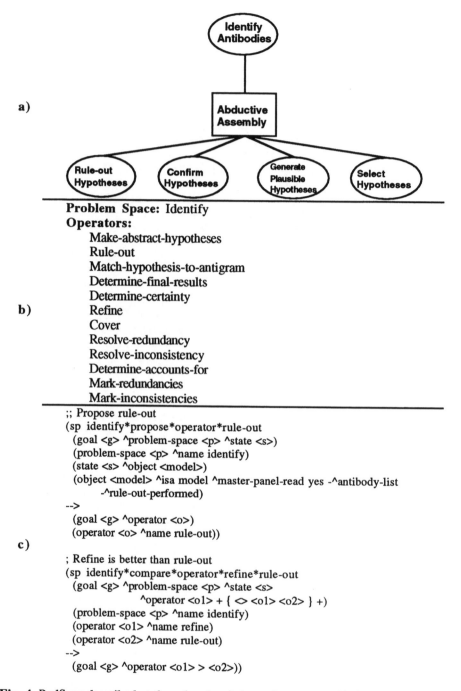

Fig. 4. RedSoar described at three levels: a) the task structure; b) the problem-space level (a computational level; and c) production rules (the symbol level).

4   Comparison to Other Work

4.1   Clancey's Model-Construction Perspective

Recently, Clancey has developed the model-construction perspective wherein systems are viewed as constructing and manipulating models of situations [25]. The knowledge in these systems is modeled using a general graph/set/operator language. By developing primitive model-construction operators, it is possible to compare systems that have very different implementations at an implementation-independent level. The model-construction perspective is related to the KADS approach in that both attempt to offer a uniform language for modeling knowledge.

In Clancey's view, knowledge systems use domain models and inference rules (contained in the knowledge base) to build a situation-specific model (SSM). Specifically, he suggests that SSM's be viewed as graphs whose nodes and links are constructed by the inference steps during problem solving. For example, consider the problem-solving graph produced by a diagnostic system whose problem solving consists of associating subsets of the symptoms with diagnostic hypotheses that explain it, and establishing the causal pathways by which the diagnoses cause the symptoms. Some of the nodes in this graph would be symptoms, some nodes would be pathophysiological states hypothesized by the problem-solving system during problem solving, and finally some nodes would correspond to diagnostic hypotheses. Many of the links would be causal links, (e.g., such and such a pathophysiological link caused such and such a symptom). Links such as "type-of" can also relate some nodes (e.g., after establishing liver disease, the problem solver might establish cirrhosis, which is a type of liver disease).

At the (successful) completion of problem solving, a subgraph of the problem-solving graph would correspond to a model of the specific case: which symptoms were caused by which pathophysiological states which in turn were caused by which disease processes which were types of which diseases, and so on. When the diagnostic job is done, not only do we have the name of a disease, but we also have an explicit record of the relation between the data and the conclusions. This subgraph is what Clancey calls the situation-specific model.

From the modeling perspective, the language in which SSM's are constructed is closely related to tasks. That is, the types of nodes and links that are constructed for a diagnostic problem are likely to be different than those for a planning problem or for a design problem. In a diagnostic task, the SSM's are couched in the language of "causes," "explained-by" and so on, while in a design task, the basic vocabulary would include terms such as "sub-function-of," "achieves-behavior" and so on. Secondly, while the terms are related to the task, the tasks would share parts of the vocabularies. To the extent that both design and diagnosis deal with devices, causal processes in them, their functions and malfunctions, many terms would occur in the SSM's of both diagnostic and design tasks. In fact, the task/method/subtask point of view that we advocate makes this clear on the following way. The task structures for design and diagnosis both have simulation as a possible subtask; and a common method for simulation is tracing of causal paths from a causal network. Thus we would expect that the problem solving activities which construct SSM's for diagnostic and design problems would, when they are engaging in the simulation subtask, be using identical terms for that portion of the SSM.

The SSM viewpoint can be sharpened by the analysis provided by the Task Structure framework. We can decompose the SSM built by a problem solver into a hierarchy of SSM's mirroring the task/method/subtask hierarchy. Thus for a diagnostic problem, the task at the highest level can be described as the construction of a problem-specific SSM of a certain type: specifically, a model in which the abnormal observations of a malfunctioning systems are linked to diagnostic hypotheses by "caused-by" or "explained-by" links, with perhaps additional causal links between hypotheses themselves. At this level we can take Clancey's proposal as a notational variant of the goal state specification in the problem space point of view. As the problem solver uses the knowledge to consider and select methods and starts executing the selected one, SSM's specific to the method chosen will be constructed. For example, if the abductive assembly method is chosen, the SSM will consist of initial hypotheses, their plausibilities, assessment of various hypothesis combinations and so on. The subtasks set up by this method will have their own characteristic SSM's, and this process will recurse, similar to the task/method/subtask recursion. The hierarchical structure of the SSM's that emerges from the Task-Structure viewpoint makes SSM's easier to comprehend and use during the problem-solving process itself. In fact, we can regard the SSM's as a well-organized working memory, which retains the structure of invocation of methods and subtasks. In this sense the hierarchical SSM's induced by the Task-Structure methodology preserve the character of an informal "proof" that Clancey attributes to SSM's, since they reflect how the agent decomposed a task and how the methods accomplish the task instance.

Let us consider the example of a problem solver engaging in the task of behavior prediction using the method of causal process simulation. There is a mapping between the following three ways of talking about the situation:

1. In the domain causal process C, the state $S1$ is causing state $S2$ because of some action $A1$.
2. The problem solver, armed with this knowledge, can transit from a problem state $P(S1)$ to $P(S2)$ by applying the operator "Action $A1$." Here $P(S1)$ stands for the problem state in which the agent's knowledge includes the information that the process C is in state $S1$.
3. The SSM has nodes $S1$ and $S2$, linked by the link "caused-by Action $A1$."

However, not all of the operators in 2 have to be "domain operators" as in 1. Some of them could be "mental" operators, such as abstraction, generalization, specialization, aggregation, and so on. In this sense, SSM's that problem solvers construct reflect both domain terms and additional abstraction terms. What is important for our perspective is that there is a close connection between the tasks, methods and the terms in the corresponding SSM's because these terms are reflected in the knowledge that is needed to implement the methods.

4.2 The KADS Approach to Knowledge Modeling

KADS [72] is a Europe-based research program for knowledge modeling which is becoming quite influential. KADS-2, the most recent version of the approach, identifies four layers:

1. *Domain layer.* In this layer the domain objects and their relations are modeled. For example, in diagnosis, presumably the device components and their connectivity relations would be included in this model. It is often stated that the domain layer in task-independent, but it is hard to imagine that one would know what entities and what relationships should be included in the domain layer without some idea of the range of tasks that we want the knowledge system to perform. Perhaps what is really meant is that the terms in the domain layer are not unique to specific high-level tasks.

2. *Inference layer.* Here the terminological differences begin to become a problem. This layer has a description of the roles played by the objects in the domain layer in the problem-solving process. For example, if "Drug d" is an object in the domain layer, and if "prescribe drug <d>" is a possible action that the problem solver can consider, this layer will make this connection explicit. They have tried to identify generic classes of such problem-solving roles such as "Available-Observation" and "Available-action" ("prescribe drug <d>" is an example of the latter), and a generic taxonomy of what might be called "elementary" goals in our terminology, e.g., "select," "classify," "compare," etc. (They call these a taxonomy of "knowledge sources," but that term has a different meaning for most researchers in this area. We think it is best to view these as types of primitive goals or primitive operators. See our earlier discussion in Section 3.2 on the duality of a goal or subtask also being an operator.) While the set of terms that they have developed is a useful one, there is no theoretical study of the orthogonality of the terms or their completeness.

3. *Task layer.* To the first degree of approximation, the task layer is really what we have called a method, namely, a series of operators that together help achieve the goal. They additionally specify that each of the operators should be one of the types that we identified as elementary goals in 2 above. There are two reasons why we would be concerned about such a requirement: One is that we would like the operators to be abstract enough that additional problem solving might be used by selecting methods. There is no reason to impose the requirement that the method's sequence of operators at the elementary level be fixed in advance. Second, given our concerns about whether the terms that they propose are orthogonal, primitive or complete, we think the development of such terms should be an on-going empirical enterprise. This is where the task-specificness of our enterprise becomes important, since we think the specification of the goal class gives us leverage in analyzing the methods and developing primitives for them. Perhaps eventually we might converge on a set of terms, but we need to have a clear idea of the role played by the terms in the performance of classes of tasks.

4. *Strategy layer.* This layer exists as a partial answer to one of the concerns that we raised in our discussion of 3 above, namely the lack of flexibility implicit in the fixed set of primitive operators. In the strategy layer, the aim is to represent meta-plans so that different combinations of operators may be generated.

From the knowledge modeling perspective, the only layer where they have made specific commitments for a vocabulary is, as we discussed above, in their proposal for a typology of primitive goal types. As we said, our preference is for these terms to emerge empirically from studies of classes of tasks.

4.3 The Componential Framework

In Steels' componential framework [66] systems are described from three perspectives: 1) the model perspective; 2) the task perspective; and 3) the method perspective. This framework is in many ways similar to the task structure framework that we have described. The model perspective corresponds to the knowledge states of problem spaces in our framework. In both frameworks tasks are decomposed via methods into subtasks to form a task structure. Likewise, both frameworks recognize that the level of the task decomposition (that is, when a particular task should be decomposed into subtasks) varies depending on the purpose of the analysis. There are, however, several differences between the two frameworks. First, Steels' task structure only includes the tasks and subtasks; ours mixes tasks, subtasks and methods. Thus our task structure makes explicit the use of methods including multiple methods for a task. Second, the componential framework makes no commitment to a technique for describing methods, whereas we have selected the problem-space paradigm because of its generality and flexibility.

4.4 Role-limiting Methods[2]

Role-limiting methods [49] identify particular paths through the task structure. A role-limiting method is described to the lowest level, i.e., all tasks, methods and subtasks are specified until the lowest subtasks can be directly implemented. The specification also includes the order in which the subtasks are accomplished. This differs from other approaches in which a system can be described at high levels of abstraction with lower level details remaining to be specified either later in the design process or dynamically at runtime. The implication of this is that a small variation of a particular role-limiting method must be viewed as a different role-limiting method.

For example, *Cover-and-differentiate* [49] is a role-limiting method for a form of abduction. McDermott defines the method as follows [49]:

1. Determine the events that potentially explain (that is, cover) the symptoms.
2. If there is more than one candidate explanation for any event, identify information that will differentiate the candidates by
   — ruling out one or more of the explanatory connections,
   — ruling out one or more of the candidate explanatory events,
   — providing sufficient support for one of the candidate explanatory events,
   — providing a reason for preferring some of the explanatory connections over others.
3. Get this information (in any order) and apply it (in any order).
4. If step 3 uncovers new symptoms, go to step 1.

Two classes of task knowledge are needed to use the *Cover-and-differentiate* method:

1. Knowledge mapping manifestations to disorders (for Step 1 of the method, generating explanations for a finding).

---

[2]This is a modified version of the anlysis appearing in [40].

2. Knowledge mapping an explanation to information that can help confirm or disconfirm the explanation (for Step 2 of the method, differentiating between competing explanations).

These two classes indicate the role that domain-dependent knowledge plays in the method.

On one hand, a role-limiting method is a domain-independent abstract method. Thus *Cover-and-differentiate*, as a method, is specified independent of whether it is going to be used for liver diagnosis or automobile diagnosis. On the other hand, the search-control knowledge that describes the behavior of the method, and hence the method's control behavior, is completely specified as part of the method specification. The knowledge engineer who is using the method for his domain has no freedom to change the control behavior to suit his domain. The philosophy is that precisely this form of pre-specification of the control strategy is needed to be able to guide the knowledge engineer on the kinds of knowledge needed to use the method. Of course, if the knowledge engineer can't even specify parts of the control strategy at system-building time, certainly, the approach does not enable the control strategy to emerge at run-time as a result of interactions between any partially specified search-control knowledge and the particulars of the problem instance. Note that the Task-Structure approach allows a full range of options in the specification of control behavior: all control knowledge does not have to be prespecified, and if some aspects of control are specific to some domains, that is fine as well. Nevertheless, the Task-Structure approach provides the same advantage as the role-limited method approach with respect to identify the role knowledge plays in a method. We will demonstrate this by showing that:

1. The role of domain-dependent knowledge is still limited even though search-control knowledge is not specified as part of a method, and
2. Domain-dependent search-control knowledge can also be role-limited.

To illustrate each of these points consider the method described for abductive assembly. This method supplies very little search-control knowledge, but since the input and output of each subtask in the method are known, the knowledge required to use the method can be specified. For example, to implement *generate-plausible-hypotheses* the system must have domain-dependent knowledge mapping a manifestation to a disorder. One direct encoding of this knowledge is a rule that maps from a particular manifestation to hypotheses that explain it. Even if this knowledge is indirectly represented using a method that implements *generate-plausible-hypotheses*, the role the knowledge plays in the abductive method remains the same. Furthermore, by specifying the task structure for the method that implements *generate-plausible-hypotheses* the role of each piece of knowledge used to generate explanations can be understood. Thus, if the subtask's input and output are known, the role and basic form of the knowledge needed to implement the subtask can be identified.

As for the second point, domain-dependent search-control knowledge is limited to the role of differentiating between competing subtasks. The form of the knowledge is a mapping from one or more subtasks to preference information for those subtasks. This knowledge can be divided into three classes:

1. Knowledge that prefers or rejects a single subtask without respect to other applicable subtasks.
2. Knowledge that prefers one or more subtasks over one or more other subtasks.
3. Knowledge that indicates that two or more subtasks are equivalent.

This might seem an overgeneral specification of the knowledge; however, it is no more general than the role of knowledge for differentiating between explanations in *Cover-and-differentiate*. Thus search-control knowledge can be given the same role-limiting status as the knowledge for differentiating explanations.

5 Shifts in Perspective and New Research Directions

The Task-Structure perspective retains many of the advantages of the GT view, but in crucial places, it reflects changes in philosophy. In this section we discuss some of these shifts in perspective.

The major shift in the point of view is about the status of the TSA's associated with the GT's. The notion of a fixed method for a task is abandoned. Furthermore, the fact that there is no finite set of distinct methods for a task implies that there is no finite set of hard-edged conceptual building blocks. But GT-based TSA's still represent a good idea technologically for a range of situations served well by the method incorporated in the TSA's.

In an earlier section, we enumerated a number of questions about GT's that motivated our reexamination: How many GT's are there? What kinds of tasks count as GT's? What are the criteria? In the current perspective, the answers is that there is no finite number of tasks or methods. They exist in some partial ordering of generality and domain-specificity, and any collection of problem instances that have some problem features in common and that is for some reason worth considering as a group is a generic task. Thus, abduction, diagnosis and medical and engineering diagnosis are all Generic Tasks. Abduction is more general than diagnosis (i.e., covers a much larger number of problem instances), and diagnosis is more general than either medical or engineering diagnosis.

The Task-Structure approach retains many of the traditional advantages of the GT perspective. The task-method-subtask characterization still conforms to the injunction not to separate knowledge from its use. The method organizes how knowledge is to be used to achieve the task. To the extent the methods are generic, useful characterizations can be made of the knowledge and strategic requirement of the methods, just as in the case of the traditional GT's. Leverage for knowledge acquisition and explanation that GT's provided is retained. In fact, because the task structure separates the task from the method, how the method helps achieve the task can be explicitly included in the explanation capability, as is done in Tanner [68]. The generic methods that are identified will play the role that generic mechanisms play in mechanical engineering: organized collections of inferences for generic types of goals. Just like generic mechanisms are not building blocks in a basic theoretical sense (that is, there is no way to argue that in principle all mechanical devices can be decomposed into a set of generic mechanisms), they still play extremely useful roles as technological building blocks. Generic methods—and method specific architectures (MSA's) indexed by tasks that they are good for—will continue to play this role in knowledge-based systems as well.

The analogy of the GT primitives to Schank's conceptual dependency primitives [64] is interesting. Schank proposed about 15 primitives in terms of which all the action verbs in natural languages can be expressed. Wilks [73] also proposed a similar idea, but the number of primitives in his scheme was in the order of hundreds. In practice, however, few natural language systems use the particular set of primitives from either system as canonical objects. There is quite a range of variation in the primitives that do get used. But what has survived is the important idea that it is useful to group verbs in such a way that inferences common to a set of verbs be shared by abstract verbs that stand for their common action quality. Similarly, in the GT view, in spite of the twists and turns about what the primitives are and at what level of genericness should they be represented, what is of long-term importance is the idea that tasks and methods provide the organizing principle for knowledge-based problem solving.

Some might argue that in moving away from a set of primitive "generic" tasks and associated preferred methods we have weakened the enterprise, i.e., that the Task-Structure approach provides fewer guidelines to researchers and system designers. To the contrary the Task-Structure approach builds upon and strengthens the GT enterprise by clearly separating analysis from implementation and by providing a framework for encompassing a multitude of task-method combinations. The task structure concept just provides the organizing principles for analyzing and describing systems, i.e., that there are tasks, methods and subtasks. In this role it is purposefully designed to be extremely general, even content-free. The content is provided by identifying and fleshing out useful task structures for important tasks, such as those we described earlier for design and diagnosis. It is these "instantiated" task structures that provide strong guidance to researchers, system designers and system users.

5.1 Research Directions

Many researchers have been associated with the GT view over time. The research directions that are currently being pursued by them cover a wide spectrum. The research issues can be broadly categorized as architectural and content issues.

Architectural Issues. The dimension in which architectural approaches differ is that of generality and flexibility. As a practical matter, there is a need for different combinations of generality and task-specificness for system-building technologies. There are many technological niches and different researchers are pursuing different ones. At one end of the spectrum, Sticklen continues to experiment with TSA's at the level of granularity of the original GT's. Punch continues to experiment with architectures that treat methods as the units to invoke. Herman [36] has similarly proposed an architecture for design which can invoke, assess and select methods for various subtasks of the design task as described in [16]. At the other end of the spectrum, Johnson and Smith are continuing their investigation into using Soar and problem spaces as the architectural medium to realize task-specific problem solvers. In this approach, TSA's (or MSA's) are constructed in the uniform framework of problem spaces. Whenever a subtask needs a new method that is not supported by an MSA, the problem-space framework is available to code up the new method.

Knowledge and Method Sharing. There are several aspects to the research on the content issues related to task structures. In one, a number of researchers are using the Task-Structure viewpoint to abstractly analyze complex tasks. We have already discussed task analyses of design and diagnosis. Goel and Chandrasekaran [31] provide a task structure for case-based design. Narayanan and Chandrasekaran [55] provide such an analysis for visual reasoning in the task of prediction of behavior of physical objects.

This type of analysis directly leads to a potentially revolutionary technological possibility: method- and knowledge-sharing. Each TSA embodies a class of strategies to solve a type of problem in addition to providing primitives in which to encode needed knowledge . In this sense each TSA is a means to share the corresponding problem-solving method. The task structure makes explicit that it is the methods that are being abstracted and made available for sharing. As research on various diagnosis and design problems is pursued around the world by numerous researchers, task structures which abstract methods and subtasks from the individual efforts and solutions can be constructed, knowledge and strategies for them identified, knowledge representation and acquisition tools for them constructed, and their computational properties analyzed. Task structures and methods in them may begin to play the role in knowledge engineering that identification and analysis of generic mechanisms played and continues to play in other engineering disciplines.

Explanation and Learning. There are a number of issues related to learning that intersect with the task structure perspective. Earlier we said that it was conceptually and practically important to have architectures which unified problem solving and learning, and pointed out that earlier GT-like architectures can be viewed as learned virtual architectures for classes of problems. Goel's work on Router [29], a system that finds routes between locations, is an instance of research in this perspective. It starts with a method that is model-based, but gradually its reasoning shifts from model-based to case-based.

There is another aspect to learning that relates, not to the learning mechanisms that architectures have, but to the content issues in learning. In [15], Chandrasekaran outlined a research agenda for explanation-based learning (EBL) in the Task-Structure framework. EBL, broadly construed, is a method of learning by constructing an explanation of why some solution was correct or incorrect, and using the explanation to refine the representation of the concept that is being learned. Weintraub [71] uses this idea to build a corrective learning component to his gait diagnosis system. When its answer to a problem is incorrect, the system attempts to identify which part of the knowledge it used and which task in the task structure may be at fault and also attempts to change it. The approach uses the fact that the task-specific view gives advantages by providing appropriate vocabularies in which explanation can be couched (Chandrasekaran, 1989). We identify three types of explanation relating to knowledge-based systems. These are: (1) trace of run-time, data-dependent problem-solving behavior, i.e., explaining the data in the current situation was used to arrive at a decision; (2) relating specific decisions to the control strategy used by the system; and (3) justifying particular pieces of knowledge by relating them to more general domain knowledge. When an error is made, Type 1 and Type 2 explanations can be constructed for the incorrect answer. These explanations together can be used to identify possible knowledge elements that could have been responsible for the error, and methods in the task structure that the knowledge elements are associated with. In this way the explanation capability associated with the task-specific view helps solve some aspects of the *credit assignment problem* for learning. Combining this ability to narrow down the error candidates with simulation of the underlying qualitative model of the gaits, Weintraub was able to both locate the source of the error and correct it. The potential of the task structure for helping solve the credit-assignment is significant.

Content Theory of Tasks, Inferences and Methods. Another important content issue is somewhat more foundational for the entire family of approaches at the task level. There is a central theoretical issue that dogs all of this type of work: GT's, task-structures, KADS, Clancey's SSM's (situation-specific models) and so on. That issue can be formulated as a series of questions about the content theory of tasks (or inferences): What are the task-level terms? In what sense are they primitives? How do they relate to one another? Is there any sense in which we can determine and agree on a set of terms that are not idiosyncratic to each research paradigm, but in fact represent some universally sharable set of analytic primitives?

Let us take some examples. KADS proposes a list of inferences as primitives in terms of which they wish to analyze the problem solving behavior of experts. That is, all information processing verbs in a natural language description of the behavior of the expert will be mapped into equivalence classes represented by these inference primitives. Similarly, while the GT view does not propose an exhaustive list of terms as KADS does, still for problems of diagnosis and design, a person trained in the GT view would be armed with terms like "classify," "assess hypothesis," "instantiate plan," and would decompose the behavior into modules like the above.

Earlier we discussed Clancey's proposal that what problem solvers do is to construct situation-specific models (SSM's) of some system in the world. He proposes that all SSM's can be expressed in terms of sets, memberships and relations. The set-relation view of the SSM is no doubt a good starting point, but it doesn't completely specify the content theory of inference operators for the task. We need to know what kinds of objects and relational operators are going to be in the vocabulary for the SSM for a given task. The set-theoretic view, or the point that what is being constructed is an SSM, does not by itself specify that in diagnosis the kinds of sets we are interested in are malfunctions, symptoms, and the kinds of relations are explanatory causal relations; or that in design, the objects of interests are components and devices, the relationships of interest are functional and physical connections. Further, we pointed out earlier the need for inferential operators (in addition to operators that stand for relations between domain objects) that arise from the strategies used in the methods. These operators are not part of the vocabulary of SSM's for the design task.

Thus whether we are following the GT/TS, KADS or SSM framework, we need a principled theory of inference operators, and how they connect to world models that we construct and the tasks that we perform. The hope that there may be small number of such operators which are in some sense primitives is present in several frameworks. But the proposals on the table for such primitives are either not complete, or not rich enough, or if nominally complete, not sufficiently well-motivated to explain why those terms and not others, or even the sense in which they are primitives at all.

Aristotle, and Kant following him, proposed rather similar content theories of fundamental categories of thought and experience: quality, quantity, order, space, causation, etc. It appears to us that when we think about the world, when we solve problems, we are trying to build models which are ultimately couched in these basic categories. Taking seriously the notion of problem solving as model building, we can say that our inference operators arise ultimately from the primitives anchored on the Kantian categories of thought and experience. Theories of generic tasks and methods will eventually have to be grounded in such a categorical content theory of our thought. Until such a thoroughgoing content theory is available, we will have to be content with pragmatic criteria as the basis for selecting from among alternative proposals for knowledge primitives.

6 Concluding Remarks

Among the many ideas that we have covered in this paper, the most important one is the emphasis on content issues in knowledge for problem solving. Clearly some of the content of knowledge is so specific to the individual or a domain that it cannot be of much interest for the theory or technology of artificial intelligence. The content issues that we have emphasized are the regularities in knowledge use that cut across individual instances of the problems, and become applicable to classes of problems. Task-level analyses are ways in which we exploit these regularities. How much of these content characterizations are part of the definition of intelligence, and how much are just analyses of knowledge that the agent has acquired, is a philosophical issue that has to do with one's prejudices about how much of intelligence has to do with form and how much with content. But from the viewpoint of creating knowledge technologies, the scientific issue is elucidation of these regularities in knowledge and its use. The original notion of Generic Tasks helped nudge the field into a consideration of content issues a decade or so ago. The notion of Task Structures, in our view, provides an analysis tool for a more sophisticated marriage of form and content in knowledge systems.

7 Acknowledgment

The work on generic tasks and task-specific architectures has been done jointly over the years with a number of colleagues to whom we offer heartfelt thanks. This paper has benefited from comments by Jack W. Smith, Tom Bylander, Susan and John Josephson, Ashok Goel, Dean Allemang, Jon Sticklen, Bill Punch and Jean-Marc David. Chandrasekaran's work on GT's has been supported over the years by AFOSR and DARPA. The preparation of this paper in particular was supported by DARPA under AFOSR contract F-49620-89-C-0110. Todd Johnson's work on this paper was supported by National Heart Lung and Blood Institute grant HL-38776, and National Library of Medicine grant LM-04298.

References

1. Allemang, D., Rothenfluh, T.E.: Acquiring knowledge of knowledge acquistion: a self-study of generic tasks. Current Developments in Knowledge Acquisition, Proc. of the Sixth European Knowledge Acquisition Workshop—EKAW 92, (ed. Wetter, T., Acthoff, K.D., Gaines, B.R., Linster, M. & Schmalhofer, F.), 353-372, Springer-Verlag, Berlin, 1992

2. Benjamins, R.V., Abu-Hanna, A., Jansweijer, W.N.H.: Dynamic method selection in diagnostic reasoning. 12th Avignon International Congress on Artificial Intelligence, 155-164, 1992

3. Breuker, J., Wielinga, B.: Models of expertise in knowledge acquisition. Topics in Expert System Design, (ed. Guida, G. & Tasso, C.), 265-295, Elsevier Science Publishers B. V., North-Holland, 1989

4. Brown, D.C.: Expert Systems for Design Problem-Solving Using Design Refinement with Plan Selection and Redesign. Ph.D. Thesis, Dept. of Computer and Information Science, The Ohio State University, Columbus, Oh, 1984

5. Brown, D.C., Chandrasekaran, B.: Expert Systems for a Class of Mechanical Design Activity. Knowledge Engineering in Computer-Aided Design, (ed. Gero, J.S.), 259-282, North-Holland, New York, 1985

6. Brown, D.C., Chandrasekaran, B.: Design Problem Solving: Knowledge Structures and Control Strategies. Morgan Kaufmann Publishers, San Mateo, California, 1989

7. Bylander, T., Allemang, D., Tanner, M.C., Josephson, J.R.: The computational complexity of abduction. Artificial Intelligence, 49(1991):25-60, 1991

8. Bylander, T., Chandrasekaran, B.: Generic Tasks for knowledge-based reasoning: The "right" level of abstraction for knowledge acquisition. Int. J. Man-Machine Studies, 26:231-243, 1987

9. Bylander, T., Johnson, T.R., Goel, A.: Structured matching: A task-specific technique for making decisions. Knowledge Acquisition, 3(1):1-20, 1991

10. Bylander, T., Mittal, S.: CSRL: A language for classificatory problem solving. AI Magazine, VII(3):66-77, 1986

11. Chandrasekaran, B.: Towards a Taxonomy of Problem Solving Types. AI Magazine, 4(1):9-17, 1983

12. Chandrasekaran, B.: Generic tasks in expert system design and their role in explanation of problem solving. Proceedings of the National Academy of Sciences/Office of Naval Research Workshop on AI and Distributed Problem Solving, National Academy of Sciences, Washington, D.C., 1985

13. Chandrasekaran, B.: Generic tasks in knowledge-based reasoning: High-level building blocks for expert system design. IEEE Expert, 1(3):23-30, 1986

14. Chandrasekaran, B.: Towards a Functional Architecture for Intelligence Based on Generic Information Processing Tasks. Proceedings of the Tenth International Joint Conference on Artificial Intelligence, (ed. McDermott, J.), 1183-1192, Morgan Kaufmann Publishers, Inc., Los Altos, California, 1987

15. Chandrasekaran, B.: Task-structures, knowledge acquisition, and learning. Machine Learning, 4:93-99, 1989

16. Chandrasekaran, B.: Design Problem Solving: A Task Analysis. AI Magazine, 11(4):59-71, 1990

17. Chandrasekaran, B.: Models versus rules, deep versus compiled, content versus form: some distinctions in knowledge systems research. IEEE Expert, April:75-79, 1991

18. Chandrasekaran, B., Mittal, S.: Conceptual representation of medical knowledge for diagnosis by computer: MDX and related systems. Advances in Computers, (ed. Yovits, M.), 217-293, Academic Press, 1983

19. Chandrasekaran, B., Mittal, S., Gomez, F., Smith, J.W.: An approach to medical diagnosis based on conceptual structures. Proceedings of the Sixth International Joint Conference on Artificial Intelligence, 134-142, IJCAI, Tokyo, Japan, 1979

20. Chandrasekaran, B., Mittal, S., Smith, J.W.: RADEX—Toward a Computer-Based Radiology Consultant. Pattern Recognition in Practice, (ed. Kanal & Gelsema), 463-474, North Holland Publishing Co., 1980

21. Chandrasekaran, B., Mittal, S., Smith, J.W.: Reasoning with uncertain knowledge: The MDX approach. Proceedings of the 1982 Congress of the American Medical Informatics Association, (ed. Lindberg, D.A.B.), 335-339, Masson Publishing, U.S.A, 1982

22. Chandrasekaran, B., Tanner, M., Josephson, J.: Explaining Control Strategies in Problem Solving. IEEE Expert, 4(1): pp. 9-24., 1989

23. Clancey, W.J.: Heuristic classification. Artificial Intelligence, 27(3):289-350, 1985

24. Clancey, W.J.: From GUIDON to NEOMYCIN and HERACLES in twenty short lessons: ORN final report 1979-1985. AI Magazine, 7(3):40-60, 1986

25. David, J.-M.: Functional architectures and the Generic Task approach. Knowledge Engineering Review, 3(3):212-215, 1988

26. David, J.M., Krivine, J.P.: Diva: An expert system for vibration-based monitoring of large rotating machinery. Technical Report, Laboratoires de Marcoussis, France, 1988

27. Eshelman, L.: MOLE: A knowledge-acquisition tool for cover-and-differentiate systems. Automating Knowledge Acquisition for Expert Systems, (ed. Marcus, S.), 37-80, Kluwer Academic Publishers, 1988

28. Goel, A., Bylander, T.: Computational Feasibility of Structured Matching. IEEE Transactions on Pattern Analysis and Machine Intelligence, 11(12):1312-1316., 1989

29. Goel, A., Callantine, T.: An Experience-Based Approach to Navigational Path Planning. Proceedings of the IEEE/Robotics Society of Japan International Conference on Robotics and Systems, 705-710, IEEE Press, 1992

30. Goel, A., Soundararajan, N., Chandrasekaran, B.: Complexity in Classificatory Reasoning. Proc. Sixth National Conference on Artificial Intelligence, 421-425, Morgan Kaufmann Publishers, Inc., Los Altos, California, 1987

31. Goel, A.K., Chandrasekaran, B.: Case-based design: a task analysis. Artificial Intelligence in Engineering, (ed. Tong, C. & Sriram, D.), 165-183, Academic Press, NY, 1992

32. Gomez, F., Chandrasekaran, B.: Knowledge organization and distribution for medical diagnosis. IEEE Trans. Systems, Man and Cybernetics, 11(1):34-42, 1981

33. Gruber, T., Cohen, P.: Design for acquisition: Principles of knowledge system design to facilitate knowledge acquistion. International Journal of Man-Machine Studies, 26(2):143-159, 1987

34. Hadzikadic, M., Yun, D.: Characterization of application domains for the expert system technology. AAAI Workshop of High Level Tools for Knowledge-Based Systems, Laboratory for AI Research, The Ohio State University, Columbus, 1986

35. Harvey, A.M.: Differential Diagnosis, The Interpretation of Clinical Evidence. W. B. Saunders, 1972

36. Herman, D.J.: An Extensible, Task-Specific Shell for Routine Design Problem Solving. Ph.D. Thesis, Department of Computer and Information Science, The Ohio State University, Columbus, Oh, 1992

37. Iwasaki, Y., Keller, R., Feigenbaum, E.: Generic tasks or wide-ranging knowledge bases? The Knowledge Engineering Review, 3(3):215-216, 1988

38. Johnson, K., Sticklen, J., Smith, J.W.: IDABLE—Application of an intelligent data base to medical systems. Working Notes of the 1988 AAAI Spring Symposium on Artificial Intelligence in Medicine, 43-44, AAAI, Stanford, Ca., 1988

39. Johnson, K.A., Johnson, T.R., Smith, J.W., Jr., DeJongh, M., Fischer, O., Amra, N.K., Bayazitoglu, A.: RedSoar—A system for red blood cell antibody identification. Proceedings of the Fifteenth Annual Symposium on Computer Applications in Medical Care, 664-668, McGraw Hill, Washington D.C., 1991

40. Johnson, T.R.: Generic Tasks in the Problem-Space Paradigm: Building Flexible Knowledge Systems While Using Task-Level Constraints. Ph.D. Thesis, Dept. of Computer and Information Science, The Ohio State University, Columbus, Oh, 1991

41. Johnson, T.R., Smith, J.W., Bylander, T.: HYPER—Hypothesis matching using compiled knowledge. Proceedings of the AAMSI Congress 1989, (ed. Hammond, W.E.), 126-130, American Association for Medical Systems and Informatics, San Francisco, California, 1989

42. Johnson, T.R., Smith, J.W., Chandrasekaran, B.: Generic tasks and Soar. Working Notes of the AAAI-89 Spring Symposium on Knowledge System Development Tools and Languages, 25-28, AAAI, Stanford University, 1989

43. Johnson, T.R., Smith, J.W., Chandrasekaran, B.: Task-specific architectures for flexible systems. The Soar Papers: Research on Integrated Intelligence, (ed. Rosenbloom, P.S., Laird, J.E. & Newell, A.), The MIT Press, In press

44. Josephson, J., Chandrasekaran, B., Smith, J., Tanner, M.: A mechanism for forming composite explanatory hypotheses. IEEE Transactions on Systems, Man, and Cybernetics, 17(3):445-454, 1987

45. Josephson, J., Josephson, S.: Abduction: Computation, Philosophy, Technology. Cambridge University Press, In Press

46. Josephson, J., Smetters, D., Fox, R., Oblinger, D., Welch, A., Northrup, G.: Integrated Generic Task Toolset—Fafner Release 1.0: Introduction and User's Guide. Technical Report, Laboratory for AI Research, The Ohio State University, Columbus, Oh, 1989

47. Laird, J.E., Newell, A., Rosenbloom, P.S.: SOAR: An architecture for general intelligence. Artificial Intelligence, 33:1-64, 1987

48. Marcus, S.: Salt: A knowledge acquisition tool for propose-and-revise systems. Automating Knowledge Acquisition for Expert Systems, (ed. Marcus, S.), 81-123, Kluwer Academic Publishers, Boston, 1988

49. McDermott, J.: Preliminary steps toward a taxonomy of problem-solving methods. Automating Knowledge Acquisition for Expert Systems, (ed. Marcus, S.), 225-256, Kluwer Academic Publishers, 1988

50. Miller, R.A., Pople, H.E., Jr., Myers, J.D.: Internist I, An Experimental Computer-Based Diagnostic Consultant for General Internal Medicine. The New England Journal of Medicine, 307:468-476, 1982

51. Minsky, M.: The Society of the Mind. Simon and Schuster, 1985

52. Mittal, S.: Event-Based Organization of Temporal Data Bases. Proceedings of the Fourth Biennal Conference of the Canadian Society for Computational Studies of Intelligence, 164-171, CSCSI, Toronto, Ontario, 1982

53. Mittal, S., Chandrasekaran, B.: Patrec: A knowledge-directed database for a diagnostic expert system. IEEE Computer, 17(9):51-58, 1984

54. Musen, M.A.: Generation of Model-Based Knowledge-Acquisition Tools for Clinical-Trial Advice Systems. PhD Thesis, Stanford, 1988
55. Narayanan, N.H., Chandrasekaran, B.: Reasoning visually about spatial interactions. Proc. 12th IJCAI, 360-365, Morgan Kaufman, Mountain View, CA, 1991
56. Newell, A.: The Knowledge Level. AI Magazine, (Summer):1-19, 1981
57. Patil, R.S.: Causal Representation of Patient Illness for Electrolyte and Acid-base Diagnosis. Ph.D. Thesis, Massachusetts Institute of Technology, 1981
58. Pearl, J.: Probabilistic Reasoning in Intelligent Systems: Networks of Plausible Inference. Morgan Kaufman, 1988
59. Peng, Y., Reggia, J.A.: Abductive Inference Models for Diagnostic Problem-Solving. Springer-Verlag, New York, 1990
60. Pople, H.: On the mechanization of abductive logic. Proc. of the International Joint Conference on Artificial Intelligence, 147-152, IJCAI, 1973
61. Punch III, W.F., Tanner, M.C., Josephson, J.R., Smith, J.W.: Peirce: A tool for experimenting with abduction. IEEE Expert, 5(5):34-44, 1990
62. Punch, W.F.: A Diagnosis System Using a Task Integrated Problem Solver Architecture (TIPS), Including Causal Reasoning. Ph.D. Thesis, Department of Computer and Information Science, The Ohio State University, Columbus, Oh, 1989
63. Reiter, R.A.: A theory of diagnosis from first principles. Artificial Intelligence, 32:57-95, 1987
64. Schank, R.C.: Conceptual dependency: a theory of natural language understanding. Cognitive Psychology, 3:552-631, 1972
65. Sembugamoorthy, V., Chandrasekaran, B.: A Representation for the Functioning of Devices that Supports Compilation of Expert Problem Solving Structures. Experience, Memory and Reasoning, (ed. Kolodner, J.L. & Riesbeck, C.K.), 47-73, Lawrence Erlbaum Associates, Hillsdale, NJ, 1986
66. Steels, L.: Components of expertise. AI Magazine, 11(2):28-49, 1990
67. Sticklen, J.: MDX2 An Integrated Medical Diagnostic System. Ph.D. Dissertation, The Ohio State University, 1987
68. Tanner, M.C.: Explaining Knowledge Systems: Justifying Diagnostic Conclusions. Ph.D. Thesis, Dept. of Computer and Information Science, The Ohio State University, Columbus, Oh, 1989
69. Van Marcke, K.: A generic tutoring environment. Proc. ECAI-90, (ed. Aiello, L.), 655-660, Pitman, London, 1990
70. Vanwelkenhuysen, J., Rademakers, P.: Mapping knowledge-level analysis onto a computational framework. Proc. ECAI-90, (ed. Aiello, L.), 681-686, Pitman, London, 1990
71. Weintraub, M.A.: An Explanation-Based Approach to Assigning Credit. Ph.D. Thesis, Dept. of Computer and Information Science, The Ohio State University, Columbus, Oh, 1991
72. Wielinga, B.J., Schreiber, A.T., Breuker, J.A.: KADS: A modelling approach to knowledge engineering. Knowledge Acquisition, 4:5-53, 1992
73. Wilks, Y.A.: A preferential pattern-seeking semantics for natural language inference. Artificial Intelligence, 6:53-74, 1975
74. Wittgenstein, L.: Proposition 560, Philosophical Investigations. McMillan, New York, 1953

The componential framework and its role in reusability

Luc Steels

Artificial Intelligence Laboratory,
Vrije Universiteit Brussel,
Pleinlaan 2, B-1050 Brussels, Belgium,
E-mail: `steels@arti.vub.ac.be`

Abstract. The paper describes a framework for constructing knowledge level models. The framework assumes that descriptions can be constructed from three perspectives: models, methods, and tasks. A workbench is introduced that supports the interactive specification of knowledge level models. The role of the symbol level is described. The problem of reuse is briefly discussed within this context.

1 Introduction

The term second generation expert systems (Steels, 1985,1987) was originally introduced to emphasise that the rules inside an expert system can be usefully decomposed into three components: tasks and subtasks, domain models which describe in a declarative way the underlying knowledge for a task and methods which describe how the knowledge is to be applied in particular circumstances. Steels (1990) contains for example an analysis of the following Dipmeter Advisor rule (taken from Smith (1984)):

```
Distributary fan rule

IF:
    1) Delta-dominated marine zone
    2) Continental-shelf marine zone
    3) Sand zone intersecting marine zone
    4) Blue pattern in intersection
THEN:
    Distributary fan  with
        Top of fan equal to top of blue pattern
        Bottom of fan equal to
                bottom of blue pattern
        Direction of flow equal to
                azimuth of blue pattern.
```

The analysis decomposes the knowledge underlying the rule into three subtasks: restrict the geological context (to delta-dominated, continental-shelf marine zone), identify the depositional structure (distributary fan), and deduce the implications (namely top and bottom as well as direction of flow in the fan). Each of these subtasks assumes a particular domain model and a method. For example, the first subtask assumes a hierarchy of geological contexts like the one in figure 1 and a top-down refinement method: Start from the most general context and refine it to a more specific one. The second subtask assumes a mapping model which maps geological features (like presence of sand or presence of a pattern on the dipmeter). The idea of second generation expert systems is

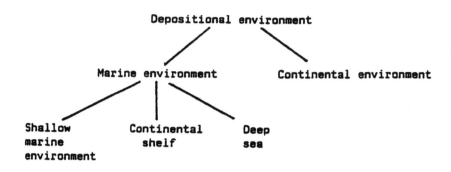

Figure 1. The Dipmeter Advisor rule assumes a hierarchy of geological contexts as domain model and uses a top-down refinement method to achieve the first subtask.

to make all this explicit in the implementation in order to give better explanations, support learning processes, have a more disciplined design, and so on. Since this early work a lot has happened and many researchers have pursued this objective. First of all the notion of the knowledge level has strongly come to the foreground although it was a very unclear and heavily debated idea only a few years ago (Steels and McDermott, 1992). The componential framework underlying our early work on second generation expert systems can in retrospect be seen as an early example of a knowledge level framework and it will be discussed in this sense later in the paper. Second many other knowledge level frameworks have emerged. One of them is the KADS framework (Wielinga, et.al. 1992) which makes different knowledge level models, particularly those emphasising inference structures, but which is nevertheless in the same line as the componential framework. Third, various attempts have been made to capture genericity for example in terms of task-specific architectures (Chandrasekaran, 1986) or role-limiting problem solving methods (McDermott, 1989).

Our own work has lead to a better worked out framework about decomposition of knowledge into models, methods, and tasks, to the development of a workbench to support design based on the framework, to a clear methodology for developing code at the symbol level organised along the basic components (models, methods, and tasks), and to work on genericity and reusability of applications by (non-)programmers.

This paper reports in particular on the framework (section 2) and the workbench (section 3). There are some comments on genericity and reusability in section 4.

2 The componential framework

This section presents our framework for describing applications at the knowledge level. The framework is also known as the *componential framework* because it decomposes a knowledge level description into many different components. Examples of the use of the framework can be found in Rademakers (1991), Vanwelkenhuysen (1991) and Jonckers, et.al. (1992).

2.1 The three perspectives

The componential framework assumes that an application can be usefully described from three perspectives: models, methods and tasks (figure 2). The task perspective focuses on what needs to be accomplished. The model perspective focuses on what is known to do the tasks, in other words what kind of models are being constructed and consulted. The method perspective focuses on how the knowledge is used to achieve the tasks. Normally the three perspectives are worked out in a kind of spiral movement each time progressively refining the description from a particular perspective. For example, the designer would first think about the task, then move to a model perspective to work out some of the models involved in the task, then think about the methods to achieve the task which typically means that more models or more subtasks are introduced, and so on.

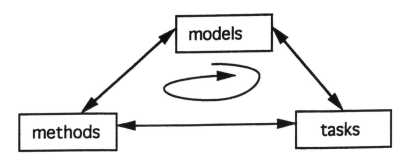

Figure 2. An application can be described at the knowledge level from three perspectives: models, methods, and tasks. These perspectives are progressively refined in a spiral movement.

2.2   The model perspective

The term model is used in its broadest possible sense. A model makes abstraction from certain aspects of reality. It identifies objects, relationships, properties and attributes of the objects, relationships between properties of objects, and so on. For example, classifying birds requires making a model of the features of the bird. The resulting classes constitute a classificatory model. A model relating features to classes is needed to perform the classification itself. Diagnosing a motorcycle requires making a model of the symptoms present in the motorcycle. A major goal of the diagnostician is to make a model of the malfunctions that are occurring and of the states in the motorcycle that caused the malfunctions. Once such a model is in place, a model can be made of the repairs that would fix the motorcycle. All this requires additional models, for example a model of the relationship between symptoms and malfunctions or a model of the relationship between malfunctions and malstates.

Two further distinctions are important. First of all a distinction can be made between a model that is fixed in a particular application, we will call this a *domain model* valid for a whole domain, and a model that is built up by the application, we will call this a *case model* because it makes a model of the specific case that the application is trying to resolve. For example, a motorcycle diagnosis application may require a model relating symptoms to malfunctions. This model would be fixed and is constructed by an expert diagnostician. On the other hand, the required model of the symptoms would obviously be specific for the case being reasoned about. This would therefore be a case model. A special class of domain models are the *ontologies* which constrain the vocabularies that can be used in other models. For example, for the motorcycle diagnosis application there will be an ontology for the possible symptoms, one for the malfunctions, one for the malstates and one for the possible repairs.

Second, a distinction can be made between the *form* and the *content* of a model. The form refers to the structure of the model, for example, whether it is a set, a sequence or a set of mappings. The content refers to the elements inside a model, for example, the mappings in a set of mappings, the members of a set, or the elements in a sequence. Thus the symptom case model might take the form of a set. The contents for a particular case are symptoms like {"black smoke comes out of exhaust", "motorcycle does not pull uphill", "starting is difficult"}. The relation between symptoms and malfunctions could be represented by a mapping model. One element in this mapping model could be: "black smoke comes out of exhaust" maps onto "fuel-air mixture too rich".

2.3   The task perspective

A task is something that needs to be accomplished. This usually means that one or more models are constructed or changed. The models that a task has an impact on are called the *target models*. The models that a task consults are called the *source models*. A task may also produce input or output from and to some *interface*. It may have one or more subtasks.

The source and target models of a task as well as its interfaces are depicted graphically in a *model dependency diagram*. Such a diagram represents the dataflow relationships between the models and the tasks. Source models and input interfaces have pointers going to a task. Target models and output interfaces have pointers coming out of a task. Figure 3 contains an example for two subtasks of a typical diagnosis application. One that acquires the symptoms from the motorcycle owner and another one that identifies malfunctions based on the acquired symptoms and a model relating symptoms to malfunctions.

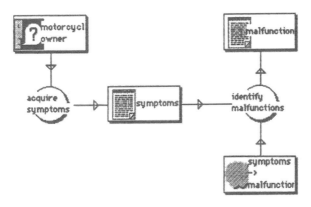

Figure 3. Model dependency diagram containing two subtasks for a diagnostic application.

The subtask relationships between different tasks are depicted graphically in task structures. Figure 4 contains an example, again for a simple diagnosis application. The graphical representation implies no ordering, it is not even necessary that all tasks are executed.

Two further distinctions are important for tasks. First there is the distinction between domain acquisition tasks and application tasks. The *domain acquisition tasks* are responsible for acquiring domain models. They should be achieved before an executable application is formed. The *application tasks* are responsible for developing the case models that are variable in an application and for inputing or outputing the contents of the case models as the application is running. There are normally two different task structures. The first one containing the domain acquisition tasks is the task structure for the knowledge acquisition tool. The second one containing the application tasks is the task structure for the application itself.

Second there is the distinction between tasks which have no further subtasks, and are therefore called *solution tasks*, and tasks which are solved by splitting the application (or the knowledge acquisition process) into various subtasks. These are called *decomposition tasks*.

278

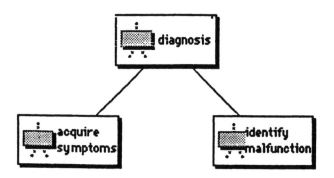

Figure 4. Task structure for a typical diagnostic application.

2.4 The method perspective

Methods specify how a task gets accomplished. A method is an algorithm. It contains a series of activities and a control flow defined over the activities. The activities consult or impact models. Each model and each interface is playing a particular *role* in the method. Some of the activities are themselves tasks. *Task decomposition methods* specify how tasks are divided up into subtasks and regulate the flow of control between tasks. *Solution methods* specify how a task without further subtasks gets accomplished. A solution method still implies a series of different activities, but they are not analysed into separate tasks at the knowledge level. It is purely a matter of grainsize how far one wants to keep decomposing tasks into subtasks or whether one wants to view an activity as primitive. This grainsize may for example depend on the size of the reusable chunks that a developer wants to address through the knowledge level description.

The control aspects of a method are depicted in *control diagrams*. These are finite state automata. The states correspond to one activity (possibly the execution of a subtask). The transitions correspond to control flow. The conditions on a transition specify the conditions under which control flows from one state to another. There is also a start point, a succeed, and a fail point. Figure 5 contains the control diagram for an instance of the generate and test method.

A method also has a set of roles to be filled by models. This information is traditionally represented in inference structures and is here represented by labeling the links in model dependency diagrams as illustrated in figure 6. Inference structures are also depicted in task inference structures, which show the roles that various subtasks play in the methods of their parent task.

There is a large variety of methods and we will come back to the problem of method definition and method selection later. The methods can in any case be split up into task decomposition methods and solution methods. The solution methods for knowledge-intensive symbolic applications fall apart into

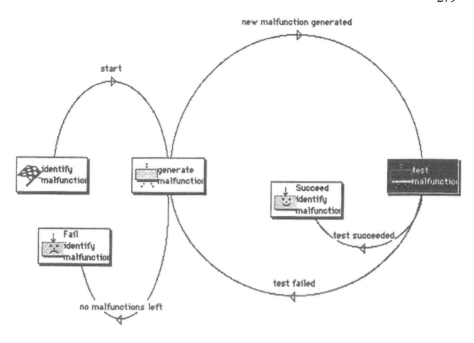

Figure 5. Control diagram imposing a control flow on different tasks which result from a generate-and-test decomposition.

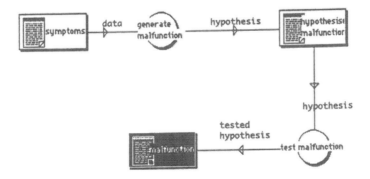

Figure 6. Model dependency diagram with labeled links. Such annotated diagrams represent the inference structure.

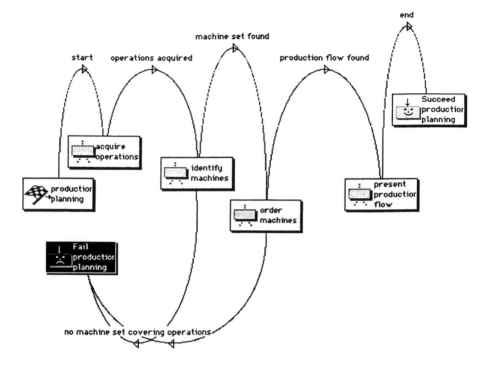

Figure 21. Control diagram for the sequential task execution of the production planning task.

because code fragments can also be data. For the purposes of the present example, a series of CLOS objects has been defined implementing various datatypes like set, ordered set (sequence), mapping model, and so on. When a particular kind of case model needs to be created, an instance of this datatype is created. A series of CLOS methods have been implemented for the various methods. For example, there is a method called cover which performs the cover as required in the identify machines subtask. This method is completely general. It works over any source and target sets and any kind of mapping model. In principle another programming language can be used even imperative programming languages like C. In such languages it is of course more difficult to support the interactive build up of an application.

To substantiate the code level, files are created that contain code to reconstruct the object when needed. In the case of the possible operations domain model the file would contain only two instructions:

(defvar possible-operations)

(setf possible-operations (make-instance 'set))

Evaluating these instructions effectively creates the required possible operations domain model and binds it to the variable internally allocated to refer to this domain model. For simplicity of the example, global variables have been used to refer to models but that is of course not at all necessary. The interaction between the execution level and the code level goes in both directions using the encode or install buttons.

bly a non-programmer) purchases an "application kit" which contains a large hierarchy of methods for a particular application domain, such as diagnosis.

3 The Workbench

This section documents the COMMET workbench that has been developed to experiment with reusability. The workbench supports the development of an application at the three levels: the knowledge level, the execution level, and the code level. The knowledge level assumes the framework outlined in the previous section. It describes the application from three perspectives: tasks, models, and methods. The execution level corresponds to a set of computational objects that implement the knowledge level components. For example, there is a computational object for a task, for a domain-model, for a case-model, for a method, and so on. The code level corresponds to a set of files. Each file contains code that can recreate the computational objects. The knowledge level model built up at the knowledge level has itself also an execution and code level but these are not discussed here in order not to complicate the paper (see Steels, 1992).

The use of the workbench is now described through an example which at the same time illustrates the componential approach.

Samuel Wilkinson owns a small company that builds parts for the automobile industry. He has a series of machines that can perform various operations over metal pieces, such as cut a left or right hole, cut the front, bend the piece, apply a rust-resistant coating, paint the outside, etc. The machines are installed at specific locations on the shop floor (figure 8). A work piece can automatically move between machines. There are certain choice points when the piece can go through one of an alternative set of machines. In some cases, the piece flows through a machine but no action is performed. Each day Samuel gets orders from a car manufacturer to construct a particular metal piece. At that moment he needs to determine which machines will be used and what the order is in which metal pieces will flow through the machine network. Samuel would like an application so that every morning he inputs the operations that need to be performed and automatically the production flow is inferred.

We will take this as a case study to construct a first simple appplication. The workbench assumes that an application is built up in the context of an *application kit*. The case study uses a very general application kit (called base) which contains some basic types of models (set, ordered-set, mapping models, etc.) as well as a series of basic methods (select subset of a set, cover, order based on a network). More specific application kits would contain many more model types and methods, as well as other kinds of generic components. An application with its descriptions at all the different levels is called a *project*. The name of the project is production planning project. The top-level window when the workbench is started looks as in figure 9. This interface makes it possible to go to the various knowledge level components: task structures, model dependency diagrams, control diagrams, or any other component.

Analysis

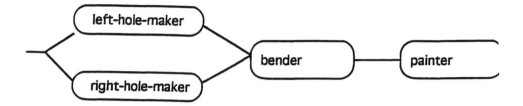

Figure 8. Position of machines on a shopfloor and flow of metal pieces between machines. Machines are lined up next to each other when their use is mutually exclusive.

The analysis phase focuses on the construction of the model dependency diagrams and the task structures. This could proceed in a top-down fashion, which means that first the source and target case models are defined of the top-level task (production planning), and then the case models for each of the subtasks. We can also do it in other ways. For example, first construct the complete task structure and only then start to fill in the models. Most often there is a continuous movement back and forth between analysis and design. Parts of the task structure and the models are worked out during analysis, decisions on form of models and methods then cause a refined task decomposition with additional models, etc.

Let us introduce immediately two subtasks for the production planning project. The first subtask is called production planning acquisition and is the top-node of the knowledge acquisition task structure. The second subtask is called production planning and is the top-node of the application itself. The model dependency diagram for the production planning task contains one source case model, namely the operations that need to be performed that day, and one target case model, namely the production flow for that day. The interface for inspecting and changing model dependency diagrams is displayed in figure 10. One can see icons for adding case models, domain models and interfaces to the diagram. The diagram itself is constructed through mouse-style interaction. For example, the arrows from and to the models are drawn with the mouse. All individual objects have their own interfaces. For example figure 11 contains the interface for inspecting a case model, in this case the one for the operations that need to be performed. The interface takes a standard form. There is a way to go to a text-file containing notes on this component and a way to go to a description of the component in terms of a set of features. Features are discussed in section 4 when we focus on application kit managers. Next there are ways to focus on the three perspectives: models, methods, and tasks. For this component it is not

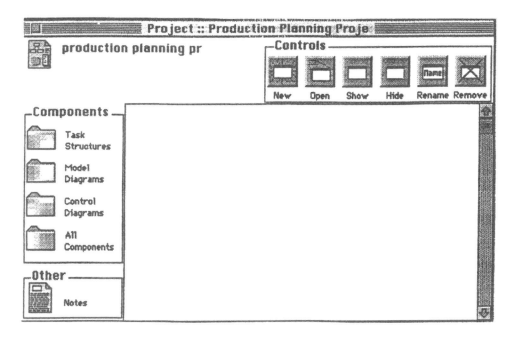

Figure 9. Overall project structure visible when starting up the workbench.

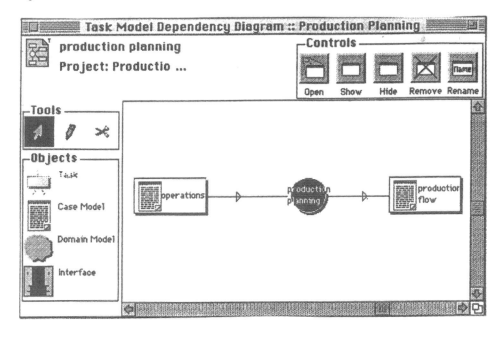

Figure 10. Model dependency diagram editing interface. The task for production
planning is visible with its source and target case model.

relevant to explore further the three perspectives but for other components, in particular tasks, there will be different icons to look at the component from each of the three perspectives. On the right side there are ways to go to the three levels: the knowledge level, the code level and the execution level. For each of these there are pulldown menus that allow various operations. All of them support a "view" which brings in a dedicated interface. Through these menus execution objects can be encoded and code installed to yield execution objects. Links can be created to code files in the application kit.

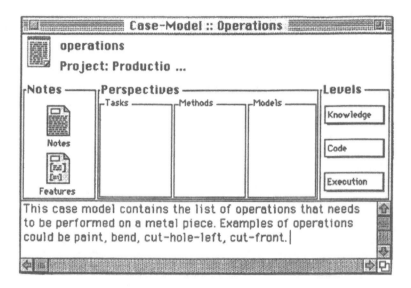

Figure 11. Interface for inspecting and editing a model.

A similar interface is available for inspecting and changing aspects of a task. Figure 12 shows the one for the top-level task so far. Notice again ways to move to the knowledge level, code level and execution level. Notice also ways to go to the three perspectives: A number of icons are now visible to go to the task structure associated with this task, the model dependency diagrams, and information about the methods, including a control diagram.

Proceeding in a top-down fashion, we now work out the production planning task. For straightforward problems, i.e. those not requiring sophisticated problem solving methods, a problem can usually be solved by introducing intermediary models which compute or infer partial information needed to formulate the case model that constitutes the final goal of the application. Concretely, to construct the production flow we obviously need to know which machines are part of the flow. So the problem could be split already in three subtasks: one to acquire the

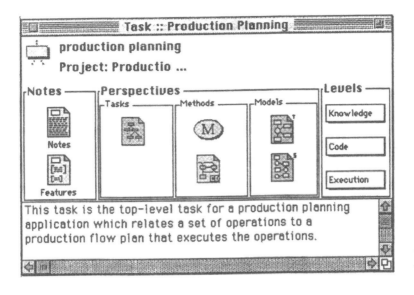

Figure 12. Interface for inspecting and editing a task

operations that need to be performed (from the plant operator), the second task to identify the machines that will be required, and the third task to determine the order on the machines. Let us also add a fourth task to present the results back to the plant operator. This gives the model dependency diagram in figure 13.

The task structure is automatically updated and now looks like in figure 14.

Each of these tasks needs information to be executable. This information is contained in the domain models that are additional sources for each task.

1. To acquire the operations, an ontology specifying which operations are possible is needed.
2. To identify the machines, a mapping model relating operations to machines is needed.
3. To construct the ordering, the constraints on ordering need to be known. They will be contained in a domain model which is called the machine network.

The tasks also involve various interfaces:

1. The acquire operations task gets input through a user interface from the plant manager.
2. The present production flow task gives output through a user interface to the plant manager. The interfaces and the various source domain models are

286

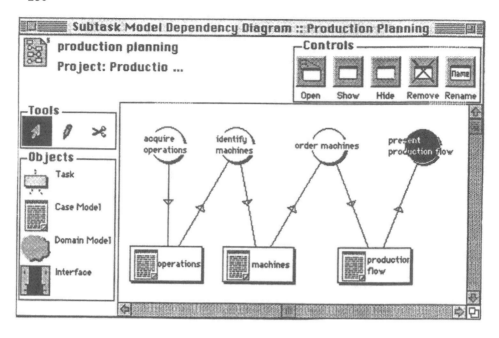

Figure 13. Model dependency diagram for the subtasks of production planning.

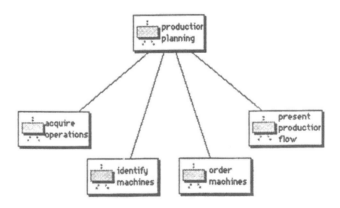

Figure 14. Task structure for production planning.

interactively added to the diagrams. For example, the model dependency diagram for identify machines is given in figure 15.

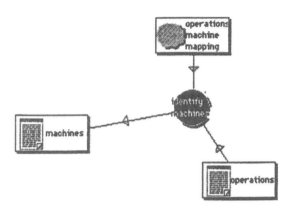

Figure 15. Model dependency diagram for identify machines with a domain model relating operations to the machines that can perform them.

Figure 16 contains the model dependency diagram for acquiring the operations that need to be done that day. There is a user interface and an ontology in the form of a list of possible operations.

The introduction of various domain models necessitates the introduction of new tasks to acquire these various domain models. These are task acquisition methods that are run by the application developer before an executable application is constructed. They are part of the production planning acquisition task structure shown in figure 17.

Figure 18 shows the model dependency diagram for knowledge acquisition. One can see that certain domain models are used to construct other domain models. In general, one needs at least ontologies that constrain the vocabulary used in a particular domain model.

Design

At the design stage decisions are made about the form of the models and the nature of the methods that achieve each task. As mentioned earlier, analysis and design are usually highly intertwined but they are presented as separately here for didactic reasons. Here are some plausible choices for the forms of the domain models and their acquisition methods.

288

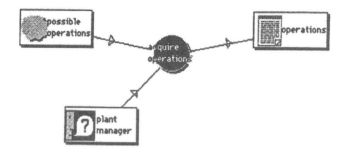

Figure 16. Model dependency diagram for the acquire operations task.

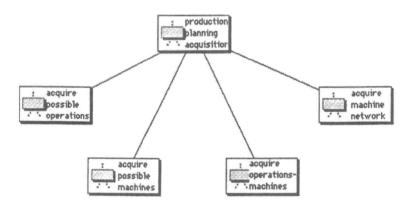

Figure 17. Knowledge acquisition task structure for production planning

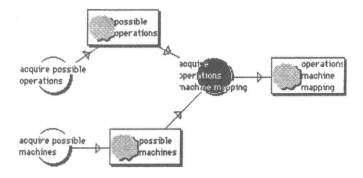

Figure 18. Partial model dependency diagram for the knowledge acquisition subtask.

1. *Possible operations*: The set of possible operations which makes up the operations ontology in this domain can be represented in the form of a set. It contains elements like paint, bend, make left hole, make two holes, cut front, etc. A user interface method that asks the user to type in the elements of the set one by one can be used to acquire the set.

2. *Possible machines*: The set of possible machines whibch makes up the machines ontology is done the same way. The type set is chosen as the form of this domain model and the "acquire set method" is used again to acquire the elements.

3. *Operations machines mapping*: This domain model relates operations with machines. The first column of the mapping contains the list of operations which the machine in the second column of the table handles. If each machine can only do one operation, the first column would be a list with a single element. An acquisition method called "acquire mapping method" will be used for the "acquire operations machines mapping task". Figure 19 contains a picture of this method in action.

4. *Machine network*. This domain model takes the form of a network, more specifically a sequence in which each element is a list of alternative machines. This domain model is acquired through the "acquire network method".

Similar decisions are made for the case models and the methods to acquire, infer, or present them:

1. *Operations*: The operations can be represented in a set which will be a subset of the possible operations. The method to acquire this set is another user interface method. For example, one that allows the user to point to those elements that need to be included. This is the "acquire subset method".

290

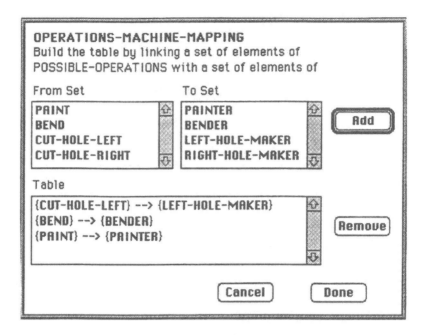

Figure 19. Window created by the acquire mapping method which is associated with the acquire operations machine mapping.

2. *Machines*: The machines to be used can also be represented as a set. The method to find the machines (in the identify machines task) is an example of a *cover method*. All the source elements (in this case operations) need to be "covered" by a list of target elements (in this case machines). This method is not so trivial because a particular machine can do several operations and so it must be checked that there are no superfluous operations. Conversely *all* operations must be covered. For the time being we assume that there is only one solution and later extend the application to handle situations where more than one solution is produced by the cover method. This variant of the cover method is called cover-one.

3. *Production flow*: This case model is clearly to be represented as a sequence. The method to find the sequence is called "order based on network". It is associated with the order machines subtask. It takes a domain model in the form of a network as explained earlier. The final subtask which presents the production flow can use a graphical presentation, although a series of instructions to the different machines and the connecting transportation bands might be more appropriate here.

All these decisions are recorded interactively by filling in parts of the knowledge level description. This process is supported by interfaces that visualise possible selections. Figure 20 contains for example an interface for selecting the methodtype of a hierarchy of methods.

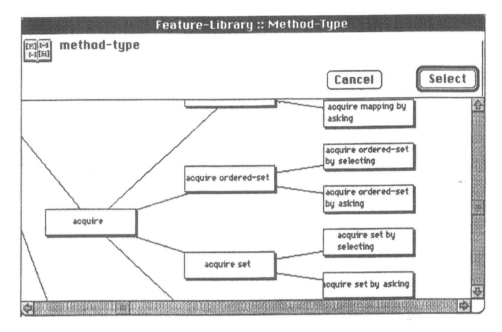

Figure 20. Interface for selecting values of features in knowledge level descriptions.

Next a decision needs to be made about the method that will be used to regulate the execution of the different subtasks in the application. Here a simple sequential task execution method is possible. The details of these task decomposition methods are typically drawn through their associated control diagrams as contained in figure 21.

The execution level and the code level

While the design decisions are made it is possible to construct at the same time objects at the execution level and files creating these objects at the code level. For example, as soon as the decision has been made that the possible operations domain model takes the form of a set, the application kit manager can create an object that will function as the possible operations domain model by instantiating the symbol level datatype associated with set. The developer can cause the creation by clicking on the object button in the domain model window and then selecting install.

In the current experimental implementation of the workbench we are using LISP as the programming language at the code level, particularly because LISP supports the progressive construction of program fragments and the easy interchange between code and execution objects. It is easy to write code generators

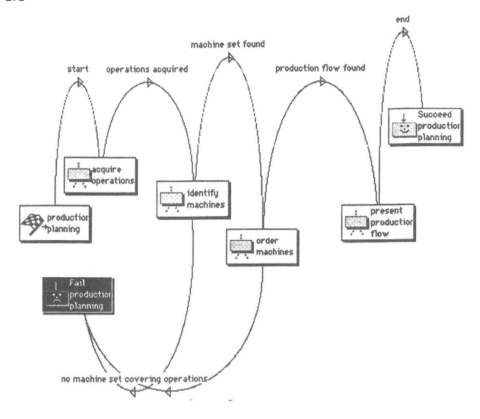

because code fragments can also be data. For the purposes of the present example, a series of CLOS objects has been defined implementing various datatypes like set, ordered set (sequence), mapping model, and so on. When a particular kind of case model needs to be created, an instance of this datatype is created. A series of CLOS methods have been implemented for the various methods. For example, there is a method called cover which performs the cover as required in the identify machines subtask. This method is completely general. It works over any source and target sets and any kind of mapping model. In principle another programming language can be used even imperative programming languages like C. In such languages it is of course more difficult to support the interactive build up of an application.

To substantiate the code level, files are created that contain code to reconstruct the object when needed. In the case of the possible operations domain model the file would contain only two instructions:

(defvar possible-operations)

(setf possible-operations (make-instance 'set))

Evaluating these instructions effectively creates the required possible operations domain model and binds it to the variable internally allocated to refer to this domain model. For simplicity of the example, global variables have been used to refer to models but that is of course not at all necessary. The interaction between the execution level and the code level goes in both directions using the encode or install buttons.

The same capabilities are present for all the components at the knowledge level, not just for domain models. The objects implementing the case models are instantiated as soon as their datatypes are known. The tasks are constructed at the symbol level as instances of the class task. Their slots (e.g. the method to be used) are filled as soon as it is specified at the knowledge level. The methods are linked at the code level to code fragments (in the present experiment CLOS-methods) that implement the methods. This code can be arbitrarily complex, as long as it executes whatever the method promises to do.

Knowledge acquisition

The knowledge acquisition phase is responsible for filling in various domain models. This turns the generic application into an executable application. The whole knowledge acquisition process is started by executing the top-level knowledge acquisition task (done by clicking on the execute button associated with the task). This invokes execution of the various subtasks that acquire all the domain models needed in the application. Execution means that the task invokes the method associated with it and applies it to the execution level objects which play specific roles in the method. The method has side effects on the contents of the target models. It may also invoke the execution of subtasks. For example, when the task *acquire operations machines mapping* is invoked, the "acquire mapping method" discussed earlier becomes active and through the interface questions are asked.

The filled-in domain models can in turn be encoded. The generated instruction should not only say which type of object is created but also what the contents are of the object. For example, in the case of possible operations the following instructions are contained in the associated code-file:

(defvar possible-operations)

(setf possible-operations (make-instance 'set :set-elements '(paint cut-hole-left cut-hole-right ...)))

Evaluating the above forms has the effect that the domain model and its contents will be re-instantiated. Running the application Running the application is technically identical to performing knowledge acquisition. The user can click on the execute button associated with the top-level application task and thus invoke the execution of the complete task structure. As the methods associated with each node in the task structure are executed the various case models are filled in. Occasionally a user interface pops up to query the user or to present certain results. For the application under investigation, the following dialog develops. First the acquire operations task queries the user for the operations that need to be performed on the workpiece - as in figure 22.

The identify machines task produces the contents of the machine case model displayed in figure 23.

The order machines task produces the contents of the machine ordering case model which are presented to the user in the final subtask - as in figure 24.

After running the application, the datastructures representing the various case models have been filled in at the execution level. For example, the operations case model now contains a specific list of operations that need to be executed.

OPERATIONS
Make a selection out of the elements of #<SET #x4EE899>

Set

| CUT-HOLE-LEFT | | Add |

Subset

| PRINT |
| BEND | Remove |
| CUT-HOLE-RIGHT |

Cancel   Done

Figure 22. Interface invoked by acquire operations task.

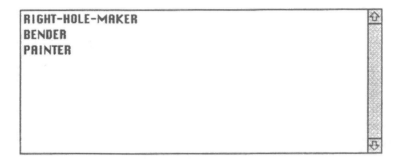

RIGHT-HOLE-MAKER
BENDER
PRINTER

Figure 23. Contents of machines case model after the application of the cover method.

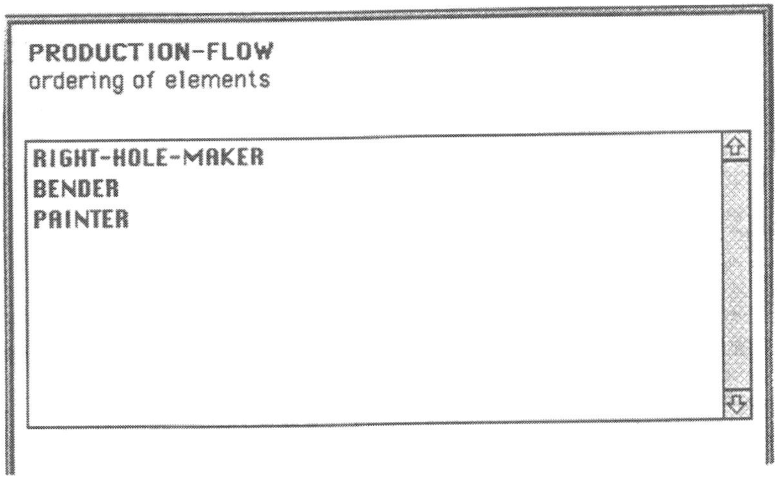

```
┌─────────────────────────────────────────────────────────────┐
│  PRODUCTION-FLOW                                             │
│  ordering of elements                                       │
│                                                             │
│  ┌───────────────────────────────────────────────────┬──┐  │
│  │ RIGHT-HOLE-MAKER                                   │⬆ │  │
│  │ BENDER                                             │  │  │
│  │ PAINTER                                            │  │  │
│  │                                                    │  │  │
│  │                                                    │  │  │
│  │                                                    │  │  │
│  │                                                    │⬇ │  │
│  └───────────────────────────────────────────────────┴──┘  │
│                                                             │
└─────────────────────────────────────────────────────────────┘
```

Figure 24. Presentation of production flow.

This information can be stored away at the code level by generating code that would regenerate the case model and its contents when installed. This makes it possible to partially run an application or re-run it from a particular point in the task structure. On the other hand, re-invocation of the complete application task structure leads to the computation of another production flow for the next series of operations.

The workbench makes it also possible to go back to the knowledge acquisition phase by simply re-executing the top-level knowledge acquisition task. It is not possible to directly edit the contents of a domain model (because this could cause undesirable errors in the domain model). But is possible to always re-execute a knowledge acquisition task and in that sense edit the domain model. For example, we can imagine that Samuel Wilkinson buys a new machine and therefore needs to extend both the possible machines domain model and the operations machines table. User driven (re-)execution of a task may induce incompatibilities, for example when one domain model (or case model) is constructed with older versions. A solution to this problem can be achieved by implementing consistency maintenance mechanisms. These are the responsibility of the application kit.

4 Opportunities for reuse

Obviously reuse implies that the developer can select parts of an application and insert them in a new application. Two observations can be made:

1. Any part of an application may in principle be reusable: an ontology, parts of the task structure, fragments of a model dependency diagram, a filled-in domain model, a filled-in case model (for example, when an application needs to be restarted), the selection of which method to use for a certain task, and so on.
2. A part may be reused at any level of genericity. For example, in the case of a domain model it could mean (1) the need for the domain model in the first place (for example that the diagnostic application needs a mapping model relating symptoms to malfunctions), (2) the form that is used to structure the domain model (for example a mapping), (3) the actual contents of the mapping, for example that it includes an entry relating the symptom "black smoke comes out of exhaust" with the malfunction "fuel-air mixture too rich".

More concretely reuse is envisioned as follows: The developer may decide during analysis or design to call upon the application kit manager to see whether any existing chunks cannot be reused. For example, the developer may be focusing on a task and may seek a decomposition with associated model dependency diagrams and methods that would be capable to perform the task. The application kit manager guides selection of the chunk by querying about the knowledge level features of the task and of associated models. Once a chunk has been found it is fused with the application under construction and the developer can adapt or edit the resulting structure. The selection of a chunk and its adaptation once it is fused, happens normally at the knowledge level, unless the developer wants to extend the run-time library.

5 Conclusions

The paper reported on work that finds its roots in the movement towards second generation expert systems which started around 1985. At that time the major goal was to introduce more structure in applications both for design as well as coding. This structure had to come from trying to understand better the knowledge contained in an application. At the moment there are completely worked out frameworks as well as workbenches to support their use. This paper has in particular focused on the componential framework and has illustrated the use of the framework for design, knowledge acquisition and the structuring of applications. It also appears that it will be possible to use the knowledge level as a basis for organising reusability.
1

Acknowledgements

This research has been directly inspired by John McDermott's visionary proposals for achieving reusability of software for knowledge systems. His support through a Digital External Research Grant has been one of the key factors that started the research efforts reported in this paper. We are grateful to Arnold Van De Brug who has acted as the liaison with Digital Equip- ment Corporation, Europe, and who has been highly supportive of the approach.

The knowledge level framework used in this paper has been under development from around 1984. Many people at the VUB AI laboratory have influenced the ideas and technologies described in this paper. Walter Van de Velde helped (long time ago) to clarify the notion of the knowledge level. Filip Rademakers, Walter Van de Velde, Kris Van Marcke, and Johan Van Welkenhuysen, early on participated in working out the "componential methodology". Their earlier experiments (around 1989) on the operationalisation of componential knowledge level models have been an important prerequisite to the ideas expressed in this paper. Important contribu- tions towards the framework have also come from Marleen Sint, Ali Hiemstra and Hans Van Ditmarsch from the Dutch Open University. The "teachability requirement" that they imposed has done a lot to refine and concretise the framework including the relationship to the symbol level. The development of the framework has further benefited from intensive discussions over the years with researchers working on the same issues, in particular with Joost Breuker, Chandrasekaran, Bill Clancey, Howard Gruber, Mark Linster, John McDermott, Mark Musen, John Sticklen, Jay Tenenbaum, and Bob Wielinga.

The design and implementation of the COMMET workbench is the work of Angus McIntyre from the VUB AI lab and Knowledge Technologies, n.v.. McIntyre is a genius programmer who single-handedly constructed the implementation of the workbench in an amazingly short time. McIntyre has contributed enormously to the further refinement of several key ideas, particularly as regards application kits and application kit managers. Some of the symbol level components needed to implement the example applications were developed together with Koen De Vroede. Important contributions have also come from other members of the CONSTRUCT project at the VUB AI lab, in particular from Sabine Geldof and Viviane Jonckers, as well as from other CONSTRUCT partners: Jean-Marc David and Alain Nguyen from Renault in Paris and Ernesto Morgado and Joao Martins from Siscog in Lissabon. Positive feedback from the CONSTRUCT project reviewers: Jean-Paul Krivine, Enric Plaza and Tim Smithers has greatly stimulated the fast progress that the project has made.

The support of the European Commission through the ESPRIT project CONSTRUCT and of the Belgian Government through the IUAP action and the ADIOS project is gratefully acknowledged.

6 References

Chandrasekaran, B. (1986) Generic Tasks in Knowledge-Based Reasoning: High-Level Building Blocks for Expert Systems. In: IEEE Expert 1(3):23-30.

Gruber, T.R. (1991) OntoLingua: A Mechanism to Support Portable Ontologies. Knowledge Systems Laboratory. KSL 91-66. Stanford University. Palo Alto.

Jonckers, V., S. Geldof, K. De Vroede (1992) The COMMET methodology and workbench in practice. VUB AI Lab Memo 92-8. Free University of Brussels. Brussels.

Scheiber, S. (1985) Introduction to unification-based approaches to grammar. CSLI Lecture Notes 85. Stanford University. Palo Alto.

Keene, S.E. (1989) Object-Oriented Programming in COMMON LISP. A Programmer's Guide to CLOS. Reading, Ma: Addison-Wesley Pub. Cy.

Klinker, G., C. Bhola, G. Dallemagne, D. Marques, and J. McDermott (1991) Usable and re-usable programming constructs. In: Knowledge Acquisition. 3, 117-135.

McDermott, J. (1989) Preliminary Steps towards a taxonomy of problem-solving methods. In: S. Marcus (ed.) Automating Knowledge Acquisition for Expert Systems. Kluwer Academic. Boston. p. 225-256.

Musen, M. (1989) Automated Generation of Model-Based Knowledge Acquistion Tools. Santa Mateo: Morgan Kaufmann.

Musen, M. (1991) Dimensions of Knowledge Sharing and Reuse. Knowledge Systems Laboratory. KSL-91-65. Stanford University. Palo Alto.

Neches, R., et.al. (1991) Enabling Technology for Knowledge Sharing. In: AI Magazine. 12(3): 36-56.

Newell, A. (1982) The Knowledge level. In: Artificial Intelligence. 18. p. 87-127.

Hooper, J.W. and R.O. Chester (1991) Software Reuse. Guidelines and Methods. New York: Plenum Publishing House.

Rademakers, P. (1991) Analysis of Expert Problem Solving Behavior Using COMMET. VUB AI Lab AI Memo 92-1. Free University of Brussels. Brussels.

Smith, R. G. (1984) On the Development of Commerical Expert Systems. p. 61-73. In: AI Magazine. Fall 1984.

Steels, L. (1985) Second Generation Expert Systems. In: Future Generation Computer Systems. Vol 2, 2.

Steels, L. (1987) The Deepening of Expert Systems. In: AI Communications. Vol. 1, nr 1.

Steels, L. (1990) Components of Expertise. In: AI Magazine. 11(2):29-49.

Steels, L. (1992) Reusability and configuration of applications by non-programmers. VUB AI Memo 92-4. Free University of Brussels. Brussels.

Steels, L. and B. Le Pape (1992) Enhancing the knowledge engineering process. Contributions from ESPRIT. Amsterdam: North-Holland Pub. Co.

Steels, L. and J. McDermott (eds) (1993) Knowledge level expert systems research in action. Academic Press. London.

Vanwelkenhuysen, J. (1991) Constructing a Knowledge Level Description of Expert Behavior in a Troubleshooting Environment. VUB AI Lab Memo 91-12. Free University of Brussels. Brussels.

Wielinga, B.J., A.Th. Schreiber and J.A. Breuker (1992) KADS: a modelling approach to knowledge engineering. In: Knowledge Acquisition 4(1) p. 5-54.

Towards a Unification of Knowledge Modelling Approaches

Bob Wielinga[1], Walter Van de Velde[2], Guus Schreiber[1] and Hans Akkermans[3]

[1] University of Amsterdam, Social Science Informatics
Roetersstraat 15, NL-1018 WB Amsterdam, The Netherlands
[2] Vrije Universiteit Brussel, AI-Lab
Pleinlaan 2, B-1050 Brussels, Belgium
[3] Netherlands Energy Research Foundation ECN
P.O. Box 1, 1755 ZG Petten, The Netherlands

Abstract. In this article we present a coherent framework for modelling reasoning processes in knowledge based systems. The aim of the framework is to integrate different lines of research and in particular, though not exclusively, the KADS approach and the Components of Expertise framework. We are especially concerned with enhanced facilities for domain modelling and with the notion of problem solving method. The resulting modelling framework, called the CommonKADS modelling framework, fits into a comprehensive methodology, called CommonKADS, that covers all aspects of knowledge based applications. In this article we first present a set of principles on which our modelling framework in founded. These are derived from a careful study of the different approaches. We then describe the modelling framework itself, illustrating it with an example. We also discuss various approaches to building models for a particular application using this framework. [†]

1 Introduction

There is little doubt about what expert systems do: they solve problems. However, what problem solving is, how we should describe it and whether there exists any systematicity in expert problem solving are questions that are still very much open. Finding the answers to these questions is important since a coherent framework for the description of problem solving will allow us to compare different expert systems, increase their quality and may lead to easier communication and re-use of problem solving methods and knowledge bases. Several researchers in expert systems are converging toward a common viewpoint on

---

[†] The research reported here was carried out in the course of the KADS-II project. This project is partially funded by the ESPRIT Programme of the Commission of the European Communities as project number 5248. The partners in this project are Cap Gemini Innovation (F), Cap Gemini Programator (S), Netherlands Energy Research Foundation ECN (NL), Eritel SA (ESP), IBM France (F), Lloyd's Register (UK), Swedisch Institute of Computer Science (S), Siemens AG (D), Touche Ross MC (UK), University of Amsterdam (NL) and Vrije Universiteit Brussel (B).

these issues. This view is emerging from various interrelated lines of research on problem solving, knowledge and its representation, and expert systems.

An important line of work concerns the representation of problem solving behaviors and the characterization of commonalities among them. This starts from an analysis in terms of explicit problem solving structures. It is then observed that commonalities exist across applications in the way that problem solving behavior is realized. This leads to the notion of generic task: a class of tasks for which a certain generic problem solving mechanism and representation scheme is appropriate [5, 7, 10, 22, 23, 32].

Newell's concept of knowledge level is another major source of ideas [25]. The knowledge level was originally introduced in an attempt to resolve some confusions in the usage of the terms 'knowledge' and 'representation' in Artificial Intelligence. Basically it provides for a means to describe problem solving behavior independent of how it is realized at the symbol (representation) level. Much of current research on models of problem solving is viewed, somewhat in retrospect, as 'operationalizing' Newell's ideas for practical purposes [37].

A third important influence comes from the usage of richer representations within expert systems [31]. Pure rule representation is considered to be no longer sufficient, neither for the purpose of system construction nor for that of knowledge acquisition. The importance of representing domain knowledge in a more adequate way is emphasized by many researchers [20, 32]. This requires stronger modelling facilities than simple attribute-value lists, if-then rules or plain logic [16, 18].

The aim of this paper is to provide a synthesis of some of these ideas. Starting from Newell's knowledge level work [25] and some interpretations of it [29, 37], a general framework is developed through a synthesis of the KADS 4-layer model of expertise [5] with aspects of the Components of Expertise [32] and work on domain modelling (e.g., [20]). The result of the synthesis is called the "CommonKADS" modelling framework. This framework is aimed at the construction of knowledge level models, or *expertise models*, and fits into a comprehensive methodology, called CommonKADS, that covers all aspects of knowledge based applications.

In the following we first formulate the principles on which the CommonKADS modelling framework is based (Sect. 2). This sets the scene for outlining the modelling framework in terms of knowledge categories, their structure and the relations between them, and the knowledge level architecture that is the basis for CommonKADS expertise models (Sect. 3). Subsequently, we give details about the individual components of expertise models and suggest constructs for a modelling language (Sect. 4). We then briefly consider the modelling process and describe the role of generic model components (Sect. 5). The paper ends by making some final remarks and by indicating further work.

2   Principles of the CommonKADS Modelling Approach

In this section we formulate the basic principles and hypotheses that are embodied in the CommonKADS modelling framework. Some of these principles are well known and generally accepted, while others are new. They capture a number of valuable basic insights in knowledge engineering that have guided this research.

2.1   Knowledge Application Principle

There are many possible views on what expert problem solving is and how it comes about. Becoming expert in a certain field clearly involves finding and consolidating ways to achieve one's goals in spite of the many epistemic and pragmatic problems posed by that field. Steels [32] views the overcoming of these problems as a major hallmark of expertise. We postulate that, for the purpose of knowledge-based systems (KBS), expertise can be expressed with the help of the knowledge application principle:

> *Effective real-world problem solving is viewed as the rational (or at least, rationalizable) application by an agent of appropriate domain- and task-specific knowledge.*

The knowledge application principle seems to be widely (albeit often tacitly) shared by the community of knowledge engineers and KBS developers, although it implies a rather specific choice in the broader context of artificial intelligence, cognitive science, and epistemology.

2.2   Modelling Principle

Knowledge engineering has traditionally been viewed as a process of extracting knowledge from a human expert, and transferring it in computational form to the machine [2, 13]. This conventional view was also reflected in the popularity of rapid-prototyping using rule-based shells. In contrast today knowledge engineering is approached as a modelling activity: the heart of the work of the knowledge engineer lies in the actual *construction* of models.

> *The development of a knowledge-based system is seen as the construction of a set of models of problem-solving behavior, seen in its concrete organizational and application context. A KBS is a computational realization associated with these models.*

> *A central model in the CommonKADS methodology is the expertise model, which models the problem solving behavior of an agent in terms of knowledge that is being applied in carrying out a certain task.*

302

Figure 1 summarizes the suite of models involved in the CommonKADS methodology (see [12] for a comprehensive description of the models and the dependencies between them). The expertise model is only one of many models that are relevant in KBS development. Other models capture relevant aspects of reality such as the task that an application supports, the organizational environment within which it takes place, the assignment of tasks to agents, their capabilities and communication, and the computational design of the KBS. It is noted that these models are engineering-type models and serve engineering purposes. An important additional point is that in the CommonKADS methodology the models are considered not only as 'steps along the way', but as independent products in their own right that play an important role during the entire KBS life-cycle.

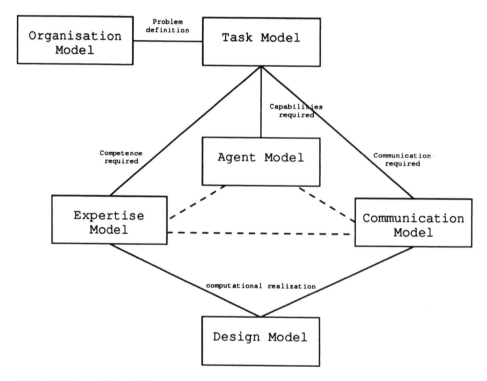

Fig. 1. The position of the expertise model in the CommonKADS suite of models. The organization model is the tool to analyse an organization. The task model captures the global task within the organization that deals with a certain function that needs support, including the assignment of tasks to agents. The agent models describe agent capabilities, the expertise model agent competence involved in realizing the overall task. The communication model describes the communication behavior among the agents. The design model describes the structure and mechanisms of the artifacts - usually knowledge based systems - involved in the task. The lines indicate direct dependencies between elements of the models.

An expertise model, like any of the other models, can be constructed for different purposes and at different moments in time. For example, in an initial situation a task may be performed by a human expert whose capabilities are modeled, while in a later stage a KBS may take over part of the task of the human expert. The expertise model for the KBS then reflects the required expertise of the system rather than that of the human expert. Of course, a model of human expertise may serve as an important input for modelling the expertise of a KBS, but is not necessarily identical to it.

2.3 Knowledge-level Principle

Allen Newell has formulated the knowledge level hypothesis in an attempt to resolve some confusions in the usage of the terms 'knowledge' and 'representation' [25]. He defined a representation as "a symbol system that encodes a body of knowledge". His knowledge level hypothesis postulates the existence of knowledge independent of its representation:

> "There exists a distinct computer systems level, lying immediately above the symbol level, which is characterized by knowledge as the medium and the principle of rationality as the law of behavior." [25, p.99]

At this so called *knowledge level* an agent is described as having a set of goals, a set of possible actions, and a body of knowledge. Its behavior is then predicted by the so called *principle of rationality*: "If an agent has knowledge that one of its actions will lead to one of its goals, then the agent will select that action" [25, p.102].[1] Knowledge is characterized as a "competence-like notion, being a potential for generating action" and completely independent from representation and implementation issues.

The *knowledge level principle* as it is taken in CommonKADS, intends to give the knowledge level hypothesis practical relevance for the development of knowledge-based systems:

> *The knowledge level is the appropriate level for modelling the competence of knowledge-based systems. It calls for the description of problem solving behavior at a conceptual level that is independent from representation and implementation decisions.*

It was Clancey [8] who first showed the relevance of modelling at the knowledge level for the development of knowledge-based systems. Subsequent research (see, e.g., [1, 6, 22, 23, 29, 32, 41]) has elaborated this point of view. In recent approaches to knowledge engineering the knowledge level idea is a recurring theme, though it is seldom being applied in its original form. Especially the separation of the conceptual, knowledge-oriented, aspects from representational and computational issues is seen as an important structuring and simplifying principle in KBS project management.

---

[1] The principle of rationality is usually not considered to be part of the knowledge level model but rather act as the 'interpreter' for it.

2.4 Role-limiting Principle

The knowledge level hypothesis does not give much guidance regarding the question *how* an intelligent agent can be described in knowledge level terms. Newell's notions of goal, action, knowledge and rationality are too coarse-grained for practical knowledge level modelling. In order to resolve this, an extension of the knowledge level principle is needed. Accordingly, an agent is thought of as imposing a structure on its knowledge by ascribing a particular role to the different components. This structure reflects the way in which an agent frames the problem it is faced with. Acting rationally within that structure leads to a class of behaviors which adequately deal with the pragmatic and epistemological problems that the agent is faced with, such as time and resource limitations or knowledge that is incomplete or inconsistent. This idea is reflected in the role-limiting principle:

> *An intelligent agent which is faced with a particular task can be modeled as imposing on its knowledge a structure, the parts of which play different, specialized and restricted roles in the totality of the problem-solving process.*

Role limitations (a term introduced by McDermott [22]) of knowledge are a basic organizing principle for modelling at the knowledge level. They delimit the class of problem-solving behaviors to those which are likely to comply with the pragmatic and epistemological characteristics of the task environment. In MYCIN for example, knowledge is configured according to the well-known heuristic classification scheme [9]. Some knowledge is used for data-abstraction, other for heuristic matching or for refinement. This leads to achieving the goals of the system and hence the employed knowledge structuring is rationally appropriate. Even when there would be a zillion ways to embark on a task a rational agent will employ one and stick to it as long as this is reasonable.[2]

2.5 Principle of Differentiated Rationality

In the knowledge level view, the behavior of an intelligent system is governed by the principle of rationality. It states that the system will take those actions that, according to its knowledge, lead to the achievement of its goals. The role-limiting principle, however, requires more elaborate principles of rationality. These must explain, first, why knowledge is structured in a certain way in order to comply with predetermined pragmatic and epistemic features of the task environment and, second, why certain knowledge is applied within the context of a specific knowledge structure. This differentiation of rationality as underlying *knowledge configuration* on the one hand and *knowledge application* on the other hand, has been called two-step rationality [37].

---

[2] The role-limiting principle has important implications for the computational tractability of complex knowledge-based systems. Epistemological role limitations of knowledge can be reflected in computational access limitations in knowledge-based systems [1, 29].

The principle of rationality must be specialized to account for the way in which the agent will structure its knowledge to approach a task in a situation with given pragmatic and epistemological characteristics.
Within the limitations of a particular structuring and role assignment of knowledge, the principle of rationality must be further specialized to account for the way in which goals are achieved by applying the appropriate type of knowledge.

The first part of the principle of differentiated rationality is concerned with modelling principles. It rationalizes the *structure* of the model of expertise. For example, the introduction into an expertise model (usually by the knowledge engineer, not by the system) of a data abstraction task can be rationalized by its capacity to reduce the size of the data space. The second part of the principle rationalizes control on knowledge application. It explains how the knowledge structure is filled in to obtain a case-specific model. For example MYCIN can be viewed as filling in the heuristic classification scheme to obtain a case-specific model that consistently explains the patient findings. The principle of rationality within the heuristic classification scheme may be phrased as 'the system uses its knowledge to reduce the size of the differential'.

2.6 Knowledge Typing Principle

The observation that different parts of the knowledge play different roles in the problem-solving process enables a distinction between different types of knowledge. In addition it appears that this differentiation does not need to be done in an ad hoc and application-dependent fashion, but rather can be characterized in generic terms. A commonly encountered notion in this respect is the separation between domain and control knowledge. In CommonKADS we employ a more refined categorization of knowledge.

A knowledge level model is usefully viewed as consisting of three different categories of knowledge: domain knowledge, task knowledge, and inference knowledge. Within these categories further generic types of knowledge can be distinguished.

The domain knowledge consists of the domain-specific knowledge relevant to a given application. This entails a description of the conceptualization of the domain in terms of its ontology as well as of the structures of and relationships between the domain concepts.

The task knowledge captures the goals of an agent and the activities that are to be carried out in order to achieve them. It consists of the decomposition of the task into subtasks (which in turn may be further decomposed into subtasks), in conjunction with knowledge concerning the control over these subtasks.

The inference knowledge describes the use of domain knowledge. This is done via so called primitive inferences, that is, small-scale coherent theories employed to make certain basic inferences. By chaining primitive inferences together one obtains an inference structure: a road map of all inferences that are possible in the domain. This specifies the competence of the system.

Our experience suggests that the above present consolidated and stable categories of knowledge that recur in many applications. They are generic in the sense that they provide a vocabulary that can be applied to describe problem solving without being dependent on the specific details of task and domain of the application.

The above three knowledge categories (domain, task, inference) are necessary and sufficient for the description of application related knowledge. Apart from application related knowledge CommonKADS also supports description of problem solving knowledge. Problem solving knowledge is not a fourth category (as was the strategic knowledge in KADS-I) but is knowledge about a specific application, namely problem solving. Accordingly, problem solving knowledge can be itself described in terms of the above three domain-task-inference categories. Here, the domain knowledge contains problem solving methods, while the task-inference aspects are an operationalization of (differentiated) principles of rationality and captured in what we now call the strategic knowledge. As a whole, this vocabulary is a further extension of the knowledge level hypothesis and is intended to turn it into a practically useful approach towards the modelling of expertise.

2.7 Interaction Hypothesis

Having distinguished different categories of knowledge, a natural question to ask is how they are interrelated. On this matter, one finds quite diverse opinions in the literature concerning knowledge modelling. In the four-layer model of KADS-I [40] the idea is that generic components related to different categories of knowledge can be modeled and represented as being independent of each other. Thus, they are thought of as 'orthogonal' dimensions of knowledge. In contrast, the Generic Task approach [7] considers them as a 'package', in which different components may be distinguished but cannot be meaningfully separated: knowledge cannot be represented independent of its use. Accordingly, in the latter view knowledge components of different types are conceived of as strongly intertwined, while in the former they do not interact at all. Judging from practical KBS experience, it now appears that neither view is really appropriate, and is to be seen as an extreme point on a continuous scale. Hence:

A good knowledge modelling methodology is able to span the whole continuum from weak to strong knowledge interaction.

There indeed seem to be varying degrees of task-domain coupling, depending on the application. Usually, task and inference knowledge presuppose a certain domain ontology or assume domain knowledge to be available in certain forms or schemata. On the other hand, these schemata often have a quite general character. For example, in the cover-and-differentiate method for diagnosis tasks as implemented in MOLE [14] it is required that the domain knowledge is present as a causal network. The interaction hypothesis implies that CommonKADS must be able to model multiple ontologies as well as to explicitly specify the forms and conditions under which they can be used in reasoning.

3 The CommonKADS Modelling Framework

This section provides an overview of the CommonKADS knowledge level modelling framework. In the first subsection the CommonKADS view on knowledge-based problem solving is put forward. In Sect. 3.2 the main categories of knowledge are being discussed: domain knowledge, task knowledge and inference knowledge. Then, in Sect. 3.3 we introduce the basic structures within these categories and the concept of knowledge role that defines the interrelationships between them. The final two subsections focus on two central aspects of CommonKADS which were not adequately covered in KADS-I [41]: domain modelling (Sect. 3.4), and problem solving knowledge (Sect. 3.5). The knowledge level modelling ingredients that are introduced here are described in technical detail in Sect. 4, while the practice of modelling is discussed in Sect. 5.

3.1 Problem solving as modelling

In his original proposal for knowledge level modelling, Newell distinguished between *goals* and *knowledge*, and postulated the *principle of rationality* stating that the agent will choose an action which, according to its knowledge, leads to the achievement of its goals [25]. A goal, in this view, is a desired state of affairs in the world. From a knowledge level perspective the 'perception' of the world is through knowledge alone. A goal is therefore equivalent to a desired state of knowledge about the system(s) in the world that problem solving is about. This is the basis of the view of problem solving as modelling:

> *Problem solving is the construction of a case-specific model of a system that summarizes the agent's understanding of the reality and should allow to "conclude" that the problem has been solved. This model is called the case model.*

The case model can be viewed as the variable part of the knowledge that an agent has about the systems it is confronted with. It is dynamically constructed during the problem solving process, based on the available knowledge and the information obtained from interacting with the world through *basic actions*, primarily transfer tasks that realize communication with other agents, say, users [11].

3.2 Categories of Knowledge

Though Newell's original notions of goal and knowledge are perhaps sufficient in principle, it is useful to impose structure on the description of the knowledge of an agent. For example, in Components of Expertise [32] knowledge is partitioned in domain models, tasks and problem solving methods. The KADS four-layer model categorizes knowledge as domain knowledge, inference knowledge, task knowledge and strategic knowledge [40, 41].

The primary epistemological categories in CommonKADS are *domain knowledge*, *task knowledge* and *inference knowledge*. In order to describe an application at the knowledge level it is *necessary* to provide knowledge in each of these categories. An application system can not be described by, for example, domain knowledge alone.

Domain knowledge. The domain knowledge expresses relevant knowledge about the systems - physical or not - that a task is about. That knowledge refers both to the specific systems that the problem solver is confronted with (i.e., the case model), and to the class of these systems (i.e., in terms of statements that, for the sake of problem solving, are assumed to hold for all systems of a certain kind).

The KADS-I framework was particularly weak in its facilities for formulating the domain knowledge. Basically no more than a KL-ONE like formalism was provided. The Components of Expertise framework, on the other hand, emphasizes the importance of domain knowledge and the guidance that its structure gives in modelling. This calls for explicit ontologies [18]. In CommonKADS these ideas are extended and incorporated in the notions of *domain ontology* and *domain model*. The *domain ontology* defines the terms in which to formulate statements about the world [19]. A coherent collection of such statements constitutes a particular view on a domain and is called a *domain model*. Causal models or hierarchical part-subpart models are examples of domain models. A domain model is itself further defined by a *model ontology* and a *model schema* that specify the language, structure and interpretation of a domain model in a concise way. For example, causal modelling views the world as 'causes' and 'effects' that are structured by one or more causal relations and uses a particular interpretation of what 'causation' means. This is described in more detail in Sect. 4.1.

Task knowledge. The task knowledge specifies tasks. Knowledge about a task relates to the goal of the task, as well as to the activities that contribute to the achievement of that goal. Basically, as explained in Sect. 3.1, a goal of a task is a specification of the case model under construction. It is assumed, however, that task knowledge is in principle independent of a domain and that references to the domain and the case model are through a task specific terminology only (see the description of roles in Sect. 3.3).

The notion of *task* is heavily overloaded in the AI and KBS literature. A common view [27] is to characterize a task by an I/O pair, and by some constraints on the relation between input and output posed by the task environment. In other fields of research concerned with the study of tasks (e.g., task analysis) a task is defined as a set of coherent activities that an agent performs in order to achieve a goal. In KADS-I a task is not much more than a name to index a particular interpretation model, leading to the quasi identification of the two. This made it impossible to talk about a task independently of the method being used to achieve a goal. In CommonKADS both the goal and activity aspects of a task are maintained in the *task definition* and the *task body*, respectively. This is described in more detail in Sect. 4.3. Moreover, the relation between the two can be - but need not be - modeled as the application of a so called *problem solving method*, a notion which is introduced in Sect. 3.3.

Inference knowledge. The inference knowledge specifies *basic inferences* that can be made in the domain knowledge. The role of inference knowledge is very similar to that of inference rules in (classical) logic. An inference rule in logic describes the ways in which axioms (domain knowledge) can be combined to derive new information. In what sequence or for what purpose such inferences are made is not described in the inference rule, but may be part of a mechanism embodied in a theorem prover. The difference between inference rules in logic and the CommonKADS basic inferences lies in the following features of CommonKADS inferences:

- Basic inferences operate on restricted parts of domain knowledge;
- Basic inferences are not necessarily truth preserving;
- Basic inferences implement an inference method that has a specific purpose in problem solving.

Inference knowledge is described in more detailed in Sect. 4.2.

The distinction between domain knowledge, task knowledge and inference knowledge is reminiscent of three views which are used in software engineering [42, p. 219]: the *data view*, the *time-dependent* or *control view*, and the *functional view*. Though not identical, the CommonKADS epistemological distinctions are similar.

3.3 Structuring a Knowledge Level Model

The role-limiting principle, which was introduced in Sect. 2, states that an agent can be modeled as imposing on its knowledge a structure, the parts of which play different specialized and restricted roles in the totality of problem solving. This structure is what in CommonKADS is the actual knowledge level model.[3] In the following subsections we describe first the structure within the three categories (Sect. 3.3), and then the structure between them (Sect. 3.3). Then we elaborate on the problem solving knowledge which underlies the process of imposing this structure itself (Sect. 3.3).

Intra-category Structure. A CommonKADS expertise model consists of domain knowledge, task knowledge and inference knowledge. It is useful to describe its structure along the same lines.

---

[3] Note that this is different from Newell's notion since it not only captures the content of the knowledge, but also the structure that emerges when the knowledge is being applied to a class of problems [37].

- The structure on task knowledge is basically contained in the task body of the top-level tasks of an application. A task body contains a decomposition of a task into a set of sub-tasks which are themselves first-class tasks. The recursive decomposition of these subtasks leads to an overall *task structure* within the task knowledge. The task structure bottoms out in tasks which are not further decomposed (and are therefore called basic tasks). The basic tasks are linked to either basic inferences or to basic actions. The task body, in addition, specifies control over the tasks in the task decomposition.
- The structure on inference knowledge is the *inference structure*, well known from KADS-I [4]. The inference structure is the most primitive functional view on the application and describes the functional dependency among all basic inferences, abstracting from control. Note that the inference structure does not contain tasks or basic actions, only basic inferences.
- The primary structure on domain knowledge is provided by the domain models and their interrelationships through the inferences in which they play a role. Basic inferences derive relationships between case-specific information items that must ultimately relate to the case model. So the inference structure has a 'dual' view in the domain knowledge, called the *domain structure*, which contains the dependencies between the various domain models.

The task structure, inference structure and domain structure provide three useful but partial views on an application. Moreover, these views can be considered as relatively independent (the relative interaction hypothesis, Sect. 2). Therefore, they also provide for a useful decomposition of the modelling task.

Inter-category Structure. Apart from structure within categories, a CommonKADS expertise model requires structure between the knowledge categories. We use the notion of *knowledge role* to describe the relations between knowledge elements of the various categories. Basically, a knowledge role is a reference to a knowledge item together with a role-specific vocabulary to talk about that knowledge item and its primary constituents.

Some concrete examples of knowledge roles are:

- A knowledge role for statements in the domain knowledge may point to a particular statement, for example wire=broken, and refer to it as a hypothesis and to its constituents wire and broken as device and state.
- A knowledge role for a relation among statements in the domain knowledge may point to a particular relation, for example influences, and refer to it as causes and to its constituents as cause and effect.
- A knowledge role for a task may point to a task find-subpart and refer to it - in a method specific way - as generate.

We distinguish two types of knowledge roles: *dynamic* knowledge roles and *static* knowledge roles. Dynamic knowledge roles point to knowledge elements that are being manipulated in the problem solving process: e.g., the input problem, the intermediate results, the solution. Static knowledge roles point to knowledge elements that are being used in the problem solving process, but that are not affected by it: e.g. causal knowledge about the normal functioning of a device, or a hierarchical decomposition of a device into its parts.

The above examples illustrate how knowledge roles allow for one category to refer to another one without making a commitment about the terms used in the latter. This is important to enable independence between and re-usability of parts of an expertise model.

Problem Solving Knowledge. In CommonKADS the knowledge about how to model a particular application is called *problem solving knowledge*. Problem solving knowledge is knowledge about modelling in the sense of the modelling principle (Sect. 2). It is knowledge about how to organize and link the task, inference and domain knowledge related to an application in order to accomplish a given class of tasks within a given task environment. Within the problem solving knowledge we distinguish two types: *problem solving methods* and *strategic knowledge*.

- A problem solving method captures a possible way of organizing the domain, task and inference knowledge. Its application therefore *generates* the knowledge structures within which the rational use of knowledge leads to meaningful problem solving behavior.
- Strategic knowledge specifies what kind of model of an application is adequate for a given task environment. The possible models are contained in the problem solving methods. Adequacy depends on availability of knowledge (epistemological adequacy) and the constraints on using or obtaining that knowledge (pragmatic adequacy).

Note that problem solving knowledge is not another knowledge category in addition to domain, task and inference knowledge. Problem solving knowledge is about a 'meta application', namely to come up with a good model in terms of application related knowledge. It would therefore be wrong and misleading to view it as a separate knowledge category. If this were done then there would be a category for knowledge about designing cars, writing programs, or curing patients. Clearly, we are using here a different categorization namely a teleological one. This categorization is orthogonal to the categorization of knowledge in task, inference and domain knowledge which is meant to be a purely epistemological one. As a consequence it is perfectly possible to analyze the problem solving knowledge in terms of the three basic categories of task, domain and inference knowledge. However, since the task here is always modelling and the method is always method selection and application it seems sufficient to provide only problem solving methods and strategic knowledge, basically the domain knowledge of strategic reasoning. The case model of strategic reasoning is formed by the application related knowledge.

Already in the KADS-I project it was recognized that the knowledge in the strategic layer is different from the knowledge in the other three layers. The strategic layer in KADS-I -when it was present at all- was linked to all of the three other layers. This indicates that it is not really another layer 'on top of' the task layer, but that it should be orthogonal to all of the three other layers. At the KADS-I strategic layer there was no particular support for modelling. No attempt was made to provide generic components (the CommonKADS problem solving methods) or ways to understand the other layers from the general principles embodied in problem solving knowledge. Incorporating such facilities was a major aim of the CommonKADS integration effort.

3.4 Domain Knowledge

The KADS-I modelling methodology was weak in the support it gave for modelling the domain. Basically, there were only two ways in which domain entities could be referred to: primitive representational terms (e.g., concepts) and metaclasses [40]. CommonKADS provides a more comprehensive domain modelling methodology, based in particular on extensible ontologies and a powerful notion of domain model. Elements of this framework have been derived from other work, in particular from [20, 32].

> An ontology for describing a particular domain contains the terms referring to the entities that must be distinguished as categories in the domain and the terms that refer to the relations that can hold between (instances of) the entities. Entities can be primitive, i.e. entities that exist and can be recognized in the domain, or can be abstracted, i.e. terms refer to abstractions of complexes of domain entities or to abstract concepts which have no direct correspondence in the domain.

Lenat and Guha [20] discuss two properties that an ontology should have: *epistemological adequacy* and *pragmatic adequacy*. An ontology is epistemologically adequate if it makes the distinctions that are required by the task environment, i.e. it allows us to talk about all the things that we need to talk about. An ontology is pragmatically adequate when it allows efficient problem solving. These criteria can be conflicting. Lenat proposes a way to solve the problem of conflicting requirements. The epistemologically adequate ontology is based on the most primitive notions of the domain. On top of this ontology a number of pragmatic abstractions are build which provide higher level constructs and allow more efficient reasoning to be performed. For example, in the domain of audio equipment an epistemologically adequate ontology could be based on the theory of electronics, i.e. by defining the workings of equipment in terms of electrical signals and components. For practical purposes (e.g. diagnosing faults in audio equipment) such a vocabulary would be too low level. A pragmatic ontology would introduce additional concepts like amplifier, volume control system, power supply etc. Domain knowledge formulated in such a pragmatically adequate ontology is more suitable for the reasoning task that has to use the domain knowledge. It thus represents a certain *viewpoint* on the domain. Such a viewpoint, is called a *domain model* [32] and it is particularly important in knowledge engineering. The way in which a domain is structured, as for example exemplified by the human expert, can provide important handles on the reasoning process.

A domain model is a coherent collection of statements about a domain that represents a particular viewpoint on the domain knowledge such that it is suitable for the problem-solving task. The domain model may therefore embody certain assumptions that are specific for the use that is made of it.

Table 1 gives a few examples of domain models. The idea of viewpoint is reflected in the usage of a coherent vocabulary and a coherent structure to refer to the individual statements in the domain model. For example, a hierarchical system decomposition can be one such viewpoint on a device. It is characterized by terms such as 'part' and 'is subpart of' to refer to items of domain knowledge. These terms are specified in the model ontology:

The model ontology of a domain model specifies the generic terms that a reasoning model may use to refer to the statements within that domain model.

Table 1. Examples of domain models

Domain model	Description
ISA-hierarchy	hierarchical structure of concepts
PART-OF hierarchy	hierarchical structure based on PART-OF relations
Causal network	a network of concepts related by CAUSE relations
Definition	An implication between an expression and a concept

The model ontology is different from the domain ontology. It does not describe entities in the domain itself, but is a description of entities in the domain model. The model ontology is a *meta description* of the elements in the domain model. For example the term 'part' in the model ontology may correspond to 'integrated circuit' in the domain ontology. The statement 'The integrated circuit IC-35K4 is mounted in PCB-A-5236' in the domain knowledge may be referred to as 'part IC-35K4 is subpart of part PCB-A-5236' when using the model ontology of a hierarchical decomposition domain model.

In the above example we intentionally avoided the use of predicates or other formal constructs. Indeed, an ontology only describes the *vocabulary* for representing a domain, but not the actual representational structure. First order logic (or even natural language) may be sufficient for describing the domain knowledge but for a domain model the representation should fit the use that is being made of it by a reasoner. For example a reasoner employing systematic diagnosis [4] requires a hierarchical decomposition of the system that is being

314

diagnosed. The representational primitives that are the building blocks for these elements of the domain model are specified in a *model schema*.

> *A model schema describes the structure of the entities that are represented in a domain model. The type of schemata that are required for a certain domain model depend on the nature of the domain of application and on the reasoning processes that make use of the domain model.*

Model ontology and model schema together provide for a mechanism to refer in a generic way to domain knowledge which can itself be stated using an arbitrary domain dependent terminology and constructs. This allows for abstracting from irrelevant details and for the sharing of individual statements by different domain models. In addition it is the basis for reusability across domains.

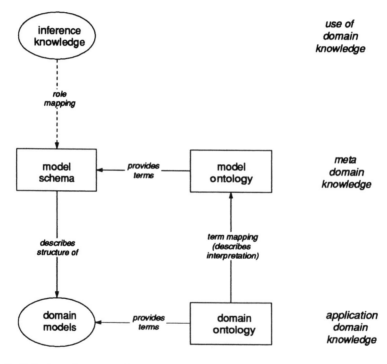

Fig. 2. Relations between the various components of the domain knowledge in an expertise model

Figure 2 summarizes the concepts that we have introduced in this section. A more powerful support for domain modelling is definitely one of the most important improvements over the original KADS-I framework.

3.5 Problem Solving Knowledge

Intuitively, a problem solving method describes a way (or ways) of solving a particular class of problems, i.e., a way of applying domain knowledge to perform a class of tasks. For example, the Cover-and-Differentiate method [15, 30] describes how a particular type of diagnostic problem can be solved by exploiting causal knowledge. However, when one searches the literature for a precise definition of 'problem solving method', it becomes clear that there are different views.

A major aspect giving rise to different notions of problem solving method is the grain-size of the tasks that they apply to. In many approaches this task is a *general performance task* [17], i.e. the overall task that a system is to perform. In earlier work by John McDermott and his group, where problem solving methods are coupled to complete execution shells, this is the only possible way [21]. Also Clancey's Heuristic Classification method, although it can can be applied to tasks of various sizes, is usually applied to such larger tasks [10]. Chandrasekaran chooses a smaller grain size [6, 7]. Here problem solving methods are embedded in so called *generic tasks*. A problem solver for a performance task is decomposed into several such generic tasks, each applying their method (and representation). Communication between such generic task problem solving components is through message passing [34]. KADS-I takes a similar approach [4]: the general performance task (or *real-life task*) is decomposed into a number of generic tasks, such as prediction, classification, diagnosis, design, planning etc. The problem solving methods were embodied in the 'interpretation models' that describe a way of solving one such a generic task. In Components of Expertise [32] problem solving methods can be applied to any task. Yet smaller grain-size is chosen for the 'mechanisms'in PROTEGE-II [27] that are only the building blocks for complete problem solving methods.

Another difference is in the way methods are described. In general a problem solving method specifies a number of possible actions and some way of determining how these actions are to be ordered in time. In KADS-I methods are embodied in Interpretation Models, descriptions of inference structure and task-level control structure in which a number of problem solving methods are 'compiled out' to components in the four layer model. In the more recent KADS literature the notion of *knowledge differentiation* was introduced to indicate the decomposition of certain knowledge components, for example meta-classes and knowledge sources, into different subtypes. Knowledge differentiation appears to be the epistemic equivalent of problem solving methods. Newell [26] defines the concept of problem solving method in the context of the *problem space hypothesis*. At any instant an agent will pursue a goal in a problem space. The problem space contains states, a problem (i.e. an initial and a desired state), and a set of operators that move from one state to another and control telling the agent how to navigate through the state space. Methods are viewed as goal structures, corresponding in a way to degenerate problem spaces: they are the result of applying operators in a state space while using the control information.

In CommonKADS we use the following notion of problem solving method:

A problem solving method is a prescription of the way in which a certain class of task definitions can be satisfied. The method may be complete with respect to a set of basic capabilities, i.e. prescribe all necessary actions in terms of the basic capabilities of the agent, or may be incomplete in the sense that the activities generated by the method my lead to new problems, which cannot be solved by basic capabilities and require the application of new problem solving methods.

In our view a problem solving method specifies the relation between a task definition and a task body. A problem solving method is applied to a task definition and after a mapping of (generic) terms used in the method description onto the task specific terms, the body of the task can be instantiated from the method description. Whether all this is being done automatically within a system (as it was done in some experiments on Components of Expertise [39]) or manually by the knowledge engineer (i.e., knowledge differentiation) is irrelevant here.

The process of problem solving is, in this view, recursive: a task that attempts to achieve a problem can generate new (sub) problems which in turn have to be transformed into goals and task definitions. Methods applied to the task definition generate a task body which in turn may generate new problems. Figure 3 represents this process in a schematic way.

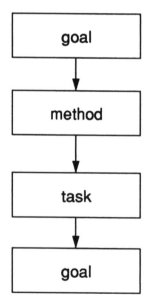

Fig. 3. Recursive nature of problem solving through the application of problem solving methods

A task is defined by an abstract input-output description. The input usually takes the form of a set of statements about some part of the world, while the output is described in terms of a goal. The task that a system must perform is not fully specified by the abstract input-output description. Additional requirements, constraints and properties can be defined. We will call this collection of information about the task the *task environment*. The task environment defines the requirements that a problem solver must satisfy in order for the solution to be valid and useful. Three types of information are part of the task environment: epistemic, computational and pragmatic [32]. *Strategic knowledge*, the second type of problem solving knowledge relates these characteristics of the task environment to problem solving methods.

3.6 Summary

In this section we have introduced the CommonKADS knowledge level modelling framework. The following points summarize the highlights of this discussion:

- Problem solving is viewed as the construction of a case model.
- A knowledge level model consists of knowledge in three knowledge categories: domain knowledge, task knowledge and inference knowledge.
- The formulation of domain knowledge is supported by the concepts of domain ontology and domain model.
- The notion of task encompasses both the goal aspect (the task definition) and the activity aspects (task body) of a task.
- A knowledge level model is a structure over the three major knowledge categories. In particular the notion of knowledge role allows for relations between knowledge in different categories.
- Problem solving knowledge is knowledge about structuring a knowledge level model. In particular problem solving methods rationalize the relation between the task definition and the task body.

In the next section, the framework is described in more technical depth, providing descriptions of each of the ingredients.

4 CommonKADS Conceptual Modelling Components

In this section we describe in more detail the different components of the CommonKADS expertise model. Figure 4 shows the top-level decomposition of this model. A major distinction is made between parts of the model that concern application-related knowledge on the one hand, and problem solving knowledge on the other hand. The application knowledge encompasses the domain knowledge, task knowledge and inference knowledge. The problem solving knowledge consists of problem solving methods and strategic knowledge. Below we will discuss the various components of the expertise model and illustrate them using a very simple example of a diagnostic application in the domain of cars. The notation used in this section is a simplified version of the CommonKADS Conceptual Modelling Language (CML) [28].

318

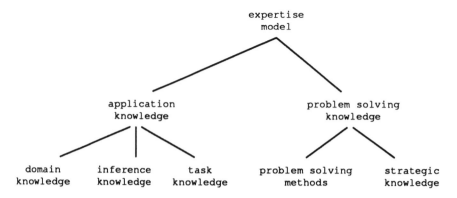

Fig. 4. Major components of the expertise model.

4.1 Domain Knowledge

The domain knowledge (Fig. 5) basically contains all the knowledge about the system (*object system*) that an application is about. Application domain knowledge comes in two flavors: static -case independent- domain knowledge and dynamic knowledge related to the case (*case model*). The static domain consists of *domain models* which are coherent collections of *domain expressions*. They capture the general knowledge relevant to the domain of application. The dynamic knowledge is grouped in the case model. It contains a number of different types of information. First there are *case initial data* available before the reasoning even starts. For example, a description of the problem or a description of a particular configuration could be part of this initial case data set. The category *user input data* represents data about the case that the user may enter during problem solving. The category *case solution* represents the solution to the problem. Additional information that is case specific and that is derived during the reasoning process is also stored in the case model *intermediate case data*).

In addition to the case and domain models, the domain knowledge also defines the vocabulary from which these are built: the *domain ontology*. The domain ontology defines the terms that can be used in the domain and case models (*domain terms*), the knowledge types that these terms have (*domain typology*, e.g., concept, attribute, value, relation) and a isa-hierarchy of terms (*domain taxonomy*). The domain ontology closely corresponds to what was called in KADS-I the 'lexicon', 'concept-base' and 'concept hierarchy'.

Knowledge elements are represented in a modelling language that uses certain modelling terms and language constructs. For example in KADS-I these were derived from KL-ONE [3] and consisted of *concepts, properties, relations* and *expressions*. This was too rigid and did not allow for multiple views on the knowledge. In CommonKADS modelling languages occur at two levels.

– First, there is the basic domain language, i.e., the one in which domain

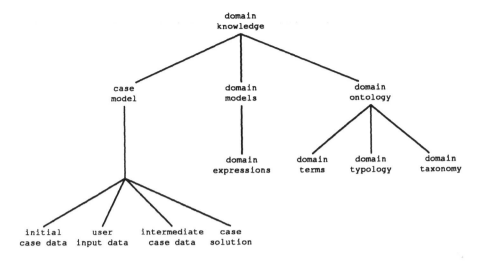

Fig. 5. Components of the domain knowledge.

expressions are stated. This is captured in the *basic model ontology* and the *basic model schemata*. CommonKADS provides the KL-ONE ontology, but allows for extending it with other language constructs, if needed. For example, a language of equations could be useful. Table 2 shows the basic CommonKADS modelling terms and constructs.

– Second there are the modelling languages used to refer to statements within a single domain model. These are captured in the *domain model ontology* and the *domain model schemata* of the domain model. The interpretation of a domain model can be captured in additional *domain model axioms*, the assumptions that a model makes about the world. For example, particular theories of time or causation can be documented in this way and imposed on the domain knowledge.

Figure 6 shows the relation between these elements, which we collectively call *meta domain knowledge*, and the domain expressions. It shows how the notion of domain model allows to talk about collections of domain expressions in a coherent and well structured way, the domain models. These domain models capture required structures for the static knowledge roles of problem solving methods.[4]

We can now define a number of example domain models and their meta description in terms of the basic domain language. Table 3 shows the domain ontology, i.e. the terms and typology of the domain.

Table 4 shows domain models for the example application and their structure in terms of the basic model terms. The names of the domain models suggest a certain type of knowledge that is represented in each model, but in actual fact

---

[4] As such the meta domain knowledge is for the domain knowledge what the problem solving methods are for the task knowledge.

320

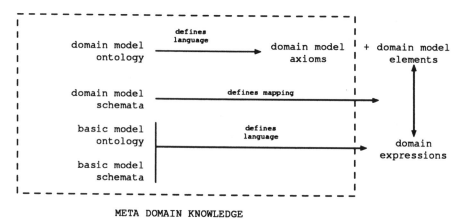

META DOMAIN KNOWLEDGE

Fig. 6. The meta domain knowledge related to the modelling languages for domain expressions and domain models.

Table 2. The CommonKADS basic modelling language

Primitive term	Structure	Example
Concept	labels (atom)	The components of an audio system
Relation	relation between concepts or other entities	Sub-type hierarchy of components of the audio system
Attribute	the name of an attribute of a concept	color, size,
Value	the value that can be assigned to an attribute constant, concept or relation	red, big.
Expression	expression between features	power-switch=pressed
relation between expressions	expression relation expression	power-switch=pressed INDICATES power-state=on

Table 3. Domain ontology for simple car diagnosis

Type	Domain Term
concept-label	no-gas battery-low no-gas-in-engine engine-does-not-run engine-stops
case-attribute	gas-dial battery-dial
value	zero medium full

these names are just pointers to a domain model. The representation chosen in the example is extremely simple. None of the domain entities has internal structure, states and parameters are represented by simple identifiers (concept-labels). A more elaborate representation would of course be possible.

Table 4. Domain models with example domain expressions and the corresponding basic model schema for simple car diagnosis

Domain Model	Domain Expression	Basic Model Schema
Fault classes	no-gas battery-low no-gas-in-engine	concept-label
Complaints	engine-does-not-run engine-stops	concept-label
Manifestations	gas-dial=zero battery-dial=zero	case-attribute = value
Explanation Model	no-gas-in-engine → engine-does-not-run no-gas-in-engine →engine-stops battery-low → engine-does-not-run	F:concept-label → C: concept-label
Behavioral Model	no-gas → gas-dial=zero battery-low → battery-dial=zero	F:concept-label → M:expression
Causal Model	no-gas → no-gas-in-engine	F1:concept-label →F2:concept-label

In addition to the basic domain language CommonKADS provides the option to extend the modelling ontology with domain or task specific terms. For example, the term *explanation* is not part of the domain ontology, it is a term that *describes* a relation between domain concepts that has a certain significance in the context of diagnostic reasoning. Table 5 shows an example of an extended model ontology for the car-diagnosis domain.

Table 5. Extended modelling ontology and structure schema for simple car diagnosis

Domain Model	Model Term	Domain Model Schema
Fault classes	fault-state(F)	fault-class: concept-label
Complaints	complaint(C)	complaint: concept-label
Manifestations	manifestation(M)	manifestation: case-attribute = value
Explanation Model	explain(F,C)	F:fault-class → C:complaint
Behavioral Model	has-manifestation(F,M)	F:fault-class → M:manifestation
Causal Model	causes(F1,F2)	F1:fault-class → F2:fault-class
Observation Model	observation(M)	M: manifestation M in case-user-input-data

It is important to note that the extended model ontology is different from the role descriptions (cf. meta-classes). The model ontology defines a vocabulary to describe the domain knowledge in abstract terms. It provides handles to the domain knowledge without having to specify all domain expressions of a certain type explicitly. It is essentially an extension of the data-modelling view with abstractions that allow easy linking to other views.

4.2 Inference Knowledge

A reasoning process in a KBS consists ultimately of a number of inference steps that derive information about the system(s) that problem solving is about. These inferences make use of static domain knowledge and relate items of information in the case model.

In CommonKADS a primitive inference is basically a relation or a function between domain knowledge roles. An *inference relation* establishes a relation between the dynamic knowledge roles that it connects. For example the inference relation *cover* establishes a pair of complaint and fault-state in the role of symptom and cause, respectively, such that the fault-state explains the complaint. Figure 7 shows a graphical representation of this basic inference. The dynamic roles (symptom and cause) are shown as white boxes, the static role causal model is shown as a grey box, while the box with rounded corners represents the relation that is established by the inference.

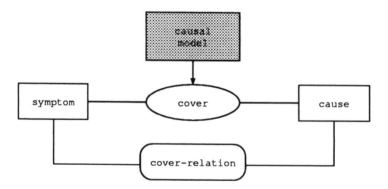

Fig. 7. The inference relation *cover*.

The definition of *cover* is given below.

inference-relation *cover(C,S)*
    goal
        ESTABLISH the cover relation between symptom and cause
    roles
        dynamic-roles
            S:symptom ↦ complaint
            C:cause ↦ fault-state

static-roles
    causal-model: cause(C,S) $\mapsto$ explains(C,S) and cause(C,S)
inference-specification
    (cause(C,S) $\vee$
    $\exists$ C1 cover(C,C1) $\wedge$ cover(C1,S)) $\vdash$ cover(C,S)

Inference relations are non-directional, i.e. the direction of the inference is not specified. *Inference functions*, on the other hand, are directional: they specify which dynamic roles correspond to input and which ones to output roles. For example, the *compute* inference (as used in KADS-I) clearly has a directional nature (see Fig. 8).

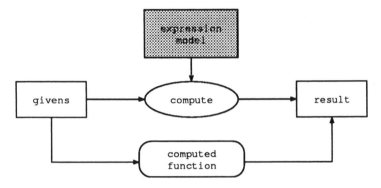

Fig. 8. The inference function *compute.*

Below an example is given of an abductive inference function for the car diagnosis example.

inference-function *generate-by-abduction(S,H)*
   goal
      FIND a hypothesis H that explains symptom S
   roles
    input-roles
      S: symptom $\mapsto$ complaint
    output-roles
      H: hypothesis $\mapsto$ fault-state
    static-roles
      implication-model: implies(H,S) $\mapsto$ explains(H,S)
   assumptions
    A1: implies(H,S) $\mapsto$ H $\vdash$ C
   inference expression
      implies(H,S) $\vdash$ hypothesis(H)

324

An *inference structure* is a structure in the inference knowledge and as such a model of a reasoning process (Fig. 9). An inference structure describes how individual inferences can be usefully related to each other. The inference structure thus specifies the inference capability or *competence* of the system.

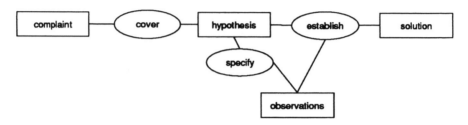

Fig. 9. Inference Structure for the car example

4.3   Task Knowledge

The knowledge category of *task knowledge* describes how a goal can be achieved. A task is characterized by two parts: the *task definition* and the *task body*. The task definition describes *what* needs to be achieved. It is a declarative specification of the goal of the task. The task body describes *how* this goal can be achieved. It is a procedural program, prescribing the activities to accomplish the task.

The *task definition* consists of:

- *Goal:* A description of the goal that can be achieved through application of the task.
- *Case roles:* A definition of the dynamic knowledge roles that the task manipulates.
- *Task specification:* A description of the logical dependencies between the case roles of the task (e.g. what is true after execution of a task, invariants).

The *task body* has the following subparts:

- *Sub-goals:* The sub-goals that the task can generate.
- *Sub-tasks:* The sub-tasks that achieve the sub-goals.
- *Task expression:* The description of control over the sub-tasks to achieve the task.

We distinguish three different types of tasks:

- Composite tasks: tasks that are further decomposed in sub-tasks, e.g. diagnosis is decomposed into generate and test.
- Primitive tasks: tasks that are directly related to inferences. E.g. a primitive abstraction task could be the computation of all solutions of an *abstract* inference, given a particular data-set and a body of domain knowledge

– Transfer tasks: tasks of interaction with the world, i.e., the user. These tasks are not further specified in the expertise model but are part of the communication model [11].

Below two examples of task descriptions are given for the car diagnosis example. The first task represents the top-level diagnostic task. It is a composite task.

task *car-diagnosis(C,F)*

> **task-definition**
>> **goal**:
>>> FIND a fault-state F that explains complaint C ∧
>>> all manifestations of F are observed
>>
>> **roles**:
>>> case-initial-input:
>>>> C: complaint
>>>
>>> case-user-input-data:
>>>> O: set of observation
>>>
>>> case-solution:
>>>> F: fault-state
>>
>> **task-specification**:
>>> explains(F,C) ∧
>>> ∀ M:manifestation has-manifestation(F,M) ⊢ observation(M)
>
> **task-body**
>> **sub-goals**:
>>> G1: FIND fault-state H with explains(F,C)
>>> G2: TEST H such that
>>>> ∀ M:manifestation has-manifestation(H,M) ∧
>>>> observation (M)
>>
>> **sub-tasks**:
>>> G1: generate(C,H)
>>> G2: test(H)
>>
>> **control-roles**:
>>> hypothesis H: fault-state
>>
>> **task-expression**:
>>> REPEAT
>>>> generate(C,H)
>>> UNTIL test(H)
>>> RESULT(H)

The top-level task *car-diagnosis* invokes a sub-task *generate* to achieve one of its sub-goals. This task is defined below. Its goal is derived from the parent task. The control role hypothesis becomes an output of the task. The task body calls the basic inference *generate-by-abduction*. The task is therefore a basic task.

task *generate(C,H)*

    task-definition
      goal:
        FIND fault-state H with explains(H,C)
      roles:
        case-initial-input
          C: complaint
        case-solution
          H: fault-state
      task-specification:
        generate(C,H) $\vdash$ explains(H,C)

    task-body
      task-expression:
        generate-by-abduction(C,H)

Figure 10 shows the task structure implied by these two example task descriptions.

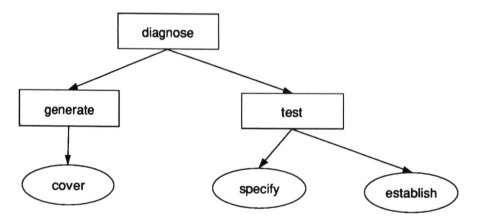

Fig. 10. Task structure for the car example. Boxes represent composite tasks; ovals primitive tasks that map to inferences.

4.4 Problem Solving Knowledge

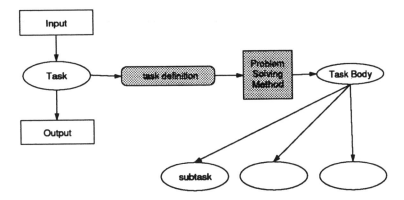

Fig. 11. Application of a problem solving method to a task definition

As explained in Sect. 3.3, problem solving knowledge consists of problem solving methods and strategic knowledge. In CommonKADS we view a problem solving method as the link between a task definition and a task body. Methods are applied to goals in the task definition and result in a decomposition of the task: the task body (Fig. 11).

A problem solving method is described as follows:

- *Goal:* a description of the goal that this method can in principle achieve.
- *Task characterization:* gives the abstract form that the the task specification of a task should have in order for the method to be in principle applicable.
- *Control roles:* any additional roles that the method introduces. These become part of the case intermediate data.
- *Sub-goals:* the sub-goals that the method sets up.
- *Definition:* a description of why the method works, what assumptions it makes and what it achieves.
- *Task expression schema:* a template for the task expression that can be used in the task definition of the task onto which the method is applied.

Below we present as an example a quite general generate-and-test problem solving method. It is the method that could be applied in the car diagnosis example to arrive at the task bodies of the two tasks that were shown previously.

> **problem-solving-method** *generate-and-test*
>   **goal**:
>   G: FIND(S:solution)
>   **task-characterization**:
>   criterium1(S) ∧ criterium2(S) ⊢ solution(S)
>   **control-roles**:
>   H: hypothesis → solution
>   **sub-goals**:
>   generate(problem, hypothesis)

test(hypothesis)

method-definition:

A1: $\forall\, x$ solution(x) $\vdash$ generate(x)

A2: $\forall\, x$ generate(x) $\wedge$ test(x) $\vdash$ solution(x)

A3: $\forall\, x$ generate(x) $\vdash$ criterium1(x)

A4: $\forall\, x$ test(x) $\vdash$ criterium2(x)

A1 $\wedge$ A2 $\wedge$ A3 $\wedge$ A4 $\vdash$ <P1> $\exists\, s$ solution(s)

task-expression-schema P1:

REPEAT

generate(C,H)

UNTIL test(H)

RESULT(H)

Basically the idea here is that the method can be applied to a task if the task specification can be interpreted as a conjunction of two criteria. The method then indicates two subgoals for generating and testing possible solutions. The method definition lists various assumptions that the method makes about the relation between these subgoals and the criteria in the task specification. Only if these assumptions are acceptable (either because they are true in the domain or it is justified to assume them) then the method should be applied. This means that the task body of the task it applies to can be instantiated according to the task expression schema. After execution of this schema, then, a solution will be found.

The approach of making explicit what the method can achieve under which conditions was first explored in the competence theories of [36]. Note that these assumptions can be translated into assumptions about the domain, depending on the way generation and testing are realized. For example, when generation is done from the subparts of the car, then it can be derived that the method is only competent to conclude about malfunctioning parts and, for instance not about faulty connections between them. Making these assumptions explicit the knowledge engineer gets an additional means of verifying the acceptability of his model.

The method definition as we have presented it allows one to check whether the method is in principle applicable. It does not say whether it is a good idea to do so. This depends on various factors related to the available knowledge and the task environment. For example, a generate and test method may be computationally too expensive even though possible, or a heuristic method that can propose erroneous solutions can be inadequate in a critical environment, and so forth. The characteristics of the task environment that determine adequacy of a problem solving method - and of a model in general - are called task features. The careful study of task features has only just begun and there does not seem to be conclusive theory about them. In CommonKADS we are approaching the problem in the context of the CommonKADS library, a library of generic models and re-usable model components. The task features are the indices into the library.

5   Building Knowledge Models

Although terminology in the various approaches to knowledge modeling differs, the knowledge types that are used in the different approaches are reasonably consistent. Where the approaches differ is in the way in which knowledge models are constructed and what knowledge types are taken as a starting point for the modeling process.

KADS emphasizes a functional viewpoint on the reasoning process: how are inferences combined in order to achieve a certain goal and what roles do domain entities play in the inference process [41]. The generic building blocks that KADS provides are at the inference level, rather than at the domain or task level [4]. The Generic Tasks approach takes a similar functional viewpoint, but the generic components are of a different grain size than the primitive inference actions in KADS [6]. A generic task realizes a functional unit that may encompass several primitive inference steps. The *role-limiting* methods developed by McDermott et al. also take a functional view: the problem solving method is fixed (e.g. Cover and Differentiate [15]) and determines what types of domain knowledge are required for a particular application [21]. This approach is similar to the use of interpretation models in KADS. An interpretation model is a fully instantiated problem solving method without the domain layer filled in. However, the models developed by McDermott's group are stronger since they impose more constraints on the domain knowledge than KADS interpretation models do.

The Components of Expertise approach emphasizes the decompositional aspects of the reasoning [32]. Its main starting point are features of the problem and correspondingly applicable problem solving methods that decompose a problem into sub problems. In the system that is being designed the resulting task structure (decomposition) can be static, i.e. the task decomposition is created during the modeling process, or it can be constructed dynamically [39].

A second aspect of the knowledge model that is considered important in the modeling approach put forward by Steels et al. concerns the domain knowledge. The types of models that are available in an application domain (structural, functional, causal models for example), are used as indication of what problem solving methods may apply to the problem.

In CommonKADS we want to support the various modeling methods through the provision of modeling tools and libraries of generic components at various levels of granularity. Below we will discuss various modeling approaches and the generic components that can support them.

5.1   Generic Components

The CommonKADS modeling framework provides a knowledge engineer with the basic constructs for defining models. However, so far we have not defined what generic components can be provided to support knowledge model construction. Such generic components can take the form of fully or partially instantiated problem solving methods, of problem solving methods that can be applied to the context of the application, or consist of components of varying grain size.

Problem Solving Methods. The most fundamental generic support for modeling is the *problem solving method*. A problem solving method is selected on the basis of a *goal description* and problem features, and is applied to the goal resulting in a decomposition of the task.

Instantiated Problem Solving Methods. Interpretation models in KADS-I can be viewed as fully instantiated problem solving models: the top-level task is decomposed through different problem solving methods until the leaves of the task tree where inference relations are referenced. In actual practice such fully instantiated problem solving methods are rarely applicable to a task that a knowledge based system must perform. However a library of such instantiated models can be a useful starting point for the knowledge engineer who through modifications of the model will create a model that is suitable for the application.

Generic Tasks. Chandrasekaran et al. have introduced the notion of *generic task*. Although a generic task is not only a specification of a task and the necessary inferences, but also includes a specification of the domain structures needed for the execution of the task, the concept will be used in CommonKADS. Generic tasks in CommonKADS are instantiated problem solving methods applied to generic task definitions at various levels of grain size. For example a generic task can be a task specification (i.e. task definition and task body) for generating hypotheses. Just as for fully instantiated problem solving models, the applicability (without modification) of the generic task is limited, as Chandrasekaran has noted too. For certain types of application domains and tasks, for example diagnosis of electronic equipment, it may be feasible to define a suite of generic tasks that can be used for configuring a problem solver.

Inference Structures. Inference structures appeared to be one of the useful tools for the knowledge engineer in KADS-I. An inference structure limits the number of possible types of inferences that occur in a model and it specifies the knowledge roles (static and dynamic) that are relevant for an application. The knowledge engineer is provided with a vocabulary for building a model and a representation of the competence of the model. The library of inference structures that was developed in KADS-I can serve as a good starting point for a more complete library of inference structures in CommonKADS.

Generic Domain Models. For certain classes of tasks, such as diagnostic tasks in certain types of domains, the required structure of the domain knowledge can be specified even if the details of the task and inference structure are still unknown.

5.2 Modeling Methods

Bottom-up Assembly from Expertise Data. One way of constructing models, albeit a tedious one, is to identify ingredients of the model in interviews and think-aloud data of an expert and assemble a model from those ingredients. The analysis of verbal data requires methods for mapping verbal statements onto the categories of the model. The problem is however, that verbal statements are usually formulated in the terminology of the application and not in generic terms. The bottom-up identification of model ingredient therefore requires a coding scheme that describes the mapping between generic components (e.g. the inference *abstract*) and natural language forms that are manifestations of such an ingredient.

Model Assembly around a Problem Solving Method. In some applications a suitable problem solving method can be identified just on the basis of problem characteristics. For example, the problem of allocating resources to agents or processes given a set of constraints, can be partially solved by a constraint satisfaction technique. However application of the problem solving method often requires additional operations in order to transform the original problem data into a format required by the problem solving method or to post-process the output of the problem solving method. For example, the resource allocation problem may be formulated as a set of requirements (e.g. incompatible persons cannot be assigned the same resource) while the constraint satisfaction method requires a constraint network as input. In that case transformation from the requirement to a network of constraints is required. In the model this means adding additional tasks and inferences.

Model assembly from Generic Components. Many modeling approaches start from a library of generic components. KADS-I relied heavily on the use of interpretation models as a basis for model refinement and adaptation. The generic task approach is based on the configuration of generic task components into a model for the application task. These and similar approaches suffer from the problem that the grain size of the library components is too coarse. A more fine grained library is needed to provide the flexibility that is needed to cover a wide range of tasks. The problem then becomes how to combine the generic components into a consistent and coherent model.

Top-down Task Decomposition. Hierarchical task decomposition is a standard form of task analysis. The top level task is decomposed through the application of decomposition methods or on the basis of empirical observations. This process results in a tree of tasks that ultimately bottoms out in primitive operations (inferences). The decomposition process is usually not guided by the nature of the domain knowledge.

Knowledge Differentiation. Knowledge differentiation is the process of introducing new knowledge roles during the modeling process. Starting point is a general knowledge model that is applicable to the task in principle, but not in practice because computational or pragmatic constraints are violated. For example in diagnostic reasoning hypotheses about the cause of a disease may be generated on the basis of any data in the case model, but this will generally result in a differential that is too large. Differentiating certain findings that are good cues for hypotheses from the ones that are indiscriminate, reduces the differential.

Structure Mapping. In some application domains the structure of the domain is available before much analysis of the reasoning processes involved has been performed. In such cases the mapping between input and output structures can be the starting point for building the knowledge model. Elements of the target structure can be compared to elements of the source structure and mapping methods can be applied. For example, in design domains where the initial requirements and the component structure of the design product are clearly defined such a mapping process can be a strong guidance for the modeling process.

6   Conclusions

The aim of the research reported in this paper was to create a unified framework for knowledge modelling in knowledge-based system development. A careful study of the various knowledge modeling approaches revealed that different approaches are not incompatible, even though terminology is often very different. A major point of disagreement that remains is the interaction hypothesis in its strong form, that states that a knowledge level model cannot be an adequate specification of a computational system without the specification of the computational constructs. We have argued against the strong interaction hypothesis and introduced a much weaker form which still allows the distinction between an analysis and a design model that is so characteristic for KADS.

A second point where the modelling framework developed here differs from the KADS-I modelling approach is the dynamics of the problem solving process. Although the strategic layer in KADS-I allowed to model very flexible problem solving behavior in principle, in actual practice such flexible models are almost never built and no library support is available. The incorporation of the notion of *problem solving method* as developed at the VUB, widens the scope of the modelling methodology. Thus, models of expert problem solving built using the CommonKADS framework can be more dynamic than the largely static models in KADS-I.

We are further developing the CommonKADS framework in two directions. The first one is toward libraries of re-usable models, called the CommonKADS library, the second one concerns the use of formal models.

- The primary role of the CommonKADS library is to support a knowledge engineer by providing generic models and re-usable building blocks. A secondary role of the CommonKADS library is to integrate the experience on modeling from the wider KBS community. Indeed, achieving a degree of re-usability is a common goal in knowledge engineering. Different views are around on how this can be realized, i.e., on what should be the nature of the re-usable components [16, 19, 24, 27, 33] and how the modeling process itself can be best characterized. As far as we know ours is the first comprehensive attempt to integrate these different views into a single library.
- In order to make our knowledge modeling framework more precise we are developing FML, a formal modeling language for CommonKADS expertise models. The advantages of a formal modeling language are in a common semantics, unambiguous models, ease of communication and the possibility to verify certain properties of the model or of the problem solving behaviors being modeled. This work extends previous results on the formalization of KADS models [38] and their operationalization [35].

Acknowledgments

Many colleagues at UvA, VUB and ECN contributed to discussions that led to this paper: Manfred Aben, Ameen Abu-Hanna, John Balder, Richard Benjamins, Bart Benus, Bert Bredeweg, Joost Breuker, Cuno Duursma, Frank van Harmelen, Wouter Jansweijer, Philip Rademakers, Johan Vanwelkenhuysen, Luc Steels, and Andre Valente. Rob Martil (Lloyd's Register), Olle Olsson and Klas Orsvarn (SICS) provided extensive comments on earlier versions.

References

1. Akkermans, H., van Harmelen, F., Schreiber, G., & Wielinga, B. (1991). A formalisation of knowledge-level models for knowledge acquistion. *International Journal of Intelligent Systems*. forthcoming.
2. Boose, J. (1985) A knowledge acquisition program for expert systems based on personal construct psychology. *Internation Journal of Man-Machine Studies*, 23:595–525, 1985.
3. Brachman, R., & Schmolze, G.J. (1985) An overview of the KL-ONE knowledge representation system. *Cognitive Science*, 9(11):216–260, 1985.
4. Breuker, J., Wielinga, B., van Someren, M., de Hoog, R., Schreiber, G., de Greef, P., Bredeweg, B., Wielemaker, J., Billault, J.-P., Davoodi, M., & Hayward, S. (1987). Model Driven Knowledge Acquisition: Interpretation Models. ESPRIT Project P1098 Deliverable D1 (task A1), University of Amsterdam and STL Ltd.
5. Breuker, J. A. & Wielinga, B. J. (1989). Model Driven Knowledge Acquisition. In Guida, P. & Tasso, G., editors, *Topics in the Design of Expert Systems*, pages 265–296, Amsterdam. North Holland.
6. Bylander, T. & Chandrasekaran, B. (1988). Generic tasks in knowledge-based reasoning: The right level of abstraction for knowledge acquisition. In Gaines, B. & J.Boose, editors, *Knowledge Acquisition for Knowledge Based Systems*, volume 1, pages 65–77. Academic Press, London.

7. Chandrasekaran, B. (1988). Generic tasks as building blocks for knowledge-based systems: The diagnosis and routine design examples. *The Knowledge Engineering Review*, 3(3):183–210.

8. Clancey, W. (1983). The epistemology of a rule based system -a framework for explanation. *Artificial Intelligence*, 20:215–251. Also: Stanford Heuristic Programming Project, Memo HPP-81-17, November 1981, also numbered STAN-CS-81-896.

9. Clancey, W. (1985a). Acquiring, representing and evaluating a competence model of diagnostic strategy. In Chi, Glaser, & Far, editors, *Contributions to the Nature of Expertise*.

10. Clancey, W. (1985b). Heuristic classification. *Artificial Intelligence*, 27:289–350.

11. de Greef, P. & Breuker, J. (1992). Analysing system-user cooperation. *Knowledge Acquisition*, 4(1).

12. de Hoog, R., Martil, R., Wielinga, B., Taylor, R., & Bright, C. (1991). Models in the kads-ii life cycle approach. ESPRIT Project P5248 KADS-II/WP1-2/TR/UvALR/018/2.0, University of Amsterdam, Lloyd's Register & Touche Ross Management Consultants.

13. Diederich, J., Ruhmann, I, & May, M. (1987) KRITON: A knowledge acquisition tool for expert systems. *International Journal of Man-Machine Studies*, 26:29–40,1987.

14. Eshelman, L. (1988). MOLE: A knowledge-acquisition tool for cover-and-differentiate systems. In Marcus, S., editor, *Automating Knowledge Acquisition for Expert Systems*, pages 37–80. Kluwer Academic Publishers, The Netherlands.

15. Eshelman, L., Ehret, D., McDermott, J., & Tan, M. (1988). MOLE: a tenacious knowledge acquisition tool. In Boose, J. & Gaines, B., editors, *Knowledge Based Systems, Volume 2: Knowledge Acquisition Tools for Expert Systems*, pages 95–108, London. Academic Press.

16. Genesereth, M. & Fikes, R.E. (1992) Knowledge Interchange Format Version 3.0 Reference Manual. Report Logic 92-1. Logic Group, Stanford University, CA.

17. Gruber, T. (1989). *The Acquisition of Strategic Knowledge*. Perspectives in Artificial Intelligence, Volume 4. Academic Press, San Diego.

18. Gruber, T. (1990). The Role of Standard Knowledge Representation for Sharing Knowledge-Based Technology. Report No. KSL 90-53. Knowledge Systems Laboratory, Stanford University, CA.

19. Gruber, T. (1992). Ontolingua: A Mechanism to Support Portable Ontologies. Version 3.0. Knowledge Systems Laboratory, Stanford University, CA.

20. Lenat, D. & Guha, R. (1990). *Building large knowledge-based systems. Representation and inference in the Cyc project*. Addison-Wesley, Reading Massachusetts.

21. McDermott, J. (1988). Preliminary steps toward a taxonomy of problem-solving methods. In Marcus, S., editor, *Automating Knowledge Acquisition for Expert Systems*, pages 225–256. Kluwer Academic, Boston, 1988.

22. McDermott, J. (1989). The world would be a better place if non-programmers could program. *Machine Learning*, 4(3/4):337–338.

23. Musen, M. (1989). *Automated Generation of Model-Based Knowledge-Acquisition Tools*. Pitman, London. Research Notes in Artificial Intelligence.

24. Musen, M. (1991). Dimensions of Knowledge Sharing and Reuse. Report KSL-91-65. Knowledge Systems Laboratory, Stanford University, CA.

25. Newell, A. (1982). The knowledge level. *Artificial Intelligence*, 18:87–127.

26. Newell, A. (1990). *Unified Theories of Cognition*. Harvard University Press, Cambridge, MA.

27. Puerta, A., Edgar, J., Tu, S., & Musen, M. (1991) A multiple-method knowledge-acquisition shell for the automatic generation of knowledge-acquisition tools. In Boose, J., & Musen, M., editors, *Proceedings of the 6th Banff Knowledge Acquisition Workshop*, pages 20/1–20/19, AAAI, University of Calgary, 1991.

28. Schreiber, G. (1992). CML language constructs. ESPRIT Project P5248 KADS-II/T1.1/TR/UvA/023/1.0, University of Amsterdan.

29. Schreiber, G., Akkermans, H., & Wielinga, B. (1991). On problems with the knowledge level perspective. In Steels, L. & Smith, B., editors, *AISB-91: Artificial Intelligence and Simulation of behaviour*, pages 208–221, London. Springer Verlag. Also in: *Proceedings Banff-90 Knowledge Acquisition Workshop*, J.H. Boose and B.R. Gaines (editors), SRDG Publications, University of Calgary, pages 30-1 – 30-14.

30. Schreiber, G., Wielinga, B., & Akkermans, H. (1992). Differentiating problem solving methods. In Wetter, T., Althoff, K.-D., Boose, J., Gaines, B., Linster, M., & Schmalhofer, F., editors, *Current Developments in Knowledge Acquisition - EKAW'92*, Berlin/Heidelberg. Springer Verlag.

31. Steels, L. (1984). Second Generation Expert Systems. *Future Generation Computer Systems*, 1(4).

32. Steels, L. (1990). Components of expertise. *AI Magazine*, Summer 90. Also as: AI Memo 88-16. AI-Lab, Vrije Universiteit Brussel, Brussels.

33. Steels, L. (1992). Reusability and configuration of applications by non-programmers. AI Memo 92-4. AI-Lab, Vrije Universiteit Brussel, Brussels.

34. Sticklen, J. (1989). Problem solving architecture at the knowledge level. *Journal of Experimental and Theoretical Artificial Intelligence*.

35. ten Teije, A., van Harmelen, F. & Reinders, M. (1991) Si(ML)2: a prototype interpreter for a subset of (ML)$\hat{2}$. Technical Report ESPRIT Project P5248 KADS-II/T1.2/TR/UvA/005/1.0, University of Amsterdam & Netherlands Energy Research Foundation ECN.

36. Van de Velde, W. (1988) Inference stucture as a basis for problem solving. In Kodratoff, Y., editor, *Proceedings of the 8th European Conference on Artificial Intelligence*, pages 202–207. Pitman, London.

37. Van de Velde, W. (1991). Tractable rationality at the knowledge-level. In Steels, L. & Smith, B., editors, *Proceedings AISB'91: Artificial Intelligence and Simulation of Behaviour*, pages 196–207, London. Springer Verlag.

38. Van Harmelen, F. & Balder, J.R. (1992) (ML)2: A formal language for kads models of expertise. *Knowledge Acquisition*, 4(1).

39. Vanwelkenhuysen, J. & Rademakers, P. (1990). Mapping knowledge-level analysis onto a computational framework. In Aiello, L., editor, *Proceedings of the 9th European Conference on Artificial Intelligence*, pages 681–686. Pitman, London.

40. Wielinga, B. & Breuker, J. (1986). Models of expertise. In Steels, L., editor, *Proceedings of the 7th European Conference on Artificial Intelligence*, pages 306–318. North-Holland, Amsterdam.

41. Wielinga, B. J., Schreiber, A. T., & Breuker, J. A. (1992). KADS: A modelling approach to knowledge engineering. *Knowledge Acquisition*, 4(1).

42. Yourdon, E. (1989). *Managing the Structured Techniques*. Yourdon Press, Englewood Cliffs, New Jersey.

On The Relationship between Knowledge-based Systems Theory and Application Programs: Leveraging Task Specific Approaches*

Jon Sticklen and Eugene Wallingford

AI/KBS Laboratory • CPS Department • Michigan State University
East Lansing, Michigan 48824-1027   USA

Abstract. The relationship between theories of knowledge-based problem solving and application-level programs is not well understood. The traditional view has been that given some knowledge-based systems theory, a successful application program built following the theory provides strong support for the theory. This viewpoint fails largely because the link between theory and application is totally through the human implementer of the application program. Insight for how to cope with this problem can be obtained from the Knowledge Level Hypothesis (KLH) of Newell. But in order for the KLH to be helpful, we must extend it to incorporate concepts of control knowledge. After describing the theory/application linkage problem, we go on to give an overview of the task specific approaches to knowledge-based system. We then discuss both Newell's KLH and an extension to it that will help in solving the AI Theory/AI application linkage problem. We end with the recommendation that knowledge-based systems theory could be grouped with those disciplines in which theory verification by experimental inquiry is the norm.

1. Introduction

The relationship between knowledge-based systems theory and application-level programs is not well understood. In the early "roaring 80's," rule-based systems were thought to be capable of expert level problem solving in any selected domain, and the link between theories of expert-level problem solving and applications was perceived to be 1:1. That is, when a researcher developed a theory of problem solving P, he "tested" P by implementing a problem solver performing some task P_1 exercising P. In many cases,

---

*   Sticklen and Wallingford gratefully acknowledge the support of DAPRA (ARPA 8673), the NSF Center for High Speed Low Cost Polymer Composites Processing at MSU (EEC-9108846), the McDonnell Douglas Research Laboratories, and generous equipment support from Apple Computer.

starting with the MYCIN applications themselves [1, 2], the implemented systems were built following a rule-based approach. The difficulty was that the theory under test when using a rule-based approach is fundamentally that "expert-level, domain-oriented problem solving can be captured in a rule-based approach."

That claim – that any problem solving can be captured in a rule based approach – is not illuminating because it only paraphrases the Turing Thesis, provided we assume that expert level problem solving is a computable function. The Turing Thesis is that an abstract computational engine (the Turing Machine) can compute anything that is computable. The Turing Machine is a bridge between mathematical theory and the realization of computational machines. Although embodying a different architecture from Turing Machines, Post Production Machines were shown to be equivalent in computational power to Turing Machines. Finally, Post Production Machines are an abstract computational model which can be realized in rule-based system shells. Given the Turing Thesis, a rule-based system can in fact compute *anything* that is computable. Thus, linking a particular AI theory to the performance of a rule-based implemented program has no justification.

In the early 80's many conference and journal papers were devoted to describing working knowledge-based systems (see AAAI-80 for example). By the end of the decade, a much smaller percentage of conference and journal papers appeared which described implemented systems (see AAAI-90 for example). In fact, in some AI quarters it is now very unfashionable to talk about implemented systems.

In this position paper, we argue that we currently risk "throwing out the baby with the bathwater" – that knowledge-based systems is an area in which experimental testing of theory is natural provided we take a high level view of problem solving. We will argue that the broad task-specific architectures (TSA) approach to knowledge-based systems supports such a high level perspective. We claim that an extension to the Knowledge Level Hypothesis of Newell is necessary to provide the link between knowledge-based system theory and program artifact, and we describe one such extension.

2. Background

The lineage of our argument lies in three areas: reflection on the first generation of knowledge-based systems, the task specific architecture (TSA) reaction to shortcomings in the first generation, and finally the attempt by Newell to free discussion of problem solving systems from vocabulary of implementation, the Knowledge Level Hypothesis.

2.1. Experience from the First Generation

The roots of knowledge-based systems are in problems of *search* . For typical problems, the use of weak problem solving methods gave rise to very high search complexity forcing the application of heuristic knowledge to control search. By encoding such control knowledge within the same "universal architecture" in which the weak methods were built, the goal was to retain many of the advantages of these architectures: modularity, uniform representation, and a single control strategy among them. The use of unitary architectures lead to unexpected disadvantages as well (see, for example, [3]). In particular, there were two difficulties:

- important control issues were hidden behind clever programming artifices at the implementation-language level, and

- system builders encountered the need to organize knowledge in the system using constructs outside the formalism provided by the architecture, such as MYCIN's *context hierarchy* [1, 2] and PROSPECTOR's *models* [4].

Even if a knowledge-based system could be built at the level of a unitary architecture, the *conceptual* problems of analysis and design would not vanish; problems at higher levels of abstraction need to be addressed.

Studies in Knowledge Acquisition (KA) yielded important advances in understanding the use of specialized vocabularies for representing knowledge-based problem solving. The knowledge acquisition problem was described in terms of the *representation mismatch* between the conceptual constructs of human experts and the implementation primitives used to analyze and build KBSs, a representational gap that limited the ability of domain experts to play a direct role in the construction and maintenance of systems [5]. This perspective led to languages and architectures that provide conceptual primitives closer to the task-level abstractions of experts "to reduce representation mismatch from the implementation side" [6]. The task-level architectures produced from this perspective provided greater power for knowledge acquisition because they incorporated explicit representations of the *types* of knowledge expected from those specializing in particular tasks. This enabled the construction of user interfaces for knowledge acquisition systems that relied on simpler syntactic techniques which presupposed the existence of the necessary conceptual structures. In the end, the high-level primitives thus employed could be mapped onto the implementation primitives of a unitary architecture without exposing domain experts to the vagaries inherent in programming such architectures.

Two intuitions grew from common experience with first generation approaches: (1) Certain knowledge and control structures may be common to a particular task (say, design or diagnosis) across different domains, and (2) the structures for different task types will likely differ. Both retrospective analysis of existing systems and prospective design of new systems indicated that an effective KBS will contain — either explicitly or implicitly — a model of the problem solving process it realizes. The evolving task-specific approach recognized the advantages of representing *explicitly* the conceptual organization of domain knowledge assembled to solve a particular type of problem following a given method. This approach denoted a paradigm shift away from use-independent, uniform knowledge bases toward a view of KBSs as collections of diverse conceptual structures organized for use in targeted ways. Weak methods are appropriate when no further knowledge of a domain is available, but typically expertise in a domain affords a more meaningful understanding of how knowledge is used to solve problems efficiently. This new outlook signified one of the central lesson of the first generation.

2.2. TSA Viewpoints

Through the 1980's there were a number of research efforts aimed at solving difficulties met in computation-universal approaches to knowledge-based systems. The *Generic Task* (GT) approach of Chandrasekaran and his colleagues has evolved as one of these efforts. The assumption of the GT approach is that knowledge takes different forms depending on its intended function [7-10]. Following the Generic Task view, a problem is analyzed according to the methods associated with solving it, where each method can be specified by the forms of knowledge and inference necessary to apply the method, and by the subproblems that must be solved to carry it out. These sub-problems can then be recursively decomposed in a similar fashion. The assumption of the GT approach is that there exist a number of ubiquitous *combinations* of method, knowledge structure, and inference structure — termed generic tasks — that serve as sub-problems for a variety of complex problem-solving tasks in a variety of domains. The totality of domain knowledge for solving a given problem is viewed as a composition of generic task "agents" that interact based upon their functions and information needs.

Another prominent view of problem solving in knowledge-based systems was due to Clancey. After recognizing that the control strategies implicit in the MYCIN/GUIDON knowledge base could be expressed independent of domain terminology [11], Clancey isolated *heuristic classification* as a method for performing diagnosis and other selection tasks [12-14]. This method decomposes selection tasks into a set of high-level subtasks that characterize the type of problem solving performed by many existing KBSs. By moving to this more abstract level of description, Clancey and his colleagues were able to reformulate MYCIN into NEOMYCIN, a system whose control knowledge made no reference to the application domain and constituted an abstract model of inference independent of implementation.

McDermott and his colleagues have formulated a view of expert problem solving, based on the notion of *role-limiting methods* (RLMs), that is strongly driven by experiences in knowledge acquisition. The RLM approach posits that a large knowledge base can be constructed, maintained, and understood more fruitfully by organizing it according to the various roles that different kinds of knowledge play. On this view, "each role-limiting method defines the roles that the task-specific knowledge it requires must play and the forms in which that knowledge can be represented" [15]. Like Chandrasekaran and Clancey, McDermott holds that families of tasks exist for which the problem solving method and its control knowledge can be abstracted away from the peculiarities of an task instance. This approach, though, focuses its concern with these methods on how they circumscribe the roles and representation of the task-specific domain knowledge on which they operate. The goal of this research program is to identify task families having these characteristics, to abstract their methods, and then to construct an architecture that assists knowledge acquisition for the corresponding tasks. For the purpose of knowledge acquisition, the RLMs represent an important class of methods because they direct the acquisition process at a more abstract level while still providing a broad coverage of tasks in a variety of domains.

Structured methodologies for the construction of application systems following the TSA viewpoint have been developed mainly in Europe. Steels [16] has advocated a framework for system analysis and development with some similarities to Chandrasekaran's task-oriented approach. Following Steels, one first conducts a thorough task analysis in which the task is decomposed into subtasks based on the nature of their inputs and outputs and on the nature of the mappings among them. Second, one constructs a model of the domain knowledge available to perform the task and subtasks. Finally, one applies problem solving methods geared to solving individual subtasks and to structuring subtasks in the pursuance of higher-level tasks. The method selected for each task depends on the kind of knowledge available to solve the task, as captured in the domain model. This methodology differs from that espoused by Chandrasekaran and McDermott, however, in that it allows for a representation of domain knowledge — in the domain model — independent of the method to be selected.

Founded on similar intuitions, KADS is a methodology for the construction of knowledge-based systems that offers an explicit software life cycle and a set of languages for describing and creating KBS structures. This methodology rests on the assumption that task methods share "ways of using knowledge" at a level of abstraction higher than that of concepts in particular domains [17]. The languages in KADS support the development of a *conceptual model* of the problem solving process and a *design model* of the target KBS at a level of abstraction corresponding to the types of knowledge employed. KADS proposes a four-layer representation of knowledge: (1) a domain layer of domain-dependent concepts, relations, and structures; (2) an inference layer that describes what inferences can be made in terms of the *roles* that domain-level entities play; (3) a task layer that controls when inferences are made in terms of goal structures; and (4) a strategy layer for goal generation and task monitoring. Like Steels' approach, KADS allows "task-neutral" representation of domain knowledge but then stresses the importance of having high-level task structures through which to view problem-solving knowledge. These structures include primitive "knowledge sources" at the inference level for solving particular subtasks and goal structures at the task level for representing task decompositions.

2.3. The Knowledge Level Hypothesis

In his AAAI presidential address of 1980 [18], Newell proposed a distinct level of analyses for problem solving systems above the symbol level. In the *Knowledge Level Hypothesis*, an implementation-free framework for analyzing problem solving agents was suggested. Since its introduction, the term "Knowledge Level" has become pervasive in the AI literature, particularly in the Expert Systems field. In broad terms, the Knowledge Level Hypothesis has been important in promoting a gradual shift in emphasis away from purely representational issues and toward implementation free descriptions of problem solving.

> *The Knowledge Level Hypothesis (KLH):* There exists a distinct computer systems level, lying immediately above the symbol level, which is characterized by knowledge as the medium and with the principle of rationality as the law of behavior.

The most important parts of Newell's hypothesis are as follows:

- The entire information processing system is identified at the Knowledge Level as the "agent." By identifying the agent as the total system at the Knowledge Level, Newell implicitly acknowledges the view that at the Knowledge Level the separability of problem solving engines and the bodies of domain knowledge they utilize is illusory. Rather, in terms that can be useful at the Knowledge Level, problem solving and domain knowledge are intimately entangled, and the agent must be analyzed on this basis. This opens the issue of the appropriate granularity at which to describe Knowledge Level agents, a discussion to which we will return.

- Knowledge has a generative flavor and cannot be captured in a static data structure; i.e., cannot be expressed at the symbol level. The emphasis that knowledge itself is unbounded and the resultant importance of the generative nature of Knowledge Level constructs is an outgrowth of Newell's goal of shifting attention away from representation issues: issues that are properly dealt with at the symbol level.

- The attribution of knowledge to an agent is via a process of simulation by self; i.e., a simulation with the "self" being the agent and an assumption by "self" of the goals and symbol-level structures of the other to produce the same actions as the other.

- The central role of self simulation in the attribution of knowledge to an agent is both a source of substantial power in the Knowledge Level Hypothesis, as well as a source of considerable weakness. The power comes *via* the identification of how we may know that an agent has certain knowledge even though we are unable to look inside that agent. The weakness comes because by using "self" as the simulator, we cannot produce reliable predictions for future behavior.

The incompleteness of the Knowledge Level Hypothesis is shown by its lack of guidance for making predictive statements for some problem solver. Suppose we subscribe to the hypothesis of the Knowledge Level and, further, also subscribe to the knowledge-level assertion of Clancey that classification problem solving involves the trivalent processes of data abstraction, heuristic match, and refinement to a problem of "...characterization of a particular case into one of a set of pre-enumerated possibilities" [13]. Further suppose that the target problem can be characterized as having a set of pre-enumerated answers. Utilizing the Knowledge Level, we assume that the processes of data abstraction, heuristic match, and refinement should exist in the Knowledge Level solution somewhere, but that is all we know. This argument that the KL as described by Newell is incomplete is more fully developed in [19].

Dietterich points out the same problem with using the Knowledge Level. In a clever example of a "perfect chess player" [20], Dietterich shows that the Knowledge Level provides a way of discussing what the chess playing agent knows, i.e., the knowledge the player has; but that the Knowledge Level gives us no clue about how to start building a chess playing agent. Indeed, although we can discuss the knowledge the agent has for any particular move, implementing such a "perfect chess player" would be infeasible. Although Dietterich is chiefly concerned with the "how to build it" issue, the "what predictions would I make" issue is inherent in his example.

The major thrust of Newell's arguments is to move away from implementation level details toward a deeper understanding of problem solving. We argue that the Knowledge Level as it stands is incomplete due to its lack of a predictive component. The question is how can we prescribe an overall problem solving scheme to make predictive statements, and at the same time avoid implementation details? The short answer is that the way of prescribing the problem solving must be stated in terms appropriate to the problem solving activity itself.

2.4. Background Synthesis

Results of first generation, unitary problem solving approaches led some researchers (Breuker & Wielinga, Chandrasekaran, McDermott, Steels, ...) to develop representational approaches which were more direct embodiments of the domain knowledge that they sought to embed in their problem solvers. At the highest level, each developed domain and control *vocabularies* specialized for some specified set of problem solving methods. In addition to very practical concerns such as knowledge acquisition, this "task specific architectures" approach emphasized the need to develop families of implementation languages tailored for specific problem solving situations and available knowledge sources. Along a seemingly different track, Newell proposed the separation of analysis of knowledge systems from implementation concerns altogether.

In fact, these two thrusts have a common denominator: the desire to analyze problem solving in "natural" terms. For Newell, this term "natural" first meant pure knowledge-level terms, with no symbols to be used at all. For the TSA schools, "natural" meant in a representation and control vocabulary tailored for the task being modeled.

3. The Knowledge Level Architecture

In [19], Sticklen proposed an extension to the Knowledge Level Hypothesis (KLH) of Newell. This extension, the Knowledge Level Architecture Hypothesis (KLAH), is in fact a generalization of the TSA viewpoint.

> ***Knowledge Level Architecture Hypothesis (KLAH):*** If a problem solving agent may be decomposed into the cooperative efforts of a number of sub-agents, the larger agent can be understood at the Knowledge Level by giving a Knowledge Level description of the sub-agents and specifying the architecture the composition follows.

Each composed agent, taken as a complete entity, can be analyzed in accord with Newell's view; each has components of goals, a body of knowledge, and primitive transducers, and each obeys the principle of rationality.

Each primitive agent also has goals, a body of knowledge, and primitive transducers that are shared with the composed agent. Here, too, the primitive agents obey the law of rationality. The only difference so far is that more primitive agents, which together composed a higher-level agent, and share primitive transducers. And further that these transducers appear to belong to the agent from the agent's perspective.

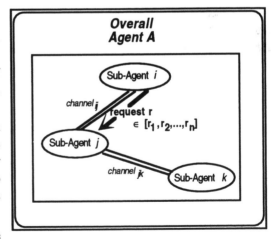

The manner in which the primitive agents are allowed to interact with one another is **restricted** by an imposed **Knowledge Level Architecture**. This architecture is defined by two ingredients. First, the Knowledge Level Architecture must fix the paths of communication along which the sub-agents agents may interact. This is a way of setting the structural relationship between the sub-agents. Put another way, decomposing the agent to sub-agents and fixing the communication paths (taking both steps together) is a way of *organizing*   the knowledge of the agent.

Second, the Knowledge Level Architecture must fix the message protocols which the sub-agents follow to communicate with one another. Assuming that sub-agents do not take independent action but rather act only when requested to, fixing the content of communications between the sub-agents is a way of expressing the goals of the sub-agents. The elements of the Knowledge Level Architecture are shown graphically below.

The hypothesis of a Knowledge Level Architecture should be taken as an adjunct to the Knowledge Level hypothesis itself; clearly if no such thing as a Knowledge Level exists, it does not have an architecture. If, however, there is a distinct Knowledge Level of the type described by Newell, then whenever the agent can be decomposed to sub-agents the Knowledge Level Architecture Hypothesis provides a framework for interpreting the actions of a composite agent by specifying the interaction of an ensemble of sub-agents.

Newell argues that the usefulness of the Knowledge Level lies in predicting and understanding behavior without having an operational model of the processing actually being done by the agent. The utility is basically to enable an implementation-free description of a problem solving agent. The Knowledge Level Architecture allows the same sort of implementation-free description while demanding an account of how the agent functions *at the Knowledge   Level*. The central issue here is what we mean by "implementation-free." Newell's original notion of the Knowledge Level limits description of how a problem solving agent functions by disallowing any discussion of problem solving control. Our extension, on the other hand, allows discussion of such questions, *but only in the vocabulary of knowledge   organization   and control*.

The vocabulary of the KLA (subagents, communication paths, communication protocols) is used to analyze a given problem solver. To the extent the analysis is successful, a particular Knowledge Level architecture will be produced, and this will be tantamount to producing a task specific architecture for performing the stated task.

It is important to distinguish three levels of description for knowledge systems:

- **The individual problem solver:**   The functioning MYCIN system is an example at this level. The vocabulary used for discussion here is the set of terms necessary in the domain of the problem solver; e.g., for MYCIN, the terms would include strep infection, patient fever, etc.

- **The problem solving type:**   MYCIN performs a type of classification problem solving. But the utility of classification is much more general. The proper epistemic terms to use at this level are the primitives for classification itself; i.e., for any system that is undertaking classification. For example, all classification systems have categories around which final answers are framed. Thus a necessary primitive for properly representing classification must be the classificatory category.

- *The Knowledge Level Architecture:* At this level, for agents which can be decomposed to an ensemble of cooperating sub-agents, we set the terms which will be used to describe the problem solving types expressed at the next lower level. These terms are in three categories: the principles for sub-agent decomposition, the organizational principles of the sub-agents (i.e., the communication channels), and the repertoire of messages which the sub-agents will understand. Note that the KLA sets the vocabulary for the description of *control* in the general problem solving types at the next lower level (the problem solving type level.

4. Link Between KBS Theory and KBS Application

There are two broad traditions for theory testing: mathematical proof and experimental testing. Some segments of AI tend more towards the mathematical-proof variant on theory testing, for example the logic school. But for Knowledge-Based Systems, the TSA viewpoint in general, and the KLAH provide a footing for the development of a experimental paradigm for theory testing.

Scientific theories must accomplish two goals. First, theory must account for known phenomena. Second, theory must make verifiable predictions about as yet unobserved phenomena. These criteria for scientific theory have been suggested by many philosophers of science, and have broad acceptance within the scientific community itself. For example, a widely used definition of science due to Conant is

> Science is an interconnected series of concepts and conceptual schemes that have developed as a results of experimentation and observation and are *fruitful* of further experimentation and observation. [21, page 25]

The "fruitful" part of Conant's definition is aimed clearly at prediction. One way for an AI theory to be predictive is for it to have a prescriptive component, where our sense of "prescription" is that the theory offers guidance in the construction of problem solving systems in the domain of the theory.

Suppose that we have an intelligent agent $\mathcal{A}$ for which we hold a theory $\mathcal{T}$. Following the above discussion, $\mathcal{T}$ should have two characteristics.

- First, given a known behavior $\mathcal{B}$ of $\mathcal{A}$, $\mathcal{T}$ should explain why $\mathcal{A}$ took the action $\mathcal{B}$ as opposed to other possible actions. For example following the observation of an agent's behavior, the Knowledge Level Hypothesis allows us to explain that behavior by ascribing to the agent compatible goals and knowledge, i.e., goals and knowledge that lead to the observed behavior.

- Second, $\mathcal{T}$ must also allow us to make predictions about future problem solving behavior $\mathcal{B}'$ of $\mathcal{A}$.

The first point above is obvious; the second requires more discussion. In science, when we say "Theory $\mathcal{T}$ predicts that $\mathcal{B}$ will be observed under conditions...," then an attempt is usually made to verify the prediction as a *test* of the theory. Of course, this is precisely why the second, predictive element of theory is important. Without the requirement that theory should predict phenomena as yet unobserved, we run the risk of simply fitting theory to known observations.

Centering now on the need to make predictions about future behavior, the next task becomes indicating *how* such predictions can be made. Let us look to a well established science for inspiration: physics. For some theories of physical phenomena, prediction becomes a matter of working out a closed form solution to some mathematical expression. However, not all situations which physical theory address have closed form solutions. Consider, for example, the astrophysical theory of stellar structure. There are five relatively simple equations of state which describe the theory of various forces in action inside a star. There is in general no closed form solution to these equations. Thus in order to make useful predictions from the current state of their theory, astrophysicists use the equations of state as the basis for a time based numerical simulation. The results of this simulation are predictions of the physical behavior of stars over time. Note that there are two bodies of knowledge which the astrophysicist utilizes to make his predictions: knowledge of the physical theory as expressed mathematically, and knowledge of how to perform a numerical simulation based on such equations. The two types of knowledge are forged into a simulation *model* of a star that is then capable of prediction.

No one would confuse a simulation model of a star with the actual star — it would be hard to get enough energy out a simulation model to energize a planetary system! But suppose that our theory concerns itself with problem solving agents, and the phenomena we want to make predictions about is the behavior of a problem solving agent. If we construct a simulation model $\mathcal{S}$ of some problem solving agent $\mathcal{A}$ which is based on a theory $\mathcal{T}$, and this model can successfully predict behavior $\mathcal{B}'$ of $\mathcal{A}$, then in fact our simulation model $\mathcal{S}$ is itself a (constructed) problem solving agent, at least if one accepts the Turing Test as a basis for calling something a problem solving agent. In the realm of information systems, a simulator of a problem solving agent is itself a problem solving agent.

Which kind of prediction (direct or simulation) do/will problem solving theories support? The "do" part is straightforward — currently there do not exist theories of problem solving that make direct detailed predictions about future behavior. But we cannot say that there will *never* be such a theory, and hence a definitive answer cannot be offered for the "will" part of the question. There are a number of research programs currently under way that will produce predictions about problem solving behavior (for example, the SOAR project) but all are based on a simulation of a problem solving agent.

If theory of problem solving is simulation-based, then another way of viewing it is that it is a statement of *how to construct* an agent to undertake the problem solving. This is a result of a strong difference between theory-based simulations that are predictive in the physical sciences, and theory-based simulations that are predictive for problem solving phenomena.

And this brings us to the bottom line for this section. Although there is not conclusive proof that we cannot construct problem solving theory capable of "direct prediction" for problem solving, current experience leads us to believe that such theory would be at best very difficult to enunciate.

Typically, we associate a prescriptive set of directions for building an artifact with an engineering discipline, not with a science. In the case of theories of problem solving, we have argued that, in order for the theory to have the important criterion of the ability to predict phenomena, the theory will be a statement of how to build a simulator for problem solving. But that simulator itself will be a problem solving agent. Hence, in addition to being a scientific statement, the theory is also a prescriptive statement for building such agents. This argument sheds light on the confusion that is often seen in arguments about whether knowledge-based systems is an engineering discipline or a science: a good KBS theory is *both*.

5. Conclusion

In this report, we have described an extension to Newell's Knowledge Level Hypothesis (KLH) called the Knowledge Level Architecture Hypothesis (KLAH). First described in [19], the KLAH is best understood as a generalization of the Task Specific Architectures view that has been gaining adherents over the last decade. A similar intuition was recently used by Van de Velde (of Steels group) to offer a different extension of Newell's Knowledge Level. While we have proposed a decomposition of the monolithic agent of Newell to the cooperative efforts of a number of subagents connected together by our KLA, Van de Velde decomposed the "principle of rationality" of Newell into a general part (similar to Newell's original) and to a second portion which would contain the control goals of particular tasks [22]. Even more recently, the SOAR community under Newell's leadership has also developed a systems description level intermediate between the symbol level and the knowledge level [23], which addresses similar concerns to our KLA level of description.

We have described how the KLAH provides a framework in which particular TSAs may be viewed as Knowledge Level constructs. A particular TSA can then be used both as

348

a prescription for building actual systems and as a statement of a problem solving theory. Once the TSA-blueprinted system is built, it may be used to predict future behavior — the TSA statement of theory is susceptible to experimental testing.

We started this report with a discussion of the shortcomings of the unitary problem solving techniques of the first generation of knowledge-based systems. Those shortcomings were typically traced to the representation of problem solving being carried out at too low a level, typically in a computation-universal framework. The bottom line of our argument for TSAs and for the KLAH framework for understanding TSAs is that by constraining what can be done in a given problem solver to targeted tasks, and doing this through limitations in representational primitives and control constructs, it is possible to forge a link between problem solving theory and problem solving application. The central facet of our argument is the *duality* for problem solving systems between a blueprint to build the system and a statement of the theory backing the problem solver.

This report owes much to the intellectual ferment and excitement of the Laboratory for AI Research at Ohio State University, and to all associated with that laboratory. In addition, recent discussions between the first author and Luc Steels have been helpful in settling these ideas. Comments of the editors, reviewers, and discussants of the original statement of the KLAH, which appeared in **JETAI**, were extremely useful in helping to clarify our proposal.

References

1. Buchanan, B. and E.H. Shortliffe, *Rule-Based Expert Systems: The MYCIN Experiments of the Stanford Heuristic Programming Project.* 1984, Addison-Wesley.

2. Shortliffe, E.H., *Computer Based Medical Consultations: MYCIN.* 1976, Elsevier North Holland Inc.

3. Chandrasekaran, B. *Towards a Functional Architecture for Intelligence Based on Generic Information Processing Tasks.* in *IJCAI-87.* 1987. Milan.

4. Duda, R.O. and J. Gaschnig, *Model Design in the Prospector Consultant System for Mineral Exploration,* in *Expert Systems in the Micro-Electronic Age,* D. Michie, Editor. 1979, Edinburgh University Press.

5. Bylander, T. and B. Chandrasekaran, *Generic Tasks for Knowledge-Based Reasoning: The 'Right' Level of Abstraction for Knowledge Acquisition.* Int. J. Man-Machine Studies, 1987. **26**(2): p. 231-243.

6. Gruber, T. and P. Cohen, *Design for Acquisition: Principles of Knowledge-System Design to Facilitate Knowledge Acquisition.* International Journal of Man-Machine Studies, 1987. **26**: p. 143-159.

7. Chandrasekaran, B. *Decomposition of Domain Knowledge into Knowledge Sources: The MDX Approach.* in *Proc. 4th Nat. Conf. Canadian Society for Computational Studies of Intelligence.* 1982.

8. Chandrasekaran, B., *Towards a Taxonomy of Problem-Solving Types*. AI Magazine, 1983. **4**(1): p. 9-17.

9. Chandrasekaran, B., *Generic Tasks in Knowledge-Based Reasoning: High-Level Building Blocks for Expert System Design*. IEEE Expert, 1986. p. 23-30.

10. Chandrasekaran, B., J.W. Smith, and J. Sticklen, *Deep Models and their Relation to Diagnosis*, in *Artificial Intelligence in Medicine*, Furukawa, Editor. 1989, Science Publishers: Amsterdam, Netherlands.

11. Clancey, W.J. *NEOMYCIN: Reconfiguring a Rule-Based Expert System for Application To Teaching*. in *Proceedings of IJCAI 7*. 1981.

12. Clancey, W.J. *Advantages of Abstract Control Knowledge in Expert System Design*. in *Proceedings of AAAI*. 1983.

13. Clancey, W.J. *Classification Problem Solving* in *Proceedings of the AAAI*. 1984.

14. Clancey, W.J., *Representing Control Knowledge as Abstract Tasks and Metarules*. 1985, Stanford University: Palo Alto.

15. McDermott, J., *Preliminary Steps Toward a Taxonomy of Problem-Solving Methods*, in *Automating Knowledge Acquisition for Expert Systems*, S. Marcus, Editor. 1988, Kluver Academic Publishers: Boston. p. 225-255.

16. Steels, L., *The Components of Expertise*. AI Magazine, 1990. **Summer, 1990**.

17. Breuker, J. and B. Wielinga, *Models of Expertise in Knowledge Acquisition*, in *Topics in Expert Systems Design: Methodologies and Tools*, G. Guida and C. Tasso, Editor. 1989, North Holland Publishing Company: Amsterdam.

18. Newell, A., *The Knowledge Level*. AI Magazine, 1982. **Summer**: p. 1-19.

19. Sticklen, J., *Problem Solving Architectures at the Knowledge Level*. Journal of Experimental and Theoretical Artificial Intelligence, 1989. **1**: p. 1-52.

20. Dietterich, T.G., *Learning at the Knowledge Level*. Machine Learning, 1986. **1**: p. 287-316.

21. Conant, J.B., *Science and Common Sense*. 1951, Yale University Press.

22. Van de Velde, W. *Tractable Rationality at the Knowledge Level*. in *Artificial Intelligence and Simulation of Behaviour (AISB)*. 1991. Leeds, GB: Springer-Verlag.

23. Newell, A., et al., *Formulating the problem space computational model*, in *Carnegie-Mellon Computer Science: A 25-year Commemorative Reading*, R.F. Rashid, Editor. 1991, ACM-Press, Addison-Wesley.

Generic Models and Their Support in Modeling Problem Solving Behavior

Philip Rademakers and Johan Vanwelkenhuysen

Artificial Intelligence Laboratory,
Vrije Universiteit Brussel,
Pleinlaan 2, B-1050 Brussels, Belgium,
E-mail: filip/johan@arti.vub.ac.be

Abstract. Generic models have received widespread attention in knowledge based systems research (KBS) as an important aid in the process of modeling "problem solving behavior". However, little empirical evidence has been presented which justifies this role. In this article, we analyze some of our experiences with using generic models of problem solving in industrial projects. In these projects, we have relied upon generic models to support the acquisition and modeling process as advocated by current modeling methodologies. Based on these experiences, we argue that there is a real danger that practitioners might be misleaded by inappropriate generic models because current modeling methodologies do not sufficiently address the issues related to selecting, refining and instantiating generic models. To avoid this costly endeavor, we argue that modeling methodologies should emphasize more the nature of the domain, the work that people do, the role of the environment and an active role of the expert. We also emphasize the importance of a tight coupling between the modeling activity and validation. Validation should be carried out with respect to the expert source and the contribution of each model construct towards the intended goal of the models. The paper concludes with remarks on a framework that we call "validation through remodeling".

1 Introduction

Similar to software engineering, knowledge engineering encompasses all activities concerned with the specification, development and integration of a computerized system. The major difference between both disciplines is that knowledge engineering achieves system specification and implementation by relying heavily on observations and analyses the problem solving behavior of human experts. Consequently, modeling (observed or intended) behavior[1] plays a central role in knowledge engineering.

Existing modeling methodologies provide the knowledge engineer with a language, a modeling framework and a library of predefined generic models to construct models of observable or intended problem solving behavior. The key idea

---

[1] When we use the term "behavior" we mean "problem solving behavior".

behind these generic models is to support the knowledge engineer in the knowledge acquisition and model construction process. In particular, generic models generally fulfill two purposes in the modeling process[2]: (i) they serve as templates for top-down knowledge acquisition and (ii) they can be used as skeletons to which observed (raw) data can be abstracted.

In spite of the widespread attention generic models receive as modeling tools, there is little empirical evidence concerning their practical applicability in large scale system development. In two industrial projects, we have applied many ideas from existing modeling approaches, in particular the use of generic modeling components. This paper reports on some problems we experienced while trying to apply these ideas. Motivated by these experiences, we argue that:

1. Generic models often mislead the knowledge engineer and/or system designer because they tend to abstract away many important details that turn out to be relevant in later stages of the life cycle. Generic models largely influence what one perceives but also what one does not perceive! To avoid this possible problem and its associated cost, we propose that modeling methodologies should put more emphasis on the nature of the domain (and the work that people do in general), the role of the environment and the active role of the domain expert.

2. Contrary to existing practice in knowledge engineering methodologies (in particular KADS [31]), we believe that the processes of modeling expert behavior and intended system behavior should be kept separate but explicit (this has also been argued by KEATS [14]). Taking this perspective, we emphasize that modeling expert behavior should be tightly coupled to validation with respect to the expert source and the intended goal of the model in knowledge engineering.

The outline of the paper is as follows. The concept of "modeling problem solving behavior" and the role that generic models play in the modeling process is presented in Sect. 2. We also clarify the ideas behind generic models and discuss the support these models provide. Section 3 presents two case studies that were used as data sources for this paper: The TroTelC project in which the goal was to develop a diagnostic system for processor boards of the System 12 digital switching system. This system is to be integrated in the troubleshooting environment of Alcatel Bell's production plant in Geel (Belgium) [26]. The second project – Schedule – [20], aims at developing a knowledge-based support system to assist expert planners with the construction of the equipment duty planning[3] of the Belgian railway company. Besides clarifying the goals of these two projects, Sect. 3 also provides a brief description of the models of problem solving that have been developed in both projects and illustrates how these models have been

---

[2] Generic models are useful beyond knowledge modeling. For example they are usually linked to re-usable implementation constructs. We will not treat these other roles in this paper, but see [12]

[3] The duty planning indicates how the railway equipment should be used.

exploited. Section 4 reports on our practical experiences with respect to the modeling activities. In particular, we describe some problems we encountered when trying to apply generic models in the acquisition and modeling process. These problems are illustrated with concrete data points from both projects. Based on this analysis, we conclude the article by formulating a number of requirements and guidelines for a practical and useful acquisition and modeling methodology (Sect. 5).

2 Modeling in Knowledge Engineering

2.1 The Role of Models of behavior

Within the work on modeling problem solving behavior, we distinguish two directions: The first direction starts from the idea that a model of the problem solving behavior exhibited by the human expert should be created. This idea is central in the KEATS methodology [14] and has also been pursued in the initial stages of the KADS project [32]. The second direction emphasizes that the modeling activity should capture the "desired" or "intended" problem solving behavior of the knowledge system to be developed. The construction of this model is usually guided by an analysis of expert behavior, but the final model is tailored towards what the prospective knowledge system should do [31, 15, 13, 3] [4].

The role of a model of expert problem solving behavior is to provide a source of information to the system designer [21, 26]. It is up to the latter to decide how to use this model during the specification of the system design (Fig. 1) [5]. KEATS tries to support the system designer in this task by offering semi-automated support for performing a mapping of the model of expert behavior onto structures in the knowledge base, i.e. the support is limited to operationalizing the model[6].

Approaches modeling the desired behavior of the prospective system (e.g, KADS) exploit the model as a *functional specification* of the system (Fig. 2). Guided by an *interpretational framework*, the knowledge engineer perceives the problem solving behavior of a human expert and abstracts the observations away from the particular details. Once this model has been developed, it is transformed into a *design model* which takes into account the technical requirements and constraints with respect to the artifact (e.g., efficiency, hardware, and so on). This transformation from the model of desired system behavior to a design model

---

[4] One could further distinguish these approaches based on whether conceptual or computational considerations underly the modeling process. This however is irrelevant for the discussion in this article. See [11] for details.

[5] In fact, how exactly a model of expert behavior might contribute to construct a system model is still an open question in knowledge engineering research. [21] and [26] discuss this topic.

[6] It is clear that such a mapping is not desirable in many cases. Contrary to the claims made in [23] one cannot expect that such a mapping preserves "functional equivalence" [21].

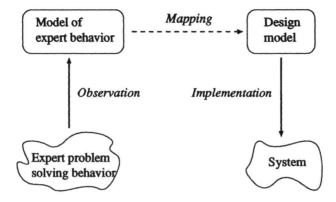

Fig. 1. The role of a model of expert behavior is to provide a source of information to the system designer. Often, these models are simply mapped onto a representational language

is usually *structure preserving*, i.e. there exist symbol level components that are a "direct operationalization" of constructs in the desired system behavior model [28, 29].

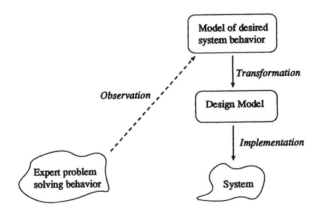

Fig. 2. A model of the desired system behavior fulfills the role of functional specification of the knowledge system. This model is usually transformed into a design model in a structure preserving manner

2.2 Generic Models and the Modeling Process

Knowledge acquisition methodologies aid the knowledge engineer in the construction of a model of problem solving behavior. These methodologies supply the knowledge engineer with a modeling language, an ontology with which to structure model components and often a library of predefined modeling constructs (generally called *generic models*). Using these generic models, the construction of a model of behavior typically involves bottom-up and top-down steps carried out in an opportunistic manner. The choice on the trajectory of these activities largely depends on the availability of pre-existing hypotheses about behavior expectations (generic models of problem solving).

We define generic models as predefined partial or abstract models about tasks, problem solving methods or domain ontologies. Generic models are typically useful for a class of application tasks and are therefore re-usable to some extent. The general idea of current modeling methodologies is that generic models are selected based on so-called *task features*. A task feature, in general, is a property of the task or problem which is indicative for the usefulness of a particular generic model.

Generic models fulfill multiple roles in the model construction process. In a bottom-up modeling approach, generic models are useful as a skeleton to which observed data (e.g., problem solving steps, domain objects) can be abstracted and generalized. Used this way, generic models assist the knowledge engineer in developing useful abstractions from specific observations of problem solving behavior (Fig. 3). In a top-down modeling approach, generic models are used as templates to focus the attention of the knowledge engineer and to formulate expectations about the problem solving behavior and the knowledge being used by the expert (Fig. 4).

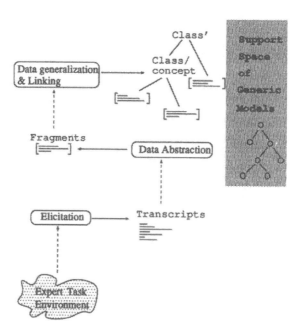

Fig. 3. Bottom-up modeling consists of data elicitation, abstractions, generalization, and linking. Generic models offer support in the latter three steps

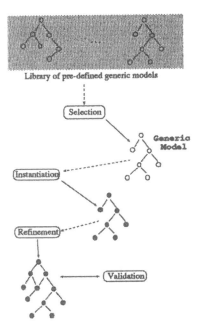

Fig. 4. Top-down modeling consists of the selection of a generic model, model instantiation, refinement, and validation

Most modeling approaches explicitly recognize the need to integrate top-down and bottom-up modeling. In such a mixed approach, generic models are used to structure the knowledge acquisition process (top-down modeling) while they also serve as skeletons to which observed data can be abstracted (bottom-up modeling).

Well-known methodologies that rely on libraries of generic models include the Generic Task Toolset [3], role-limiting methods [13], Musen's and his co-workers' multiple method methodology [15] and the KADS' interpretation models [31]. These methodologies differ along two dimensions: the kinds of generic models they provide, and the granularity of these generic models. Nevertheless, the principles behind them are basically the same: based on task features, generic models are selected and subsequently filled in and combined to arrive at a complete model of problem solving behavior.

As an illustration consider the approaches based on role-limiting methods. The modeling components in the role-limiting methods library are *problem solving methods*. They supply the knowledge engineer with classes of tasks, a control structure, domain-independent knowledge roles and assumptions (constraints) presupposed by the model. A class of tasks covers all tasks and actions contributing to the goal defined with the class. For example, in the generic model *Cover and Differentiate* [8] (which is suitable for diagnostic tasks), there are two classes of tasks: *Cover* and *Differentiate*. The class *Cover* groups all tasks and actions which contribute to finding a set of candidate explanations for the events or states that need to be explained. This problem solving method relies upon the exhaustivity assumption (i.e. if a symptom has at least one potential explanation, the final diagnosis must include at least one of these potential explanations). An iterative control structure is defined by the *Cover and Differentiate* method.

The integrated framework consisting of SPARK, BURN, and FireFighter is a workbench for non-programmers based on the role-limiting methods methodology [12]. The selection of a generic model of problem solving is supported by SPARK. SPARK manages a library of methods that cover a task. The number of possible methods associated with a task is deliberately limited (of the order of one or two). A few questions about particular task features are asked to disambiguate between multiple methods[7]. Based on the selected method, BURN selects a specialized knowledge acquisition tool. This tool exploits the assumptions and roles of the problem solving method allowing it to elicit and encode the specific knowledge that will fill these roles.

Musen and his co-workers have defined a "multiple method methodology" which extends the library of models of problem solving methods with finer grained modeling components (so-called *mechanisms*) [15, 19]. These mechanisms are building blocks that can be combined to construct problem solving methods of arbitrary complexity. A mechanism imposes requirements on the type of knowledge that must be available to solve the task with that mechanism. In contrast to SPARK, the tool that supports the multiple method methodology (PROTEGE II [19]) does not define a strong relation between task features and appropriate modeling components. However, the PROTEGE II environment offers an indexing mechanism which allows the knowledge engineer to filter out particular mechanisms of interest (based on the domain ontologies presupposed by the mechanism, their input/outputs, and the mechanism's task relation). The decision on which method to select or what set of mechanisms to configure is left to the knowledge engineer. The output of PROTEGE II is a specialized knowledge acquisition tool which elicits the domain specific knowledge that will fill the roles presupposed by the problem solving method.

3 Description of the Case Studies

In two of our industrial projects, we have followed attentively the advice of current modeling methodologies: Based on some task features we have selected generic models to support the acquisition and model construction process. Before analyzing these experiences, we briefly introduce these two industrial projects.

3.1 TroTelC

For three years, we have been involved in a joint project with Alcatel Bell in which a diagnostic knowledge system for digital processor boards – called

---

[7] The relation between task features and problem solving methods is not established yet.

TroTelC – has been developed.

Alcatel Bell is a telecommunications company producing the System 12 digital switching system for application in public and special networks. System 12 has a distributed architecture consisting of a large number of subscriber line circuit boards and (combined) processor, memory, and terminal interface boards (generally called *Printed Board Assemblies (PBAs)*). Each PBA is manufactured and extensively tested in Alcatel Bell's production environment before it is installed in the final customer's configuration.

After assembly, each PBA undergoes three test stages: the *manufacturing defect analyzer test (MDA), functional board test (FBT)* and *functional unit test (FUT)*. A MDA test inspects the board to identify process faults. In principle, all open connections or shorts between lines are detected during this test phase. After MDA test, each PBA undergoes a FBT. The PBA is subjected to a system functional test under different operating conditions (e.g., the test environment's temperature can be increased). The FBT checks that the PBA realizes its design functionalities correctly. Lastly, the PBA is installed into a rack assembly and the entire system is tested during FUT.

When a board fails the FBT, a fault listing reporting the failed test is generated. The failing PBA, together with the fault listing, are forwarded to a troubleshooter whose task is to identify the component(s) causing the observed misbehavior.

The goal of the project was to introduce a knowledge system (KS) into this troubleshooting environment. This KS should be operatable by an electronics technician. The technician is not required to be an expert troubleshooter. He or she is expected to be able to operate the resources offered by the environment to control and to observe the PBA's behavior. The KS should provide the technician with specific knowledge about the UUT such as the design functionalities, the available test programs, schematics, etc. In addition, it must also provide problem solving capabilities to assist diagnosis of the UUT. Whenever the KS fails to provide the technician with the required knowledge in a particular situation, the UUT is forwarded to an expert troubleshooter.

We have constructed a model of expert problem solving behavior through a combined top-down and bottom-up approach, relying heavily on predefined generic models [25]. The problem solving behavior is viewed as a hierarchical diagnosis on functional design models: we ascribed to the expert knowledge of the intended use of the processor board at different levels of detail [27]: (1) The *circuit operations level* which describes the processor board in terms of all the operations that can be performed onto the board (e.g., Reset the board); (2) the *hardware module functions level* covers for each hardware module the functions this module is designed for (e.g., decode address, generate interrupts); and (3) the *logical primitive functions level* defines for some logical primitives (gates) the functions it is supposed to realize (e.g., and, nand, or, inversion).

Given an initial symptom description, we observed that three major tasks might be pursued at each of these three levels of board description (see [26] for more details on this knowledge level model of expert behavior). This task decomposition and their input and outputs are shown in Fig. 5:

symptom verification: The reliability of the symptoms are verified.
suspect generation: Based on test results, a visual inspection or on other
   kinds of observations, it is deduced which suspects can account for all the
   observations whereby a suspect might have different degrees of plausibility.
suspect testing: During suspect testing, the expert selectively focuses on plausible suspects and executes tests or performs other operations and observations on the board to reduce the set of suspects.

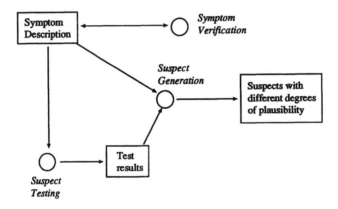

Fig. 5. Diagnosis of processor boards involves *symptom verification, suspect generation,*
and *suspect testing* at multiple levels of board descriptions

We have exploited the model of expert problem solving behavior to guide
the system modeling process. In particular, it allowed us to identify the tasks to
be carried out by the problem solving system, offered alternative approaches to
some problems and suggested the design of relevant domain ontologies [26]. The
resulting system model of desired behavior was operationalized via the computational framework CML (as discussed in [28]).

3.2   Schedule

The SCHEDULE project is a joint project between the Belgian national Railway
Company NMBS, Knowledge Technologies N.V. and the laboratory for Artificial
Intelligence of the University of Brussels. The project aims to construct a knowledge based support system which should provide assistance to expert planners
during the development of the "equipment duty planning".

The input to equipment duty planning consists of timetables which meet the
requirements of passengers and freight transport. These tables thus specify the
trains that should be available. They contain information such as the station
of departure and arrival, the train number, the time of departure and arrival,

the days of the week when the train actually runs, the period of the year when it runs, etc. Table 1 shows some examples of trains that are specified in the timetables[8]. The equipment duty planning is a specification of how the railway equipment (electrical and diesel engines; motor vehicles) should be used in order to actually run these trains.

Table 1. Examples of entries in the timetables.

train	charac teristic		period	dept. station	arr. station	dept. time	arr. time
155	1111111	R	09	ASD	FBMZ	06:22	09:30
157	1111111	R	09	ASD	FBMZ	07:24	10:30
178	1111110	N7	09	FBMZ	ASD	06:10	09:10
179	1111111	R	09	FBMZ	ASD	07:10	10:08
3370	1111100	N67	09	FLV	FM	07:02	07:33
6428	1111111	R	09	FLV	FM	05:30	05:55

The construction of the equipment duty planning is performed in three steps:

development of the basic roster: This amounts to determining sequences of trains that are driven by particular types of equipment (e.g., motor vehicles). A set of sequences that are related to a particular type of equipment is called a *basic roster*.

filling in local operations: "local operations" are imposed on the sequences. These local operations are the actions that a particular piece of equipment should perform (besides the actual driving of trains). Examples of such actions include shunting, (de)coupling, startup, shutdown, break tests, etc. The result of this step is a daily plan for each piece of equipment that is being used. This plan indicates all the actions that a particular piece of equipment should perform within a time scale of 24 hours. Such a plan is called a *duty*.

construction of rotations: In a third step, the duties are organized into "rotations". A rotation is a sequence of duties, organized in the time dimension, between two maintenances.

The equipment duty planning must satisfy different − often conflicting − constraints. In the first place, the equipment must be used as "rationally" and "economically" as possible. A rational use entails, among other things:

− that the equipment is maintained regularly such that the probability of errors and the cost of eventual repairs is low,

---

[8] Stations are often described by means of an abbreviation. ASD = Amsterdam, FBMZ = Brussels South Station, FLV = Leuven, FM = Mechelen.

- that the equipment is allocated in such a way as to maximize ease of daily use (e.g., take into account that certain stations may not be able to perform certain operations with the equipment during rush hours).

An economic usage entails, among other things:

- that the number of pieces of equipment used is as low as possible,
- that the number of "empty rides" is as low as possible[9],
- that the number of effective versus non-effective kilometers is as high as possible.

In the Schedule project, we have so far concentrated primarily on the first of the three steps mentioned above (the development of the basic rosters). The input for this first task consists of a set of trains that have been planned in the timetables. The output of this task is (i) a specification of types of equipment that will be used to drive certain trains, (ii) for each type of equipment, the number of pieces of equipment that are needed and (iii) for each piece of equipment, the sequence of trains that it will drive.

In order to obtain a model of the expert's problem solving behavior, we studied a representative number of duty planning examples. For each example, a protocol was collected which contained a detailed account of the steps that the expert had taken in order to arrive at a solution for the problem. A bottom-up analysis of these protocols revealed three basic steps that were being taken by the expert (see [20] for a detailed description of the model):

1. repeated partitioning of the initial set of trains (input) into subsets,
2. development of the basic roster for each subset,
3. integration of the basic rosters into a basic roster for the complete initial set of trains (output).

The specific observations from the protocols fitted into a problem solving framework that is known as "design by decomposition" [4]. It can be considered as a problem solving method which contains the following steps or subtasks.

1. repeated decomposition of a problem into independent subproblems,
2. solving subproblems independently of each other,
3. recomposition of subsolutions into a global solution.

The process of design by decomposition is depicted in Fig. 6.

4 Practical Experiences with Using Generic Models

In this section, we present an analysis of our experiences in applying current modeling methodologies in the TroTelC and Schedule project. We highlight some problems which emerged while using generic models in the process of modeling problem solving behavior. These problems can be summarized as follows:

---

[9] An empty ride is a ride between two stations in which the equipment does not carry an actual load.

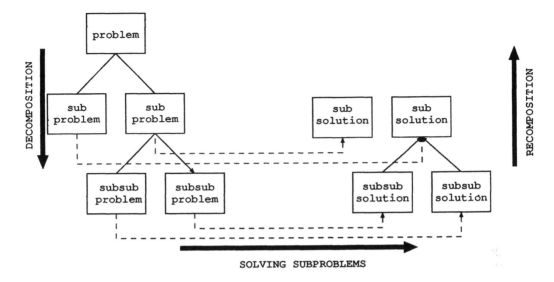

Fig. 6. Design by decomposition.

1. The appropriateness of a model depends on its contributions to the intended goal;
2. Multiple generic models apply, but with different degrees of appropriateness;
3. Generic models are often too general to give useful support and guidance;
4. Generic models can seldom be used "as it is" and may need to be adapted or combined;
5. Terminology of generic models may be hard to tailor to the audience to which it is to be communicated;
6. The consequences of selecting a wrong model can be very costly;
7. Viewing knowledge acquisition as a knowledge transfer process misleads the knowledge engineer into focusing solely on the human expert.

In subsequent sections, these problems are discussed in more detail and illustrated with examples from both projects:

4.1 The Appropriateness of a Model Depends on its Contributions to the Intended Goal

There exists no unique way to describe and model expert problem solving behavior. The appropriateness of a particular model depends on the model's usefulness and contributions to the intended goal: If a model of expert behavior is needed as discussion material for multiple domain experts (so that they can converge on the same problem solving process or eventually improve upon it), the model should be very detailed and expressed in an application specific terminology, familiar to all these experts.

If the purpose of the model is to explain the problem solving process to managers (e.g., in order to point out bottlenecks or costly activities or to argue for the purchase of some resources) different aspects need to be emphasized. If you want to use the model of problem solving to explain your observations to an AI community, you should make use of a well-known generic problem solving method.

Modeling expert behavior in knowledge engineering is not a goal on its own. In knowledge engineering, we try to build useful systems. With respect to this goal, a model of expert behavior can fulfill two important purposes:

- The model can be considered as a high level design (blueprint) for the system that needs to be built,
- The model can be considered as a source of information for specifying the design.

We argue that during the model construction process, the model creator must continuously validate whether the added model constructs contribute to and, in particular, do not conflict with the prospective system and characteristics of the desired task environment.

For example, the problem solving behavior of experts observed at Alcatel Bell's troubleshooting environment can be described in terms of the *cover and differentiate* [8] problem solving method: possible misbehaviors are related to all entities that might explain this misbehavior. Problem solving actions are carried out to collect a set of candidate explanations for the events or states that need to be explained. Another category of actions aims to discriminate between candidate explanations. This model construct, however, violates features of the desired target environment, limiting its support during the functional specification of the system: Each time knowledge of a new type of processor board is to be elicited, the informant has to have troubleshooting experience with this new board. He or she has to be knowledgeable about what misbehavior the board exhibits when a particular chip fails in a certain way. Given the short product life cycles and the project goal to unburden the expert's involvement, this is an undesired property.

In the Schedule project, the model of expert behavior actually served two purposes. We exploited the model to define the functional requirements of a user interface which assists the end users in manipulating graphical representations of the equipment duty plans. The model of the expert's problem behavior thus served as a source for structuring the different types of manipulations on this representation. Although this was initially not an explicit goal for developing the model, it turned out to be quite useful for this purpose.

A goal explicitly put forward was that the model of the expert's problem solving behavior should be suitable as a blueprint design for a prototype problem solving system. Although we are still in the process of evaluating the model we have already seen that it is too weak for this purpose. Our first intuitions are that there are two major difficulties. First, the model is not completely suitable for actually producing adequate solutions. The main reason is that there are subtle interactions among the problems and subproblems of the problem decomposition hierarchy (see Fig. 6). This means that the solutions for these subproblems cannot be constructed independently of each other, even taking into account the interactions during the recomposition step. These interactions became visible after showing the prototype to the end users. Second, the solutions that were developed by the prototype were not transparent[10] to the end users of the system in the sense that they had substantial difficulties in understanding what had been produced. Although they knew the different problem solving steps that the prototype could/would take and the domain knowledge which it would bring to bear in the different steps they had – even for the simplest problems – difficulties in relating these individual steps to the overall solution because this solution is very complex. As a blueprint for an automated problem solving support system, the model thus turned out to be inadequate. Although we have to analyze this in more detail, the end user's perspective on the problem turns out not to be as hierarchical as indicated by the model.

4.2 Multiple Generic Models May Apply

Given a library of predefined model constructs, methodologies suggest selection of a model by verifying associated task features. This requires a bottom-up analysis of the problem domain, searching for particular knowledge constructs and investigating the applicability of the assumptions underlying the generic model. We found that, based on these criteria only, all generic models of problem solving related to the task of diagnosis were applicable. All required knowledge constructs could be created by the domain experts, although some were more easily constructed than other ones.

For example, in the TroTelC project, we initially identified the following models as potential candidates: *Heuristic Classification* [5], *Cover and Differentiate* [8], *Hierarchical Diagnosis* [10], *Model-based Diagnosis based on functional design models* [1] (which we call *design-functionality-based method* throughout the text), *Systematic Diagnosis*, and *Heuristic Diagnosis* [2]. All knowledge requirements of the candidate models were satisfied in the troubleshooting task environment:

– Heuristic classification is applicable since the diagnosis problem can be represented as a classification problem. Domain knowledge can be identified to support the abstraction, match, and refinement tasks.
– Cover and Differentiate is applicable since knowledge is available that can fulfill the role to cover the explanations. The domain also provides event-qualifying and connection-qualifying knowledge to differentiate between the alternatives.
– Hierarchical diagnosis is also applicable: In [10], the author shows how a model of a processor board in terms of the device's structure, local behaviors, faults and misbehaviors qualifies to perform diagnosis through behavior

---

[10] Transparency is an important issue because the end users have to build upon the solutions that are produced by the system.

prediction, candidate generation, discrimination and decomposition. Similar knowledge can be created in TroTelC's problem domain.

- Model-based diagnosis based on functional design models can be applied. According to [1] schematics about the processor boards under focus and documentations regarding the board's design and functional specification can fulfill the roles required by this method. This knowledge is available to TroTelC's domain expert.

In the Schedule project, we initially attempted to formulate the problem as a constraint satisfaction problem (CSP). Later, we introduced the decompositional model (Sect. 3.2).

- The constraint satisfaction approach is applicable: If the problem of constructing the basic rosters is viewed as a CSP problem, the constraints relate to the order of trains within the sequences of trains that are driven by one particular engine. The domain expert could easily list many constraints that should be taken into account (e.g., turning an electrical engine in a head station[11] requires at least 5 minutes).
- The model based on the decomposition of problems into subproblems is applicable: Here, decompositions relate to the various ways in which the expert groups trains together (e.g., based on weekdays).

Given this multiple applicability, it seems to be useful to discriminate between the applicable methods by considering their degree of contribution towards the intended goal. This requires a discrimination between the applicable methods based on the ease with which the expert can formulate the required knowledge constructs, on the detail of the focus of attention defined by the method and on the compliance of the model with the desired target system and task environment characteristics (as discussed before). But even considering these additional criteria, we found that the relative appropriateness models is often determined by conflicting features:

- Hierarchical diagnosis [10] relies upon a behavioral model in which temporal abstractions are introduced (such as change, cycle and frequency). It requires a lot of engineering work to describe a processor board this way. Through a close and very time-intensive cooperation between the designer of the board and the knowledge engineer, such a behavioral model could be created. This, however, conflicts with desired task features of the application task: "No knowledge engineer should be involved in the elicitation process" and "The aim is not to exceed three weeks to provide the KS with its required knowledge". To understand the observed expert behaviors, hierarchical diagnosis is thus an appropriate model, but the support it can give to create a functional specification is very limited. In addition, it turned out that an expert troubleshooter does not necessarily know all these details for

---

[11] A head station is a station in the form of a dead end, i.e. equipment cannot pass through it but has to drive out in the opposite direction.

a given processor board. Hierarchical diagnosis therefore does not support the use of the expert's representations. This limits the focusing power of this method during the modeling process.

- Cover and differentiate relies upon a relation between possible misbehaviors and all entities that might explain this misbehavior. Diagnosing processor boards, the set of entities which might cause one specific misbehavior is very large. For example when the primary communication with a board fails, ca. 80 % of the board is suspected. We found it very difficult for the domain expert to come up with this information. Therefore, in the TroTelC project, this generic model is not suited for guiding the elicitation process.
- Some of the undesired properties of these selected problem solving methods are resolved by the model based diagnosis method based on the functional design model. However, not all the observations fitted in this model. It was observed, for example, that the expert sometimes investigates chips which fall outside the set of components contributing to the correct working of the function under focus [27]. This observation conflicts with an assumption underlying the model based method based on the functional design model.

In the schedule project, the models are also conflicting:

- The CSP model requires a careful formulation of the different constraints that apply. However, many constraints require complex procedures for their evaluation. It is unreasonable to expect that the end users would actually fill in these constraints themselves. This conflicts with the requirement that the knowledge base should be maintainable by the domain experts themselves.
- The "design by decomposition" model requires that the subproblems that are generated are (at least to a great extent) independent from each other. Although the expert could provide us with different kinds of decomposition steps, it is clear that certain combinations of these steps do not yield independent subproblems. This conflicts with the philosophy of the model itself. To alleviate this, complex backtracking should be incorporated into the model such that solutions for subproblems could be partially re-constructed during the decomposition phase.

Clearly, these experiences strengthen our conclusion derived in the previous section: A selection of generic models based only on knowledge availability is too weak. Features related to the intended goal of the model should also be taken into account. From the experiences presented in this section, we conclude that these features should include the complexity of the domain model creation (e.g., creating a behavioral model of a processor board), the reliability of the information and features of the desired target environment.

It seems to be extremely useful to precede the model selection process with a bottom-up analysis to understand better the real potential of applying certain problem solving methods. In the TroTelC project, a bottom-up analysis would have immediately emphasized the appropriateness of functional approach methods. If we had analyzed the representations used by the domain expert better (in particular the test programs and design documentation), we would have had a strong indication of the functional view adopted by the expert.

4.3 Generic Models May Be Too General

The main role of a generic model in knowledge engineering is to provide guidance during the acquisition phase. Important requirements imposed on a generic model are therefore that the model should sufficiently constrain the knowledge roles to allow the knowledge engineer to limit his focus of attention and the model should identify and discriminate between the relevant issues in a task environment as much as possible. Some generic models are too general to provide any practical contribution to this role.

Two examples of this kind of generic models are systematic diagnosis [2] and heuristic classification [5]. Systematic diagnosis requires a decomposable model of the device under focus. Many type of models have this property: a behavioral, functional, causal, or structural model. In heuristic classification, the abstraction hierarchies used in the abstraction and refinement steps can be based on a variety of types of knowledge. One of the most difficult issues in knowledge engineering is to find out how the expert views the device, i.e. what kind of representations he creates or uses and how they are structured. Once this is known, it is much easier to understand and rationalize the behaviors of the expert. Some generic models (such as systematic diagnosis or heuristic classification) are too general to provide good support to suggest which domain models to look for during knowledge acquisition.

Although heuristic classification might not be suited to fulfilling the role of an acquisition template, the model turns out to be very useful to clarify some aspects of a model of behavior to an AI community. Plentiful articles can be found which describe a model of behavior using this generic problem solving method (e.g., [8]).

Similar experiences were encountered in the Schedule project. The model based on the decomposition of an equipment planning problem into independent subproblems describes the expert's problem solving behavior, but only at an intermediate level of abstraction. As we continued to add more and more details we encountered significant difficulties because it turned out that there were complex interactions between these seemingly "independent" subproblems. As an example, one decomposition step is "focusing on the trains of a particular day of the week" and then producing a duty plan for that day. However, if there is a train which continues to run after 12pm then (part of) this train "belongs" to the next day. In order to come up with a duty plan for the selected day, certain aspects of the solution of the next day should be taken into account. If all these kinds of interactions could be taken into account during the recomposition step it would not be problematic but unfortunately, many of these interactions lead to substantial reconstruction during the recomposition step. This is simply outside the scope of the model.

4.4 Generic Models May Need to be Adapted or Combined

Generic models seldom consistently match all observations in the task environment. (refer to similar experiences with the GT approach or role-limiting methods). They might be used to describe certain aspects of an expert's behavior but they may fail to describe other aspects. Often, these models need to be adapted or combined.

As pointed out in Sect. 4.2, the design-functionality-based method best agrees with the observations and the task features of the target environment, as characterized in the TroTelC project. In particular, during the acquisition phase, this model drew our attention to the fact that the expert performs a verification task before the actual diagnosis is started, something which we were not aware of before. However, some conflicts with the observed expert behaviors were identified: the expert sometimes investigates chips which fall outside the set of components contributing to the correct working of the function under focus. Adapting constructs of this generic method allowed us to remove the conflicts: We introduced an additional task and slightly modified the control knowledge so that causal reasoning is performed after no faulty components have been found within the set of components contributing to the correct working of a function. In spite of this and some other conflicts, we still consider this method as appropriate in our experience because it allowed us to adapt the model easily to make it consistent with the observations.

Similarly, in the Schedule project, the "design by decomposition" model is inadequate because many equipment duty planning problems cannot be decomposed in subproblems that are sufficiently independent from each other. To resolve this problem, the model could be extended to incorporate some form of backtracking in case of subproblems that are highly dependent. In practise, this could mean that the solutions of subproblems may need to be substantially modified during the recomposition phase in order to account for the interdependencies.

4.5 Terminology Difficulties

One of the major difficulties we experienced in our knowledge engineering project was related to communication and terminology. These difficulties arise from the fact that:

- Different types of generic models are distinguished, each introducing its own model-specific terminology. These model-specific terminologies have to be related to each other and re-formulated in an application-specific vocabulary;
- The model of expert behavior must be expressed in different vocabularies, depending on the audience to which it is to be communicated.

Generic primitives, constituting the predefined models used for knowledge acquisition, apply to a class of applications and are therefore formulated in a language that is not specific to a single application. In addition, different types of generic models introduce their own application-independent but model-specific terminology:

In the TroTelC project, for example, we have relied upon the generic model of problem solving, cover and differentiate. Some vocabularies used by that method are candidates, hypothesis, explanations, evidence. A generic model of the diagnosis task was also studied. This task model is expressed in terms of symptoms, misbehaviors, device, and so forth. A causal model as an applicable domain ontology, relies on a cause and effect vocabulary. A difficult task was to relate these different vocabularies to each other such that all applicable generic models fit together and can be used as a consistent entity to guide the acquisition efforts.

Even more important than relating the different model-specific terminologies is an appropriate reformulation of the generic model vocabulary in terms of entries in the application-specific lexicon. The KL model, often created through a generic model, should reflect the observations in the expert task environment as closely as possible and the model should be familiar to the domain expert because it is a means of communication between the knowledge engineer and the domain expert. Matching these two vocabularies is not an easy task. This is also true in particular because often some application-specific lexicon entries (although sometimes really relevant, but see Sect. 4.6) cannot be classified in or distinguished by the generic model vocabulary.

4.6 Selecting the Wrong Model May be Costly

A role of generic models in the acquisition process is to express expectations about the problem solving behaviors and the representations created and used by the expert. A generic model thus functions as primary source for perception. A danger which we actually experienced is that the model largely influences what we perceive[12]. It makes us look for certain data, neglecting other issues, which finally turn out to be very relevant. Consequently, a knowledge engineer might be convinced that he is working with an appropriate generic model because of all evidence found in the observed data. It requires a critical review and it can take quite some time before a knowledge engineer realizes that the selected generic model might not be as appropriate as he first thought. The selection of an inappropriate generic model can have a number of costly consequences:

1. A re-design of the model of expert behavior: All abstracted observations have to be reconsidered, generalized into new classes, and the relations between the findings have to be redefined.
2. Before a new model can be created, a re-adjustment of the knowledge engineer's primary data of perception and of the expert's view of his own behavior has to be carried out.
3. All activities relying on the model of expert behavior as a source of information have to be reconsidered. In the case of prototyping, this involves a re-specification of the system's functionality, a re-design and re-implementation

---

[12] *The Logic of Perception* [22] is entirely devoted to the impact of the mind on what one is able to perceive.

In the TroTelC project, we were faced with rejecting the initial generic model and instantiating a new one. After working with the *Cover and Differentiate* [8] model of problem solving for 7 man-months and following a structured prototyping approach, we realized that important behaviors and representations could not be captured by the model. Instead, for the purpose of guiding the acquisition phase and contributing to meeting the desired target system and environment characteristics, we found that the diagnosis method based on functional design models [1] was more appropriate. The whole re-design, re-adjustment, and re-implementation[13] of the prototype occupied approximately two man-months[13].

In the Schedule project we have not yet performed a detailed evaluation of the "design by decomposition" model which is embedded in the prototype problem solving system that has been constructed so far. However, if the model turns out to be inadequate, this could be very costly. Even incorporating some forms of backtracking in order to resolve problems with dependent subproblems is not likely to be an easy way out. As in the TroTelC project, if the model is really wrong, this could easily mean that the whole prototype must be re-designed and re-implemented.

4.7 Knowledge Acquisition is Viewed as a Knowledge Transfer Process

Numerous methodologies view knowledge acquisition as a process to transfer knowledge from a human knowledge source to a machine usable representation [30, 9, 14, 34]. Taking this perspective, knowledge acquisition involves sensing data (the so-called *phenomenonly* or *raw data*), collecting and generalizing this data to obtain knowledge primitives, free from the specific circumstances (context) in which the data was observed. These primitives are related and assembled to obtain knowledge constructs which become transformed into computational representations.

The underlying epistemology is the physical symbol hypothesis [16]. This hypothesis states that knowledge consists of symbols of reality and relationships between these symbols. Intelligence is the appropriate logical manipulation of the symbols and their relations. To put it in different words, this hypothesis argues that one can retrieve from an expert problem solver a rigorous knowledge structure and transfer this to a computational medium to obtain similar intelligent behavior.

Arguments have been put forward by many researchers that question this philosophy of knowledge [24, 33, 6, 7, 18]. We too can point out some experiences supporting these arguments:

1. What is being perceived, i.e. the observed data, depends on the context in which the perception takes place. Among other things, this context is also

---

[13] We experienced great support from the computational framework CML to minimize the re-implementation overhead [28]. CML establishes a close connection between entities of the model of behavior (tasks, methods, domain models) and objects on the implementation level.

determined by the expectations of the knowledge engineer, his familiarity with similar problems and his awareness of the different kinds of generic models that have been proposed. Our experience suggests that the more models one knows about, the quicker one is persuaded to apply such a model. This may, or may not, be successful. In Sect. 4.6, we described how the cover and differentiate model misleaded us for some time although evidence was found in the phenomenonly data making that particular model applicable. After recovering from this track, we easily found new evidence in favor of another model which defined our expectations. From this experience, we have difficulties viewing the observed data as an objective source out of which knowledge (viewed as a rigorous context-free structure) can be built.

2. An interesting observation (and this is not novel. See [7].) is that the knowledge provided by an expert often has to be extensively manipulated to fit into the model of behavior without corrupting the structures already contained. If fact, we learned that an expert comes up with different justifications for the same case depending on his awareness of all the bits and pieces already communicated during the acquisition phase.

3. To create a model of expert behavior, we have observed five different experts. Sometimes, these experts gave different reasons underlying certain approaches to solve a similar problem. When bringing them together and asking them which approach is correct, a very complex discussion ensued, which they resolved by agreeing that their approaches apply in different contexts and are complementary. This illustrates that the knowledge structures communicated by these expert are justifications in a particular context instead of context-free rationalizations.

4. After some time, we had difficulties in keeping the model consistent with new cases or examples that were being considered. The physical symbol hypothesis suggests that there should be an underlying rationalization that provides an absolute foundation for the knowledge. Up to now, we have not found this rationalization. Although we believe that one can probably persevere and finally find this rationalization, it at least raises the question of whether there may be a better philosophy of knowledge than one whereby knowledge is made up from some sort of absolute primitive elements.

Based on these experiences, we too believe that the perspective of viewing knowledge acquisition as a knowledge transfer process misleads the knowledge engineer into focusing solely on the human expert. It underestimates the importance of the context in which problem solving takes place. This context includes more than the "knowledge" that the knowledge engineer is primarily interested in. Trying to create conceptually adequate representations to provide a cognitive account of the expert's knowledge is almost an impossible task when relying on the current hypothesized epistemology.

5 Guidelines

Based on practical experiences, we have pointed out some problems in relying on generic models as advocated by current modeling frameworks. These problems are due to the limited attention drawn upon the nature of the domain and the strong impact of a predefined model on what one does and does not perceive. When constructing a model of behavior, the model designer should realize that the model is a subjective description of regularities and patterns that emerge during the interaction between an agent and his task environment and that the role of the model is to inspire the system developer.

In this section, we present some guidelines for knowledge engineering. These guidelines seem to us to be important to avoid the problems discussed in this article.

Support for mixed modeling: Although current modeling approaches recognize the need for combining bottom-up and top-down modeling few of them present concrete hints about how this problem should be approached. However, this kind of support is crucial. If top-down modeling is applied too early during the modeling process, it often misleads the knowledge engineer because the model does not focus on important details. On the other hand, continuous bottom-up modeling is infeasible because the individual observations may fit many model constructs so that the resulting abstractions are too observation specific.

Distinguish between observable expert behavior versus desired system behavior: We argue for an explicit distinction between a model of observable expert behavior and a model of desired system behavior (similar to the KEATS methodology [14]). This takes into account that the physical structure of the problem solver and its structural coupling [33] to the task environment constrain the space of behaviors that the agent can exhibit. Since a human expert, a computer system and the combination user/system have a different embedding, neither of them can exploit the information coming from the task environment in a similar way. This also implies that none of them is functionally equivalent (as is suggested in [23]). Consequently, system construction must be explicitly viewed as a design problem (designing intended system behavior), not as a process of operationalizing a model of expert problem solving behavior [21]. Generic models may be used to model either expert behavior or intended system behavior but it is not necessarily the case that these models can be used for both purposes. On the contrary, our experience suggests that this is frequently not the case. Generic models from current modeling methodologies are strongly biased towards modeling intended system behavior but are less suitable for modeling expert problem solving behavior.

Modeling expert problem solving behavior alone is insufficient: A model of the problem solving behavior exhibited by the human expert is definitely a useful source of information for system specification and design. However, that model must be complemented with additional types of models, in particular a model of the task environment and the resources that are being used during the problem solving process. This is required because the environment in which the systems are employed is complex and subject to constant change. Generic models from current modeling methodologies do not provide adequate support for modeling these aspects because they implicitly assume that "knowledge" is the only resource which is important during problem solving. In addition, other issues such as communication or cooperation between the actors in the work space is often completely neglected.

A model of expert behavior positions or orients the consultant to understand the behavior or to exploit contingencies and to avoid others: A model of expert problem solving behavior describes regularities in that behavior and takes into account the total problem solving agent, i.e. it includes the environment in which the agent is embedded. Such a model allows the consultant to rationalize the problem solving actions in the expert task environment. Rationalization is obtained by allowing the consultant to position or orient himself to understand the behaviors or to exploit contingencies of the task environment and to avoid others. In other words, we view a model of expert behavior as an abstract representation over problem solving actions. The purpose of this representation is not to serve as a specification for behavior generation, but rather to enable the consultant to understand the behavior or to exploit certain contingencies. Consequently, we believe that the model of expert behavior should be deliberately kept vague by omitting control knowledge over the intended goals. In fact, we found that these control issues are often related to personal preferences of the problem solver or they depend on situation-specific circumstances which are not always captured by the model.

A model of expert behavior is a source of information for system specification and design: The role of modeling expert behavior in knowledge engineering is to create a source of information for system specification and design. The model should inspire the system developers: (i) to identify tasks for automation and/or support or to point out lacunae which should be bridged via a new resource; (ii) to envision alternative approaches to some problems; and (iii) to distinguish and design relevant domain ontologies. In the TroTelC project, the knowledge engineer has taken large structures from the model to create the desired system model which should function as a routine problem solver. In the Schedule project, on the other hand, the model inspired the knowledge engineer to create a new resource (dedicated graphical interface) allowing the domain expert to manipulate the representations of the duty plans in a more flexible way.

Domain characterization should precede the model construction phase: Before deciding on and applying an acquisition technique, an analysis investigating the nature of the domain is required (this has also been argued by [34, 17]). This analysis should come up with a domain characterization which includes the construction of a domain lexicon, a description of the representations used or created during problem solving, an indication of the kind of faults the problem solver expects, the resources he has available, and so forth.

Models should be simple and transparent to its users: If the participants (e.g., end users) of the project are to be explicitly confronted with the problem solving models, then these models should be simple, transparent and easy to understand. If the model includes generic components, then these components must be tailored to the participant's requirements (see also previous point) and the scope and limitations of the model should be clearly indicated.

Modeling vocabularies should be extended: Existing methodologies for modeling problem solving behavior exploit a modeling vocabulary in terms of "goals", "tasks", "problem solving methods" and "domain models". However, such a vocabulary is too limited because it depicts problem solving processes as a bunch of functional objects capable of precise (formal) description. What we need to understand in the first place is the "work" that people do. Obviously, "problem solving" is a crucial part of "work" but it can not be straightforwardly isolated from things such as communication, cooperation, negotiation. These aspects should be included in a more encompassing analysis. Current methodologies have not yet even included vocabularies for describing such processes.

Modeling and validation should be tightly coupled: By distinguishing observable from desired behavior, one runs the risk of unremunerative efforts and useless model constructs with respect to the role of these models in knowledge engineering. Consequently, the modeling activity should be tightly coupled to validating the model with respect to its intended goal. Also, we believe that the expert should play a central and active role in the model construction process. Therefore, validation should also concern the faithfulness of each model construct with respect to the expert source.

6   Conclusion

In this article, we presented an analysis of some experimental data concerning the use of predefined generic models in the acquisition and modeling process. The experiences gained in two industrial projects tempered our enthusiasm about the actual support offered by these generic models. We argue for a more constructive modeling approach guided by a domain characterization and an active involvement of the expert. This modeling activity should explicitly distinguish between observable expert behavior and desired system behavior, keeping in mind that the first model may assist in constructing the latter.

Acknowledgements

The authors wish to thank all members of the VUB AI-Lab and in particular Walter Van de Velde, Agnar Aamodt and Cuno Duursma for their instructive discussions.

References

1. Abu-Hanna, A., Benjamins, R., & Jansweijer, W. (1991). Device understanding and modeling for diagnosis. *IEEE*, 6(2).

2. Breuker, J., Wielinga, B., van Someren, M., de Hoog, R., Schreiber, G., de Greef, P., Bredeweg, B., Wielemaker, J., Billault, J.-P., Davoodi, M., & Hayward, S. (1987). Model driven knowledge acquisition: Interpretation models. ESPRIT Project P1098 Deliverable D1 (task A1), University of Amsterdam and STL Ltd,.

3. Bylander, T. & Chandrasekaran, B. (1988). Generic tasks in knowledge-based reasoning: The 'right' level of abstraction for knowledge acquisition. In B. Gaines & J. Boose (Eds.), *Knowledge Acquisition for Knowledge Based Systems* (pp. 65–77). Academic Press.

4. Chandrasekaran, B. (1990). Design problem solving: A task analysis. *AI Magazine*, 11(4), 59–71.

5. Clancey, W. J. (1985). Heuristic classification. *AI Journal*, 27(4), 289–350.

6. Clancey, W. J. (1989). The knowledge level reinterpreted: Modeling how systems interact. *Machine Learning*, 4(3/4), 285–291.

7. Compton, P. & Jansen, R. (1990). A philosophical basis for knowledge acquisition. *Knowledge Acquisition*, 2(3), 241–257.

8. Eshelman, L. (1988). Mole: A knowledge-acquisition tool for cover-and-differentiate systems. In S. Marcus (Ed.), *Automating Knowledge Acquisition for Expert Systems*. Kluwer Academic Publishers, Massachusetts.

9. Gaines, B. (1987). Advanced expert system support environments. In *Proceedings of the Second Knowledge Acquisition for Knowledge-Based Systems Workshop*: Banff. Canada.

10. Hamscher, W. (1988). *Model-Based Troubleshooting of Digital Systems*. PhD thesis, MIT Lab.

11. Karbach, W., Linster, M., & Voss, A. (1990). Models of problem-solving: One label - one idea ? In B. Wielinga, J. Boose, B. Gaines, G. Schreiber, & M. van Someren (Eds.), *Current Trends in Knowledge Acquisition* (pp. 173–189). IOS Press.

12. Klinker, G., Bhola, C., Dallemagne, G., Marques, D., & McDermott, J. (1991). Usable and reusable programming constructs. *Knowledge Acquisition*, 3(2), 117–135.

13. McDermott, J. (1989). Preliminary steps towards a taxonomy of problem-solving methods. In S. Marcus (Ed.), *Automating Knowledge Acquisition for Expert Systems* (pp. 225–255). Kluwer Academic Publishers.

14. Motta, E., Rajan, T., Domingue, J., & Eisenstadt, M. (1991). Methodological foundations of keats, the knowledge engineer's assistant. *Knowledge Acquisition*, 3(3), 21–47.

15. Musen, M. & Tu, S. (1991). *A Model of Skeletal-Plan Refinement to Generate Task-Specific Knowledge Acquisition Tools*. KSL-Report 91-05, Knowledge Systems Laboratory, Stanford University, Stanford, CA.

16. Newell, A. & Simon, H. (1981). Computer science as empirical enquiry: symbols and search. In J. Haugeland (Ed.), *Mind Design*. Cambridge, MA: MIT Press.

17. Nwana, H., Paton, R., Bench-Capon, T., & Shave, M. (1991). Facilitating the development of knowledge based systems: a critical review of acquisition tools and techniques. *AI Communication*, 4(2/3), 60–73.

18. Pfeifer, R. & Rademakers, P. (1991). Situated adaptive design: Toward a new methodology for knowledge systems design. In W. Brauer & D. Hernandez (Eds.), *Verteilte Künstliche Intelligenz und Kooperatives Arbeiten. Proceedings of the 4th International GI-Congress on Knowledge Based Systems* (pp. 53–64). Berlin: Springer.

19. Puerta, A., Egar, J., Samson, T., & Musen, M. (1991). A multiple-method knowledge acquisition shell for the automatic generation of knowledge-acquisition tools.

In *IV reunion tecnica de la asociacion espanola para la inteligencia artificial, AEPIA-91* (pp. 205–230).: ACTAS.

20. Rademakers, P. (1991). *Task Analysis of an Equipment Assignment Problem.* Technical Report 91-1, Laboratory for Artificial Intelligence, University of Brussels.

21. Rademakers, P. & Pfeifer, R. (1992). The role of knowledge level modeling in situated adaptive design. To appear in the proceedings of ECAI-92, Vienna.

22. Rock, I. (1983). *The logic of perception.* Cambridge, MA: MIT Press.

23. Sandberg, J. & Wielinga, B. (1991). How situated is cognition. In *Proceedings of the 10th International Joint Conference on Artificial Intelligence,* (pp. 341–346).

24. Suchman, L. (1987). *Plans and Situated Actions.* Cambridge University Press.

25. Vanwelkenhuysen, J. (1990). *Modeling and Implementing the Task of Diagnosing PCBs: A Task-Oriented Approach.* AI-Memo 90-6, AI-Lab VUB.

26. Vanwelkenhuysen, J. (1992a). *Attentive knowledge engineering in practice: The development of a diagnostic system for processor boards in a production environment.* PhD thesis, Vrije Universiteit Brussel. (forthcoming).

27. Vanwelkenhuysen, J. (1992b). Scaling-up model-based troubleshooting by exploiting design functionalities. In *Proceedings of the 5th International Conference on Industrial and Engineering Applications of Artificial Intelligence and Expert Systems.* Paderborn (Germany).

28. Vanwelkenhuysen, J. & Rademakers, P. (1990). Mapping a knowledge level analysis onto a computational framework. In *Proceedings of the 9th European Conference on Artificial Intelligence* London: Pitman Publishing.

29. Voss, A., Karbach, W., Drouven, U., Lorek, D., & Schukey, R. (1990). Operationalization of a synthetic problem. German National Research Center for Computer Science. Task I.2.1 report, ESPRIT Basic Research Action REFLECT.

30. Waterman, D. (1986). *A Guide to Expert Systems.* MA: Addison Wesley.

31. Wielinga, B., Akkermans, H., Schreiber, G., & Balder, J. (1989). A knowledge acquisition perspective on knowledge-level models. In J. Boose & B. Gaines (Eds.), *Proceedings Knowledge Acquisition Workshop KAW'89, Banff:* University of Calgary SRDG Publications.

32. Wielinga, B. & Breuker, J. (1986). Models of expertise. In *Proceedings of the 7th European Conference on Artificial Intelligence, Brighton, UK.*

33. Winograd, T. & Flores, F. (1986). *Understanding Computers and Cognition.* Addison Wesley.

34. Woodward, B. (1990). Knowledge acquisition as the front end: Defining the domain. *Knowledge Acquisition, 2(2),* 73–94.

Building and Maintaining a Large Knowledge-Based System from a 'Knowledge Level' Perspective: the DIVA Experiment

Jean-Marc David[1]*, Jean-Paul Krivine[2]* and Benoit Ricard[3]

[1] RENAULT - Service Systèmes Experts
860 Quai de Stalingrad
F - 92109 Boulogne Billancourt, France

[2] EDF - Direction des Etudes et Recherches
1, Av. du Général de Gaulle
F - 92141 Clamart Cedex, France

[3] EDF - Direction des Etudes et Recherches
6, Quai Watier
F - 78401 Chatou Cedex, France

Abstract

Designing knowledge-based systems from a knowledge level perspective is becoming an increasingly widespread practice. Expected benefits from using this approach have been extensively described in literature. The purpose of this paper is to throw light on actual benefits based on a project aiming to design a diagnostic system for rotating machinery: DIVA.
DIVA is a large and complex application. The project started several years ago and is now in an advanced state of industrialisation. Moreover, it has addressed most of the issues related to second generation expert systems: knowledge acquisition, explanation of reasoning and maintainability.
For each of these issues, we will discuss and demonstrate practical benefits of the chosen approach.

1. Introduction

The introduction of a knowledge level for designing knowledge-based systems has been an important step forward in knowledge engineering during the last decade. The term "knowledge level" was first introduced by Newell [27]; it is now widely used to denote a more abstract level for describing problem solving behaviour. Recently, a large discussion has started on the accuracy of this term according to Newell's initial definition [37] [41]. In this paper, the term "knowledge level" will be used

---

* Part of the work described in this paper was carried out while these authors were at Alcatel-Alsthom-Recherche, former Laboratoires de Marcoussis.

in the latter sense, i.e. as a more abstract representation level for describing problem-solving behaviour, supposed to fill the gap between the expert's discourse and the implementation. Motivations for such an approach have been extensively described in literature. In particular, Chapters 3, 4 & 5 of this volume describe various approaches and summarise their benefits.

This paper is based on an industrial project whose aim was to design a diagnostic system for a specific kind of rotating machinery (turbine-generators in electrical power plants): DIVA. From this experiment, we will show the benefits that have been drawn from using a knowledge level approach for building a large and complex knowledge-based system. Most of these benefits have already been described elsewhere during the course of the project. This paper tries to summarise them; it also attempts to give a coherent presentation and vocabulary for the different facets of the project. The main objective of this paper is to put together arguments that should convince knowledge engineers to adopt a knowledge level approach as opposed to the now outdated first generation expert systems approach.

Results from the DIVA experiment are interesting for at least two reasons:

• Firstly, DIVA is a large and complex industrial application. Problems encountered during the project were non-trivial; the results presented here are thus significant. Moreover, the project has addressed most of the issues related to second generation expert systems: knowledge acquisition, explanation of reasoning, maintainability, etc. For each of these issues, we will discuss and demonstrate practical benefits of the chosen approach.

• The second reason is that the project was started several years ago. A first prototype was designed from 1985 to 1987. DIVA is now in an advanced state of industrialisation. Over the years, we have gathered a lot of experience and feedback. It is thus interesting to discuss the benefits of the approach, not just those we expected to gain when we designed the system, but the benefits we actually obtained.

Initial motivations for designing DIVA at the knowledge level were to benefit from a structured model-driven knowledge acquisition process, to provide enhanced explanations of reasoning, to improve maintainability and, lastly, to enable the design of a hybrid system combining knowledge-based modules with more classical programming modules. These motivations have been described in [14] [16]. Most of these issues will be discussed again in the following sections. Section 2 describes the application domain − the monitoring of large rotating machinery − and the DIVA project. Section 3 then introduces what we mean by modeling DIVA at the knowledge level. Benefits of this approach for knowledge acquisition and explanation of reasoning are presented and discussed in Section 4 and Section 5 respectively. Finally, Section 6 describes the validation of the system and the ongoing industrialisation.

2. Monitoring of Turbine-Generator Vibrations

2.1. The application domain

Turbine-generators play a critical role in electrical power plants: steam passes through turbines, which drive a generator to produce electricity. These large rotating machines – typically 70 meters long, weighing about 700 tons and with a normal speed of 1,500 rpm – need very careful surveillance. Condition monitoring of turbine-generators has two main objectives: 1) prevention of catastrophic failures to ensure the safety of both workers and the plant, and 2) early detection and diagnosis of developing faults to optimise the overhaul and maintenance programs. The diagnosis of a developing fault is necessary to predict further deterioration and anticipate this by acting appropriately: *"Will I have to shut the machine down? Should we continue using it, and if so under what conditions?"*

A good image of the internal state of a rotating machinery can be obtained by observing the vibrations induced by its rotation. Faults on such machines often produce an abnormal vibratory behaviour. It is thus important to monitor these vibrations along the whole length of the shaft line to detect and interpret changes. In France, automated monitoring of turbine generator vibrations dates from the end of the 1970s. Electricité de France has progressively fitted out more than 60 plants with monitoring systems that continuously measure and record the main working parameters, process these data, and set off alarms when the situation is considered abnormal. Unfortunately, experience has shown that the interpretation of data released by such monitoring systems is a tricky task for a non-specialist of the problem. On the other hand, turbine generator faults are not frequent enough – thankfully – for specialists to be needed in every plant. This may explain why rotating machinery has been the target of so many computer-based advisory systems [2] [10] [20] [22] [26] [28] [33] [38].

2.2. The DIVA* project

In 1985, GEC-Alsthom (French turbine generator maker), the Direction des Etudes et Recherches (R&D Division) of Electricité de France and Alcatel-Alsthom-Recherche (research laboratory for the Alcatel-Alsthom group) launched a joint AI project for the diagnosis of turbine generator faults [17] [32]. The aim of this system is to help plant maintenance staff to interpret changes in vibrations and to diagnose developing faults.

DIVA is a module that will be included in a more global surveillance and diagnosis assistance architecture for nuclear power plants: PSAD [23]. When requiring assistance in interpreting the abnormal behaviour of a turbine-generator, a maintenance engineer will start DIVA. DIVA will

---

* DIVA is an acronym for *DIagnostic de Vibrations d'Arbres* (Diagnosis of Shaft Vibrations).

acquire information on the incident – both by querying the user and by consulting data collected by monitoring systems within the PSAD – and will either identify and characterise the fault, or conclude that no fault is present.

The diagnosis of turbine generator faults is primarily based on the interpretation of monitored data. Such a diagnosis encounters all the usual difficulties of interpretation problems:

(i) Data have to be interpreted *globally*. The purpose of interpretation is to infer a consistent description that accounts for the observed phenomenas. Data do not have any meaning of their own and can only be explained within the framework of the inferred interpretation.

(ii) A great variety of information is necessary: vibratory measurements along the whole length of the shaft line, but also other running parameters: load, oil temperature of the bearings, hydrogen pressure, vacuum measurement, etc. The diagnosis also requires technological and historical information about the plant, e.g. *"what was done during the last overhaul?"*

(iii) Information is often uncertain or incomplete: monitored data, as well as information retrieved from the plant operator or databases, are often incomplete or uncertain. The use of redundancy and a careful analysis of inconsistencies are thus necessary.

(iv) Multiple faults are often present at the same moment and their manifestations may mask one another.

Furthermore, the types of problems DIVA has to deal with can vary greatly: instantaneous problems (e.g. a turbine blade loss will provoke a vibration step), short-term or long-term problems (e.g. a movement of the foundations will cause an upward trend over a period of months), recurrent problems (e.g. increasing difficulties in starting the machine), etc.

The project was launched in 1985; the first stage was completed in 1987 with the design of a first prototype. During the two following years (1988 & 1989), the knowledge base was continuously extended and completed; this led to minor modifications and refinements of the initial problem solving model. In 1990, an extensive validation of the second prototype was launched: about two years were spent testing and validating this prototype. Conclusions were very positive. It was decided to start the industrialisation of DIVA at the beginning of 1992. This industrial version should be installed in 1994.

The total effort, from the beginning of the project till the end of the industrialisation, can be estimated to approximately 25 man-years.

2.3. Overview of DIVA

DIVA diagnosis activity can be described through three high-level tasks: the *Diagnosis* task, the *Situation Recognition* task and the *Information Retrieval & Data Abstraction* task.

DIVA has to provide explanations for – potentially – abnormal symptoms. The role of the **diagnosis task** is to determine the cause of the problem. Given a list of possible faults, it has to establish which are the most plausible. Each established fault is then characterised in terms of severity, cause, location, etc. The Diagnosis task should also advise the user of possible interventions on the machine.

However, performing a diagnosis by directly mapping symptoms onto the set of possible faults would undoubtedly lead to a complex and even intractable task. The same fault may occur in various forms according to the context in which it appears (speed-up, steady conditions, etc.) which results in a very large combination of possible symptoms. Thus, before diagnosis, the system will try to assess as precisely as possible the context of the abnormal behaviour. This is the role of the **Situation Recognition** task, to provide an accurate characterisation of the problem situation. The *diagnosis task* will be based on faults evoked by the established situations. More precisely, the *Situation Recognition* task should (1) assess whether the situation really is a problem situation or not; (2) *recognise* the problem situation, i.e. detect atypical problems or problems outside the domain of expertise to ensure that DIVA's diagnosis knowledge is relevant to the problem at hand; and (3) elaborate a description of the problem to be used in the diagnosis. It has already been stated that DIVA has to deal with very different problems and that fault manifestations may vary considerably depending on the context; established situations will be used as contexts for diagnosing faults.

Lastly, both the *Diagnosis* task and the *Situation Recognition* task have to deal with a description of the considered case. The required information is not always directly available. The role of the **Information Retrieval & Data Abstraction** task is to retrieve the required information, either by sending requests to the user or to various databases, or to infer it through a data abstraction process (rule-based inferences or computations). This task should also maintain a coherent representation of the problem.
There is often more than one way to retrieve information, as illustrated by the following – simplified – example.

> *If we need to know whether or not the vibration is sensitive to the hydrogen pressure, the best way might be to send a request to the monitoring system; but, because the monitoring system has very precise and severe criteria, it may be unable to answer (for instance because too many parameters were changing).*
> *Another way is to ask the user: "did you get the impression that the vibration was sensitive to hydrogen?" If he cannot answer, a third way*

might be to retrieve the information from a database: "is the machine known to be sensitive to hydrogen?" Lastly, we can again ask the user for an experimentation: "stabilise the conditions, modify the hydrogen pressure and observe the vibration behaviour".

From this example, we can see that the methods cannot be used indifferently; the last query – if possible – will certainly deliver the most precise answer but will considerably disrupt operation. On the other hand, a request to the historical database is quite cheap but is obviously rather less informative. The different ways to retrieve the value of an attribute – i.e. the different methods we can use – and the strategy to follow are expert knowledge that should be explicitly represented.

3. Designing DIVA at the Knowledge Level

The complexity of the problem, and the level of competence expected of DIVA obviously require more than a small knowledge-based system. Designing DIVA as a pure first generation rule-based expert system would have undoubtedly led to most of the difficulties normally associated with this technology: brittleness of the system, knowledge acquisition as a bottleneck, poor explanation capabilities and, last but not least, difficulties of maintaining the knowledge base [19] [34] [36].

DIVA has thus been built using 2 main principles:

1) modelling DIVA at the knowledge level, i.e. in terms of what the system does, what kind of knowledge is processed, etc. We paid particular attention to making explicit the domain models and the different tasks to be achieved;

2) ensuring an implementation that reflects, as much as possible, this knowledge level model.

We shall first describe how DIVA has been modelled before commenting on the second design principle.

3.1. Characteristics of the knowledge level model

DIVA modelling was centered around the use of two concepts: *problem solving tasks* and *domain models*:

- *problem solving tasks* explicitly describe what has to be done. Solving a non-trivial problem can rarely be reduced to performing a single, simple task; on the contrary, there are various tasks that *should be made explicit. DIVA's problem solving tasks are largely indebted to Chandrasekaran's Generic Tasks [4] [15]; they combine both a goal and the method of reaching this goal. Actually, most of the tasks have only one associated method – hence the confusion. We will discuss at the end of this section the problems raised by not distinguishing between these two concepts.

Tasks can either be directly executed or decomposed into subtasks; DIVA's problem solving activity is thus described using a collection of about 30 tasks and subtasks.

- *domain models* contain the knowledge needed by the tasks: taxonomies of domain objects, taxonomy of problem situation prototypes, mapping knowledge that associates situation descriptions to hypothesis, etc.

The task structure

Problem solving tasks describe what has to be done. They have their own knowledge either to achieve their goal or to split themselves up into subtasks. The decomposition of complex tasks into simpler ones enables us to describe DIVA at various levels of detail.

As suggested earlier, DIVA's problem solving mechanism is a recognition process. DIVA first tries to recognise the problem among the typical problem situations it knows and, once a situation – or possibly several situations – have been recognised, DIVA elaborates its diagnosis. DIVA's root task, namely *Diagnosis of Large Rotating Machinery* is thus decomposed into three subtasks: *Situation Recognition, Diagnosis* and *Information Retrieval & Data Abstraction* [Figure 1]. The *Situation Recognition* and *Diagnosis* tasks are achieved through particular classification methods; both make use of the *Information Retrieval & Data Abstraction* task. These three subtasks are then further decomposed into more elementary subtasks.

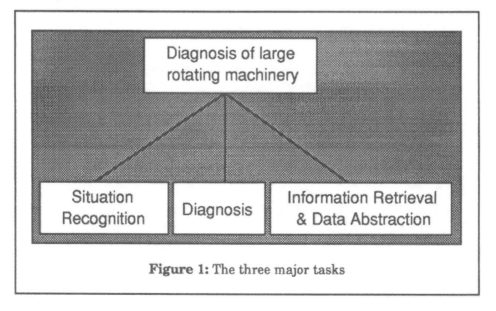

Figure 1: The three major tasks

One of the subtasks of the *Situation Recognition* task is the *Establish Situation* task. Its role is to consider a typical situation, represented within a prototype, and to judge how this hypothetical situation can account for the observed one. This task will thus either establish the prototype as a possible candidate or, on the contrary, reject it. The method used follows three steps. In other words, the *Establish Situation* task is decomposed into three subtasks that are executed sequentially: *Acquisition of Typical Features, Evaluation of Correspondence* and *Evocation of sub-prototypes* [Figure 2].

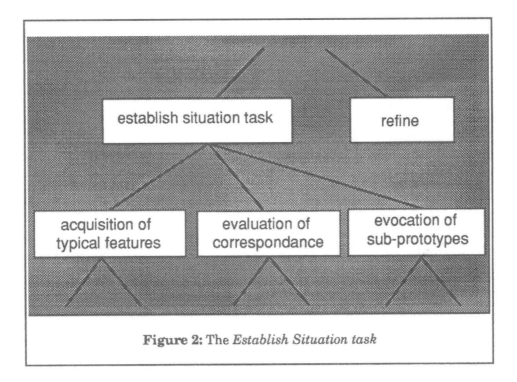

Figure 2: The *Establish Situation task*

- The role of the *Acquisition of Typical Features* task is to collect the most relevant features of the situation in question before trying to evaluate it.

- Then the *Evaluation of Correspondence* task tries to evaluate the match between the prototypical situation and the observed one. This may require additional information on the actual situation.

- Finally, the *Evocation* task suggests which of the sub-prototypes should or should not be considered next in order to refine the established situation. These evocations will be used by the *Refine* task to guide the reasoning and to prune the search.

These three subtasks are then further decomposed.

A task-level representation of control

Tasks not only decompose themsleves into subtasks; they also control the execution of their subtasks. Let us use the previous examples to illustrate this point.

One of DIVA's high level strategies is to recognise the problem before diagnosing it; if the problem is not sufficiently well identified – because the problem is an atypical one or is outside the domain of expertise – DIVA should not try to make a diagnosis. This strategy is directly expressed in the *Diagnosis of large rotating machinery* task as a condition for linking the two subtasks: *Situation Recognition* and *Diagnosis* [Figure 1]. Not only will DIVA decide to stop the reasoning process because the problem situation is not sufficiently well assessed, but it will also be able to explain the control decision at this level of abstraction. Section 5, on explanation of reasoning, discusses this aspect in greater detail as well as it provides other examples.

The second example concerns the *Establish Situation* task [Figure 2]. These three subtasks should normally be executed sequentially; however:

1) the *acquisition of typical feature* task may be interrupted if *reject values* are encountered;

2) if key data are missing, or not enough information has been gathered during the *acquisition of typical feature* step, DIVA may decide not to evaluate the correspondence and to stop considering this hypothesis;

3) if the prototype has not been sufficiently well established, it may be decided not to evoke the sub-prototypes.

The important point here is that these control decisions are expressed at the task level. Representing control at the task level provides a more abstract representation of the system's strategy that will be fully exploited in explaining reasoning. But it is already of particular use in understanding the system's behaviour, anticipating and predicting the consequences of modifications in the knowledge base and more generally keeping control of a large knowledge base.

Multiple competing methods

DIVA does not distinguish between tasks and methods. This limitation has not been a problem, since for most tasks there is only one associated method. However, it may be that several methods are in competition for the same task as there may exist a number of different ways of achieving this task. For instance, to determine the value of an attribute, several methods can be used: a question put to the user, a query to a particular database, an inference or a computation. Moreover, there can be several possible questions to the user, several possible queries – if we can access several databases – or several computations. Similarly, different methods can be used to evaluate the correspondence between a prototype and the actual situation. Lastly, multiple competing methods are also very useful while building and debugging the knowledge base. It is thus possible to complement a method whose domain models are still incomplete with another method – e.g. interactive simulation – in order to run complete cases even when some parts of the knowledge base are still missing. Distinguishing between methods and tasks has proved to be a clean and useful distinction [3] [35]; if DIVA were to be remodelled now, such a distinction should apply.

3.2. Implementation of the knowledge level model

The second design principle we have followed is to implement DIVA in such a way that its actual structure reflects, as precisely as possible, the knowledge level model. Each concept described at the knowledge level should have a correspondence at the implementation level. This principle is now known as the *structural correspondence* principle [30].

The DIVA prototype was written in a sophisticated object-oriented language. This enabled us to construct a framework for representing DIVA. Domain models have been easy to represent through the various taxonomies and relations provided by the language. Tasks have been defined as particular objects, with their own behaviour. This has been useful for the explanation module as well for tracing tasks while debugging the system (see section 4.3. on debugging at the knowledge level).

4. A Model-driven Knowledge Acquisition Process

Knowledge acquisition has undoubtedly been one of the most challenging tasks in designing DIVA. Moreover, several experts have been involved in the knowledge acquisition process. Basically, those from EDF tended to be specialists in diagnosis while those from GEC-Alsthom were specialists in the design of the machine. The construction of the knowledge base required the combination of several types of expertise.

Knowledge acquisition consists principaly of 2 activities:

- modelling, i.e. constructing a knowledge level model of the system;

- building the knowledge base, i.e. filling the previously defined model.

Interviews with experts, analysis of cases encountered in the past, simulations of the diagnosis activity, etc. were used as a basis for constructing the model. Knowledge of generic models also played a role in

386

guiding modelling. In this sense, DIVA is indebted to Centaur [1] and MDX [6], among others. We will not describe the modelling process any further; modelling is a creative activity and is still an open issue for knowledge acquisition [24] [29] [40].

Part of the model has already been described in the previous section. We will now focus on building the knowledge base. This has been achieved through a model-driven knowledge elicitation process.

4.1. Activities for building the knowledge base

The actual process of building the knowledge base, once the model has been constructed, can be split up into four different activities [Figure 3].

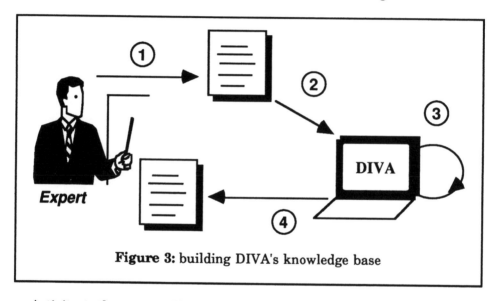

Figure 3: building DIVA's knowledge base

• Activity 1: the experts fill in forms corresponding to the knowledge to be acquired. [Figure 4] shows an example of a form corresponding to the prototype described in [Figure 5].

• Activity 2 consists of translating the acquired knowledge into the system; the translation is done using a specific editor that has been developed during the project. This activity, usually a tricky task in first generation expert systems, is here semi-automatic due to the correspondence between the forms that have been filled in and the knowledge base structure. However, ambiguities may remain and need to be detected. This is due to the fact that these forms are simplified as regards the knowledge level model, and our knowledge level model is not a formal one. Hence, the knowledge engineer will still have to *interpret* part of the knowledge provided by the experts. However, these interpretations are simpler and fewer – by orders of magnitude – than when building first generation expert systems.

Name of the prototype: **Instability during a transitory**
Father: **Vibration evolution during a transitory**
Sons:

Definition: Frequency most concerned

Feature 1

Value:	$\Omega / 2$	*Weight:*	0.6
Value:	$\neq \Omega / 2$	*Weight:*	- 0.5
Value:		*Weight:*	

Condition:

Definition: Date of the last speed-up

Feature 5

Value:	< 1 day	*Weight:*	0.6
Value:	else	*Weight:*	0
Value:		*Weight:*	
Value:		*Weight:*	

Condition: This speed-up was a cold start

Figure 4: Excerpt from the form to be filled by the experts

Activities 3 and 4 can be achieved concurrently; in fact, they are complementary.

• Activity 3 corresponds to tests and simulations that are carried out either by the experts or by the knowledge engineers. The most important aspect here is the possibility of debuging the knowledge base at the knowledge level. The explanation mechanism described in Section 5 has also proved particularly useful during this activity.

• Activity 4 illustrates another facet of the knowledge acquisition process that we have carried out. A module has been developed that automatically generates documents from the system's knowledge base. A complete generation of the knowledge base will produce several hundred pages of forms. Thanks to the correspondence between the implemented knowledge base and the knowledge level model, these generated forms [Figure 5] are closed enough to the initial forms to be presented to the experts for comparison. Experts are thus able to check what knowledge engineers have understood from what they write down and what has actually been entered in the system; they can suggest modifications if necessary.

This generation module was extensively used during the validation of DIVA (Section 6.).

4.2. Model-driven knowledge elicitation

The initial construction of a knowledge level model leads to a precise identification of *what* knowledge is to be acquired. The knowledge that is to be represented in the system and the way in which the system will use this knowledge are clearly understood by both the knowledge engineers and the experts. For instance, when asked to describe typical situations and the different kinds of knowledge associated with them, the experts know exactly what to provide and the role each piece of knowledge will play in the problem solving process. Moreover, because we have a global picture of what is to be acquired, it is possible to assess the progress of knowledge acquisition, to estimate what has already been done and what still remains to be done.

However, although a clear identification of what is to be acquired is an important step, it is not sufficient. We also need to define *how* to acquire it. Indeed, knowledge cannot be acquired just anyhow and in any order. We thus need to structure the knowledge elicitation process in such a way that it appears natural to the experts [25]. In particular, we need to consider which piece of knowledge might help to acquire another piece of knowledge, i.e. we need to *plan* the acquisition steps.

We have thus defined a methodology to guide the knowledge elicitation process [16]. This methodology defines the different steps to follow; it is supported by specific forms to be filled in by the experts and specific tools we have developed. Before discussing this approach any further, let us illustrate with an example this step-by-step knowledge elicitation process. The knowledge elicitation process related to the Situation Recognition task will proceed through the following four steps:

1. **defining a skeleton of the prototype taxonomy**: the recognition process proceeds through the identification of the current situation using a taxonomy of typical situations. This first step is thus an important and crucial one; indeed, experts must agree on a common basis before sharing out the work that remains to be done.

2. **representing the typical features:** all previously identified situations, from the most general to the most specific, now have to be precisely described through their typical features. This often leads to a modification of the previously established skeleton.

Prototype:
instability of the shaft in a bearing during a power transitory

refine: sudden changes in vibration pattern during a power transitory

refined by: problem of instability related to a condenser pressure variation
problem of instability related to movements of the foundations;
...

description:

• type of the vibration change	expected value: cf. Figure 5
• frequency most concerned by vibration change	expected value: $\Omega / 2$
• amplitude of the $\Omega / 2$ frequency change	expected value: > 100 m
• instability is a recurrent problem on this machine	expected value: yes
• date of the last speed-up	expected value: < one day ago
• size of the power transitory	expected value: large
• technology of the bearings concerned	expected value: coussinets-patins
• loading of the bearings concerned	expected value: rather low
• date of last modification of the bearings concerned	expected value: recent

condition to evaluate the correspondence:
at least 30 % of the typical features
and the change in the $\Omega / 2$ frequency should be known

Establish / reject rules:
R1: if the vibration change looks like Figure 5 then establish the prototype (0.7)
R2: if the vibration change looks like Fig 2 or Figure 4 then reject the prototype (0.6)
R3: if the frequency most concerned is $\Omega / 2$ then establish the prototype (0.6)
R4: if the frequency most concerned is not $\Omega / 2$ then reject the prototype (0.5)
R5: if the $\Omega / 2$ frequency is not concerned in the change then reject the prototype (1)
R6: if the change in $\Omega / 2$ frequency is greater than 100 m then establish prototype (0.7)
R7: if instability is a recurrent problem on this machine then establish prototype (0.5)
R8: if instability is a recurrent problem on this kind of machine then establish ... (0.3)
R9: if the last speed-up happened less than one day ago and was a *cold* one then ...
R10: if large power transitory during the last hour then establish prototype (0.4)
R11: if the technology of the bearings concerned is "coussinet à patins" then...
R12: if the technology of the bearings concerned is "coussinet elliptique" then reject...
R13: if the loading of the bearings concerned is low then establish the prototype (0.5)
R14: if the bearings concerned have been recently modified then establish ... (0.5)
R15: if the bearing oil has been recently changed for a more viscous one then ...
R16: ...

Evocation rules:
R1: if there has been a recent variation in condenser pressure
then evoke "problem of instability related to condenser pressure vibration"
with priority 0.8
R2: ...

Related diagnosis:
bearing fault ...

Figure 5: Excerpt of a prototype description
in a early stage of completion

3. **representing "matching" knowledge:** once steps 1 and 2 have been terminated, prototypes are completed with the knowledge they need to establish or reject themselves. The acquisition of this knowledge is guided by the typical features represented in step 2: at the start, decisions will be based on a simple interpretation of these features [figures 4 & 5]. As acquisition progresses, rules will become more and more sophisticated to account for more complex cases.

4. **representing control knowledge:** this is the "final touch" to the picture. Reject values may be added on some typical features; the condition under which the correspondence can be evaluated is specified; evocation rules may be added. These evocation rules provide suggestions about the prototypes to consider next, suggestions that will be used by the *Refine* task to better control the reasoning.

4.3. Debugging at the knowledge level

Debugging requires, as does explaining reasoning, to understand and to reason on what the system does, why it does it and how it has achieved a particular behaviour. In addition, debugging also requires to compare a abnormal behaviour with the expected behaviour. Debugging a knowledge-based system at the implementation level, i.e. by tracing rule firing or message passing, is a laborious and tedious task. The behaviour of the system is obscured by the low level of abstraction and the important steps in problem solving are often hidden by numerous irrelevant details. The structural correspondence between DIVA's implementation and its knowledge level model has, on the contrary, enabled us to debug it at a much more abstract level. By tracing the different tasks that are achieved, we can trace system behaviour at various levels of detail. Tracing the main tasks enables the main steps in the reasoning to be followed; when necessary, the tracing of specific subtasks enables us to detail specific parts of the reasoning. We are thus able to determine the cause of the abnormal behaviour and to correct it accordingly.

For instance, suppose a fault has not been correctly assessed. There are several possible causes: the problem situation might have not been correctly assesed; a characteristic symptom of the fault has not been correctly inferred; etc. Each of these causes can be easily linked to DIVA's behaviour and the corresponding task be traced.

Tracing tasks is done using a very general mechanism associated to the task meta-class. There are almost no overheads in system construction. On the contrary, this function has proved to be of considerable value for debugging and tuning the knowledge base.

4.4. What the experts should know about the model

Knowledge level modelling is supposed to fill the gap between the experts' discourse and the implementation. One of the assumptions behind this approach is that the constructed model should provide an intermediate framework, precise enough to enable a straightforward and non-ambiguous implementation while remaining *natural* enough to be easily understood and used by the experts. So the question is: *how well did the experts appropriate the DIVA model?*

First of all, it should be stressed that the experts have rapidly integrated the main points of the model. And while they recognise that the model does not correspond to their way of reasoning, they acknowledge they found it natural enough to be at ease with.
It was clearly not our intention to account for the way an expert reasons – actually, given the complexity of the processes involved, the current state of the art in AI would have probably not enabled us to achieve such a goal anyway. The important point is that they have been able to appropriate this model and that they have been able to use this framework to express their knowledge.
It might be interesting to add that during the knowledge elicitation phase, while we were building the knowledge base, the experts decided independently to use a large part of the model in documents external to the project to explain how diagnosis should be performed. This convinced us that they had fully integrated the model and that they have adopted the model as a way of communicating about their job. This story had a beneficial side-effect for the project since future users heard about the main concepts of DIVA and were familiar with them long before they saw the first demo.

Obviously, a few subtle points have been more difficult to assimilate. For instance, the distinction between a prerequisite condition for an attribute and multiple conditions in a rule premise has long been a point of confusion. Inevitably, acquired knowledge may still contain ambiguities that will need to be detected by the knowledge engineers.

4.5. Conclusions on knowledge acquisition

We have focused our discussion on knowledge elicitation, assuming the model to be already constructed. However, building the knowledge base, i.e. filling up the model, often leads to its modification or refinement. This is what happened in our case. For instance, the *Diagnosis* task was added only when it appeared impossible to represent all the knowledge in the situation prototype taxonomy; diagnosis could thus no longer be simply attached to the different situations but was the result of a new problem solving task. Not only was it possible to easily modify the model but the way the model was implemented also ensured an easy modification of this implantation, and without unwanted side-effects.

In its current version, DIVA knows more than 85 problem situations and 35 faults. By adopting a well principled design (both a knowledge level modelling approach and the structural correspondence principle), it has been possible to acquire – and then to maintain – a large knowledge base. We are convinced that this would have been intractable – if not completely impossible – with a first generation expert system approach.

5. Explaining Reasoning

DIVA has addressed two different kinds of explanations: explanations of reasoning, i.e. explanations of the behaviour of the system, built from a trace of its reasoning, and *reconstructive* explanations, mostly concerned with justifying the conclusions by adopting another point of view [11] [12] [13] [18] [39] [42].

Reconstructive explanations were used to build *causal scenarios* supposed to account for the system's diagnosis by reconstructing the story of what happened in the machine. This requires two knowledge bases: one to infer the diagnosis (the one which contains DIVA's competence) and another one to support the causal reasoning. The role of these causal explanations was both to check the coherence of the diagnosis and to convince the user that the diagnosis was well founded, through the use of a different, more understandable, knowledge. This particular kind of explanation is no longer part of the system; it will not be described here.

We will now discuss how explanations of reasoning can be greatly enhanced and abstracted by relating them to the knowledge level model of the system.

5.1. Principles

The implementation of DIVA reflects its knowledge level model. The structural correspondence principle enables us to closely map the system's behaviour onto the model its designers or users have in mind. The DIVA experiment has demonstrated the efficiency of such an approach for debugging and maintaining a large knowledge base (see Section 4). But the most obvious advantage of this structural correspondence principle is surely the explanation of reasoning.

Explaining reasoning requires to reason on a representation of the system's activity. DIVA's explanations of reasoning is based on 1) the explicit task structure and 2) a trace of the tasks that are performed. This trace usually contains – for an average session – more than one thousand task instances. Such a trace provides a structured representation of behaviour at a much more abstract level than the one provided by conventional implementations.

Every query about the system's activity will be expressed and interpreted in terms of the knowledge level model tasks. Thus, the three general types of queries often found in KBS are:

- why do (did) you perform this task? e.g. *why are you asking me this question? why are you considering this situation? why are you trying to find out the value of this attribute?*

- how did you perform this task? e.g. *how did you evaluate this attribute? how did you conclude on this situation? how did you diagnose this fault?*

- why didn't you perform this task? e.g. *why didn't you consider this situation? didn't you evoke this fault?*

Actually, the way we profit from the explicit representation of the task structure to build explanations is very similar to what Clancey has done with NEOMYCIN [8] [9] [21]. Potentially, every task can be explained through a general explanation mechanism. However, not all tasks have the same interest for the user who often perceives the system's activity through just a few particular tasks. We therefore preferred to restrict queries and to tailor explanations to these specific tasks. This enabled us to build more easily *global* explanations. We will now illustrate some of the capabilities of the explanation module in a set of examples.

5.2. Four commented examples

Let us begin with a very simple "why" example (Figure 6) that takes advantage of the explicit representation of the *check-prerequisites* task.

```
-   Did you stop the machine after the incident?

-   Why this question?

-   I need to know whether there have been [...] (any abnormal vibrations) during a
slow down after the incident. This is meaningless if you did not stop the machine.


            Figure 6: First example of a "why" explanation
```

The second "why" example (Figure 7) is a more complex one. For the sake of simplicity, specific domain knowledge has been ruled out and replaced by generic terms. An excerpt of the corresponding trace of tasks is given in [Figure 8]. This excerpt should not be confused with a simple goal/sub-goal stack (as in Teiresias, for instance); the way methods can decompose a task into subtasks is much more rich and complex.

- *Why are you asking me this question? (Question 23)*

- I am gathering the typical features of the situation Y. (1)

I am trying to identify the problem situation before elaborating a diagnosis. (2)
I have already recognised the situation X and I am trying to refine it in Y. (3)
The first step when considering a situation is to gather the relevant information in the
context. (4). Therefore, I am asking a question in order to establish the value of A. (5)
This may help to infer the value of B (6) which is a typical feature of the situation Y.
In this context, I expect the value V for B.

Figure 7: Second example of a "why" explanation

The explanation provided by DIVA in this particular example is built as
follows. First, (1) is a short summary of the problem solving process
whose role is to specify the context. The second part details the
relationship between question 23 and a higher level task, here the
Situation Recognition task (2). The most relevant tasks are then quoted:
establish Y (3), gather relevant features (4), evaluate attributes B (6) and
A (5). Note that this explanation makes use both of knowledge of the task
structure (identifying the problem before diagnosing, establish/refine as
a way of classifying) and domain knowledge (Y refines X, expected
value V for parameter B).

Ask question 23
(...)
Select an evaluation method for A
(...)
Evaluate A
(...)
Evaluate premise P1 of rule R1
(...)
Use the rule base BR1 to evaluate B
(...)
Select an evaluation method for B
(...)
Evaluate B
(...)
Acquisition of typical features for prototype Y
(...)
Establish prototype Y
(...)
Situation recognition
(...)
DIVA: session 1

Figure 8: Stack of active tasks

The "how" explanation [Figure 9] also combines strategic and domain knowledge. The evaluation of attribute A has been decomposed into several subtasks, but most of them have been considered as irrelevant for explanation in this case (no specialisation of the object in its taxonomy, prerequisite true, no constraints on this attribute, etc.). Thus, the explanation focuses on how different methods can be used to achieve this task. The three different methods available for this particular attribute are listed.

- *How did you get the value for attribute A of object O?*

- I could use one of 3 different methods to evaluate A:

      - inference from the rule base: BR1;
      - access to the historical database: BD1;
      - question to the user.

These methods should be used in this order. I tried to apply the rule base BR1, but no likely value has been inferred. I sent a request to the database BD1 where I found the value V for A.

Figure 9: Example of a "how" explanation

The last example [Figure 10] refers to the *situation recognition* task. Basically it is a "why-not" explanation, but note that it also includes an explanation of *how* the ancestor situation was rejected.

-   *Why didn't you consider the situation Y?*

-   The situation Y refines the situation X which has not been recognised. Thus, it is not useful to consider the situation Y.

The situation X was not recognised because, when collecting its characteristic features, I found value V for the feature F; V is a reject value for this situation hypothesis.

Figure 10: A "why-not" explanation

5.3. Conclusions on explaining reasoning

These four examples illustrate the quality of the explanations produced by DIVA. The explicit representation of problem solving tasks and associated domain models is the basis for elaborating enhanced and more abstract explanations. Because we restricted explanation facilities to only a subset of the tasks, it was possible to tailor the explanation generation so as to obtain very impressive and relevant explanations. From an application point of view, such a restriction is reasonable; it offers a good compromise between the quality of produced explanations and the required development effort.

6. Validation and Industrialisation

Putting DIVA into actual operation required a two-stage approach: first, a thorough validation of the prototype had to be undertaken; then, specifications of the *industrial* version had to be written down.

6.1. Validation of DIVA

In order to ensure that DIVA was indeed able to perform the expected service, it was necessary to carefully validate its capacities and its knowledge base [7] [31]. Doing this, we intended to answer three main questions: *is DIVA able to handle turbo-generator incidents correctly? how easy is it to correct and/or expand the knowledge base? would the reasoning and the questions asked by DIVA be accepted by its users?*

DIVA tested by the experts

A preliminary task in the validation process was to evaluate whether or not the knowledge expressed by the experts had been correctly represented in the DIVA's knowledge base. A two-fold protocol was thus established: a static verification of the knowledge base had to be performed by the experts – who should appreciate how well their knowledge had been transposed – and a series of dynamic tests were conducted, in which case-studies were submitted to DIVA, and the results compared to expert expectations according to predefined criteria. These two steps are very similar to Activities 3 and 4 of knowledge elicitation; however, the motivations are slightly different.

Static verification

Static verification relies on DIVA's ability to generate forms that describe the content of the knowledge base in a similar way to how the knowledge was expressed by the experts. Expert static analysis was first focused on exhaustive comparison of the content of the prototypes in DIVA (characteristic information, confirmation and evocation rules) with what had been provided by the experts during knowledge acquisition. Similar analyses were performed for fault and complex parameter descriptions. Automatic checks were also defined to detect errors or inconsistencies in the knowledge base. These automatic verifications are systematically performed prior to releasing a new version of the knowledge base.

Dynamic validation

To test DIVA in its various configurations, a matrix of the main probable or possible faults in each operation condition was established. A test-case was defined for each fault in the matrix, adapted when possible from a real case observed on a machine, so as to represent a typical malfunction case. A two-part form was filled in for each test case. The first part of the form, filled in prior to the experimentation, contained the description of the anomaly, the technological and historical background of the machine, and the diagnosis, from the most probable to the least probable possible faults. The second part, filled in after the test, contained the expert's remarks on the session. Two criteria were emphasised:

- quality of the diagnosis, in terms of comparison between what the expert expected and what DIVA found (either in a positive form, viz. expected faults, or in a negative form, viz. impossible faults),

- pertinence of the diagnosis path followed. As the behaviour of DIVA is built upon a progressive recognition mechanism, the correctness of this progression – as much as possible avoiding pointless searches – is considered by experts as an essential feature of DIVA.

More than 100 cases were used in this validation stage.

DIVA tested by future users

The prototype was then evaluated by future users of operational services in order to validate the industrial product specifications as regards the users' needs in power stations. The evaluation consisted of testing the expert system with more than 30 concrete examples of failures detected on site. The main objectives were to give an overall assessment of the system's aid to diagnostic fields, to analyse its suitability to user competence, to understand user's reactions to the questions asked, to validate the method, to rate its diagnostic quality and finally to evaluate DIVA's ability to give explanations.

Most of the participants in the evaluation were impressed by DIVA's diagnosis ability. The competence required to use the system seemed adequate as regards the user profile. As the questions require a good knowledge of turbogenerators, users felt in a way "flattered" by the level of dialogue that could be established with the system. Pertinent questions were also asked which the user might have overlooked. Consequently, DIVA was perceived as a useful tool for an on-site diagnosis of faults. Evaluation showed a high sensitivity of DIVA's diagnosis to key questions concerning the definition of the phenomenon. It seemed necessary to specify some important definitions and to check the validity of the most critical answers. Finally DIVA's ability to provide explanations for its reasoning and precisions on its questions appeared to be of great value.

6.2. Industrialisation

Validating DIVA has been a large-scale project. A rough estimate indicates that about 4 man-years were spent on it. Results were very positive: DIVA correctly handled more than 90% of submitted cases in terms of accuracy of diagnosis. Based on the results of this validation phase, the decision was taken to industrialise DIVA.

7. Conclusion

The DIVA experiment has demonstrated the benefits of adopting a knowledge level approach for building knowledge-based systems. Benefits discussed in this paper are real ones that have been gained on a complex industrial problem over more than 6 years; they reside in the following points:

• *a more principled design:* DIVA was constructed using a top-down refinement process rather than the first generation bottom-up approach; this has eliminated many unecessary development iterations;

• *a model-driven knowledge aquisition process:* what knowledge is to be acquired, and the role of each chunk of knowledge in the problem solving process, are precisely defined by the knowledge level model. This has greatly facilitated the constitution of a large knowledge base;

• *enhanced debugging facilities:* DIVA takes full advantage of the correspondence between its knowledge level model and its implementation structure. Tracing problem solving tasks and inspecting explicit domain models should be contrasted with tracing message passing or rule firing while debugging first generation expert systems;

• *enhanced explanations:* the explicit representation of the task structure and domain models have enabled us to explain reasoning at a higher level of abstraction. Explanations have played a major role in making DIVA's results understandable and thus in the acceptance of DIVA by its users.

DIVA was mostly designed between 1985 and 1987. Since then, much of the effort has been spent on extending, refining and validating the knowledge base. Maintaining and improving DIVA during these years has not been the intractable task that it could have been – given the size and complexity of the system. DIVA is now about enter service on real plants. We are confident that the approach we have adopted will ensure the perennity of the system.
While knowledge level modelling and second generation expert systems are now increasingly used, we do hope results steemming from this project will constitute convincing arguments for adopting and spreading this approach.

Acknowledgements

DIVA has been an exciting project, mainly because of the enthusiasm of the people involved. We would like to thank the experts: Benoit Michau, Eric Veith, Roger Chevalier – especially for his patience in debugging the knowledge base – and

Jacques Morel, who acted as lead expert in the DIVA project and is now responsible for the PSAD project. We would also like to thank all the people who contributed to the project, especially Bernard Monnier and Pierre Vaudrey. Last, special thanks to Jean-Pierre Tiarri for his invaluable contribution to the design and the implementation of the prototype.

We also thank Philippe Laublet and Marc Linster for their comments on a previous version of this paper.

References

[1]   Aikins J.: "Prototypical Knowledge for Expert Systems"; Artificial Intelligence 20 (2); 1983.

[2]   Bannister R., Moore M.: "General Rotating Machinery Expert System"; Expert Systems 86; Brighton, UK; December 1986.

[3]   Chandrasekaran B., Johnson T.: "Generic Tasks and Task Structures: history, critique and new directions"; in *Second Generation Expert Systems*; JM. David, JP. Krivine & R. Simmons (Eds); Springer-Verlag, 1993.

[4]   Chandrasekaran B.: "Towards a Functional Architecture for Intelligence based on Generic Information Processing Tasks"; 10th IJCAI; Milano, Italy; 1987.

[5]   Chandrasekaran B.: "Towards a Taxonomy of Problem-Solving Types"; AI Magazine 1983.

[6]   Chandrasekaran B.: "Decomposition of domain knowledge into knowledge sources: the MDX approach"; Fourth CSCSI conference, Canada, May 1982.

[7]   Chevalier R., Ricard B., Morel J.: "Validation of Diva, a turbine-generator diagnosis expert system", International Joint Power Generation Conference, San Diego (USA), 1991.

[8]   Clancey W.: "From GUIDON to NEOMYCIN and HERACLES in Twenty Short Lessons"; AI Magazine, Summer 1986.

[9]   Clancey W., Letsinger R.: "NEOMYCIN: Reconfiguring a rule-based expert system for application to teaching"; 7th IJCAI; Vancouver, Canada; 1981.

[10]   Clapis A., Gallanti M., Stefanini A.: "Sistemi Esperti nella diagnostica di impianto: un'applicazione sperimentale" (in Italian); Automazione E Strumentazione; March 1984.

[11]   David J-M., Krivine J-P., Simmons R.: "Second Generation Experts Systems; a step forward in knowledge engineering"; in *Second Generation Expert Systems*; JM. David, JP. Krivine & R. Simmons (Eds); Springer-Verlag, 1993.

[12]   David J-M., Krivine J-P.: "Explaining Reasoning from Knowledge level Models"; European Conference on Artificial Intelligence (ECAI-90), 1990.

[13]   David J-M., Krivine J-P.: "Augmenting Experience-Based Diagnosis with Causal Reasoning"; Applied AI Journal, Special Issue on Causal Modelling (Hemisphere Publ.); 1989.
        also in: "Causal AI Models: steps towards applications" (Hemisphere Publ.).

[14] David J-M., Krivine J-P.: "Designing KBS within Functional Architectures: the DIVA experiment"; 5th IEEE Conf. on AI Applications; Miami, FL; 1989.

[15] David J-M.: "Functional Architectures and the Generic Task Approach"; the Knowledge Engineering Review, vol. 3 (3); 1988.

[16] David J-M., Krivine J-P.: "Acquisition of Expert Knowledge from Prototypical Situations" (in French); 8th International Workshop on Expert Systems and their Applications; Avignon, France; May 1988.

[17] David J-M., Krivine J-P.: "Using Prototypes in a Diagnosis Expert System: the DIVA Project" (in French); 7th International Workshop on Expert Systems and their Applications; Avignon, France; May 1987.

[18] David J-M., Krivine J-P.: "What Happened? Causal Reasoning in DIVA"; First European Workshop on Fault Diagnostics; Rhodes, Greece; August 1986.

[19] Davis R.: "Expert Systems; where are we and where do we go from here"; AI Magazine, 1982.

[20] Finn G., Hall J.: "An Expert System for Rotating Equipment Vibration Diagnosis"; EPRI Seminar; Boston, MA; May 1987.

[21] Hasling D., Clancey W., Rennels G.: "Strategic explanations for a diagnostic consultation system"; International Man-Machine Studies 20; 1984.

[22] Korteniemi A.: "An expert system for fault diagnostics of rotating machines", 2nd symposium on Expert Systems Applications to Power Systems, Seattle, Wash., USA, July 17-20, 1989.

[23] Mazalerat J-M., Morel J., Puyal C., Monnier B., Zwingelstein G., Legaud P.: "PSAD, An integrated tool for global vibratory and acoustic surveillance of EDF nuclear plants in the near future". SMORN 6 (Specialist Meeting On Reactor Noise), Gatlinburg, USA, May 19-24, 1991.

[24] Musen M.: "An overview of knowledge acquisition"; in *Second Generation Expert Systems*, JM. David, JP. Krivine and R. Simmons (Eds); Springer Verlag; 1993.

[25] Musen M. et al.: "Use of a domain model to drive an interactive knowledge eliciting tool"; International Journal of Man-Machine Studies (26); 1987.

[26] Milne R.: "Artificial Intelligence for Rotating Machinery Monitoring"; 12th IMACS World Congress; Paris; July 1988.

[27] Newell A.: "The Knowledge Level"; Artificial Intelligence, 1982.

[28] Osborne R.: "Online Artificial Intelligence-Based Turbine Generator Diagnostics"; AI Magazine; fall 1986.

[29] Rademakers P., Vanwelkenhuysen J.: "Generic Models and their Support in Modeling Problem Solving Behavior"; in *Second Generation Expert Systems*, David J-M., Krivine J-P. and Simmons R. (Eds); Springer Verlag; 1993.

[30] Reinders M., Vinkhuyzen E., Voss A., Akkermans H., Balder J., Bartsch-Spörl B., Bredeweg B., Drouven U., van Harmelen F., Karbach W., Karssen Z., Schreiber G. and Wielinga B.; "A

conceptual Modelling framework for Knowledge level Reflection"; AI-Communications, Vol 4, n°2/3, 1991.

[31] Ricard B., Chevalier R., Bonnet J-C., Tiarri J-P.: "Test and validation of DIVA, a turbine-generator diagnosis expert system"; Advanced Information Processing in Automatic Control (AIPAC 89), IFAC/IMACS/IFORS, Nancy (France), 1989.

[32] Ricard B., Monnier B., Morel J., David J-M., Krivine J-P., Tiarri J-P.: "Overview of DIVA: an expert system for turbine-generator diagnosis"; American Nuclear Society Conference on Artificial Intelligence and Other Innovative Computer Applications in the Nuclear Industry; Snowbird, Utah; 1987.

[33] Skatteboe R., Lihvod E., Hystad R.: "DIAMON: a Knowledge-Based System for Fault Diagnosis and Maintenance Planning for Rotating Machinery"; 6th International Conference on Expert Systems and their Applications; Avignon, France; May 1986.

[34] Soloway E., Bachant J., Jensen K.: "Assessing the Maintainability of XCON-in-RIME: Coping with the Problems of a VERY Large Rule-Base"; Proc. of the National Conference on AI, Seattle, Washington; July 13-17, 1987.

[35] Steels L.: "The Componential Framework and its Role in Reusability"; in *Second Generation Expert Systems*, David J-M., Krivine J-P. and Simmons R. (Eds); Springer Verlag; 1993.

[36] Steels L.: "Second Generation Expert Systems"; Future Generation in Computer Systems, (1) 4; 1985.

[37] Sticklen J., Wallingford E.: "On The Relationship between Knowledge-Based Systems Theory and Application Programs: Leveraging Task Specific Approaches"; in *Second Generation Expert Systems*, David J-M., Krivine J-P. and Simmons R. (Eds); Springer Verlag; 1993.

[38] Stuart J., Winson J.: "Turbomac: an expert system to aid in the diagnosis of cause of vibration-producing problems in large turbomachinery"; Radian Technical Report; August 1985.

[39] Swartout B., Moore J.: "Explanation in Second Generation Expert Systems: Depth and Dialogue"; in *Second Generation Expert Systems*, David J-M., Krivine J-P. and Simmons R. (Eds); Springer Verlag; 1993.

[40] Terpstra P., van Heijst G., Shadbolt N., Wielinga B.:"Knowledge Acquisition Process Support Through Generalised Directive Models"; in *Second Generation Expert Systems*, David J-M., Krivine J-P. and Simmons R. (Eds); Springer Verlag; 1993.

[41] van de Velde W.: "Issues in Knowledge Level Modelling"; in *Second Generation Expert Systems*, David J-M., Krivine J-P. and Simmons R. (Eds); Springer Verlag; 1993.

[42] Wick M.: "Second Generation Expert System Explanation"; in *Second Generation Expert Systems*, David J-M., Krivine J-P. and Simmons R. (Eds); Springer Verlag; 1993.

Part IV

Knowledge Acquisition

An Overview of Knowledge Acquisition

Mark A. Musen

Knowledge Systems Laboratory
Departments of Medicine and Computer Science
Stanford University
Stanford, CA 93205-5479 USA

musen@camis.stanford.edu

Abstract. The process of knowledge acquisition is central in the development of intelligent computer programs. In the second generation of expert systems, the elicitation, modeling, and representation of human problem-solving knowledge remain principal barriers that development teams must overcome. This overview surveys some of the major barriers to the construction of expert-system knowledge bases and reviews current and emerging knowledge-acquisition methods. The common thread that runs through research on knowledge acquisition is the creation of models of problem-solving behavior and the use of those models to guide further knowledge elicitation and model formulation.

Knowledge acquisition was first identified as a central concern in the development of first-generation expert systems nearly three decades ago. Since that time, various investigators have proposed explanations for why building a knowledge base is so difficult. Some authors attribute the problem to the lack of a formal theory for knowledge engineering, stressing the need to establish more principled methodologies that can be used by system builders. Others point to the impalpable nature of human expertise, claiming that the limited ability of experts to introspect on their problem-solving behavior and the difficulty of encoding their behavior within a computer may represent insurmountable barriers to the creation of truly "expert" systems. As we shall see, both perspectives are important.

Any discussion of knowledge acquisition compels us to consider approaches from computer science, from psychology, from philosophy, and from the social sciences. In this brief survey of the field, it is impossible to describe all the insights that any one of these points of view can offer—let alone to form a completely satisfactory integration. Consequently, my goal is to provide a rather broad survey of the salient issues, and to refer the reader to the individual research reports in this volume to observe how the field of knowledge acquisition can be sounded from many perspectives and to many different depths.

1 Impediments to Knowledge Acquisition

Developers of expert systems have spoken so much of the knowledge-acquisition "bottleneck" that the expression has become cliché. Nevertheless, knowledge acquisition remains the major difficulty in the creation of most practical knowledge bases. The nature of human knowledge, the problems associated with communicating knowledge, and the limitations of our languages for encoding knowledge within computers all contribute to the difficulties. Our emerging understanding of these potential barriers not only helps us to establish an agenda for research in the area of knowledge acquisition, but also can inform our adoption of practical second-generation knowledge-acquisition methods and tools.

1.1 The Problem of Tacit Knowledge

Human cognitive skills appear to be acquired in at least three generally distinct phases of learning [1]. Initially, there is the *cognitive* stage, in which the actions that are appropriate in particular circumstances are identified, either as a result of direct instruction or from observation of other people. In this stage, learners often rehearse verbally information needed for execution of the skill. Next comes the *associative* phase of learning, in which the relationships noted during the cognitive stage are practiced, and verbal mediation begins to disappear. With repetition and feedback, the person begins to apply the actions accurately, fluently, and efficiently. Then, in the final *autonomous* stage, the person "compiles" [2] the relationships from repeated practice to the point where she can perform them without conscious awareness. Suddenly, the person performs the actions appropriately, proficiently, and effortlessly—"without thinking." The knowledge has become *tacit*.

Philosophers have long made a distinction between the concepts *knowing how* and *knowing that* [3]. In recent years, it has become clear to cognitive psychologists that *knowing how* generally involves tacit knowledge, whereas *knowing that* requires knowledge accessible to consciousness. Tacit knowledge governs activities that are skilled, smooth, and efficient—behaviors that are neither easily decomposed into their components nor easily modified. The knowledge of which we are conscious, on the other hand, can be inspected, abstracted, and applied in totally novel contexts—albeit without the deftness associated with skilled behavior. Many psychologists, struck by the correspondences between human expertise and knowledge representation in AI, refer to tacit, compiled knowledge in humans as *procedural;* analogously, they refer to knowledge available to consciousness as *declarative* [4].

Although there certainly is no consensus regarding how knowledge is encoded physiologically in human memory, the evidence that problem solving by experts involves some degree of tacit knowledge has enormous implications for those researchers concerned with knowledge acquisition for expert systems. As humans become experienced in an application area and repeatedly apply their know-how to specific tasks, their declarative knowledge becomes procedural. Experts lose awareness of what they know. Consequently, the special knowledge that we would most like to incorporate into our expert systems often is the knowledge about which experts are least able to talk. Johnson [1] has identified this phenomenon as "the paradox of expertise."

The problem for knowledge engineers is that experts do not introspect reliably. Although human beings may have some declarative knowledge of the extent of their procedural memory, the two types of memory appear to be handled quite separately by the nervous system. For example, Cohen [5] has investigated patients with neurologic amnesia to learn more about the mechanisms of human memory. In one experiment, 12 such patients were taught how to solve the Tower of Hanoi puzzle. The patients with amnesia became proficient at the task just as quickly as did control subjects without amnesia and learned rapidly to perform the necessary sequences of moves "without thinking." However, despite their obvious acquired expertise at solving the Tower of Hanoi problem, *not one of the amnesia patients would ever state that he was familiar with the puzzle or knew its solution!*

In normal subjects with intact declarative memory, the distinction between procedural knowledge and declarative knowledge becomes even more important. Whereas declarative memory may continue to hold traces of knowledge that later is compiled procedurally, the declarative knowledge may well be imperfect. In a classic review article, Nisbett and Wilson surveyed evidence that suggests that people have "little or no introspective access to higher order cognitive processes" [6, p. 231]. In experimental situations, subjects have been shown to be frequently (1) unaware of the existence of a stimulus or cue influencing a response, (2) unaware that a response has been affected by a stimulus, and (3) unaware that a cognitive response has even occurred. Instead, subjects give verbal reports of their cognition based on prior causal theories from their declarative memory. These prior theories may or may not be accurate. In a given situation, a subject's verbal report of cognitive behavior is likely to be accurate only if the influential stimuli are salient enough to be *available* in declarative memory [7]. The stimuli also must be plausible causes of the response and must not be accompanied by other available, plausible, noninfluential factors.

Nisbett and Wilson's conclusions may be troubling to many of us simply because Western culture mistakenly teaches that accurate introspection somehow should be possible [8]. Yet despite our confident attempts at introspection, compiled knowledge is not accessible to our conscious awareness. Human beings frequently explain and rationalize their compiled behaviors without recognizing that their declarative explanations frequently are wrong. Consequently, knowledge engineers must seek ways to build expert systems by using techniques that do not force experts to answer questions that these experts cannot answer reliably.

1.2 The Problem of Miscommunication

People who develop expert systems often emphasize the communication difficulties that beset application specialists and knowledge engineers [9,10]. At least initially, the experts in the application area and the computer scientists building the knowledge base rarely speak the same language.

To represent the relevant knowledge in the computer, knowledge engineers must familiarize themselves with the domain of application. In some ways, the knowledge engineers must become experts. They must learn a new vocabulary and, perhaps, a new way of looking at problems. In the traditional view of knowledge-engineering, knowledge is said to flow from the domain expert to the knowledge engineer to the computer [11]. In this light, the accuracy of the knowledge base depends on the effectiveness of the knowledge engineer as an intermediary. Construction of optimum knowledge bases requires the knowledge engineer to understand the application area at a sufficient level of detail. Psychological studies of comprehension suggest that a person's prior knowledge of an application area is critical for assimilating new information correctly and for recognizing the need to clarify areas of misinterpretation. Knowledge engineers must either make an effort to learn the expert's problem area or risk suffering the consequences of misunderstanding what the expert is trying to convey.

Communication of knowledge is perceived as a stumbling block by domain experts as well. Because experts typically do not understand programming, they have little appreciation for what knowledge might be relevant for computer-based models of their behavior. They do not know what information they should volunteer.

The precision, explicitness, and consistency with which knowledge must be programmed may be at odds with the way experts talk about their fields—even in highly formalized application areas. This apparent lack of consistency does not necessarily mean that domain experts are capricious or irrational. Rather, these discrepancies point out fundamental differences between the ways that people and computers process information and indicate that much of human cognition—including the use of language—is influenced by factors that are unavailable to consciousness. Knowledge engineers cannot *a priori* expect domain experts to explain their specialized knowledge in precise, unambiguous terms, as no spoken language (including jargon) contains invariant definitions for what the words denote.

Winograd and Flores [12] were among the first authors to make the significance of these observations clear to workers in computer science. In their view, a primary objective of knowledge acquisition is the explicit construction of a *systematic domain*—a formal description of the expert's task in words that have unequivocal, agreed-on meanings. The systematic domain is created during the interactions of the expert and the knowledge engineer. Until these people identify the relevant concepts, label them, and decide unambiguously what the labels mean, it is impossible for domain experts to relate their knowledge in a consistent fashion. Thus, in the MYCIN domain, the use of terms such as "compromised host," "sterile site," and "significant organism" allowed both infectious-disease specialists and computer scientists to speak without confusion about the contents of the knowledge base and the behavior of the program. Equally important, these systematic terms allowed users to interact with MYCIN and to understand the intention of the questions the program asked. Knowledge acquisition "is often described as a process of 'capturing' the knowledge that experts already have and use. In fact, it is a creative design activity in which a systematic domain is created, covering certain aspects of the professionals' work" [12, p. 175]. In this perspective, knowledge acquisition is difficult not because experts and knowledge engineers do not speak the same language, but rather because they must work together to create a language.

1.3 The Problem of Using Knowledge Representations

In addition to the cognitive and linguistic barriers, there is the issue of how knowledge is encoded in the computer. Knowledge acquired from a human expert cannot be captured within a knowledge base if the representation language to be used lacks sufficient expressive power. McCarthy and Hayes [13] introduced the notion of *epistemological adequacy* as the ability of a knowledge-representation formalism to express the facts that a person knows about some aspect of the world. Since that time, substantial work in AI has concentrated on the development of representation languages that are epistemologically adequate for various types of problems. Knowledge-representation languages and, as a result, tools for building expert systems, differ in the ease with which they can describe particular concepts. The differences often are a matter not of epistemological adequacy, but rather of *usability*. With current tools, certain abstractions will always be easier to represent than are others.

The canonical example of this phenomenon is described in the book *Building Expert Systems* [14]. In 1980, teams of experienced knowledge engineers, each well versed in the use of a particular expert-system shell, were assembled as part of a workshop on expert systems. Each team spent 3 days developing a prototype expert system designed (1) to classify possible toxic spills at Oak Ridge National Laboratory, and (2) to identify and to apply an appropriate strategy to contain such a spill within the intricate drainage system installed at that site. Two domain experts were brought in specifically for this experiment, and written documents also were made available to the knowledge engineers. Prior to the workshop, not one of the participants knew what the application area would be.

Although this exercise was not a well-controlled experiment, the results were illuminating. The spill-containment task had been delineated in advance by one of the workshop organizers, yet each knowledge-engineering team interpreted that task somewhat differently. The exercise showed that knowledge engineers, when using preselected formalisms for knowledge representation, may model *different aspects of the same task* on the basis of what is easy to express in the given representation language; the conceptual-modeling primitives provided by a tool necessarily affect the way developers think about a problem. For example, rule-based shells such as EMYCIN lacked facilities to model interrelationships among objects directly, and thus the Oak Ridge drainage-system network could not be described explicitly. The Stanford team, using EMYCIN, consequently downplayed the subtask of applying a containment strategy for a spill; the SRI team, using KAS, avoided that part of the problem entirely; the Rutgers team, using the EXPERT rule-based shell, implemented a strategy for spill containment, but did so using a FORTRAN program invoked by the expert system. As not one of the knowledge-engineering teams worked with a language that could explicitly represent the passage of time, temporal constraints were ignored in all the systems [14].

Since the time of the oil-spill experiment, many more knowledge-representation formalisms have become widely available, including languages for representing probabilistic and causal relationships, and for supporting blackboard architectures, nonmonotonic inference, and case-based reasoning. Although the options available to system builders have increased significantly, the effort required to implement a knowledge-based system has not declined comensurately. Just as human thought is limited by our language and by our mental models of the world, the knowledge bases of expert systems are restricted both by the expressiveness of our computer languages for knowledge representation and by our cleverness in using those languages.

1.4 The Problem of Creating Models

Current expert systems make major assumptions about their task domains; they become "brittle" when reasoning about unusual cases, and are unable to arrive at a reasonable conclusion. It would be incorrect to conclude that the epistemological inadequacies of our representation languages are primarily responsible for our systems' failures. Our knowledge bases often are imperfect for more fundamental reasons.

Knowledge bases are *models*. Like all abstractions of reality, they are approximate. They are unavoidably selective in what they contain. In the study reported by Waterman and Hayes-Roth, for example, it would be misleading to say that the KAS team did not implement a spill-containment strategy *because* it was difficult to represent the necessary knowledge. (After all, the team using EXPERT was faced with the same task, and they ended up solving the problem with FORTRAN.) Rather, we should simply conclude that the KAS team chose not to model that portion of the problem. We should not say that the KAS program was less expert than were any of the others; it merely incorporated a different model. All models are imperfect approximations.

When an expert system fails often or is brittle, the knowledge base is a model that makes too many simplifying assumptions. System builders often maintain that the way to overcome brittleness in expert systems is simply to add more knowledge [15]. Such a response, however, begs the question of exactly what knowledge should be added. It may be more helpful to view the problem as the need to develop a different or more comprehensive *model* of the application area.

As a consequence of interacting with an expert, knowledge engineers develop their own mental models of the application area. Although the knowledge engineers and experts tend to have very different models at the outset, they eventually reach a compromise through a process of convergence that Regoczei and Plantinga [16] refer to as *harmonization*. Harmonization is possible primarily because knowledge engineering forces all parties to commit their mental models to a fixed, publicly examinable form—typically the emerging knowledge base. Both the experts and the system builders continually revise their mental models of the domain as the system is constructed. The experts must work to fill in the large gaps where their knowledge is tacit. The knowledge engineers constantly struggle to revise their naive theories of how the experts solve problems.

Many authors continue to describe knowledge acquisition as the *transfer of expertise* from an expert to a knowledge engineer to a knowledge base. Such a view, however, is misleading. The model of expertise encoded in the knowledge base is not simply transferred from one locus to another. It is *created*. Much of the expert's mental model is initially fragmented and tacit; the flaws must be filled in and the compiled knowledge must be made declarative. There is initially no language with which the knowledge engineer and expert can speak unambiguously; they must construct a systematic domain and must use it to build the model. Knowledge acquisition clearly involves more than knowledge transfer. It is a dynamic and inventive activity. Like all processes that require creativity and ingenuity, knowledge acquisition is difficult [17].

2 Strategies for Knowledge Acquisition

Given all these impediments to knowledge acquisition, we can appreciate why early observers such as Dreyfus [18] continue to be pessimistic about the possibility of building comprehensive expert systems. The obstacles are inherent in the nature of human cognition, of human language, and of the creative process itself. Dreyfus is correct; these problems will not go away. The goal of research on second-generation knowledge-acquisition techniques is to develop mechanisms by which these problems can be confronted and contained.

Many of the research results described in this book speak directly to the difficulties of knowledge acquisition experienced during development of the first generation of expert systems. These experimental approaches build directly on strategies for knowledge elicitation that are now well entrenched in the expert-systems community. Understanding the research frontier consequently requires an appreciation for current, more conventional knowledge-acquisition methods.

2.1 Knowledge-Elicitation Techniques

Most of the model building that takes place during traditional knowledge engineering is under the direction of the knowledge engineer. Although creating a knowledge base is necessarily a collaborative process, the domain expert typically remains illiterate in the language being used to build the model. The expert consequently assumes a more passive posture, responding to the knowledge engineer's questions as a model of the informant's expertise is filled out.

Techniques used to interview domain experts have received increasing attention in the literature [19]. Many interviewing strategies have been borrowed from original work in psychology and cognitive anthropology, disciplines in which the methods that people use to categorize their world and to solve problems have been focal points of investigation.

2.1.1 Direct Questioning
The simplest way to elicit information from experts is to ask them questions. Unfortunately, direct questioning has a number of major limitations. An expert's response to a question may depend in subtle ways on how the question is asked. The reply may assume implicit background information that is not directly articulated.

The words used to phrase a question can have an enormous effect on an expert's response. For example, La France [20] cites work by Loftus demonstrating that eyewitnesses to an automobile accident, when asked "How fast was the car going when it *crashed* into the wall?" reported significantly higher velocities than did witnesses asked, "How fast was the car going when it *ran* into wall?" Similarly, more headaches were revealed when survey respondents were asked "Do you get headaches *frequently*, and if so, how often?" than when asked "Do you get headaches *occasionally*, and if so, how often?" To ensure the accuracy of reported information, La France advocates posing large numbers of questions using different formats to elicit the same knowledge. Many of the strategies she describes are reminiscent of the interviewing techniques employed by successful ethnographers.

A knowledge engineer may ask myriad well-formed questions and still elicit misinformation. Much of skilled knowledge is tacit and is thus unavailable to consciousness (see Section 1.1). When asked direct questions about tacit processes, experts volunteer plausible answers that may not reflect their true behavior. Johnson [1] refers to these believable, although sometimes inaccurate, responses as *reconstructed* reasoning methods. Reconstructed methods are "socially acceptable" problem-solving procedures that are acknowledged and endorsed by entire professional communities. These methods form the basis of most major textbooks. However, "the disadvantage of these methods of reasoning is that they do not always work, sometimes not even in the hands of those who devise them" [1, p. 82]. Johnson, among other authors, has argued for the elicitation of *authentic* methods of reasoning. The goal is determination of the behaviors actually used by experts in performing relevant tasks. Acquisition of authentic knowledge, not surprisingly, requires more than just asking direct questions.

2.1.2 Protocol Analysis The most extensively studied methods designed to elicit authentic knowledge all involve *protocol analysis*, a technique developed by cognitive psychologists [21]. Protocol analysis requires subjects to be studied while they are in the process of solving problems. The subjects are encouraged to "think aloud" while working on either real or simulated cases. They are asked to report their problem-solving goals and the data they are considering at each point, but are asked not to rationalize or justify their actions. The result is a *verbal protocol* that traces execution of the particular task.

Knowledge engineers then can use the recorded protocols to create a model of problem solving. Substantial anecdotal evidence suggests that this method of knowledge acquisition can be effective. Nevertheless, many authors remain concerned that asking experts to speak out loud during their problem solving may cause distortion of these experts' behavior, resulting in less-than-authentic protocols.

2.1.3 Psychometric Methods Researchers interested in psychological testing frequently are concerned with how people classify elements in the world and solve problems. Just as protocol analysis has been adopted from the methods of cognitive psychologists, formal psychometric techniques also have worked their way into the knowledge engineer's tool box.

Perhaps the most important contribution has been George Kelly's [22] *personal construct theory*. Kelly was a clinical psychologist who developed special interviewing techniques to elicit the idiosyncratic characterizations (*personal constructs*) that patients may have used to classify people and other entities in the world. Kelly's structured interviews began by selecting a set of entities—called *elements*—from the patient's personal experience (for example, psychologically important people such as the patient's parents, friends, and teachers). The interviewer identified a patient's personal constructs by asking the patient to volunteer distinguishing features of the various elements. For example, a patient might report that one of his friends is "easy to talk to" whereas his parents are "not understanding"; this distinction would represent one of the patient's personal constructs. Ultimately, the interviewer asked the patient how *each* construct applied to *each* element. The result was a matrix of personal constructs and elements, which Kelly called a *repertory grid*. Analysis of the grid revealed associations and dependencies among the patient's constructs—interactions that Kelly found valuable in targeting his psychotherapy.

Personal construct theory soon became an important focus for work in psychometry, particularly because Kelly's interviewing strategy and repertory-grid analysis were so straightforward to automate [23]. Cognitive anthropologists saw the technique as a useful way to learn how people in other cultures form distinctions among entities in the world and then act on those distinctions. In the past decade, knowledge engineers have begun to use Kelley's methods to learn how domain experts make and act on distinctions. Furthermore, personal construct theory has formed the basis for a number of important computer-based knowledge-acquisition tools (Section 2.2.2.2).

Other psychometric techniques have been used for knowledge acquisition, primarily in experimental settings. Many authors, for example, advocate the use of multidimensional scaling techniques such as cluster analysis [24,25]. These investigators argue that formal statistical approaches offer considerable precision in knowledge elicitation without the biases that are introduced when experts are asked to introspect.

2.1.4 Ethnographic Methods Because the ability of human experts to introspect on their problem-solving behavior is faulty, and because abstract discussions of human behaviors outside of the situations in which those behaviors take place frequently omits salient information [26], several workers have sought alternatives to traditional laboratory-based knowledge-acquisition techniques. These researchers have adopted the field methods of anthropologists and perform ethnographic observations of human experts directly in the workplace, hoping to identify the authentic methods by which these experts solve actual problems.

Belkin and colleagues [27], for example, concluded that the task of assisting people with accessing on-line information sources could not be analyzed "in vitro," but rather required knowledge engineers to observe and audiotape real interactions between clients who wished to search bibliographic databases and specialists in information retrieval. Belkin's group transcribed the audiotapes and analyzed the recorded discourse to determine (1) the tasks that were being carried out, (2) the knowledge required to perform the tasks, and (3) the structure of the interactions between clients and experts. Belkin argues that analysis of these interactions at the level of discrete utterances is crucial if researchers are to learn how the clients and experts work together to build a shared model of the information that needs to be retrieved.

Suchman and Trigg [28] argue that discourse analysis alone is insufficient for understanding the complexities of modern work practices. Their research in an airline operation room highlights the value of videotaping workers in the course of their routine interactions and the value of reviewing those videotapes later with the aid of the workers themselves to understand the nuances of dynamic work settings. Such study of workers directly in the environments in which they perform their jobs is becoming increasingly important in the design of many types of computer systems. The considerable inconvenience and expense of ethnographic field work, however, is a major barrier to widespread adoption of these techniques.

2.2 Creation of Computational Models

From simple interviews, to protocol analysis, to the use of psychometric and ethnographic approaches, there are many techniques available to knowledge engineers for the elicitation of the basic data required to build knowledge-based systems. Transcripts of protocols and other verbal data alone, of course, are insufficient for creating a knowledge base; developers must use these elemental data to create computational models of the professional behavior that given expert systems ultimately will carry out. Whereas the knowledge-acquisition literature is replete with discussion of how knowledge engineers might collect their basic data, much less has been written about how developers can gain insight into the data and construct appropriate models. Authors may tend to ignore the model-creation step not because it is unimportant (indeed, it is crucial), but rather because the development of models is so dependent on human ingenuity and inventiveness that it is often difficult to understand how such models are formed.

2.2.1 Model-Specification Techniques The Knowledge Acquisition and Design Structuring (KADS) system, developed by workers at the University of Amsterdam and by other European partners, attempts to address the problem of model formulation head on [29,30]. KADS is a methodology for the structured and systematic development of knowledge-based systems, which aims to provide software-engineering support for the knowledge-engineering process—from the first exploratory interviews with experts to the development of an operational system. KADS is a manual, nonformal method that divides the development process into a suite of models the represents the transformation of knowledge from the initial, informal phases into an operational system. Within the models, knowledge is represented using four distinct *layers* that represent the different types of expertise that developers must represent within a knowledge-based system.

Four types of knowledge may be distinguished: domain-layer, inference-layer, task-layer, and strategy-layer knowledge. The **domain layer** describes all the knowledge of the application domain in the form of concepts, structures, and relations. The domain layer thus captures the fundamental ontologies relevant in the application area. The **inference layer** describes the "canonical inferences" of the application area. The developer who uses KADS represents these inferences in terms of *meta-classes* (roles that components of the domain-layer knowledge may play in problem solving) and *knowledge sources* (functional descriptions of the inferences that operate on the meta-classes). Thus, to model a portion of the behavior of the MYCIN expert system [31], a meta-class denoting "bacteria potentially causing a patient's infection" might be related to another meta-class denoting "potential antibiotics to prescribe" by a knowledge source that infers the appropriate antibiotics to administer for given bacterial infections. The third layer of a KADS model is the **task layer**. Here, the developer specifies the sequence in which the expert system should invoke specific inference-layer knowledge sources to achieve a solution to a given problem. The task layer consequently models the control knowledge required by the problem solver. Finally, KADS allows for a **strategy layer**, with which developers can specify how the problem solver might wish to choose dynamically among alternative task-layer control sequences.

Using either paper-and-pencil sketches or a computer workbench [32], system builders apply the terms provided by the KADS methodology to create models of expertise that address each of these four layers. KADS itself provides little guidance that can aid developers in the creation of this model [33]. The principal advantages of using KADS come from the set of knowledge-structuring primitives associated with the four different layers, which can help knowledge engineers to specify problem-solving behaviors and domain ontologies in a consistent fashion. Because there is no intrinsic semantics associated with the meta-classes and knowledge sources in a KADS model, the methodology does not provide a prescriptive means to transform a four-layer model drawn out on paper into a functioning expert system. As evidenced by research reported in this volume [34,35], development of extensions to KADS that include a defined semantics for the knowledge-structuring components has become an area of intense investigation. By defining such a semantics, researchers hope to provide builders of knowledge-based systems with both a software-engineering methodology with which to construct models of expertise, and a formal system that can transform those models into practical expert systems.

The system–model–operator metaphor recently introduced by Clancey [17], like KADS, attempts to provide a modeling framework for describing intelligent behavior. Clancey's approach concentrates on modeling the control knowledge required for problem solving (incorporating elements that a KADS' user would represent both in the task layer and in the inference layer). The system–model–operator metaphor attempts to clarify how a problem solver might use *operators* (akin to KADS' knowledge sources) to refine a *situation-specific model* (a component of KADS' domain layer) when executing a given task.

2.2.2 Use of Predefined Models Concomitant with the development of the KADS methodology in Europe, many workers in the United States began to experiment with alternative means for constructing operational expert systems from initial verbal data [36,37,38,39]. Whereas the originators of KADS hoped to define a broad methodology with which knowledge engineers potentially could describe abstract models of expertise with minimal distortion, these North American researchers concentrated on knowledge-engineering techniques that would be guaranteed to yield executable systems—albeit systems in which the model of expertise might not be authentic. The latter techniques relied on computer-based interviewing tools with which system builders can supply the domain knowledge required to automate given application tasks. To use one of these tools, developers relate components of the pertinent domain knowledge to the manner in which that knowledge ultimately will be used by the target expert system.

Each knowledge-acquisition tool embodies a different model that it uses to generate expectations about the knowledge to be entered and to construct a functional knowledge base on the basis of a user's entries. The model thus defines the manner in which the contents of the knowledge base are both displayed by the program and referred to by the user. Following terminology advocated by Norman [40], we refer to the set of terms and relationships that defines the semantics of the knowledge-base elements that the program displays as the program's *conceptual model*. (Developers of the KADS system, among other workers in the knowledge-acquisition community, also use the term *conceptual model* to refer to a developer's abstract formalization of the task that a given knowledge-based system will perform; in this chapter, however, I use the term to refer to only a model that defines the semantics of a given user interface.)

Every computer program, regardless of its purpose, is written with particular assumptions about the data on which it operates. These assumptions, which are reflected in the way that users interact with the program, form the conceptual model of the data. For example, simple text editors generally employ a conceptual model in which the data represent characters in a document; such programs accept commands whose semantics relate to modifying characters or lines of text. In spreadsheet programs, on the other hand, data are viewed as rows and columns of interdependent numbers.

Similarly, knowledge-acquisition programs must adopt conceptual models that frame their presentation of the contents of a knowledge base. Whereas most knowledge-acquisition tools have modeled the knowledge in terms of the symbol-level representations required by particular inference engines (for example, production rules in EMYCIN), many recent programs use a more abstract kind of model—that of the problem-solving method in which the knowledge is ultimately brought to bear. Alternatively, some knowledge-acquisition tools adopt a conceptual model based on the semantics of the application task itself. Whatever its form, the conceptual model guides the knowledge-acquisition process by determining precisely those concepts that a user may articulate during knowledge elicitation. For this reason, van Heijst et al. [35] use the term *directive model* when referring to the prevailing conceptual model of a knowledge-acquisition tool.

When knowledge-acquisition tools adopt a conceptual model of the acquired knowledge that is based on the problem-solving method in which the knowledge is used, the conceptual model typically is based on a predefined, *explicit* model, such as Clancey's [41] description of heuristic classification. Entering knowledge then requires the user to apply the terms and relations of the model to the domain task at hand. Alternatively, it is possible to shield the user from the specific details of the problem-solving model. Such an approach, however, often requires that the knowledge-acquisition program make major assumptions about the knowledge a user has entered. We now consider the use of tools with conceptual models based on explicit and implicit models of problem-solving methods. Note that, for our purposes, the expression *problem-solving method* can be viewed as roughly equivalent to the term *generic task,* as used by workers at Ohio State University [42] and to the term *interpretation model*, as used by developers of the KADS methodology [29].

2.2.2.1 Explicit Models of Problem-Solving Perhaps the first tool to adopt a method-oriented conceptual model was ROGET [36], a program designed to assist knowledge engineers and domain experts in developing EMYCIN-based expert systems. Using an explicit model of classification problem solving that was akin to heuristic classification, ROGET conducted a dialog with its user, asking what kinds of evidence might be gathered during a consultation and how that evidence might relate to possible hypotheses.

The dialog was driven by the terms and relations in ROGET's model of problem solving. For example, ROGET knew that hypothetical "problems" might be concluded on the basis of classes of evidence, such as "directly observed signs," "predisposing factors," "reported symptoms," and "laboratory tests." The program prompted the developer for information regarding the evidence that end users would enter into an advice system by asking the developer which of the various categories best described the anticipated data. Based on the developer's responses, the program could solicit additional knowledge. Thus, if the ROGET's user indicated that "laboratory tests" are required to support a particular hypothesis, the program would ask what the *names* of the tests were and what the tests' possible *values* were, as well as how the values bore on the hypotheses under consideration. Once the conceptual knowledge had been entered through ROGET, the program generated portions of the corresponding EMYCIN rule base.

ROGET's model of classification provided a mechanism by which a knowledge engineer could describe an expert system's behavior at the knowledge level. ROGET asked how primary data were abstracted into "problems," and how "problems" were associated with "causes" of the disorder under consideration; particular symbols that might be used to *encode* such relationships never entered into the human–computer discussion. A dialog with ROGET thus resulted in a knowledge-level specification of the application task. Unlike pencil-and-paper specifications, however, the knowledge-level analyses produced by ROGET were in machine-readable form. Bennett wrote complex LISP programs to translate these knowledge-level descriptions into EMYCIN symbols that could form the basis of working expert systems.

There are now numerous computer-based tools that have conceptual models for expert-system knowledge based on explicit models of problem solving. Many of these systems were developed by John McDermott's research group at Carnegie–Mellon University during the 1980s [38].

A tool called MORE [43], for example, adopted a model of classification problem solving not unlike that of ROGET. MORE asked its user to specify knowledge in terms of *symptoms, hypotheses*, and *conditions* that might modulate the strength of associations between symptoms and hypotheses. Unlike ROGET, MORE did not take at face value its user's knowledge-level description of an application; instead, MORE used various knowledge-acquisition heuristics to probe the knowledge engineer for possible deficiencies in the entered knowledge. For example, MORE would point out instances in which given symptoms would not permit competing hypotheses to be distinguished adequately. The program would then suggest locations where the user could augment the knowledge by entering additional symptoms that might discriminate among possible hypotheses more completely. MORE, however, was difficult to use because the program would typically ask for an overwhelming number of potential enhancements to the knowledge base. A successor system, called MOLE [44], incorporates a more detailed model of classification problem solving called *cover-and-dif-*

ferentiate. MOLE consequently can use heuristics that are more refined than those of the MORE program when suggesting changes to the knowledge.

Unlike ROGET, MORE, and MOLE, which model classification problem solving, a system called SALT [45] models a strategy for *constructing solutions.* SALT assumes that a task can be mapped onto a *propose-and-revise* method of problem solving, in which a partial plan is incrementally extended while the program constantly verifies that the extensions are consistent with known constraints. SALT requires a structured language for entry of specific concepts, such as methods for determining values, constraints on values, and corrections for constraint violations. The program then converts the resulting knowledge-level description of the application into rules in OPS5. SALT has been used by engineering experts to specify knowledge for configuring electromechanical elevators in new buildings and for scheduling a variety of manufacturing processes. Like other method-oriented knowledge-acquisition tools, SALT presumes that the user will be able to conceptualize the solution to the problem in terms of the method provided by the system.

Although not the basis of automated knowledge-acquisition tools, the KADS methodology incorporates a library of *interpretation models*—KADS conceptual models that include only a task layer and an inference layer—that can help developers to structure their descriptions of domain-layer knowledge [29]. The interpretation models are thus like models of problem-solving methods that can guide a developer's (manual) representation of domain knowledge. Recent work in the ACKNOWLEDGE project [36] has attempted to endow KADS interpretation models with an operational semantics that could allow a computer-based workbench to use the interpretation models both to direct interactive dialogs with knowledge engineers and, given the results of those interactions, to produce implemented knowledge bases.

To a great degree, the usefulness of model-based tools such as SALT and ROGET—and of the interpretation models in KADS—is limited by the ability of system builders to recognize correctly whether the corresponding model pertains to the task at hand. For example, classification problem solving probably is of no value in configuring elevators, because a solution set cannot be pre-enumerated. On the other hand, the strategy of *propose-and-revise* might be satisfactory (albeit inefficient) for choosing antibiotics in a system such as MYCIN. A knowledge engineer might be able to use SALT to describe a portion of MYCIN's task, but would be hard pressed to specify how to design an elevator using ROGET or MOLE. Each of these programs presumes that the user has performed a preliminary task analysis and thus somehow knows *a priori* that the program's model of problem solving is applicable. Moreover, these knowledge-acquisition tools also presuppose that the user will be able to apply the relevant terms and relationships of the problem-solving model to an application task correctly and consistently. ROGET, for example, requires that the user appreciate the difference between a "cause" and a "problem," a distinction that is not necessarily obvious at first blush. Before developers can use a tool whose conceptual model is based on an explicit problem-solving method, they must learn a systematic domain of terms that allows them to relate domain knowledge to the particular model of problem solving assumed by the tool. Because these systematic domains may be confusing and arcane, many investigators are searching for ways to insulate developers from the need to understand the corresponding problem-solving methods in their entirety.

2.2.2.2 Implicit Models of Problem Solving   A growing number of knowledge-acquisition programs based on personal construct psychology [22] solicit knowledge in a manner that largely conceals the problem-solving model from the user.

ETS, for example, is a now-classic system that acquired knowledge directly from application specialists during the early stages of expert-system development [37]. ETS automated the structured interview and repertory-grid analysis originally developed by Kelly to elucidate an individual's system of personal constructs. After ETS conducted an initial dialog to elicit the constructs used by an application specialist to classify elements in the selected domain, the program would present visually as a repertory grid the knowledge that it had acquired. Analysis of the grid allowed the program to determine the implied hierarchical relationships among the expert's constructs and to display these relationships graphically. ETS then could use the manner in which particular constructs seem to entail the presence of other constructs to generate knowledge bases for prototype expert systems using a variety of rule-based shells.

ETS assumed a model of classification problem solving in which solutions are selected from a pre-enumerated set by the abstraction of primary data. The method is one of hierarchical (that is, decision-tree) classification. Unlike a user of programs such as ROGET, the user of ETS did not need to understand the problem-solving model, because the classification hierarchies in ETS were generated *indirectly*. The user merely had to answer the simple questions generated during the structured interview, indicating what the possible diagnostic solutions were and how well the various constructs pertained to each member of the solution set. The program—not the user—attempted to fit the answers to the questions into the problem-solving model. The advantage is that ETS could be used almost immediately by computer-naive application specialists after only minimal training. The major limitation is that it was impossible for the program itself to generate a robust model of the application based on the often spurious and incomplete relationships implied by the repertory grid. An imperfect model, however, often is better than no model at all.

A large number of other computer-based knowledge-acquisition tools have been based on repertory-grid analysis [46]. Several commercial products now facilitate knowledge elicitation using repertory grids.

Like the knowledge-acquisition tools based on *explicit* models of problem solving, those tools using personal construct psychology assume that the user knows *a priori* that his task can be solved via a form of classification. More important, these programs presuppose that the model of classification provided will be sufficient for representing the task. As with all knowledge-acquisition programs that adopt method-based conceptual models, knowledge that falls outside of the problem-solving model generally cannot be entered by the user.

2.2.2.3 Task-Based Conceptual Models   Unlike the knowledge-acquisition tools that require their users to define an application in terms of some predefined problem-solving method, some programs instead incorporate directly the semantics of a class of domain tasks. Rather than presenting the user with the terms and relations of a model of problem solving (such as heuristic classification), these knowledge-editing programs present the terms and relations of predefined models of general application tasks to be performed. Defining a particular application then requires applying the terms and relations of a general task model to a specific problem. Thus, in the case of OPAL, a *general* model of cancer-treatment plans is used by the program to elicit the details of *specific* cancer-treatment plans from physicians [47]. The specific plans entered into OPAL then form the basis of the treatment advice offered by the ONCOCIN expert system [48].

Tool builders increasingly recognize the utility of creating knowledge-acquisition programs with conceptual models that closely mirror the way developers seem to think about the knowledge to be entered [49]. The result has been several recent tools that incorporate task-oriented conceptual models. P10, for example, is a tool that adopts a conceptual model of the task of protein purification [50]. P10 asks developers to enter knowledge for generating plans for purifying different classes of proteins that chemists might wish to isolate from biological samples. The P10 conceptual model takes into account protein characteristics, skeletal purification procedures, laboratory samples, and reagents. Developers use this conceptual model to frame all their statements regarding processes by which a laboratory technician might refine various proteins.

In all task-oriented programs, the *methods* required to solve the application tasks are predetermined. For example, OPAL contains no explicit model of the planning steps needed to produce a cancer-therapy recommendation; in P10, the strategies needed to execute a laboratory procedure are transparent. Moreover, users of the programs are insulated from the mapping between the task models and the problem-solving methods used by the underlying expert systems. Implicitly, those mappings have already been established by the developers of the task-oriented tools; users need only to acquiesce to the systematic domains and general task models created in advance by the tool builders. Knowledge-level analysis of the task area consequently must precede development of any task-oriented knowledge-acquisition tool.

2.2.2.4 Metalevel Knowledge Acquisition Tools   Whenever a developer uses a model-based knowledge-acquisition tool, he assumes that the conceptual model embraced by the tool is appropriate for the knowledge that he must enter.   When a tool's conceptual model relates to a specific class of application tasks (as is the case with OPAL and P10), the developer can predict reasonably well whether the particular tool is suitable for a task at hand; when the terms and relations embodied by the tool match those with which domain specialists seem to talk about the application task, there is a good chance that the tool incorporates an appropriate model. On the other hand, when a tool adopts a conceptual model that is abstract—such as *propose-and-revise* in SALT or *cover-and-differentiate* in MOLE—it is less obvious in advance whether a given tool will be applicable. A principal lesson of the past decade of research is that, when a tool happens to contain the correct conceptual model, knowledge acquisition can be simplified greatly [38]; when a user happens to select a tool with an inappropriate conceptual model, however, knowledge acquisition will be impeded. How to measure the "appropriateness" of a conceptual model for a given task is a crucial issue that is not well understood, unfortunately.

There is a clear need the for the models that direct knowledge acquisition to be better suited for the task knowledge to be entered. As models become more general—and thus potentially usable in more situations—they may become too abstract to guide knowledge acquisition effectively. For example, the heuristic-classification model

[41] is so abstract that, in practice, it may be of only modest help to developers when acquiring actual domain knowledge.

Recently, several researchers have begun to study the use of knowledge-acquisition programs that contain conceptual models that developers can *tailor* to the needs of classes of application tasks by using separate metalevel tools. For example, PROTÉGÉ [39] is a metalevel program that generates task-oriented knowledge-acquisition tools like OPAL. PROTÉGÉ itself adopts a conceptual model based on a problem-solving method called *episodic skeletal-plan refinement* (ESPR) [48]. The ESPR method assumes that the problem solver will refine a hierarchy of plan components in a top–down manner. Developers enter into PROTÉGÉ the elements of the task domain that correspond to the abstract data on which the ESPR method operates. Thus, in the domain of cancer-therapy administration, the planning hierarchy might consist of generic cancer-treatment plans and their component chemotherapies and radiotherapies. The PROTÉGÉ system applies such entries to generate programmatically an OPAL-class knowledge-acquisition tool whose conceptual model reflects the particular domain knowledge. The tools that PROTÉGÉ constructs thus incorporate the semantics of the target application area—provided that the tasks to be automated can be solved using the ESPR problem-solving method that is built into PROTÉGÉ.

A knowledge-acquisition–tool generator called DOTS [51] allows developers to create task-oriented knowledge-acquisition tools without imposing a particular problem-solving model. Rather than incorporating a method-oriented conceptual model, as does PROTÉGÉ, DOTS maintains a symbol-oriented view of the developer's entries. The DOTS user thus has considerable freedom to define arbitrary graphical interface components for the generated knowledge-acquisition tool and to relate the entries that application experts will make into the generated tool to arbitrary knowledge-base structures. Although the DOTS approach offers the developer enormous flexibility when defining the conceptual model of a target knowledge-acquisition tool, the user loses the benefit of the guidance offered by PROTÉGÉ's method-oriented metaview [52].

The tension felt by builders of metalevel knowledge-acquisition architectures mirrors the unease that developers of more traditional knowledge-acquisition tools have experienced for many years: There is a clear trade-off between providing users with the flexibility that they desire to represent unanticipated concepts and providing users with sufficient structure to assure the semantic clarity and integrity of entered knowledge [49]. Current research on metalevel knowledge-acquisition tools seeks to explore potential ways to achieve the necessary balance.

For example, investigators at Digital Equipment Corporation are building a metatool called Spark [53], which asks users to perform a detailed analysis of the work settings in which knowledge-based systems might be deployed; Spark then uses the results of the workplace analysis to select applicable problem solvers (and their associated, predefined knowledge-acquisition tools) from a prespecified library. The Spark approach favors the use of rather simple tools for entry of domain knowledge, while offering a quite flexible metalevel environment for performing task analysis. The developers of Spark hope that these design decisions will make their system extremely easy to use—even by nonprogrammers.

The PROTÉGÉ-II system [54], on the other hand, is viewed as a metalevel environment for use by experienced developers and provides a flexible means for programmers to create extremely specialized graphical knowledge-acquisition tools. Unlike the initial version of PROTÉGÉ [39], the new system does not presuppose any particular problem-solving method (such as ESPR). Instead, PROTÉGÉ-II allows developers to select arbitrary problem-solving methods from a library and to compose those methods to meet the requirements of intended application tasks. The PROTÉGÉ-II environment additionally allows developers to create and retrieve frame hierarchies that represent the ontologies of application domains, and to link the elements of those ontologies to the input–output requirements of the relevant problem-solving methods [55]. On the basis of the knowledge engineer's representation of the ontology of the application domain, PROTÉGÉ-II creates prototype knowledge-acquisition interfaces programmatically. As with the initial version of PROTÉGÉ, an important goal is the automated generation of task-oriented knowledge-acquisition tools that application specialists can use independently. An additional goal for the new architecture is to provide a metalevel environment in which developers can select predefined domain ontologies and problem-solving methods from libraries, with the potential to reuse those methods and ontologies to create new classes of knowledge-based systems [56].

3 Conclusions

Researchers in the knowledge-acquisition community seek to understand more fully the nature of human expertise and communication and to develop techniques to assist developers in building the computational models of problem solving that form the basis of expert systems. Many early workers in the knowledge-acquisition community argued that a primary research goal must be to eliminate the role of the knowledge engineer as the "middleman" who stands between the expert's knowledge and the emerging knowledge base. Contemporary workers recognize increasingly, however, that there are frequent gaps in an expert's knowledge, that volunteered explanations of professional behavior may be inaccurate, and that special skills are required to create robust models of expertise that ultimately can perform well in a variety of situations— many of which may be difficult for the developers to anticipate. Current research no longer concentrates on a quest to eliminate intermediaries from the knowledge-acquisition process; instead, the emphasis is on development and refinement of methodologies that can help system builders of all backgrounds to collaborate in the construction of intelligent systems.

Elsewhere in this volume, contributors describe current research on knowledge-level modeling (Section III) and architectures for second-generation expert systems (Section VI). In many ways, these topics are at the core of much current knowledge-acquisition research. Knowledge acquisition can no longer be regarded as rule acquisition, and the development of techniques that allow system builders to create models of expert behavior at the knowledge level—and to translate those models into computational architectures that can preserve the structure of those knowledge-level models—is a principal research objective. Although interviewing experts and working with a variety of knowledge sources remain vital knowledge-acquisition activities, much current research focuses on the initial models (both conceptual and computer-based) that can guide developers as they gather the primary verbal data and on the translation of models of human activities into operational expert systems.

This overview has touched on the problems of building expert systems and on the current avenues of knowledge-acquisition research. Although there are important distinctions among the approaches that different research groups have taken, there is increasing consensus regarding long-term objectives. We need more descriptive methods that can allow us to observe how human expertise is applied in practice, to write down our observations using unambiguous representations, and to create authentic models of human knowledge. We need more expressive tools for representing knowledge— tools that aid both knowledge engineers and application specialists in viewing and editing emerging knowledge bases in ways that are natural, intuitive, and precise. We need to discern more completely the social contexts in which human expertise is applied and, equally important, those in which our expert systems will be invoked. Although knowledge acquisition may still be bottlenecked, builders of second-generation expert systems are beginning to understand why development of knowledge bases is so difficult and can turn to a variety of emerging knowledge-acquisition methods to ease their work and to facilitate construction of operational systems.

Acknowledgments

Jean-Marc David, Lyn Dupré, and Marc Linster provided valuable comments on an earlier draft of this manuscript. This work was supported, in part, by grants LM05157 and LM05208 from the United States National Library of Medicine. Dr. Musen is recipient of National Science Foundation Young Investigator Award IRI-9257578.

References

1. Johnson, P.E.: What kind of expert should a system be? Journal of Medicine and Philosophy **7**, 77–97 (1983)

2. Neves, D.M., Anderson, J.R.: Knowledge compilation: Mechanisms for automatization of cognitive skills. In: Anderson, J. (ed.): Cognitive Skills and Their Acquisition. Hillsdale, New Jersey: Lawrence Erlbaum Associates 1981, pp. 57–84

3. Ryle, G: The Concept of Mind. New York: Barnes and Noble 1949

4. Anderson, J.R.: Skill acquisition: Compilation of weak-method problem solutions. Psychological Review **94**, 192–210 (1987)

5. Cohen, N.J.: Preserved learning capacity in amnesia: Evidence for multiple memory systems. In: Neuropsychology of Memory. New York: Guilford Press 1987, pp. 83–103

6. Nisbett, R.E., Wilson, T.D.: Telling more than we can know: Verbal reports on mental processes. Psychological Review **84**, 231–259 (1977)

7. Tversky, A., Kahneman, D.: Judgment under uncertainty: Heuristics and biases. Science **184**, 1124–1131 (1974)

8. Lyons, W.: The Disappearance of Introspection. Cambridge, Massachusetts: MIT Press 1986

9. Davis, R.: Interactive transfer of expertise: Acquisition of new inference rules. Artificial Intelligence **12**, 121–158 (1979)

10. Buchanan, B.G. et al.: Constructing an expert system. In: Hayes-Roth, F., Waterman, D.A., Lenat, D.B. (eds.): Building Expert Systems. Reading, Massachusetts: Addison-Wesley 1983, pp. 127–167

11. Feigenbaum, E.A.: Knowledge engineering: The applied side of artificial intelligence. Annals of the New York Academy of Sciences **246**, 91–107 (1984)

12. Winograd, T., Flores, F.: Understanding Computers and Cognition: A New Foundation for Design. Norwood, New Jersey: Ablex 1986

13. McCarthy, J., Hayes, P.J.: Some philosophical problems from the standpoint of artificial intelligence. In: Machine Intelligence, **vol 4.** Edinburgh, United Kingdom: Edinburgh University Press 1969, pp. 463–502

14. Waterman, D.A., Hayes-Roth, F.: An investigation of tools for building expert systems. In: Hayes-Roth, F., Waterman, D.A., Lenat, D.B. (eds.): Building Expert Systems. Reading, Massachusetts: Addison-Wesley, Reading, Massachusetts 1983, pp. 169–215

15. Lenat, D., Prakash, M., Shepherd, M.: CYC: Using common sense knowledge to overcome brittleness and knowledge acquisition bottlenecks. AI Magazine **6**, 65–85 (1986)

16. Regoczei, S., Plantinga, E.P.O.: Creating the domain of discourse: Ontology and inventory. International Journal of Man–Machine Studies **27**, 235–250 (1987)

17. Clancey, W.J., Barbanson, M.: Using the system-model-operator metaphor for knowledge acquisition. In: David, J.-M., Krivine, J.-P., Simmons, R. (eds.): Second Generation Expert Systems. Berlin: Springer-Verlag 1993

18. Dreyfus, H.L.: From micro-worlds to knowledge representation: AI at an impasse. In: Haugeland, J. (ed.), Mind Design. Cambridge, Massachusetts: MIT Press 1981, pp. 161–204

19. Scott, A.C., Clayton, J.E., Gibson, E.L.: A practical guide to knowledge acquisition. Reading, Massachusetts: Addison–Wesley 1991

20. La France, M.: The knowledge acquisition grid: A method for training knowledge engineers. International Journal of Man–Machine Studies **26**, 245–255 (1987)

21. Ericsson, K.A., Simon, H.A.: Protocol Analysis: Verbal Reports as Data. Cambridge, Massachusetts: MIT Press 1984

22. Kelly, G. A.: The Psychology of Personal Constructs. New York: Norton 1955

23. Shaw, M.L.G. (ed.): Recent Advances in Personal Construct Technology. New York: Academic Press 1981.

24. Cooke, N.M., McDonald, J.E.: The application of psychological scaling techniques to knowledge elicitation for knowledge-based systems. International Journal of Man–Machine Studies **26**, 533–550 (1987)

25. Myer, M., Booker, J.: Eliciting and Analyzing Expert Judgement: A Practical Guide. London, United Kingdom: Academic Press 1991

26. Suchman, L.A.: Plans and Situated Actions. Cambridge, United Kingdom:Cambridge University Press 1987

27. Belkin, N.J., Brooks, H.M., Daniels, P.J.: Knowledge elicitation using discourse analysis. In: Gaines, B.R., Boose, J.H. (eds.), Knowledge Acquisition for Knowledge-Based Systems. London: Academic Press 1988, pp., 107–124

28. Suchman, L.A., Trigg. R.H.: Understanding practice: Video as a medium for reflection and design. In: Greenbaum, J., Kyng, M. (eds.), Design at Work: Cooperative Design of Computer Systems. Hillsdale, New Jersey: Lawrence Earlbaum Associates 1991, pp. 65–89

29. Wielinga, B., Schreiber, A.T., Breuker, J.: KADS: A modeling approach to knowledge acquisition. Knowledge Acquisition **4**, 5–53 (1992)

30. Wielinga, B. et al: Towards a unification of knowledge modeling approaches. In: David, J.-M., Krivine, J.-P., Simmons, R. (eds.): Second Generation Expert Systems. Berlin: Springer-Verlag 1993

31. Buchanan, B.G., and Shortliffe, E.H.: Rule-Based Expert Systems: The MYCIN Experiments of the Stanford Heuristic Programming Project. Reading, Massachusetts: Addison–Wesley 1984

32. Anjewierden, A., Wielemaker, J. Toussaint, C.: Shelley—computer aided knowledge engineering. Knowledge Acquisition **4**, 109–125 (1992)

33. Linster, M., Musen, M.A.: Use of KADS to create a conceptual model of the ONCOCIN task. Knowledge Acquisition **4**, 55–88 (1992)

426

34. Linster, M.: Explicit and operational models as a basis for second generation knowledge acquisition tools. In: David, J.-M., Krivine, J.-P., Simmons, R. (eds.): Second Generation Expert Systems. Berlin: Springer-Verlag 1993

35. van Heijst, G. et al.: Using generalized directive models in knowledge acquisition. In: David, J.-M., Krivine, J.-P., Simmons, R. (eds.): Second Generation Expert Systems. Berlin: Springer-Verlag 1993

36. Bennett, J.S.: ROGET: A knowledge-based system for acquiring the conceptual structure of a diagnostic expert system. Journal of Automated Reasoning 1, 49–74 (1985)

37. Boose, J.H.: A knowledge acquisition program for expert systems based on personal construct psychology. International Journal of Man–Machine Studies 23, 495–525 (1985)

38. McDermott, J.: Preliminary steps toward a taxonomy of problem-solving methods. In: Marcus, S.(ed.): Automating Knowledge Acquisition for Expert Systems. Boston, Massachusetts: Kluwer Academic 1988, pp. 225–255

39. Musen, M.A.: Automated Generation of Model-Based Knowledge-Acquisition Tools. London, United Kingdom: Pitman 1989

40. Norman, D.A.: Cognitive engineering. In: Norman, D.A., Draper, S.W. (eds.): User-Centered System Design. Hillsdale, New Jersey: Lawrence Erlbaum Associates 1986, pp. 31-61

41. Clancey, W.J.: Heuristic classification. Artificial Intelligence 27, 289–350 (1985)

42. Chandrasekaran, B.: Generic tasks in knowledge-based reasoning: High-level building blocks for expert system design. IEEE Expert 1, 23–30 (1986)

43. Kahn, G., Nowlan, S., McDermott, J.: Strategies for knowledge acquisition. IEEE Transactions on Pattern Analysis and Machine Intelligence PAMI-7, 511–522 (1985)

44. Eshelman, L. et al.: MOLE: A tenacious knowledge-acquisition tool. International Journal of Man–Machine Studies 26, 41–54 (1987)

45. Marcus, S., McDermott, J.: SALT: A knowledge acquisition tool for propose-and-revise systems. Artificial Intelligence 39, 1–37 (1989)

46. Shaw, M.L.G., Gaines, B.R.: KITTEN: Knowledge initiation and transfer tools for experts and novices. International Journal of Man–Machine Studies 27, 251–280 (1987)

47. Musen, M.A. et al.: Use of a domain model to drive an interactive knowledge-editing tool. International Journal of Man–Machine Studies 26, 105–121 (1987)

48. Tu, S.W. et al.: Episodic monitoring of time-oriented data for heuristic skeletal-plan refinement. Communications of the ACM **32**,1439–1455 (1989)

49. Musen, M.A.: Conceptual models of interactive knowledge-acquisition tools. Knowledge Acquisition **1**, 73–88 (1989)

50. Eriksson, H.: Domain-oriented knowledge acquisition tool for protein purification planning. Journal of Chemical Information and Computer Sciences **32**, 90–95 (1992)

51. Eriksson, H.: Meta-Tool Support for Knowledge Acquisition. Ph.D. Thesis, Department of Computer and Information Science, Linköping University, Linköping, Sweden. Technical Report Number 244, 1991

52. Eriksson, H., Musen, M.A.: Conceptual models for automatic generation of knowledge-acquisition tools. In: Wetter, T. et al. (eds.): Current Developments in Knowledge Acquisition—EKAW'92. Lecture Notes in Artificial Intelligence **599**. Berlin: Springer–Verlag 1992, pp. 14–36

53. Marques, D. et al.: Easy programming: Empowering people to build their own applications. IEEE Expert **7**(3), 16–29 (1992)

54. Puerta, A.R. et al.: A multiple-method shell for the automatic generation of knowledge-acquisition tools. Knowledge Acquisition **4**, 171–196 (1992)

55. Walther, E., Eriksson, H., Musen, M.A.: Plug and play: Construction of task-specific expert-system shells using sharable context ontologies. Proceedings of the AAAI'92 Workshop on Knowledge Representation Aspects of Knowledge Acquisition, San Jose, California. American Association for Artificial Intelligence 1992, pp. 191–198

56. Musen, M.A.: Dimensions of knowledge sharing and reuse. Computers and Biomedical Research (in press)

KA Process Support Through Generalised Directive Models*

Peter Terpstra[1], Gertjan van Heijst[1], Nigel Shadbolt[2], Bob Wielinga[1]

[1] Social Science Informatics, Department of Psychology, University of Amsterdam,
Roeterstraat 15, 1018 WB Amsterdam, The Netherlands
[2] AI Group, Department of Psychology, Nottingham University, University Park,
Nottingham NG7 2RD, United Kingdom

Abstract. In this paper we describe Generalised Directive Models and their instantiation in the ACKnowledge Knowledge Engineering Workbench. We have developed a context sensitive rewrite grammar that allows us to capture a large class of inference layer models. We use the grammar to progressively refine the model of problem solving for an application. It is also used as the basis of the scheduling of KA activities and the selection of KA tools.

1 Introduction

As part of the ACKnowledge ESPRIT II Project (P2576) [9] we have been designing and building an integrated knowledge engineering workbench (KEW). KEW provides the knowledge engineer with operational support for knowledge acquisition in the development of knowledge-based systems [23]. KEW is an integrated environment that allows the combination of a variety of knowledge acquisition tools and techniques, ranging from interactive elicitation techniques to machine learning [1]. The knowledge engineer can take advantage of the differential efficacy of the various tools and techniques for acquiring different kinds of knowledge.

KEW allows to progressively formalise knowledge. The KEW elicitation techniques use intermediate representations that are supportive of human ways of describing knowledge. The acquired informal descriptions are gradually reformulated and refined into the standard AI formalisms of frames and first order logic. KEW facilitates the integration of the results of several acquisition techniques. Thus KEW provides support for merging partial knowledge bases into a consistent knowledge base.

KEW embodies a variety of types of knowledge about knowledge engineering: knowledge about the knowledge acquisition process, knowledge about the effective use of particular acquisition tools and techniques, knowledge about how to integrate knowledge from different tools, knowledge about how to validate the results of acquisition, and knowledge about the types of the components of expertise (for example, what is involved in a typical diagnostic application).

The description above illustrates that KEW is a complicated system, both technically and conceptually. To effectively manage the combination of functionality, KEW

---

* This paper is partially a reprint of [25] but with an extended knowledge acquisition scenario (Sect. 4)

provides the knowledge engineer with active advice for constructing a model of the expert task, for selecting appropriate techniques, for planning of his/her knowledge acquisition (KA) work and for organising the final knowledge base (KB). It is this directive and active component of KEW which we will discuss in this paper.

KEW views knowledge acquisition as a model driven activity. It uses models of the knowledge acquisition process and the task of the target system to suggest what to do next in the KA process. In the sequel we will call these models *directive models*.

These directive models contain information about typical inference steps that are used in a particular task, information about the type of domain knowledge that is required to make these inferences, information about the way this domain knowledge can be elicited and information about alternatives for particular subtasks. KEW uses these directive models for the following purposes:

- To figure out how to discover the nature of the task that the target system has to perform.
- To decide which domain knowledge is required to perform that task.
- To structure the target knowledge base in a way that mimics the inference structure of the task at hand. This aids partial evaluation of the knowledge base and it also aids maintenance once the system has been delivered.

In Sect. 2 we will discuss in detail how directive models can guide the knowledge acquisition process and we will introduce the notion of *generalised directive models*. Section 3 is about the top level control loop that drives KEW's advice and guidance module and about the tools that realise this loop. In Sect. 4 we will illustrate by means of a scenario how our models can direct and organise the KA process. In Sect. 5 we will relate out work to other approaches and draw some conclusions.

2 Model Driven Approaches to Knowledge Acquisition

Currently the main theories of knowledge acquisition are all model based to a certain extent. The model based approach to knowledge acquisition covers the idea that abstract models of the tasks that expert systems have to perform can highly facilitate knowledge acquisition. These abstract models have taken the form of interpretation models [26], generic tasks [4] and task specific shells and tools [16,15,14].

Abstract models can be used as high level templates that put constraints on the required domain knowledge. They direct knowledge acquisition because they make explicit what kind of knowledge is used in the problem solving process and they structure the knowledge base. This is exactly what is needed in an environment like KEW. In ACKnowledge we have chosen the KADS type of abstract models as a starting point for our exercise. These seemed a good candidate because KADS provides a semi formal language for the description of arbitrary models [10]. However, the approach that has evolved could also be adapted to model types that reflect other theories about knowledge acquisition.

According to KADS, the construction of a KBS goes through a fixed set of stages. Each of these stages results in a particular model. KADS discerns the following milestones in the KA process: First there is the *task model*. This is a high level description of the task that the system has to perform. The next important milestone in the KA process is a construction of the reasoning to be done by the system — this is the construction of a *model of expertise*. This describes the reasoning of a human expert at the conceptual level. The *conceptual model* is then produced through a transformation and synthesis of the model of human expertise and the model of cooperation. The conceptual model is real-world oriented in that it describes the competence in expert problem solving. The next model in the process, the *design model*, is a model at the same level of abstraction as the conceptual model, but is a model of the artifact, not of the real world. The design model is undertaken from two viewpoints: the functional viewpoint, whereby the functions to be performed by the system are discussed; and the physical viewpoint, where discussion focuses on the realisation of those functions in the physical system to be built.

KADS supplies a library of interpretation models that can be used to bridge the gap between the task model and the model of expertise. These interpretation models describe the inference structures of prototypical tasks. Interpretation models are abstract in the sense that they do not contain domain knowledge. They consist of knowledge sources, representing "primitive" inference steps, and meta classes, which index domain knowledge according to its role in the problem solving process. A conceptual model is an instantiation and adaptation of an interpretation model for a particular domain.

In ACKnowledge we have limited our scope to the first three stages of the KADS view on KBS construction. That is, the output of KEW is a conceptual model. Moreover, in KEW we have taken the view that the conceptual model should be executable.

2.1 Task Identification and Model Selection

The first step in the knowledge acquisition process in KADS is the identification of the task that the target system should perform. Since the task description will be used to select an interpretation model from the library this library is indexed on features that discriminate between tasks. Figure 1 (taken from [27]) shows a part of the decision tree that is used to select an interpretation model. The interpretation models are associated with the leaves of this tree.

In the upper part of the decision tree the task features are very general and they are used to discriminate between different types of tasks, (e.g. analysis versus synthesis). Features like these are usually easy to establish without actual elicitation of domain knowledge. In the lower parts of the decision tree the discriminating features are more specific. These features are used to discriminate between models that realise the same type of task but have different task decompositions and control regimes. Features like these are usually closely related to characteristics of the domain knowledge that realises the inferences of the directive model. Here issues like the structure of the domain concepts, the use of uncertain information, the number of components etc. are relevant. Unfortunately it is difficult to answer questions like these without actual elicitation of domain knowledge.

We can conclude from the foregoing discussion that, although it is certainly possible to elicit relevant features of the task that the system should perform, in general it will not be possible to select a single model without eliciting domain knowledge.

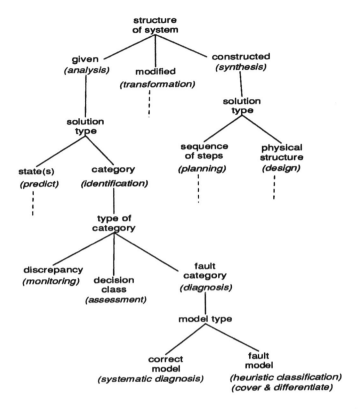

Fig. 1. Partial decision tree for interpretation models

2.2 Model Driven Knowledge Elicitation

When a directive model is selected the "semantics" of this model put constraints on the knowledge that is to be elicited. These constraints can be exploited to guide the acquisition process in two ways.

The first constraint is related to the structure of the directive model. This structure can be used to define a structure on the target knowledge base that mimics the structure of the directive model. That is, for every knowledge source and for every metaclass in the directive model there is a partition in KEW's *Core Knowledge Base* (CKB from now on). The interdependencies in the directive model can then be used to suggest an optimal time sequence for the elicitation of the domain knowledge in the different partitions. Several "optimality principles" have been identified to guide this operation. These will be described in Sect. 3.2.

The second way the directive model can be exploited has to do with the semantics of the primitive knowledge sources. Every primitive knowledge source puts constraints on the structure of its input and output metaclasses and on the syntactic structure of its domain rules. For example, if there is a knowledge source *taxonomic abstraction* in a directive model, the domain knowledge for the input metaclass of that knowledge source must have a hierarchical structure.

2.3   Generalised Directive Models

In model driven knowledge acquisition directive models are used to advice the knowledge engineer about usage of tools for eliciting domain knowledge. If there is no directive model only limited advice is possible. However, in Sect. 2.1 we pointed out that usually domain knowledge is needed to select an appropriate model. This is recognised as a dilemma in ACKnowledge. If there is no directive model, there can only be limited advice; on the other hand, selecting the most appropriate directive model requires some knowledge of the domain. Eliciting domain knowledge to select the model will be difficult if there is no model to direct its selection! ACKnowledge has attempted to resolve this dilemma by the use of what have been called *generalised directive models* (GDM's). These are directive models, but they leave parts of the problem-solving process underspecified. These underspecified parts are represented by *generalised knowledge sources*, which describe non-primitive problem-solving steps. The idea is that these can then be used to describe problem-solving processes which we understand at only a coarse-grained level. However, there will still be enough structure to guide elicitation of domain knowledge sufficient to reveal new information about the domain which will then be used to "fill in" the underspecified portions of the model.

Another way of saying this is that a generalised knowledge source describes a set of similar extensions. These extensions could be primitive knowledge sources but they could also be partial models that consist of multiple generalised and primitive knowledge sources and intermediate meta classes. However, these extensions do have in common that they describe the same relation between the input and the output of the generalised knowledge source.

The use of GDM's is based on three related principles:

- *knowledge acquisition is a cyclic process*
  We view knowledge engineering as an iterative process of elicitation of domain knowledge, integration of the elicited knowledge with previously acquired knowledge and evaluation of the acquired knowledge to assess the current state of the acquisition process [21]. Model construction is an integral part of this cycle.

- *compositionality*
  A directive model describes a relation between inputs and outputs. With the extension of a (partial) model we mean the set of input /output combinations for which that relation holds. The compositionality principle states that the extension of a model only depends on the extensions of its parts and the way they are related. This implies that model parts with equal extensions can be exchanged, leaving the extension of the model as a whole unaffected.

- *a delayed commitment strategy*
  The third principle states that the knowledge engineer should only commit himself to a particular model if there is sufficient evidence that it is the "right" model. This reflects the idea that backtracking on abstract model construction is difficult and should be avoided.

The GDM's enable us to interleave model selection and knowledge elicitation. Although it is still required that there is an abstract model of the problem solving process before the domain knowledge is elicited, this initial GDM may be very general, leaving all parts that depend on properties of the domain knowledge unspecified. This initial model can then be used to direct acquisition of domain knowledge. Formally a GDM could be described in the following way:

```
GDM --> {input-metaclass}+ GKS output-metaclass
GKS --> {knowledge-source}+ {{meta-class}+ knowledge-source}*
```

In KEW the library of GDM's is represented as a generative grammar, where the final directive models are sentences, the generalised knowledge sources are non terminal symbols and the knowledge sources and meta classes are terminal symbols. The model construction steps in each acquisition cycle correspond to the application of rewrite rules. Each of the rewrite rules has associated conditions that have to be true before the rule may be applied. These conditions are the link between the abstract model and the features of the domain knowledge. In Sect. 4 we give some examples of grammar rules that we used.

In summary, in this section we have argued that an abstract model of the problem solving task can highly facilitate knowledge acquisition. We have also argued that such a model can only be selected after a certain amount of domain knowledge has been elicited. Finally, we have suggested a way out of this dilemma based on the observations that on the micro level knowledge elicitation is a cyclic process and that model construction should be a stepwise process that is part of this cycle. In the next section we will show how these ideas are realised in KEW.

3 KEW Top Level Control Loop

In the previous section we described the theory of knowledge acquisition that KEW exploits to give active support for the KA process. In this section we will show how this theory is supported by the different subtools of KEW's advice and guidance module.

The KEW advice and guidance module is implemented as a top level control loop on the workbench. This loop can be viewed as an instantiation of the knowledge acquisition cycle as described in [21] and shown in Fig. 2. The cycle occurs throughout the life cycle, and so forms part of most KA activities. However, the emphasis will vary depending on the KA context. The cyclic nature of the KA process can be captured by a number of basic processes, which we can now briefly discuss:

- *Planning* takes into account the current activity in which KEW is engaged, available information about the task or domain, and possibly an assessment of the current state of the KB. Output of the planning process is a goal.

- Usually, a goal may be achieved in any one of a number of different ways. Hence many factors (e.g. the availability of an expert, the nature of the task and domain, the state of the KB) are relevant to *selection* of an operation.

- KEW can *apply* the selected operation.

- KEW then *stores* and *assimilates* the results into an information repository.

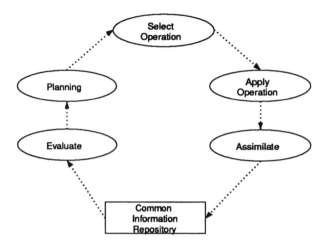

Fig. 2. The generic KA cycle

– Finally in the cycle, the resulting state of the KB is *evaluated* in terms of consistency, completeness, correctness, etc.. When problems emerge during evaluation, those problems are communicated to the planning component, which attempts to set up remedial goals.

Figure 3 gives an overview of the different steps in the KEW top level control loop. In the remainder of this section we will describe each of the steps in this control loop. Some of these steps are done automatically but others have to be done by the knowledge engineer. For each of the steps in the loop KEW delegates control to a tool of the advice and guidance module.

3.1 Select Initial GDM

The first step in the acquisition process is the selection of an initial GDM. As described in Sect. 2 we assume that we can select an initial GDM without eliciting domain knowledge. To select this initial GDM KEW contains an interview facility that asks multiple choice questions to establish features of the task that the target system has to perform. The interview is structured in a way that mimics the decision tree in Fig. 1. Every node in the decision tree has an associated interview question and a generalised directive model. For example, one of the questions in the interview is "What is the task of the System?", and a possible answer to this question is "Analytic (i.e. diagnosis or classification)". Associated with this answer are the GDM *diagnosis* and another interview question. If the interviewee is able to answer this next interview question the interview proceeds, but if the interviewee is unable or unwilling to answer this new question, the interview finishes and the GDM diagnosis is selected as the initial GDM.

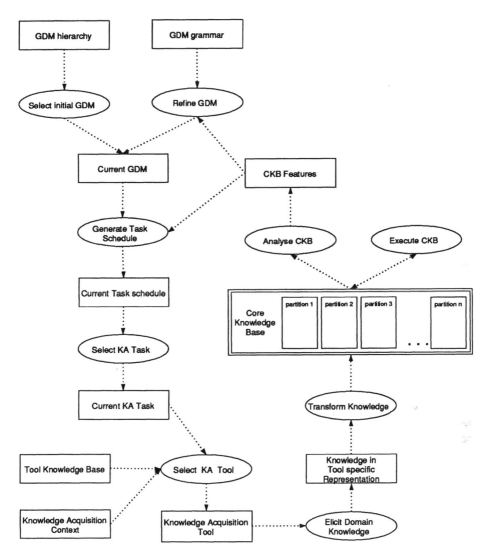

Fig. 3. KEW's top level control loop

3.2 Generate a Task Schedule

In Sect. 2.2 we pointed out that the partition structure of the CKB should mimic
the form of the directive model. So the next step in the KA process is to generate
a sequence of KA tasks that must be performed to build the CKB that corresponds
to the current GDM. For this purpose KEW contains a scheduling tool. The KA
task scheduler analyses the current GDM and suggests a task break down for the
knowledge acquisition process, the *task schedule*.

When using GDM's there are two types of knowledge acquisition tasks: tasks to
acquire domain knowledge that is used in the problem solving process, and tasks to

acquire domain knowledge for GDM refinement. The function of the task scheduler is to identify these tasks and to suggest a temporal ordering. In order to do this the scheduler has to know about the constraints that are imposed on the acquisition process, and about the guiding principles that can be exploited to choose between legal alternatives. We will now describe some assumptions and heuristics used by the scheduler.

- *Work on one CKB partition only at each cycle.*
  This assumption allows KEW to associate one task with every component of the directive model.

- *Focus acquisition around primitive knowledge sources.*
  The directive model can be broken up in partial models that consist of a knowledge source and its related input and output meta classes. Since the domain knowledge for a partition is constrained by the role that the knowledge fulfills in the problem solving process, that is, by the semantics of the associated knowledge sources, it makes sense to start with partial models whose knowledge source is primitive. Moreover, if the knowledge source is primitive, and all the components of such a partial directive model have been filled in, the submodel can be evaluated on consistency and completeness. That is, it can be checked whether the knowledge source supplies a complete mapping of its inputs on its output.

- *Start with partial directive models whose inputs/output are known.*
  The third principle is concerned with the order in which the partial directive models are filled with domain knowledge. If a partial directive model has been marked as complete there are two ways to undo this fact. Either an input or an output meta class can be modified. Both types of modifications imply that the partial directive model is no longer complete so the primitive inference action has to be adapted and evaluated again. It is clear that this implies a lot of extra work that should be avoided when possible. However, knowledge acquisition is a difficult process so every once in a while a situation like this will occur. The only way to ease the pain is to work systematically, and to start with the partial directive models that depend least on the contents of other partial directive models. These are the partial directive models that require user input or generate system output. The next partial directive model would be the one whose inputs/outputs are the inputs/outputs of partial directive models that already have been filled in, and so on.

Based on the above principles the task scheduler generates a diagram of tasks with their interdependencies. Each task corresponds either to a knowledge source or to a meta class. The dependencies can be exploited to check whether a partial directive model is still complete, when another part of the directive model has been modified. At the same time, the dependencies can be considered as a suggested time schedule.

3.3 Select a Knowledge Acquisition Task

The output of the scheduling tool is a set of tasks that must be performed to build the executable knowledge base, and a suggested time schedule for these tasks. The next step in the top level control loop is the selection of one of these tasks to work on. In KEW this decision is made by the knowledge engineer. The task scheduler visualises the current schedule as a PERT diagram. The user can select one of the tasks in the diagram and tell KEW to analyse the task. The analysis in the task will reveal the constraints that the GDM puts on the domain knowledge for the corresponding domain partitions. For example, if the CKB partition that corresponds to the selected task is the input partition for the knowledge source partition for *taxonomic abstraction*, the analysis will reveal that the required knowledge should be organised in a taxonomy. The results of this analysis are put in a temporary knowledge base that contains all the information that is available about the selected task. This knowledge base is then handed over to the tool selector.

3.4   Select a Knowledge Acquisition Tool

The next step is the selection of a knowledge acquisition tool (or a sequence of tools) to perform the selected KA task. In order to do this the selected KA task is passed to the tool selector of KEW. This tool selector exploits three types of information to suggest an appropriate KA tool.

The first type of information are the constraints that the semantics of the directive model put on the knowledge that is to be elicited. This is the knowledge that resulted from the analysis in the previous step. secondly, there is contextual information about the knowledge acquisition situation. This type of information refers to things as "the availability of experts", "the time constraints" and so on. The third type of information is knowledge about the tools that are available in KEW and about their functionality and requirements.

Based on this information the tool selector will come up with a set of appropriate tool configurations to elicit the knowledge for the partition that we are currently working on. We speak of tool configurations instead of tools because the tool selector does also suggest the transformation and integration operations that are needed to merge the new knowledge in the CKB.

3.5   Elicitation, Transformation and Integration

After a tool configuration has been selected KEW hands over control to the selected KA tools. KEW's knowledge acquisition tools are not the subject of this paper. For the reader who is interested in this subject we refer to [9]. Here we just remark that the elicited knowledge is will be put in the appropriate CKB partition.

3.6   Execute the CKB

In Sect. 2 we mentioned that we considered KEW's CKB as an executable conceptual model. In this section we will say a bit more about the internal organisation of the CKB and the way it is executable. A conceptual model contains three types of knowledge: domain knowledge, inference knowledge and control knowledge. In KEW's CKB domain knowledge can be represented in two languages: a frame language (SFL, [8]) and first order predicate logic (NTP, [18]). We have explained already that the partition structure of the CKB corresponds to the structure of the directive model, that is, the inference structure of the system task. We have used ideas from the $(ML)^2$ language [24] to specify how domain knowledge is used by the inference knowledge and how to use the partition structure of the CKB.

To be executable, the CKB does also require *control* knowledge: when to make which inference. In the KADS four layer model [27] this kind of of knowledge resides at the *task layer*. KEW contains a control knowledge editor COMEX [1] that supports the elicitation of this control knowledge. Control knowledge is specified by means of a mixture of dataflow between knowledge sources, constraints between these dataflows and execution modes for knowledge sources. The tool has a facility to transform the inference model corresponding to a GDM automatically into a data flow model. The user only has to specify the constraints between different dataflows and the type of computations within a knowledge source to specify the task layer control. This knowledge can be entered using a simple graphical (boxes and arrows) language. Once the control knowledge is specified, the user can execute the CKB to test if the combination of task-layer control, the specification of the inference layer and the contents of the domain layer partitions works as intended.

Although the issue of control knowledge is related to the use of directive models, the elicitation of the control knowledge itself is not model driven at the moment. The GDM grammars that we have at the moment do not specify "typical" control structures that can be associated with the right hand sides of rewrite rules.

3.7   Analyse CKB

When the CKB is modified, it is analysed and evaluated. The results of this evaluation are expressed as *CKB features*. These features are used to plan the next cycle of the top level control loop. We distinguish three types of CKB features:

- *GDM independent features.*
  With this we mean features like the completeness of the partitions. They are called "GDM independent" because these features are not used to evaluate or refine the current GDM. Knowledge source partitions can be evaluated on the criterion that they realise a complete mapping of the input partitions on the output partition. That is, for every input there is an output and for every output there is an input. This type of evaluation is only meaningful when all the related meta class partitions are "filled" with domain knowledge.

- *Features that are characteristic for the current (G)DM.*
  These are the features that are mentioned in the conditions of the rewrite rules of the GDM grammar. A rewrite rule is only applied when its conditions are true. After the application of the rule the Model Selection Tool continues to check whether the conditions remain true. If this is no longer the case this might imply that the current GDM is wrong after all.

- *Features that are useful for GDM refinement.*
  The features are similar to the features of the type mentioned above, but they have another function. If there are some rewrite rules available to refine the current GDM, these features are used to decide which rewrite rule is applicable. If there is a rewrite rule applicable the GDM will be refined and the update will be

forwarded to the KA-Task Scheduler. The scheduler makes a new decomposition of the input and output dependencies and constructs a new agenda of KA-tasks. When this is all done the knowledge engineer can select the next task in the updated KA-task schedule.

3.8 Refine GDM

When the CKB has been analysed, the next step in the top level control loop is GDM refinement. If the GDM contains non primitive components (generalised knowledge sources), it is usually the case that there were multiple applicable rewrite rules in the GDM grammar. The reason that there were more rules applicable was that there was not enough domain knowledge (or more precisely, meta knowledge about the domain knowledge) available to rule out some of these rewrite rules. It might be that this is not longer the case, since the most recent knowledge acquisition cycle might have revealed new CKB features. Because the conditions on the rewrite rules in the GDM grammar are formulated in terms of CKB features this has a direct impact on the applicability of the rules. If there is only one applicable rule for a certain generalised knowledge source in the GDM, this must be the correct refinement. In this situation the knowledge engineer is expected to apply the rewrite rule and start with the next knowledge acquisition cycle. Refining the GDM will automatically cause an update of the task schedule.

4 A Scenario in the Domain of Respiratory Medicin

In this section we will show how the differentiation of generalised directive models (GDMs) can be used to direct and organise the KA process. The scenario is an idealised reconstruction of how a knowledge acquisition process previously done with domain experts would be implemented in KEW. The scenario is incomplete in the sense that we highlight only those parts which demonstrate the interaction between models for problem solving and features of domain knowledge and how this interaction can be used to guide the knowledge acquisition process. In Sect. 3 and Fig. 3 the KA process was described as a cycle consisting of (1) the generation of a task schedule, (2) selection of an KA task, (3) selection of an KA tool (4), application of that KA tool, (5) analysis of the CKB and (6) the refinement of the GDM. We will describe the scenario as much as possible in terms of this top level cycle.

The domain chosen is that of respiratory medicine. This domain is of real world complexity and has sufficient richness to demonstrate how progressive refinement and instantiation of GDMs can act as a means of informing KA and organising the emerging knowledge bases.

4.1 Select Initial GDM

The first step in the scenario is to select an initial GDM by trying to ascertain certain key properties of the domain and task. This is supported through the use of the discrimination tree shown in Fig. 1. The decision tree is traversed by asking global features of the task. This interview reveals that we are building an *analytic* application where the solution is a diagnosis (finding the cause of a respiratory complaint of a patient). The diagnosis is done by means of a fault model (as opposed to Reiter's principled diagnosis). We assume a single fault model[3]. This enables KEW to select the GDM in Fig. 4 and start the KA top level cycle.

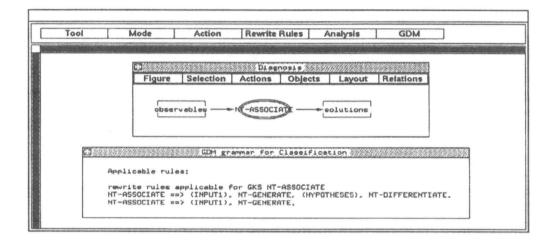

Fig. 4. The top level GDM and its possible expansions

4.2 Refining the initial GDM

Generate Task Schedule Given the initial GDM, the task scheduler sets up an agenda with three global tasks: (1) the elicitation of domain knowledge for **observables** and (2) for **solutions**. The third task is the elicitation of meta knowledge about **nt-associate** to determine which of a number of models of single fault diagnosis is most appropriate to the domain.

Select KA Task The more refined a GDM is, the more support it gives for knowledge acquisition. Therefore we decide to elicit knowledge that can be used to refine **nt-associate**. In Fig. 4 we see that there are two possible ways to refine the current GDM. There is a choice between a class of models which generate a set of hypotheses which are afterwards differentiated and others that directly compute the right solutions. The grounds for applying the first rewrite rule would be evidence of an intermediate problem solving step of hypothesis formation and subsequent differentiation between the hypotheses.

Select KA Tool Given the discriminative conditions of the GDM rewrite rules, the goal for the tool selector is to suggest configurations of tools which could provide information whether which conditions are satisfied. The key ingredient in our

---

[3] Although in our domain it is quite likely that experts will be confronted with patients suffering from multiple conditions we are assuming a single fault model for the sake of exposition.

GDM formulation is the presence of hypotheses as intermediary constituents of problem solving. Where might such evidence originate? It could arise in protocols or interviews. This expectation is itself the kind of knowledge that drives our KEW advisor. The advisor has canned text which it presents to the knowledge engineer as a way of resolving the conflict between the rewrites shown in Fig. 4.

Tool Application Taking the advice of the system we decide to invoke protocol analysis on recorded diagnostic sessions of the expert with his patients (Fig. 5).

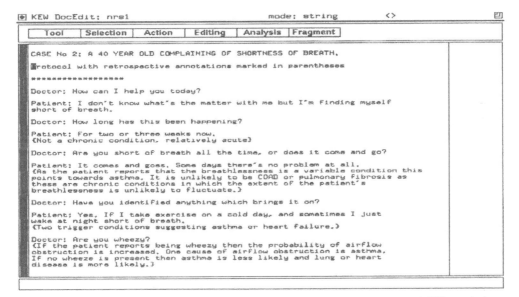

Fig. 5. The protocol editor revealing evidence for hypothesis generation and differentiation

Analyse CKB Inspecting the protocols we find that the fragments in the protocol editor are strong evidence for the generation and differentiation of hypotheses.

Refine GDM We will therefore follow through the refinement of our GDM by choosing the first expansion rule for **nt-associate** in Fig. 4. The result is the GDM in Fig. 6.

4.3 Exploring **NT-Generate** in Generate and Differentiate

Generate Task Schedule The task schedule which is being dynamically generated as we refine our GDMs is shown in Fig. 7. The schedule indicates a default linearisation of how the various model components might be instantiated. The first of which is the fragment consisting of the metaclass **observables**, the non-terminal knowledge source **nt-generate**, and the metaclass **hypotheses**.

Select KA Task We decide to continue with elicitation of meta-knowledge about **nt-generate** which is useful to make a distinction between the two possible expansions (Fig. 6) of this GKS. The crucial difference between the possible expansions is whether hypothesis generation makes appeal to a *structural model*

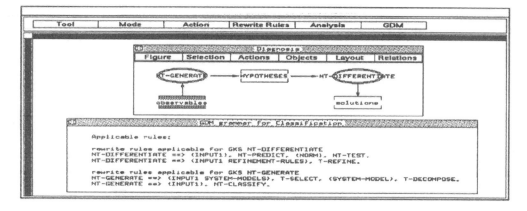

Fig. 6. Generate-and-Differentiate model of diagnosis

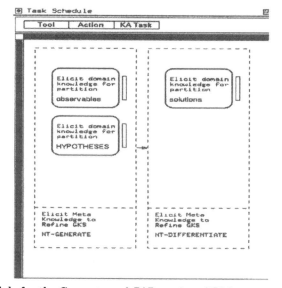

Fig. 7. Task schedule for the Generate-and-Differentiate GDM

of the system. Is such a model of the system used, for example through recursive decomposition of its components, to generate hypotheses about faulty parts of the system?

Select KA Tool The laddering tool of KEW (ALTO [11]) is configurable in such a way that it elicits part-of hierarchies instead of the default isa hierarchies. The KEW tool selection knowledge base contains a rule that such a configuration of the laddering tool is useful to build system models. Alternatively one can use a tool which poses questions in canned text to elicit meta knowledge for the refinement of generalised knowledge sources directly.

Tool Application We decide to use the interview tool. The existence of a structural model is actually a difficult question to answer categorically. One is always likely, if pushed, to find such models of the system under investigation. The point is whether such a model is routinely used to generate the initial hypotheses - and whether such a model is explicitly available to be acquired.

We make the assumption in this case and in conjunction with the expert that no such model is routinely used in hypothesis formation.

Refine GDM Applying the second rule of the **nt-generate** conflict set results in a new set of rewrites for a new intermediate non-terminal knowledge source which has substituted for **nt-generate** - namely, **nt-classify** in Fig. 8.

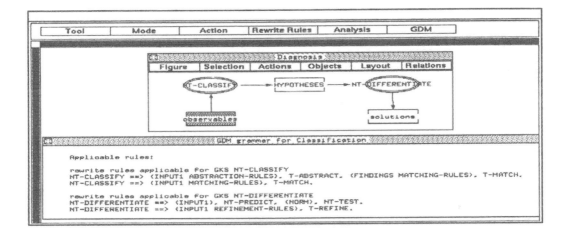

Fig. 8. The GDM further refined

4.4 Detecting Abstraction in NT-Classify

Generate Task Schedule The task schedule is updated in a similar way as in Fig. 7.

Select KA Task We decide to elicit meta knowledge about **nt-classify**. Discrimination between the two rewrites for **nt-classify** is dependent on whether there is significant abstraction of observables.

Select KA Tool The existence of abstraction can quickly be determined using KA techniques which are known to reveal abstraction steps. Such techniques include laddering and sorting.

One source of KA material which is particularly useful for determining the processes which might be applied to the universe of observables is contained in case descriptions. Such a typical case structure for our domain is shown in Fig. 9.

A goal for the system with such information is to decompile the information that is often *flattened* out in simple attribute–value case descriptions. In order

breath-sound = diminished breathlessness = grade 3 breath-degree = worse
respiratory rate = 120   cough = absent   sputum-colour = yellow
sputum = exist   sputum-quantity = little weight = standard
general-feeling = ill   ankle = normal   finger-clubbing = normal
lips-shape = normal   lips-colour = blue   jugular-vein-pressure absent
neck-muscles = normal   barrel-chested = normal heart-position = normal
heart-state = normal   heart-sound = normal   sex = male
smoker = 20pd   age = 48   employment = carpenter

Fig. 9. Typical *flat* case description

to reinstate structure in the case description one thing we can do is ask the expert to ladder on the case descriptors.

Tool Application It appears that the expert makes a distinction between **symptoms**, **signs**, **tests**, **triggers** and **case history**, each divided in several subclasses.

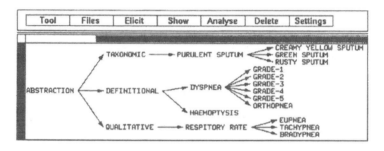

Fig. 10. Identifying abstraction types

With the help of the knowledge engineer this abstraction hierarchy is further refined into different types of abstraction. This results in a partially configured laddered grid of the sort shown in Fig. 10. To more thoroughly explore these abstraction steps we can ask the expert to describe the rules that allow him to infer the superordinate nodes of the figure from subordinate ones. This results in abstraction rules like

- Definitional - dyspnoea is breathlessness, central cyanosis is a blue hue to the tongue, tachypnea is increased respiratory rate
- Taxonomic - creamy yellow sputum is ako purulent sputum, green sputum is ako purulent sputum
- Qualitative abstraction - FEV1/FVC ratio < 70% is obstructive, peak expiratory flow rate = 500L/min is normal, respiratory rate > 20 is increased respiratory rate

Analyse CKB The above discussion clearly shows that there is abstraction involved in the various concepts of this hierarchy.

Refine GDM Figure 11 shows the GDM after expanding **nt-classify**.

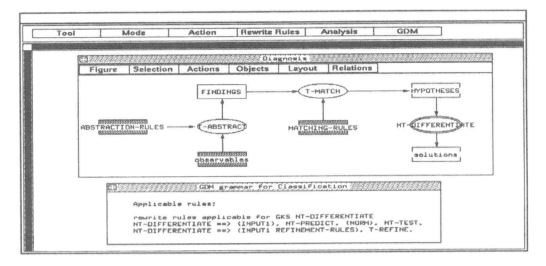

Fig. 11. The GDM with terminal abstraction and match

4.5 Exploring the solution space of the GDM

Generate Task Schedule Using the KA schedule heuristics as mentioned in Sect. 3 the taskscheduler updates the latest task sequencing for our current GDM. It introduces new tasks for acquisition of domain knowledge for matching-rules.

Select KA Task However although at this moment the lefthand side of the GDM is almost instantiated, we know very little yet about the righthand side, that is about the type of hypotheses, the differentiation of these hypotheses and the resulting solutions. Therefore we decide to find out a little about the nature of the solution metaclass.

In [28] we noted that in any diagnosis task the size and structure are important properties of the solution space, helpful to discriminate between intermediate candidate knowledge sources. We learn from the expert that in terms of common diseases of the upper and lower respiratory tracts there are 10's of possibilities but less than 100, and that they are organised into hierarchies.

Select KA Tool With this contextual information KEW could again use a technique such as laddering to elucidate the solution space itself.

Tool Application A KA session in this domain would yield the sort of knowledge shown in Fig. 12. Moreover KEW translation tools (described in [19,20]) now can transform this knowledge into first order logic to begin to build up the beginnings of domain level knowledge partitions as in Fig. 13.

Analyse CKB Evidently there is clear hierarchical organisation in this domain.

Refine GDM We can reasonably expect with this amount of structure in the solution space that there is a likelihood that the generalised knowledge source nt-differentiate in our current GDM (Fig. 11) contains an explicit refine knowledge source. The choice is between simple refine and a more complex GDM. We will continue with the elaboration on nt-differentiate in Sect. 4.7.

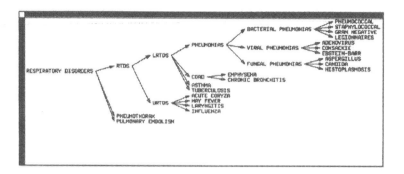

Fig. 12. Laddering solutions

```
((exists x) (pneumococcal x))
((exists x) (legionnaires x))
......
((all x) (=> (pneumococcal x) (seasonal x winter)))
((all x) (=> (legionnaires x) (seasonal x summer)))
((all x) (=> (pneumococcal x) (~(legionnaires x))))
........
((all x) (=> (pneumococcal x) (bacterial_pneumonia x)))
........
((all x) (=> (COAD x)  (V (emphysemia x) (chronic_bronchitis x))))
.......
```

Fig. 13. Solution domain partition 1

4.6   Acquisition of match rules

Select KA Task For the selection of the next KA Task we apply the KA heuristic, that we should where possible always provide some instantiation of a terminal knowledge source. The underlying principle being that KA data will always constrain the classes of model available, and provide a basis for minimal evaluation of the overall topology of problem solving. This means looking at the instantiation of the terminal knowledge source **t-match** in Fig. 11, along with its associated meta-classes. This is now facilitated by the fact that we have some idea of what the **solution** and **hypothesis** elements are.

Select KA Tool What KA tool properties might be used to establish the associational links between **findings** and **observables**? Repertory grids and machine learning tools implemented in KEW like KEW-SBL and CNN [1] are all able to produce rules of association. One example is invoking the repertory grid tool with solutions (respiratory diseases) as elements and constructs that correspond to general observables categories identified in Sect. 4.4.

Tool Application In figures 14, 15 and 16 we see the result of an expert rating some of the diseases elicited in the previous section in terms of signs and symptoms.

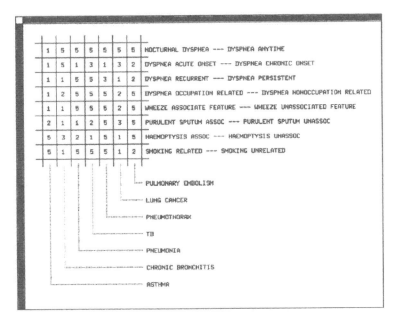

Fig. 14. The repertory grid data for signs, symptoms and diseases

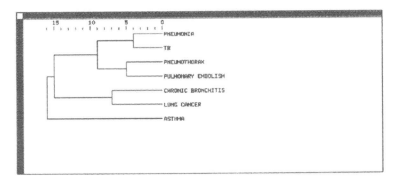

Fig. 15. The repertory grid data analysed into element similarities

Analyse CKB What is interesting about this exercise is that the clusters and entailments that arise as a result of the ratings produce clusters of diseases which are similar in terms of presenting observations. Of course, they may be quite distinct in the solution hierarchy - but in terms of the expert's initial evidence we can see which diseases are likely to be difficult to tell apart.

Select KA Task Thus a second round of acquisition could now attempt to elicit constructs which do discriminate diseases which are quite clearly distinct in the solution space and yet cluster on presenting symptoms. It is these new constructs that are likely to form the basis of hypothesis differentiation.

Analysis by Execution At this stage in the process the knowledge sources t-match and t-abstract are instantiated with domain knowledge. The *animation* of

Entail	Truth	Information	Constructs
L5 -> L4	100	61	DYSPNEA OCCUPATION RELATED -> WHEEZE ASSOCIATE FEATURE
R4 -> R5	100	49	WHEEZE UNASSOCIATED FEATURE -> DYSPNEA NONOCCUPATION RELATED
L3 -> L8	100	46	SMOKING RELATED -> DYSPNEA RECURRENT
L3 -> L5	100	46	WHEEZE ASSOCIATE FEATURE -> DYSPNEA RECURRENT
R8 -> R3	100	42	DYSPNEA PERSISTENT -> SMOKING UNRELATED
R5 -> R3	100	42	DYSPNEA PERSISTENT -> WHEEZE UNASSOCIATED FEATURE
L3 -> L4	100	41	DYSPNEA OCCUPATION RELATED -> DYSPNEA RECURRENT
L4 -> L1	100	40	NOCTURNAL DYSPNEA -> DYSPNEA OCCUPATION RELATED
R4 -> R3	100	39	DYSPNEA PERSISTENT -> DYSPNEA NONOCCUPATION RELATED
L5 -> L1	100	26	NOCTURNAL DYSPNEA -> WHEEZE ASSOCIATE FEATURE
R1 -> R4	100	19	DYSPNEA NONOCCUPATION RELATED -> DYSPNEA ANYTIME
L7 -> R1	100	17	NOCTURNAL DYSPNEA -> HAEMOPTYSIS UNASSOC
L3 -> L1	100	17	NOCTURNAL DYSPNEA -> DYSPNEA RECURRENT
L2 -> L1	100	17	NOCTURNAL DYSPNEA -> DYSPNEA ACUTE ONSET
R1 -> R5	100	16	WHEEZE UNASSOCIATED FEATURE -> DYSPNEA ANYTIME
L1 -> R7	100	13	HAEMOPTYSIS ASSOC -> DYSPNEA ANYTIME
R1 -> R3	100	13	DYSPNEA PERSISTENT -> DYSPNEA ANYTIME
R1 -> R2	100	13	DYSPNEA CHRONIC ONSET -> DYSPNEA ANYTIME
L8 -> R1	100	12	NOCTURNAL DYSPNEA -> SMOKING UNRELATED
L3 -> R8	100	10	SMOKING RELATED -> DYSPNEA ANYTIME

Fig. 16. The repertory grid data analysed in terms of construct entailments

fragments of the KBS acquired so far gives a way of characterising the *dynamic* properties of the knowledge base and also of assessing sufficiency. How might evaluation work in such a context? One of the principles we appeal to is the idea that knowledge acquired should be sufficient to cover the relevant input and output metaclasses. In this context are the **findings** we know about derivable from the knowledge source **t-abstract**. In terms of **t-match** are the solution classes we know about covered by the rules of association? Conversely are all findings used in the rules of association?

4.7 Refining Hypothesis Differentiation

In this section we will show how the GDM grammar supports the non grounded part of the GDM, the hypothesis differentiation. Due to space constraints we will only show how the rewrite rules are applied and skip the acquisition of domain knowledge.

Refine GDM Moving on to consider refinement of the remaining non-terminal knowledge source of Fig. 11 we see that **nt-differentiate** can expand either as simple refinement which gives us the traditional model of heuristic classification, or else as a more complex set of models which attempt to **predict** and **test** the expected values of hypothesis parameters.

The clusters derived from the repertory grid tool in Fig. 15 give an impression how the differential of diagnoses might look like. The fact that these clusters are very different from the solution hierarchies of Fig. 12 may well indicate that the process of differentiation is more complex than simple refinement. Moreover in the the protocols we see clear evidence that hypotheses are tested by predicting an observable manifestation (a norm) that is expected when the hypothesis is true. Therefore we decide to use the first rewrite rule in Fig. 11 which results in the GDM in Fig. 17.

The figure shows four possible ways to rewrite **nt-predict**. The conditions for each of the rewrite rules to be applicable are

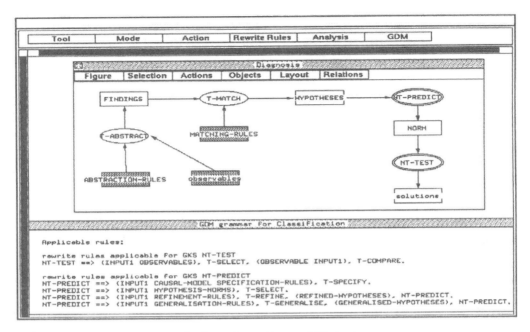

Fig. 17. **NT-differentiate** refined as **NT-predict** and **NT-test**

1. there is a `causal model` in the domain that can be used to derive observable effects of deficiencies in the system that is reasoned about.
2. Every hypothesis in `?input1` has an associated `hypothesis norm` that must be true if the hypothesis is true.
3. Not every hypothesis in `?input1` has an associated norm, but can be `refined` to another hypothesis with an associated norm that must be true if the refined hypothesis is true.
4. Not every hypothesis in `?input1` has an associated norm, but can be `generalised` to another hypothesis with an associated norm that must be true if the generalised hypothesis is true.

Analyse CKB The think aloud protocols we have for this domain indicate that no causal model is used to predict the norms for hypotheses. This rules out the first rule in Fig. 17. Since many rules have unique identifiers the knowledge engineer could reasonably suspect that the second rule is the correct rule. For this reason one might attempt to elicit the associated norms for the possible hypotheses. Given our KA material the knowledge engineer discovers that not every possible hypothesis has an obvious associated norm that can be used to decide if the hypothesis is true. This proves that rule 2 is not the correct rule either. However, every hypothesis can be refined to a more specific hypothesis that has an associated norm.

Refine GDM The fact that every hypothesis can be refined makes the third rule for `nt-predict` applicable. The result of applying this rule is shown in Fig. 18.

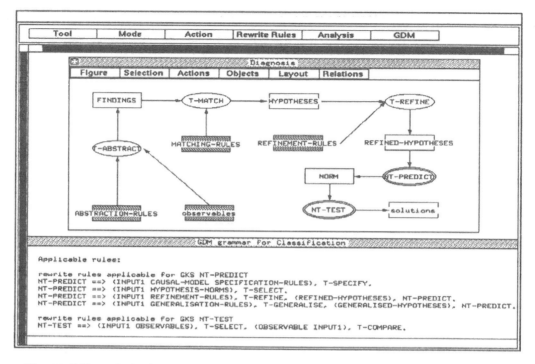

Fig. 18. Differentiation by `T-Refine`, **NT-Predict** and **NT-Test**

Analyse CKB The directive model still contains the non terminal `nt-predict`.
However, now the refined hypotheses are the input for `nt-predict` and we know
that all the refined hypotheses have associated norms.

Refine GDM Rule 2 can be applied directly after rule 3 resulting in Fig. 19[4]. There
is only one rule applicable for `nt-test`. Applying this rule results in the GDM
in Fig. 20.

From here on we have a fully grounded GDM, and the knowledge engineer will
proceed to instantiate the various metaclass and knowledge source partitions.

---

[4] It is worth mentioning that application of both rule 4 and rule 3 would have caused
our system to mimic the behaviour of NEOMYCIN [6]. NEOMYCIN evaluates hypotheses by first testing a generalised form of the hypothesis under consideration and then
subsequently refine this hypothesis.

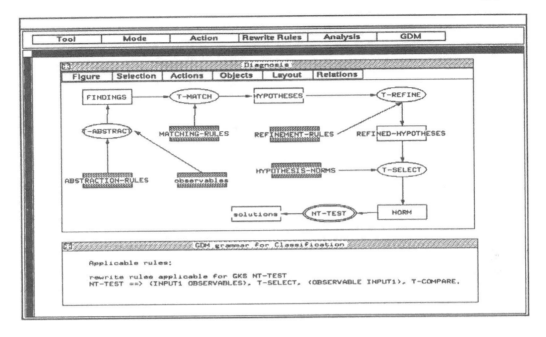

Fig. 19. Differentiate by **T-Refine, T-Select** and **NT-Test**

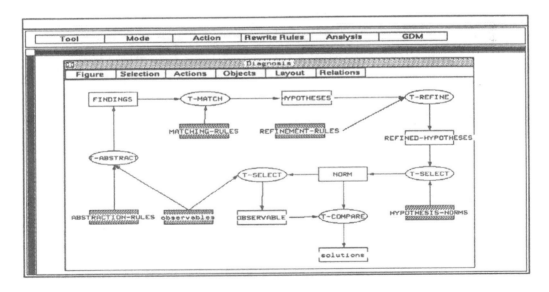

Fig. 20. The final directive model

5 Conclusions

In this paper we have described a method and a set of tools that differ from earlier approaches in two ways. First, the development of the model and the acquisition of static domain knowledge are interwoven. Initially a highly abstract model of the reasoning task is used to acquire some basic domain knowledge. Subsequently the model is refined using properties of the already acquired domain knowledge. This approach allows a much more flexible and iterative knowledge acquisition process than the two-stage process used in other approaches. Second, knowledge about the use of knowledge acquisition methods and tools is coupled to specific transitions in the model search space. When a specific refinement of a model is required, the nature of the required domain knowledge is used to select a particular knowledge acquisition tool. Thus, the model is not just a guide to the acquisition of the domain knowledge, but also supports the choices that a knowledge engineer has with respect to methods and tools. The scenario that we have presented clearly shows how a system like KEW can actively support the knowledge acquisition process without making strong concessions to the flexibility and task specificity.

5.1 Relation To Other Approaches

The approach taken by Musen in OPAL and PROTEGE [15] starts from the view that a task-specific model of the domain knowledge that is to be acquired is necessary to support the acquisition of the static domain knowledge. In PROTEGE such models are derived from a template (skeletal plan refinement) through interaction with the knowledge engineer, while the acquisition of the static domain knowledge is done in interaction with the domain expert. McDermott and co-workers [14,12,7] also developed knowledge acquisition tools based on models for specific tasks. The MOLE system for example [7] uses a model of the Cover-and-Differentiate method for diagnostic reasoning to acquire domain knowledge from an expert. Compared with KEW these approaches are powerful in the sense that knowledge acquisition with the expert is strongly focussed, but suffer from the severe limitation that the approach and the supporting tools are entirely task specific and thus limited in scope. Moreover, the task specificity puts a strong emphasis on task identification at an early stage in the acquisition process.

The use of KADS interpretation models [27] is more flexible. Models can be selected for a wide variety of tasks. However, the models in KADS are less explicit with respect to the required domain knowledge than the models in OPAL. Moreover, KADS interpretation models generally require substantial modification for a specific application and this in turn requires information about the nature of the static domain knowledge. KADS does not offer any support for model modification.

In PROTEGE-II [17] the limitation of using a fixed template is removed. In this system the knowledge engineer can create his own template. However, the system does not actively support model construction or model editing. The functionality of PROTEGE-II resembles that of the Inference Structure Editor in the SHELLEY workbench [2].

The GDM approach combines the advantages of the approaches mentioned above. Because of the dynamic model construction process the GDM approach offers the strong guidance of task specific models while it still covers a wide range of tasks. Moreover, the delayed commitment strategy allows incremental task identification.

More recent developments based on KADS and the "Components of Expertise" approach [22,26] introduce the notion of *problem solving methods* [3] as a way of generating task-specific models. A problem solving method describes how a particular goal can be decomposed in primitive and/or non-primitive subgoals. Application of one or more methods to a goal results in a full model of the task. In addition to the knowledge about goals and how to decompose them, requirements for the domain knowledge are associated with each method. While these requirements are in general used for determining the applicability of methods, they could also be used for knowledge acquisition. Methods can thus be viewed as similar to the rewrite rules in a GDM grammar.

The idea of using a grammar to represent abstract models of problem solving fits quite well with the recent work of Chandrasekaran [5]. The task analysis for design that he presents can easily be reformulated as a GDM grammar. The work on advice and guidance in KEW is also quite similar to the approach recently presented by [13]. Their workbench consists of three tools: SPARK, which is intended for model selection, BURN which selects the appropriate KA tools, and FireFighter, which functions as an application debugger. The SPARK/BURN approach is similar to ours in the sense that an abstract task model is used to select appropriate knowledge acquisition tools. However, this work is also based on the two stage assumption mentioned before. Moreover, tool selection is a very simple process in BURN: there is a more or less one to one mapping between the inference steps in the model (mechanisms, as they call it) and knowledge acquisition tools. KEW takes also into account information about the knowledge acquisition context. The advice and guidance model in KEW does not have a debugging tool comparable with FireFighter.

Acknowledgements The research reported here was performed in cooperation with Han Reichgelt and Fano Ramparany.

It was carried out in the course of the ACKnowledge project partially funded by the ESPRIT Programme of the Commission of the European Communities as project number 2567. The Partners in this project are GEC-Marconi, University of Nottingham (both UK), Cap Gemini Innovation (F), Sintef, Computas Expert Systems (both N), Telefonica (ES), and the University of Amsterdam (NL).

References

1. S. Adey et al. KEW user manual (A4 deliverable). deliverable ACK-GEC-DL-A4-001-A, ACKnowledge Consortium, 1992.
2. A. Anjewierden, J. Wielemaker, and C. Toussaint. Shelley - computer aided knowledge engineering. In B. Wielinga, J. Boose, B. Gaines, G. Schreiber, and M. van Someren, editors, *Current Trends in Knowledge Acquisition*, pages 173–189. IOS Press, Amsterdam, 1990.
3. V.R. Benjamins, A. Abu-Hanna, and Wouter Jansweijer. Dynamic method selection in diagnostic reasoning. In *the 12th Int. conf. on Artificial Intelligence, Expert Systems, Natural Language, Avignon'92*, Avignon, 1992. EC2. SKBS/A2/92-1.

454

4. B. Chandrasekaran. Towards a functional architecture for intelligence based on generic information processing tasks. In *Proceedings of the 10th IJCAI*, pages 1183–1192, Milano, 1987.

5. B. Chandrasekaran. Design problem solving: a task analysis. *AI Magazine*, Winter:59–71, 1990.

6. W.J. Clancey and R. Letsinger. NEOMYCIN: Reconfiguring a rulebased expert system for application to teaching. In W.J. Clancey and E.H. Shortliffe, editors, *Readings in Medical Artificial Intelligence: the first decade*, pages 361–381. Addison-Wesley, Reading, 1984.

7. L. Eshelman. MOLE: A knowledge-acquisition tool for cover-and-differentiate systems. In S. Marcus, editor, *Automating Knowledge Acquisition for Expert Systems*, pages 37–80. Kluwer Academic Publishers, The Netherlands, 1988.

8. I. Norbo G. Aakvik, A. Aamodt. A knowledge representation framework supporting knowledge modelling. In *Proceedings of the fifth EKAW*, University of Strathclyde, 1991. Not Published.

9. C. Jullien et al. ACKnowledge final report. Technical Report ACK-CSI-WM-DL-007-A-pre4, Cap Gemini Innovation, 1992. Final report of ESPRIT Project 2567.

10. W. Karbach, M. Linster, and A. Voß. Model-based approaches: One label - one idea? In B. Wielinga, J. Boose, B. Gaines, G. Schreiber, and M. van Someren, editors, *Current Trends in Knowledge Acquisition*, pages 173–189. IOS Press, Amsterdam, 1990.

11. N. Major and H. Reichgelt. ALTO: An automated laddering tool. In *Current Trends in Knowledge Acquisition*, pages 222–235. IOS, 1990.

12. S. Marcus and J. McDermott. SALT: A knowledge acquisition language for propose-and-revise systems. *Artificial Intelligence*, 39(1):1–38, 1989.

13. D. Marques, G. Dallemagne, G. Klinker, J. McDermott, and D. Tung. Easy programming: Empowering people to build their own applications. Technical report, Digital Equipment Corporation, 1991. submitted to the IEEE Expert.

14. J. McDermott. Preliminary steps towards a taxonomy of problem-solving methods. In S. Marcus, editor, *Automating Knowledge Acquisition for Expert Systems*, pages 225–255. Kluwer Academic Publishers, The Netherlands, 1989.

15. M.A. Musen. *Automated Generation of Model-Based Knowledge-Acquisition Tools*. Pitman, London, 1989. Research Notes in Artificial Intelligence.

16. M.A. Musen, L.M. Fagan, D.M. Combs, and E.H. Shortliffe. Use of a domain model to drive an interactive knowledge editing tool. In J. Boose and B. Gaines, editors, *Knowledge-Based Systems, Volume 2: Knowledge Acquisition Tools for Expert Systems*, pages 257–273, London, 1988. Academic Press.

17. A. Puerta, J. Egar, S. Tu, and M. Musen. A multiple-method knowledge acquisition shell for the automatic generation of knowledge acquisition tools. Technical Report KSL-91-24, Stanford University, Knowledge Systems Laboratory, Medical Computer Science, Stanford University, Stanford, California, 94305-5479, May 1991.

18. H. Reichgelt. *Logic-Based Knowledge Representation*, chapter Assertion Time Inference. The MIT Press, Cambridge, MA, 1989.

19. H. Reichgelt and N. Shadbolt. Knowledgeable knowledge acquisition. In *Proceedings of the Conference of the Society for the Study of Artificial Intelligence and Simulation of Behaviour AISB-91*, Leeds, 1990.

20. H. Reichgelt and N. Shadbolt. ProtoKEW: a knowledge based system for knowledge acquisition. In Sleeman and Burndsen, editors, *Research Directions In Cognitive Science Volume 5*, Leeds, 1990. Lawrence Erlbaum.

21. N. Shadbolt and B.J. Wielinga. Knowledge based knowledge acquisition: the next generation of support tools. In B. J. Wielinga, J. Boose, B. Gaines, G. Schreiber, and

M.W. van Someren, editors, *Current Trends in Knowledge Acquisition*, pages 313–338, Amsterdam, 1990. IOS Press.

22. L. Steels. Components of expertise. *AI Magazine*, Summer 1990. Also as: AI Memo 88-16, AI Lab, Free University of Brussels.

23. P. Terpstra, G.J. van Heijst, I. Nordbo, F. Ramparany, H. Reichgelt, N. Shadbolt, and B. Wielinga. KA process support in KEW. Deliverable ACK-UVA-A2-DEL-002-B, SWI University of Amsterdam, 1992.

24. F. van Harmelen and J. Balder. $(ML)^2$: A formal language for KADS models of expertise. Technical Report ESPRIT Project P5248 KADS-II/T1.2/PP/UvA/017/1.0, University of Amsterdam & Netherlands Energy Research Foundation ECN, 1991. This paper is published in *Knowledge Acquisition Journal*, 1992.

25. J. Vanwelkenhuysen and P. Rademakers. Mapping knowledge-level analysis onto a computational framework. In L. Aiello, editor, *Proceedings ECAI–90, Stockholm*, pages 681–686, London, 1990. Pitman.

26. B. J. Wielinga, A. Th. Schreiber, and J. A. Breuker. KADS: A modelling approach to knowledge engineering. *Knowledge Acquisition*, 4(1), 1992. Special issue 'The KADS approach to knowledge engineering'.

27. B.J. Wielinga, N. Shadbolt, and T1.4 partners. Conceptualization of a knowledge engineering workbench. deliverable ACK-UvA-T1.4-010-A, University of Amsterdam, 1990.

Using the System-Model-Operator Metaphor for Knowledge Acquisition

William J. Clancey[1] and Monique Barbanson [2]

[1] Institute for Research on Learning, 2550 Hanover Street, Palo Alto, CA 94304 USA
[2] Metaphor Computer Systems

Abstract. The systems-model-operator perspective provides a unifying perspective for the ways that expert systems represent, organize, and apply knowledge representations. We use this metaphor to develop Topo, an expert system for configuration of computer networks. Generalizing Topo, we show that its modeling language and operators can be adapted to other tasks that require relating a physical/organizational structure to a service-supply network. This experiment demonstrates how expert systems can be generalized and more easily related to each other if we express control knowledge in terms of operators for constructing system models.

1 Task-Specific Architectures

The techniques for building expert systems have advanced from tools that provide an "empty knowledge base," with a backward-chaining inference engine, such as EMYCIN [10], to tools that allow for an explicit representation of the domain-general control knowledge necessary for a specific task, such as diagnosis or design [1, 2, 4, 5, 8]. Task-specific tools incorporate a way of organizing knowledge and an inference procedure for applying this knowledge. As researchers analyze these tools to generalize and integrate different methodologies, we need to understand the relation between specific problems and general ways in which knowledge representations can be organized and applied. In essence, how should we formalize the reusable part of the knowledge base so its capabilities and limits can be related to new problems?

Task-specific architectures need to address the following distinct issues [3]:

❑ What *system* in the world is being modeled?

❑ For what purpose, or *task*, is the system being modeled?

❑ What subsystems and *subprocesses* are represented in the general model (that is, in the knowledge base)?

❑ What subsystems and subprocesses are represented in a *situation-specific model* (that is, in a problem solution)?

❑ What *relational networks* (what kinds of hierarchies and transitional graphs) are used to represent processes?

❑ What are the *operators*, or inference procedures, for constructing situation-specific models?

❑ How are the relational networks and inference procedures implemented in a *programming language* (for example, in frame and rule-based languages)?

1.1 The system-model-operator metaphor

To introduce the idea of this metaphor, we begin with the idea of describing knowledge bases in terms of tasks, systems in the world, and situation-specific models, presented several years ago as heuristic classification [2]. We extend that idea to describe inference as a process of constructing and comparing situation-specific models of processes for some purpose. Situation-specific models are usually chained: One system's model (for instance, a diagnostic model of physiological processes) feeds into decisions for constructing another system or process (for example, therapy). We can view each situation-specific model as a graph, and inference subprocedures as operators for manipulating the nodes and relations within this graph and across graphs representing other situation-specific models. Clancey explores this idea in detail and relates it to other control paradigms such as blackboards [3].

We can illustrate this idea in the medical-diagnosis context of Heracles-DX, the diagnostic shell developed from Neomycin. Heracles uses *subtasks* and *metarules* to represent the inference procedure. Subtasks are procedures that order and control the application of conditional statements, called metarules. Metarules are stated in a language of relations for representing the modeled system's structures and processes (for example, causal and subtype relations). The general model of the domain is expressed as a set of propositions over these relations. Metarules themselves use variables rather than domain terms (so we say they are domain general). A given set of propositions about a particular situation in the world constitutes a situation-specific model. The relations and operators are the reusable knowledge contained in Heracles-DX, constituting a language for representing general and situation-specific models, plus an inference procedure. According to the system-model-operator view, subtasks are *operators* for manipulating situation-specific *graphs* that represent *structures and processes* in the system being modeled.

This perspective provides a unifying basis for analyzing expert systems by reducing the dimensions of domain, problem type, and problem-solving method to a graph representation. As a general architecture, Heracles lets us define subtasks, metarules, or relations, but does not contain any specific operators or relations. But can we use the Heracles architecture to efficiently write new subtasks and metarules for a different, non-diagnostic task? We designed an experiment to find out: We developed Topo, an expert system for configuration using the Heracles shell.

2 Blackboards and Operators for Computer Network Layout

Topo explores the problem of writing new subtasks and metarules for the logical topology design of computer networks. The problem is relevant to efforts to develop a front end for the programs developed by Digital Equipment Corporation's programs for computer system configuration. For example, an expert system like Topo might provide a sales person with a language for modeling a potential client's business and information-processing requirements. Topo is designed to propose a layout of generic components and connections, suitable for input to sizing and configuration programs such as Xcon [9]. The program we describe in this paper is a prototype that runs on one example case. Our interest here is not in solving the logical topology problem, but in determining how the system-model-operator perspective and the availability of the subtask/metarule language help or hinder knowledge acquisition.

458

2.1 Designing Topo in Terms of Process Models

Topo first constructs a model of the client's business and then produces a corresponding network design (see Figure 1). The program reasons as follows:

1. Construct a model of the physical and organizational structure of the client's business. Describe business sites and floor locations of workgroups at each site.

2. Determine the information-processing requirements, leading to a preliminary sizing (for instance, the number of printers required).

3. Design the network topology:
   a. Derive the backbone from the physical layout.
   b. Represent the components and connections.

Following the lessons learned from heuristic classification, we first conjectured that Topo would contain three kinds of situation-specific models corresponding to these three steps. However, we found that a separate case-based reasoning system could estimate the type and number of devices more conveniently. Therefore, we did not require a separate model for information-processing requirements. In the final design, Topo's information processing requirements were directly represented as properties of workgroups within the physical and organizational structure, rather than as two separate models chained together.

In effect, elements of the physical and organizational structure (such as sites and buildings) are related, as are elements of the network topology (for instance, segments and backbones).

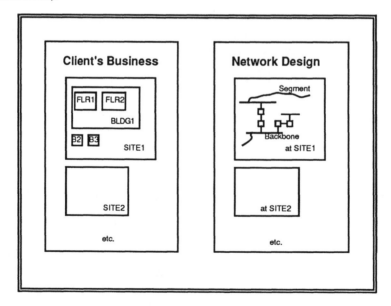

Figure 1. Two blackboards in Topo: a client's business (left); network design (right).

Conceptually, the inference procedure of Topo defines subtasks that construct a situation-specific model for each connected system. Each subtask defines metarules, each of which characterizes a set of domain rules that can be applied to construct a piece of the situation-specific model, such as Business-at-site-1 or Network-at-site-2, shown in Figure 1. The two blackboards (business and network) contain a panel for each site (corresponding to a situation-specific model), and the levels in each panel correspond to hierarchical connnections (for instance, segments on a backbone).

2.2 Defining Operators for Constructing Configuration Models

Generalizing from the representations used in Topo, we can define configuration-specific inference operators as follows:

1. Draw separate pictures for each real-world system being modeled.

2. Specify class structure of nodes in each situation-specific model, and draw separate situation-specific models for unconnected systems (for example, different sites).

3. Draw links showing the information mapping between models of different types (for example, from workgroup to equipment layout).

4. Describe operators for placing nodes in each model, linking them, and specifying their spatial and process attributes.

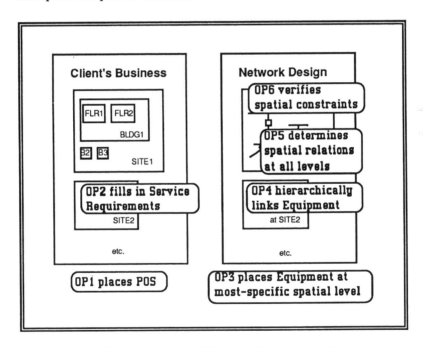

Figure 2. The six operators of Topo's inference procedure.

In practice, we abstract descriptions of Topo's operators (see Figure 2) from the subtasks/metarules that carry out the necessary computations. A given operator typically corresponds to a single Heracles subtask (and hence several metarules). Higher-level subtasks control when the operators are performed (just as Process-Hypothesis in Neomycin determines that the operator Test-Hypothesis is executed before Refine-Hypothesis). As shown in Figure 2, the six operators of Topo's inference procedure place different nodes and links in the situation-specific models.

Another program computes the sizing table used by Op3 (quantifying the amount of equipment).

Based on the perspective of Clancey's analysis of blackboard systems [3], in which he shows the correspondence between the blackboard paradigm and the system-model-operator view, we can describe Topo's operators in more detail in terms of the nodes and relations they manipulate on the blackboards (see Table 1). The relations of the situation-specific model are specializations of the general domain model. For example, the general domain model can indicate a USES/CONSUMES relation between types of organizational-structures and types of services. A client-business situation-specific model indicates that a particular organizational structure uses or consumes a particular service (for example, "Work-Group-3 USES/CONSUMES Information-storage"). Topo implements operators as Heracles subtasks; therefore the relations of Table 1 appear in metarule premises. The situation-specific model's nodes (terms of the relations) appear as variables in the metarules.

OPERATOR	(RELATION Node1 Node2)
1) "Determine Position"	(**LOCATED-IN/AT** POS \<place\>)
2) "Determine Service Requirements"	(**USES/CONSUMES** Organizational-Structure Service)
3) "Process Sizing Data"	(**USED-BY** Organizational-Structure Equipment) (**PROVIDES** Equipment Service) (**AMOUNT-SUPPLY** Service Sizing-data-table) (**SIZING.DATA.TABLE** Equipment \<number\>)
4) "Derive Logical Topology from POS and Equipment "	(**PROVIDE-SERVICE-FOR** Physical-Structure Logical-Service-Components)
5) "Transfer properties from POS to Service"	(**PROVIDE-SERVICE-FOR** Physical-Structure Logical-Service-Components) (**LINEAR-SPAN** Physical-Structure \<number\>)
6) "Verify Skeletal Design"	\<Various relations represented in constraint rules\>

Table 1. Domain relations used by Topo's operators.
(POS is the Physical/Organizational-Structure, and sizing is the capacity of a service or supply.)

2.3 Generalizing Topo's Models and Operators

Building Topo in Heracles was an incremental process in which we shifted attention back and forth between the details of writing metarules and the high-level definition of blackboards and operators. Just as we were able to build another program quickly using Neomycin's relations and operators [9], we conjecture that expert systems similar to Topo can be constructed more quickly than Topo itself.

Toward this end, we need to describe Topo's reasoning and representations at a more general level than computer network layout. Topo's blackboards and operators are suitable, for instance, for "social services network configuration." This characterizes a wide variety of potential expert systems that map from a model of social structure, such as a university or business description, to a network of services or suppliers, such as a telecommunication network (see Figure 3). We can reuse existing physical/organizational structure models in expert systems that design different kinds of systems or processes (for example, an insurance policy configuration). In each of these expert systems, we follow similar steps: determine the physical/organizational-structure; determine service and local-resource sizing requirements, and finally, place and connect servers and suppliers. The relations and operators shown in Table 1 provide a useful level of abstraction for building such expert systems. Put another way, we don't simply give the knowledge engineer the subtasks and metarules used in Topo; we provide the design of the blackboards in terms of the domain relations of Table 1 and a description of what the operators do.

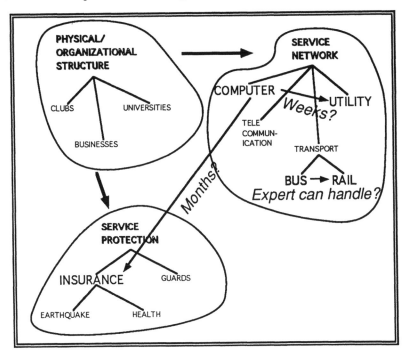

Figure 3. Generalizing of Topo's inference structure. The terms in italics designate the knowledge-engineering effort required to generalize and to specialize existing knowledge bases.

We are also building up a language for describing kinds of *systems*. Physical and organizational structures different from service networks, in that the latter involves a distribution of resources rather than a single, roving supplier. For example, Topo's blackboards and operators are probably inadequate for solving the traveling salesman problem. Other expert systems that provide "service protection" also start by constructing a models of physical/organizational structures. For example, an expert system to configure an earthquake insurance policy for a univeristy would develop a model of the university's physical and organizational structure, including a description of buildings and distribution of work groups. This model will contain new distinctions (relations) that are useful for configuring service protection but not for configuring a service network. This suggests that an ultimate library of system models and operators will be roughly hierarchical, with sharing and specialization of descriptions for different tasks.

Figure 3 shows how we use a classification of system types to describe the relationships among specific expert systems, and what knowledge engineering effort (in italics) is required to generalize and specialize existing knowledge bases. As always, we use the term "system" very generally; an earthquake insurance policy is a kind of system. We conjecture that it takes much more time to shift between systems of different abstract types (for example, shifting from service networks to service protection). It should be much easier to reuse blackboards and operators for systems that are of a similar type, such as converting operators developed for bus route configuration to rail configuration.

Figure 3 also illustrates the research task of developing future knowledge acquisition tools. While showing just a small part of the space of potential expert systems, the diagram illustrates the kinds of conversions and adaptations that we expect to find. The system-model-operator metaphor suggests that classifying our tools in terms of system models—for example, telecommunication—will facilitate sharing and reuse of representations and inference procedures.

3 Other Task-Specific Frameworks

Other researchers have advocated the analysis and decomposition of knowledge bases in terms of general, or generic, components. How do these analyses compare? McDermott's role-limiting methods [6], Chandrasekaran's generic tasks [1], and the inference operators described here are related as follows:

❑ A (role-limiting) problem-solving method is a procedure composed of several inference operators that, through controlled interaction, form a situation-specific model that satisfies task constraints. For example, Neomycin's subtasks together implement a variant of the Mole system's Cover-and-Differentiate method.

❑ A subtree in Neomycin's subtask hierarchy (such as Explore-and-Refine) is packaged and distributed separately in what Chandrasekaran calls a *generic task*. Such subtasks appear in several problem-solving methods,

Thus, from the perspective of the model-construction operator, researchers have pursued different levels of generality in formalizing control knowledge: Single operators for constructing a situation-specific model correspond to a Heracles-DX subtask; subprocedures of one or more operators correspond to generic tasks; and a complete inference procedure corresponds to a role-limiting method.

4 Conclusion

It is productive to view knowledge engineering as a modeling methodology in which systems are modeled qualitatively in terms of causal, temporal, and spatial relations. From this perspective, control knowledge consists of the procedures for constructing situation-specific models. Different representations, problem-solving architectures, knowledge acquisition tools, and specific expert systems can then be systematically related in terms of types of relational networks, process models, inference operators, domains, and tasks.

Each time we write a new procedure for interpreting a Heracles representation, we define new relations that classify its constructs. For example, we find that classifications and procedures are defined in terms of each other. When we state control knowledge abstractly, using variables in place of primitive terms, the resulting representation is not domain independent, but domain general; that is, by using spatial, temporal, causal, and subtype distinctions—a perspective by which all systems can be described—we can make the language and relations more general than any one system being modeled.

The system-model-operator paradigm can be used as the basis for analyzing the models and inference procedures in any expert system. It helps us develop new programs, like Topo, but its strength lies especially in helping us relate different research terminology. We can relate blackboards to metarules, Neomycin to Mole, heuristic classification to qualitative process simulation, and generic tasks to role-limiting methods. Put another way, we can now relate representational constructs, expert systems in a given domain, inference methods, knowledge acquisition programs, and reasoning strategies, all from a system-model-operator perspective.

Given any expert system, we can *ask*, "What are the systems being modeled? What are the structure and process characteristics of this system? What kind of relational network is used to represent these structures and processes? What is the inference procedure for constructing a situation-specific model? How is this model employed by later reasoning phases, evaluated, or conveyed to the user?" Rather than simply asking about a new problem domain, "Is there real-world knowledge that allows classification?" we might ask, "Must the system be modeled as open in its interactions with its environment? Is there a known etiological hierarchy? Are there stages or developmental descriptions involving trends and frequency of behaviors? What experience have people had with this system in rebuilding, modifying, assembling it in different situations?" Thus, knowledge engineering is a form of systems analysis that emphasizes the qualitative modeling of processes.

Acknowledgements

Topo was designed and implemented with the help of David Marques at Digital Equipment Corporation. Partial support for this research was provided by gifts from the DEC and Xerox Corp. Aside from minor corrections, this paper first appeared in *IEEE Expert*, 6(5)61-65, October 1991. Reprinted with permission.

References

1. Chandrasekaran, B.: "Expert systems: Matching techniques to tasks," in *AI Applications for Business*, W. Reitman, ed., Ablex Publishing, Norwood, NJ, (1984) 116-132.

2. Clancey, W. J.: Heuristic classification, *Artificial Intelligence* **27** (1985) 289-350.

3. Clancey, W. J.: Model Construction Operators, *Artificial Intelligence* **53** (1992) 1-115.

4. Hayes-Roth, B., Hewett, M., Vaughan Johnson, M., and Garvey, A.: "ACCORD: A Framework for a Class of Design Tasks," Tech. Report KSL-88-19, Stanford Univ., Palo Alto, CA (1988).

5. Marcus, S.: *Automating Knowledge Acquisition for Expert Systems*, Kluwer Academic Publishers, (1988).

6. McDermott, J.: "Preliminary steps toward a taxonomy of problem-solving methods," in *Automating Knowledge Acquisition for Expert Systems*, S. Marcus, ed., Kluwer Academic Publishers, Norwood, MA (1988) 225-256.

7. McDermott, J.: R1: A rule-based configurer of computer systems, *Artificial Intelligence* **19** (1982) 39-88.

8. Musen, M.: Automated support for building and extending expert models, *Machine Learning* **4** (1989) 347-377.

9. Thompson, T. and Clancey, W.J.: A qualitative modeling shell for process diagnosis, *IEEE Software* **3** (1986) 6-15.

10. van Melle, W.: *A Domain-Independent System that Aids in Constructing Knowledge-Based Consultation Pprograms*, doctoral dissertation, Stanford Univ., Computer Science Department, Palo Alto, CA,1980.

Explicit and operational models as a basis for second generation knowledge acquisition tools

Marc Linster

AI Research Division, GMD
D-5205 St. Augustin 1, FRG
email: marc.linster@gmd.de

Abstract. The paper describes the transition from a first generation knowledge acquisition approach towards a second generation, model-based one. Firstly, we depict the first generation knowledge acquisition tool KRITON with its components *interview, protocol,* and *text analysis* and we render the underlying assumptions of the tool. Then, we make a point for second generation, model-based knowledge acquisition tools and discuss their architecture. We focus on the role of explicit models of problem-solving methods in automated knowledge acquisition tools and on the guidance that models of methods can provide. We give a short description of the KADS-oriented knowledge-modeling language OMOS that we developed, among others, to analyze the facet of guidance. We combine aspects of the KRITON-based development with features of the modeling language OMOS, thus obtaining a second generation view on knowledge engineering, supported by a special architecture for computer supported model-based knowledge acquisition. Finally, we highlight future developments that exploit the guidance of the method models for automated knowledge acquisition.

1 Introduction

This paper describes a change in perspective in the knowledge acquisition project at GMD. It describes how we moved from a first generation *knowledge transfer* paradigm to a second generation *knowledge modeling* point of view. Section 2 describes the assumptions and techniques of the first generation knowledge acquisition tool KRITON; Section 3 discusses the reasons for the paradigm shift towards a second generation model-based approach to be described in Section 4. Section 5 outlines our current work and delineates future developments.

2 KRITON: A first generation knowledge acquisition tool

The knowledge acquisition tool KRITON [19; 20; 38] has been developed as an acquisition front end for the hybrid, general-purpose representation and inference environment BABYLON [14; 18]. Section 2.1 delineates some assumptions about knowledge and knowledge acquisition that were the basis for the design of KRITON. Section 2.2 describes the tool, the techniques, and their interaction. Section 2.3 is a critical reconsideration of KRITON and the assumptions that underlie its design.

2.1 Underlying assumptions of KRITON

KRITON was built upon three assumptions:

1. Knowledge can be acquired from an expert in the form of symbolic expressions and can be *transferred* in terms of rules, frames, or clauses from the human mind into a knowledge base. The *knowledge transfer assumption* was shared by several other tools, for example ETS (*Expertise Transfer System*) [4] or MACAO [2].
2. Knowledge engineering consists of acquisition followed by representation. It is an incremental process, which does not require the definition of explicit meta-structures (see Figure 1 for the architecture of KRITON, which results mainly from this assumption).
3. No single (automated) acquisition technique is powerful enough to acquire all the knowledge that a knowledge-based system needs.

2.2 The tool KRITON

KRITON consists of three knowledge acquisition components working on an internal intermediate representation (see Figure 1). Three separate generators use the contents of the intermediate representation to write BABYLON-specific rules, frames, and constraints.

The knowledge acquisition components KRITON's acquisition components implement three standard elicitation techniques that cooperate in the task of incremental knowledge acquisition:

- *Text analysis* and *interview* acquire knowledge about static domain features, such as concepts, structures, attributes, and their values.
- *Protocol analysis* acquires knowledge about procedural and associative aspects of the application task.

Text analysis Knowledge acquisition often starts out with the analysis of background literature. The knowledge engineer gains a basic understanding of the domain elements and this allows him to ask meaningful questions during the first interviews. This has motivated us to include a text analysis feature in KRITON. Texts are read from a file, nouns are highlighted and made mouse-sensitive. This relies on dictionaries and on specific properties of the German language. The knowledge engineer can include the nouns into a hierarchy (or heterarchy) describing the way the text presents the organization of the concepts of the domain, or the way the expert sees their organization.

The text analysis is a computer support to get started in a knowledge acquisition process. A simple example illustrates this (adapted from [38]). An excerpt of an introductory text on programming languages is analyzed and transformed

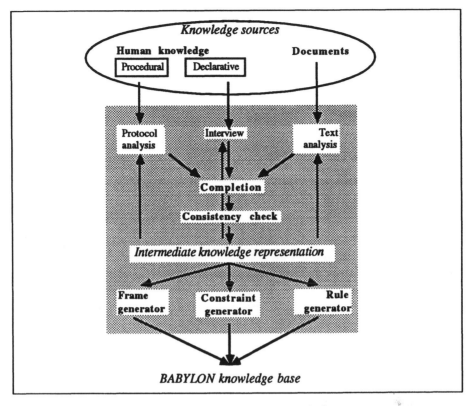

Fig. 1. The basic KRITON architecture (adapted from [20]). The acquisition components of KRITON (protocol analysis, text analysis, and interview) acquire knowledge from different sources. It is represented in a common intermediate representation format (a semantic net of concepts, labeled edges, attributes, and rules). Dedicated generators produce BABYLON-specific formalisms.

into one of many possible taxonomies (see Figure 2) representing aspects of the domain[1]:

> ...languages that can be selected are : **LISP, COBOL, ADA, PAS-CAL, ASSEMBLER, C, C++,** and **FORTRAN. FORTRAN, COBOL,** and **ASSEMBLER** are blockfree languages, **LISP** is highly functional, **ADA** and **PASCAL** are procedural ...

Interview The interview component edits and completes the initial information gathered by the text analysis. It uses the Repertory Grid technique [4; 25; 32; 48]

---

[1] Nouns will be printed in bold here. In the KRITON system they are highlighted to indicate their mouse sensitivity. Screen copies are not included as KRITON's text analysis and protocol analysis are limited to German texts.

468

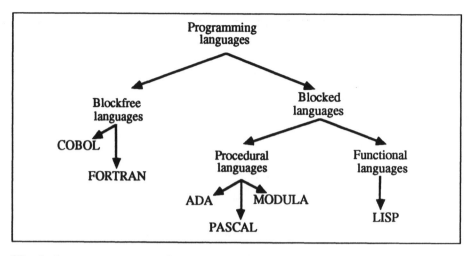

Fig. 2. A taxonomy generated with the text analysis component representing a particular's view on programming languages (adapted from [38]). ADA, MODULA, and PASCAL belong to one context as they have a common super concept.

to acquire attributes and values describing the concepts of the domain. Questions are asked about differentiating attributes between concepts:

What do MODULA and ADA have in common that differentiates them from PASCAL?

What differentiates PASCAL from ADA?

The answers to these questions are given by indicating an attribute that is applicable to the concepts mentioned in the questions and that has differentiating attribute values for the different concepts. If no sensible answer can be given the system changes into a laddering mode to explore potentially implicit hierarchical relations among the concepts.

The concepts used for the phrasing of the differentiating questions are chosen from a common context. This means that they have a common super concept in the taxonomy. The relation the concepts have with the super concept does not matter for this purpose; it does not even have to be specified. We assume that the expert groups the concepts in the given manner because they have a common context.

The user can select between two modes of interview. A text-oriented mode puts forward questions such as those discussed above. A graphical mode (see Figure 3) allows to answer the same questions by filling out a grid. The user adds concepts as rows and properties as columns. In the grid a bullet (•) indicates that the property applies to the concept, a cross (×) indicates that the negation of the property applies.

Note here that KRITON does not provide scales to indicate degrees of fit for attributes and values, as it is done for example in KSS0 [23] or ETS.

Several other techniques are used in the interview component to elaborate the description of the concepts.

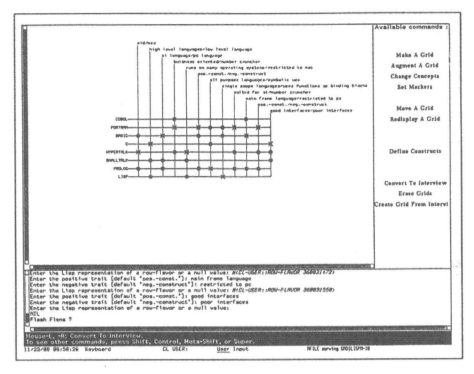

Fig. 3. A screen dump of the KRITON repertory grid interview component. After initial questions about concepts and properties have been answered, the grids can be managed graphically.

Explicit inheritance: If the attribute DATASTRUCTURE is defined for BLOCKFREE_LGS the system will inquire about the corresponding attribute value for COBOL and FORTRAN, to account for the possibility that the latter two could be refinements of the first one (see Figure 2).

Explicit generalization: In a taxonomy such as the one rendered in Figure 2 the system will inquire about the value for the attribute DATASTRUCTURE for the concept PROGRAMMING_LANGUAGES. If this attribute is not known or if the attribute is not applicable then the user does not have to indicate it.

Completion operation: Let's assume it is known in the taxonomy that PRO-CEDURAL_LGS has *pointers*, *strings*, and *chars* as DATASTRUCTURES and that none of ADA, PASCAL, or MODULA has *strings* as a value of that attribute. The system will inquire about a concept comparable to ADA, PASCAL, and MODULA that has *strings* as DATASTRUCTURES.

In KRITON these operations must be explicit as the user wants to edit and change the semantic net during the interview. If inheritance, generalization, or completion happened implicitly, nothing could be said about the values assumed if the edge that triggered the operation was erased or changed, for example, from

IS-A to SUBSET-OF. Making these operations explicit does not guarantee their truth or consistency either, but it makes sure that the expert agrees with their results.

An *elicitation councelor* indicates the appropriate actions in the interview component. It compares the attribution of concepts closely related in the graph and proposes differentiating questions and completion techniques.

Protocol analysis Protocol analysis is a technique that helps acquire procedural and associative knowledge. It is based on the work of Ericsson and Simon [21] and concentrates on the analysis of transcripts of thinking-aloud recordings. The result of a protocol analysis can be considered as a path through successive knowledge states of a problem solving process. If a knowledge-based system uses this sequence of state transitions in a consultation, the human problem-solving process is remodelled superficially.

To analyze the protocols, they are transcribed with the pauses of speech. Based on the assumption that pauses of speech represent delimiters that separate the transcript into coherent segments, these segments are transformed into operator-argument structures that are then combined into rules to explicate the inference steps that are implicitly contained in the protocol. Protocol analysis is a partially automated and partially computer-supported feature of KRITON. Operator-argument structures are generated automatically using linguistic techniques such as lemmatization to identify verbs, combined with dictionnaries and look-up tables, and specific properties of German, such as the capitalization of nouns. The structures can be post-edited by the user, which is necessary if pronouns could not be resolved or if the subject or the object of a verb had not been identified properly. He must then combine them into rules to explicate associative and procedural information contained in the protocol. A simple example illustrates the features of protocol analysis. An excerpt of a thinking-aloud protocol is analyzed :

> . . .⋆⋆ large company ⋆⋆ they do some research ⋆⋆ got a good software department ⋆⋆ what they want are COBOL code generators ⋆⋆ they have used LISP before ⋆⋆ let them use LISP ⋆⋆ . . .

It is transformed by the system into operator-argument structures, that have been post-edited by the expert :

> (large D1^2 company), (do D2 research), (software-department D3 good) (need D4 Cobol-code-generators), (used-before D5 Lisp), (recommend D6 Lisp)

These are then combined into rules to make the inferences described in the protocol explicit :

---

[2] The markers point to the phrase in the protocol used to generate the operator-argument structure. They serve documentation purposes.

```
If    (size-company D1 large)
      (do-research D2 t)
      (quality-software-dept D3 good)
      (used-before D5 Lisp)
      (task D4 Cobol-code-generators)
then (recommend D6 Lisp)
```

The interaction of the components The knowledge acquisition components work on an intermediate knowledge representation: a semantic net consisting of concepts, labeled edges, and attributes, combined with rules. Text analysis and interview operate on the semantic net. The user is free to define relationships between concepts as edges or as attributes. The protocol analysis produces rules describing how the concepts in the semantic net are used in a problem-solving process.

In a prototypical acquisition session the user starts with analyzing a background text and building a taxonomy representing the most important and frequently used concepts of a domain. These will then be attributed and described in the interview component. The taxonomy can be edited to fit new facets of the domain unraveled during the interview. Then one can go back to the text analysis to complete the taxonomy by analyzing a second chapter of the background text, or directly go into the protocol analysis. Prior to protocol analysis one must analyze texts or perform an interview. This allows to refer to a well-defined vocabulary and to well-defined concepts of the domain which can then be used as a basis for the analysis of the operator-argument structures.

New concepts appearing in rules are introduced into the taxonomy using the interview component. The result of an acquisition process with KRITON is a dense network of relations between concepts describing structural relations (stemming from interview and text analysis) or associative relations (stemming from protocol analysis).

2.3   A critical analysis of KRITON

Experiences with KRITON (e.g., in the diagnosis of gear boxes [19]) showed that it provides good analysis facilities to define an initial vocabulary and to get started when building a knowledge-based system. However, to move beyond the early stages in knowledge acquisition, a tool needs guidance—it must be goal driven. In KRITON it is not clear in which direction the semantic net should be extended or which new protocols should be analyzed to elaborate the procedural knowledge, as there is no meta-knowledge about the goal to be achieved with the knowledge base.

In subsequent developments we focussed on making KRITON goal driven, giving it meta-knowledge to allow for knowledge-based knowledge acquisition. We introduced pre-defined domain templates that had to be filled in and meta-rules about anticipated structures of the domain knowledge, for example: *classes and instances must be discernible on the basis of their attributes and values.*

472

These rules were then used to guide actively the interview component. However, a reconsideration showed that these rules were not universally valid; they express the knowledge needs of certain problem solving methods. For example, the rule given above expresses requirements of a hierarchical classification problem-solving method. Thus we concluded that guidance for the knowledge-acquisition process emanates from the problem-solving method. To analyze this correlation in greater depth, we developed specialized tools that combine one problem-solving method with knowledge acquisition tools from KRITON. For example we analyzed the combination of the problem-solving method *heuristic association* [27] with the repertory-grid based interview tool of KRITON (see Figure 4). This combination was implemented as IRA-Grid (Interpretation, Representation and Acquisition on the basis of Grids) [37].

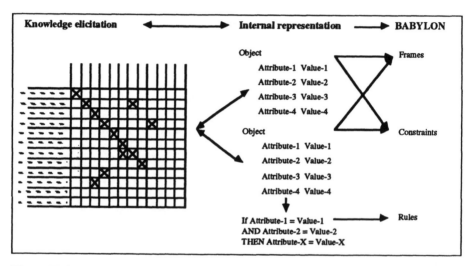

Fig. 4. IRA-grid uses the repertory grid mechanisms of KRITON to acquire knowledge about objects, attributes, and values. The internal representation consists of objects and implication rules deduced from the object descriptions. The internal representation is compiled into operational BABYLON representation formalisms to test the knowledge base (adapted from [37]).

The heuristic association problem-solving method relates descriptive elements of situations with each other, thus inferring a more complete description of a situation from a partial description. Situations are represented as concepts, described by attributes with values. Heuristic association uses rules between attribute-values to associate partial descriptions. It is used, among others by Hyper-KSE [23]. This method has well-defined knowledge needs: it requires concepts, attributes for each concept, and values for the attributes such that the concepts can be distinguished easily on the basis of the attribute values. Furthermore, it needs *meaningful* attributes, that is, attribute values must vary between concepts. This definition of knowledge needs is used to guide the

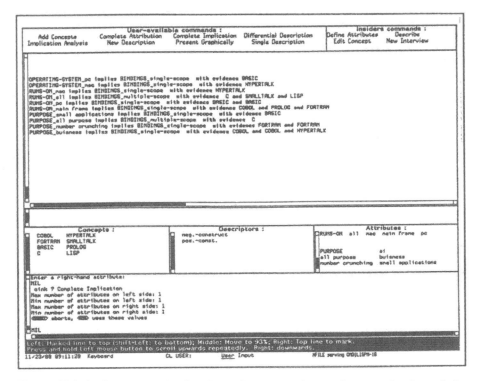

Fig. 5. IRA-Grid generates implication rules among the attributes and values of the concepts of a grid.

grid-based interview tool of KRITON. With its grid-based interview component IRA-Grid acquires descriptions of prototypical situations (represented as concepts with attributes and values). From these situation descriptions the tool deduces ENTAIL-like [25] rules between attributes and values (see Figure 5). These rules and objects are then compiled into BABYLON representations used in a shell-like consultation mechanism that implements a simple type of heuristic classification. The knowledge needs serve as meta-knowledge, specifying a goal that the automated knowledge acquisition tool must obtain.

IRA-Grid shows that strong guidance emanates from the problem-solving method. Analyses of other tools confirm that indeed the guidance for the knowledge acquisition process (e.g., which question to ask next) does come from the exploitation of the properties of the methods of problem solving (see for example [29; 39; 43] for such analyses).

Concurrently with the development of the automated tools KRITON and IRA-Grid, we had first hands-on experiences with acquisition approaches that use explicit higher-level meta-structures, such as KADS inference structures [28]. The exposure to KADS [54], combined with the reflections on KRITON and IRA-Grid set the stage for the work described in the next sections: the exploitation of the properties of explicit models in the context of automated knowledge acquisition, which in the terms of this book will be referred to as *second generation knowledge acquisition*.

3   A case for modeling and a change of perspective

Whereas the previous section has shown that meta-structures are needed to guide automated knowledge acquisition tools like KRITON, this section discusses which kinds of meta-structures are required (Section 3.1) and how they can be described (Section 3.2). Section 3.3 gives a brief introduction to the design of the experimental modeling language OMOS and describes it with a simple application.

3.1   The need for models in automated knowledge acquisition

Models of problem solving. Consider the following example (adapted from [38]): A mushroom classification system knows about a set of unequivocally described mushrooms, with properties such as *taste, color, grows-in-season, root-shape*, etc.

Toadstool

. . .

    Taste: (bitter, sickening)

Champignon

. . .

    Taste: sweet

Let us assume that the problem solver uses a classification procedure to categorize a sample mushroom and that at some point in the problem-solving process *toadstool* and *champignon* are two alternatives. A straightforward classification system could then ask for the property *taste* to discriminate among its alternative choices. However, the property *taste* should only be inquired about if poisonous or sickening mushrooms have been reliably eliminated from the set of considered alternatives. On the one side, such knowledge can be represented as deep domain knowledge, but on the other side, the method must reflect this distinction between different kinds of properties of mushrooms together with possible interdependencies. This simple example showed us that we need an explicit modeling of the problem-solving method and of the roles that knowledge elements play in the method. Concurrently, Chandrasekaran argued that *the representation level of conventional formalisms, e.g., rules or frames, obscures the essential nature of the information processing tasks that current knowledge based systems perform* [12, p. 23].

The end of the transfer view. At the same time new perspectives were delineated by Clancey, Breuker, and Wielinga. Clancey states that *knowledge is something that an observer ascribes to a human agent in order to describe and explain recurring interactions that the agent has with its environment* [15, p. 288]. Breuker and Wielinga criticize the mining view of knowledge acquisition by stating that *even if we were able to obtain the detailed data of the knowledge that drives human expert behavior, we would not know how to handle it* [10, p. 267]. Morik emphasizes the importance of viewing knowledge acquisition as a process of interactive model *creation* [45, p. 112].

Re-evaluation of the assumptions about knowledge acquisition. On the basis of these arguments we reconsidered KRITON's underlying assumptions. According to Morik and Clancey, the knowledge transfer hypothesis is not acceptable, as on the one side a model is *created* when acquiring knowledge, and on the other side not all knowledge exists per se but often is dependent on purpose and context. According to Breuker, Wielinga, McDermott, and our own experience with IRA-Grid, the model of the problem-solving method defines the knowledge requirements of the knowledge-based system.

Thus the decision to frame the acquisition of knowledge with methods of problem-solving is motivated by three arguments:

1. Knowledge is not composed of discrete symbol-level elements that each on their own, independently of purpose, context, or interpreter are *knowledge*.
2. It is pointless to try to acquire knowledge that one cannot represent in a machine.
3. Knowledge elicitation, without the documentation of a purpose, gets stuck all too soon.

This implies a temporary shift of attention: away from cognitive-science motivated acquisition techniques such as interviewing or protocol analysis, towards explicit modeling of problem-solving methods[3]. The next section discusses several properties that we deem essential for knowledge modeling languages.

3.2 A case for multi-faceted models of problem solving

As discussed above, modeling of problem-solving methods is required in automated knowledge acquisition for two reasons: (1) knowledge acquisition is a creative process of model construction, thus we need models; and (2) automated tools for knowledge acqusition are best driven by properties derived from models of problem-solving methods, thus the models must be of methods. From this we can derive a set of requirements that should be met by modeling languages and model-based approaches:

1. **Epistemologic modeling constructs.** The modeling language must provide a vocabulary that supports the knowledge engineer in the bottom-up process of conferring meaning to new situations by allowing him to construe such situations in the terms of the modeling vocabulary. To be truly general-purpose and thus application-independent, and applicable to a wide range of different application domains, the components of the modeling language must be of epistemological nature (epistemological in the sense of Brachman [6]).

---

[3] For the purpose of this article we define models as *purposeful abstractions that allow us to reduce complexity by focussing on certain aspects* [29].

2. **Reusable templates.** We need template-like structures that the knowledge engineer can use when interpreting different situations that share structural aspects. For example, systematic diagnosis is a problem-solving method that has been identified in many domains.

   The reusable templates must be selectable and configurable. Obviously they must be coined in terms that abstract from application specifics. Arguments for the developments of such templates can be found in [13]—where they are called *generic tasks*—and in [54]—where they are called *interpretation models*.

3. **Multi-faceted modeling.** To promote insight, response, discussion, and to provide a focus of attention, model building should distinguish between naturally occurring facets of a real-world task, such as, modality, task sharing, procedural aspects, static structures. Besides merely distinguishing between these facets, a modeling approach must promote the exploitation of the interaction between these facets. Linster and Musen [42] show that the interaction between different points of view facilitates the creation of a new model by providing insights into complex behavior. This multiple-facet modeling is used by other approaches too, such as COMMET [51].

4. **Formal properties.** Automated knowledge acquisition tools need guidance, which is derived from the model descriptions. This implies that the models must have formal properties from which we can derive additional information, such as the knowledge needs of the method.

5. **Operational models.** Models of knowledge-based systems are too complex to anticipate their behavior on the basis of non-operational—pictorial or textual—descriptions. Non-operational systems exclude the effects of insight—resulting from the feedback that a running system provides—from the ongoing model elaboration. Thus, the model constructs and the resulting models must be executable.

6. **Model equals system.** The model that results from the knowledge acquisition process and the final system must be identical to *integrate knowledge acquisition with system operation to facilitate a heavy activity of continuing system maintenance and upgrade as knowledge changes* [22]. This appears to us to be an essential capability that knowledge-based systems must have.

The last point deserves elaboration. It is based on two assumptions. First, we assume that the construction of a knowledge-based system never ends; such a system must always be modifiable to suit the ever changing requirements coming from the outside world. Moreover, a system should be able to learn from its own performance and should even be able to reflect upon its own (in)competence [30]. For that purpose the model must reflect all knowledge-based aspects of the system; any non-modelled aspects cannot be maintained within the paradigm of continuing knowledge acquisition.

Second, we assume that a conceptual model (for example a KADS model) can be *refined* into a running system by continuously adding detailed information, thus resolving ambiguities of the conceptual model to make it unambiguous and give it those semantics that characterize a computer executable program. Thus we assume that conceptual models—which get their semantics from a human observer—will always have the same structure as operational models; except that operational models are more concise.

The continuous refinement view is not shared by all other modeling aproaches, such as, MODEL-K [30; 31] which implements building blocks of the conceptual model with manually developed code bodies to combine KADS-oriented modeling with prototyping.

Obviously there are tradeoffs to this approach. Manual implementations of conceptual models—as it is done in the KADS approach—result in more efficient code and allow a more efficient encoding of issues of control. However, every change in the knowledge of such a system may require a manual reimplementation of parts of the system. Moreover, a conceptual model can contain other kinds of knowledge, characterized by being represented on other media and not being accessible to symbolic inferencing (e.g., pictures, graphics, sounds, etc.). However in [23; 24] we have shown that one can integrate multi-media based knowledge with symbolic knowledge used for inferencing.

3.3   Design of a multi-faceted modeling language

A comparison of several approaches to modeling for knowledge-based systems on the basis of methods of problem solving—Generic Tasks [12], PROTÉGÉ [46], Role-Limiting Methods [43], and KADS [54]—shows that none of them fulfill *all* the requirements given above [29; 39]. What is essential for the kind of modeling delineated in Section 3.2 is a combination of the modeling flexibility of KADS with the properties of computerized approaches such as PROTÉGÉ (i.e., operational knowledge bases and formal modeling constructs from which knowledge needs can be derived).

To get a better understanding of the properties described in Section 3.2, we defined the experimental modeling language OMOS. The development of OMOS aims at combining major properties of KADS with those of automated approaches. OMOS is but one development in a larger venture to analyze method-oriented models of problem solving; MODEL-K and MoMo [53] tackle similar problems from other points of view.

General modeling principles of OMOS This section gives an overview of the underlying principles of OMOS' design. Detailed examples of OMOS applications can be found elsewhere [34; 39; 40; 41]. Section 3.3 illustrates OMOS with excerpts of an operational model for clamping tool selection.

In the context of OMOS, we distinguish two facets of building a model of a real-world task. On the one hand we analyze static structures of the domain; on the other hand we examine aspects of change (i.e., dynamic aspects) occurring in the real-world task. Thus, OMOS models consist of two partial and relatively independent (sub-)models: the *model of the domain* and the *model of the method*. Combined, they form the *model of the task*[4] (see Figure 6).

---

[4] The term *model of the task* is used here in Musen's sense [46, p. 70], meaning a

478

Both partial models (i.e., method and domain) are developed in parallel and in relative independence. However, the fact that they must combine into a coherent model of the task makes sure that they converge. One might argue that a more powerful, or more flexible mapping between both models would allow the combination of heterogeneous partial models into a task model. But this would not be helpful from a model-construction point of view, as the domain provides those distinctions that the method uses, and vice versa, the method indicates distinctions that the domain must provide. For example, a hierarchical classification problem-solving method makes sense only if the domain provides a natural hierarchy of diagnoses that the method can use.

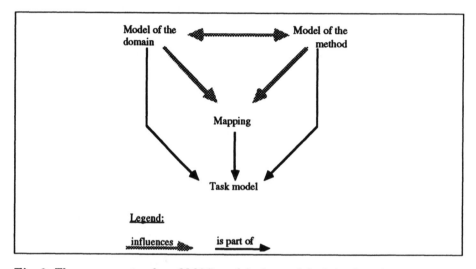

Fig. 6. The components of an OMOS model: the model of the domain, representing static and structural domain knowledge, the model of the method, representing aspects of change, and the model of the task, which relates the knowledge about change to the knowledge about the domain to constitute the operational problem solver.

In both partial models, OMOS provides the knowledge engineer with a set of

---

method combined with the knowledge of the types and structures of a domain of application, for example the application of skeletal-plan refinement to cancer-chemotherapy admininstration. This does not coincide with the meaning of the term in the KADS approach, where a task model describes the sharing of a task between the user and a system [17], nor with the way it is used in the COMMET workbench [51] where tasks are things that need to be accomplished.

Note however, that we use the term *model* of the task to express that we do not assert anything about the real world-task itself. We abstract from its complexity by purposefully introducing structure. Where others might structure a task from the point of view of agents accomplishing things, or from the point of view of goals needing to be achieved, we look at tasks from the points of view of the method and the application data involved in performing that task.

epistemological knowledge structuring primitives. For the representation of the domain knowledge we use *classes, instances, supers* relations (comparable to *is-a* relations), *relations* between instances, and *attributes with values* to structure knowledge and to describe concepts.

In the model of the method, change is represented as consisting of (intermediate) states and of operations realizing transitions between these states. This view is very similar to the KADS view. In OMOS, states are represented as *roles* (corresponding to KADS metaclasses); transitions are called *inference actions* (comparable to KADS knowledge sources). Combined, the roles and inference actions of a model form the *inference structure*. To attribute clear-cut semantics to inference actions, we took a similar view as the KADS developers do. In KADS one distinguishes four kinds of change-inflicting operations: generation of concepts, modification of attribute values, differentiation, and structure manipulation. This typology of operations is motivated by enumerating the kinds of change that one can effectuate on a KL-ONE–oriented domain representation [54, p. 28].

KADS is generally applicable to a broad range of tasks, which is partially due to the fact that it is a conceptual, non-operational language. For OMOS—an operational language—we had to define unambiguous modeling primitives with well-defined semantics. To simplify this task, and to establish a clear domain of applicability for our language, we defined boundaries. OMOS can only be used to model real-world tasks that do not require the dynamic creation or deletion of concepts or instances. Along the lines of the KADS typology argument, one can limit the description of change-inflicting operations in OMOS to two kinds: (1) the assignment of values at the domain; and (2) the modification of states of the problem solver (i.e., roles). However limited this may appear, OMOS has been used to model several applications from varying domains and problem-solving methods: allocation of offices in the Sisyphus project (an assignment task) [41], selections of clamping tools for lathe turning (an analytic task) [34; 40], and the cancer-chemotherapy administration task of ONCOCIN (a synthesis task) [39].

OMOS' knowledge structuring primitives allow a purely declarative description of the inference actions, roles, domain concepts, and relations; similarly, the mapping that connects both models is phrased declaratively. This is a precondition for analysis tools that check, for example, how domain knowledge is used by components of the method.

The knowledge structuring primitives are represented in an object-oriented way. Besides being an implementation technology, object-orientedness has many advantages for knowledge-modeling environments. This issue is discussed in detail in [29]. For example, if the knowledge engineer defines an OMOS inference action, then this corresponds to an instantiation of the class *inference action*, the definition of parameters and the inheritance of the abstract interpreters (defined in a message-passing paradigm). This allows us to define local interpreters for each knowledge structuring construct[5].

---

[5] This is different from the COMMET approach [51], where the developer selects code elements from a library to operationalize knowledge elements in the model.

OMOS models are configured from simple building blocks (e.g., role, inference action). The results of a configuration process can be reused. This is especially true for models of the problem-solving method, whose building blocks are domain independant. In applications of OMOS we have reused aspects of models of problem solving. For example, the core of the model for clamping tool selection (to be described later in this section) consists of two different selection inferences: the first one performs a selection of possible clamping tools for the task at hand by using *discrete* criteria; the second selection inference uses the result of the first one to make an optimal choice on the basis of *continuous* criteria. This complex selection process had been identified on the basis of psychological evaluation of experts' behavior in the domain of production planning. We reused that template in the problem-solving model for the office allocation task, as we could observe similar behavior. It allowed us to identify known structures in newly observed behavior.

As OMOS models are directly operational and as they provide for certain kinds of user interaction (e.g., inference actions can query the user for missing knowledge), we think that OMOS shows that one can have declarative models that result from a constructive modeling process and that are operational systems. Thus, an approach like OMOS allows to combine system operation and system update in an environment where knowledge changes continuously.

An example of an OMOS application We give a brief description of an OMOS application, to illustrate the general design decisions described above. A detailed description can be found elsewhere [34; 40].

Clamping tool selection for lathe turning is part of a larger task of generating production plans for the manufacturing of rotational parts [3]. A clamping tool centers a workpiece in the lathe and transmits the rotational forces. Among others, one distinguishes lathe dogs, lathe centers, clamping jaws, and collet chucks. Clamping tools are characterized by the ways they fasten the workpiece in the lathe and the types of access that they allow the cutting tools. For example, lathe dogs hold the workpiece from the side and allow free access to all surfaces except the left and the right vertical planes. The types of access define the kinds of turning that can be effectuated to shape the workpiece. Besides the accessibility of different sections of the workpiece surface there are other criteria. We will consider the set-up time, that is, the time needed to mount the clamping tool on the lathe, and the clamping time, that is, the time it takes to close the clamping tool when a new mold is inserted into the lathe.

The model of the domain. In the domain model, the knowledge engineer represents the concepts, instances (see Figure 7) and relations (see Table 1 for an example of a relation) of the domain of the real-world task.

The model of the problem-solving method. We give a high-level description of the problem-solving method. The choice of a good clamping tool to turn a workpiece is a selection process that observes (1) discrete criteria that eliminate unsuitable

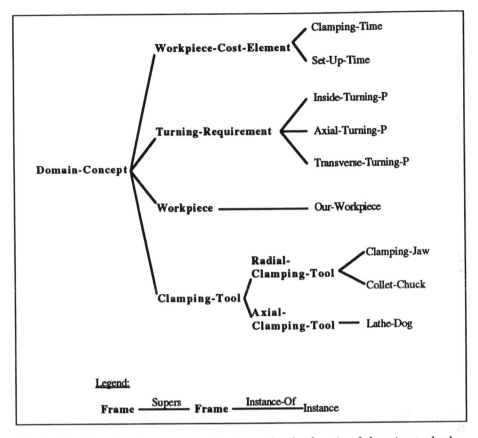

Fig. 7. The hierarchy of concepts and instances for the domain of clamping tool selection.

alternatives from the set of possible clamping tools (e.g., inside turning is a knock-out criterion for collet chucks); and (2) optimization criteria that are used to single out a best choice on the basis of numerical ratings (e.g., best set-up time).

The use of the discrete criteria happens in two ways: (1) criteria can be used rigorously to select an ideal clamping tool; or (2) criteria can be relaxed somewhat to make a less than optimal choice, which is called a feasible choice. The second alternative is used if the first one does not result in a solution.

This problem-solving method is called *selection by elimination and optimization*. Using the terms of the inference structure of Figure 8, the method proceeds as follows:

1. In the first step, the description of the workpiece to be turned (i.e., the situation parameter in generic method terms) is used to instantiate a set of criteria, which will be the basis for the selection of the clamping tool.
2. In the next step, one tries to make an ideal choice of those clamping tools

482

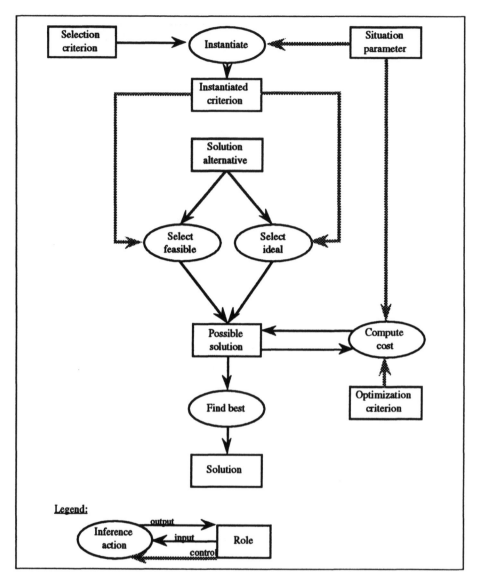

Fig. 8. The inference structure for the problem-solving method *selection by elimination and optimization* (adapted from [34]).

Table 1. The domain relation `optimal-clamping-tool` with one of its tuples. It is a binary relation (arity = 2), that relates instances of the concept *clamping tool* with a list of instance-attribute-value triplets of the concept *turning-requirement* (EXTENSION-* Turning-Requirement). The tuple indicates that a collet chuck is an optimal clamping tool if the turning operation requires transverse turning and if inside turning is not needed.

```
(DEFINE-DOMAIN-RELATION Optimal-Clamping-Tool
 WITH ARITY = 2
      TYPE-SEQUENCE = (((INSTANCE Clamping-Tool)
                          (EXTENSION-* Turning-Requirement)))
      ARGUMENT-SEQUENCE =
                     ((Clamping-Tool Important-Turning-Requirements))
      TUPLES = ((
                ((Optimal-Clamping-Tool
                    Collet-Chuck
                     ((Transverse-Turning-P Required-Value = Yes)
                      (Inside-Turning-P Required-Value = No))))

           ...
```

(i.e., the solution alternatives) that totally fulfill the instantiated criteria.

3. If this fails to produce possible solutions, a less than optimal choice is made through the inference action SELECT FEASIBLE.
4. On the basis of the workpiece description (i.e., the situation parameters in the abstract method terms), numerical costs are computed for all the possible solutions. This involves factors such as set-up time, clamping time, etc.
5. The inference action FIND BEST selects the clamping tool with the lowest costs.

The model of the task. The model of the task results from the combination of the model of the method with the model of the domain (see Figure 6). The model of the task is not defined explicitly, it results from the definition of the mapping of the method elements onto the elements of the domain model. The inference actions are mapped onto the domain relations; the roles are mapped onto domain concepts and their instances. Figure 9 shows how the clamping-tool task model is combined from the method model (see the inference structure in Figure 8) and the domain model (see Figure 7 for the definition of the concepts and instances), by establishing a mapping between roles and concepts, and between inference actions and domain relations.

The following roles of the problem-solving method are initialized with elements of the domain (see the shaded links between concepts and roles in Figure 9):

484

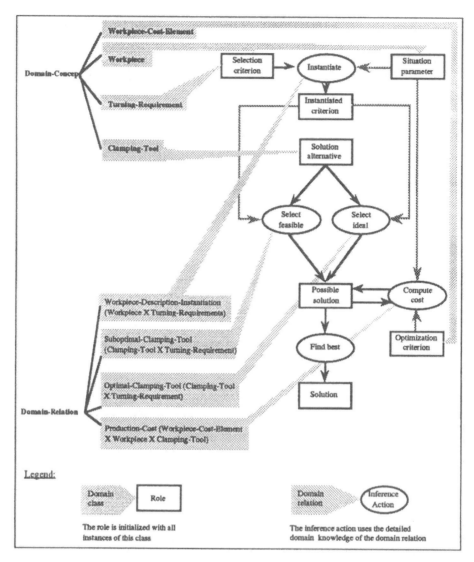

Fig. 9. The domain model (left side), with the concepts (on top) and the relations (below), combines with the method model (right side) to form the task model. The links between both models represent the mapping (adapted from [40]).

1. Optimization criterion is initialized with all instances of the concepts *work-piece cost element*. Initially, the instances *clamping-time* and *set-up-time* play this role.
2. Situation parameter is initialized with the description of the workpiece to be turned.
3. Selection criterion denotes the turning requirements, that is, *inside turning*, *axial turning*, and *transverse turning*.
4. Solution alternative is the role that all the instances of the frame *clamping tool* play initially.

The roles instantiated criterion, possible solution, and solution are not initialized.

The inference actions of the method get their detailed knowledge from the tuples of domain relations (see the shaded links between the domain relations of the domain model and the inference actions of the method model in Figure 9).

Analysis tools in the framework of the task model. OMOS provides several tools to analyze the use of the domain knowledge in the framework of the problem-solving method. The *dead-end analysis* looks for intermediary role-assignments that are not used by any of the subsequent inferences. For example, the concept *clamping jaw* can play the role solution-alternative (see Figure 8), but neither SELECT-FEASIBLE nor SELECT-IDEAL can access it, as they do not have the necessary detailed knowledge in their domain relations. Table 2 renders the result of an analysis of the role solution alternative. Other tools focus on the definition of domain relations (coverage analysis) and inference actions (loop-hole analysis).

Table 2. The result of a dead-end analysis for the role solution alternative.

```
The domain concept CLAMPING-JAW can be assigned to the role
SOLUTION-ALTERNATIVE, but it is not used by any of the inference
actions SELECT-IDEAL, SELECT-FEASIBLE that use
SOLUTION-ALTERNATIVE as control- or as input-role.

To change this do AT LEAST ONE of the following:

    Add a tuple to the relation OPTIMAL-CLAMPING-TOOL, which is used
    by the inference action SELECT-IDEAL. CLAMPING-JAW must be
    mentioned in the 0. argument of the tuple, which is of type
    (INSTANCE CLAMPING-TOOL) and is called CLAMPING-TOOL.

    Add a tuple to the relation SUBOPTIMAL-CLAMPING-TOOL, which is
    used by the inference action SELECT-FEASIBLE. CLAMPING-JAW must be
    mentioned in the 0. argument of the tuple, which is of type
    (INSTANCE CLAMPING-TOOL) and is called CLAMPING-TOOL.
```

3.4 Summary

We have shown that the transfer view on knowledge acquisition is not a consensus in the research community anymore; there has been a paradigm shift (in the sense of Kuhn [35]); knowledge acquisition is now considered to be a creative modeling process. Moreover, this section has spelled out that explicit models of problem-solving are needed in knowledge-based systems. In the framework of that paradigm we discussed certain requirements that we deem a modeling environment should fulfill to support knowledge engineering. OMOS illustrates how a language can be designed to ensure these properties.

The next section combines these results into a general view on the development process of knowledge-based systems and sketches an architecture for second generation knowledge-acquisition environments.

4 A revised view on knowledge engineering

Our first view—the one underlying KRITON—saw the knowledge engineering process as consisting of two distinct phases: acquisition and interpretation (see Section 2.1). Section 2.3 shows how a method of problem solving can guide the ongoing knowledge acquisition process. Section 3 shows that explicit models of knowledge play a major role in knowledge engineering. Requirement 6 of Section 3.2 stressed the need for integrating continuous knowledge acquisition with system operation.

These points are reflected in the following list of knowledge acquisiton subtasks representing the central part of a second generation knowledge-based systems development cycle[6]:

1. **Initial knowledge acquisition.** The knowledge engineer goes through initial interviews with the domain expert, records first protocols, and if possible he uses techniques such as the knowledge acquisition grid [36], repertory grids [25], clustering techniques [16], protocol structuring tools [1], or hybrid tools such as KRITON to obtain initial structures and to get a first overview of the application task [11].
2. **Data interpretation and knowledge structuring.** The knowledge engineer identifies recurring and potentially more abstract structures in the domain. These structures can be of different kinds.
   (a) **Identification of domain structures.** The knowledge engineer develops a structured terminology for the domain, for example he can define a T-box in KL-ONE–like approaches [5] or a set of classes in an object-oriented approach [9]. A host of tools can be used for the acquisition of a domain model, for example MOBAL [44; 55] or KITTEN [49; 50].

---

[6] We neglect aspects that are less important in this context, such as requirements analysis and systems integration. They are discussed in [27].

(b) **Identification of inferences and roles that knowledge elements play in the problem-solving process.** The knowledge engineer defines the actions, goals, and decision criteria to give an abstract (possibly knowledge level) description of the problem-solver.

One can use approaches such as KADS, MODEL-K, or GT in this phase. An approach such as GDM (Generalized Directive Models) [52] would provide active guidance in the elaboration of the method structures.

(c) **Identification of other structures,** such as, task sharing, task decomposition, data flow, or modality.

(d) **Integration and mapping of the different structures into a coherent model of the task.** The different knowledge structures, identified in the previous phases, must be merged into a coherent model. This phase is most important, as it represents the creative interaction between the different points of view represented by the different knowledge structures. For example, abstract goals identified in the problem-solving method must have an equivalent in the domain.

3. **Acquisition of the detailed knowledge in the framework defined by the task model.** The model of the task provides structures that are now stuffed with detailed knowledge about the application. The task model must provide the guidance for this process; it must be *strong*—in the sense of McDermott [43]—to allow for automated analysis techniques and dedicated knowledge editors, so that the domain expert can have an active part in the extension of the task model.

Such editors have for example been developed for D3/Classika [26; 47].

4. **Testing and debugging.**

5. **Knowledge maintenance after system delivery.** The system delivered and the model are identical. Conceptually, the system consists of two parts: the structures and their contents. The maintenance is organized along these lines.

(a) **Maintenance of the structures that constitute the framework of the task model.** If structures are modified, then this changes the task model. Such modifications require re-engineering of the task model, and if necessary, restructuring of the detailed knowledge. For example, if a hierarchical diagnosis model that uses *part-of*-relations is changed so that it performs the same task, but using *is-a*-relations, then the domain structures—and thus the task model—must be redefined. Large parts of the detailed knowledge must be reacquired or restructured.

(b) **Maintenance of the detailed knowledge in the structures of the task model.** Within the framework of the task model, maintenance of the detailed knowledge is similar to the acquisition of the detailed knowledge. It is supported with the same tools and techniques.

The knowledge-acquisition subasks must not be realized in a waterfall-oriented series of phases; we see them as being the central activities of a spiral development cycle, so that all phases can be repeated and previous results can be refined if indicated by the ongoing elaboration process [56].

488

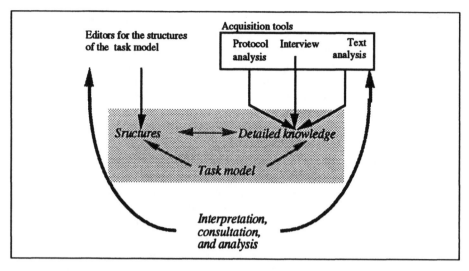

Fig. 10. The architecture for a model-based knowledge support system reflecting the development cycle aspects spelled out in Section 4. Knowledge acquisition tools function in the framework defined by the structures of the task model. Special editors work on these task structures. The task model is operational and is the basis for analysis tools. Consultation and analysis provide feedback for acquisition and modeling components.

Figure 10 depicts the architecture of a model-based knowledge support environment realizing our view on the development cycle of a knowledge-based system. A set of knowledge-acquisition tools (e.g., repertory-grid based interviews, protocol analysis, graphical knowledge editors, text analysis tools, etc.) operate on the representation of the detailed knowledge in the framework of the model of the task. The model of the task is the meta-information that guides the knowledge acquisition tools. In the early phases, the knowledge acquisition tools can be used in the identification or elaboration of the different structures. For example, clustering techniques are helpful in the elaboration of the domain model. The structures of the task model, assembled from the structures of several other specialized models (e.g., the model of the domain, the model of the method) are edited separately. Analysis tools—operating on the detailed knowledge in the framework of the task model—provide feedback and guidance for the model-structure editors and for the acquisition tools for the detailed knowledge. The task model is directly operational.

The architecture separates the acquisition (and maintenance) of the detailed knowledge from the editing of the task model. This allows a separation of the roles of those involved in the development process: the knowledge engineer performs systems-analysis–like tasks and manages the task model (comparable to a data-base administrator managing the data-base schema); the domain expert is responsible for the acquisition and maintenance of the detailed knowledge (comparable to a clerk in charge managing the tuples within the relational schema).

This separation of roles has first been proposed by Musen [46]. Other approaches, such as SBF (Spark, Burn, Firefighter) [33] or COMMET [51] put both responsabilities in the hands of non-programmers.

5 Current status and future developments

The architecture sketched above is our long-term goal. This section will point out were we are on the way to reaching that goal, and what are the open research questions.

With OMOS we developed a modeling language from which one can derive guidance in the form of knowledge needs for the detailed knowledge-acquisition process. In [34] we illustrated how OMOS' diagnostic messages (such as the one rendered in Table 2) provide topics for the agendas of subsequent focussed knowledge-acquisition interviews. The same information can be used to prompt a knowledge acquisition session with the KRITON interview component (Figure 3). For example, the diagnostic message of the analysis tool (see Table 2) indicates that the relation optimal-clamping-tool must be extended by at least one tuple, having *clamping jaw* as its first argument. The other argument types can be looked up in the definition of the relation (see Table 1). Thus an editor like the one rendered in Figure 11 could be called upon, indicating exactly what the knowledge needs of the method are, and how the user could fill them in.

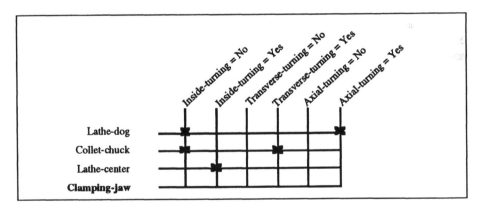

Fig. 11. A (proposed) graphical editor for the relation optimal-clamping-tool. Clamping jaw must be inserted in the relation, as the dead-end analysis of the role solution-alternative (see Table 2) determined that the concept *clamping jaw* is not used by any inference action, because it is—among others—not mentioned in the relation optimal-clamping-tool.

Thus, we have modeling languages that could guide automated knowledge acquisition tools, which in turn operate in the framework of the modeling languages. Further work will concentrate along the following lines:

1. How does one develop the structures of a model, that is, how can a knowledge engineer identify inference actions, roles, etc., in the documents that result from the first, initial knowledge acquisition phase? We are currently analyzing how one could generate models from cases recorded in media such as video, pictures, or text [7; 8]. This could be combined with GDM (Generalized Directive Models) [52].

2. The KRITON knowledge acquisition tools showed that they are practical and can be used to build a knowledge base. They must be reimplemented and completed with table-driven and graphical knowledge editors so that they can handle more complex knowledge constructs.

3. OMOS is an experimental language, developed to validate our assumptions about modeling. It has shown that they are valid and can be realized. But OMOS is limited to tasks that do not require the dynamic creation or deletion of instances or concepts. We are currently working on the implementation of new modeling languages, that are not constrained and can be applied to a wider range of tasks, but that nevertheless have properties comparable to those of OMOS.

4. Even though we realized all the important aspects of the architecture for second generation knowledge support systems rendered in Figure 10, we must still come up with an integrated environment supporting the whole life cycle as described in Section 4.

6 Summary

This paper describes several stages in our knowledge acquisition project, starting out from the first generation, knowledge-transfer oriented tool KRITON, via IRA-Grid—a first attempt to use methods of problem solving as meta-knowledge—to the declarative method-oriented modeling language OMOS, built to guide automated knowledge acquisition.

Besides describing the different stages of the project, we concentrated on explicating the underlying assumptions that motivated the design decisions for the different software systems. Even though we shifted the focus of attention away from automated techniques, towards explicit models we want to emphasize that this was motivated by the need for meta-knowledge to guide the automated knowledge acquisition tools, and not by arguments against automated tools. Now that we have shown that we can develop task models that guide knowledge acquisition, we will study the interaction between KRITON-type knowledge acquisition tools and operational modeling languages.

Finally, we have suggested an architecture for a second-generation—and thus model-based—knowledge support environnment. It combines acquisition, modeling, and maintenance with system operation and knowledge consultation.

Acknowledgements

Otto Kühn and Gabi Schmidt helped in the development of the application example. Barbara Schmidt-Belz, Otto Kühn, Jean-Paul Krivine, and Karin Lagrange gave very helpful comments on earlier versions of this article. Joachim Diederich and Ingo Ruhmann deserve the credit for the development of the concepts of KRITON and its first implementations. Many of the ideas discussed in this paper originated in the discussions with Wolfgang Gräther, Werner Karbach, Angi Voß, Jürgen Walther and other members of GMD's knowledge modeling team.

References

1. Anjo Anjewierden and Jan Wielemaker. Shelley - computer aided knowledge engineering. In Bob Wielinga, John Boose, Brian Gaines, Guus Schreiber, and Maarten van Someren, editors, *Proceedings of EKAW90*, pages 41 – 59, Amsterdam, 1990. IOS Press.

2. Nathalie Aussenac. *Conception d'une méthodologie et d'un outil d'acquisition de connaissances expertes*. PhD thesis, Universite Paul Sabatier, Toulouse, November 1989.

3. Ansgar Bernardi, Harold Boley, Christoph Klauck, Philip Hanschke, Knut Hinkelmann, Ralf Legleitner, Otto Kühn, Manfred Mayer, Michael Richter, Franz Schmalhofer, Gabi Schmidt, and Walter Sommer. ARC-TEC: Acquisition, representation and compilation of technical knowledge. In Jean-Paul Haton and Jean-Claude Rault, editors, *Proceedings of Avignon 91*, volume 1, pages 133 – 145, Avignon, France, 1991. EC2.

4. John H. Boose. A knowledge acquisition program for expert systems based on personal construct psychology. *International Journal of Man-Machine Studies*, 23:495 – 525, 1985.

5. R. Brachman and G.J. Schmolze. An overwiev of the KL-ONE knowledge representation system. *Cognitive Science*, 9(11):216–260, 1985.

6. Ronald J. Brachman. On the epistemological status of semantic networks. In N.V. Findler, editor, *Associative Networks: Representation and Use of Knowledge by Computers*, pages 3 – 50 50. Academic Press, New York, 1979.

7. Sonja Branskat. Case-based knowledge acquisition in the preformal phase. In John Boose and Brian Gaines, editors, *Proceedings of the 6th Banff knowledge acquisition for knowledge-based systems workshop*, pages 5–1/5–20, Calgary, Canada, 1991. AAAI, University of Calgary.

8. Sonja Branskat. Fallbasierte Wissensakquisition. Working paper 606, GMD, St. Augustin, FRG, 1992.

9. Harry Bretthauer and Juergen Kopp. The meta class system MCS: A portable object system for Common Lisp. Technical Report 554, GMD, St. Augustin, July 1991.

10. Joost Breuker and Bob Wielinga. Models of expertise in knowledge acquisition. In Giovanni Guida and Carlo Tasso, editors, *Topics in Expert System Design, Methodologies and Tools*, Studies in Computer Science and Artificial Intelligence, pages 265 – 295. North-Holland, Amsterdam, 1989.

11. D.C. Brown. A graduate-level expert system course. *AI Magazine*, Fall 1987.

12. B. Chandrasekaran. Generic tasks in knowledge-based reasoning: High-level building blocks for expert system design. *IEEE Expert*, pages 32 – 30, Fall 1986.

13. B. Chandrasekaran. Generic tasks as building blocks for knowledge-based systems: The diagnosis and routine design examples. *The Knowledge Engineering Review*, 3(3):183 – 210, Octobre 1988.

14. Thomas Christaller, Franco di Primio, and Angi Voß. *The AI workbench BABY-LON*. Academic Press, London, 1992.

15. William J. Clancey. The knowledge level reinterpreted: Modeling how systems interact. *Machine Learning, Special Issue on Knowledge Acquisition*, 4(3, 4):285 – 292, 1989.

16. Nancy Cooke and James McDonald. The application of psychological scaling techniques to knowledge elicitation for knowledge-based systems. *International Journal of Man-Machine Studies*, 26:533 – 550, 1987.

17. Paul de Greef and Jost Breuker. Analysing system–user cooperation in KADS. *Knowledge Acquisition*, 4(1):89 – 108, 1992.

18. Franco di Primio and Karl Wittur. BABYLON, a meta-interpretation model for handling mixed knowledge representations. In *Proceedings of the 7th International Workshop on Expert Systems and Their Applications*, volume 1, pages 821 – 833, Avignon, 1987.

19. Joachim Diederich and Marc Linster. Knowledge-based knowledge elicitation. In Giovanni Guida and Carlo Tasso, editors, *Topics in Expert System Design*, pages 323 – 352. North-Holland, Amsterdam, 1989.

20. Joachim Diederich, Ingo Ruhmann, and Mark May. KRITON: A knowledge acquisition tool for expert systems. *International Journal of Man-Machine Studies*, 26:29 – 40, 1987.

21. A. Ericsson and Herbert Simon. *Protocol-Analysis - Verbal Reports as Data*. MIT Press, Cambridge, 1984.

22. Brian R. Gaines. Second generation knowledge acquisition systems. In John H. Boose, Brian R. Gaines, and Marc Linster, editors, *Proceedings of EKAW88*, pages 17/1–17/14, Sankt Augustin, 1988. GMD. GMD-Studie 143.

23. Brian R. Gaines and Marc Linster. Integrating a knowledge acquisition tool, an expert system shell and a hypermedia system. *International Journal of Expert Systems*, 3(2):105 – 129, 1990.

24. Brian R. Gaines, Marc Linster, and Mildred L. G. Shaw. An integrated knowledge support system. In *Proceedings of FCGS: International Conference on Fifth Generation Computer Systems*, pages 1157 – 1164, Tokyo, 1992. ICOT.

25. Brian R. Gaines and Mildred L.G. Shaw. New directions in the analysis and interactive elicitation of personal construct systems. In Mildred L. G. Shaw, editor, *Recent Advances in Personal Construct Technology*, Computers and People, pages 147 – 182. Academic Press, London, 1981.

26. Ute Gappa. CLASSIKA: A knowledge acquisition tool for use by experts. In John H. Boose and Brian R. Gaines, editors, *Proceedings of the 4th Banff Knowledge-Acquisition for Knowledge-Based Systems Workshop*, pages 14/1–14/15. AAAI, University of Calgary, 1989.

27. Werner Karbach and Marc Linster. *Wissensakquisition für Expertensysteme: Techniken, Modelle und Softwarewerkzeuge*. Hanser Verlag, München, June 1990.

28. Werner Karbach, Marc Linster, and Angi Voß. OFFICE-Plan, tackling the synthesis frontier. In Dieter Metzing, editor, *Proceedings of GWAI89*, volume 216 of *Informatik Fachberichte*, pages 379 – 387, Heidelberg, 1989. Gesellschaft fuer Informatik, Springer Verlag.

29. Werner Karbach, Marc Linster, and Angi Voß. Models, methods, roles and tasks: Many labels - one idea? *Knowledge Acquisition*, 2(4):279 – 300, 1990.

30. Werner Karbach and Angi Voß. MODEL-K for prototyping and strategic reasoning at the knowledge level. In Jean-Marc David, Jean-Paul Krivine, and Reid Simmons, editors, *Second generation exppert systems*. Springer, 1992, Forthcoming.

31. Werner Karbach, Angi Voß, Ralf Schukey, and Uwe Drouven. MODEL-K: Proto-typing at the knowledge level. In *Proceedings of the First International Conference on Knowledge Modeling and Expertise Transfer*, Sophia Antipolis, France, 1991.

32. George Kelly. *The Psychology of Personal Constructs*. Norton, New York, 1955.

33. Georg Klinker, C. Bhola, Geoffrey Dallemagne, David Marques, and John Mc-Dermott. Usable and reusable programming constructs. *Knowledge Acquisition*, 3(2):117 – 135, 1991.

34. Otto Kühn, Marc Linster, and Gabi Schmidt. Clamping, COKAM, KADS and OMOS. In *Proceedings of EKAW91*. University of Strathclyde, 1991. Also published as Technical Memo TM-91-03 of DFKI, Kaiserslautern.

35. Thomas Kuhn. *The structure of scientific revolutions*. University of Chicago Press, Chicago, 1970.

36. M. LaFrance. The knowledge acquisition grid: A method for training knowledge engineers. *Int. Journal of Man-Machine Studies*, 26:245–255, 1987.

37. Marc Linster. Integrating acquisition, representation, and interpretation. In John H. Boose, Brian R. Gaines, and Jean-Gabriel Ganascia, editors, *Proceedings of EKAW89*, pages 565 – 577, Paris, 1989.

38. Marc Linster. Towards a second generation knowledge acquisition tool. *Knowledge Acquisition*, 1(2):163 – 183, 1989.

39. Marc Linster. *Knowledge acquisition based on explicit methods of problem-solving*. PhD thesis, University of Kaiserslautern, Kaiserslautern, February 1992.

40. Marc Linster. Linking modeling to make sense and modeling to implement systems in an operational environment. In Thomas Wetter, Klaus-Dieter Althoff, John Boose, Brian Gaines, Marc Linster, and Franz Schmalhofer, editors, *Current developments in knowledge acquisition: EKAW92*, volume 599 of *LNAI*, pages 55 – 74, Heidelberg, 1992. GI, ECCAI, Springer-Verlag.

41. Marc Linster. Using the operational modeling language OMOS to tackle the Sisy-phus'92 office-planning problem. In Marc Linster, editor, *Sisyphus'92: Models of problem solving*, volume 630 of *Technical report of GMD*, St. Augustin, 1992. GMD.

42. Marc Linster and Mark Musen. Use of KADS to create a conceptual model of the ONCOCIN task. *Knowledge Acquisition*, 4(1):55 – 88, 1992.

43. John McDermott. Preliminary steps toward a taxonomy of problem-solving methods. In Sandra Marcus, editor, *Automating Knowledge Acquisition for Expert Systems*, pages 225 – 256. Kluwer Academic, Boston, 1988.

44. Katharina Morik. Acquiring domain models. *International Journal of Man-Machine Studies*, 26:93–104, 1987.

45. Katharina Morik. Sloppy modeling. In Joerg Siekmann, editor, *Knowledge Representation and Organization in Machine Learning*, volume 347 of *LNAI*, pages 107 – 133. Springer Verlag, Heidelberg, 1989.

46. Mark A. Musen. *Automated Generation of Model-Based Knowledge Acquisition Tools*. Research Notes in Artificial Intelligence. Pitman Publishing, London, 1989.

47. Frank Puppe. *Problemlösungsmethoden in Expertensystemen*. Studienreihe Informatik. Springer Verlag, Berlin Heidelberg, 1990.

48. Mildred L. G. Shaw. *On Becoming a Personal Scientist*. Computers and People Series. Academic Press, 1980.

49. Mildred L.G. Shaw and B. Gaines. An interactive knowledge elicitation technique using personal construct technology. In A. Kidd, editor, *Knowledge Acquisition for Expert Systems*. Plenum Press, New York, 1987.

494

50. Mildred L.G. Shaw and Brian R. Gaines. KITTEN: Knowledge initiation and transfer tools for experts and novices. *International Journal of Man-Machine Studies*, 27(3):251 – 280, 1987.

51. Luc Steels. The componential framework and its role in reusability. In Jean-Marc David, Jean-Paul Krivine, and Reid Simmons, editors, *Second Generation Expert Systems*. Springer, 1992, Forthcoming.

52. Gertjan van Heijst, Peter Terpstra, Bob Wielinga, and Nigel Shadbolt. Using generalised directive models in knowledge acquisition. In Thomas Wetter, Klaus-Dieter Althoff, John Boose, Brian Gaines, Marc Linster, and Franz Schmalhofer, editors, *Current developments in knowledge acquisition–EKAW92*, volume 599 of *LNAI*, pages 112 – 132, Heidelberg, 1992. GI, ECCAI, Springer-Verlag.

53. Jürgen Walther, Angi Voß, Marc Linster, Thomas Hemmann, Hans Voš, and Werner Karbach. MoMo: Initial specification of the alpha version. Technical report, GMD, St. Augustin, FRG, 1992.

54. Bob Wielinga, Guus Schreiber, and Jost Breuker. KADS: A modelling approach to knowledge engineering. *Knowledge Acquisition*, 4(1):5 – 54, 1992.

55. Stefan Wrobel. Design goals for sloppy modeling systems. *International Journal of Man Machine Systems*, 24(4):461 – 477, October 1988.

56. Edward Yourdon. *Decline and fall of the American programmer*. Prentice Hall, Engkewood Cliffs, 1992.

ACTE: a Causal Model-Based Knowledge Acquisition Tool

Jean Charlet

DIAM, INSERM U194 & Service d'Informatique Médicale de l'AP-HP
91, Bd de l'Hôpital – 75634 Paris Cedex 13 – France
charlet@frsim51.bitnet

Abstract. In this paper, knowledge acquisition is presented as the instantiation of the so-called conceptual model by domain knowledge. In this framework we describe ACTE, a causal model-based knowledge acquisition tool designed to assist in knowledge acquisition for a heuristic classification problemsolver.

Our approach is based on the interpretation of an initial causal model. By exploiting problem-solving methods of the problem-solver to be built, ACTE is able to generate heuristic knowledge. Depending on its nature – i.e. the nature of the causal relationships and problem-solving methods which have generated this heuristic knowledge – this knowledge may be checked and refined by the expert. Thus, the causal model is interpreted with regard to the conceptual model and produces an operational knowledge-base.

1 Introduction

Knowledge acquisition (KA) is a modelling activity (Boose & Bradshaw, 1987). In current *knowledge base systems* (KBS) knowledge is acquired and organized according to its use in the reasoning process. In a prototypical approach (Clancey, 1986), a qualitative model is built in two steps. The first step consists in modelling the domain in order to identify relevant concepts and describe the objects. The second step consists in modelling the reasoning in order to ascertain any mutual relationships these objects may have and describe the problem-solving behavior. Once this modelling act is done, the model is used to guide the KA process. Hence, the task to be realized structures the knowledge base (Karbach *et al.*, 1990; Wielinga *et al.*, 1992).

KA is now modelled using a broader perspective and can be described in four steps (Aussenac-Gilles *et al.*, 1992; Charlet *et al.*, 1992): (i) identifying relevant concepts in the knowledge sources – *knowledge elicitation* in (Motta *et al.*, 1990) –, (ii) building the schema of a conceptual model of the problem-solver behavior, (iii) instantiating this conceptual model in order to acquire the knowledge defined by the preceding step, and (iv) operationalization of the conceptual model in the implemented system.

In this paper we focus primarily on the domain knowledge which is modelled in a causal model, on its interaction with a model of the problem-solving behavior (the interpretation model), and on the consequent development of the knowledgebase system. We present KA as the interpretation of the domain knowledge by the interpretation model. We use this framework to describe ACTE, a KA tool designed to assist in KA for a heuristic classification problem-solver. We show how ACTE uses the problem-solving methods of the interpretation model in order to interpret the causal model of the domain knowledge and produces an operational knowledge-base. Moreover, we investigate the nature of the causal model and its role in the KA process.

This paper is organized as follows: section 2 first recalls the terminology of KA systems with regard to causal and interpretation models, then outlines our proposals for enhancing the KA process; sections 3 and 4 present the ACTE tool, section 5 presents a medical application of ACTE, the LÉZARD system, and section 6 discusses some features of the approach with respect to the causal model.

2   Models and Interpretations

Although there is increasing acceptance of the importance of the modelling approach, the KA literature is just beginning to define a general terminology for this topic. In this paper, we try to be congruent with the terminology proposed by the authors of the KADS methodology (Wielinga *et al.*, 1992) and by Karbach *et al.* in a review paper (1990). In this paper we assume that the expert is the only knowledge source[1] and that the final KBS is the output of a KA process which can be described, as a cognitive task, as follows (see fig. 1) :

- In the beginning there is the *source activity*, the cognitive process we want to model (e.g. diagnosis or design); in some cases (e.g. diagnosis) this cognitive activity is performed on a real system (e.g. a biological or (patho)physiological system in medicine).
- The expert then has a *mental representation* of the real system which includes the behavior of this system and his reasoning activity about it. This representation can be more or less complete and multiple. The principal feature of this representation is to be unavailable to an observer[2].
- In the field of KA and in the body of this article, the *conceptual model* is the model that is reflected in communicating the representation of the expected behavior of the KBS to be built[3]. The *domain knowledge* or *domain model* refers to the communication of the knowledge about the real system. The structure of the domain model is a part of the conceptual model. The model which describes the behavior of the KBS independently of the domain knowledge is the *interpretation model* (Wielinga *et al.*, 1992).
- The *knowledge base* of the built KBS is inseparable from its *control*. They are both produced by the interpretation of the domain knowledge by the interpretation model.

---

[1] This hypothesis is a reduction of the reality but for our purposes it causes no problem to assume it.

[2] Some authors use the term *mental model* for the representation of the real system and its behavior. Features of these mental models are discussed in (Johnson-Laird, 1980) and (Gentner & Stevens, 1983).

[3] In the cognitive psychology area, the conceptual model is the model that is reflected in communicating the mental model to other entities (Norman, 1983).

– The *validation* of the KBS is an essential step of the KA process because there is a fundamental distortion between the mental representations of the expert and the symbolic representation of the conceptual model in a KBS. This distortion deals with interpretation problems (see 2.3) and has to be reduced with the observation of the KBS activity by the expert. This observation and the corrections which can be done correspond to the beginning of the validation.

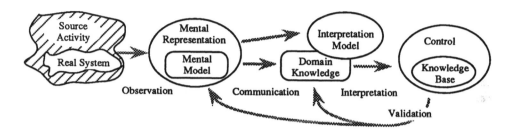

Fig. 1. The knowledge acquisition process.

This description of the KA process as a cognitive task is different from but not contradictory with Aussenac (1992) which describes a step of instantiation of the conceptual model followed by its final operationalization in the KBS (steps (iii) and (iv) of the KA process described in section 1). Our purpose is to integrate these two steps into one unique step of interpretation of the domain knowledge – e.g. a causal model in our approach – by the interpretation model. *The advantage of this approach is the integration of the operationalization step in the knowledge acquisition process performed in interaction with the expert. As we will discuss it below (see 2.3) this is the only way to check the interpretation performed by the expert and then to complete the knowledge acquisition process* .

2.1 Interpretation Model

When developing a knowledge-base, the system builder aims at describing a model of expert behavior. This model attempts to approximate – not reproduce – the problem-solving steps of human reasoning (Clancey, 1986). This model is thus an interpretation model, which refers to a set of (problem-solving) methods which work towards the problem solution.

Artificial intelligence researchers have identified a number of problem-solving methods, either domain-independent (e.g. Clancey's "heuristic classification" (1985) and Chandrasekaran's "generic tasks" (1987)) or domain-dependent (e.g. Szolovits *et al.* for medical diagnosis (1988)). Clancey's method of heuristic classification relies upon "data-abstraction", which consists in using hierarchies which allow the problem-solver to generalize from specific input data. Conversely, most medical decision making systems are based upon the two following strategies: (i) "focus on the highest abstraction levels", i.e. try to decide if classes of the most widespread diseases are present before deciding on more specific classes; and (ii) "unicity of the fault process", i.e. attempt to create a unique plausible chain of causally-related events to explain the observed symptoms (Szolovits *et al.*, 1988).

The development of KA tools based on problem-solving methods dates back to the completion of recent work (Eshelman, 1988; Marcus, 1988; Musen, 1989). These KA tools generate a model of a specific task from a fixed set of pre-existing problem-solving methods. A user of such a tool has at his disposal methods and their organization – i.e. a conceptual model – in order to perform a given task. Through the use of this tool and specific knowledge of the domain, an operational knowledge-base can be built for a defined problem-solver.

MOLE[4] and SALT (Eshelman, 1988; Marcus, 1988) are KA systems which use the paradigm of the *role-limiting method*: as oppose to the *weak method*, which is constrained only by the task to be achieved, the role-limiting method is an algorithmic description of how a task can be performed. The hypothesis underlying this paradigm is that only such a method can be used successfully in the KA process; a weak method cannot provide much help in determining what knowledge needs to be collected or how it should be encoded (Karbach *et al.*, 1990). Like MOLE or SALT, the ACTE tool fits in with this approach: *using clearly defined methods of the interpretation model in order to guide the knowledge acquisition process.*

This interpretation model is the same as in the KADS methodology (Wielinga *et al.*, 1992). The authors of this methodology have proposed a four-layer model with (i) domain knowledge, (ii) inference layer where some problem-solving methods are described, (iii) task layer, and (iv) strategic layer. This four-layer model is called the *model of expertise* and the definition of the interpretation model is the following:

> *A model of expertise from which the domain-specific knowledge layer is removed can be used by the knowledge engineer as a template for a new domain and thus support top-down knowledge acquisition. In KADS such partial models are called interpretation models because they guide the interpretation of verbal data obtained from the expert* (Schreiber *et al.*, 1991).

In ACTE, we use the term "interpretation model" for an additional but not contradictory reason: it is used to signify the interpretation of the domain knowledge.

2.2 Causal Model

Let us define what we call causal models. First, we reject the terms "deep models" and "shallow models". These notions are relative. As quoted by Sticklen *et al.*. (Sticklen *et al.*, 1988), one model is deep with respect to another, and may well be shallow compared with a third. Another point of view concerns the function of the expressed knowledge (the "teleology"). What we term "causal models" are models that *express causality at a certain level of abstraction, without referring to the aim of the final system in which they will be used* – e.g. diagnosis or classification in a

---

[4] "MOLE is both a performance system (MOLE$_P$) that interprets a domain-dependent knowledge base and a knowledge acquisition tool (MOLE$_{KA}$) for building and refining this knowledge base..." (Eshelman, 1988). In this paper we refer to MOLE as MOLE$_{KA}$.

medical knowledge-based system. Intuitively, causal models express knowledge that can be relevant over a wide class of applications and so appear to be "generic". They often try to represent "domain theory". For this reason, the term "deep knowledge" is sometimes applied. This kind of knowledge seems to be naturally available, often appearing as a background to a number of interviews for KA ("why are you telling me that?"). They also serve to justify acquired knowledge and to provide new clues and new directions for broadening the KA process itself.

According to Davis (1989) we note that increasing use of model-based systems has demonstrated the utility of using first principles to reason from a model of structure and behavior; along with this has grown a desire to combine the robustness of these systems with advantages offered by other paradigms such as rule-based systems. Additionally, for our KA framework we conclude that *a causal model seems to be the best way in order to express domain knowledge and can be very useful for knowledge acquisition.* But a causal model is not totally specified knowledge; it must be integrated in a KA workbench in order to build a knowledge-base system. Several issues have been quoted: (i) the use of justifications of expert knowledge for the validation of acquired knowledge or for the extension of an existing knowledge-base (Neches *et al.*, 1985), (ii) the acquisition of heuristic knowledge (Davis, 1989), and (iii) the acquisition of strategic knowledge (Gruber, 1991).

Our aim is to build an operational and totally specified knowledge-base. To achieve this aim we must acquire heuristic knowledge. Additionally, heuristic knowledge has certain characteristics; in particular it is a partially instantiated conceptual model (Charlet *et al.*, 1992). Therefore, our proposal is to formulate this instantiation and also *to use the interpretation model for interpreting the causal model in order to acquire heuristic knowledge.*

However, the ACTE tool is expected to enable the development of a well-suited system. The problem of the representation of the expert knowledge in the system must be pointed out.

2.3 Symbols, Interpretation and Knowledge

An artificial intelligence system manipulates symbols. We (people) are able to interpret these symbols. And we give them meaning. The system also interprets symbols. However, this interpretation does not mean that the system has access to anything other than an interpretation in the mathematical sense – i.e. a syntactic manipulation. Therefore, the symbols do not have an internal semantics but rather an external one: the interpretation given by an agent (Pylyshyn, 1987). Checking their external semantic impose to interpret them. And because they represent expert knowledge they must be interpreted by the expert[5].

Therefore the expert has to intervene in the KA process in order to check the interpretation of the symbolic system. But, checking the interpretation of the system does not only mean reading the formal representation of knowledge: this means observing the interpretation – i.e. the syntactic manipulations – performed by the system.

---

[5] These interpretation problems between the expert and a symbolic system deal with the *Knowledge Level* and the *Symbol Level* from Newell (1982). This problem is also discussed by Vinkhuyzen (1992).

So, our proposal is to have the system interpret the acquired knowledge and propose to the expert the interpreted knowledge at a non-ambiguous level. In that step, *the expert intervenes in the* KA *process in order to check the generated knowledge as well as to generate new one (both interpretations of the causal model). He intervenes in the validation process, an essential step in the* KA *process.*

3   ACTE: conceptualization

ACTE is a KA tool which take into account the observations and thoughts made above. The principal aim of this tool is: (i) allowing the expert to express its knowledge in a causal model framework and (ii) using a fixed interpretation model so as to interpret the causal model and having the expert to intervene in order to check this interpretation.

3.1   Problem-solving methods

So, in ACTE we choice some problem-solving methods typically defined in order to solve diagnostic problems. These methods can be all described independently of the medical domain but the choice is made in order to solve diagnostic problems in a medical area. So the descriptions and motivations are supported by medical considerations.

This choice is guided by the descriptions and studies developed in (Clancey, 1986; Bylander & Mittal, 1986; Szolovits *et al.*, 1988; Eshelman, 1988). Let us now give the principal methods used in acte for building the interpretation model of the final system.

Tangled taxonomies. Szolovits and Clancey (1986; 1988) have studied the necessity of the representation of the diseases in taxonomies and have concluded that multiple tangled taxonomies are useful to represent knowledge and to enable the program to explore disease features while preserving clarity:

> *It is better therefore, to organize the programs knowledge in a number of pure hierarchies, and to allow the program to choose among them or intermix them as needed during the process of diagnosis* (Szolovits *et al.*, 1988).

In the ACTE framework, the diseases are represented in two tangled taxonomies, a pure hierarchy of anatomical localization – e.g. DIGESTIVE-DISEASE or URINARY-DISEASE – and another pure hierarchy of pathophysiological processes – e.g INFLAMMATION. These hierarchies build a lattice.

This representation paradigm is not exactly a method. It is rather the *support* of methods than a method itself: for example, hierarchies are the support for the "data-abstraction" of the "heuristic classification" defined by Clancey (1985).

Data-abstraction. In diagnostic problems, data are often not directly solution features. These solution features must be inferred by "data-abstraction". Among the three basic relations for abstracting data – i.e. definitional abstraction, qualitative abstraction and, generalization (Clancey, 1985) – the qualitative abstraction is often used in the medical domain. For example, we can infer a HIGH-TEMPERATURE from a temperature of 38.5 degrees. More generally, grouping signs (data) in hierarchy defines some syndromes or clinical features.

Evocation signs. The abductive reasoning is accepted to be useful in medicine and more generally in diagnostic tasks: suppose there is a disease P which may cause the presence of the sign s. If I know that the sign s is present, then by abduction, I can suppose that the disease P is a good hypothesis which explains the presence of the sign s. The sign is the "trigger" of the hypothesis (Szolovits *et al.*, 1988). Such a mechanism is acceptable only if another mechanisms limit the number of hypotheses that need to be considered (by the program). The precedings hierarchies that enable the system to evoke diseases at the right abstraction level is a way to prevent the abusive growth of the set of hypotheses; another way is to link the disease to the signs (if they exist) necessary to take into account the disease as an assumption. The *qualifying conditions* from MOLE (Eshelman, 1988) play this role.

Hypothesis of the unicity of the fault process. Some expert systems, especially the medical ones (Long *et al.*, 1984; Szolovits *et al.*, 1988), rely on the hypothesis of the unicity of the fault process. This hypothesis is that a patient can suffer from more than one disease but that all these diseases are the expression of one unique pathophysiological process. Using this hypothesis supposes that the relationships linking the diseases are known. It is possible to refine this description by taking into account the eventual presence of other chronic diseases. For example, a patient can suffer from a CHRONIC-ULCER in addition of a PERITONITIS without any causal link between the two diseases.

3.2 Dealing with uncertainty

Despite using such problem-solving methods, representing uncertainty cannot be avoided. Moreover, these methods show the necessity to explicitly represent uncertainty: hypotheses triggering, heuristic classification or focusing on the highest abstraction levels... are symptomatic of this uncertainty.

The principal source of uncertainty is the reliability of information (signs) about a patient: these uncertainty of the signs can be due to inaccuracy and poor reliability of the instruments used to make the observation (the expert is one of these instruments) or to analyse these observations (its deals for example with biological analysis). Another kind of uncertainty is caused by the incompleteness of the information (Bonissone, 1987). Numerous works have also emphasize the necessity to explicitly represent uncertainty (Clancey, 1986; Szolovits *et al.*, 1988).

To take into account this uncertainty, three strategies are used in ACTE. They aim at solving conflicts which appear between two (or more) reasoning in the inference system. For example, there is a conflict when a reasoning $\mathcal{R}_1$ concluding c and a reasoning $\mathcal{R}_2$ concluding ¬c. These strategies use a notion of specificity developed by Gascuel *et al.* (1985) and specified in more recent works (Moinard, 1987).

The principal strategies used in the final system are:

- **Defining exceptions with a "shunt" rule[6].** when a reasoning $\mathcal{R}_1$, bringing into play almost two rules concluding C and a reasoning $\mathcal{R}_2$, bringing into play one rule concluding ¬C, $\mathcal{R}_2$ is an exception of $\mathcal{R}_1$, and is a "better" reasoning.
- **Keeping the most simple reasoning.** When a reasoning $\mathcal{R}_1$ concludes C and a reasoning $\mathcal{R}_2$ concludes ¬C with signs which are sufficient to conclude C, then $\mathcal{R}_1$ is "better" than $\mathcal{R}_2$ and the conclusion is C. $\mathcal{R}_2$ is a parasitic reasoning of the system.
- **Keeping the most reliable reasoning.** This strategy represents uncertainty through certainty factors as MYCIN. A reasoning concluding an object has a certainty which depends on the signs and rules building this reasoning. Between two reasonings concluding the same object, the best one is the one whose certainty factor is the greatest.

These strategies are applied in this order. The strategy which deals with numerical factors is the latest used. It is a priori less justified than the others which are based upon a qualitative analysis of the reasoning[7].

These strategies are a part of the system control. They must be presented and explained to the expert during the KA *phase. This presentation is included in the* ACTE *method.*

3.3 ACTE

ACTE is a KA tool in a medical diagnosis domain. The resulting knowledge-base system is aimed at doing a heuristic classification. The approach is based on the interpretation of a causal model. The aim of this interpretation is twofold: on one hand, it facilitates the checking of the causal model, on the other hand, it generates heuristic knowledge which is usable for a specific task.

ACTE deals with two knowledge-bases: the *causal knowledge-base* (CKB) – i.e. the causal model – which is the input to the KA process, and the *heuristic knowledge-base* (HKB) which is the output of this process and will constitute the operational knowledge-base. The following steps describe ACTE's KA process:

1. The conceptual model, and therefore the interpretation model, is first defined so as to describe the problem-solving methods that accomplish the diagnostic task. These methods deal, for example, with "data-abstraction" or the "unicity of the fault process".
2. The expert provides domain knowledge in a causal model framework. This causal model is the CKB.
3. The CKB is taken as a whole and globally analysed in interaction with the expert in order to check its consistency.
4. Each relation is analysed separately and interpreted by the problem-solving methods of the interpretation model. This generates both immediate (obvious) and heuristic knowledge. Depending on the nature of the heuristic knowledge – i.e. the nature of the causal relationships and problem-solving methods which

---

[6] The term "rule" refer here to an atomic inference and not to a production rule.

[7] We do not want here to discuss about certainty factors and their cognitive property. In our simplistic approach, they are actually less justifiable than the other strategies.

have generated this heuristic knowledge – it may be checked and refined by the expert.

The CKB is therefore interpreted by the interpretation model and the final HKB is built.

ACTE has been applied to LÉZARD, a medical diagnosis reasoning system for discriminating between diseases in the domain of acute abdominal pain. We illustrate various features of ACTE with examples from the knowledge-base of the LÉZARD system (Charlet, 1989).

4 ACTE: implementation

4.1 Knowledge Representation

Causal Knowledge Base. We have seen that CKB is a model of the domain knowledge. This knowledge is a pathophysiological and semiological knowledge. Both semiological and pathophysiological knowledge are represented in a causal network.

The pathophysiological part of the network is made up of causal and hierarchical relationships between diagnoses. Causal relationships describe the etiology of diagnoses. Hierarchical relationships are tangled taxonomies based on anatomical or pathological considerations. These taxonomies express multiple viewpoints on the same set of diseases. In ACTE we chose both an anatomical description of the diseases – e.g. DIGESTIVE-DISEASE or URINARY-DISEASE – and a description by the process – e.g. OBSTRUCTION or INFLAMMATION.

Semiological knowledge is described by relationships between signs and diagnoses. These signs are symptoms (input-data) or syndromes (abstracted data). Furthermore, the nature of these relationships is twofold: some qualifying conditions which express that a sign must be observed before evoking a disease (Eshelman, 1988) or some triggering conditions which evoke some hypotheses (Szolovits *et al.*, 1988). Figure 2 gives an illustration of such a knowledge.

At this step, the expert has built a causal model of the domain. The expression of this model is less constraint by the conceptual model; it just respects the support of the methods – e.g. taxonomies.

Heuristic Knowledge Base. The main aim of ACTE is to enable the interpretation of a CKB in a non-ambiguous fashion. So, the result of this interpretation must be non-ambiguous. In order to represent this result we did the choice of the production rule which (i) has the good level of abstraction to be comprehensible by the expert and (ii) represents clear and univocal relationship between the domain objects – e.g. taxonomies consist of some relationships between the objects which belong to them ; conversely, the production rule represents one unique relationship (see 4.2)

About uncertainty, after choosing the production rule as knowledge representation carrier, it is evident that the uncertainty representation support is this rule, so managing precisely the interpretation reliability of knowledge. As saw before (3.2) the uncertainty representation is done by certainty factors like thus used in the MYCIN system with a simplistic propagation algorithm.

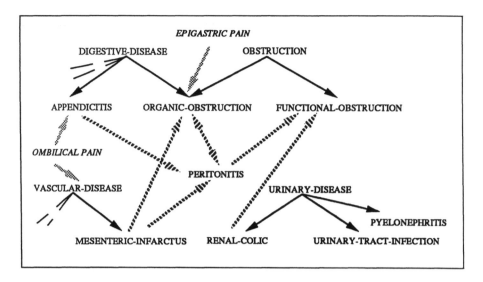

Fig. 2. Causal network representation. Dotted lines represent causal links, Black lines taxonomic links and gray lines evocation links

As we will see after (6.2) the CKB include heuristic knowledge while heuristic knowledge base include obvious knowledge. Nevertheless, the CKB is a domain theory mainly including taxonomies and causal relationships, while the HKB include heuristic mainly interpretations of these relationships.

4.2 Knowledge Interpretation

Let us now describe the problem-solving methods which are implemented in ACTE and how they contribute to the interpretation of the CKB.

Pathophysiological Knowledge Interpretation.

Exclusions calculus. ACTE interprets the causal network based on the hypothesis of the unicity of the fault process. The interpretation algorithm is *the exclusions calculus.* The basic idea is to use the unique fault process in two ways: either to seek diagnoses which may appear in the same causal process or to seek diagnoses which may not appear in the same causal process; a simplified formulation is: "two concepts without causal relationships are exclusive".

Practically, the results of this interpretation consist of *mutual-exclusions* – i.e. two concepts of the domain cannot belong to the same solution – as opposed to *mutual-compatibilities.*

The reality is obviously more complex insofar as the causal relationships may be transitive or not: "A may cause B" and "B may cause C" do not imply "A may cause C". These problems of "weak transitivity" have been treated in cognitive science by Johnson-Laird (1980) as well as in the AI framework (Szolovits *et al.*, 1988;

David & Krivine, 1989). Our choice is to ask the expert about the plausibility of chains of causally-related events such as A and C. Also, mutual-exclusion or mutual-compatibilities are retained conditional to the transitivity (or non-transitivity) attributed by the expert to the successive causal relationships.

The benefit of this interpretation is twofold:

- The causal network is validated. For example, the expert may not agree with the result of the system – e.g a mutual-exclusion relation between two diagnoses – and be led to add new causal relationships to justify its position – e.g. that the two concepts above are compatible.
- The unique fault process hypothesis is operationalized in heuristic knowledge through mutual-exclusions.

The exclusion calculus algorithm is optimized for computing this knowledge at the highest level in the hierarchical representation of the domain concepts (Charlet & Gascuel, 1989). For example, based on the causal network represented in figure 2, we have the interaction between the expert and the system described in figure 3.

Abduction on causal relationships. This method proposes a different but direct logical interpretation of causal relationships. It is accepted to be useful in medicine (Szolovits *et al.*, 1988) and more generally in diagnostic tasks. Its principle – the principle of the abduction – is as follows: "if I know that Q is true and P may cause Q, then I can suppose that P is true". The abduction process transforms "P may cause Q" into "Q $\Rightarrow$ P".

For example, if ACTE knows that APPENDICITIS may cause PERITONITIS, it proposes to the expert the following rule: "PERITONITIS $\Rightarrow$ APPENDICITIS". The implicit purpose is to ask the expert whether PERITONITIS always has APPENDICITIS as a cause.

Formal derivation. The interpretation of taxonomic links is performed by a rewriting process, the formal derivation. In a standard context no any condition is required in order to perform this rewriting process. In our uncertain context some conditions appear: as for the causal relationships, the meaning of the taxonomic links depends on the domain object which are linked and the task to be realized. Explicit formulation of underlying relationships of low granularity of the taxonomic link allows a precise parametrization of the meaning of this link. This parametrization is performed by the expert in accepting or discarding and/or giving a certainty factor to the production rules which represent interpretations of taxonomic links. So, ACTE enables the expert to control precisely how the knowledge is used for the task which has to be performed.

Let us consider an example. How can the taxonomic knowledge K: "A is-a S, B is-a S, and C is-a S" of which an interpretation could be (S $\Leftrightarrow$ A OR B OR C), be used? The formal derivation of K give the 10 following production rules:

Do you agree with the following mutual-compatibilities:
APPENDICITIS and OBSTRUCTION are compatible (y/n)? y
VASCULAR-DISEASE and FUNCTIONAL-OBSTRUCTION are compatible (y/n)? y
ORGANIC-OBSTRUCTION and FUNCTIONAL-OBSTRUCTION are compatible (y/n)? n
Caution. Refusing this compatibility may question the model or generate an exclusion relationship between the two above diagnoses. (1) You refuse the model, (2) you refuse only the compatibility, (3) you agree with the compatibility (1/2/3)? 2

Do you agree with the following mutual-exclusions:
DIGESTIVE-DISEASE and URINARY-DISEASE are exclusive (y/n) ? y
VASCULAR-DISEASE and URINARY-DISEASE are exclusive (y/n) ? y
OBSTRUCTION and URINARY-TRACT-INFECTION are exclusive (y/n) ? y
OBSTRUCTION and PYELONEPHRITIS are exclusive (y/n) ? y
RENAL-COLIC and URINARY-TRACT-INFECTION are exclusive (y/n) ? y
URINARY-TRACT-INFECTION and PYELONEPHRITIS are exclusive (y/n) ? n
RENAL-COLIC and PYELONEPHRITIS are exclusive (y/n) ? y
VASCULAR-DISEASE and APPENDICITIS are exclusive (y/n) ? y
ORGANIC-OBSTRUCTION and URINARY-DISEASE are exclusive (y/n) ? y
PERITONITIS and URINARY-DISEASE are exclusive (y/n) ? n

Generated mutual-exclusions :

ORGANIC-OBSTRUCTION and FUNCTIONAL-OBSTRUCTION are exclusive
DIGESTIVE-DISEASE and URINARY-DISEASE are exclusive
VASCULAR-DISEASE and URINARY-DISEASE are exclusive
OBSTRUCTION and URINARY-TRACT-INFECTION are exclusive
OBSTRUCTION and PYELONEPHRITIS are exclusive
RENAL-COLIC and URINARY-TRACT-INFECTION are exclusive
RENAL-COLIC and PYELONEPHRITIS are exclusive
VASCULAR-DISEASE and APPENDICITIS are exclusive
ORGANIC-OBSTRUCTION and URINARY-DISEASE are exclusive

Fig. 3. Interaction between ACTE and the expert about the causal network described in the preceding figure

$P_1 : A \Rightarrow S$
$P_2 : B \Rightarrow S$
$P_3 : C \Rightarrow S$
$P_4 : \neg S \Rightarrow \neg A$
$P_5 : \neg S \Rightarrow \neg B$
$P_6 : \neg S \Rightarrow \neg C$

$P_7 : S \wedge \neg B \wedge \neg C \Rightarrow A$
$P_8 : S \wedge \neg C \wedge \neg A \Rightarrow B$
$P_9 : S \wedge \neg A \wedge \neg B \Rightarrow C$
$P_{10} : \neg A \wedge \neg B \wedge \neg C \Rightarrow \neg S$

After interpretation these rules could be used by the inference system. But, in our uncertain medical domain a plain formal derivation (replacing K by P_1 to P_{10}) is not always possible. Let us illustrate this with a medical example; given S, A, B and C :

S : URINARY-DISEASE

A : RENAL-COLIC

B : URINARY-TRACT-INFECTION

C : PYELONEPHRITIS

The knowledge K is therefore "the specializations of URINARY-DISEASE are RENAL-COLIC, URINARY-TRACT-INFECTION, and PYELONEPHRITIS". K can be considered as acceptable (it is true 9 times out of 10); URINARY-CANCER however, not represented here, could also lead to abdominal acute pain syndromes. Conversely, the proposition P_9: "URINARY-DISEASE $\wedge$ ¬RENAL-COLIC $\wedge$ ¬URINARY-TRACT-INFECTION $\Rightarrow$ PYELONEPHRITIS" is not acceptable: in fact, in the context of URINARY-DISEASE, PYELONEPHRITIS and URINARY-CANCER are both diagnoses of the same weak occurrence with regard to the other diagnoses. The proposition "URINARY-DISEASE $\wedge$ ¬RENAL-COLIC $\wedge$ ¬URINARY-TRACT-INFECTION $\Rightarrow$ URINARY-CANCER" is true (or false) like P_9 and both are true 1 time out of 2: they are not acceptable.

The syntactic manipulation which produces P_9 from K has a poor reliability when K is uncertain. The solution is to allow the expert to intervene in the interpretation in accepting or discarding and/or giving a certainty factor to the production rule – i.e. allow the expert to check the interpretation process. But, if we know that some taxonomies are not exhaustive, why propose interpretations exploiting exhaustiveness? It is worth remembering that we are in an uncertain framework but that we should maximize the use of our knowledge within this framework: these interpretations are efficient inference carriers and it would be a pity to do without them. It is necessary to select the valid derivation from several possibilities. In this case we should ask the expert to validate a derivated knowledge. But the questions asked to the expert should be opportune and the number of these questions should be as small as possible. Knowledge guiding these questions is sometimes logical but most of the time it is heuristic. Examples of heuristics are (i) *when a taxonomy is believed non-exhaustive it is necessary to ask the expert about generated rules exploiting exhaustiveness of this taxonomy* or, (ii) *when two elements A_i and A_j (some diseases) of a taxonomy such as $S \Leftrightarrow \bigvee_{i=1}^{n} A_i$ are causaly-related events (as in 4.2) it is necessary to ask the expert about generated rules such as $S \bigwedge_{i=1, i \neq j}^{n} \neg A_i \Rightarrow A_j$*. Obviously, taking into account these links supposes their preliminary validation by the exclusion calculus (see 4.2).

Such heuristics lead to a non-optimal number of questions. Some of the question may not be necessary to avoid non-relevant interpretations; but we prefer too many questions rather than generating non-relevant rules or leaving relevant rules out. In our example, the expert has been asked about interpretations P_7 to P_{10}; he discarded P_9 and P_{10}, and accepted P_7 and P_8.

One might put forward the argument that giving precise knowledge straightaway would be better. But it is generally difficult to acquire and organize knowledge especially when it is dynamic (such as inference rules). From our experience, it seems better to let the expert give rough knowledge and to help him to refine it[8]. Formal derivation of taxonomic links is an example of this process.

---

[8] In the KADS methodology, the best way seems too to build a model and refine it (Wielinga & Breuker, 1986).

Semiological Knowledge Interpretation. The interpretation of semiological knowledge deals with (i) data-abstraction (Clancey, 1986) and (ii) abduction paradigms.

Data-Abstraction. This data-abstraction paradigm is used in the following ways:

- On abstractions given by the expert. The expert may declare some abstraction as a syndrome or clinical features. In this case ACTE aims at checking these abstractions and their use in the causal network – e.g. by asking the expert about the relevance of such an abstraction if it's not used in order to trigger hypotheses.
- In order to generate new abstractions. ACTE may generate new data-abstraction depending on the use of the signs – i.e. data – in the semiological relationships. For example, by proposing a new abstraction of a sign conjunction if this sign conjunction is used several times in order to trigger hypotheses; the expert may name this new "syndrome" in order to re-use it.

Abduction. The abduction method applied on the semiological knowledge gives the same results than on the pathophysiological knowledge (see above). For example if ACTE knows that "OMBILICAL-PAIN evokes APPENDICITIS" it proposes to derive the implication: "OMBILICAL-PAIN ⇒ APPENDICITIS". The implicit purpose consists in asking the expert if OMBILICAL-PAIN is almost always sign of APPENDICITIS.

Organization. The different steps of the KA process are organized in a logical way. For example, pathophysiological knowledge is acquired before semiological knowledge, the latter depending on the former at the level of the disease. In the same way, the interpretation of the causal relationships is possible only if they have been validated by the exclusion calculus: actually, exclusion calculus may modify the the causal model and discard some causal relationships.

In a general way, the implementation of the problem-solving methods generate two types of interaction with the expert: (i) consistency checking of knowledge given by the expert and (ii) validation by the expert of the interpretation proposed by the tool. Obviously, the former should be performed before the latter.

5 Medical Application

5.1 Implementation

ACTE has been applied to LÉZARD, a medical diagnosis reasoning system for discriminating between diseases in the domain of acute abdominal pain. This application is described in (Charlet, 1989). We recall the main characteristics of this experiment and interesting facts which appeared during the KA phase.

In the project definition our goal was to create a medical diagnosis reasoning system for discriminating between diseases in emergency conditions. We had at our disposal a surgery data-base[9] of 6732 patients in the domain of acute abdominal pain. This domain seemed a good test for ACTE as it provided: (i) important and real complexity of the domain, (ii) knowledge incompleteness justifying an explicit account of uncertainty, and (iii) a large sample of data.

We now discuss the results of this application from the viewpoint of both the KA process and the performance of the final system.

5.2 Results

The declaration of the taxonomies was easy for the expert to do: The choice of the leaf diseases – i.e. leaf nodes in the taxonomies – was imposed by the classification of the ARC & AURC data-base. The causal model was described by the expert with 135 objects linked by approximately 145 relationships. These objects were signs (90), syndromes (11) and diseases (34). The links between the diseases were taxonomic links (27) and causal links (39). The signs were linked by 48 abstraction relationships (creating also syndromes and clinical features) and linked to the diseases by approximatively 200 links.

ACTE interpreted the causal model and generated about 500 questions which were put to the expert. Among these questions, some were asked about the types of the objects and their reliability ($\approx$ 250). Other questions were illustrated in the exclusion calculus step (cf. section 4.2). Figure 4 does the same at the formal derivation step.

Two remarks could be made about the acceptance by the expert of the questions and generated rules:

- Some rules about exclusion seemed strange to the expert ($\approx$ 20 to 80 generated rules). Actually, these rules are generated at the highest level of abstraction and do not correspond to the expert expertise because the abstraction level of the two objects involved in the rules are different. Nevertheless some of them were accepted.
- The number of questions ($\approx$ 500) seemed high. But it is necessary to consider this number with regard to the pertinence of these questions. Half the questions tend to structure the knowledge area of the expert: he did not doubt their relevance. The situation regarding the other questions is more complex (cf. supra).

1200 rules were included in the final knowledge base. Less than 100 rules were used by the inference engine during a diagnostic run on each case of the data-base. The 2000 rules which would have been included in the knowledge base if the expert had accepted all the generated rules is a good indicator of the total number of possible interpretations of the causal model.

The results of the LÉZARD system on the ARC & AURC data-base (with the knowledge base generated with ACTE) have been compared with those of a bayesian system: we can note that they are close to but lower than those of the bayesian system. Conversely, on the diseases with a low occurrence in the data-base LÉZARD gives better results. This is a first – pragmatic – justification of our approach[10]. Nevertheless, we noted that this domain was not well suited for a modelling task. Actually, in the acute abdominal pain domain we are faced with a unit of localization, the abdomen, but multiple physiological systems are taken into account. In contrast,

---

[9] This data-base has been provided to us by the Association pour la Recherche Chirurgicale & Association Universitaire pour la Recherche Chirurgicale (ARC & AURC).

Certain generated rules (Automatically):

◇ APPENDICITIS ⇒ DIGESTIVE-DISEASE
◇ ORGANIC-OBSTRUCTION ⇒ DIGESTIVE-DISEASE
◇ ¬DIGESTIVE-DISEASE ⇒ ¬APPENDICITIS
◇ ¬DIGESTIVE-DISEASE ⇒ ¬ORGANIC-OBSTRUCTION
◇ ORGANIC-OBSTRUCTION ⇒ OBSTRUCTION
◇ FUNCTIONAL-OBSTRUCTION ⇒ OBSTRUCTION
◇ ¬OBSTRUCTION ⇒ ¬ORGANIC-OBSTRUCTION
◇ ¬OBSTRUCTION ⇒ ¬FUNCTIONAL-OBSTRUCTION
◇ URINARY-TRACT-INFECTION ⇒ URINARY-DISEASE
◇ RENAL-COLIC ⇒ URINARY-DISEASE
◇ PYELONEPHRITIS ⇒ URINARY-DISEASE
◇ ¬URINARY-DISEASE ⇒ ¬URINARY-TRACT-INFECTION
◇ ¬URINARY-DISEASE ⇒ ¬RENAL-COLIC
◇ ¬URINARY-DISEASE ⇒ ¬PYELONEPHRITIS
◇ MESENTERIC-INFARCTUS ⇒ VASCULAR-DISEASE
◇ ¬VASCULAR-DISEASE ⇒ ¬MESENTERIC-INFARCTUS

Uncertain generated rules exploiting exhaustiveness of taxonomies (questions):

◇ ¬FUNCTIONAL-OBSTRUCTION ∧ ¬ORGANIC-OBSTRUCTION
  ⇒¬OBSTRUCTION
◇ ¬FUNCTIONAL-OBSTRUCTION ∧ OBSTRUCTION
  ⇒ORGANIC-OBSTRUCTION
◇ ¬ORGANIC-OBSTRUCTION ∧ OBSTRUCTION
  ⇒FUNCTIONAL-OBSTRUCTION
◇ ¬URINARY-TRACT-INFECTION ∧ ¬RENAL-COLIC
  ∧ ¬PYELONEPHRITIS ⇒ ¬URINARY-DISEASE
◇ ¬RENAL-COLIC ∧ ¬PYELONEPHRITIS
  ∧ URINARY-DISEASE ⇒ URINARY-TRACT-INFECTION
◇ ¬PYELONEPHRITIS ∧ ¬URINARY-TRACT-INFECTION
  ∧ URINARY-DISEASE ⇒ RENAL-COLIC
◇ ¬URINARY-TRACT-INFECTION ∧ ¬RENAL-COLIC
  ∧ URINARY-DISEASE ⇒ PYELONEPHRITIS

Fig. 4. Rules generated from the preceding semantic network.

the cardio-vascular system is for example a unique physiological system and is well suited for a modelling task. These results are discussed in (Charlet, 1989).

---

[10] These results come from the fact that even if the learning sample is large some diagnoses are always insufficiently represented in order to be learned by the bayesian system. ACTE does not have such problems and this is due to the "expert system" approach.

6 Discussion

6.1 Related works

In this section we discuss features of ACTE with regard to two systems: MOLE, developed by Eshelman (1988), and ADÈLE, a KA tool (Cordier & Reynaud, 1991; Reynaud, 1993) currently applied to a medical diagnosis reasoning system for electromyography – i.e. diagnosing muscle and peripheral nerve disorders by electrical measurements.

Mole. The underlying modelling technique of MOLE is characterized by the "role-limiting method" approach (see 2.1). Our work has also been influenced by some consequent features of this approach: for example, the fact that the expert is not required to describe anything more than an under-specified network before starting the KA process or the efforts which have been directed toward not bothering the expert with unnecessary questions.

Like MOLE, ACTE makes heuristic assumptions about the world, allowing limits and constraints in the determination of the knowledge to be acquired. Some of these assumptions play a similar role in the KA process of the two systems. Nevertheless, similar assumptions may lead to different expressions of the corresponding problem-solving methods. It may also be interesting to compare the results – in knowledge base terms – given by the assumption of *Exclusivity* in MOLE and the assumption of *unicity of the fault process* in ACTE.

Nevertheless, the main difference between the two systems is the use of the causal model: in MOLE this model is constructed during the KA process without constraints on its structure. In ACTE an explicit causal model is defined with a hierarchical structure. This description is more restrictive but allows global checking and validation about the knowledge to be acquired.

Adèle. ADÈLE is used for the refinement and the extension of an already existing heuristic knowledge-base by using causal models. ADÈLE is composed of two knowledge-bases: the HKB which is represented by production rules (and will form the operational knowledge-base) and the CKB which is composed of causal models and is represented in a semantic network formalism. The KA process within ADÈLE is as follows: the expert expresses a production rule encoding heuristic knowledge. Abductive reasoning based on the causal knowledge-base provides justifications that can be regarded as proofs of the association between the premises and the conclusion of the rule. An analysis of the justifications provides the expert with information on the nature of the link between premises and conclusion, the strength of this link, the roles played by the conditions, and the discriminating power of the conditions over the conclusion.

ADÈLE and ACTE are closely related; in particular their CKB and HKB are the same with regard to the nature of the modelled links. Nevertheless, specific differences must be quoted. They do not refer to the interpretation model of the task being modelled in the same way. ACTE assumes a fixed interpretation model and interprets the causal model in this framework in order to create heuristic rules. Conversely,

ADÈLE takes heuristic rules and verifies that these rules are plausible interpretations of a causal model. Both of these approaches are complementary: ACTE instantiates a conceptual model in order to build a heuristic and operational knowledge-base while ADÈLE validates chunks of an implicit conceptual model included in new heuristic rules.

6.2 About Causal Models

In this section we discuss the nature of the causal model used in the ACTE tool. Three viewpoints will be emphasized: the nature of the causal model (i) in terms of deepening of knowledge, (ii) in terms of global signification of the causal model and, (iii) in terms of origin of the causal model.

Compilation vs. Acquisition. The KA process of the ACTE tool may appear a priori as a compilation of deep knowledge into shallow knowledge. But the terms deep and shallow knowledge are not appropriate for describing the KA process as noted by Davis (1989):

> *They are still vague to the point of meaninglessness, engender pointless arguments, and say nothing technical. There are* models of structure and behavior, *organized by components and connections, that attempt to capture the causality in a device; models can also be organized by process. As an alternative we might reason from* empirical association *that reflect useful inferences without capturing structure, behavior, or causality.*

Moreover, a compilation – i.e. a rewriting –, without a precise goal is without interest. What is interesting is taken to be refining knowledge or generating new knowledge from the causal model (Davis, 1989; Pitrat, 1990).

In this context, ACTE has some interesting features: firstly, it allows to generate operational empirical associations directed by the specific task – e.g. diagnostic – to be realized; secondly, it proposes a new description of the behavior of the final system at a good level of abstraction in order to take into account the interpretation and uncertainty problematics.

Fault vs. Correct behavior Model. We have seen in section 2.2 that causal models attempt to represent the domain theory. Let us define two types of causal models, each of them referring to a different domain theory. The first type is related to *models of correct behavior*. These models are usually characterized by their completeness. The ability to obtain models of correct behavior proves that the domain is well defined. In such a domain – e.g. in qualitative physics – the KA process is easier to perform and the models of correct behavior are helpful for design systems as well as for diagnostic systems, among others. The second type, dealing with *fault models*, characterizes domains in which no model of correct behavior can be obtained. In such domains, which is often the case in medicine, only partial models are available because of the incomplete understanding of the underlying processes. Therefore in such domains, fault models are necessary to perform diagnostic tasks[11]. In this work, the only causal models which we refer to are fault models. As pointed out above, these fault models can be used for reasoning, justification as well as for KA. ACTE is a good illustration of a fault model which is used for KA.

Causal vs. Heuristic Knowledge. From our experience, we distinguish two classes of causal models in KA. Each of them has its own interests, raises different kinds of difficulties, and solves different kinds of problems as well (Charlet *et al.*, 1992):

- **Bottom-up-designed causal models.** These models are designed independently of the KA process. They generally come from pre-existing models (design models, handbooks or tutorial manuals). They often describe "how things work" or "how things fail". ADÈLE fits in with this definition.
- **Top-down-designed causal models.** These models are directly issued from the main KA process. They frequently appear as justifications of elicited knowledge ("why are you telling me that?"). Thus, using top-down-designed causal models often leads to simultaneously run two distinct KA processes: the main KA process (to acquire what we have called "heuristic knowledge") and the design of the causal model itself. Therefore, top-down-designed causal models are more useful to extend the knowledge-base over a broader domain area.

Bottom-up-designed causal models provides a different viewpoint of the domain (different with regard to the HKB and because its source is different from the source of heuristic knowledge, usually an expert). The combination of these two visions of the same domain may be very fruitful, especially in terms of validation of the heuristic level, but may also be difficult to achieve. Let us note that, in ACTE applied to LÉZARD, the same expert was the source of both the causal model and the heuristic knowledge. It is worth noting that top-down designed causal models and heuristic knowledge are also two different viewpoints. However the former is derived from the latter, and thus its role is rather a role of "internal consistency in the expert discourse" than a validation of what is acquired.

The causal model in ACTE can be qualified as a "bottom-up-designed causal model" because CKB may well come from existing models directly extracted from medical textbooks. Nevertheless, this model has been designed for a particular discrimination diagnostic task, with well known signs and diagnoses. Moreover, the CKB is checked during the KA process. In this way, we can say that the term causal model, in ACTE, mainly refers to a "top-down-designed causal model". These problems are discussed in (Charlet *et al.*, 1992). The causal model of MOLE, built during the KA process, refers to a "top-down-designed causal model".

7   Conclusion

We have presented ACTE, a tool designed to assist in KA for a diagnostic task. We have illustrated how the conceptual model guides the KA process and structures the knowledge base. Moreover, we have shown how causal knowledge – i.e. a causal

---

[11] In that case the fault model does not totally respect the definition of the causal model from the section 2.2. It includes knowledge about the diagnostic task to be performed by the KBS.

514

model – which is not diagnostic specific may be interpreted by the interpretation model in order to build an operational knowledge base dedicated to a specific task. Another feature of ACTE is to have the system interpret the acquired knowledge and propose to the expert the interpreted knowledge at a non-ambiguous level; our claim being that the expert must intervene in the KA process in order to check the interpretation – i.e. to reinterpret – of the knowledge symbolic system.

In the ACTE workbench the causal model plays a role in the KA process from the state where an interpretation model exists. In the KA framework defined in the introduction this corresponds to the step of instantiation of the conceptual model (iii). Nevertheless, causal models can play a role in other steps of the KA process: for example, in order to help defining the problem-solving methods of the interpretation model (step ii). Actually, these methods depend on the concepts – and their role – defined in the causal model and consequently this causal model influences these method definitions. Some experiments should be done in this direction.

Acknowledgments

Discussions with Jean-Paul Krivine, Chantal Reynaud and Bruno Bachimont helped to shape and direct the above thoughts. Thanks to Jacques Bouaud for his comments on this paper.

References

AUSSENAC-GILLES, N., KRIVINE, J.-P. & SALLANTIN, J. (1992). Introduction to the special issue on knowledge acquisition. *Revue d'Intelligence Artificielle*, 6(1–2), 7–18. (In French).

BONISSONE, P. (1987). Reasoning, plausible. In S. SHAPIRO, Ed., *Encyclopedia of Artificial Intelligence*. J. Wiley & Sons, Inc.

BOOSE, J. H. & BRADSHAW, J. M. (1987). Expertise transfer and complex problems: using aquinas as a knowledge acquisition workbench for expert systems. *International Journal of Man-Machine Studies*, 26(1), 3–28.

BYLANDER, T. & MITTAL, S. (1986). CSRL: A language for classificatory problem solving and uncertainty handling. *The Artificial Intelligence Magazine*.

CHANDRASEKARAN, B. (1987). Towards a functional architecture for intelligence based on generic information processing tasks. In *Proceedings of the 10th International Joint Conference on Artificial Intelligence*, pp. 1183–1192. Milan, Italy.

CHARLET, J. (1989). *LÉZARD : Knowledge Acquisition and Uncertainty Management in a Second Generation Expert System*. PhD thesis, Université Paris VI. (In French).

CHARLET, J. & GASCUEL, O. (1989). Knowledge acquisition by causal model and meta-knowledge. In J. H. BOOSE, B. R. GAINES & J. G. GANASCIA, Eds., *Proceedings of the 3rd European Workshop on Knowledge Acquisition for Knowledge-Based Systems*, pp. 212–225. Paris, France.

CHARLET, J., KRIVINE, J.-P. & REYNAUD, C. (1992). Causal model-based knowledge acquisition tools: Discussion of experiments. In *Proceedings of the 6th European Workshop on Knowledge Acquisition for Knowledge-Based Systems*. Heidelberg, Germany.

CLANCEY, W. J. (1985). Heuristic Classification. *Artificial Intelligence*, 27(3), 289–350.

CLANCEY, W. J. (1986). From GUIDON to NEOMYCIN and HERACLES in twenty short lessons: ORN final report 1979-1985. *The Artificial Intelligence Magazine*.

CORDIER, M.-O. & REYNAUD, C. (1991). Knowledge acquisition techniques and second generation expert systems. *Applied Artificial Intelligence*, 5(3), 209–226.

DAVID, J.-M. & KRIVINE, J.-P. (1989). Augmenting experience-based diagnosis with causal reasoning. *Applied Artificial Intelligence*, 3(2-3), 239–248.

DAVIS, R. (1989). Form and content in model based reasoning. In *Proceedings of the IJCAI workshop on Model-Based reasoning*.

ESHELMAN, L. (1988). MOLE: a knowledge acquisition tool for cover-and-differentiate systems. In S. MARCUS, Ed., *Automating Knowledge Acquisition for Expert Systems*. Kluwer Academic Publishers.

GASCUEL, O., CHARLET, J., GENETET, S. & MARI, B. (1985). The LÉZARD system: a work on uncertain reasoning. In *Proceedings of the 5th International Workshop Expert Systems & their Applications*. Avignon, France: Gerfau. (In French).

D. GENTNER & A. L. STEVENS, Eds. (1983). *Mental Models*. Lauwrence Erlbaum Associates, Publishers.

GRUBER, T. (1991). Learning why by being told what. *IEEE-Expert*, x, 65–75.

JOHNSON-LAIRD, P. N. (1980). Mental models in cognitive science. *Cognitive Science*, 4, 71–115.

KARBACH, W., LINSTER, M. & VOSS, A. (1990). Models, methods, roles and tasks: many labels – one idea? *Knowledge Acquisition*, 2, 279–299.

LONG, W., NAIMI, S., CRISCITIELLO, M. G., PAUKER, S. G. & SZOLOVITS, P. (1984). An aid to physiological reasoning in the management of cardiovascular disease. In *Proceedings of the Computers in Cardiology Conference*.

MARCUS, S. (1988). SALT: a knowledge acquisition tool for propose-and-revise systems. In S. MARCUS, Ed., *Automating Knowledge Acquisition for Expert Systems*. Kluwer Academic Publishers.

MOINARD, Y. (1987). Donner la préférence au défaut le plus spécifique. In *Proceedings of the 6th Conference RFIA-AFCET*, pp. 1123–1132. Antibes, France: Dunod.

MOTTA, E., RAJAN, T. & EISENSTADT, M. (1990). Knowledge acquisition as a process of model refinement. *Knowledge Acquisition*, 2, 21–49.

MUSEN, M. A. (1989). *Automated generation of Model-Based Knowledge Acquisition Tools*. Research notes in Artificial Intelligence. Los Altos, California: Morgan Kaufmann Publishers.

NECHES, R., SWARTOUT, W. & MOORE, J. (1985). Explainable (and maintainable) expert systems. In A. JOSHI, Ed., *Proceedings of the 9th International Joint Conference on Artificial Intelligence*, pp. 382–389. Los Angeles, CA: M. Kaufmann, Inc.

NEWELL, A. (1982). The knowledge level. *Artificial Intelligence*, 18, 87–127.

NORMAN, D. A. (1983). Some observations on mental models. In D. GENTNER & A. L. STEVENS, Eds., *Mental Models* chapter 1, pp. 7–14. Lauwrence Erlbaum Associates, Publishers.

PITRAT, J. (1990). *Métaconnaissance, Futur de l'intelligence artificielle*. Paris: Hermès.

PYLYSHYN, Z. W. (1987). Cognitive science. In SHAPIRO, Ed., *Encyclopedia of Artificial Intelligence*, pp. 120–124. Wiley-Interscience.

REYNAUD, C. (1993). Acquisition and validation of expert knowledge by using causal models. In J.-M. DAVID, J.-P. KRIVINE & R. SIMMONS, Eds., *Second Generation Expert Systems*. Springer Verlag. *In this book*.

SCHREIBER, A. T., WIELINGA, B. J. & BREUKER, J. A. (1991). The KADS framework for modeling expertise. In J. H. BOOSE, B. R. GAINES & D. SMEED, Eds., *Proceedings of the 5th European Workshop on Knowledge Acquisition for Knowledge-Based Systems*. Glasgow, UK: Springer Verlag. *(To appear)*.

STICKLEN, J., CHANDRASEKARAN, B. & BOND, W. E. (1988). Distributed causal reasoning for knowledge acquisition: A functional approach to device understanding. In

516

Proceedings of the 3rd *Banff Workshop for Knowledge Acquisition.* Banff, Canada. (Revised version: *Applied AI* 3(2-3):275–304,1989).

SZOLOVITS, P., PATIL, R. S. & SCHWARTZ, W. B. (1988). Artificial intelligence in medical diagnostic. *Annals of Internal Medicine*, 108, 80–87.

VINKHUYZEN, R. E. (1992). On the non-existence of knowledge level models. In B. NEUMANN, Ed., *Proceedings of the 10*th *European Conference on Artificial Intelligence*, pp. 620–622. Vienna, Austria.

WIELINGA, B. J. & BREUKER, J. A. (1986). Models of expertise. In *Proceedings of the 7*th *European Conference on Artificial Intelligence.* Brighton, UK.

WIELINGA, B. J., SCHREIBER, A. T. & BREUKER, J. A. (1992). KADS: a modelling approach to knowledge engineering. *Knowledge Acquisition*, 4(1), 5–54.

Acquisition and Validation of Expert Knowledge by using Causal Models

Chantal Reynaud

Laboratoire de Recherche en Informatique, Bât. 490, Université Paris-Sud
91405 Orsay Cedex – France
cr@lri.lri.fr

Abstract. In this paper, we present techniques to support knowledge acquisition and validation within the framework of SGES. Our approach can be called a causal model-based knowledge acquisition process. It applies to a KBS composed of two knowledge bases : the expert knowledge base referring to the heuristic level is represented by production rules and will form the operational knowledge base, and the causal knowledge base composed of causal models. When new expert knowledge (a production rule) is acquired, abductive reasoning based on causal models provides justifications which are then analyzed with appropriate criteria. These justifications are useful for refining and extending an initial expert knowledge base: they can be used to propose explanations, to comment on rules, to control them, to suggest modifications or other rules. Our approach has been applied to the design of a medical diagnostic reasoning system for electromyography. Examples in this field are used in the paper.

1 Introduction

The design of a Knowledge Based System (KBS) is a laborious process. One step is to build a model of expertise. The aim is to specify the knowledge of the domain, the problem-solving methods and the tasks of a KBS. This is a question of knowledge acquisition. This problem is particularly difficult because of the conceptual gap between the form in which knowledge is described in the natural discourse by experts and the form it is represented in an operational KBS.

To make the process easier, knowledge acquisition is more and more considered as a modelling task in four steps: knowledge elicitation, conceptual model design, conceptual model instantiation, operationalization (Aussenac-Gilles *et al.*, 1992). The conceptual model defined in step two is a very solid foundation for knowledge acquisition. The role and place of the specific domain knowledge to be acquired is clearly defined (Clancey, 1985; Wielinga & Breuker, 1985; Chandrasekaran, 1987). For this reason, many tools exploit this fact and belong to a family of knowledge acquisition tools which get their power by taking particular care of the problem-solving method used by performance systems: (MOLE (Eshelman, 1988), MORE (Kahn *et al.*, 1985), SALT (Marcus, 1988)). All these tools play a major role during the step of instantiation of a conceptual model (step three) because their aim is to provide an instantiated conceptual model of an application. The designed model refers to the modelization of the heuristic level which will be operationalized in the KBS.

Here, we present an alternative approach to support the knowledge acquisition activity. It is similar with respect to its role in the knowledge acquisition process (it contributes to the design of an instantiated conceptual model although not any explicit conceptual model is used) but is very different regarding the ways of contributing to the conceptual model instantiation step. The original feature of our approach is to consider the problem of knowledge acquisition (confined to step three) within the framework of Second Generation Expert Systems (SGES). SGES aim firstly, at providing expert systems with a better understanding of the domain in which they must work and secondly, at making problem-solving methods more explicit. Because a real-life problem can only be solved by implementing various problem-solving models and methods, SGES try to instigate cooperation of all these different models and methods (Chandrasekaran & Mittal, 1983; Chittaro et al., 1989; Console et al., 1989b; David & Krivine, 1989). They are more structured systems and consequently important advantages lie in knowledge acquisition and explanation (Reynaud, 1991). Our approach applies to such systems (SGES) and tries to benefit from all these advantages.

Several approaches to knowledge acquisition within the framework of SGES have been proposed in the last few years. Apparently, as SGES are composed of several models, several different phases of knowledge acquisition are necessary to build such systems. In this paper, we shall focus only on heuristic knowledge acquisition.

Surprisingly, some contributions within the framework of SGES have shown that, in such systems, the choice of deeper rather than empirical[1] models can simplify the problem of knowledge acquisition. As some models (or knowledge bases) may be more easily described and in a more natural way than others, a solution is to acquire only one of the knowledge bases from the domain expert and to derive the other one(s) from it. Obviously, the only acquired knowledge will be the most easily acquired one.

So, some proposals have been made in the last few years to derive heuristic from causal knowledge. In (Steels, 1985), heuristic knowledge acquisition is seen as a learning process and new rules can be learned by examining results of deep reasoning. In (Console et al., 1989a), heuristic knowledge is automatically derived from causal one, the only knowledge base acquired from the domain expert. Such a causal knowledge base is introduced in the diagnostic system using NEED, a graphical causal network editor with many facilities to simplify the phase of knowledge acquisition. In (Charlet & Gascuel, 1989; Charlet, 1993), the expert provides domain knowledge in a causal model framework. The causal model, just obtained and taken as a whole, is firstly analyzed while interacting with the expert so as to check its consistency. Secondly, in order to generate heuristic knowledge, each relation is analyzed separately and interpreted in the light of the problem-solving methods of the performance system. Finally, the generated heuristic level may be refined by the expert.

Previously mentioned in other works, our approach considers the problem of knowledge acquisition within the framework of SGES and particularly in the framework of systems in which heuristic and causal models cooperate. Yet, we don't try to generate a heuristic from a causal level but to validate a heuristic level using

---

[1] This kind of model refers to heuristic knowledge (experience-based knowledge) which models the expert-like kind of reasoning. Each piece of knowledge encodes associationnal or derivative links.

causal models. In our approach, the causal and the heuristic knowledge base are totally independent. This is not the case in approaches described above. Heuristic knowledge is acquired independently of the acquisition of causal knowledge and we assume it is possible to acquire an initial heuristic knowledge base. Yet, the initial heuristic knowledge base or pieces of heuristic knowledge may be incomplete, and require to be checked. So, we take advantage from a modelization of another view point (causal models which generally develop out of existing models) which provides interesting results to validate acquired heuristic knowledge.

More precisely, our approach can be called a causal model-based knowledge acquisition process (CMBKAP) and it has been applied to the design of ADELE, a causal model-based knowledge acquisition tool. It applies to a KBS composed of two knowledge bases: the expert[2] knowledge base (EKB) refering to the heuristic level, is represented by production rules and will form the operational KB, and the causal knowledge base (CKB) composed of causal models. When new expert knowledge (a production rule) is acquired, abductive reasoning based on causal models provide justifications which can be regarded as proofs of the association between the conditions and the conclusion of the rule. These justifications are useful to support the knowledge acquisition process: they can be used to propose explanations, to comment on the rule, to control it, to suggest modifications or other rules.

Our approach has been applied to the design of a medical diagnostic reasoning system for electromyography[3]. Examples in this field will be used in the paper. Other applications to this specific domain are developed, among these, the project P599 supported in part by the EEC Esprit Program (Andreassen et al., 1987). It also involves knowledge acquisition particularly estimating conditional probabilities in a causal probabilistic network for interpretation of electromyographic findings. The method restricts possible choices of probabilities by using "deep knowledge" i.e. models of pathophysiological processes as found in medical textbooks and papers.

This paper is organized as follows. We first give a general description of our approach. In section 3, we describe the Causal Knowledge Base, CKB, according to its structure and the way it must be designed. Then (section 4) we outline how CKB is used to compute explanations for pieces of expert knowledge. In section 5, appropriate criteria for analysing explanations are identified whilst the last section (section 6) focuses on the way the knowledge acquisition activity can take advantage of the analysis on explanations of expert knowledge and presents an example of a session with the ADELE system in the field of electromyography.

2 Overview of the approach

ADELE is composed of two knowledge bases: the Expert Knowledge Base denoted EKB and the Causal Knowledge Base denoted CKB.

---

[2] This kind of knowledge can only be obtained from domain experts unlike causal knowledge (in our approach). This is why it is called "expert" knowledge.

[3] Electromyography is a diagnosis of muscles and peripheral nerves disorders by electrical measurements.

EKB is composed of production rules[4] noted "Cond $\rightarrow$ Cl" where Cond = $cond_1$ AND $cond_2$ AND ... AND $cond_n$ and Cl = cl_1 AND cl_2 AND ... AND cl_m. Cond and Cl refer respectively to conjunctions of conditions and conclusions. For the sake of simplicity, in this paper, we will consider the case where m = 1. A production rule, "Cond $\rightarrow$ Cl", encodes an association between conditions and one conclusion which is purely operational. It suggests that "if conditions belong to the fact base, then conclusion can be added to the fact base". Production rules are shortcuts of an expert reasoning. The record of inference steps that ties conditions to a conclusion has been left out. The underlying process upon which rules are based is not explicit as in the well-known example "if the patient is less than 8 years old, don't prescribe tetracycline" (Clancey, 1981). So, we often refer to rules as "compiled knowledge" and as knowledge containing tacit knowledge, which is sometimes interesting to explain.

The CKB stems from pre-existing models extracted directly from textbooks (essentially medical textbooks for the application in electromyography). The causal knowledge acquisition process is independent of the heuristic knowledge acquisition process. Such causal knowledge is generally available. ADELE considers this kind of knowledge as acquired and does not offer any help for its acquisition.

Knowledge acquisition techniques are used in ADELE when the expert gives a production rule, "Cond $\rightarrow$ Cl", encoding a piece of expert knowledge. Each production rule is considered separately. The objective is to try to prove the association between Cond and Cl or between Cl and Cond, with the causal knowledge base, CKB. The main function of CKB is to produce some proof(s) of "Cond $\rightarrow$ Cl". This can be formalized:

For each rule "Cond $\rightarrow$ Cl", try to prove:
CKB, Cond $\models$ Cl
or
CKB, Cl $\models$ Cond.

CKB is represented in a formalism closely related to that of the semantic network and appears as a graph. Getting proofs of "Cond $\rightarrow$ Cl" doesn't use a logical approach but rather involves getting paths in a semantic network. A proof of "Cond $\rightarrow$ Cl" is a sub-graph of CKB.

The proofs or justifications of "Cond $\rightarrow$ Cl" are the basic material for knowledge acquisition techniques used in ADELE. We argued that a precise analysis of these explanations produce interesting results on the nature of the link between conditions and conclusions and its strength, roles played by conditions (reinforcing conditions will increase the strength of the link in the studied rule, other nonexplainable conditions will reflect a heuristic context, etc) and the discriminating power of conditions over the conclusion. The acquisition module can take advantage of this analysis to explain the rule, analyze it, check it, suggest modifications or other rules.

The Expert Knowledge Base of ADELE, applied to medical diagnosis, was built in cooperation with an INSERM[5] group. It was used as a diagnostic tool and has

---

[4] We consider here the restricted case where a rule does not contain any variables or quantifiers.

[5] INSERM means "Institut National de la Santé et de la Recherche Médicale".

been validated. 95 production rules have been written. A complete description of the project can be found in (Reynaud, 1989) and (Cordier & Reynaud, 1991). Subsequently, we will use the following simple rule relative to this diagnosis to illustrate the method: "if Paresthesie in the median distal region then Carpal channel syndrome". It expresses the relation between the symptom "Paresthesie" (prickling) confined to a part of the arm and the disease "Carpal channel syndrome" being an obstruction of the channel of the median nerve at the wrist.

3 The Causal Knowledge Base (CKB)

CKB is represented in a formalism closely related to that of the semantic network. In order to keep some advantages of abstraction without losing any information, the modelization has been made on two levels and has given rise to two kinds of models. We are going to describe its structure and the way CKB has to be designed.

3.1 Structure of CKB

The semantic network restricted to objects and relations between objects is termed the *Instantiated Causal Model*. These objects refer directly to the conditions and conclusion of the production rules of EKB.

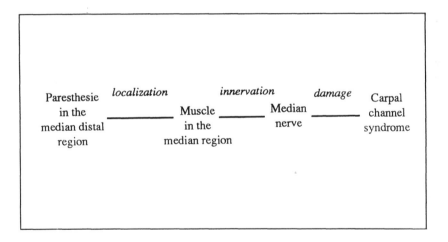

Fig. 1. Instantiated Causal Model.

The semantic network restricted to classes of objects and relations between classes of objects is termed the *Generic Causal Model*[6].

Relations in the Instantiated Causal Model and in the Generic Causal Model are described by:

---

[6] The original term used in ADELE is "Conceptual Model". Conceptual Model is now a term largely used. To avoid any confusion, we prefer to use the term "Generic Causal Model" in this paper.

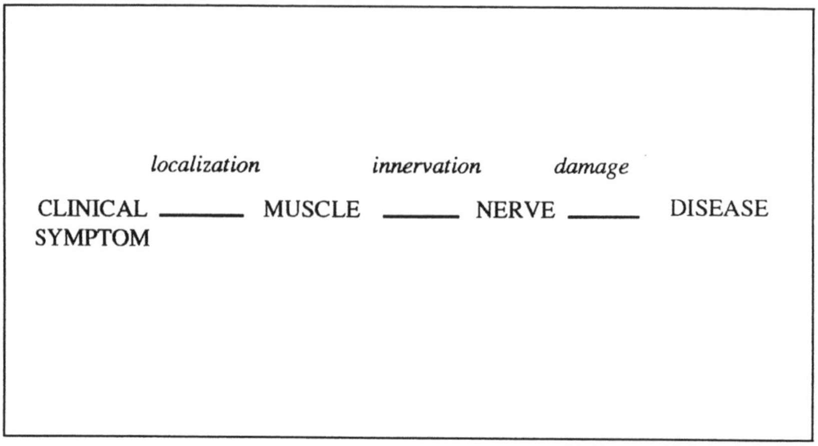

Fig. 2. Generic Causal Model.

- **A name:** the name of the relation will be used to describe, in a litteral form, links between objects or classes of objects ; a relation between X and Y denoted R(X,Y) corresponds to two litteral forms, one relating X to Y and one relating Y to X. For example, *innervation* is a relation between NERVE and MUSCLE ; it can be described as "a MUSCLE *is innervated by* a NERVE" or "a NERVE *innervates* a MUSCLE".
- **A type or viewpoint** which can be: neuro-anatomical, pathophysiological, clinical and denotes the type of domain knowledge the relation refers to.
- **A nature:** a relation can be hierarchical (the relation *is-a* between an object and its class), descriptive (the relation *localization*), functional (the relation *innervation*), or causal/evocative (the relation *damage/is damaged by*). A causal relation needs to be oriented. It will be causal (from causes to effects) or evocative (from effects to causes) according to its orientation.

For example:

- The relation innervation between NERVE and MUSCLE corresponds to an anatomical view point ; it is a functional relation.
- The relation between a DISEASE and the EXPECTED CHANGES ON NERVES corresponds to a pathophysiological view point ; it is a causal relation.
- The relation between a DISEASE and PRESENCE OF CLINICAL SYMP-TOMS corresponds to a clinical view point ; it is a causal relation.

3.2 CKB Design

Instantiated Causal Models model objects and relations between objects of the domain. These objects refer directly to conditions and conclusions of production rules of the EKB. Let us recall that the process of CKB acquisition is totally independent of the process of EKB. Consequently, at first, the connection between CKB and

EKB is not established whereas it is essential in our approach. A causal model can be useful to the heuristic knowledge being acquired only if it is connected with EKB. So, in ADELE, the extraction of pre-existing Instantiated Causal Models is preceded by a connection step in order to connect CKB with HKB. Design of CKB and HKB is completely separate from the initial stages. The need for a connection step is not surprising. The knowledge engineer is responsible for the connection phase. He has to select the most appropriate Instantiated Causal Models, considering that those most closely related to the heuristic knowledge are acquired.

Generic Causal Models are obtained from selected Instantiated Causal Models. Classes of objects stem from grouping objects together. Relations between classes of objects stem from generalizing relations between objects. Consequently:

Assumption 1: for each relation R between two objects of the domain, there exists a generalized relation R (its conceptual ascent) between classes these objects belong to. This generalized relation is of the same nature, the same type as the basic relation but it applies in different domains. For sake of simplicity, they will both be denoted: R.

Links between Generic and Instantiated Causal Models are exclusively is-a relations between classes of objects and objects to which they belong (see fig. 3).

The structure of CKB is very interesting both from a methodological (see section 4) and from a computational viewpoint (see conclusion).

CKB is not a pure causal model. Causal relations coexist with descriptive or definition relations.

CKB is not composed of a unique causal net but may contain several competitive models. Indeed, in a same application domain, a variety of models is available. A model is always designed from a particular viewpoint and a variety of viewpoints is possible. There exists as many competitive models as authors with particular viewpoints on models. According to which sources of knowledge (essentially books in our application) are preferred to build CKB, models of CKB will be very different. Our choice, in ADELE, has been to take advantage of the multiplicity of available domain models. Therefore, CKB can contain a variety of models which refer to multiple view points and which can be divided into Instantiated and Generic Causal Models. Once more, the knowledge engineer is responsible for choosing the most appropriate among all available ones.

Sometimes, we need to represent objects (or classes of objects) in relation with another $n+1^{th}$. For example, a symptom s_1 and a symptom s_2 are in relation with a disease d because s_1 is always associated with s_2 when the disease d appears. This can be represented so:

For this reason, CKB can be seen as an AND/OR graph or more exactly a hypergraph. Each relation R(X,Y) is a n-ary relation between X and Y where we can have $X = \{x_1, x_2, \ldots, x_n\}$ and $Y = \{y_1, y_2, \ldots, y_p\}$. All sub- graphs of CKB related in this paper are in fact sub-hypergraphs of CKB. Nevertheless, for simplicity, in most examples of the paper, X and Y will be reduced to one element.

4 Explanations

As seen in section 2, production rules do not make the semantic link between conditions and conclusions, explicit. When a rule "Cond → Cl" is added to EKB, ex-

524

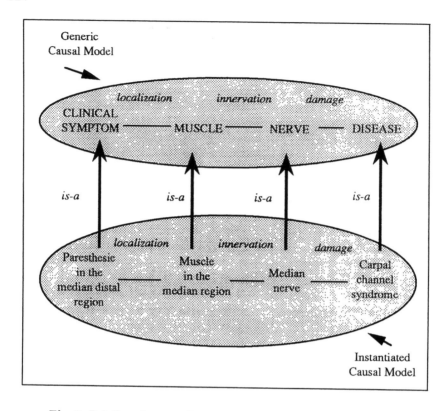

Fig. 3. Relations between Instantiated and Generic Causal Model.

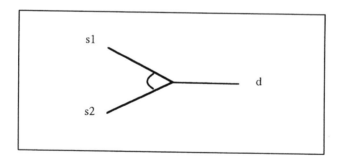

Fig. 4. Representation of a relation between s1, s2 and d.

planations (or justifications) for "Cond → Cl" are searched in the causal knowledge base CKB to make it explicit. Explanations of a rule refer to explanations of a pair (a,b) as described below.

4.1 Explanations of a pair (a,b)

We essentially consider explanations of a pair (a,b) where $a = \{a_i, \ldots, a_n\}$ and b is a singleton. E will be an explanation of (a,b) iff E is a sub-graph such that:

$\forall a_i \in a, a_i \in E$

$b \in E$

$\forall a_i \in a$, there exists a path in E between a_i and b.

By definition, a path between two objects must contain only objects. A path between two classes of objects must contain only classes of objects.

An explanation of a pair (a,b) where a and b are objects will be called an instantiated explanation ; an explanation of a pair (A,B) where A and B are classes of objects will be called a generic explanation.

4.2 Operations on explanations

Abstraction and instantiation are two operations we have defined on explanations. We give their definition below.

Abstraction. Abstraction applies to an instantiated explanation F of a pair (a,b). It provides a generic explanation of a pair (A,B), called the abstraction of F, such that:

A is a set of classes of objects, B is a class of objects.
Each node of the instantiated explanation can be projected in the generic explanation of the pair (A,B) with a relation is-a.
Each relation of the instantiated explanation of the pair (a,b) exists in the generic explanation of the pair (A,B).

So, A and B are obtained this way: For $a = \{a_i\}$, $A = \{A_i \ / \ is\text{-}a \ (a_i, a_i); \ is\text{-}a \ (b,B)\}$.

Instantiation. Instantiation applies to a generic explanation G of a pair (A,B). It provides an (or several) instantiated explanation(s) F, called instances of G, such that G is an abstraction of F. Instances of the same generic explanation are called *Brother-Explanations*.

Consequences. Two assumptions can be derived from the previous definitions:

Assumption 2: If E is an explanation of (a,b), there exists an abstraction of E (see assumption 1), but an instance of an abstraction of E is generally not an explanation of (a,b).

Assumption 3: if E is an instance of an abstraction of an explanation F of (a,b), such that $\forall a_i \in a, a_i \in E$ and $b \in E$, then E is an explanation of (a,b).

Fig. 5 is a graphic representation of abstraction and instantiation taking into account the assumptions to which they are related.

526

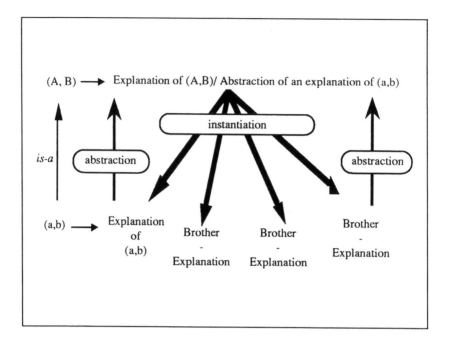

Fig. 5. Schema of abstraction and instantiation.

4.3 Some generic and instantiated explanations

We present some generic and instantiated explanations in the domain of electromyography. Figure 6 below is an explanation F[7] between DISEASE and CLINICAL SYMPTOM, two classes of objects. It is a generic explanation which suggests that: "a DISEASE modifies the ELECTRICAL MEASUREMENT FROM A NERVE; An ELECTRICAL MEASUREMENT FROM A NERVE depends on an ELECTRICAL MEASUREMENT and on a NERVE. NERVES are damaged by DISEASES. a NERVE innervates a MUSCLE; a MUSCLE is a place where CLINICAL SYMPTOMS are localized. Figures 7, 8, and 9 are instances of F.

Figures 7 to 9 represent instantiated explanations which are three instances of the generic explanation above (figure 6).

Figure 7 suggests that "Carpal channel syndrome modifies Amplitude sensitivity of the median nerve; Amplitude sensitivity of the median nerve depends on Amplitude sensitivity and on the Median nerve; the Median nerve innervates the Muscle in the median nerve; the Muscle in the median nerve is a place where Paresthesie in the median distal region is localized".

Figure 8 suggests that "Carpal channel syndrome damages the Median nerve; the Median nerve innervates the Muscle in the median nerve; the Muscle in the median nerve is a place where Paresthesie in the median distal region is localized".

---

[7] In fact, the links between nodes are represented by arcs and not lines. Yet, at first, we will use explanations without taking direction into account. So, the latter doesn't appear on the examples.

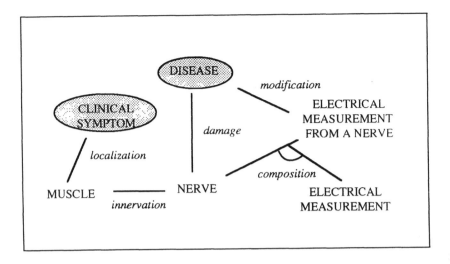

Fig. 6. A generic explanation F between DISEASE and CLINICAL SYMPTOM.

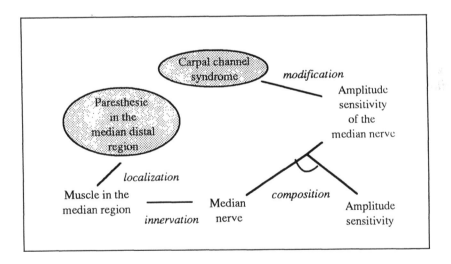

Fig. 7. Instance 1 of F.

Figure 9 suggests that "Carpal channel syndrome damages the Median nerve; the Median nerve innervates the Muscle in the median nerve; the Muscle in the median nerve is a place where Hypoesthesie in the median region is localized".

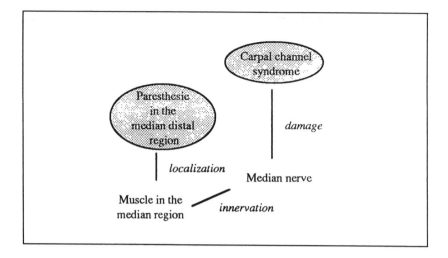

Fig. 8. Instance 2 of F.

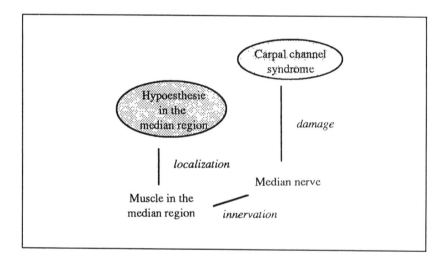

Fig. 9. Instance 3 of F.

4.4 Explanations for a rule "Cond → Cl"

E will be an explanation for a rule "Cond → Cl" iff there exists Cond' ⊆ Cond such that E is an explanation of (Cond',Cl)[8] Explanations of (Cond,Cl) are obtained by

---

[8] The Expert Knowledge Base EKB and the Causal Knowledge Base CKB do not share the same representation language. When a rule "Cond → Cl" composed of its conditions Cond and its conclusion Cl is added to EKB, "Cond → Cl" then has to be translated into a pair (a,b) where "a" results from translation of Cond and "b" from translation of Cl. This translation process is not detailed in this paper.

looking for abstractions of explanations of (Cond,Cl) and by retaining the explanations of (Cond',Cl) with Cond ⊆ Cond.

For example, to explain the rule "if Paresthesie in the median distal region then Carpal channel syndrome", we are looking for explanations of (Paresthesie in the median distal region, Carpal channel syndrome). These explanations are obtained the following way:

1. firstly, we are looking for their abstractions. We obtain the only generic explanation described figure 6. In general, several explanations are possible.
2. secondly, instantiations of the generic explanation looked for, are calculated: see figures 7, 8, and 9.
3. finally, explanations of (Paresthesie in the median distal region, Carpal channel syndrome) are the only instances retained. In our example, this refers to explanations in figures 7 and 8.

5   Analysis of explanations

These "brute" explanations are the basic material for expert knowledge acquisition. It is assumed a precise analysis of these explanations can produce interesting results through following: the nature of the link between conditions and conclusions, the strength of this link, the roles played by conditions, the discriminating power of conditions over the conclusion. The acquisition module will exploit this analysis to explain the rule, analyse it, check it, suggest modifications or other rules.

In this section, criteria for analysing explanations are defined and illustrated. In the next section, it will be shown how these criteria are used in the expert knowledge acquisition process.

The criteria for analysing a rule can be divided into two types: criteria for analysing an explanation per se, or criteria for analysing a set of explanations. Before explaining in detail these criteria, we need to define what we call an *oriented explanation*. A rule is oriented from conditions to conclusions. Relations between objects in an explanation have not, until now, been considered as oriented relations; now we need to explain how an explanation can be oriented to "mimic" a rule more closely.

5.1   Oriented explanation

An explanation is oriented by labelling the nodes of an explanation: nodes corresponding to conditions are first labelled as sources. By propagation of markers, an algorithm divides the nodes of the explanation in three classes as this is shown on figure 10 below: O: the set of sources, I: the set of intermediate nodes and X: the set of extremities. For an oriented explanation of a rule "Cond → Cl", we have: Cond ⊆ O and Cl ⊆ X.

5.2   Criteria for analysing an explanation

We present four criteria which we consider very useful to guide the process of expert knowledge acquisition.

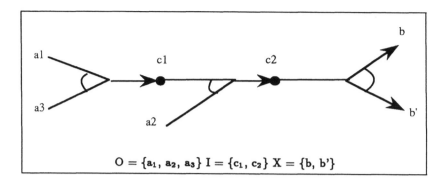

Fig. 10. Identification of different kinds of nodes.

The nature of an explanation. The nature of an explanation can be used to evaluate the strength of the deductive link of a rule. It results from the nature of the constituant relations: descriptive, functional, causal or evocative. In an oriented explanation, it is possible to decide whether a relation is causal or evocative. An explanation is said to be causal if the corresponding relations are descriptive, functional or causal and if it contains at least a causal relation; an explanation is said to be evocative if it is not causal and if it contains at least an evocative relation; in the other cases, it is said undefined.

For example, the explanation below is an evocative one for the rule "if Paresthesie in the median distal region then Carpal channel syndrome".

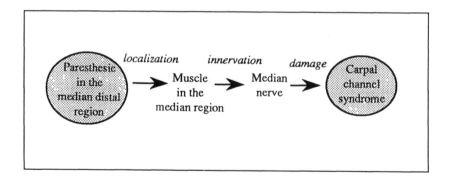

Fig. 11. An evocative explanation.

The explanation for "if Carpal channel syndrome then Paresthesie in the median distal region" will be causal one as can be seen below:

Coverage of a rule by an explanation. A rule "Cond → Cl" is *α-covered by an explanation* E iff:

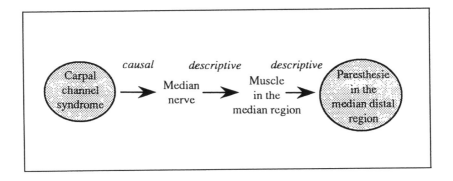

Fig. 12. A causal explanation.

- E is an explanation of (a, Cl) with $a \subseteq$ Cond and
- $\forall$ Cond", $a \subset$ Cond", E is not an explanation of (Cond", Cl).

An explanation E is said to be total for "Cond $\rightarrow$ Cl" iff R is Cond-covered by E; an explanation E is said to be partial for "Cond $\rightarrow$ Cl" iff R is a-covered by E and a $\subseteq$ Cond.

This criterion, as well as the next one, is useful to analyse conditions of a rule and the strength of the link between conditions and conclusion of a rule.

As an illustration, the explanation of figure 11 is partial for the rule "if Paresthesie in the median distal region and Woman then Carpal channel syndrome" because "Woman", a factor in favour of the disease, isn't covered.

Adequacy of an explanation to a rule. The set O of sources of an explanation can contain nodes which do not correspond to conditions of the explained rule "Cond $\rightarrow$ Cl". The set {O - {Cond}} contains the objects (or classes of objects) which are not explicitly stated as conditions in the rule but are required to explain the conclusion. When this set is empty, it means that conditions are sufficient to explain the conclusion; if not, it means that supplementary conditions are necessary to explain the conclusion.

Thus, the explanation represented on figure 10 is adequate for a rule whose conditions are {a_1, a_2, a_3} but inadequate for a rule whose conditions are {a_1, a_2}.

Brother-explanations. They are used to suggest other rules. Let E, the analysed explanation, be an explanation of (Cond,Cl):

- if E_1 is an explanation of (Cond,Cl') and E_1 is a brother-explanation of E, it means that E_1 can explain a distinct conclusion from the same conditions with the same scheme of explanation;
- if E_2 is an explanation of (Cond',Cl) and E_2 is a brother-explanation of E, it means that E_2 can explain the same conclusion from a set of distinct conditions with the same scheme of explanation.

5.3 Criteria for analysing a set of explanations

We present four criteria which allow to compare some explanations in relation to others.

Coverage of a rule by a set of explanations. Using the concept of coverage of a rule by an explanation, it is possible to define the coverage of a rule by a set of explanations $\{E_i\}$. Let us note α_i the coverage of the rule "Cond $\rightarrow$ Cl" by the explanation E_i. $\cup \alpha_i$ will be the coverage of the rule "Cond $\rightarrow$ Cl" by $\{E_i\}$. A rule can then be totally or partially covered by a set of explanations. We can distinguish between:

- conditions covered by all the explanations of a rule: central conditions,
- conditions not covered by any explanation: un-explainable conditions,
- others, only covered by some explanations: partially-explainable conditions.

Complementary explanations. Let us note α, the coverage of the rule "Cond $\rightarrow$ Cl" by the explanation E_1 and β, the coverage of the rule "Cond $\rightarrow$ Cl" by the explanation E_1; E_1 and E_2 are complementary explanations if: $\alpha \subset \alpha \cup \beta$ and $\beta \subset \alpha \cup \beta$. The coverage of both is greater than the coverage of each of them. E_1 and E_2 are totally complementary iff $\alpha \cup \beta = \text{Cond}$.

Comparable explanations. E_1 and E_2 are two comparable explanations if the coverage of "Cond $\rightarrow$ Cl" by E_1 and E_2 is the same.

Refined explanations. E_2 is said to be a refinement of an explanation E_1 iff

- they have the same sources and the same extremities and
- $\exists\ R(X,Y) \subset E_1$, $\exists\ r_1,\ r_2,\ \ldots\ r_p \in E_2$, $X,\ Y \in E_1$ and $X,\ Y \in E2$ and E_2 is obtained by replacing $R(X,Y)$ in E_1 by: $r_1\ (X,Z_2)\ o\ r_2\ (Z_2,Z_3)\ o\ldots o\ r_p\ (Z_p Y)$.

A refined relation is transitive.

   In the example below (figure 13), the first explanation is a refinement of the second which is more general.

6 Use of explanations in the acquisition phase

The knowledge acquisition activity can benefit from the analysis of explanations to check a rule, justify and analyse it and to suggest other rules. All these points are detailed in this section.

6.1 Checking a rule

The existence or non existence of explanations can be used to check a rule and suggest errors in its formalization.

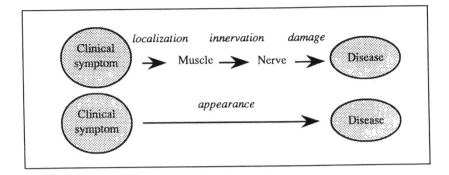

Fig. 13. A refined explanation of an other more general.

Absence of generic explanations. The absence of generic explanations (and then of instantiated explanations) means that no link can be found in the causal models between any of the conditions and the conclusion.

For example, there is no explanation for "if Paresthesie in the median distal region then Cardal channel syndrome" because of a spelling mistake.

Existence of a generic explanation and absence of instantiated explanations. The existence of a generic explanation and absence of instantiated explanations mean that a link has been found between classes of objects representing the conditions and the conclusion, but this link cannot be instantiated as it is established within the rule. For example, a generic explanation exists for the rule "if Amplitude sensitivity of the cubital nerve = reduced then Carpal channel syndrome", but there is no instantiated explanation. The latter would be obtained with "Amplitude sensitivity of the **median nerve** = reduced".

It is important to remember that CKB is not considered as complete and that HKB is not merely a compiled form of CKB: the absence of explanations does not mean that the rule is false, but that it could be false and must be checked. The kind of error seen in the example just above, can easily be detected and corrected (suggestions can then be made by the system as explained further).

6.2 Justifying a rule

Explanations of a rule are justifications that make explicit the semantic link between conditions and a conclusion. ADELE can propose different explanations for a rule and for each of these explanations, generic explanations or instantiated explanations. One of the problems is then to decide which explanations are more appropriate for the user. Some of the criteria seen in the previous section will help to make this choice.

- the type (or view point) of the explanation,
- the coverage of explanations: the best covering explanations are often the most appropriate,

- complementary explanations: in order to cover all conditions of a rule,
- the degree of detail of an explanation: it seems natural to begin with giving general explanations before giving refined ones.

In ADELE, the adopted solution is to propose a menu to the user who can then decide to display one or all explanations or to select detailed or general explanations. In all cases, general explanations are given first. Obviously this problem is a classical problem of man-machine communication and a user model is needed to decide the best choice.

6.3 Analysing a rule

The analysis of explanations for a rule "Cond → Cl" can provide interesting information about it.

Conditions of the rule.

Non-explainable conditions: they are conditions which are not covered by any explanation. Often, they are conditions reflecting a heuristic context, but do not belong to CKB.

For example, the two conditions which are written in italic style in the rules presented below cannot be explained by CKB:

"if *Post-christmas period* and ... then suspect ...".

"if Pregnancy and Paresthesie in the median distal region then Carpal channel syndrome".

Reinforcing conditions: when the adequacy of the explanation is not total (see previous section). They correspond to nodes of an explanation which are sources in the oriented explanation but are not conditions in the rule. These objects contribute to the explanation but have been "forgotten" in the rule. Adding them as conditions will restrict the applicability of the rule, but will increase the strength of the deductive link existing between conditions and conclusion.

If these objects appear in all the explanations of a rule, it is very likely that they are necessary and "forgotten" conditions.

Strength of the deductive link. Oriented explanations can shed light on the nature of the deductive link between conditions and conclusion. They can be helpful to evaluate the strength or the certainty of the deduction, especially when certainty factors are needed.

- The strength of the deduction can be evaluated using the kind of elementary relations: a causal link is stronger than an evocative link; a definitional link is stronger.
- The strength of the deduction can be evaluated taking into account reinforcing conditions.

— The strength of the deduction can be evaluated considering brother-explanations. The brother-explanations of the conclusion, if it exists, i.e. explanations of (Cond, Cl') with Cl ≠ Cl', reveals that other conclusions can be explained by the same conditions and according to the same explicative scheme. When the nature of the link is evocative, it means that Cond is a symptom (or a set of symptoms) of Cl, but also of Cl', Cl", etc. The discriminating power of Cond for Cl is clearly inversely proportional to the number of brother-type explanations. When the nature of the link is causal, Brother-explanations of the conclusion can be used in the same way.

6.4   Suggesting variant rules

Brother-Explanations can be used to suggest variant rules. These suggested rules are analogous to the analysed rule in the sense that they have exactly the same generic explanation but different instantiations.

Brother-explanations for conditions are explanations of the conclusion by an other set of conditions (following the same scheme of explanation). For example, analysing: "if Paresthesie in the median distal region then Carpal channel syndrome" suggests the following rule: "if Hypoesthesie in the median distal region then Carpal channel syndrome".

Brother-explanations of the conclusion are explanations of other conclusions using the same set of conditions (following the same scheme of explanation). For example, analysing: "if Amplitude sensitivity of the Median nerve = reduced then Carpal channel syndrome" suggests this new rule: "if Amplitude sensitivity of the median nerve = reduced then Axonal suffering".

6.5   An example of session

Here, we present an example of session with the ADELE system in the field of electromyography (fig 14).

7   Conclusion and perspectives

7.1   Conclusion

The goal of this paper was to show how a structured model can be used to refine an expert knowledge base. In doing so, we have shown how explanations for heuristic rules are built from causal models, and how these explanations can be analyzed according to a set of criteria. In ADELE, they are used to support knowledge acquisition; they could also be used for reasoning but we have only focussed on knowledge acquisition, in this paper.

Our approach has been applied to a medical diagnosis task in electromyography. This experiment has shown that the approach was very interesting both from a methodological and a computational viewpoint. Indeed, as the instantiated causal model was composed of 134 nodes and of 168 relations, the generic causal model built from the instantiated causal model was very small: 18 nodes and 12 relations.

The knowledge engineer gives the rule described below. ADELE immediately operates on it.

If not   Paresthesie in the median distal region
and if   Woman
then   Carpal channel syndrome

This rule expresses the relation between paresthesie (prickling) confined to a part of the arm, the fact that the patient is a woman and carpal channel syndrome being an obstruction of the channel of the median nerve at the wrist.
The results of ADELE are:

This rule is not valid, it can not be explained.
(Not any explanation has been found for the association between the conditions and the conclusion of the rule in instantiated causal models)

Nevertheless, one (partial) generic explanation exists: "A clinical symptom is localized in a muscle; a muscle is innervated by nerves; a nerve can be damaged by diseases".
(This generic explanation has been provided by generic causal models)
. . .

Not any explanation has been found for "woman". Is "woman" a condition which reflects heuristic context?
. . .

ADELE has identified generic concepts which can be associated with the terms of the rule: clinical symptom for Paresthesie in the median distal region and disease for Carpal channel syndrome. Its justifies the association between these concepts. This helps the knowledge engineer by providing understanding of the rule being acquired. Let us note that the explanation is partial. No concept has been found for the condition "woman" and then, no explanation which refers to this condition, has been delivered. ADELE deduces that the condition "woman" could reflect a heuristic context.
Results of ADELE are analyzed. The knowledge engineer decides to modify the rule (to remove the "not" in the conditions of the previous rule) and proposes ADELE to validate the modified rule.

If   Paresthesie in the median distal region
and if   Woman
then   Carpal channel syndrome

The results of ADELE are:

This rule is partially valid.
(One partial explanation has been found in instantiated causal models)
"Paresthesies in the median distal region are localized in the muscle in the median nerve; the muscle in the median nerve is innervated by the median nerve; the median nerve can be damaged by carpal channel syndrome"
. . .

According to this explanation, no additive condition is required to explain the conclusion of the rule.
. . .

The explanation below suggests the rule is an evocative one.
. . .

Here is an analogous rule:
If   Hypoesthesie in the median distal region
then   Carpal channel syndrome
. . .
etc.

Fig. 14. An example of session with the ADELE system, in the field of electromyography.

Our approach, and particularly the small size of the generic causal model, makes the search for generic explanations easy and, consequently, considering our methodological choice of explanation search, the search for explanations of rules as well.

Testing a medical diagnosis application has been totally satisfactory. We think that this domain is suitable because it is relatively well delimited and the knowledge can easily be organized and structured.

A second test has been performed , this time, in a very different domain, bidding in the game of Bridge. This domain was more difficult to modelize because no pre-existing causal model was available. Nevertheless, causal models have been built and an experimentation has been carried out. Explanations have been obtained but, very often, they were numerous and complex. This has led us to study and work on the content and the nature of explanations to make them useful in a context of Knowledge Acquisition. We have defined ways to simplify explanations (Reynaud, 1989). We have studied criteria to select the more appropriate explanations for a user when facing multiple explanations (cf. section 6.2.). This problem is relative to man-machine communication and can only be solved by using a model of the user. Such a model has not been implemented in ADELE.

From these tests, we will draw your attention on a few specific points. Firstly, such techniques can only be used when causal models are available. A typical example of use of various models, is technical systems such as vehicles, electronic devices, etc. They are artefacts constructed to perform a particular function. All components are known and the behavior of the whole can theorically be predicted from the behavior of the parts. Another illustration (the one we used in our experiments) is medical applications. In such context, structural and functional models would be too complex although a lot of information about dysfunction is listed in medical textbooks or papers and can easily be represented with causal models. Secondly, our approach is based on schematic causal models describing the domain entities and their relations. These models represent one semantic of the domain. Using such models can support knowledge acquisition activity but we must be aware that our results have to be viewed as helpful comments or warnings and no more. According to these two points, we think our approach is applicable to all diagnostic problems. In particular, justifications can be required for all rules suggesting hypotheses i.e. troubles, badly working components or diseases from observations of abnormalities or symptoms. Such rules are important because they control the system's reasoning and specify which assumptions are more likely to be solutions to a problem. Their derivative process is far from being clear. Justifications help to control the rules, then anyone is able to understand their meaning. Note that such explanations can also be very beneficial when teaching rules to students. It is easier to memorize a rule when we are aware of its underlying derivative process.

7.2   Perspectives

In its actual version, ADELE contributes to the design of a heuristic knowledge base. This heuristic knowledge base is an equivalent to an instantiated Conceptual Model but, in no way, the approach benefits from an explicit Conceptual Model.

In recent years, however, a new and fruitful paradigm for Knowledge acquisition (KA) has emerged. KA has become a modelling task requiring abstraction, organi-

538

zation and transformation of knowledge. The KA process is currently described as composed of several steps which one important step is the design of a Conceptual Model (Musen, 1989). A Conceptual Model describes the problem-solving process at a better level of abstraction and is important to make communication easy between designers of Knowledge Based Systems and experts of the domain (Aussenac, 1989). Nevertheless, designing a Conceptual Model is difficult; What must be modelized? How? At which level of abstraction? To help in this phase, some approaches recommend to select and to refine Conceptual Models from predefined libraries of generic tasks rather than building them from scratch (Bylander & Chandrasekaran, 1987; Breuker *et al.*, 1987).

Viewing knowledge acquisition in terms of "acquiring knowledge for a specific task in a specific conceptual model" means that another step forward is necessary, compared to "acquire rules" as in the first generation of expert systems. Furthermore, making the underlying conceptual model explicit appears to be a promising path of research, particularly in KA. So, actually, we are currently trying to reconsider our approach within this new framework. We want to find out if our approach can help refine and make more precise a "brute" Conceptual model. We want to redefine our approach so as to show how it can help the instantiation of an explicit Conceptual Model.

References

ANDREASSEN, S., WOLBYE, M., FALCK, B. & ANDERSEN, S. (1987). Munin - a causal probabilistic network for interpretation of electromyographic findings. In *Proceedings of the 10th International Joint Conference on Artificial Intelligence* (pp. 366–372). Milan, Italy.

AUSSENAC, N. (1989). A mediating representation to assist knowledge acquisition with MACAO. In J. H. BOOSE, B. R. GAINES & J. G. GANASCIA, Eds., *Proceedings of the 3rd European Workshop on Knowledge Acquisition for Knowledge-Based Systems* (pp. 516–529). Paris, France.

AUSSENAC-GILLES, N., KRIVINE, J.-P. & SALLANTIN, J. (1992). Introduction to the special issue of knowledge acquisition. *Revue d'Intelligence Artificielle*, 6(1–2), 7–18. (In French).

BREUKER, J., WIELINGA, B., VAN SOMEREN, M., DE HOOG, R., SCHREIBER, G., DE GREEF, P., BREDEWEG, B., WIELEMAKER, J. & BILLAULT, J.-P. (1987). *MUNIN - A Causal Probabilistic Network for Interpretation of Electromyographic Findings*. Technical Report 1, University of Amsterdam and STL Ltd. Esprit Project P1098 Deliverable D1.

BYLANDER, T. & CHANDRASEKARAN, B. (1987). Generic tasks for knowledge-based reasoning : the right level of abstraction for knowledge acquisition. *International Journal of Man-Machine Studies*, 26, 231–243.

CHANDRASEKARAN, B. (1987). Towards a functional architecture for intelligence based on generic information processing tasks. In *Proceedings of the 10th International Joint Conference on Artificial Intelligence* (pp. 1183–1192). Milan, Italy.

CHANDRASEKARAN, B. & MITTAL, S. (1983). Deep versus compiled knowledge approaches to diagnostic problem-solving. *International Journal of Man-Machine Studies*, 19, 425–436.

CHARLET, J. (1993). ACTE: a causal model-based knowledge acquisition tool. In J.-M. DAVID & J.-P. KRIVINE, Eds., *Second Generation Expert Systems*. Springer Verlag. *In this book.*

CHARLET, J. & GASCUEL, O. (1989). Knowledge acquisition by causal model and meta-knowledge. In J. H. BOOSE, B. R. GAINES & J. G. GANASCIA, Eds., *Proceedings of the 3 rd European Workshop on Knowledge Acquisition for Knowledge-Based Systems* (pp. 212–225). Paris, France.

CHITTARO, L., CONSTANTINI, C., GIOVANNI, G., CARLO, T. & TOPANNO, E. (1989). Diagnosis based on cooperation of multiple knowledge sources. In *Proceedings of the 9 th International Workshop Expert Systems & their Applications* Avignon, France.

CLANCEY, W. (1981). The epistemology of a rule-based expert system : a framework for explanation. *Artificial Intelligence*, 27(3), 289–350.

CLANCEY, W. J. (1985). Heuristic Classification. *Artificial Intelligence*, 27(3), 289–350.

CONSOLE, L., FOSSA, M. & TORASSO, P. (1989a). Acquisition of causal knowledge in the check system. *Computers and Artificial Intelligence*, 8(4), 323–345.

CONSOLE, L., FOSSA, M. & TORASSO, P. (1989b). Heuristic and causal reasoning in check. In J. DAVID, R. HUBER, J. KRIVINE & C. KULIKOWSKI, Eds., *AI and Expert Systems in Scientific Computing*: J.C. Baltzer Scientific Publ. Co.

CORDIER, M.-O. & REYNAUD, C. (1991). Knowledge acquisition techniques and second generation expert systems. *Applied Artificial Intelligence*, 5(3), 209–226.

DAVID, J.-M. & KRIVINE, J.-P. (1989). Augmenting experience-based diagnosis with causal reasoning. *Applied Artificial Intelligence*, 3(2-3), 239–248.

ESHELMAN, L. (1988). MOLE: a knowledge acquisition tool for cover-and-differentiate systems. In S. MARCUS, Ed., *Automating Knowledge Acquisition for Expert Systems*. Kluwer Academic Publishers.

KAHN, G., NOWLAN, S. & McDERMOTT, J. (1985). MORE: an intelligent knowledge acquisition tool. In A. JOSHI, Ed., *Proceedings of the 9 th International Joint Conference on Artificial Intelligence* (pp. 581–585). Los Angeles, CA: M. Kaufmann, Inc.

MARCUS, S. (1988). SALT: a knowledge acquisition tool for propose-and-revise systems. In S. MARCUS, Ed., *Automating Knowledge Acquisition for Expert Systems*. Kluwer Academic Publishers.

MUSEN, M. (1989). Conceptuals models of interactive knowledge acquisition tools. *Knowledge Acquisition*, 1, 73–88.

REYNAUD, C. (1989). ADELE, *A Knowledge Acquisition Tool based on Justifications*. PhD thesis, Université Paris Sud. (In French).

REYNAUD, C. (1991). Where does knowledge acquisition interfere with explanation. In D. HERIN-AIME, R. DIENG, , J. REGOUD & J. ANGOUJARD, Eds., *Proceedings of the 1 st conference on Knowledge Modeling & Expertise Transfer* Sophia-Antipolis: IOS Press. (In French).

STEELS, L. (1985). Second-generation expert systems. *Journal of Future Generation Computer Science*, 1(4).

WIELINGA, B. & BREUKER, J. (1985). KADS : Structured knowledge acquisition for expert systems. In *Proceedings of the 5 th International Workshop Expert Systems & their Applications* Avignon, France.

Part V

Explanation

Explanation in Second Generation Expert Systems

William R. Swartout[1] and Johanna D. Moore[2]

[1] USC/Information Sciences Institute
4676 Admiralty Way
Marina del Rey, CA 90292

[2] University of Pittsburgh
Computer Science Department and
Learning Research and Development Center
Pittsburgh, PA 15260

Abstract. What is needed for good explanation? This paper begins by considering some desiderata for expert system explanation. These desiderata concern not only the form and content of the explanations, but also the impact of explanation generation on the expert system itself— how it is built and how it performs. In this paper, we use these desiderata as a yardstick for measuring progress in the field. The paper describes two major developments that have differentiated explanation in second generation systems from explanation in first generation systems: 1) new architectures have been developed that capture more of the knowledge that is needed for explanation, and 2) more powerful explanation generators have been developed in which explanation generation is viewed as a problem-solving activity in its own right. These developments have led to significant improvements in explanation facilities: the explanations they offer are richer and more coherent, they are better adapted to the user's needs and knowledge, and the explanation facilities can offer clarifying explanations to correct misunderstandings.

1 Introduction

The need for explanation in expert systems has been recognized from the start. Expert systems operate in domains that are imprecise and use problem-solving knowledge that is heuristic. Formal methods, such as program verification, cannot guarantee that an expert system's advice is correct, because the underlying knowledge behind that advice is inherently imprecise. For an expert system to be trusted, it must be accountable. It must be able to explain its reasoning and justify its conclusions, as a human expert can. An explanation facility makes an expert system more transparent. If an expert system's advice is based on sound knowledge and reasoning methods, then an explanation system can reassure the user that the system's advice is appropriate. On the other hand, if an expert system has been pushed beyond the bounds of its expertise, an explanation facility can also make that more apparent to the user, thus alerting him that the system's advice may not be correct.

Even early expert systems, such as MYCIN [35] could provide a rudimentary explanation capability by translating the rules they used to solve problems into natural language. As research in expert system explanation has progressed, researchers have discovered that explanation concerns need to be taken into account while a system is being designed, otherwise the system is unlikely to produce good explanations. As a consequence, advances in explanation capabilities and expert system architectures have been closely linked. Some of the important advances of second generation expert system architectures over first generation systems can be directly attributed to the need to address explanation concerns.

1.1 Themes for Second Generation Systems

Explaining something to a user requires constructing an expository text, or "story" that relates the things that the user does not understand to general facts, plans and goals that he knows and accepts. For example, a good explanation of a specific step taken by a diagnostic system should show how that step is motivated by the domain facts and diagnostic strategies that the system is following. All explanation systems have attempted to construct such stories. However, because first generation systems produced explanations by paraphrasing the rules used to solve a problem directly into natural language, they suffered from two problems. First, critical parts of the "story" were often left out because these systems did not represent the abstractions behind the rules [43, 4, 8]. Thus, the system could not justify the specific actions it took in terms of general strategies that the user understood. Second, the explanations that the system produced often sounded unnatural and were unclear, because they followed very closely the trace of rule firings that occurred as the system solved the problem.

Two themes have been apparent in the development of second generation explanation capabilities that address these problems. The first theme concerns knowledge representation. Many of the limitations of early expert system explanations can be attributed to the failure of first generation architectures to represent knowledge that is needed to support explanation. Researchers now have a better understanding of what kinds of knowledge need to be represented to support good explanations, and second generation expert system architectures have been developed to represent that knowledge and make it available for explanation. The second theme has been the development of improved techniques for the generation of explanations. An important step toward improved explanations has been the realization that explanation generation is a problem-solving activity in its own right, worthy of its own problem-solving architecture.

In this paper, we assess some of the advances that have been made in second generation explanation facilities. To help in that assessment, we begin by describing some desired characteristics, or desiderata, for explanation systems. Using these desiderata to measure progress, we discuss the major research themes and key research efforts that have characterized the development of second generation explanation capabilities.

1.2 Desiderata for Expert System Explanation

What makes a good explanation? It has become clear that an explanation facility imposes some strong requirements on the design of an expert system and it can be difficult or impossible to provide a system with adequate explanations unless those requirements are taken into account during system design [8, 43]. But what are these requirements? What implications do they have for expert system architectures? In this section, we outline a set of desiderata for explanation facilities and discuss how they can affect the design of such a facility. We do not claim that the set of desiderata presented here is exhaustive, or the best possible set conceivable. Nevertheless, they have helped us evaluate progress in the field, and understand better the requirements that explanation poses on expert system design and construction.

The five general desiderata below fall into three classes. The first desideratum is concerned with how the explanations are produced. The second and third are requirements on the explanations themselves. The fourth and fifth concern the effect of an explanation facility on the construction and execution of an expert system.

1. **Fidelity.** The explanation must be an accurate representation of what the expert system really does. An inaccurate or misleading explanation is worse than no explanation at all. A strong implication of this desideratum is that explanations must be based on the same underlying knowledge that the system uses for reasoning. Explanations produced from canned text or 'fill-in-the-blank' templates do not meet this requirement because there can be no guarantee that such explanations have anything to do with the program's behavior.

   A less obvious implication is that the expert system's interpreter (or inference engine) should be as simple as possible with a minimal number of special features (such as mechanisms for reasoning about uncertainty). Special features built into the interpreter are not part of the system's knowledge base. Thus, they will not be explainable unless they are shadowed by special procedures built into the explanation routines. These shadowed features introduce the potential for inaccuracy in explanations because any changes made to the interpreter must also (independently) be made to the explanation routines.

2. **Understandability.** Clearly, to be useful, the explanations that a system produces must be understood. Understandability is not a single factor, but rather a composite of several factors involving the content of the explanations, their production, and the context in which they are produced. Consequently, understandability will affect the design of many parts of an expert system.

   Identifying the factors involved in understandability is an on-going research effort. Some of the factors that we have identified are:

   - **Terminology.** Terms used in the explanation must be familiar to the user or the system must be able to define them in familiar terms.

- **User Sensitivity.** The system should be able to present explanations that take into account the user's knowledge, goals, preferences, and concerns.
- **Abstraction.** The system must be able to provide explanations at different levels of abstraction. By level of abstraction, we are referring to the level of terminology used in the explanation. For example, in describing a patient's problem, the system should be able to describe it either abstractly as a bacterial infection or specifically as an *e. coli* infection.
- **Summarization.** The system must be able to give explanations at different levels of detail. The level of detail refers to how much has been left out of the explanation. Changing to a different level of detail does not necessarily require a change in terminology and therefore it is not the same as, and should not be confused with, changing level of abstraction. For example, a very detailed explanation of why the patient has a particular disease might list the primary symptoms and all the secondary ones while a less detailed one would mention only the primary symptoms.
- **Perspectives.** The system should be able to explain its knowledge from different perspectives, e.g., form vs. function in a biological domain, or safety vs. profitability in a financial domain.
- **Linguistic Competence.** The explanations the system generates should sound "natural" and adhere to linguistic principles and constraints. The explanations should cohere, reflecting things that the user has already been told. If several things must be conveyed to the user in an explanation, the text should flow smoothly from one topic to the next. These properties may be difficult to achieve if simple canned text or template-based generators are used because they are inflexible and cannot adapt the fragments they assemble to reflect context.
- **Feedback.** It must be possible for the user to indicate that he doesn't understand part of an explanation and receive further clarification on that point.

3. **Sufficiency.** The system has to know what it is talking about. Enough knowledge must be represented in the system to answer the questions users have. As we mentioned above, the explanations of first generation systems were limited, in part because they failed to represent some of the knowledge needed for explanation.

   In creating an expert system, one has to identify the kinds of knowledge that will be represented in the system. Because systems are used in various different contexts, these requirements will vary from system to system. We have found that a useful technique for identifying the required knowledge is to consider what sorts of explanations a system should offer, and in turn what sorts of knowledge are needed to support those explanations. Some of the more useful explanations include:

   - **Explanations about the system's behavior.** These include explanations of how the system solved a particular problem, how a parameter affected the outcome, and what would be the effect of a change in some of the data. These explanations can be produced by paraphrasing the system's methods and an event history of their application to particular problems.

- **Justifications.** These explanations provide the rationale behind the system's actions and recommendations. Although first generation systems represented the goals they were achieving, they often failed to represent the knowledge needed for justifications, that is, why the goals were needed in the first place. Much like a cook following a recipe, an expert system can often *perform* adequately without understanding the rationale behind the actions it takes. As a result, expert systems have trouble explaining why particular actions are appropriate. To provide such justifications, one needs to understand the design decisions underlying the artifact to be explained.

- **Preferences.** These explanations describe why one strategy or recommendation is preferred over another. Providing them requires knowledge of the tradeoffs and preferences that were involved in making a selection.

- **Domain explanations.** These describe the problem domain itself. For example, in the domain of digitalis therapy, a user might ask for the system to describe possible adverse effects of digitalis therapy. These explanations don't involve the system's problem-solving knowledge, but users may request them either to understand the domain better, or as a way of assessing the depth of the system's knowledge about a particular topic as a way of determining its applicability to a particular problem.

- **Terminology definitions.** These answer questions about the meanings of terms the system uses, e.g. 'What is a drug sensitivity?'

4. **Low Construction Overhead.** If it turns out to be much more difficult to design an expert system with explanation capabilities than without, system designers may well avoid providing such facilities. Thus, explanation must either impose a light load on the construction of an expert system, or any load that is imposed should be recovered, for example, by easing some phase of the expert system life cycle, such as maintenance or evolution.

5. **Efficiency.** The explanation facility should not degrade the runtime efficiency of the expert system.

In the next section, we discuss the limitations of first generation explanations. Section 3 describes how second generation expert system architectures provide better support for explanation. Section 4 then describes how advances in explanation generation techniques have improved the explanatory capabilities of expert systems.

2 First Generation: Explanations Based on Rules

First generation systems based their explanations directly on the rules that the system used to solve a problem and traces of their execution. Such systems produce explanations by paraphrasing the rules or execution traces into natural language using fill-in-the-blank templates (see [34]). For this approach to work, the terms used in the rules must be understood by the user. In addition, the rules themselves must follow lines of reasoning that are familiar to the user. A major advantage of this approach is its simplicity: once the expert system is working, relatively little additional work is required to produce explanations. Because these explanations follow the system's processing very closely, they have proved to be useful for debugging and augmenting a knowledge base (see [11]).

However, the limitations of the "paraphrase-the-rules" approach to explanation have been well documented (see [4, 8, 42, 43]). Fundamentally, these limitations all stem from a common source: the use of a representation (rules) that is too low-level, that fails to capture all the information needed for explanation, and fails to distinguish the roles that different kinds of knowledge play.

Inadequacy of low level rules. Each rule by itself solves a small, local part of the problem. Because the system's overall behavior results from complex interactions among these rules, it is not possible to see the general problem-solving strategy that the system uses by looking at rules in isolation. For example, a diagnostic system may use an establish-and-refine approach to diagnosis, but this general algorithm may not be stated anywhere. Instead, behavior that can be *characterized* as establish-and-refine emerges from the interactions of many specific rules. Because the explanation facility is limited to working with the operational rules, it is impossible for it to explain the general algorithm that the system is following. Thus, the user may be able to understand each of the rules *locally* but still not understand the overall approach that the system is taking.

Failure to distinguish roles of knowledge. An additional problem comes from the intertwining of different types of knowledge in the rules. The operational rules in an expert system come from the designer's efforts to integrate several orthogonal concerns. For example, it may only be appropriate to fire a particular rule during one stage of the problem-solving process, so there needs to be a clause in the rule reflecting that *control* constraint. If the rule involves obtaining information from the user, it may only be appropriate to fire it after certain other information has been obtained, so the rule must have a clause for this *user interface* constraint.[3] Finally, some clauses in the rule will reflect domain inferences that the rule makes. In producing an explanation, the rule paraphraser will translate all of the clauses in each rule into natural language. Thus, clauses intended to constrain the system's control strategy or the user interface may be explained along with those supporting domain-level inference. The resulting explanations can be difficult to understand because the different roles that the

---

[3] For example, to avoid irritating users, systems generally ask a general question (e.g. "Does the patient have lung disease?") before specific questions (e.g. "Is the lung disease viral?") because the answer to the general question may obviate the need to ask the specific question. In first generation systems, a clause was added to each rule associated with a specific question. This clause prevented the rule from firing unless the general question had been asked.

clauses play is not explicitly stated and it may be impossible for the user to infer them.

Insufficient knowledge. A more serious problem is that the rules often fail to contain enough knowledge to support some kinds of explanations, particularly justifications of the system's actions (see [4, 8, 43]). This is because much of the reasoning about which actions should be performed and when they should be performed is actually done by the system's designer as he structures the system. Because this reasoning is not recorded, it cannot be explained. For example, when Silverman built a system to advise physicians about dosages for the drug digitalis (see [38]), he knew that it was necessary to check for an increased level of serum calcium in the patient because it could interact badly with digitalis and cause dangerous heart arrhythmias. He also knew that to reduce the risk of these problems, the drug dosage should be reduced in the presence of increased serum calcium. All of that knowledge could be needed to explain why the system asked about serum calcium, or why it reduced the dose in the presence of elevated serum calcium. However, this knowledge stayed in the system builder's head and was not represented in the system itself (and was thus not available for explanation) as it was not needed for the system to give correct recommendations about dosage: the system just checked if the level of serum calcium was above a threshold, and reduced the dosage if it was.

First Generation Systems and the Desiderata. Because first generation systems based their explanations on the rules used to solve a problem and the traces of their firings, they provided reasonable *fidelity*. However, they were less successful in providing good *understandability* for several reasons. Because the explanations were based on low-level rules, they lacked the *abstractions* needed to explain the system's general problem-solving approach. Because the systems lacked *terminology* definitions, they could not explain the meaning of a term if the user did not understand it. As we will discuss in Section 4, because first generation explanation generators typically followed the reasoning trace closely, the explanations they produced were not structured following principles of *linguistic competence*. For the same reason, these systems were also severely restricted in their ability to offer explanations that took into account different *perspectives* or *user sensitivities*, although some clever techniques were developed to provide explanations at different levels of detail [47]. Finally, because the systems had no conceptual model of the explanations they produced, and usually had only one way to answer a question, they could not respond to *feedback* from the user requesting elaborating or clarifying text.

First generation systems failed to represent some of the knowledge that is important for explanation, and thus only partially satisfied the desideratum of *sufficiency*. While they could provide explanations of what the system did by paraphrasing rules, justifications and explanations about the domain could not be provided because that information was not represented in the rules. Finally, first generation systems can be given good ratings for *low construction overhead* and *efficiency*. Providing explanation for a first generation system required constructing appropriate templates for paraphrasing the rules, concepts and relations used by the system and this was generally not too difficult. First generation systems receive a good rating for *efficiency* because the only cost imposed by explanation was the overhead of storing the trace of rule firings during system execution.

In summary, first generation systems could provide limited kinds of explanations. The chief advantage of these systems was their simplicity. In the next section, we will consider more sophisticated expert systems architectures that come closer to meeting our desiderata.

3   Enhanced Expert System Architectures for Explanation

As described earlier, producing explanations in expert systems involves constructing an expository text that shows how the item to be explained relates to concepts, methods, facts or terms that the user understands. Thus, to support explanation, the expert system architecture needs to represent two general kinds of information:

1. It must represent concepts, methods, facts and terms that are potentially familiar to the user and that underlie the system's actions. These are the *starting points* for an explanation. They are the points where the explanation connects with the user's current knowledge.
2. It must represent the inferential *linkages* between the starting points and the item to be explained. These linkages show how the object to be explained relates back to things the user understands. The linkages provide an abstract "story line" for the explanation.

Research in second generation architectures has tried to increase the kinds and breadth of *starting points* that the architecture represents (so that a broader range of users and topics can be accommodated), and provide more *linkage pathways* between the starting points and the system's structure and behavior (so that a broader range of explanations can be generated). These efforts have led to improvements in the desiderata, particularly to *abstraction, summarization,* and *sufficiency.*

Second generation frameworks have primarily focused on explanations that involve placing a system's specific actions (e.g., its recommendations or requests for information) in context. This involves 1) showing how an action relates to the overall goals of the system and other actions that the system may have taken or plans to take in the future, 2) describing the general method that the system is following, and 3) justifying why the action is appropriate. To support such explanations, these frameworks have had to increase the possible starting points for explanation by abstracting from the rule representations of first-generation expert systems, and they have had to provide ways of linking the starting points to the system's specific actions.

In this section, we discuss four architectures that support better explanation. The first, NEOMYCIN [7, 14], builds on conventional rule-based systems by using metarules to provide higher-level representations for the general problem-solving strategy a system employs. The second approach, Generic Tasks [3], is based on the idea that these general problem-solving strategies recur across systems, and that a common set of abstract strategies can be identified for solving particular tasks. For each abstract strategy, explanation routines are developed that incorporate knowledge about what sorts of information should be presented in an explanation of that strategy. The third approach, the Explainable Expert Systems framework [44, 28], is intended to capture more of the design information about an expert system, which is needed to provide good explanations but is missing from first generation systems. In this approach, a high-level knowledge base is created that represents domain facts, terminology, and problem-solving methods expressed as plans. An automatic programmer is used to derive an expert system from this knowledge base. As it creates the expert system, the program writer leaves behind a trace of the design decisions it makes. This trace provides explanation routines with the linkages needed to show how specific actions taken by the system can be justified by the high-level knowledge in the knowledge base. The fourth approach, Reconstructive Explanation [49], is quite different from the first three. In this approach, the knowledge base that was used to solve the problem is not used to explain the result. Instead, after the problem has been solved, the system constructs a *post hoc* explanation that justifies the result by using a separate explanation knowledge base. We will consider each of these systems in turn.

3.1 NEOMYCIN: Abstraction Through Metarules

Clancey developed NEOMYCIN to address some of the problems he found in his analysis of MYCIN's explanatory limitations [8]. In particular, NEOMYCIN provided an abstract and explicit representation for the control structures that were implicit in MYCIN's rules. In analyzing MYCIN, Clancey noted that it goes through several distinct processing phases, or tasks, in performing a diagnosis, such as gathering information about the patient and establishing and refining a hypothesis. In MYCIN, these tasks were implicit—the flat structure of the rules did not support their explicit representation.

NEOMYCIN made these tasks more explicit by altering the conventional rule-based system architecture in several ways. First, rules that performed processing associated with a particular task were grouped together into a ruleset. Rules within a ruleset together achieved the task associated with the ruleset. For example, NEOMYCIN associated a set of rules with the task EXPLORE-AND-REFINE, which was concerned with developing and refining hypotheses, and another set with the phase FINDOUT, which was concerned with question-asking. Rules within a ruleset could only fire if the ruleset was active. Metarules were used to provide control across rulesets by activating them. In addition to activating rulesets, metarules could recommend specific domain rules to apply or findings to request from the user [7].

Figure 1 shows a NEOMYCIN metarule (from [7]). As an example of how this metarule could be used, suppose that NEOMYCIN's knowledge base in-

```
METARULE001
TASK: EXPLORE-AND-REFINE
ARGUMENT: CURRENT-HYPOTHESIS

(IF (AND (CURRENT-ARGUMENT $CURFOCUS)
         (CHILDOF $CURFOCUS $CHILD)
         (THNOT (PURSUED $CHILD)))
    (NEXTACTION (PURSUE-HYPOTHESIS $CHILD)))
```

Paraphrase:

IF the hypothesis being focused upon has a child that has not been pursued,
THEN pursue that child.

Fig. 1. A NEOMYCIN Metarule

cluded the facts that viral-meningitis and bacterial-meningitis were subtypes of
meningitis. If it were exploring the hypothesis that the patient had meningitis,
METARULE001 would cause it to post the new task of pursuing the subhy-
potheses that the patient might have either bacterial or viral meningitis. If the
system were asked to explain why it was asking about viral meningitis, it could
explain that it was exploring the hypothesis that the patient had meningitis and
trying to refine that hypothesis by pursuing viral meningitis, which is one of the
subtypes of meningitis. By clustering rules into rulesets corresponding to processing phases and using metarules to specify control between phases, NEOMYCIN
abstracted away from the low-level rules of MYCIN.

Figure 2 shows an abstract NEOMYCIN explanation from another situation
(from [14]). In this case, NEOMYCIN is engaged in the task of ESTABLISH-
HYPOTHESIS-SPACE, and the user asks how that task is being accomplished.
NEOMYCIN's task structure and its use of abstract metarules for control allow
it to produce a high-level explanation giving an overview of the general strategy
that it is following in accomplishing this task. Such an explanation would not
be possible in MYCIN, because it lacks NEOMYCIN's abstract representations for
control.

NEOMYCIN and the Desiderata. The major contribution of NEOMYCIN
was better *abstraction* for control knowledge. NEOMYCIN's rulesets clustered
rules concerned with particular tasks together, and thus abstracted away from
the individual rules to provide an explicit representation for the major processing steps in an expert system. NEOMYCIN's metarules allow explicit representation of control for moving between processing stages. These abstractions allowed
NEOMYCIN to give better explanations of the overall strategy it was following in
performing diagnosis.

** HOW 25.0

[i.e. HOW are we trying to develop the differential using basic history and pertinent physical exam?

We did the following:

[26.1] Got a general idea of the problem: categorized it into one of several pathogenic classes or disease loci, or both.

[26.2] Confirmed and refined the differential diagnosis through specific questions.

We are now:

[26.3] Rounding out the diagnostic information by looking generally into past medical history and by reviewing systems.

Fig. 2. An Abstract NEOMYCIN Explanation

As we have argued, explanation in expert systems often involves showing how a particular action the system is taking relates to a general strategy that the user accepts. Thus, the abstractions included in NEOMYCIN were important because they provided an explicit representation for the general strategies that was missing in first generation systems. Without such a representation, it is difficult to give explanations that show how specific actions relate to a general strategy.

However, because NEOMYCIN still uses a rule-based architecture, all the problems of flat rule-bases can exist *within* a ruleset. Also, while NEOMYCIN could show how a specific action related to an abstract strategy, it did not address the problem of *justification*, that is, showing how a particular action can be justified by knowledge of domain facts, terminology and problem-solving strategies.

3.2 Generic Tasks

NEOMYCIN gained explanatory power by providing representations for abstract problem-solving strategies. The Generic Task approach builds on that by noting that a handful of abstract strategies are reused across many expert systems to solve certain classes of problems. These techniques are characterized by the general steps they take and the way they process information. For example, Clancey [9] showed how a number of different systems built within the EMYCIN framework could all be seen as performing the same general abstract task, which he called *heuristic classification*. Heuristic classification involves selecting the most appropriate answer to a problem from a set of pre-determined answers, based on the evidence presented. Some of the kinds of operations that occur in a heuristic classification system include *data abstraction, generalization, heuristic match*, and *refinement*. Chandrasekaran and his colleagues[4] have developed the

---

[4] The authors would like to thank Michael Tanner and B. Chandrasekaran for providing valuable material for this section. Most of Tanner's work has been done in the context of planning methods for a Mission Planning Assistant [5, 45]. The example used here shows how the same techniques could be applied to the task of hierarchical classification.

554

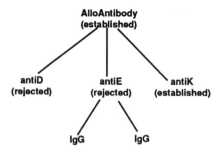

Fig. 3. Hierarchical Classification in RED

most extensive set of these abstract methods, which they call *Generic Tasks* [3], and they have characterized several general approaches that can be taken to solve problems in diagnosis and design.

Chandrasekaran's group uses their analyses of generic tasks to benefit explanation and system construction. They begin by defining a language for each type of generic task. This language directly supports the expression of the abstract operators (e.g., *data abstraction*) that occur in that generic method. Knowledge of these operators is then built in to explanation routines that are especially constructed for each generic method. Thus, they construct one set of explanation routines for heuristic classification, another for abduction (which is another kind of generic task), and so forth. The primary advantage of this approach is that because the explanation routines "understand" the task they are explaining at an abstract level, they can abstract away from specific details and provide more focused and understandable explanations. Their work has primarily concentrated on identifying and representing the *content* that needs to be conveyed in an explanation, and they have used relatively simple template-based generators to produce the explanation text.

Consider an example from RED [16], a system designed to help select compatible donor blood for patients who need a blood transfusion, by finding out what antibodies a patient has.

RED is organized as a hierarchical classification system, one of the diagnostic generic tasks. Hierarchical classification works by starting at the top of a tree structure such as the one in Figure 3. Each node in the tree represents a possible diagnosis for the patient. Subnodes represent hypotheses that are specialized versions of the hypothesis represented by the parent node. The hierarchical classification method works by starting at the top of the tree and attempting to *establish, reject* or *suspend* nodes based on the available evidence. If a node can be established, then its children are explored. If a node is rejected, the children are not explored. Suspended nodes are in an intermediate state where there is not enough evidence to either reject or establish them. They are not pursued further, but might be reactivated if further evidence becomes available.

Suppose that after processing, the system was in the state shown in Figure 3. The state of each node is indicated in parentheses under the node. IgG and IgM have no state associated with them because they were not considered.

To construct an explanation generator to explain why a particular node was in a particular state, we note that for this task two situations need to be considered:

1. Explaining why a particular node was rejected or established
2. Explaining why a particular node was not explored

For case 2, a sample explanation for IgG would be:

> IgG was not considered because it is a type of antiE which was rejected. The establish-and-refine strategy only examines successors of established classes.

This would be produced using the following template, which would be associated with the generic task establish-and-refine.

```
NODE was not considered because it is a type of ANCESTOR
which was rejected. The establish-and-refine strategy only
examines successors of established classes.
```

To generate an explanation, the capitalized words are replaced by information that is specific to the node in question. Note that the fixed text in this template reflects specialized knowledge about how the establish-refine strategy works. This illustrates how, in generic tasks, specialized knowledge about the things to be explained is built into the explanation generator itself.

An explanation for case 1 is more involved, and requires having access to the classes of evidence the system considers in making its decisions. A hierarchical classification system is organized into "knowledge groups" which are clusters of rules that are concerned with making a particular kind of decision. In RED, a RuleOut knowledge group tries to find evidence for ruling out a particular hypothesis. Similarly, other knowledge groups consider history information and evidence of the presence of an antigen. The explanation is produced by stating the results produced by each of these knowledge groups, and then giving the inputs that led to the decision. A possible explanation for why antiK was established appears in Figure 4.

The explanations in this section represent a considerable improvement over what would be possible with a flat rule-based system. The improvement comes from two sources. First, knowledge about the generic methods the system uses is built into the explanation routines. This knowledge is used to organize the explanations and improves their overall coherence. Second, the rules are organized into knowledge groups and the groups correspond to high-level terms (like "rule out") that the user is likely to understand.

Generic Tasks and the Desiderata. Like NEOMYCIN, the improvements in explanation provided by this approach come from *abstraction* of problem-solving

In the context of AlloAntibody established, the plausibility of antiK was examined.

- RuleOut evidence is negative because,
    - ProfileEmpty is F
    - ProfileZero is F
    - SignificantNonReaction is F
    - NonReactingCell is F
- History evidence is uncertain because,
    - PatientPossessesAntigen is unknown
    - PatientPossessesAntibody is unknown
- Presence evidence is positive because,
    - RuleOut is negative
    - History is uncertain

AntiK has plausibility value +2 because,

- Presence is positive
- Prevalence is common

So, antiK is established.

Fig. 4. Explaining an Established Node in RED

knowledge. However, in NEOMYCIN, the abstract control structure was represented by the task structure and metarules, and a general purpose method produced explanations by examining those structures. In contrast, in the Generic Task approach, the abstract methods are not explicitly represented as part of the system, but instead knowledge of those methods is embedded in the explanation routines. As a result, the explanation routines are not general purpose, but instead are especially constructed to explain particular kinds of tasks.

Ironically, the major limitations of this approach also come from one of its sources of strength. Because a lot of knowledge about a particular generic method is built into the routines that explain it, it will be impossible to use explanation routines for generic methods other than the one for which they were designed. This could introduce significant *construction overhead*. A related problem concerns *fidelity*. If one decides to change the abstract method the system is following (i.e., make a change to the establish-and-refine strategy) then that change needs to be made to both the problem-solving component of the system and the explanation routines. If the changes are not made consistently, the explanations will not accurately reflect what the system does.

3.3 The Explainable Expert System Framework (EES)

As we have discussed, first generation systems failed to capture knowledge about how an expert system was designed, and thus they could not provide good justifications for their actions. The Explainable Expert Systems framework was

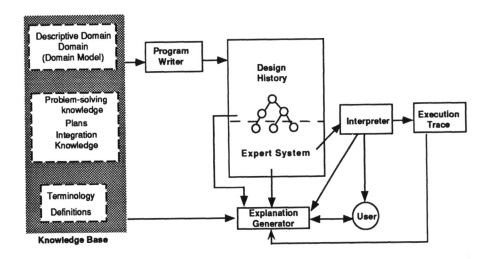

Fig. 5. The EES framework

designed to capture design information and improve explanations by providing a new approach to the construction of expert systems. In EES, system builders do not write directly executable code. Instead, they collaborate with domain experts to construct a high-level knowledge base that captures facts about the domain, its terminology, and general problem-solving strategies (see Figure 5). The knowledge base can be thought of as an abstract specification for the expert system that is to be created. An automatic program writer then constructs an executable system from this high-level specification. As the program writer constructs the expert system, it records its design decisions in a Design History. The code produced by the automatic program writer is linked to the Design History. At runtime, the expert system code is executed by an Interpreter. When the user requests an explanation of the expert system's behavior, the explanation facility uses the Design History to determine what design decisions were behind that part of the system and produces an explanation that not only tells the user what is happening, but also justifies the actions the system is taking in terms of the design decisions that were made and the higher-level knowledge sources in the knowledge base. EES thus captures the reasoning *behind* the system's actions.

The architectures presented earlier allow one to represent various links between specific actions and general methods. In contrast, EES actually derives the specific actions from an abstract specification of general methods and properties of the domain. Because the links are automatically derived, they are more likely to be consistent.

The EES architecture provides support for explanation in several ways:

- Abstract (and specific) control knowledge is represented in the high-level specification as plans. This gives EES a mechanism for representing the sorts of task structures that are captured in NEOMYCIN and Generic Tasks.[5]

- The use of a high-level specification allows the representation of a broad range of knowledge about the domain, its principles and its terminology. Different kinds of knowledge are separated and can be represented at various levels of abstraction. A broader knowledge base increases the number of possible "starting points" for an explanation and enhances understandability.

- The Design History captured by the automatic programmer provides the "connective tissue" that is needed to explain the relation between knowledge the user may know (the high-level specification) and specific actions that need to be justified.

The EES Knowledge Base. An EES knowledge base distinguishes three different kinds of knowledge: *terminological knowledge*, a *domain model*, and a library of *plans for problem solving.* EES's terminological knowledge expresses how the terms in the domain are defined and gives these terms an explicit semantics. These terms and their definitions are represented using Loom[20], a KL/ONE-style knowledge representation language. These terms are used as the building blocks for EES's problem-solving knowledge and the domain model. The domain model contains the "facts" of the domain that specify how different objects in the domain relate to one another. For example, in an electronics diagnosis domain, the model might include information about the components that make up a device, the circuit schemata, and the failure modes of the device.

While the domain model describes the domain, it does not describe how to solve problems in the domain. That is done by the problem-solving knowledge in the knowledge base. Problem-solving knowledge in EES is represented as strategies (called *plans*) for achieving particular goals (see Figure 6). Each plan includes a *capability description* which states what the plan can do (e.g., "diagnose a component"), and a *method body* which is a sequence of abstract steps that attempt to achieve the advertised capability of the plan. The steps can post further subgoals for the system to achieve. The language used in the method bodies is somewhat richer than in most planners, since it allows conditional expressions and iteration.

The EES Automatic Programmer. The EES automatic program writer works in a refinement-driven fashion. Initially, the program writer starts with a high-level goal that specifies what the expert system is supposed to do. The program writer searches its library of problem-solving knowledge to find a plan whose capability description matches[6] the goal. If no plan is found, the program writer attempts to reformulate (i.e., transform) the goal into a new goal or set of

---

[5] The EES project has been concerned with providing mechanisms for representing generic problem-solving methods, but has not performed the extensive analyses of generic task structures that Chandrasekaran and his associates have done.

[6] This match is performed by translating the goals and capability descriptions into Loom concepts and using the Loom classifier. A plan is applicable to a goal if its capability description subsumes the goal.

```
(define-plan diagnose-component
 :capability (DIAGNOSE (obj (c is (inst-of COMPONENT))))
 :method
   (let
    ((actual-symptoms
      (loop for each symptom in (POTENTIAL-SYMPTOM c)
        when
          (DETERMINE-WHETHER-DESCRIBED (obj c) (by symptom))
        collect symptom)))
      (FIND-CAUSES (obj actual-symptoms) (of c))))
```

Paraphrase (manual):

> To diagnose a component, the system finds the potential symptoms of the component. For each symptom, the system determines whether the component exhibits the symptom. These are called the actual symptoms. The system then finds the causes of the actual symptoms and returns them.

Fig. 6. An EES plan for diagnosing a component

goals that have the same underlying intent as the original goal but are expressed differently. It then attempts to find plans for achieving these new goals. This reformulation process is important for explanation, because the reformulation process does much of the reasoning that is needed to provide justifications for specific actions.

EES's reformulations allow it to derive from its abstract knowledge base of domain facts, terminology and problem-solving methods, *specific* problem-solving methods that would otherwise have to be written by hand. For explanation, this captures the reasoning behind how the abstract goals of the system were operationalized—reasoning that would otherwise stay in the head of the system builder. For example, in building a medical system to administer a drug, one abstract goal that would arise would be to adjust the drug dosage for any factors that would make the patient abnormally sensitive to the drug. To make this abstract goal operational, specific methods are needed that will check particular sensitizing factors and make appropriate adjustments. To produce that specific code, one needs to understand the criteria that make something a sensitizing factor for the drug, what particular physiological factors meet those criteria, and so forth. Reformulations are intended to capture the reasoning required to produce such specific methods. Once that reasoning is captured, it can be used to explain, for example, why the user is being asked the value of a particular physiological factor, or why that factor is considered to be a sensitizing factor for the drug.

In this section, we will discuss three of the reformulations that EES provides: *covering, redescription,* and *individualization.* For a more complete discussion of

EES's reformulations see [28].

A *covering* reformulation occurs when a goal can be transformed into several new goals that together *cover* the intent of the initial goal. In Loom, a set of one or more terms is said to *cover* another term if, taken together, the set of terms denotes all the things that the term denotes. For example, the terms "boy" and "girl" together *cover* the term "child".

A covering reformulation is a form of divide-and-conquer. If a goal involves performing an operation on a set of objects, but no method can be found for performing the operation, the covering reformulation splits the set into subsets, which allows the system to use more specialized methods to perform the operation on the subsets.

Performing a covering reformulation on a goal involves examining each of the terms that make up the goal, and for each term, trying to find a covering set for that term. If the system is successful in finding a covering set, it creates a new goal for each of the terms in the covering set by replacing the original term in the original goal with one of the terms in the covering set. Together, the resulting set of goals will cover the intent of the original goal, so if the system can find a way of achieving the new goals, it will have achieved the original goal.[7]

Consider an example from the domain of the Program Enhancement Advisor (PEA) [28]. PEA is a system that examines Lisp programs and suggests ways of transforming the program to improve its readability or maintainability. If one were to write PEA using conventional expert system technology, one would simply write a number of transformations that would enhance a Lisp program's style and create a mechanism that would apply the transformations where they were applicable. Such a system would work but it would not be able to explain why a particular transformation was appropriate. Below, we discuss how the EES approach provides such explanations.

Suppose at some point in the program-writing process the program writer is supposed to write code to achieve the following goal:

goal1: Apply maintainability-enhancing transformations to program-1.

Further, suppose that the system had two methods for applying transformations and that one of these could apply a single local transformation, while the other could apply a single distributed[8] transformation. The capabilities for these two plans would appear as:

capability-description: Apply a local transformation to a program.

---

[7] In performing both covering and individualization reformulations, part of the reformulation process involves finding a way to combine the results produced by each of the reformulations into a result that can be returned by the original goal. For a discussion of some of the issues involved see [43].

[8] Local transformations are ones whose applicability can be determined by looking at a single s-expression (e.g. transforming SETQ to SETF), while distributed transformations require looking at several places in the program to determine whether or not they are applicable (e.g. replacing CAR and CDR accessors to a data structure by a record facility.)

capability-description: Apply a distributed transformation to a program.

Neither of these plans can be directly used to achieve our goal of applying maintainability-enhancing transformations because 1) neither local nor distributed transformations subsume maintainability-enhancing transformations and 2) the plans apply *single* transformations while the goal calls for applying a *set* of transformations. The reformulation problem is to find a way of transforming the original goal so that these plans can be used to achieve it.

When the writer failed initially to find a plan, it would then try to reformulate the goal into new goals. Suppose the domain model contained the fact:

> TRANSFORMATION is covered by LOCAL-TRANSFORMATION and
> DISTRIBUTED-TRANSFORMATION

Using that fact, the writer could reformulate the original goal into two new goals:

goal2: Apply local maintainability-enhancing transformations to program-1.

goal3: Apply distributed maintainability-enhancing transformations to program-1.

For explanation, the reasoning behind this reformulation would allow EES to explain how it achieves the goal of applying maintainability-enhancing transformations:

> Since transformations can be classified as either distributed transformations or local transformations, the goal of applying maintainability-enhancing transformations to a program can be accomplished by first applying all the local maintainability-enhancing transformations to the program and then applying all the distributed maintainability-enhancing transformations to the program.

Unfortunately, the reformulated goals still won't match the available plans because the goals still involve applying a set of transformations while the plans apply single transformations. Normally, an individualization reformulation would be used to resolve this. Individualization reformulations are similar to covering reformulations, except that they decompose a goal over a set of objects into a set of goals over individual objects. However, this reformulation cannot be applied here, because there are no individual transformations indexed under maintainability-enhancing transformations in the knowledge base. But another way of describing maintainability-enhancing transformations is as "transformations whose right-hand side use is more general than their left-hand side use," that is, a transformation is maintainability enhancing if produces a more general construct. This alternative definition is stored in the knowledge base. Individual transformations *are* indexed under that alternative description. To get to them, the system performs a *redescription* reformulation.

A redescription reformulation transforms a goal into a new goal by transforming terms used in the goal based on definitions of those terms stored in the knowledge base. Using the alternative definition of maintainability-enhancing transformations cited above, a redescription reformulation transforms goal2 into:

562

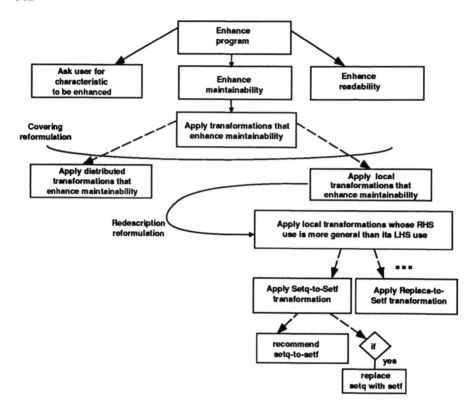

Fig. 7. A Portion of the EES Design History for PEA

goal4: Apply local transformations whose right-hand side use is more general than their left-hand side use to program-1.

Once this redescription has been done, the program writer can use an individualization reformulation to set up goals for applying individual transformations, such as the transformation of replacing SETQ with SETF.

Figure 7 shows the Design History that is left behind by the EES automatic programmer. This record provides explanation routines with the additional knowledge they need to justify the system's actions. For example, to explain why the system recommends replacing occurrences of SETQ with SETF, the system uses information recorded during the redescription reformulation to produce the following explanation:

> I am trying to enhance the maintainability of the program by applying transformations that enhance maintainability. A transformation that enhances maintainability is defined as a transformation whose right-hand side's use is more general than its left-hand side's use. SETF can be used to assign a value to any generalized variable. SETQ can only be used to assign a value

to a simple variable.

EES and the Desiderata. EES moves us closer to achieving the desiderata in several ways. First it improves *fidelity* because not only are explanations of the operation of the system produced from the code, but justifications of the system's actions are based on the Design History produced by the automatic program writer. Thus, changes that are made to the knowledge base will be directly reflected both in explanations of *what* happened and justifications of *why* it happened. Like the other systems described in this section, EES improves understandability by providing better *abstractions* for problem-solving knowledge. Because EES supports explicitly defined *terminology*, it can provide definitions for terms that a user may not know. From the standpoint of *sufficiency*, the primary contribution of EES is its approach to capturing the design rationale needed to support *justifications*. For *construction overhead* the situation is mixed. On one hand, EES increases construction overhead because it requires a system builder to represent more information in the knowledge base than would be required to build a simple first generation system that would solve the problem. This is a direct consequence of providing better explanations: more information is required to explain a solution to a problem than to simply solve it. It can also be argued that there are ways that the EES approach reduces construction overhead. Because knowledge is represented more abstractly in EES, there is a greater possibility for re-using knowledge across systems. For example, some of the diagnostic strategies EES uses are quite general and are not restricted to specific domains.

Finally, consider *efficiency*. A system that provides good justifications for its actions by always reasoning at runtime from first principles will probably run too slowly—in essence, such a system re-derives its expertise on every run. Although EES derives its expertise from general domain knowledge and principles, it avoids these efficiency problems because it performs the reasoning about how to reduce abstract plans to specific actions *once* when the automatic programmer produces the actual executable code of the expert system. Experts not only know more than non-experts, they also reach conclusions more rapidly. Part of becoming an expert is deriving useful reasoning "shortcuts" from more general principles. Most expert systems contain just the shortcuts, which limits their explanatory capabilities. The trick is to build an expert system that reasons efficiently using shortcuts and maintains a record of how the shortcuts were derived, for explanation.

3.4 Reconstructive Explanation

In each of the approaches to explanation that we described above, explanations were produced by generating text from the same knowledge structures that were used to solve a problem. As we discussed in the introduction, such an approach helps assure our desideratum of *fidelity*, that is, that the explanations accurately reflect what the system actually does. However, to produce *understandable* explanations (another desideratum) using this approach, the system must be structured in such a way so that it uses terms the user understands and reasons in ways that are familiar or that can be explained. But sometimes the best way to solve a problem on a computer requires using techniques that are totally foreign to users. How can such systems be explained?

Wick and Thompson [49] have proposed using *reconstructive explanation* to solve this problem. In their approach, a problem is first solved using techniques that may not be easily explainable. Once the problem is solved, a second knowledge base, with different techniques, is used to assemble a plausible story that will justify the conclusions that were reached, even though this story may have little to do with the actual processing that solved the problem in the first place. The second knowledge base does not have to be as powerful as the first. Since it is given the right answer, it just has to assemble a plausible line of reasoning from the inputs to the answer. This may involve substantially less search that was required to find the answer in the first place. Thus, this approach makes it possible to tailor the first knowledge base to problem-solving efficiency at the expense of explainability, while stressing explainability rather than efficiency in the second.

REX. Wick and Thompson's REX system implements reconstructive explanation. REX has been used to provide explanations for classification-based diagnostic systems. It has been used in two domains. We will use one of those domains, analysis of problems with concrete gravity dams, to illustrate its capabilities.

A key idea in REX is to allow for variability in the degree of coupling between the path the expert system took to reach a conclusion and the explanation that is given. By changing certain parameters, REX can be required to give an explanation that follows the solution path closely, or it can be given the freedom to generate an explanation that plausibly justifies the system's conclusion, but does not follow its solution path at all.

In the REX approach, a conventional expert system is first used to solve a problem. The expert system keeps a trace of the solution process which records the temporal order of processing, the data that was used, the hypotheses that were generated, and whether they were accepted or rejected.

This trace is then passed through a filter which can be set to one of four states:

1. *No-Restrict:* None of the trace (except the answer) is passed through the filter.
2. *Direct-Only:* Only direct cues are passed though. Hypotheses that the system may have generated are removed.
3. *Indirect-Only:* Only hypotheses are passed through.
4. *Direct-Indirect:* The trace is passed through without modification.

This filter is one of the mechanisms REX provides for controlling the degree of coupling between the expert system's processing and the explanation. The more information that is passed through the filter, the more closely the explanation will follow the expert system's line of reasoning.

Once the trace has been filtered, it is mapped onto an explanatory knowledge base. The content of this knowledge base is similar to the one used by the expert system to solve the problem, except that it is tailored to explanation concerns. Thus, it is stated at a more abstract level and removes many of the "implementation concerns" that are present in the expert system's knowledge base. The explanatory knowledge base consists of links between data and hypotheses and techniques for determining the plausibility of hypotheses.

When the trace is mapped onto the knowledge base, nodes that are present in the trace cause corresponding nodes in the explanatory knowledge base to be highlighted (these are called *reasoning cues*). The job of another module in REX, called the *explainer*, is to find a path through the nodes in the knowledge base that leads to the final conclusion. The degree to which the explainer must use the highlighted nodes in the knowledge base is determined by another switch, which can be set in four ways:

1. *No-RC:* Reasoning cues can be ignored by the explainer.
2. *RC:* The explainer can only consider lines of reasoning in which the hypotheses visited are directly supportable with the reasoning cues used by the expert system. Additional cues that support those lines of reasoning can be added.
3. *Only-RC:* Only the cues used by the expert system may be used. The explainer is not free to add additional cues.
4. *All-RC:* All of the reasoning cues used by the expert system must be used, and additional cues may be added.
5. *All-Only-RC:* All of the cues used by the expert system must be used, and the explainer is not free to add additional ones.

As Wick and Thompson point out, these settings are not independent of the settings of the filter described earlier. For example, it appears that the setting of the explainer's switch won't matter much if the filter has been set to *No-Restrict*, and similarly, the filter's setting won't have a big effect if the explainer is set to *No-RC*.

To get an idea of the kind of variation that is possible, consider the following two explanations (from [49]). If the explanation system is set to follow the expert system's processing as close as possible (*Direct-Indirect* and *All-Only-RC*) the following explanation results:

> I attempted to find the cause of an excessive load on a concrete dam. Based on the water marks on the abutments and the debris on top of the dam, I made an initial hypothesis. In looking at causal relationships, I found that a flood would cause the water marks and debris. This led me to hypothesize a flood was the problem. However, based on the duration of recent floods I was able to refute this hypothesis. In evaluating the hypothesis, I found no floods of sufficient duration to have caused the observed problems. As floods and settlement often have similar symptoms, I hypothesized that settlement

was the problem. After evaluating the hypothesis and determining causing relationships, I was able to further support this hypothesis. In evaluating the hypothesis, I found the drainage and uplift pressures were consistent with settlement as settlement will cause slow drainage in turn causing high uplift pressures. This led me again to hypothesize settlement. However, based on the selective breaking of the broken pipes in the foundation, I was able to refute this hypothesis. Again in looking at causal processes, I noted that settlement would cause crushed-like damage to the drainage pipes whereas erosion of soil would cause selective breaking. Therefore, I concluded erosion was causing the excessive load.

In contrast, the explainer produces a much more direct explanation that leaves out intermediate hypotheses when the settings are *Direct-Indirect* and *No-RC*):

I attempted to find the cause of an excessive load on a concrete dam. Based on the broken pipes in the foundation, the sliding of the dam, the uplift pressures, and the slow drainage, I was able to make an initial hypothesis. In studying causal relations, I found that the erosion of soil from under the dam would cause broken pipes, resulting in slow drainage, thereby creating increased uplift pressures and eventually sliding of the dam downstream. This led me to conclude erosion was the cause of the excessive load.

REX and the Desiderata. The primary contribution of REX is to *understandability*. By separating the explanation knowledge base from the 'performance' knowledge base, much more flexibility is possible. The explanations can easily abstract away from implementation details, in fact they do not need to follow the system's line of reasoning at all: the solution can be justified by knowledge and a derivation that is entirely different from the one used to obtain the solution. The major risk with the reconstructive approach is *fidelity*. Because the explanation can be so completely de-coupled from the process used to solve the problem, there is a risk of constructing a misleading explanation. *Construction overhead* can also be significant with this approach, because essentially two knowledge bases must be built: one to solve the problem, the other for explanation. *Efficiency*, however, can be good. The separation of explanation and problem-solving allows one to construct a highly optimized problem-solver without being concerned about how the optimizations might affect explainability.

In this section, we have examined a number of different expert system architectures that improve over first generation systems by capturing more of the knowledge that is needed to support explanation. In the next section, we will consider how more advanced explanation *generation* techniques can make use of that knowledge for better explanation.

4 More Sophisticated Approaches to Explanation Production

As we argued in the introduction, explanation is a process of constructing a coherent story that relates the expert system's concepts and results to things the user understands and accepts. First generation systems assumed that satisfactory stories could be produced with clever techniques for traversing, pruning, and translating the system's execution trace. But, as we have seen, this approach proved inadequate for first generation systems. It is even less viable for producing explanations from the more complex knowledge bases of second generation systems because they confront explanation components with new choices about what information to include and how to present it. Thus, the richer knowledge bases of second generation systems provide both an opportunity and a challenge for explanation generation.

Producing good explanations is a complex problem-solving task requiring its own expertise. We advocate the view that explanation must be freed from slavishly paraphrasing portions of the expert system's knowledge structures; explanation requires its own body of knowledge, in addition to the knowledge used by the expert system. In particular, to construct explanations that meet our desiderata, a system must have the following capabilities.

1. It must be *linguistically competent*, i.e., it must be able to construct a coherent multisentential text to achieve a communicative goal.
2. Its explanations must reflect *knowledge about the user*. That is, it must employ knowledge about what the user already knows, as well as the user's goals, plans and preferences to tell a story that relates to the user's existing knowledge and desires.
3. It must be able to *recover* if the user's feedback indicates that an explanation was unclear or otherwise inadequate.

These issues have been studied extensively by researchers in computational linguistics and natural language processing. This section describes some of the results from that literature and illustrates how techniques from computational linguistics and natural language processing can be used to improve the explanation capabilities of expert systems.

4.1 Generating Coherent Multisentential Responses

To produce coherent multisentential explanations, systems must adhere to discourse conventions, and explanations must flow smoothly from topic to topic (*linguistic competence*). McKeown (1985, pp. 1–2) argues that "people have preconceived ideas about the means with which particular communicative goals can be achieved as well as about the ways in which these means can be integrated to form a text." If systems were to produce explanations that match these preconceived ideas, their explanations would appear natural.

In Section 2, we saw that the explanations produced by paraphrasing the sequence of rules (or procedures) that led to a conclusion were often unnatural.

The problem is that these paraphrases follow the structure of a program, and there is no reason to assume that the computationally efficient reasoning strategies used by programs to produce results will form natural explanations. In fact, as we discussed in Section 2, many researchers have noted that they often *do not* provide a good basis for understandable explanations (e.g., [8, 11, 30, 43, 48]). However, in Section 3, we saw that with appropriate enhancements to a knowledge base, rule paraphrasing can lead to good explanations. For example, by paraphrasing its meta-rules, NEOMYCIN is able to produce good explanations its overall problem-solving strategy. This is because NEOMYCIN's metarules were specially designed to represent the system's problem-solving tasks in the way that humans talk about these tasks.

In general, paraphrasing a system's knowledge structures can be used to produce coherent explanations whenever these knowledge structures can be engineered to mirror the structure of natural explanations of the domain knowledge they represent. By studying naturally occurring explanations, computational linguists have identified types of text for which text structure closely follows the conceptual relations (e.g., causal, temporal, spatial) connecting the domain entities being described. If a system's knowledge representation captures these conceptual relations, coherent explanations can be generated by traversing links in the system's knowledge base. However, other types of explanations require organization that is not inherent in the domain knowledge. These texts are structured according to rhetorical considerations reflecting patterns of human discourse. To produce these texts, a system must have organizing strategies based this rhetorical knowledge. These rhetorical techniques can then guide the search through the system's knowledge sources to select information and structure it appropriately.

Here we describe these two text types and the generations techniques that can be used to produce them.

Exploiting inherent domain structure. For some text types, the organization of understandable texts should be dictated primarily by the inherent structure of the knowledge being communicated [29, 36, 41]. For example, Paris observed that one strategy for describing a complex physical object is to trace through the process that allows the object to perform its function. When text structure follows domain structure, Suthers argues that the most appropriate generation mechanism is *graph traversal*, which selectively follows existing links in a knowledge base [41]. Paris' *process trace* strategy, shown in Figure 8[9], exemplifies this technique. It traverses causal links to describe how an object functions.

Graph traversal mechanisms rely on the assumption that tracing certain types of domain links will produce a coherent explanation. This assumption will only be valid if the domain knowledge is represented in the way that people naturally talk about this knowledge. Furthermore, traversal mechanisms do not allow communicative strategies that differ significantly from the organization of the knowledge base, and therefore restrict the types of explanations that can be produced. To alleviate this problem, researchers turned to domain-independent

---

[9] In this figure, optional steps are enclosed in "{}".

Given a chain of causal links, for each object:
1. Follow the next causal link
2. {Mention an important side link}
3. {Give attributive information about a part just introduced}
4. {Follow the substeps if there are any
    (These substeps can be omitted for brevity.)}
Go back to 1.
(This process can be repeated for each subpart of the object)

Fig. 8. Paris' Process Trace Strategy (from [29])

rhetorical strategies that control both what is said and how it is structured. Such strategies have two major advantages. First, because they de-couple explanation strategies from low-level details of knowledge representation, knowledge engineers have more flexibility to design knowledge bases to satisfy other desiderata, such as maintainability and runtime efficiency. Second, explanation strategies based on rhetorical knowledge enable systems to generate a range of different explanations from the same knowledge representation. We now turn to a discussion of these techniques.

Rhetorical Structuring Techniques. Linguists and computational linguists (e.g., [13, 15, 22]) have proposed that there are domain-independent rhetorical predicates and relations that characterize the organization of coherent texts, and they have identified the effects that these relations can be used to achieve. McKeown operationalized a set of such predicates to build a system capable of generating coherent descriptions of domain entities [23]. From an examination of naturally occurring texts, she identified patterns of rhetorical predicates that were typically used to describe and compare entities. For example, she found that speakers frequently describe an object in terms of its constituent parts by:

1. Identifying the object as a member of some generic class.
2. Introducing constituents of the object being defined.
3. Providing characteristic information about each constituent in turn.
4. Providing attributive or analogical information about the object being defined.

McKeown encoded these standard patterns of discourse structure as partially ordered sequences of rhetorical predicates, called *schemata*. The above pattern is embodied in the *constituency schema*, shown in Figure 9.[10]

---

[10] In this figure, the "{}" indicate optionality, "/" indicates alternative, "+" indicates that the item may appear 1 or more times, and "*" indicates that the item is optional and may appear 0 or more times.

Constituency Schema

> Identification/Attributive
> Constituency
> Cause-effect*/Attributive*/
>   {Depth-identification/Depth-attributive
>   {Particular-illustration/Evidence}
>   {Comparison; Analogy/Renaming} }+
>   {Amplification/Explanation/Attributive/Analogy}

A Text Generated using Constituency Schema:

> (1) A guided projectile is a projectile that is self-propelled. (2) There are two types of guided projectiles in the ONR database: torpedoes and missiles. (3) The missile has a target location in the air or on the earth's surface. (4) The torpedo has an underwater target location. (5) The missile's target location is indicated by the DB attribute DESCRIPTION and the missile's flight capabilities are provided by the DB attribute ALTITUDE. (6) The torpedo's underwater capabilities are provided by the DB attributes under DEPTH (for example, MAXIMUM OPERATING DEPTH.) (7) The guided projectile has DB attributes TIME TO TARGET & UNITS, HORZ RANGE & UNITS and NAME.

Fig. 9. TEXT Constituency Schema and Sample Text from [23]

By associating each rhetorical predicate with an access function for an underlying knowledge base, schemata enable McKeown's TEXT system to select information from a knowledge base, order that information, and include discourse markers (e.g., "for example") in the final text. To produce a text, schema components are sequentially instantiated by using the access functions to match the rhetorical predicates against propositions in the underlying knowledge base. In McKeown's theory, each entry in the schema can be filled by an instantiated predicate or a full schema of the same name.

As shown in Figure 9, schemata contain many options and alternatives. To fully determine the content and order of a response, McKeown's system appeals to a set of constraints on how focus of attention shifts in natural discourse [37]. From the possible propositions that could come next in a text (as dictated by the chosen schema), these focus constraints select the alternative that fits in best with the previous discourse according to the following priorities:

1. Shift focus to a topic just introduced.
2. Maintain the current focus.
3. Return to a topic previously introduced.
4. Shift focus to a topic with the greatest number of implicit links to the list of topics just introduced.

A sample text generated with the CONSTITUENCY SCHEMA from a knowledge base of naval concepts appears in Figure 9.

To use schemata for generating responses, one must provide the system with knowledge about which schemata can be used to achieve each communicative goal. In general, there may be more than one schemata that can be used to achieve a particular explanatory goal. For example, the TEXT system had two schemata for achieving the goal *define entity*: the IDENTIFICATION SCHEMA defines an entity by identifying the entity as a member of a generic class and then providing attributes or examples of the entity; the CONSTITUENCY SCHEMA, illustrated above, defines an entity in terms of its constituent parts. Therefore, a schema-based system must have strategies for choosing among the applicable candidates. One influencing factor is the knowledge available for answering the question. For example, when defining an object, TEXT chooses the CONSTITUENCY SCHEMA when the knowledge base contains rich information about an object's constituents and less information about the object itself. The IDENTIFICATION SCHEMA is used otherwise. In this way, semantic information interacts with discourse structure to influence the choice of explanation strategy.

Schemata and the Desiderata. Schemata represent domain-independent discourse strategies. Each schema is a global organizing mechanism that directs the search through the underlying knowledge base for information appropriate to achieving a given communicative goal. Schemata thus preserve *fidelity* since they can be used to select content from the same knowledge bases that are used in problem-solving. Augmented with the focus constraints, schemata dictate the organization of a text while allowing the structure of a given response to be sensitive to "local" considerations, i.e., the available knowledge and the previous discourse. Thus, they satisfy the desideratum of *linguistic competence*.

To handle the range of explanations required of an expert system, an explanation component requires both graph traversal mechanisms (for tracing a system's causal or reasoning chains) and also discourse strategies that embody standard rhetorical techniques for achieving communicative goals. In some cases, strategies of both types may be available for answering a given type of question. Thus, the system also needs guidelines for choosing among these options. One source of such guidance is information about the current user's background knowledge and goals. We now consider how some explanation generators use knowledge about the current user to make these and other choices.

4.2 Generating Customized Explanations

Explanations are more likely to be understood and accepted if they are tailored to the user's knowledge of the domain, and take into account the user's goals, plans, and preferences. Information about the user is typically stored in a *user model*. One problematic issue is the question of where such models come from. Hand-crafting models for individual users is prohibitively time-consuming and error-prone. Recent research has produced several proposals for how a user model

can be built or refined from interactions with the user (e.g., [1, 17, 18, 19, 39, 50].
However, Sparck Jones questions the feasibility of acquiring detailed user models
and verifying their correctness, as well as the tractability of utilizing such models
to affect an expert system's reasoning and generation of responses [40]. She
advises system builders to be conservative about their expectations concerning
user modeling, and suggests that techniques based on *stereotypical models* should
be used whenever possible.

Assuming a user model is available, an explanation generator must be capable
of employing the information stored therein when planning its explanations. In
addition, the capability to customize explanations requires support from the
underlying domain knowledge representation. For example, the system can only
provide justifications of its actions in terms of the user's goals if the system
represents the relationship between user-level goals and the actions it takes.

Customizing the Level of Detail. Grice argues that good explanations
should be as informative as is required for the current purposes, but should not
include unnecessary detail [12]. A common approach to the problem of deciding
how much detail to include is a scheme involving double stereotypes. First, user
classes are identified, and then facts and rules in the knowledge base are marked
(e.g., [6, 43, 47]) or the knowledge base is partitioned (e.g., [10]) to indicate what
knowledge is appropriate for each user class. The most common user stereotypes
have been based on the user's level of expertise. For example, Wallis and Shortliffe developed a technique for customizing explanations of causal chains to the
user's level of expertise [47]. Expertise is represented as an integer ranging from 1
to 10, which the user declares. Each inference rule and concept in the knowledge
base is also marked with a measure of *complexity* ranging from 1 to 10. When
generating an explanation, the user's expertise value acts as an upper bound
on the complexity of concepts that will be included in the explanation. If two
concepts are linked by a rule deemed too complex for the current user's level
of expertise, canned text associated with the rule is included instead. Similarly,
a rule is also omitted from the explanation if its measure of complexity is too
far *below* the user's level of expertise, so that a user will not be overwhelmed by
things he is presumed to know.

An advantage of this method is that it is straightforward, and therefore easy
to implement. Moreover, because this scheme relies on users to indicate their
level of expertise, it does not require sophisticated methods for inferring this
information. However, this approach is limited by two assumptions: that the
difference between explanations for experts and novices is just the complexity
of the steps described, and that a user's expertise is uniform across domain
concepts and rules. If explanations for experts and novices differ in the *kinds*
of information to be presented, this approach cannot provide them. Also, this
approach will not work well if a single explanation must span both areas that the
user knows well and areas in which the user is a novice. Finally, this approach
requires marking each item in the knowledge base by hand to indicate its level
of complexity. This may involve considerable additional work during knowledge

engineering, and because all of the power of this technique comes from the hand marking, it does not ease system maintenance or evolution.

Tailoring to the User's Knowledge. In later work, Paris showed how a system could exploit more detailed information about a user to vary explanations in more sophisticated ways [29]. In order to determine what information should be included in explanations to users with different domain expertise, Paris compared the descriptions of several complex physical objects as given in adult and junior encyclopedia. She found that in addition to varying the *amount* of detail given to the two types of readers, the naturally occurring descriptions varied according to the *kind* of information provided. In particular, she found that the adult entries describe objects in terms of their subparts and properties, while the junior entries focus on how an object works.

To produce customized descriptions, Paris' TAILOR system employs two distinct discourse strategies. For experts, a parts-oriented description is produced using McKeown's CONSTITUENCY SCHEMA (see Figure 9.) For naive users, the process-trace strategy is used (see Figure 8). Paris does not assume that users fall into one of several stereotypical classes, e.g., novice vs. expert. Rather, she recognizes that users may have *local expertise* about some objects in the knowledge base while being naive about others. TAILOR assumes a user model that contains knowledge of which specific objects in the knowledge base are known to the user as well as an indication of whether or not the user understands the "underlying basic concepts." Given such a model, TAILOR can mix the two discourse strategies to cover cases where the user has significant knowledge about some aspects of the object being described and is naive about others.

For example, Figure 10 shows TAILOR's description of a telephone. In this example the user model indicates that the user knows about loudspeakers, but does not know about microphones or how they work in conjunction with loudspeakers in a telephone. Because the user knows about one of the two parts of the telephone (a receiver is a kind of loudspeaker), the CONSTITUENCY SCHEMA is selected, and the description begins by identifying the telephone by stating its purpose and introducing its parts. Structural information about each of the subparts is presented next. However, when the system consults the user model and learns that the user has no local expertise about transmitters (a type of microphone), the system switches momentarily to the process-trace strategy to describe the transmitter. The description of the transmitter is italicized in Figure 10.

Paris' approach shows how detailed knowledge about a user can be used to select among alternative explanation strategies. This approach requires that system builders identify the types of explanations that are suitable for users in different classes, and encode explanation strategies for producing these different types of explanations. This approach also assumes that the system has knowledge about which concepts are known to an individual user. Thus, the system must have a way of acquiring this information.

The telephone is a device that transmits soundwaves. The telephone has a housing that has various shapes and various colors, a transmitter that changes soundwaves into current, a curly-shaped cord, a line, a receiver to change current into soundwaves and a dialing-mechanism. *The transmitter is a microphone with a small diaphragm. A person speaking into the microphone causes the soundwaves to hit the diaphragm of the microphone. The soundwaves hitting the diaphragm cause the diaphragm to vibrate. The vibration of the diaphragm causes the current to vary. The current varies, like the intensity varies.* The receiver is a loudspeaker with a small aluminum diaphragm. The housing contains the transmitter and it contains the receiver. The housing is connected to the dialing-mechanism by the cord. The line connects the dialing-mechanism to the wall.

Fig. 10. Description Generated by Mixing Two Strategies (from [29])

Tailoring to User's Goals. A good explanation should indicate to the user that his goal(s) were taken into account [24]. In addition, the system should recognize cases in which the user's query indicates that his plan is suboptimal or invalid, and provide a response that points out the problem and informs him of better alternatives [32, 31, 46]. Finally, good explanations should address not only the goals stated in an individual query, but should take into account previously expressed goals or preferences as well as goals that can be inferred from the user's background [46].

In order to provide such responses, a system must be provided with knowledge about the user's goals and plans *a priori*, or must be able to infer this information, and then must be capable of using this information to affect the explanations it produces. In some cases, it is feasible to associate default goals and preferences with user stereotypes.[11] For example, Cohen *et al.* developed a system to assist in the diagnosis of students' learning disabilities. They found that in this domain all users shared the high-level goal of properly diagnosing the student, but users in different groups had different preferences for choosing the tests to be used in the diagnosis process. In particular, parents prefer tests that minimize the stress to the student, psychologists prefer to administer standard tests, and principals prefer tests that can qualify for funding. This information can be acquired during the knowledge engineering phase and incorporated into the stereotypes for these user classes.

Assuming that a model of the user's current goals, plans, and preferences can be obtained, the system must have mechanisms for using this information when computing its results and constructing its explanations. Cohen *et al.*'s system uses information about the user's preferences to add information to the response

---

[11] For application domains where users' goals cannot be determined *a priori*, the system must have a mechanism for inferring users' goals and plans from their queries. Computational linguists have provided several approaches to the *plan recognition* problem. For a good survey of this field, see Chapter 2 of [2].

being constructed. When a user asks the system to justify a recommendation, the system computes a response indicating how the recommended action will take the user closer to the higher domain goal of accurately diagnosing the student. The system then uses the following strategy to determine whether or not this response should be augmented to reflect its relationship to the user's preferences.

1. If the computed result satisfies the user's preference, state the preference in the explanation.
2. If the computed result does not satisfy the user's preference, identify the factor that overrode the preference, and state this factor in the explanation.
3. If the preference cannot be satisfied by any of the possible solutions satisfying the higher domain goal, state that the preference need not be considered because there are no solutions that satisfy the preference.

Figure 11[12] illustrates how this strategy enables user's preferences to affect the system's explanation.[13]

4.3 Feedback

One of the desiderata is that a system be able to respond to feedback from the user about the suitability of its explanations. By feedback we mean follow-up questions evoked by previously generated responses (e.g., "What is an X?", "Why?"), indications that a clarification of a response is desired (e.g., by asking a question again), or simple indications that a response was not understood (e.g., "Huh?", "I don't understand.").

This capability is crucial for two reasons. First, studies of naturally occurring advisory interactions show that experts and novices must negotiate the problem to be solved as well as a solution that the novice understands and accepts [33, 26]. Second, the completeness and accuracy of user models cannot be guaranteed in practice. Thus, unless systems can compensate for incorrect or incomplete user models, the impracticality of building user models will prevent much of the work on tailoring from being successfully applied in real systems [27]. The ability to recover when the user is not satisfied with an explanation alleviates some of the burden placed on user modeling. With this capability, a system does not *require* a detailed and correct user model in order to supply users with the information they seek. It is not forced to attempt to provide a response that will be understood and that will be the most appropriate in *one shot*. Instead, the system can rely on the user to provide feedback when necessary. By responding to this feedback, the system can overcome the limitations of its user model.

---

[12] These examples are based on those in [10]. The original examples do not show English input and output. We have provided the English glosses to make the example more readable.

[13] In this system, the user's preferences affect only the explanations, not the recommendations. In other systems, preferences affect the recommendations as well (e.g., see [24]). However, the issues raised by those systems go beyond the explanation concerns of this article.

System: Administer the NEAL Analysis of Reading Test.
User: Why is this test being recommended?

Un-augmented Answer: `NEAL-appropriate-for-reading`

Parent prefers tests which are low stress to the student.

Response to Parent:
   The NEAL is appropriate for diagnosing reading disorders and
   is low stress.

Psychologist prefers to administer common standardized tests
with which he or she is familiar.

Response to Psychologist:
   The NEAL is not a standardized test, but it is a high accuracy test.

Principal prefers to administer tests which can be used in
government funding formulae.

Response to Principal:
   The NEAL is appropriate for diagnosing reading disorders.
   We do not need to consider whether funding is available
   because there is no evidence to suggest that this student
   will qualify for additional funding.

Fig. 11. Generating Explanations Customized to a User's Perspective (from [10])

Requirements for handling feedback. To respond to feedback, a system must "understand" the text it generates. Users' follow-up questions must be interpreted in the context of the ongoing interaction, and the system's previous explanations make up part of this context. When the user does not fully understand a response, the generation facility must be able to determine what portion of the text failed to achieve its purpose, so that it can clarify misunderstood explanations and elaborate on prior explanations. To provide these capabilities, the system must keep a record of the communicative goals that it is trying to achieve as well as the strategies it used to achieve them.

In addition, the system must have several strategies for achieving its communicative goals. Making oneself understood often requires the ability to present the same information in multiple ways or to provide different information to illustrate the same point. Without multiple strategies for responding to a question, a system cannot offer an alternative response even if it understands why a previous explanation was not satisfactory.

Finally, a system needs *recovery strategies* that tell it how to respond if an initial explanation is not understood.

EES: A System That Responds to Feedback. To be capable of responding to users' feedback, the EES framework adopted a plan-based approach to explanation generation. As described in Section 4.1, previous systems made use of schemata to produce multisentential texts. However, schemata are insufficient for use as a representation of the system's previous utterances. A schema can be viewed as the result of a "compilation" process where the *rationale* for all of the steps in the process has been compiled out. What remains is the top-level communicative goal that invoked the schema, and the sequence of actions (i.e., instantiated rhetorical predicates which cause sentences to be generated) that can achieve that goal.

Because of this compilation, schemata provide a computationally efficient way to produce multisentential texts for achieving discourse purposes. However, because information about the intended effects of the components of a schema and how these intentions were achieved has all been compiled away, a system using schemata does not have the information it needs to respond to feedback. It cannot determine which goal failed or what other strategies could be used. Therefore, the system cannot recover from the failure by planning another response to achieve this goal using an alternative strategy.

To address this problem, the authors of this paper, working with Cécile Paris, have developed a plan-based approach to explanation for the EES framework described in Section 3.3 above. This work was guided by the lessons learned in improving the problem-solving architectures of first generation systems to support explanation. Recall that in first generation systems, much of the control knowledge needed to support explanations was compiled away. To improve the architectures, researchers moved towards systems that explicitly represented and reasoned about their own control structure. By recording the rationale behind the system's construction, systems had the knowledge needed to support explanations of their problem-solving strategy and justifications of their actions. In a similar vein, by explicitly representing knowledge about communicative intentions and the rhetorical means that may be used to achieve them, the EES explainer can produce text plans that record the "design rationale" behind its own explanations. In this way, it provides increased flexibility and the record of intentional structure that is needed to handle feedback.

In EES, communicative goals are represented in terms of the effects that the speaker intends the text to have on the hearer's beliefs or goals (e.g., make the user know a certain concept, persuade the user to perform an action). To produce text, the planner makes use of explanation strategies that map communicative goals to the linguistic resources for achieving them. These strategies are encoded in a set of plan operators that were derived by studying naturally occurring explanations.

Figure 12 shows an example plan operator to persuade someone to do an act. It captures the common sense notion that if the act needs to be done to achieve a goal that the user shares, then one way to persuade the user to do the act is to *motivate* the act by relating it to the shared goal.[14]

---

[14] For example, one can persuade a researcher to write an interim research report by

In Plan Language Notation:

> EFFECT: (PERSUADED ?hearer
>   (GOAL ?hearer (DO ?hearer ?act)))
> CONSTRAINTS: (AND (STEP ?act ?goal)
>   (GOAL ?hearer ?goal)
> NUCLEUS: (FORALL ?goal
>   (MOTIVATION ?act ?goal))
> SATELLITES: nil

English Translation:

> To achieve the state in which the hearer is persuaded to do an *act*,
> IF the *act* is a step in achieving some *goal(s)* of the hearer,
> THEN motivate the *act* in terms of those *goal(s)*.

Fig. 12. Plan Operator for Persuading User to Do An Act

When a communicative goal is posted, the text planner searches its library of explanation operators looking for those that can achieve the goal. In general, there will be several candidate strategies for achieving a goal. The planner employs a set of *selection heuristics* to determine which strategy is most appropriate in the current situation. These selection heuristics take into account information about the user's knowledge and goals (as recorded in the *user model*), and the conversation that has occurred so far (as recorded in the *dialogue history*). Once a strategy is selected, it may in turn post subgoals for the planner to refine. Planning continues in a top-down fashion until all goals are refined into speech acts, such as INFORM and RECOMMEND.

As the system plans explanations, it records its decisions in a text plan. This text plan captures the "design rationale" behind the explanation, by recording the goal structure of the text produced, the relationships between parts of the text, and an indication of the roles played by individual clauses in the explanation. The text plan is also input to a sentence generator, the Penman system [21], which performs the process of realization into English text.

After it has generated an explanation, the system waits for feedback from the user. The recorded text plan gives the system the dialogue context it needs to interpret the user's follow-up questions in context, and to plan explanations that elaborate on previous explanations or correct misunderstandings. Thus capturing the design rationale behind the explanation is as important to providing good explanatory capabilities as capturing the design rationale behind the expert system itself.

Figure 13 shows a sample dialogue with the Program Enhancement Advisor

---

pointing out that the report is required to receive continued funding.

SYSTEM (1) What characteristics of the program would you like to enhance?
USER (2) Maintainability.

$$\vdots$$

SYSTEM (3) You should replace (setq x 1) with (setf x 1).
USER (4) Why?
SYSTEM (5) I'm trying to enhance the maintainability of the program by applying transformations that enhance maintainability. Setq-to-setf is a transformation that enhances maintainability.
USER (6) Why?
SYSTEM (7) Transformations that enhance maintainability are defined as transformations whose right-hand-side use is more general than its left-hand-side use. Setf can be used to assign a value to any generalized-variable. Setq can only be used to assign a value to a simple-variable.
USER (8) What is a generalized variable?
SYSTEM (9) Simple-variables are storage locations named by symbols. This concept can be generalized to a storage location that can be named by any accessor function. These storage locations are called generalized-variables.
USER (10) Huh?
SYSTEM (11) For example, the *car* and *cdr* of a cons are generalized-variables, named by the accessor functions car and cdr.

Fig. 13. Sample Dialogue from [25]

(PEA), an expert system built in the EES framework. After the user supplies PEA with the program to be enhanced, PEA begins the dialogue by asking what characteristics of the program the user would like to improve. In this example, the user chooses maintainability. PEA then recommends transformations that would enhance the program along this dimension. After each recommendation is made, the user is free to ask questions about the recommendation.

To illustrate the text planning process, consider how the system produces its response on line 4. First, the system interprets the user's "why?" on line 4 as a request to be persuaded to perform the action recommended on line 3 (i.e., replace SETQ with SETF). The system must thus plan an explanation to achieve the goal (PERSUADED USER (GOAL USER (DO USER REPLACE-SETQ-WITH-SETF))). It uses the operator shown in Figure 12 to achieve this goal. When attempting to satisfy the constraints of this operator, the system first checks the constraint (STEP REPLACE-SETQ-WITH-SETF ?goal). This constraint states that, in order to use this operator, the system must find a domain goal, ?goal, that is a super-goal of REPLACE-SETQ-WITH-SETF. To find such goals, the planner searches the design history that has been recorded by the EES automatic programmer. In this example, the applicable expert system goals are all of the ancestors of the node "Replace SETQ with SETF" in the design history shown in Figure 7.

The second constraint of the current plan operator, (GOAL ?hearer

580

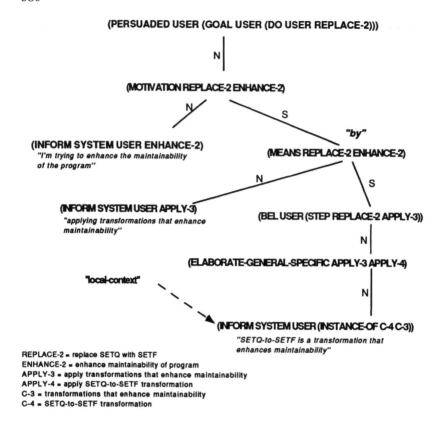

Fig. 14. Explanation Text Plan

?goal)), is a constraint on the user model stating that ?goal must be a goal of the hearer. In this example, since the user is employing the system to enhance a program and has indicated a desire to enhance the maintainability of the program, the system infers the user shares the top-level goal of the system (ENHANCE-PROGRAM), as well as the more specific goal ENHANCE-MAINTAINABILITY. Therefore, the two goals that completely satisfy the constraints of the operator shown in Figure 12 are ENHANCE-PROGRAM and ENHANCE-MAINTAINABILITY. EN-HANCE-MAINTAINABILITY is a refinement of ENHANCE-PROGRAM. In order to avoid explaining parts of the reasoning chain that the user is familiar with, when one goal is a subgoal of another, the most specific goal is chosen. Therefore, EN-HANCE-MAINTAINABILITY is now the preferred candidate binding for the variable ?goal.

The nucleus of the chosen plan operator is now posted, resulting in the subgoal (MOTIVATION REPLACE-SETQ-WITH-SETF ENHANCE-MAINTAINABILITY). In this example, this subgoal is achieved by operators that explain how a specific action (i.e., REPLACE-SETQ-WITH-SETF) is a step in a method for achieving the user-level goal (i.e., ENHANCE-MAINTAINABILITY). Planning continues in a top-down fashion until all subgoals have been refined to speech acts. The final text plan for the system's response on line 5 is shown in Figure 14.

There are several other important things to note about the dialogue shown in Figure 13. After the system produces the justification on line 5, the user asks "why?" again (line 6). Note that, this time, "why?" must be interpreted differently than the "why?" on line 4. In this case, the "why?" is ambiguous. Among other things, it could be a question about the super-goal, that is: "Why are you trying to enhance the maintainability of the program?" This is in fact the way that MYCIN would interpret this question. However, most people interpret this "why?" as a question about the statement that is currently the focus of attention (i.e., the thing most recently said). That is, people interpret the question on line 6 as: "Why is setq-to-setf a transformation that enhances maintainability?" Our system is able to make this interpretation because it understands the structure of the explanations it has produced (shown in Figure 14) and because it has heuristics for interpreting such questions based on its dialogue context (see [25]).

Third, to produce the answer on line 7, the system uses the domain model and the fact that the goal was reformulated using a redescription as recorded in the design history. This illustrates how the explanation component makes use of the enhanced knowledge provided in the design history.

Next, on line 8, the user asks the system "What is a generalized variable?" In response, the system defines a piece of its terminology using a strategy that abstracts from a concept the user knows about (simple variable) to define the new concept (generalized variable). This is one of many strategies the system has for defining concepts. It is chosen because it relates the new concept to a concept the user already knows. However, on line 10, the user indicates that he doesn't understand this definition. On line 11, the system produces a follow-up explanation to that clarify the definition by giving examples of this term (line 11). The system is able to recover from such failures because it understands and can reason about the text it previously produced. In this case, the system needed to know what communicative goal it was trying to achieve (i.e., to make the user know about generalized variables) and how it achieved this goal (by abstracting from the concept of simple variables). In addition, the system has alternative strategies for defining terms and recovery heuristics that allow it to choose the "most appropriate" strategy when an alternative explanation is required [26]. In this case, the recovery heuristic used says that when the goal that failed was to define a term, examples should be tried next.

The Desiderata Revisited. The EES text planner satisfies many of the desiderata for producing understandable explanations. First, the plan operators used to construct explanations encode standard ways that communicative goals are achieved by rhetorical means, thus providing *linguistic competence*. Second, each operator contains applicability constraints that specify the knowledge that must be available if the operator is to be used. These constraints direct the explanation planner to search the expert system's knowledge bases and user model for the information it needs to achieve its communicative goals. Planning using these operators allows the system to produce coherent explanations directly from the expert system's domain knowledge, thus preserving *fidelity*. In addition, because operator constraints can refer to a user model, the system can tailor the content and organization of its explanations to the individual user (*user sensitivity*) [27]. Finally, as we have shown in this section, because the EES text planner explicitly records the planning process behind the explanations it produces, it is able to *respond to the user's feedback* about the suitability of its explanations.

5   Conclusions

In this paper, we argued that explaining something to a user requires constructing a story relating things the user does not understand to general facts, plans and goals that he knows and accepts. The stories told by first generation systems were inadequate. They were often missing important parts, because the knowledge needed to explain these parts was not represented in the system. Moreover, because these explanations closely followed the trace of the system's rule firings, there was only one type of story that could be told, and this story was often unnatural and difficult for users to understand.

Second generation systems addressed these problems with new architectures that capture more of the knowledge needed to support explanation, and more powerful explanation generators that are able to exploit these richer knowledge structures to produce more understandable explanations. By providing more comprehensive knowledge bases that include the concepts, methods, and facts known to the user, second generation systems increase the range of starting points for explanations. By representing the linkages between the starting points and the system's structure and behavior, second generation systems can produce the broader range of explanations that users desire. In explanation generation, these systems moved toward explanation strategies encoding knowledge about standard patterns of human discourse structure. To tell stories from different starting points, several different strategies may be represented. By taking into account knowledge about the user and dialogue context, second generation systems can choose the strategy most suited to the user's needs and knowledge. Finally, by recording the rationale behind the explanations they generate, some systems can answer users' follow-up questions in the context of the ongoing explanation dialogue and offer clarifying explanations when needed. Thus, better explanation comes from capturing more knowledge: about the domain, the user, the expert system and its design, and about the generation of explanations themselves. This insight is the key contribution of second generation explanation systems.

Acknowledgments

The work on the Explainable Expert Systems framework was supported by the Defense Advanced Research Projects Agency under contract DABT63-91-C-0025, and under NASA Ames cooperative agreement number NCC 2-520. The authors would particularly like to thank Eduard Hovy, Cécile Paris and Ramesh Patil for comments on drafts of this paper.

References

1. H. C. Bunt. Modular Incremental Modelling of Belief and Intention. In *Proceedings of the Second International Workshop on User Modeling*, 1990.
2. Sandra M. Carberry. *Plan Recognition in Natural Language Dialogue*. MIT Press, 1990.
3. B. Chandrasekaran. Generic tasks in knowledge-based reasoning. *IEEE Expert*, 1(3):23–30, 1986.
4. B. Chandrasekaran and S. Mittal. Deep versus compiled knowledge approaches to diagnostic problem-solving. In *Proceedings of the National Conference on Artificail Intelligence*. AAAI, 1982.
5. B. Chandrasekaran, M. C. Tanner, and J. R. Josephson. Explaining control strategies in problem solving. *IEEE Expert*, 4(1):9–24, Spring 1989.
6. David N. Chin. Exploiting user expertise in answer expression. In *Proceedings of the Seventh National Conference on Artificial Intelligence*, pages 756–760, St. Paul, Minnesota, August 1988. Morgan Kaufmann.
7. W. Clancey. The advantages of abstract control knowledge in expert system design. In *Proceedings of the National Conference on Artificial Intelligence*, 1983.
8. W. Clancey. The epistemology of a rule-based expert system: A framework for explanation. *Artificial Intelligence*, 20(3):215–251, 1983.
9. W.J. Clancey. Heuristic classification. *Artificial Intelligence*, 27(3):289–350, 1985.
10. Robin Cohen, Marlene Jones, Amar Sanmugasunderam, Bruce Spencer, and Lisa Dent. Providing responses specific to a user's goals and background. *International Journal of Expert Systems*, 2(2):135–162, 1989.
11. R. Davis. *Applications of meta-level knowledge to the construction, maintenance, and use of large knowledge bases*. PhD thesis, Stanford University, 1976.
12. H. P. Grice. Logic and conversation. In *Syntax and Semantics III: Speech Acts*, pages 41–58. Academic Press, New York, NY, 1975.
13. Joseph E. Grimes. *The Thread of Discourse*. Mouton, The Hague, Paris, 1975.
14. D.W. Hasling, W. J. Clancey, and G. Rennels. Strategic explanations for a diagnostic consultation system. *International Journal of Man-Machine Studies*, 20(1), 1984.
15. Jerry R. Hobbs. On the coherence and structure of discourse. Technical Report CSLI-85-37, Center for the Study of Language and Information, Leland Stanford Junior University, Stanford, California, October 1985.
16. J. R. Josephson, B. Chandrasekaran, J. W. Smith, Jr., and M. C. Tanner. A mechanism for forming composite explanatory hypotheses. *IEEE Transactions on Systems, Man, and Cybernetics*, 17(3):445–454, 1987.
17. Robert Kass. Building a User Model. *User Model and User Adapted Interaction*, 1(3):203 – 258, 1991.

584

18. Alfred Kobsa. Generating a User Model from WH-Questions in the VIE-LANG System. Technical Report 84-03, Department of Medical Cybernetics, University of Vienna, 1984.

19. Jill Fain Lehman and Jaime G. Carbonell. Learning the User's Language: A Step Towards Automated Creation of User Models. In Alfred Kobsa and Wolfgang Wahlster, editors, *User Models in Dialog Systems*. Springer Verlag, Berlin—New York, 1989.

20. Robert M. Mac Gregor. A deductive pattern matcher. In *Proceedings of the Seventh National Conference on Artificial Intelligence*. AAAI, 1988.

21. William Mann. An overview of the Penman text generation system. Technical report, USC/Information Sciences Institute, 1983.

22. William C. Mann and Sandra A. Thompson. Rhetorical Structure Theory: Towards a functional theory of text organization. *TEXT*, 8(3):243–281, 1988.

23. Kathleen R. McKeown. Discourse strategies for generating natural-language text. *Artificial Intelligence*, 27:1–41, 1985.

24. Kathleen R. McKeown. Generating goal-oriented explanations. *International Journal of Expert Systems*, 1(4):377–395, 1988.

25. Johanna D. Moore. *A Reactive Approach to Explanation in Expert and Advice-Giving Systems*. PhD thesis, University of California, Los Angeles, 1989.

26. Johanna D. Moore. Responding to "huh?": Answering vaguely articulated follow-up questions. In *Proceedings of the Conference on Human Factors in Computing Systems*, pages 91–96, Austin, Texas, 1989.

27. Johanna D. Moore and Cécile L. Paris. Exploiting user feedback to compensate for the unreliability of user models. *User Modeling and User-Adapted Interaction*, in press.

28. R. Neches, W. R. Swartout, and J. D. Moore. Enhanced maintenance and explanation of expert systems through explicit models of their development. *IEEE Transactions on Software Engineering*, SE-11(11):1337–1351, November 1985.

29. Cécile L. Paris. Tailoring object descriptions to the user's level of expertise. *Computational Linguistics*, 14(3):64–78, September 1988.

30. Jasmina Pavlin and Daniel D. Corkill. Selective abstraction of AI system activity. In *Proceedings of the National Conference on Artificial Intelligence*, pages 264–268, Austin, Texas, August 6-10 1984.

31. Martha E. Pollack. *Inferring Domain Plans in Question-Answering*. PhD thesis, University of Pennsylvania, May 1986. Published by University of Pennsylvania as Technical Report MS-CIS-86-40.

32. Martha E. Pollack. A model of plan inference that distinguishes between the beliefs of actors and observers. In *Proceedings of the Twenty-Fourth Annual Meeting of the Association for Computational Linguistics*, pages 207 – 214, New York, NY, June 1986.

33. Martha E. Pollack, Julia Hirschberg, and Bonnie Lynn Webber. User participation in the reasoning processes of expert systems. In *Proceedings of the Second National Conference on Artificial Intelligence*, Pittsburgh, Pennsylvania, August 18-20 1982.

34. A. Scott, W. Clancey, R. Davis, and E. H. Shortliffe. Methods for generating explanations. In B. Buchanan and E. H. Shortliffe, editors, *Rule-Based Expert Systems*. Addison-Wesley, 1984.

35. Edward H. Shortliffe. Mycin: A rule based computer program for advising physicians regarding anti-microbial therapy selection. Technical Report AI Lab Memo AIM-250, Stanford University, October 1974.

36. Penelope Sibun. Generating text without trees. *Computational Intelligence*, 8(1):102–122, 1992.

37. Candace L. Sidner. *Toward a Computational Theory of Definite Anaphora Comprehension in English Discourse*. PhD thesis, Massachusetts Institute of Technology, Cambridge, Mass., 1979.

38. H. Silverman. A digitalis therapy advisor. Technical Report TR-143, Massachusetts Institute Technology Project MAC, 1975.

39. D. H. Sleeman. UMFE: A User Modelling Front End SubSystem. *International Journal of Man-Machine Studies*, 23:71–88, 1985.

40. Karen Sparck Jones. Realism about user modelling. In *User Models in Dialog Systems*. Springer-Verlag, Symbolic Computation Series, Berlin Heidelberg New York Tokyo, 1989.

41. Daniel D. Suthers. Task-appropriate hybrid architectures for explanation. *Computational Intelligence*, 7(4), 1991.

42. W. Swartout. Explaining and justifying expert consulting programs. In *Proceedings of the Seventh International Joint Conference on Artificial Intelligence*. IJCAI, 1981.

43. W. R. Swartout. XPLAIN: A system for creating and explaining expert consulting systems. *Artificial Intelligence*, 21(3):285–325, September 1983.

44. William R. Swartout, Cécile L. Paris, and Johanna D. Moore. Design for explainable expert systems. *IEEE Expert*, 6(3):58–64, June 1991.

45. M. C. Tanner and A. M. Keuneke. Explanation in knowledge systems: The roles of the task structure and domain functional models. *IEEE Expert*, 6(3), June 1991.

46. Peter van Beek. A model for generating better explanations. In *Proceedings of the 25th Annual Meeting of the ACL*, Palo Alto, California, 1987. Association of Computational Linguistics.

47. Jerold W. Wallis and Edward H. Shortliffe. Customized explanations using causal knowledge. In *Rule-Based Expert Systems: The MYCIN Experiments of the Stanford Heuristic Programming Project*, chapter 20, pages 371–388. Addison-Wesley Publishing Company, 1984.

48. Bonnie Lynn Webber and Aravind Joshi. Taking the initiative in natural language data base interactions: Justifying why. Technical Report MS-CIS-82-1, University of Pennsylvania, 1982.

49. Michael R. Wick and William B. Thompson. Reconstructive expert system explanation. *Artificial Intelligence*, 54(1-2), March 1992.

50. Dekai Wu. Active Acquisition of User Models: Implications for Decision-Theoretic Dialog Planning and Plan Recognition. *Journal of User Model and User Adapted Interaction*, 1(2):149 – 172, 1991.

Explanation Using Task Structure and Domain Functional Models

Michael C. Tanner[1], Anne M. Keuneke[2], and B. Chandrasekaran[3]

[1] Computer Science Department, George Mason University, Fairfax VA 22030, USA
[2] Computer Science Department, California State University, Chico CA 95929, USA
[3] Department of Computer and Information Science, The Ohio State University, Columbus OH 43210, USA

Abstract. In this paper we present some of the work and ideas developed at the Ohio State Laboratory for AI Research on explaining the behavior of knowledge systems. The first part of the paper presents an analysis of the explanation problem and the aspects of it that we have concentrated on (briefly, we are concerned more with the form and content of the representations than the explanation form or presentation). Then we describe a generic task-based approach to explanation, including relating the explanation to the logical structure of the task. Finally, we show how causal models of a domain can be used to give explanations of diagnostic decisions.

1 Aspects of Explanation

As described by Chandrasekaran, Tanner, and Josephson [8], we can separate the explanation generation problem in knowledge systems into three top-level functions: generating the content, being responsive, and interacting with human users.

Generating an explanation's basic content. Given user queries about a system's decisions, we need to generate an information structure containing the elements needed for an explanation.

Shaping explanations to match user knowledge. It may not be necessary to communicate all the available explanation content to users. Systems apply knowledge of user goals, state of knowledge, and the dialog structure to filter, shape, and organize the output of the above *content* process so that explanations respond to user needs.

Interacting with users. The two preceding functions produce all the information needed conceptually and logically for the required explanation. However, presentation issues remain; specifically, how an appropriate human-computer interface effectively displays and presents information to users.

---

* Parts of this paper appeared in B. Chandrasekaran, M. C. Tanner, and J. R. Josephson, "Explaining control strategies in problem solving," *IEEE Expert*, 4(1), pp. 9–24, 1989, and M. C. Tanner and A. M. Keuneke, "The role of the task structure and domain functional models," *IEEE Expert*, 6(3),1991, pp. 50-57. Reused by permission of IEEE Computer Society.

If explanation content is inadequate or inappropriate – no matter how good theories for responsiveness and interface functions are – then correspondingly poor explanations will be presented. Thus, generating the correct explanation content is the central problem in explanation generation. We can break this down into the following types:

Step explanation. Relating portions of the data in a particular case to the knowledge for making specific decisions or choices, i.e., explaining the steps in the solution process.

Strategic explanation. Relating decisions to follow particular lines of reasoning to the problem solver's goals.

Task explanation. Relating the system's actions and conclusions to the goals of the task it performs.

Knowledge justification. Relating conclusions and problem-solving knowledge to other domain knowledge, possibly showing how they were obtained.

These four kinds of explanation are related to the act, or process, of solving problems. A knowledge system might be asked questions about many other relevant things, including requests for definition of terms and exam-like questions that test the system's knowledge. Answers to these questions may or may not be explanations, as such, but a knowledge system should still be able to produce them. All of these kinds of explanation correspond to structures that must be examined when constructing explanations, even though some of the structures may not be needed to solve problems in the system's domain.

Often explanations are produced by introspection, i.e., a program examines its own knowledge and problem-solving memory to explain itself. Step and strategic explanations are most often done this way. But sometimes explanations are concocted, i.e., they do not relate to how the decision was actually made, but independently make decisions plausible. Constructing such *post facto* justifications or explanations is necessary when problem solvers have no access to their own problem solving records, or when the information contained in those records is incomprehensible to users. The explanation may argue convincingly that the answer is correct without actually referring to the derivation process, just as mathematical proofs persuade without representing the process by which mathematicians derive theorems. Task explanations and knowledge justifications are often done this way. Generating explanations of this sort is an interesting problem solving process in its own right [23, 39].

2 Tasks, Methods and Explanations

In this section we give a brief outline of the notion of a task analysis as developed by Chandrasekaran [3]. Explaining a knowledge system's solutions requires, among other things, showing on one hand how the logical requirements of the task were satisfied by the solution and, on the other hand, showing how the method adopted (the strategy) achieved the task in the problem-solving instance. In principle there may be more than one method for a task. Most knowledge systems have "hard-wired" specific methods for the tasks. Thus Mycin can

588

be understood as solving the diagnostic task by the method of heuristic classification, which in turn performs the subtasks of data analysis, heuristic match,
and refinement [9]. In the generic task (GT) framework, developed at Ohio State,
we have identified a number of task-method combinations that can be used as
building blocks for more complex tasks. Thus, for example, the task of diagnosis
is associated with a generic method called abductive assembly, which in turn
sets up a subtask of hypothesis generation. In our GT work, a generic method
called hierarchical classification is proposed for exploring certain types of hypothesis spaces. This in turn sets up subtasks for evaluating hypotheses in the
hierarchy for which a generic method called hierarchical evidence abstraction is
proposed. What we have called GTs are in fact task-method combinations. The
method is particularly appropriate to the task because it is commonly used in
many domains for that task and it gives significant computational advantages.
Two of the GTs we have identified are Hierarchical Classification and Design by
Plan Selection and Refinement.[4]

Hierarchical Classification

> **Task:** If a hypothesis hierarchy is available, generate hypotheses that match
> the data describing a situation.
>
> **Method:** For each hypothesis, set up a subtask to establish or reject it. If
> it is established, test its successors. If it is rejected, it and its successors
> are rejected. The top-down control strategy, called Establish-Refine, can
> be varied under specific conditions. Bylander and Mittal [2] elaborate on
> this simplified account.

Design by Plan Selection and Refinement

> **Task:** Design an object that satisfies certain specifications.
>
> **Method:** Design is separated into a hierarchy of subdesign problems, mir-
> roring the object's component structure. For each node in the hierarchy,
> there are plans for making commitments for some component param-
> eters. Each component is designed by choosing a plan, based on some
> specifications, which instantiates some design parts and designs further
> subcomponents to fill in other parts. We describe this task in more detail
> in Sect. 3, but Brown and Chandrasekaran [1] is the definitive reference
> on this topic.

Each GT method is explicitly supported by a high-level language that aids knowledge system development by giving the knowledge engineer access to tools that
work closer to the problem level, not the rule or frame level. However, it may
be necessary to divide non-trivial problems into subproblems such that each
matches some GT. This way of building complex knowledge systems also means
that knowledge engineering environments should provide a tool set rather than
a single tool. Consequently, some of our recent work has concentrated on developing the Generic Task Toolset [21].

---

[4] The following description differs from descriptions in earlier papers [4], since we have
separated the task and the method explicitly.

In using the GT theory for explanation we need to show how the method-specific high-level language helps in explicitly and directly generating explanations of strategy at the right level. This is what our early work involved, and is described in Sect. 3. In general, however, we also need to relate the logical structure of the task to the strategy employed. Issues involved in this are discussed in Sect. 4. Then in Sects. 5 and 6 we describe work on justifying problem-solving knowledge by reference to the more general knowledge on which it is based.

3 Generic Tasks and Explanation – An Example

GTs make strategic explanation possible for systems built using this theory [8]. Additionally, any explanation facility should be able to explain the steps a problem solver takes in reaching a solution. In this section we describe MPA (a Mission Planning Assistant) [18], a GT program capable of explaining its problem-solving steps and its strategy. We transferred the techniques developed on this system to the Generic Task Toolset [21] so that any system built using those tools could explain its steps and strategy.

MPA is a GT implementation of Knobs [13], a system that plans a particular kind of Air Force mission.[5] The type of planning required can be viewed as design, i.e., designing the plan. So we used the GT of Design by Plan Selection and Refinement, and implemented MPA using the generic task tool DSPL (Design Specialists and Plans Language) [1].

3.1 Overview of DSPL

A design problem solver in DSPL is a hierarchy of specialists, each responsible for a specific design portion (see Fig. 1). Specialists higher up in the hierarchy deal with the more-general aspects of devices being designed, while specialists lower in the hierarchy design more-specific subportions. The organization of the specialists, and the specific content of each, is intended to capture design expertise in the problem domain.

Each specialist contains design knowledge necessary to accomplish a portion of the design (see Fig. 2). Each specialist has several types of knowledge but, for simplicity, we will describe only three. First, explicit design plans in each specialist encode sequences of possible actions to successfully complete that specialist's task. The plans consist of design steps, each of which chooses a value for one parameter of the design. Second, specialists have design plan sponsors associated with each plan to determine that plan's appropriateness in the runtime context. And third, each specialist has a design plan selector to examine runtime judgments of sponsors and to determine the plan most appropriate to the current problem context.

In a DSPL system, control proceeds from the topmost design specialist to the lowest. Each specialist selects a plan appropriate to the problem's requirements.

---

[5] MPA actually implements a very simplified version of the problem.

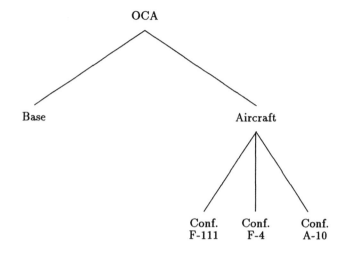

Fig. 1. Organization of MPA, a DSPL Problem Solver

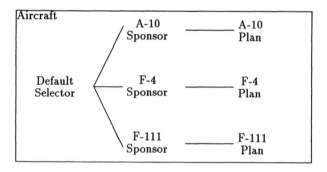

Fig. 2. Inside a DSPL Specialist

The system executes plans by performing design actions that the plan specifies (which may include computing and assigning specific values to device attributes, checking constraints, or invoking subspecialists to complete another portion of the design).

3.2 Description of MPA

In MPA the top-level specialist is OCA (for Offensive Counter Air, the type of mission MPA works on), which has design plans for producing the mission plan. Subcomponents of the mission are the Base and the Aircraft (see Fig. 1). The Base specialist chooses the air base (actually a list of bases) using the requirements of the mission. The Aircraft specialist chooses an aircraft type, and then configures the aircraft for the mission using subspecialists.

As an example of a specialist, consider Aircraft (shown in Fig. 2). It contains a selector, in this case it is the default selector built into DSPL. The default selector simply chooses the best plan, according to ratings assigned by the sponsors, and if there are no good plans it fails.[6] Aircraft also contains three sponsors, one for each of its plans. It has a plan for each aircraft type (A-10, F-4, and F-111).

The DSPL code for Aircraft's A-10 Plan is given in Fig. 3. MPA decides whether A-10 is the appropriate aircraft type for the mission using its sponsor-selector mechanism described above. If A-10 is appropriate, this plan is executed. The **BODY** contains a list of the steps in the plan. It first notes the aircraft type, then chooses a squadron. The base is determined from the chosen squadron and then the range to the target is computed. Finally, the aircraft is configured for the mission (bomb and fuel load) by calling the subspecialist Configure-A-10.

```
(PLAN
    (NAME A-10)
    (SPONSOR A-10-Sponsor)
    (PURPOSE ''considering the feasibility of an A-10 for the mission'')
    (ACHIEVED ''chose an A-10 for the mission'')
    (BODY
        AssignAircraftType
        ChooseSquadron
        AssignBase
        GetRange
        (DESIGN Configure-A-10)))
```

Fig. 3. MPA's A-10 Plan

One of the steps, ChooseSquadron, is shown in Fig. 4. Steps in DSPL set the value of a single design attribute, so the step first identifies the attribute it sets

---

[6] DSPL contains a mechanism, not described here, for dealing with failures. Brown and Chandrasekaran [1] provide the details.

(SQUAD). The DSPL functions **KB-FETCH** and **KB-STORE** fetch and store attribute values of the design. The **KNOWN** section of the body is a facility for defining local variables for known attributes. **REPLY** contains the main work of the step. In this case the **REPLY** simply stores an attribute value but, in general, it could do more work to decide on the value. The Lisp function **squad-select** implements the expert's method of choosing a squadron given the aircraft type and bases available. Since this is done in a Lisp function, it will not be easily explainable. A better implementation of MPA would include this decision process in DSPL, rather than in Lisp.

```
(STEP
   (NAME ChooseSquadron)
   (ATTRIBUTE-NAME SQUAD)
   (PURPOSE ''selecting a squadron for the mission'')
   (ACHIEVED ''selection of & as the squadron for the mission'')
   (BODY
     (KNOWN
        plane      (KB-FETCH AIRCRAFT)
        base-list  (KB-FETCH BASELIST))
     (REPLY
        (KB-STORE SQUAD (squad-select plane base-list))
```

Fig. 4. MPA's ChooseSquadron Step

In the end, MPA produces a list of attributes for the mission with the values it decided upon. For example:

Aircraft Type	A-10
Number of Aircraft	4
Squadron	118TFW
Airbase	Sembach
⋮	⋮

This list is actually a menu, from which users can select any value and ask MPA to explain how that value was decided.

3.3 Explanation in MPA

We implemented explanation in MPA on the organizing principle that the agent that makes a decision is responsible for explaining it. For our purposes, we consider the things we have described – specialists, selectors, sponsors, plans, and steps (Figs. 2–4) – to be problem-solving agents in DSPL. The current implementation of MPA contains nearly 100 of these agents, which call upon each other during the problem-solving process. All of these agents have well-defined roles, so the system can explain an agent's decisions in terms of the goals of its calling agent, the agent's own role in the pursuit of those goals, and the roles of other agents it called upon. To do this we added slots called PURPOSE and ACHIEVED to the agent definitions in DSPL to hold text strings for describing the agents' goals. Then to explain how MPA decided on a particular attribute value, the explanation module puts these strings together in an order that depends on the runtime context in which the decision was made. Given such an explanation users can select any of the other agents and ask for further elaboration from them.

Suppose a user selected the value "118TFW" of the attribute "Unit". The only question users can ask MPA, the only explanation it can give, is a form of "How was it decided?" Thus, the user's selection in this case implicitly asks, "How was it decided that the Unit should be 118TFW?" The explanation is given in Fig. 5. This decision was made by the ChooseSquadron step so the explanation comes from that agent. The explanation first gives the purpose of the calling agent (shown in italics), which comes from the A-10 plan in this case. Then it gives the values of the local variables. Finally, it gives the value it chose for its attribute.

The context of *considering the feasibility of an A-10 for the mission* determined that:

- plane was **A-10**
- base-list was **Ramstein, Bitburg, Sembach**

So **118TFW** was an appropriate choice for Unit.

Fig. 5. Explanation for a Step

This explanation may be unsatisfying. A better explanation in this case might be:

Assuming that we are to use A-10s and that the only bases available are Ramstein, Bitburg, and Sembach, then 118TFW is the only unit that flies A-10s out of these bases.

Some of the difference between this and Fig. 5 is the quality of the English text. The only content difference, and content has been our focus, is in connecting the assumptions (values of local variables) to the final decision. MPA could do this better if the final decision were made using DSPL rather than the Lisp function squad-select. A slightly improved version of the explanation would appear as in Fig. 6. Because the explanation module is essentially just translating DSPL code into text, the quality of the programming affects the quality of the explanation. This is a little bit undesirable but also unavoidable in a system that has to explain itself using only its own problem-solving knowledge.

Users can select any of the local variables given in the explanation (i.e., plane and base-list) for further elaboration. For example, to find out why plane is A-10. This would result in getting an explanation from another step,

The context of *considering the feasibility of an A-10 for the mission* determined that:

- plane was **A-10**
- base-list was **Ramstein, Bitburg, Sembach**
- units-with-A10 was **118TFW**

So **118TFW** was an appropriate choice for Unit.

Fig. 6. Improved Explanation for a Step

since attribute values are determined by steps. Or users can select the calling agent for further explanation. This would result in an explanation from the **A-10** plan, shown in Fig. 7. As with the step explanation, the context comes from the calling agent, the Aircraft specialist here. The bulleted items are the purposes from the called agents. Additionally, the explanation shows where the agent was in its procedure. In this explanation, since the user arrived here from the ChooseSquadron step, the plan had completed the **AssignAircraftType** step, was in the process of doing the **ChooseSquadron** step, and had yet to do the **AssignBase** and **GetRange steps** and complete the configuration.

In the context of *selecting an appropriate aircraft for the mission* I:

- Assigned A-10 as the aircraft type.

I was in the process of:

- Selecting a squadron for the mission.

and was about to do to following:

- Select a base for the mission.
- Determine the range for the mission.
- Choose a configuration for the A-10 on this mission.

Fig. 7. Explanation for a Plan

The explanations shown here are generated from explanation templates. Each agent type has a standard representation form from which we derived its explanation template. A simplified version of the standard form for plans is shown in Fig. 8 (the simplification is that in addition to steps, plans can contain **DESIGN** calls to subspecialists as in Fig. 3). Figure 9 shows a correspondingly simplified explanation template for plans, assuming that it is entered from step i. Thus, a plan's explanations are put together out of the goals of its calling specialist and the goals of the steps it calls.

Putting explanations together out of "canned" text, the way MPA does, is not a very sophisticated method of text generation. However, the important point here is that the roles of the various agents – specialists, plans, steps, etc. – and their relationships define the kinds of things that can be said and how these things go together to make sensible explanations. These roles and relationships

```
(PLAN
    (NAME (plan name))
    (SPONSOR (sponsor name))
    (PURPOSE (purpose string))
    (ACHIEVED (achieved string))
    (BODY
        (step 1)
          .
          .
          .
        (step i)
          .
          .
          .
        (step n)))
```

Fig. 8. Standard Plan Representation

In the context of ⟨purpose of containing specialist⟩ I:

- ⟨achieved string from step 1⟩
- .
  .
- ⟨achieved string from step $i - 1$⟩

I was in the process of:

- ⟨purpose string from step i⟩

and was about to do to following:

- ⟨purpose string from step $i + 1$⟩
- .
  .
- ⟨purpose string from step n⟩

Fig. 9. Plan Explanation Template

are defined by the GT, in this case Design by Plan Selection and Refinement. We have more work to do on developing a taxonomy of PURPOSEs for the various agents, and then showing how to use the taxonomy for explaining. However, our aim for MPA was to demonstrate that GT programs provide the structures needed to generate explanations of strategy and steps.

4 Explanation Based on the Logical Structure of a Task

GTs combine tasks with appropriate methods, which enables explanations to show how strategic elements combine to achieve the task's major goals. However, as described by Chandrasekaran [3] (see Sect. 3), for any task there are many possible methods. To properly explain how a program's knowledge, strategy, behavior, and conclusions relate to its problem-solving task, we need to separate the task's requirements from those of the methods that perform it. For example, one diagnostic goal is to find a disease that explains the symptoms. One method would produce explanatory hypotheses using disease hierarchies, another would produce them using causal models. Each method imposes its own requirements and has a distinctive behavior, but both serve the same diagnostic subgoal – generating explanatory hypotheses. An explanation should relate their behavior to their subgoal in spite of the detailed differences between them. So it is important to identify tasks' logical structure, independent of particular solution methods, to be used in designing explanation components for systems that perform them. In this section we describe Tanner's work on task explanation in diagnosis [36].

4.1 The Logical Structure of Diagnosis

Diagnosis is usually considered an abduction problem [12, 17, 20, 28, 29, 30]. That is, the task is to find a disease, or set of diseases, that best explains the symptoms. Accordingly, a diagnostic conclusion is supported, perhaps implicitly, by the following argument:

- There is a principal complaint, i.e., a collection of symptoms that sets the diagnostic problem.
- There are a number of diagnostic hypotheses that might explain the principal complaint.
- Some of the diagnostic hypotheses can be ruled out because they are: (1) unable to explain the principal complaint in this instance, or (2) implausible independent of what they might explain.
- The diagnostic conclusion is the best of the plausible hypotheses that are capable of explaining the principal complaint.

This argument form is the logical structure of the diagnostic task. It can be thought of as a means of justifying diagnoses. As such, it suggests specific ways a diagnostic conclusion might be wrong.

Suppose the diagnostic conclusion turns out to be wrong. What happened to the true answer? That is, why did the true, or correct, answer *not* turn out to be the best explanation? Based on the logical structure of diagnosis, given above, the diagnostic conclusion can only be wrong for one or more of the following reasons:

1. There is something wrong with the principal complaint. Either it is (1) not really present or does not need to be explained, or (2) incomplete, there are other things that should be explained by the diagnostic conclusion.
2. The true answer was not on the list of diagnostic hypotheses thought to have the potential of explaining the principal complaint.
3. There is an error in ruling out.
   (a) The true answer was ruled out. It was mistakenly thought (1) to be implausible or (2) not to explain the data.

(b) The wrong answer (the one given) was not ruled out. It was mistakenly thought (1) to be plausible or (2) to explain the data.
4. There is an error in choosing the best of the plausible explanations. Either (1) the wrong answer appears to be better than it is, or (2) the true answer appears to be worse than it is.

The source of these errors might be found in either missing or faulty knowledge as well as in various problems with the data itself.

Many users' questions can be interpreted as attempts to ensure that the conclusion is correct. Thus, corresponding to each source of potential error there is a class of questions, each seeking reassurance that a particular kind of error was not made. This analysis tells us that if we build a knowledge-based system and claim it does diagnosis, we can expect it to be asked the following kinds of questions.

1. Is the principal complaint really present or abnormal?
2. Does the principal complaint contain all the important data?
3. Was a broad enough set of explanatory hypotheses considered?
4. Has some hypothesis been incorrectly ruled out?
5. Could some hypothesis explain a finding that the system thought could not?
6. Was some hypothesis not ruled out that should have been?
7. Is it possible that the hypotheses in the diagnostic conclusion do not really explain the findings?
8. Might the hypotheses in the diagnostic conclusion be rated too high?
9. Has some hypothesis been underrated?

Furthermore, these questions express the only reasonable concerns that arise *solely because* it is a diagnosis system. We are not suggesting that all questions will be in exactly one of these classes, some may refer to many of these concerns, others are not specifically about diagnosis.

4.2 Using the Logical Structure for Explanation

Any diagnostic system will have some means of achieving the diagnostic goals specified in the logical structure given above. Otherwise it will fail, in some respect, to be a diagnostic system. The diagnostic question classes are derived from the diagnostic goals, so the first step in building an explanation component is to map the diagnostic question classes onto the program. That is, each question class (say, "Is it possible that the hypotheses in the diagnostic conclusion do not really explain the findings?") is mapped onto the the part of the system responsible for achieving the corresponding goal (in the example, the part that determines the symptoms a diagnostic hypothesis explains). This way the questions can be answered by the part of the system that made the relevant decisions to explain how the decision helps achieve the goal. In order for this to work, the explainer needs a way of mapping users' questions into the appropriate question classes.

598

User: What antibody in the conclusion explains the following test result:

(164 Coombs 3+)

Red: The finding:

(164 Coombs 3+)

is explained by:

antiS

Fig. 10. An Explanation From RED

Let us briefly consider an example from a diagnostic system called Red. In order to give blood to patients who need it, a hospital blood bank must select compatible donor blood. A part of this decision involves finding out what antibodies a patient has. Red is a system that aids in this antibody-identification problem. This is a kind of diagnostic problem since the data is a set of test results to be explained and the antibodies are used to explain them. One type of question that people ask of Red is what antibody in Red's conclusion explains a particular test result. This question is an instance of the question class defined by: "Is it possible that the hypotheses in the diagnostic conclusion do not really explain the findings?" This is derived from the potential error that the answer given does not actually explain the data. This, in turn, is derived from the diagnostic goal of explaining the data. So the question ("What explains a particular test result?") is directed to the component of Red that chooses antibodies to explain particular elements of data. It produces an explanation such as the one in Fig. 10. The "(164 Coombs 3+)" is the notation for a test result and "antiS" is shorthand for "antibody to the S antigen". This process of mapping the question to the part of the system that can answer it is not done automatically in Red. The logical structure of diagnosis was used in building Red's explanation component, but the mapping is hard-coded in the program. Tanner [36] describes explanation for Red in more detail while Red itself was fully reported by Josephson, et al. [20]

The logical structure of diagnosis presented here is a common view of the diagnostic task [12, 17, 20, 28, 29, 30]. Not all approaches to diagnosis will share this view. In fact, there is one common competing view – diagnosis as description, i.e., the goal of diagnosis is to describe the patient's state, not to find a cause for the symptoms. But if users and systems agree to a logical structure, it can be used to develop explanation for diagnosis in the manner we describe. The details will change if the model changes, but the method, and the idea, of using the logical structure to develop explanations remains.

5 Knowledge Justification: Relating Problem Solving to Causal Models

The integration and use of causal models in compiled problem-solving systems has become increasingly prevalent. Xplain was probably the first system to provide explanations of problem-solving knowledge by showing how it was obtained by compilation from other knowledge about the domain [26, 35]. Our work on functional representations (FR) [31] is similar in showing how to compile diagnostic programs from functional representations of mechanical devices. Following on this, Keuneke's work [23] showed how to use FR for justifying diagnostic conclusions, which we describe in this section.

5.1 Background

Methods that carry out problem-solving tasks need knowledge of certain kinds and in particular forms. For example, establish-refine, a method for hierarchical classification, requires knowledge relating descriptions of situations to descriptions of classes (see Sect. 2). If knowledge is not available in this form, it must be derived from some other knowledge. We refer to this derivation process as compilation [31, 35, 15], and to knowledge in the desired form as compiled knowledge [7]. The "other knowledge" has sometimes been called deep knowledge, but it is not necessarily deeper or better, only less compiled relative to the method that needs it. The compiled knowledge can be justified by referring to the knowledge from which it was compiled.

As with any compiled knowledge, compiled diagnostic knowledge can be justified by referring to the compilation process. Diagnosis also admits an interesting variation on this type of justification. If a system for diagnosing faults in a mechanical device is compiled from a causal model of the device, then its diagnostic conclusions can be related to observations using the causal model. This justifies the conclusion and validates the compiled knowledge that produced it. The causal model could be used to perform diagnosis, and systems have been built that do this [11, 27, 38], but for complex devices the large amount of causal information makes the diagnostic task very difficult. In most diagnostic systems, the causal knowledge is compiled for greater expertise and optimum diagnostic performance. Then, if a causal story can be put together, using the hypothesized diagnostic answer as a focus, we get the advantages of both worlds: the computational benefits of compiled knowledge to obtain the diagnostic answer, as well as the causal model to validate it.

In a diagnostic context, given the symptoms and the diagnostic conclusion, Keuneke showed how to use a causal model to justify the diagnosis at various levels of detail. In many situations a similar method will work to justify individual rules in the knowledge base. Wick [39] developed a related idea: justifying a conclusion in terms of the standard arguments used by domain experts. Both Wick and our work using FR produce justifications by reference to knowledge not used, perhaps not even needed, to produce the solution. However, one important difference is that justifications come from knowledge that, in principle, could be used to compile diagnostic problem solvers while Wick is not committed to any particular relationship between justification knowledge and problem-solving knowledge. The intent of Keuneke's [23] research was to continue efforts in the development of a device- and domain-independent representation capable of modeling the core aspects of device understanding; the extended goal is a cognitive model of device understanding. Although this work was driven by the task of explanation, the representation was designed to provide the basic primitives and organization for a variety of problem-solving tasks.

The Functional Representation. Initial efforts to generate causal justifications [5, 6, 18, 24] focused on enhancing Sembugamoorthy and Chandrasekaran's FR [31] to provide a representation with the needed organization and primitives[7].

Functional Representation is a representational scheme for the functions and expected behavior of a device. FR represents knowledge about devices in terms of the functions that the entire device is supposed to achieve and also of the sequence of causal interactions among components that lead to achievement of the functions. FR takes a top-down approach to representing a device, in contrast to the bottom-up approach of behavior-oriented knowledge representation and reasoning schemes [10, 14]. In FR, the function of the overall device is described first and the behavior of each component (its causal process) is described in terms of how it contributes to the function[8]. Figures 11 and 12 illustrate the top-level representation of a chemical processing plant.

In this representation, a device's *function* is its intended purpose. Functions describe a device's goals at the device level. For example, the function of a chemical processing plant is to produce a certain product. It has components for supplying the reactants, stirring the substance, extracting the product, and so forth. But generating the product is a function of the device as a whole.

Functions are achieved by *behaviors* or *causal processes*. In the chemical processing plant example, the substance is produced by the causal sequence of (1) input of the reactants into the reaction vessel, (2) allowing reactant contact, and then (3) extracting the product from the reaction vessel. In short, the functions are *what* is expected; the behaviors are *how* this expected result is attained. In FR, behaviors are represented as causal sequences of transitions between partial states or predicates (e.g., (present reactants rxvessel)).

The device is represented at various levels. The topmost level describes the functioning of the device by identifying which components and more detailed causal processes are responsible for bringing about the various state transitions. If a transition is achieved using a function of a component, the next level describes the functioning of this component in terms of the roles of its subcomponents, and so on. Ultimately, either by tracing through more detailed causal processes or by expanding the causal processes of functional components, all the functions of a device can be related to its structure and the function of the components within this structure.

Enhancing the Functional Representation. Early explanation work [5] simply used the FR as a tool to answer questions such as: (1) Why is this device

---

[7] For a more current formal treatment of the representation, see [19]

[8] A function's causal process is represented in the machine by its causal process description (CPD).

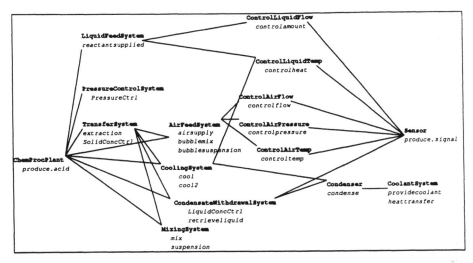

Fig. 11. Functional Component Hierarchy

needed? (2) What subcomponents does this device require? (3) What does this function accomplish? (4) Why or where is this function used in the device? (5) How is this function achieved?

Later, enhancements to the FR allowed the representation of state and behavior abstractions [25, 23]. Abstract schema specifications, and the ability to make transitions between abstraction levels, is useful for providing different levels of explanation.

For example, suppose there exists a solid/liquid mixture in which action is being taken to keep the solid from the bottom of the container. One might witness the following causal loop:

$$\text{(solid falls)} \quad \begin{array}{c} \text{by stirring} \\ \xrightarrow{\hspace{3cm}} \\ \xleftarrow{\hspace{3cm}} \\ \text{by gravity} \end{array} \quad \text{(solid rises)}$$

Here an observer could follow the loop any number of times, but somewhere one takes a conceptual jump and identifies the dynamic process (solid fall, solid rise, solid fall, solid rise...) as a *state* at a different behavioral level, i.e., identification of the process state (solid suspended). In doing so, one is identifying a new phenomenon; the observer is packaging a process and seeing it from a higher

602

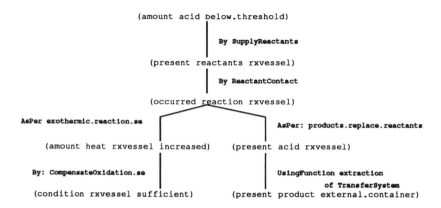

Fig. 12. CPD *oxidation* for Function *produce.acid* of a Chemical Processing Plant

conceptual viewpoint. These types of conceptual transitions are commonplace in one's understanding of a device's behavior – especially in cyclic or repeated behaviors. Nevertheless, past methods of behavior abstraction (detail suppression) did not explicitly address the representation of such phenomenon.

For researchers interested in building models of devices solely to predict behavior at a given level of detail, these abstractions will not be helpful. Instead, these abstractions provide the ability to tell a higher level story. Prediction is not driven solely by constraints of structure and low-level processes, but can be enriched and focused by knowledge of abstract processes and the inferences they dictate.

Additional enhancements include establishing a taxonomy of function types. Each function type indicates different procedures for simulation, different functional capabilities, different expectations, and thus different knowledge specifications for representation and explanation. Function types include:

1. **ToMake:** achieves a specific partial state
2. **ToMaintain:** achieves and sustains a desired state
3. **ToPrevent:** keeps a system out of an undesirable state
4. **ToControl:** gives a system power to regulate changes of state via a known relationship.

More details on the knowledge distinguishing each type, explicit specifications of the function types, and the information processing distinctions each type makes is provided in [23, 22].

The structure of the functional representation, organized around functional packages, provides focus through which simulation and the identification of structural cause can be determined (i.e., given changes in function, what changes in structure could be hypothesized to account for them?). Since, at some level, most problem-solving tasks dealing with devices are concerned with either the achievement of function, or consequences of the failure to achieve function, a functional description and reasoning power proves useful. The use of the representation in diagnosis seems especially appropriate since diagnosis centers around determining the change in structure that resulted in some malfunction.

6   Causal Explanation: The Problem Statement

To illustrate the use of the representation, we pose the following problem: Given a set of observations and a diagnostic hypothesis, attempt to construct an explanation in the form of a causal story which starts with a diagnostic hypothesis and ends with one or more of the observations to be explained. In the following, we examine how a functional representation can be used for this purpose. Technical definitions of a few terms may be useful:

Observations: observable states, including a subset which are malfunctions of the device subsystems or components. The following distinctions about observations are useful:

- **Symptoms:** abnormal states which are indicative of malfunctions and trigger the diagnostic process, e.g., specification of a drop from normal pressure.
- **Malfunctions:** observations which *are* malfunctions, e.g., specification of a faulty pressure regulator. Malfunction observations are generally also symptoms.
- Observable states which provide information about the device but do not directly correspond to abnormalities, e.g., specification of temperature or pressure readings. Typically in a complex system, a large number of observations are used in the diagnostic process which provide focus for the problem-solving but do not necessarily indicate problems (e.g., sensor readings).

Diagnostic Hypotheses: the set of malfunctioning components or missing (but expected) relationships between components. Each in the latter should sooner or later, manifest itself as the malfunction of a subsystem within which the components lie.

Causal Explanation: Normally one expects a diagnosis to causally "explain" the symptoms, even though in general the diagnosis actually should explain all the observations. The explanation provided here takes any given set of observations to be explained and tries to propose a causal path from the diagnostic hypothesis to these observations.

The explanation sought can be formally stated as follows:

$$\text{diagnostic hypothesis} \rightarrow x_1 \ldots \rightarrow x_i \ldots \rightarrow x_N$$

where each x_i is either (1) an internal state which is causally relevant in producing an observation, but is itself not a malfunction, (2) a component or subsystem malfunction, or (3) an observation at the device-level. The explanation system developed in this work produces explanation chains where the members are limited to the last two, i.e., malfunctions or observations, *unless* the causally relevant internal state has been provided explicitly as a state that needs to be explained, i.e., as input to the casual explanation system.

6.1 Generating the Malfunction Causal Chain

In the same way a functional representation provides an organization to allow simulation of how *expected* functionalities are achieved, it can also serve as a backbone to trace the effects of not achieving certain functions – thus identifying potential malfunctions.

The organization of a functional representation gives both forward and backward reasoning capability, i.e., it can trace from the hypothesized malfunction to the observed malfunctions and symptoms (forward), or it can trace from observed malfunctions to the hypothesized malfunction (backward). Because both the observations and the diagnostic hypotheses have been identified once diagnosis is complete, the functional representation could potentially be used to perform either form of control. This section provides an algorithm which demonstrates the forward simulation potential[9].

Specifically, if device A is malfunctioning, then devices which use device A (say devices B and C) have a high probability of malfunctioning as well. Similarly, devices which use B and C may malfunction, etc. The malfunction causal chain is achieved through the following algorithm which has been condensed to illustrate main points.

1. – Set Observations to the symptoms and malfunctions to be explained,
   – Set MalfunctionList to the hypothesized malfunction set provided by the diagnosis,
   – Initialize MalfunctionObject to an individual malfunction in this set (diagnosed hypotheses and their relationship to observations are considered individually)
2. Find all functions which made use of the function which is malfunctioning (MalfunctionObject), call this set PossibleMalfunctions,
3. For each element in PossibleMalfunctions (call the specific function PossMal) consider the significance of the effect of MalfunctionObject on the function.
   – if no effect on PossMal then remove from PossibleMalfunctions – MalfunctionObject is not causing future problems. Consider the next element in PossibleMalfunctions.
   – else maintain (Malfunction → Malfunction) explanation chain; MalfunctionObject is now known to cause a malfunction to PossMal. Specifically MalfunctionObject → PossMal is appended to chain. Note that this step will ultimately place any potential malfunctions in a malfunction chain, including those which are in the set of Observations. Continue.
4. Check the states in the causal process description of the affected PossibleMalfunction. Would noncompletion of these states explain any symptom(s) in Observations?

---

[9] Note that since the explanation generation mechanism uses expected functionalities and their causal processes rather than all behaviors that could possibly be generated, the problem space is bound and thus focused.

- if yes, append to ExplainedSymptoms and print the chain which led to this symptom. Complete the malfunction explanation chain by continuing.
5. Set MalfunctionObject to PossMal. (MalfunctionObject $\Longleftarrow$ PossMal)
6. Repeat process from step 2 until all symptoms are in ExplainedSymptoms or the top level causal process description of the device has been reached.
7. The Process from step 1 is repeated until all elements of MalfunctionList have been considered.

Step 2 is easily accomplished through the component hierarchy of the functional representation (example in Sect. 6.2). Step 3 and 4 are more intricate and involve knowledge of function type and the achievement of the intended causal processes.

For example, in step 3, to determine the effects of a malfunction on other functions, one must consider the possible consequences of malfunctioning components. In general, the malfunction of a component in a device can cause one or more of the following three consequences:

NOT Function: expected results of the function will not be present. Given that the malfunction is not producing the expected results within the causal process, what states in those causal processes will not occur, and will lack of this functionality cause the malfunctions of functions in which the malfunctioning component was used?

Parameter Out-of-Range: expected results of the function are affected, but behavior is still accomplished to a limited degree. Sometimes components may be considered malfunctioning yet can still perform the behavior (or value of some substance parameter) to the extent needed for future use.

New Behaviors: the malfunction results in behaviors and states which were not those intended for normal functioning.

The determination of whether a proposed malfunction can explain a symptom, step 4 in the explanation algorithm, can be established by a number of means:

1. Check each state in the causal process description where the malfunctioning component is used to see if there is a direct match between a symptom and *not* achieving an expected state.
2. Check to see if the function which is malfunctioning has an explicit malfunction causal process description and if the symptom is included therein. [10]
3. Check to see if side effects of the functions causal process description refer to the symptoms.
4. Check each state in the malfunction causal process description and its provided clause to see if expected states point to general concepts or generic

---

[10] See [23] for knowledge of function type and detail on functions with explicit malfunction causal processes.

classes of behavior (such as leak, flow, continuity) and if the symptom pertains to or is explained by such concepts.

5. If the malfunction is a malformation, i.e., the malfunction is described as a malformation of a particular physical component, perform deep reasoning (e.g., qualitative physics) to see if malformation could cause the symptom.

The first three are implemented and currently used for the explanation generation; the means to perform the last two are research in progress.

6.2 Representation of a Chemical Processing Plant

This section provides the output for an example explanation in the domain of Chemical Processing Plants. Reference to Fig. 11 (in Sect. 5.1) will assist the reader in following the causal explanation chains given by the algorithm. The hierarchy in Fig. 11 shows a partial representation of the functional components with their intended functions (functions are specified under component names). The top level function, *produce.acid*[11], is achieved by the causal process *oxidation* shown in Fig. 12. It should be noted that the function hierarchy is *generated* given the causal processes used to achieve functions of the functional component. For example, the Chemical Processing Plant uses the functional components LiquidFeedSystem, AirFeedSystem, TransferSystem, etc. in the process *oxidation* which represents the causal chain used to achieve the function *produce.acid*; the TransferSystem uses the functional components AirFeedSystem, MixingSystem, etc. in its causal process to achieve the function *extraction*, and so on.

The Problem. The Coolant System (identified at the right of Fig. 11) is used to provide coolant water to a Condenser so that it can be used to transfer heat from the vapor in the Condenser (see Fig. 13). Suppose the coolant water has been completely cut off. A diagnostic system has concluded that a malfunction of the function *provide.coolant* of the Coolant System explains the symptoms of NOT (present product external.container) and NOT (temperature rxvessel at.threshold). Specifically, MalfunctionObject is {*provide.coolant* of Coolant System} and the Observations to be explained are {NOT (present product external.container), NOT (temperature rxvessel at.threshold) }. The system produces the following three casual stories.

Causal Story 1: Generation of Causal Connections. The causal process SupplyReactants uses the functions *retrieveliquid* and *LiquidConcCtrl*, in addition to the LiquidFeedSystem and AirFeedSystem. The explanation system generates the following:

```
The symptom
NOT (present product external.container)
is explained by the following chain:
```

---

[11] The acid produced is a solid, terephthalic acid.

```
NOT provide.coolant causes
malfunction in condense causing
malfunction in retrieveliquid causing
malfunction in LiquidConcCtrl causing
problems in behavior SupplyReactants
which is used in behavior oxidation and
indicates malfunction of the top level
function and results in
NOT (present product external.container)
---
  The following symptoms are not explained:
NOT (temperature rxvessel at.threshold)
```

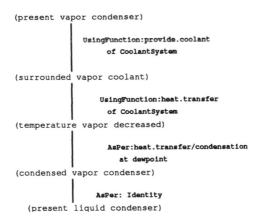

Fig. 13. CPD: *RemoveHeat* of Function *Condense*

The idea here is that if the required amount of reactants is not available, the product is not produced as desired and thus can not be retrieved. The explanation system generates this chain by using the following information: *Provide.coolant* caused a malfunction in *condense* because it caused a failure in *condense*'s behavior. A malfunction in *condense* caused a malfunction in *retrieveliquid* because its achievement was required to attain the desired behavior for *retrieveliquid*. *Retrieveliquid* caused a malfunction in *LiquidConcCtrl* because it was needed to provide the preconditions for *LiquidConcCtrl* and it preceded the use of *LiquidConcCtrl* in the behavior SupplyReactants. SupplyReactants was used in the causal process Oxidation, Fig. 12, to achieve the state (present reactants rxvessel). This state was necessary for the completion of the behavior and thus non-achievement here denotes non-achievement of further states in the behavior, particularly NOT (present product external.container).

Causal Story 2: The Use of Side Effect Inspection. The explanation system continues and finds a causal connection for the second symptom, NOT (temperature rxvessel at.threshold).

```
The symptom
NOT (temperature rxvessel at.threshold)
is explained by the following chain:
  NOT provide.coolant causes malfunction
  in condense causing problems in behavior
  removeheat of function cool
```

Since *cool* is not a top level function of the chemical processing plant, the trace continues until all consequences are determined.

```
The symptom
NOT (temperature rxvessel at.threshold)
is explained by the following chain:
  NOT provide.coolant causes
  malfunction in condense causing
  malfunction in cool causing problems
  in behavior compensate.oxidation.se
  a notable side effect behavior used in
  oxidation and indicates
  NOT (temperature rxvessel at.threshold)
---
  The following symptoms are not explained
  (present product external.container)
```

Notice that this explanation identifies that the symptom was observed in a *side effect* behavior (compensation for effects of the reaction) rather than a behavior of the main functionality (production of acid).

The statement of which symptoms are not explained indicates those that were not explained in the specific causal chain. A final statement is made when the system has inspected all pertinent causal chains (as seen in the next causal story).

Causal Story 3: Using Subfunction Connections for Causal Focus. The final causal path is achieved via causal connections obtained specifically through the knowledge of subfunctions. In its specification, the function *extraction* has a provided clause which specifies that the solid acid slurry must have the proper consistency so that flow through the extraction tube is possible. The function *SolidConcCtrl* is present in this device for the sole purpose of producing these conditions for *extraction*.

The purpose of *SolidConcCtrl* is to keep the solid suspended and the concentration in the reaction vessel at the proper consistency. In the Condensate-WithdrawalSystem, the *retrieveliquid* function uses the Condenser to retrieve the condensate from the vapor produced. The *MixtureLevelCtrl* function then uses a feedback controller to maintain the flow and thus the desired amount of liquid in the reaction vessel – which ensures that the acid slurry has the proper consistency. If the liquid is not retrievable, then obviously the condensate flow cannot be controlled and consistency of the acid in the vessel is not maintained. The explanation system provides this explanatory story as follows:

```
One function affected by provide.coolant
is SolidConcCtrl which is a necessary
subfunction of extraction


 The symptom
NOT (present product external.container)
is explained by the following chain:
 NOT provide.coolant causes
 malfunction in condense causing
 malfunction in retrieveliquid causing
 malfunction in MixtureLevelCtrl causing
 malfunction in SolidConcCtrl causing
 malfunction in extraction causing
 malfunction in produce.acid causing
 NOT (present product external.container)
---
 All symptoms have been explained.
```

6.3 Discussion

The intrinsic limitations of a functional representation for explanation arise from its intrinsic limitations for simulation. The representation uses prepackaged causal process descriptions which are organized around the expected functions of a device. Simulations of malfunctioning devices are thus limited to statements of what expectations are "not" occurring.

This limitation effects the capabilities for explanation in two significant ways. First, the functional representation is not capable of generating causal stories of malfunctions which interact unless the device representation has this interaction explicitly represented. Similar problems regarding the interactions of malfunctions arise in diagnosis [33]. Secondly, "new" behaviors, i.e., behaviors which are not those intended for normal functioning but which arise due to a change in device structure, could potentially lead to symptoms which cannot be explained using the functional representation. Current research efforts focus on how a functional organization might be used to determine these new behavioral sequences, in addition to how conventional methods of qualitative reasoning may be integrated.

7 Additional Applications of a Functional Model

The idea of considering how devices work is a generally useful concept which provides a focus for reasoning about objects. Since goals can be attributed to many types of objects, a general representational language, focused around functionality, can potentially model an understanding of a variety of object types, i.e., truly a "device-independent" representation. In addition, the organization around functions helps to focus a reasoner's attention toward expected goals; something works like it does because it is meant to achieve a specific purpose. The practical uses of having a functionally oriented understanding of how something works can be seen in the following applications:

diagnosis: How something works provides information about what functions to expect from working models, and thus implicitly knowledge of malfunctioning models. This helps to enumerate malfunction modes and to derive what observable consequences follow for a given malfunction.

learning: In diagnosis, if a hypothesis has been made and a causal chain cannot be found that connects the hypothesis to the symptoms, a learning process could be triggered. Specifically, a diagnosis which cannot be causally connected to the symptoms might cause suspicion, not only about the diagnostic result, but also about the knowledge used in the diagnostic process. Use of the malfunction causal explanation capabilities can help explicate erroneous malfunction hypotheses and aid in pointing to alternatives. [37]

repair/replacement: Knowledge of how a device works indicates knowledge of its teleology. Replacement with objects of like teleology can be considered.

design/redesign: Knowledge of what functionalities are desired can point the designer to necessary components. [16, 19]

planning: The representation of plans (as devices) provides an understanding of how the plan's goals are achieved. [5]

determination of optimum use: Knowledge of how a device works can provide information regarding how to use the device to its maximum potential.

analogy: Organizing knowledge of how one object works provides links for determining how a similar object might operate.

prediction: Knowledge of expected functionalities focuses reasoning for determining what will happen in a device. [32]

simulation: Simulation of expected device behavior is useful for problem solving, in particular, design. [34, 19]

explanation: Having the knowledge of how something works allows one to simulate and explain the mechanism, i.e., tutorial purposes.

8 Conclusion

In this paper we have surveyed the work done at the Ohio State Laboratory for AI Research on knowledge systems explanation. We consider the explanation problem to have three aspects: the explanation content, the form of presentation, and the manner of presentation. We have concentrated on the explanation content, which we see as having four parts: explaining problem-solving steps, strategy, and task, and justifying knowledge. Most of our work on these has been guided by GT theory – any task can be accomplished by many different methods, the combination of a particularly appropriate, domain-independent, method with a task is called a generic task. GT research has identified several generic tasks and a knowledge system that uses a generic task can explain its steps and its strategy, since strategy is an aspect of the method. By combining generic tasks with a theory of tasks, independent of method, it is possible to give explanations that show how a system's method achieves the task goals. Using the functional representation, also developed at the LAIR, to represent general purpose knowledge in the knowledge system's domain we can justify its problem-solving knowledge by showing how it was derived. Individually, each of the efforts described here solves a few problems and leaves many issues unaddressed. Taken as a whole, they represent an attempt to explore the wide range of roles that knowledge plays in explanation – knowledge about tasks, methods and strategies, system design, background domain knowledge, and memory for particular problem-solving instances – and the benefits of explicitly representing these kinds of knowledge.

9 Acknowledgments

This work has been supported by the Air Force Office of Scientific Research (grant 89-0250), the Defense Advanced Research Projects Agency (contracts F30602-85-C-0010 and F49620-89-C-0110), and the National Heart Lung and Blood Institute (grant HL-38776). In addition we would like to thank John Josephson who led the MPA project and provided insightful comment on the rest of the work reported here; the other members of the MPA team: Dean Allemang, Matt DeJongh, Ron Hartung, and Dave Herman; and our friends and colleagues at the LAIR who have contributed to the ideas presented here through their work, discussions, and friendship. We also thank Bill Swartout and Cecile Paris for their helpful comments on an earlier draft. These individuals do not necessarily endorse the entire contents of this paper, however. The authors accept full responsibility for that, including any inadvertent errors.

References

1. Brown, D. C., Chandrasekaran, B.: Design Problem Solving: Knowledge Structures and Control Strategies. Morgan Kaufmann, Inc., San Mateo, CA, 1989
2. Bylander, T., Mittal, S.: CSRL: A language for classificatory problem solving and uncertainty handling. AI Magazine, 7(3):66–77, August 1986
3. Chandrasekaran, B.: Design problem solving: a task analysis. AI Magazine, 11(4):59–71, Winter 1990
4. Chandrasekaran, B.: Generic tasks in knowledge-based reasoning: High-level building blocks for expert system design. IEEE Expert, 1(3):23–30, Fall 1986

5. Chandrasekaran, B., Josephson, J., Keuneke, A.: Functional representation as a basis for explanation generation. Proceedings of IEEE International Conference on Systems, Man, and Cybernetics, pages 726–731, 1986

6. Chandrasekaran, B., Josephson, J. R., Keuneke, A. M., Herman, D.: Building routine planning systems and explaining their behavior. International Journal of Man-Machine Studies, 30:377–398, 1989

7. Chandrasekaran, B., Mittal, S.: On deep versus compiled approaches to diagnostic problem solving. International Journal of Man Machine Studies, 19:425–436, 1983

8. Chandrasekaran, B., Tanner, M. C., Josephson, J. R.: Explaining control strategies in problem solving. IEEE Expert, 4(1):9–24, Spring 1989

9. Clancey, W. J.: Heuristic classification. Artificial Intelligence, 27(3):289–350, December 1985

10. Crawford, J., Farquhar, A., Kuipers, B.: QPC: a compiler from physical models into qualitative differential equations. Proceedings of the 8th National Conference on Artificial Intelligence, pages 365–372, 1990

11. Davis, R., Shrobe, H., Hamscher, W., Wieckert, K., Shirley, M., Polit, S.: Diagnosis based on description of structure and function. Proceedings of the 2nd National Conference on Artificial Intelligence, pages 137–142, Pittsburgh, PA, 1982

12. deKleer, J., Williams, B. C.: Diagnosing multiple faults. Artificial Intelligence, 32(1):97–130, April 1987

13. Engelman, C., Millen, J. K., Scarl, E. A.: Knobs: An Integrated AI Interactive Planning Architecture. Technical Report DSR-83-162, The MITRE Corporation, Bedford, MA, 1983

14. Falkenhainer, B., Forbus, K.: Setting up large-scale qualitative models. Proceedings of the 7th National Conference on Artificial Intelligence, pages 301–306, 1988

15. Goel, A.: Knowledge compilation: a symposium. IEEE Expert, 6(2):71–73, April 1991

16. Goel, A., Chandrasekaran, B.: Functional representation of designs and redesign problem solving. Proceedings of the 11th International Joint Conference on Artificial Intelligence, 1989

17. Harvey, A. M., Bordley, J. III: Differential Diagnosis, the Interpretation of Clinical Evidence. W. B. Saunders, Philadelphia, 1972

18. Herman, D., Keuneke, A., Tanner, M. C., Hartung, R., Josephson, J.: MPA: A mission planning assistant in the Knobs domain. Expert Systems: Proceedings of a Workshop, pages 103–116, Pacific Grove, CA, April 16–18 1986

19. Iwasaki, Y., Chandrasekaran, B.: Design verification through function- and behavior-oriented representations: bridging the gap between function and behavior. Proceedings of the Conference on Artificial Intelligence in Design, 1992

20. Josephson, J. R., Chandrasekaran, B., Smith, J. W. Jr., Tanner, M. C.: A mechanism for forming composite explanatory hypotheses. IEEE Transactions on Systems, Man, and Cybernetics, SMC-17(3):445–454, May/June 1987

21. Josephson, J. R., Smetters, D., Fox, R., Oblinger, D., Welch, A., Northrup, G.: Integrated Generic Task Toolset: Fafner Release 1.0, Introduction and User's guide. Technical Report 89-JJ-FAFNER, Lab. for AI Research, Ohio State Univ., Columbus, OH, June 1 1989

22. Keuneke, A.: Device representation: The significance of functional knowledge. IEEE Expert, 6(2):22–25, April 1991

23. Keuneke, A.: Machine Understanding of Devices: Causal Explanation of Diagnostic Conclusions. PhD thesis, The Ohio State University, Columbus, Ohio, 1989

24. Keuneke, A., Allemang, D.: Exploring the "No-Function-In-Structure" Principle. Journal of Experimental and Theoretical Artificial Intelligence, 1:79–89, 1989

25. Keuneke, A., Allemang, D.: Understanding Devices: Representing Dynamic States. Technical Report, The Ohio State University, 1988

26. Neches, R., Swartout, W. R., Moore, J. D.: Enhanced maintenance and explanation of expert systems through explicit models of their development. IEEE Transactions on Software Engineering, SE-11(11):1337–1351, November 1985

27. Patil, R. S.: Causal Representation of Patient Illness for Electrolyte and Acid-Base Diagnosis. PhD thesis, MIT Lab for Computer Science, TR-267, Cambridge, Massachusetts, 1981

28. Pople, H. E.: The formation of composite hypotheses in diagnosic problem solving. Proceedings of the 5th International Joint Conference on Artificial Intelligence, pages 1030–1037, Cambridge, MA, 1977

29. Reggia, J.: Diagnostic expert systems based on a set covering model. International Journal of Man-Machine Studies, 19(5):437–460, November 1983

30. Reiter, R.: A theory of diagnosis from first principles. Artificial Intelligence, 32(1):57–95, April 1987

31. Sembugamoorthy, V., Chandrasekaran, B.: Functional representation of devices and compilation of diagnostic problem solving systems. J. L. Kolodner and C. K. Riesbeck, editors, Experience, Memory, and Reasoning, pages 47–73, Lawrence Erlbaum Assoc., Hillsdale, New Jersey, 1986

32. Sticklen, J.: MDX2, An Integrated Medical Diagnostic System. PhD thesis, The Ohio State University, 1987

33. Sticklen, J., Chandrasekaran, B., Josephson, J.: Control issues in classificatory diagnosis. Proceedings of the 9th International Joint Conference on Artificial Intelligence, pages 300–306, IJCAI, 1985

34. Sun, J., Sticklen, J.: Steps toward tractable envisionment via a functional approach. Second AAAI Workshop on Model Based Reasoning, pages 50–56, 1990

35. Swartout, W. R.: Xplain: A system for creating and explaining expert consulting programs. Artificial Intelligence, 21(3):285–325, September 1983

36. Tanner, M. C.: Explaining Knowledge Systems: Justifying Diagnostic Conclusions. PhD thesis, Dept. of Computer and Information Science, Ohio State University, Columbus, OH, March 1989

37. Weintraub, M.: An Explanation Approach to Assigning Credit. PhD thesis, The Ohio State University, Columbus, Ohio, 1991

38. Weiss, S. M., Kulikowski, C. A., Amarel, S., Safir, A.: A model-based method for computer-aided medical decision-making. Artificial Intelligence, 11:145–172, 1978

39. Wick, M. R., Thompson, W. B., Slagle, J. R.: Knowledge-Based Explanation. TR 88-24, Computer Science Dept., Univ. of Minn., Minneapolis, MN, March 1988

Second Generation Expert System Explanation

Michael R. Wick

Computer Science Department, University of Wisconsin - Eau Claire, Eau Claire WI 54702, USA

Abstract. Explanation has long been cited as one of the key advantages of the expert system methodology. Most current approaches to expert system explanation view explanation as an "add-on" to the expert system's domain problem solving. This is in direct conflict with findings on human explanation. For humans, explanation is a complex problem-solving process of reconstructing an explanation based on a partial memory of the problem-solving episodes. Further, this process of explanation is at the same level as the original domain problem solving; working on the current state to reconstruct a plausible explanation. Recently, a new direction has emerged in expert systems, namely the study of second generation expert systems. These new expert systems view domain problem solving as an interaction and combination of several explicit reasoning processes or representations (i.e., causal, heuristic, planning). This chapter discusses two related projects that investigate the natural role of explanation in such second generation expert systems.

1 Introduction

During the last two decades, expert systems have grown from a novel idea to a well-defined and practical technology. The major focus in expert systems during these years has been on *classification* problems. As a result, the problem of classification as well as methods for solving classification problems have become well-understood and form the basis of most practical applications of expert systems. The primary means through which expert systems solve classification problems is called *heuristic classification* [5]. In this problem-solving approach, heuristic rules are used to bridge the gap between various classification hierarchies. These heuristics generally take the form of "rules-of-thumb" or empirical associations. The expert system uses these heuristics in an attempt to move the search space of possible classifications to the final conclusion.

It was realized very early in expert system development [20] that explanation was to play a key role in the construction and execution of expert systems. In fact, explanation has been found to be one of the most important characteristics of automated expert problem solving [23]. For this reason, much attention has been given to the problem of how to explain the actions and conclusions of an expert system. This research has led to well-established methods of generating an explanation of an expert system's execution. The basis of nearly all these methods is that the explanation should be an augmented, pruned, or in some other way translated version of a trace of the expert system's execution (line of reasoning).

Recent developments in expert systems stand to present a new frontier of research on explaining an expert system's actions and conclusions. As discussed earlier, expert systems for heuristic classification have become commonplace in both academics and industry. However, many forms of expert problem solving do not fit into this narrow scope. In fact, researchers have found that heuristic classification is just one of a number of generic expert problem-solving methods [3], [5]. The result is an evolving direction in expert systems in which expert problem solving is modeled as a collection of cooperating problem-solving specialists. Each problem-solving specialist is responsible for a certain aspect of the overall problem solving. For example, one problem-solving specialist might be a classification specialist while another might be a planning specialist. The key point is that the overall problem is broken down into a collection of interacting specialized problems. Expert systems designed around this notion are often called *second generation* or *hybrid expert systems*.

This article attempts to establish the potential role of explanation in such second generation expert systems. The onset of second generation expert systems offers a significant opportunity for new and exciting directions in explanation research. It is the proposal of this paper that expert system explanation be promoted from simply a communicative device to a reasoning and communicative device.

2 Second Generation Expert Systems

Before discussing the proposed role of explanation it is worth taking a moment to more carefully examine what constitutes a second generation expert system. To date, the term "second generation expert systems" has been used to mean significantly different things to different people. However, there appear to be three common features that characterize most second generation expert systems.

The overall problem-solving process is decomposed into a collection of specialized information processing systems. In second generation expert systems, problem solving is decomposed into a collection of specialized information processing systems (IPSs) that take input, perform some internal processing operations and produce a final output.

Each information processing system uses a specialized reasoning method or representation. In this way, it is not enough to have simply delegated the problem solving to a collection of information processing systems. Instead, the "process" element for each IPS must be qualitatively different. This is the key distinction between second generation expert systems and blackboard-style expert systems. A blackboard system typically involves a collection of *knowledge sources* each designed to perform one aspect of the overall problem-solving process [11]. However, these knowledge sources need not be qualitatively different in form. A blackboard architecture is not enough to classify an expert system as second generation. Clearly, though, a blackboard system could be designed with diverse knowledge sources thus qualifying as a second generation expert system. Therefore, a second generation expert system depends on the nature of the IPSs used to solve the problem and not on the specific architecture (for example, a blackboard) used to implement that system. It should be noted that the distinction in the process may be defined solely by the level of knowledge being used. For example, several second generation expert systems use two basic IPSs: a shallow reasoner and a deep reasoner.

Each information processing system plays an active role in the overall problem-solving process through the sharing of data with other information processing systems. It is not enough that the expert system simply use different reasoning strategies, but those reasoning strategies must work together and interact in such a way as to form the overall problem-solving process. Thus, each IPS must be a "first-class" problem solver, working in conjunction with the other IPSs to solve the overall problem.

These three features serve to illustrate the common characteristics of a second generation expert system that seem to be emerging. For examples of second generation expert systems see [3], [7], [21], and [25].

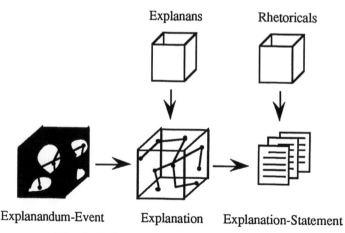

Fig. 1: Philosophy of Science Explanation

3 The Generic Problem of Explanation

Figure 1 presents a generic view of the problem of explanation. The terminology of the figure corresponds to the terminology of many studies in philosophy of science literature. As shown in the figure, explanation involves the observation of portions of an event. The task of explanation involves finding (or postulating) connections between the observed items in such a way that the connected whole forms a consistent description of process responsible for the observed items. This "explanation" of the event is then presented, using techniques from rhetoric, in the final explanation statement. Based on this interpretation of explanation, the following definition emerges:

> **Explanation.** A problem-solving process that takes the possibly incomplete operation of a system as input and generates a more complete description of that system's operation as an output.

It is interesting to consider traditional "expert system explanation" in light of this definition. Figure 2 illustrates the resulting representation. Notice that the process of observing partial items from an event and postulating plausible connections between those items has been removed. This is largely because, in expert systems, the entire reasoning chain is available and need not be postulated. However, we claim that explanatory power can be gained from re-introducing this aspect of explanation into expert system explanation.

Domain Knowledge   Rhetoricals

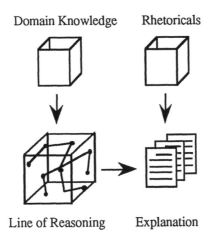

Line of Reasoning   Explanation

Fig. 2: Expert System Explanation

618

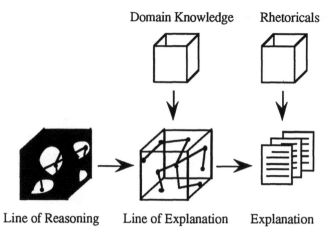

Domain Knowledge · · · Rhetoricals

Line of Reasoning · · · Line of Explanation · · · Explanation

Fig. 3: Reconstructive Expert System Explanation

Figure 3 illustrates the problem of expert system explanation when viewed as an instance of the complete problem of explanation. Notice the distinction between the *line of reasoning* as followed by the expert system and the *line of explanation* postulated by the explanation process. Expert system explanation becomes a complex problem-solving process of reconstructing plausible connections between observed elements of the expert system's line of reasoning. This representation appears to be consistent with phenomena observed in many of the explanation protocols we have collection [26]. Consider the following transcript of an expert attempting to classify the needs of a client requesting an experimental design.

> ...the client claims to need only 5 factors and therefore 32 treatments... suggests to me a factorial design might be appropriate. Let's see, oh, he only needs first order interactions... should be able to find something cheaper...looks like the maximum block size is reasonable, I think a balanced incomplete block design would be best...

Later, in explaining this problem solving, the expert reconstructed the reasoning steps that lead to the hypothesis of an *incomplete balanced block* design. In the reconstructed version, the data of the case is used to lead directly to the current hypothesis, thus giving the impression that the reasoning went from the initial problem state directly to the hypothesis of an *incomplete balanced block* design.

> ...the client needs 32 treatments with first order interactions. This suggests an inexpensive design, like a balanced incomplete block where only a few treatments are wasted from off block size... umm... I wonder if a fractional factorial could be used? How many units are required for each treatment?...

This example illustrates two important properties of explanation inconsistent with the traditional view of expert system explanation. First, the expert's line of explanation and line of reasoning are significantly different. The line of explanation results from a retrospective *reconstruction* that connects key items from the actual line of reasoning. In reconstructing the explanation, the expert reinterprets the data of the case so as to create a smooth and direct flow to the current hypothesis. Thus, the explanation does not move from *factorial* to *balanced incomplete block*, but instead moves directly to *balanced incomplete block*. Second, in so doing, the expert generalizes this case to fit with the typical case in which a direct movement to *balanced incomplete block* would be found. In particular, the expert talks of "off block size", a generalization typical of *balanced incomplete block* designs but not present during the original problem solving. As a direct effect of this generalization, an alternative hypothesis is suggested and leads to additional questions regarding the particulars of the current case. This example illustrates the *active* role decision explanation can play in problem solving.

Expert system explanation can therefore be described as an information processing operation that uses an explanatory strategy (or strategies) to explain the problem solving of other information processing operations and, in so doing, provides direction to those information processing operations. In other words, explanation is an information processing operation that actively participates in the overall problem-solving process. But this is just the characteristics of a generic problem solver in second generation expert systems. Thus, explanation in second generation expert systems is an IPS, on the same level as the other IPSs.

The following two sections discuss in detail our research which aims at investigating both the use of reconstructive expert system explanation and the active role such a system can play in second generation expert systems.

4 Reconstructive Expert System Explanation

The underlying premise of previous work is that the basis of the explanation is the trace of the expert system's line of reasoning. We believe another approach is possible that, for certain audiences, will overcome many of the problems evident in earlier explanations. A human expert, when asked to account for complex reasoning, rarely does so exclusively in terms of the actual process used to solve the problem [9]. Instead, an expert tends to reconstruct a "story" that accounts for the problem solving. This story reflects the expert's line of explanation [15] that is not necessarily the same as the original line of reasoning. For example, consider the following line of reasoning taken by an inspector attempting to find the cause of the excessive load on a concrete dam (based on [10]).

> ...the debris on top of the dam suggests a recent flood. The water markings on the abutments do, too. I suspect the flood is the cause of the excessive load. No, the duration of the flood wasn't long enough. Sometimes settlement has these same features. Perhaps settlement is involved. That would account for the high uplift pressures suggested by the slow drainage over time. But the damage to the drainage pipes isn't right. It must be erosion causing the dam to drop more at the toe. Yes, erosion is causing the excessive load...

Note that the inspector is using a heuristic, data-driven problem-solving process. Later, the field inspector is asked to explain the reasoning that led to the conclusion.

> ...the symptoms led me to believe the problem is internal erosion of soil from under the dam. See, erosion would cause the selectively broken pipes under the dam, therefore slowing drainage and causing high uplift pressures that cause the dam to slide downstream...

Notice how the line of explanation is different from the line of reasoning. During problem solving, the line of reasoning is directed to settlement through a heuristic association with flood , and then on to erosion. However, the line of explanation moves to erosion directly. The line of explanation is not simply a version of the line of reasoning pruned for dead-ends. The heuristic association between flood and settlement that eventually led to the conclusion erosion has been replaced by relationships that bond the symptoms directly to erosion.   Data introduction is another interesting feature of this explanation. During explanation, evidence not used during problem solving is introduced as additional support. This includes not only the underlying causality of many of the items, but also the introduction of new symptoms that further support the final conclusion (i.e. the movement of the dam). This type of data introduction is common in domains marked by non-exhaustive problem solving. In such domains, an expert will use a small set of cues from the data to reach a conclusion. Once this conclusion has been made, the expert will support it with additional data items. In some explanations, the initial data cues are replaced with new more directly supporting data. In our example, the triggering data (i.e. the duration of the flood) is dropped as it is not needed to directly support the conclusion. As illustrated by this example, the line of explanation and the line of reasoning are often considerably different in both form and content. In contrast to previous work, our research aims at creating the explanation as a product of a problem-solving activity largely distinct from the expert system's problem-solving process. This breaks the tight bond between explanation and problem solving. With this bond broken, the explanation system has freedom to reconstruct the explanation to create a more direct account of the expert system's conclusion.

4.1 Different Kinds of Explanation

The nature of an effective explanation depends heavily on the user. Knowledge engineers and others involved in the design and maintenance of an expert system require an explanation facility that elaborates on precisely what the system did to accomplish a specific result. This reflects the common thought that "justification must remain true to the expert system". However, an explanation for an end-user is intended to increase the user's confidence in the system and to aid the user in understanding the consequences of the system's conclusion. A system designer clearly needs a traced-based explanation that accurately reflects the line of reasoning used in the expert system. This line of reasoning may be inappropriate, however, for an end-user. A line of reasoning often proceeds to a conclusion via an obscure and indirect path. For instance, as illustrated earlier, many complex domains involve heuristic reasoning [5]. An effective explanation of the conclusion erosion, although arrived at from a heuristic association with flood, may not only require a substantial reorganization of the line of reasoning, but may require the use of additional supporting information not part of the original reasoning process. Generating such an explanation is possible only within a reconstructive explanation

There are obvious costs associated with the adoption of a reconstructive explanation strategy. However, these costs may not be as great as might at first be supposed. A clearer separation between problem solving and explanation reduces the need to trade problem-solving competence for comprehensibility that often arises with conventional explanation systems. Another possible problem with reconstructive explanation is the potential inconsistency between problem solving and explanation. However, better separation of problem solving and explanation might improve consistency. A recent study has shown that non-experts are not likely to catch reasoning errors when presented with trace-based explanations [8]. This may be because a non-expert, such as an end-user, often will not catch reasoning errors in a difficult to understand line of reasoning. Reconstructive explanation can aid the end-user in a better understanding of the problem and thus provide a basis for the user independently evaluating a system's actions. Overall, quality end-user explanation is not free, and the designers of an expert system must determine if they require extensive end-user explanations.

4.2 Intuitive Support for Reconstructive Explanation

As reconstructive explanation is significantly different from previous explanation paradigms, we present some intuitive support for its use. Research in psychology has discovered that, in certain situations, recall is reconstructive [6]. That is, during recall of an event, details are filled in that are not available from the memory of that particular event. This same notion of reconstruction has be shown to carry over to complex problem solving [9]. In expert problem solving, many of the details of how and why things happened are not available from a memory of the problem solving [1]. When asked to report this information, the expert will reconstruct an explanation that integrates the elements of a partial memory trace with the memory of other related entities (for example, textbook information). We believe this freedom to reconstruct an explanation based on information in addition to the information and processes used during problem solving is in part responsible for the high quality of human explanations. Reconstructive expert system explanation is the study of how to give an expert system this reconstructive ability.

4.3 The Rex System

Rex (Reconstructive EXplainer) is a system capable of producing reconstructive explanations for expert systems. Rex is designed to answer retrospective queries in an attempt to obtain the end-user's ratification of the expert system's conclusion. Such retrospective queries have been shown to be a useful context for reconstructive explanation techniques [9]. Rex provides an explanation of the movement within the competitor set of conclusions, thus showing how the final conclusion was reached.

4.3.1 A Model of Reconstructive Explanation

The Rex system is built on a model of reconstructive explanation that maps the execution of the expert system onto a textbook representation of the domain. Here a textbook representation is simply a representation of the information presented in human explanations, much of which comes from domain textbooks. The process of explanation then becomes the process of mapping over key elements from the execution trace and expanding on them using the more structured textbook knowledge. This should not be confused with "decompiling" the rules used by the expert system. Decompiling results in an explanation of the relationship between the antecedent and consequent of a rule. Reconstruction results in textbook knowledge that accounts for the data uncovered by the expert system. The execution trace is passed from the expert system to **Rex** where it is mapped into a high-level specification of expertise that represents the knowledge required for this problem-solving task. The specification points to structures in the textbook knowledge base that represent methods and relationships involved in performing each particular problem-solving task. A search is conducted within the textbook knowledge base to find the information necessary to answer the end-user's query. In the traditional approach to explanation the execution trace is mapped directly to the explanation text. Sometimes pruning is done to remove unnecessary information and auxiliary knowledge (called support knowledge) is added. However, the line of the explanation is based exclusively on the trace or line of reasoning. In our reconstructive explanation approach the execution trace is mapped through a high-level specification to the textbook knowledge of the domain. As the trace is mapped through the specification, information on the processes and reasons used by the expert system (the "how" knowledge) is filtered out. This leaves only information on the data used during problem solving (the "what" knowledge). Using this "what" knowledge as an index, textbook methods and relations are found that represent well-organized "how" knowledge. This textbook information, as opposed to the more obscure information found in the trace, forms the content and organizational structure of the explanation text.

An obvious question arises. Why go through all the extra work of mapping the trace into the textbook knowledge? Why not simply use the "textbook justifications" attached to the rules in the trace? The answer rests in the realization that explanation is a complex problem-solving task in its own right, requiring at a minimum a significant reorganization of the knowledge used for problem solving. For example, in medical school, knowledge is presented and explained as symptoms given disease. In the real world, problems are solved as disease given symptoms. However, conclusions are still explained as symptoms given disease as the explanation is then easier to understand and follow. Likewise, when an expert is asked to explain complex problem-solving methods, what can be given is the textbook method of solving the problem, instantiated for the specific case at hand. This method explains the process for the same reason that it was used to teach the process, it is easier to understand than the more obscure and ad hoc method used during real problem solving. This raises yet another question. If the textbook methods are so easy to explain, why not use them directly to solve the problem? The answer rests in the realization that real-world problem solving is also a complex task. Experts often proceed from symptoms to conclusions through long diverted paths. It is rarely possible to identify what method of solving the problem is appropriate from the beginning. It is much easier to reconstruct an appropriate method once the answer is known. Thus, explanation and problem solving are two largely distinct tasks, each requiring its own methods and knowledge.

4.3.2 Specification of Expertise

Before describing how **Rex** reconstructs an explanation, it is first necessary to briefly describe the representation used for the high-level specification. The specification represents what knowledge is required to solve the problem. In particular, this representation of expertise takes the form of a graph of hypotheses, each connect to other hypotheses by one or more "transitions". Associated with each transition are two sets. A set (called the condition set) of cues defines the data that must be found for the transition to be valid. In other words, this set represents information from the problem solving that can lead to a movement between the two hypotheses. Secondly, another set (called the goal set) defines the goals that must be posted in moving between the two hypotheses. These two sets combine to define what knowledge (cues and goals) is required to move between two hypotheses in the knowledge specification. At first, this representation may sound like a representation of how to solve the problem. However, the representation is neither procedural or deterministic. In other words, each transition tells what information is required to move between two hypotheses, but does not enforce how that information will be used. For example, the condition and goal elements of a transition are supersets of the cues and goals needed to make the transition. Different subset(s) of cues and goals can be used to move between the two hypotheses. The following section will illustrate the use of such a specification for reconstructing explanations.

4.3.3 Reconstruction of How from What

To illustrate the process of explanation, consider the line of reasoning given in concrete dam example earlier. In that example, the domain expert was trying to identify the cause of the excessive load on a concrete dam. In the explanation, the expert was attempting to answer how that cause was determined. The expert's problem-solving leaves a trace of data corresponding to symptoms and inferences. The trace for this example contains the following: debris on dam, water marks, drainage, uplift pressure, and broken pipes. In **Rex**, the data in this trace are used to "activate" the same data in the high-level specification of the knowledge required to solve the problem. This enables **Rex** to determine what data cues were used by the expert system in moving to the conclusion. The line of reasoning follows a path from the initial empty hypothesis through the hypothesis flood , onto the hypothesis settlement and stopping at the final solution erosion. However, the line of explanation (as given earlier) moves from the initial empty hypothesis directly to erosion, using the data cues uplift pressure, drainage, broken pipes and sliding. **Rex**, when given access to the expert system to find additional supporting knowledge that was not activated from the expert system's problem-solving trace, reconstructs an explanation that closely resembles this line of explanation. This reconstruction involves three core elements of the **Rex** design: the textbook knowledge base, the explainer, and the story teller. The following paragraphs will describe how each of these elements helps reconstruct a line of explanation for the concrete dam example. The Textbook Knowledge Base is represented in **Rex** as a collection of relationships between cues, hypotheses, and goals as illustrated in Figure 4. The cues, hypotheses, and goals themselves represent the domain objects that other relationships and methods manipulate. In **Rex**, each relationship is represented as a cue script and each method is represented as a goal script as shown in Figure 4.

Each frame and script has text slots for English presentation. Using the representations illustrated in Figure 4, a transition from one hypothesis to another is possible when a method and relationships are found such that each goal and cue used is a member of the goal and condition sets defined between the two hypotheses in the knowledge specification graph. In **Rex** , the structure built by combining the method and the relationships is called an explanation structure as it serves as an explanation of the movement between the hypotheses. The Explainer is responsible for constructing the line of explanation that will eventually be presented to the end-user. This line of explanation represents a movement from the initial problem-solving state to the final conclusion reached by the expert system. In **Rex** , this corresponds to finding a path through the knowledge specification from the conclusion of the expert system to the empty hypothesis. Each transition in this path must be supported by the existence of a valid explanation structure. **Rex** uses the A* algorithm to search through a space of knowledge specification transitions for which a valid explanation structure has been found. The search is carried out backwards from the final conclusion of the expert system towards the empty hypothesis. Each state in this search corresponds to an emerging line of explanation that uses certain cues and a hypothesis as data, establishes other cues and a hypothesis as conclusions and traverses certain edges in the specification. Transitions between states in the A* search correspond to expanding the bottom hypothesis by finding each edge with a valid explanation structure that moves to this hypothesis. As the precise explanation structure chosen will determine the cues included in the explanation, a separate transition in the A* search is constructed for each valid explanation structure on each incoming edge of the bottom hypothesis. A complete line of explanation represents a path from the initial problem state (the empty hypothesis) to the final conclusion reached by the expert system.

CUE uplift
    Value   : true
    Type   : direct
    Name   : the high uplift pressures acting on the dam
    Nickname   : uplift pressures
    Valuename   : *cue*

HYPOTHESIS erosion
    Value   : true
    Name   : the erosion of soil from under the dam
    Nickname   : erosion
    Valuename   : *hypothesis*

GOAL det-cause
    Name   : determine causal relationships
    Nickname   : determine causes

CUE SCRIPT erosion-to-sliding
    Uses   : (drainage uplift sliding)
    Supports   : erosion
    Achieves   : det-cause
    Vconstraint : (and drainage uplift   sliding)
    Text   : (erosion causes broken-pipes causing drainage resulting in uplift
                  and in turn sliding)

GOAL SCRIPT causal
    Holds   : (det-cause)
    Text   : (simply det-cause)

Fig. 4 : A sample knowledge representation from Rex.

```
LOE          ::= {problem description} {problem statement} Story Resolution
Story        ::= Setting Theme Plot Resolution |
                 Setting Theme Plot Resolution Story
Setting      ::= {hypothesis}
Theme        ::= Event Goal
Event        ::= {cue} | {cue} Event
Goal         ::= {make initial hypothesis} | {refute hypothesis} | {generalize hypothesis}
                 {support hypothesis} | {refine hypothesis}
Plot         ::= Strategy Relations Outcome
Strategy     ::= {goal} | {goal} Strategy
Relations    ::= {explanatory relation} | {explanatory relation} Relations
Outcome      ::= {hypothesis}
Resolution   ::= {hypothesis}
```

Fig. 5: A story grammar.

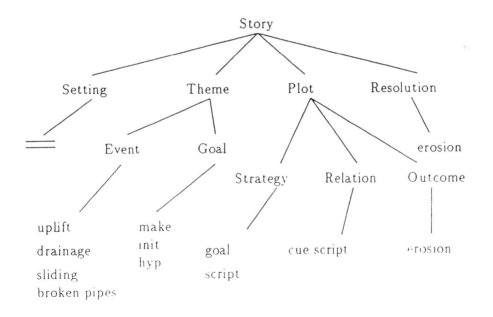

Fig. 6: An example story tree.

The Story Teller takes the path found by the explainer and formats it for English presentation using the grammar of Figure 5, thus creating a story tree. Figure 6 shows the story tree for our example. The **Rex** system translates this story tree to produce the following explanation[1]:

> We have a concrete dam under an excessive load. I attempted to find the cause of the excessive load. Not knowing the solution and based on the broken pipes in the foundation of the dam, and the downstream sliding of the dam, and the high uplift pressures acting on the dam, and the slow drainage of water from the upstream side of the dam to the downstream side I was able to make an initial hypothesis. To achieve this I used the strategy of striving to simply determine causal relationships. In attempting to determine causes, I found that the internal erosion of soil from under the dam causes broken pipes causing slow drainage resulting in uplift and in turn sliding. This led me to hypothesize that internal erosion was the cause of the excessive load. Feeling confident in this solution, I concluded that the internal erosion of soil from under the dam was the cause of the excessive load.

The expert system, using a reconstructive explanation system, is able to present a line of explanation that leads directly to the solution. Whereas the expert system using a traditional explanation system would be restricted to a line of explanation moving first to flood , through settlement to erosion. Even when the explanation system is not given access to the expert system and thus can not ask for additional supporting data (such as sliding), the reconstructive paradigm can still create a more direct explanation than is possible within the traditional paradigm. **Rex** can find the shortest path of "activated" data from the solution hypothesis to the initial empty condition. In other words, **Rex** can find the most direct path to the solution using only information uncovered by the expert system during problem solving. In our example, this path is found by moving from the initial empty set directly to settlement and on to erosion. This line of explanation, although less direct than the previous line of explanation, is still more direct than the path followed by the traditional explanation paradigm as it by-passes the need for the heuristic association with flood.

5 Active Expert System Explanation

Our generic view of explanation also points to another area of interesting research on explanation in second generation expert systems. Typically, problem solving can be

---

[1]The verbose nature of the English output is a result of our focus on the content and structure of the story tree and not on its presentation.

thought of as a combination and intermingling of three major activities: investigation, hypothesis formation, and explanation. During investigation, data is collected in order to develop patterns of information. In hypothesis formation, these patterns are interpreted and hypotheses are made concerning possible solutions to the problem. Explanation then involves linking these possible problems with the patterns of data found earlier. Problem solving consists of a intermixed sequence of these three activities that leads the problem solver from the initial data of the problem to the final solution.

Most problem-solving programs use some variation of this three-phase approach to problem solving. This seems to suggest that explanation is already an active element of automatic problem solving and, in a sense, this is true. Explanation does play an active role in many automatic problem-solving systems. However, the use of explanation by those systems is significantly different than the use of explanation illustrated in the examples of Section 1. In the explanation phase of problem solving described above, the explanation concerns the nature of the interaction between elements of the problem. For example, in the concrete dam domain, such an explanation might link an observed symptom such as crushed concrete to a possible cause, for instance high uplift pressures. In the examples of Section 1, the explanation concerns the problem solving itself. Clearly, these are two different types of explanation (this distinction has been made by other researchers as well [4]). The first concerns the explanation of some phenomenon in the problem. The second concerns the explanation of the process used to solve the problem. As the example of Section 1 illustrates, the process of constructing this second type of explanation can play an important role in providing feedback to the original problem solving.

In attempting to harness the active feedback of the explanation, the first step is to identify a specific type of feedback on which to focus. In our preliminary research on reconstructive explanation, we found several examples of active feedback typified by the protocol shown in Section 1. As discussed earlier, this feedback occurs through the instantiation of *prototypical explanation patterns*. In attempting to explain previous problem solving, the human expert often appealed to standard methods of explaining certain findings and hypotheses. It is during this instantiation that feedback to the original problem solving occurs. In the example of Section 1, when the expert attempts to adapt the standard explanation pattern to the specific case at hand, a generalization is made that suggests other hypotheses that deserve further consideration. Other examples of active explanation from our previous research include the incorporation of extra supporting information not present in the original line of reasoning, but present in prototypical explanation patterns [26].

We see this earlier research as supplying substantive support for a *case-based approach to explanation* [17]. In this approach, explanation is viewed as the task of retrieving from memory relevant explanation patterns that address the anomaly confronting the system (i.e., unexplained hypotheses or data). The retrieved explanation patterns are then "tweaked" and "evaluated" to fit the current problem. We believe that the "tweak" and "evaluation" phases of this process offer powerful areas of feedback to the original problem solving.

Although heavily based on Schank's theory of explanation patterns, this research offers a significant new application and advancement of those ideas. In particular, the explanation patterns used by Schank are explanations of the world, not explanations of complex decision making. This distinction is relevant in that the algorithms for tweaking and evaluating that Schank has proposed are aimed toward explanations of people's plans and not towards the explanation of problem-solving decisions. As is discussed in the following subsection, Schank's research provides an excellent starting point for our research, however, many open issues remain.

Before describing in detail the proposed architecture of explanation, two questions are worth explicitly addressing. First, why would the expert ever receive feedback from explanation to problem solving? Isn't the knowledge used during explanation known during problem solving? The answer to this question lies in the nature of the domain problem solving and the problem solving that must occur during explanation. In our example from Section 1, the expert clearly knows the generalization during domain problem solving. However, that generalization is not made until explanation begins. Why? The expert, during the domain problem solving, is using heuristic classification [5]. This type of problem solving is typified by non–hierarchical jumps between or within classification hierarchies. An example of such a jump is the switch from settlement to erosion. This type of heuristic association enables the expert to begin working part way down the new hierarchy, based on associations that have been learned with other hierarchies. However, these associations are not perfect (i.e., the name "heuristic") and the entry into the new hierarchy is not guaranteed to be at the correct level. In our example, the association led directly to erosion, skipping the more general entries above. Although this association is correct most times, in this particular case it was not. In explaining problem solving, heuristic associations are often replaced with domain knowledge that more directly leads to the conclusion [26]. In our example, this involves mapping the current problem onto the prototypical movement to erosion.

In so doing, the generalization (upward movement within the erosion hierarchy) is made and the feedback occurs. Thus, it is not the lack of knowledge that causes the feedback from explanation to problem solving, but rather the manner in which the available knowledge is used. Another reason for feedback from explanation to problem solving is that information is considered during explanation that is not considered during problem solving. Ericsson and Simon [9] have found that reasons and processes are not heeded during problem solving but do play an important role in retrospective descriptions of that problem solving. The incorporation of such information offers significant potential for feedback during explanation.

The second question that comes to mind from this discussion is that if case–based reasoning (explanation) provides guidance to the problem solving, why not use it to begin with? In many cases, one could. However, in more difficult problems, the adaptation of earlier cases to fit the new problem is too difficult and experts appeal to a deeper knowledge to solve the problems. This argument centers on the tradeoffs between rule–based and case–based problem solving and space does not allow an exhaustive treatment of those issues here (for more information on this topic, see [16]). However, it is interesting to note that intuitively explanation offers the most potential for feedback during the solution of difficult problems. Rarely does one appeal to explanation for guidance when the solution is forth-coming. It is, in part, the distinction between the deep problem solving and the case-based explanation during these difficult problems that provides the foundation for active feedback.

5.1 RAX - A Proposed Architecture of Explanation

An important aspect of the proposed research is the design and implementation of an architecture of explanation. In contrast to previous research in expert problem solving, the architecture must support explanation as a complex problem-solving activity in its own right. Numerous problem-solving architectures have been proposed based on the importance of explanation (for example, [22]). However, these architectures are best described as architectures *for* explanation as opposed to our focus on an architecture *of* explanation. The distinction being that an architecture of explanation must support explanation as a problem-solving task analogous to the task of a traditional domain problem solver whereas an architecture for explanation must simply support the explanation of problem solving on that architecture. This section discusses the nature of such an architecture of explanation in light of the preceding discussion on case–based explanation.

632

Figure 7 shows an overview of how the proposed architecture of explanation will interface with the expert system. For this study, we have selected an implemented and tested heuristic classification system called GALEN as the expert system [24]. GALEN is a heuristic classification system that diagnoses congenital heart disease in children. GALEN has been selected for several reasonings including its maturity (over 70 diseases), its portability, its inherent reliance on the type of heuristic associations demonstrated earlier, and its internal structure which uses a scratchpad (blackboard). The scratchpad provides a natural forum for communicating feedback from the explanation system to the expert system. The proposed architecture, called RAX (Reconstructive Active eXplainer), takes reasoning cues (hypotheses and data) from the expert system and attempts to explain the problem solving that lead to those cues. Again, any information that results from the process of explanation that was not already posted by the expert system will be placed on the scratchpad for later review by the expert system.

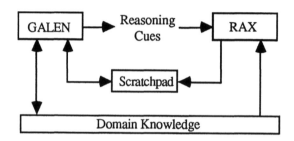

Fig. 7: An Overview of RAX/GALEN Interface

Figure 8 gives a detailed block diagram of the RAX architecture[2]. The reasoning cues obtained by the expert system are inspected by the *anomaly detector (AD)*. The reasoning cue representing the "largest" anomaly is selected and passed to the *explanation pattern searcher (XPS)*. The XPS selects retrieval cues for use in finding relevant explanation patterns in the *episodic memory*. All explanation patterns (xp) found in the episodic memory are returned. The XPS then selects an explanation pattern that is evaluated by the *explanation pattern evaluator (XPE)* for plausibility. If the explanation pattern does not pass the basic plausibility tests, it is

---

[2]This architecture is heavily based on the process of case-based explanation demonstrated by Schank [Schank,1986]. However, the nature of the processes involved will need to be changed to reflect the shift from the explanation of everyday plans to the explanation of complex problem solving.

passed to the *explanation pattern tweaker (XPT)* which attempts to patch the problems. The resulting explanation pattern is then returned to the XPE. This process cycles until one of the patterns found by the XPS is accepted by the XPE, resulting in that explanation pattern being passed to the *explanation pattern indexer (XPI)* for storage in the episodic memory. That same explanation pattern is then passed back to the AD for inclusion in the emerging complete explanation. This process continues until all anomalous reasoning cues have been incorporated into the complete explanation. Finally, the complete explanation (which is itself an explanation pattern) is passed to the XPI for indexing. Feedback can occur from either the XPE or the XPT subsystems. As such, they are both linked to the shared scratchpad.

To aid in understanding the proposed architecture, a few definitions are necessary. *Reasoning cues* are either data or hypotheses known in the domain. An *anomaly* is any reasoning cue that has not been both linked to the evolving complete explanation and grounded. A data cue is linked to the evolving complete explanation by showing that is was used in supporting a given hypothesis, whereas a hypothesis is linked by showing that it led to another hypothesis or is the current hypothesis. An *explanation pattern* is a transition between two or more hypotheses showing what data was used in the movement and why certain other paths (possible hypotheses) were not pursued further. The explanation pattern in this context is similar to a derivational history [2]. *Episodic memory* is a MOP-based memory system used for the storage of basic, and generalized explanation patterns [13]. Explanation patterns are generalized by removing overly restrictive information from their representation using explanation-based learning techniques [14]. The *complete explanation* produced by the RAX system is a composite explanation pattern (a graph of hypotheses) that links the initial problem state to the current hypothesis and accounts for (uses) all reasoning cues given by the expert system.

The following paragraphs discuss in more detail the major elements of the RAX architecture. Clearly, during the course of this research, the ideas forming the foundation of this architecture may need to be changed and the architecture updated. However, based on research in human explanation, this architecture provides a sound starting point for the design and implementation of an active explanation system.

634

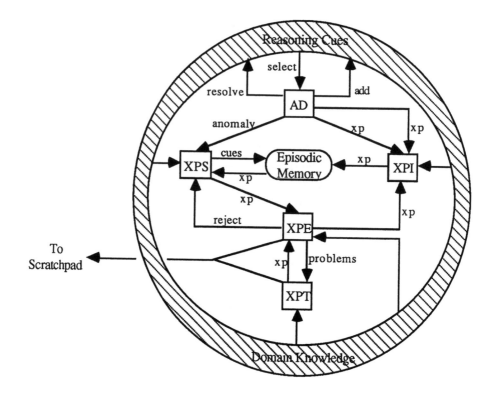

Fig. 8: A Block Diagram of the RAX Architecture.

The anomaly detector (AD) subsystem is responsible for selecting anomalous reasoning cues, using a model of the end–user receiving the explanation. It may appear odd to incorporate a user model in a system that is primarily being designed for meta-level feedback. However, the user model provides a basis for the selection of which reasoning cues represent the largest anomaly and as such provide a perspective from which the explanation can be constructed. The AD system attempts to explain the reasoning cues based on the user model's domain rule base. Those that cannot be resolved are marked as anomalous. The size of the anomaly can be roughly judged by the degree of isolation from the other elements of the reasoning cues. The AD system then operates as a means-ends analysis problem solver, attempting to create one large explanation structure. As an explanation pattern can introduce new anomalies, for example indirect data that must be linked to the direct data, the AD system can also add elements to the set of reasoning cues that must be resolved.

The explanation pattern searcher (XPS) subsystem attempts to find explanation patterns that might be useful in resolving a given anomaly. Clearly, the main retrieval cue is the anomaly itself. However, other information can also be used. For example, other data cues used by the expert system might be useful in locating explanation patterns that stand a good chance of being relevant to the current problem. Also, anomalies that are "hierarchically close" to the given anomaly might be tried. Techniques similar to those used by Schank [18] will be useful starting points for search strategies.

The explanation pattern evaluator (XPE) subsystem is responsible for checking the validity and plausibility of a given explanation pattern. Each explanation pattern may make certain assumptions or require certain data. The XPE system checks to make sure this information is met in the current problem. In doing so, new knowledge about the problem may be generated (i.e., new data may be obtained that was not previously needed). Any such knowledge is posted on the shared scratchpad for possible use by the expert system.

The explanation pattern tweaker (XPT) subsystem attempts to alter the structure and/or assumptions of a given explanation pattern to fit the current problem. Examples of tweaking strategies include trying to find alternative data that can support intermediate hypotheses, and searching for alternative hypotheses that can be used to support other intermediate results. Many of the tweaking strategies developed by Schank's work [12] will be useful, but more research is needed to exploit information particular to explanation of decisions. Again, any new information proposed by this process is placed on the scratchpad for subsequent review by the expert system.

Finally, the explanation pattern indexer (XPI) takes a given explanation pattern and places it into the episodic memory for future retrieval and adaptation. Initially, this subsystem will simply be a re-indexing program. However, more advanced systems are possible.

6 Significance

This paper has discussed the design of second generation expert systems and the implications of that design on expert system explanation. Explanation was found to have many of the same characteristics as other problem-solving activities, thus defining explanation as a first-class problem solver in second generation expert system reasoning. In this light, explanation was shown to be consistent with observed phenomena in human explanation that are not obviously supported through the traditional approach to explanation. Both reconstructive explanation and active explanation have significance to second generation expert system explanation.

6.1 Reconstructive Explanation

Reconstructive explanation is a significantly new approach to the automatic generation of expert system explanations. The feasibility of using the reconstructive explanation paradigm has been shown by the **Rex** system. Such a reconstructive explanation paradigm has several advantages that show its desirability: (1) The textbook methods and relations used to integrate the information uncovered during problem solving serve to reorganize the flow of the explanation to be more direct. (2) Different methods and relations can be used to allow the explanations to be tailored to the needs of specific user types. (3) A reconstructive explanation system can provide independent feedback on the performance of the expert system. For example, if the explanation system can not find an explanation for the conclusion, this could suggest an error in the problem solving of the expert system. (4) An expert system with a reconstructive explanation facility will have the ability to use one approach for problem solving and another for explanation. Thus, the system can be implemented with less concern for the tradeoff between problem-solving ability and end-user explanation. (5) Under certain constraints, a reconstructive explanation has the freedom to present multiple lines of explanation leading to the same conclusion. (6) Reconstructive explanation provides more flexibility than conventional explanation systems allowing explanations to be built on information other than a subset of the execution trace.

Another advantage to using the reconstructive approach is that the *line of explanation* can be tailored to the particular user requesting the explanation. In traditional explanation, the line of explanation was by necessity a subset (pruned) or a superset (augmented) of the line of reasoning [15]. Thus the explanation was forced to move through the data in much the same manner as the original problem solving. Wick and Thompson have shown that this significantly restricts the quality of the explanations that can be produced [26]. In the reconstructive paradigm, movement through the data can be reconstructed to appear as natural as possible to a wide range of end-user audiences. Further, this process of reconstructing a line of explanation may require introducing new information (data) not used during the original problem solving. This data introduction can motivate even more feedback to the other problem solvers.

6.2 Active Explanation

Active expert system explanation also has several advantages over more traditional roles of explanation in second generation expert systems. Perhaps the most important and exciting is the potential *feedback* from explanation to problem solving. It is a well-known phenomenon in human explanation that the act of giving an explanation of problem solving can improve that problem solving. Nearly everyone has experienced a time in which they were stuck on a problem, but when explaining their approach to a colleague, a "light bulb" goes off and you see something in the problem that you had missed before. It is not at all clear how traditional methods of expert system explanation could achieve such feedback. However, in second generation expert system explanation, this type of feedback is not only possible, but is directly supported by the second generation expert system architectures that are designed to handle the cooperation and interactive of diverse reasoning techniques. For instance, in the blackboard example, when the explanation module posts "off block size" this would trigger knowledge on units per treatment in the empirical module, thus bringing alternative hypotheses into consideration.

A related advantage of the second generation expert system explanation methodology is the concept of *interference*. When humans give explanations, that process often will interfere with subsequent problem solving [9]. This interference is not the direct form as discussed above but is a more subtle influence. In particular, the process of explanation in humans uses working memory. Any concepts entered into working memory that are not erased during explanation are still in working memory when explanation terminates. This reminisce of the explanation process is therefore part of the current state of the system and thus is considered when the next problem solver is initiated. For example, when giving an explanation many items are brought into awareness (working memory) that would not otherwise have been considered [9]. By focusing attention on these items, they (and knowledge associated with them) may become primed so that later problem solving will more easily find these items than others. In this way, the process of explanation may make certain knowledge more accessible than it would have been without giving an explanation. As the knowledge is more accessible, problem solving would require less search and can be performed faster. In our example architecture, this would correspond to explanation posting items on the blackboard that later can be used by the other problem solvers.

These first two consequences are a result of viewing explanation as an active information processing system. However, other advantages exist that do not depend

638

of this feature. In second generation expert systems, problem solving is viewed as an interaction of several diverse reasoning techniques. Even within the traditional approach to explanation, this implies an increased diversity in the kind of explanations that can be given. However, using the reconstructive approach to explanation, even more *diverse explanations* can be generated. As the explanation routine is responsible for reconstructing the reasoning of the system for explanatory purposes, this reconstruction can be slanted so as to allow explanations to be generated in several of the reasoning paradigms. For example, a causal explanation (using the causal IPS) could be generated for the empirical reasoning process. In this way, reconstruction allows even more diversity than the traditional expert system explanation methodology.

References

1. Anderson, J.: Acquisition of Cognitive Skill, Psychological Review, **89:4** (1982) 369-406
2. Carbonell, J.: Derivational Analogy: A Theory of Reconstructive Problem Solving and Expertise Acquisition, In R.S. Michalski, J.G. Carbonell, and T.M. Mitchell (eds) Machine Learning: An Artificial Intelligence Approach, vol. II, (1986) 371-392
3. Chandrasekaran, B.: Generic Tasks in Knowledge-Based Reasoning: High-Level Building Blocks for Expert System Design, IEEE Expert, Fall (1986) 23-30
4. Chandrasekaran, B., Tanner, M., and Josephson, J.: Explaining Control Strategies in Problem Solving, IEEE Expert, **4** (1989) 9-24
5. Clancey, W.: Heuristic Classification, Artificial Intelligence, **27** (1985) 289-350
6. Dawes, R.: Cognitive distortion, Psychological Reports, **14** (1964) 443-459
7. David, J. and Krivine, J.: What Happened? Causal Reasoning in DIVA, In System Fault Diagnostics, Reliability and Related Knowledge-Based Approaches, S. Tzafestas *et al.* (eds.), **2** (1987) 23-27
8. Erdman, P.: A Comparison of Computer Consultation Programs for Primary Care Physicians: Impact of Decision Making Model and Explanation, Ph.D. Thesis, University of Wisconsin - Madison (1983).
9. Ericsson, K. and Simon, H.: Protocol Analysis: Verbal Reports As Data, Cambridge, Mass: The MIT Press, (1984)

10. Franck, B.: Preliminary Safety and Risk Assessment For Existing Hydraulic Structures - An Expert System Appraoch, Ph.D. Thesis, Mechanical Engineering Department, University of Minnesota, (1987)

11. Hayes-Roth, B.: A Blackboard Architecture for Control, Artificial Intelligence, **26** (1985) 251-321

12. Kass, A.: Adaptation-Based Explanation: Explanation as Cases, Proceedings of the Sixth International Workshop on Machine Learning, (1989) 49-51

13. Kolodner, J.: Reconstructive Memory: A Computer Model, Cognitive Science, **7** (1983) 281-328

14. Mitchell, T. and Keller, R.: Explanation-Based Generalization: A Unifying View, In Machine Learning, R.S. Michalski, J.G. Carbonell, and T.M. Mitchell (eds.), Boston, Mass: Kluwer Academic Press, (1986)

15. Paris, C., Wick, M., and Thompson, W.: The Line of Reasoning Versus the Line of Explanation, Proceedings of the 1988 AAAI Workshop on Explanation, (1988) 4-7

16. Riesbeck, C. and Schank, R.: Inside Case-Based Reasoning, Hillsdale, NJ: Lawrence Erlbaum Associates, (1989)

17. Schank, R.: Explanation Patterns: Understanding, Mechanically and Creatively, Hillsdale, N.J.: Lawrence Erlbaum Associates, (1986)

18. Schank, R. and Leake, D.: Creativity and Learning in a Case-Based Explainer, Artificial Intelligence Journal, **40** (1989) 353-385

19. Schulman, R. and Hayes-Roth, B.: ExAct: A Module For Explaining Actions, Technical Report KSL-87-8, Stanford University, (1987)

20. Shortliffe, E.: Computer-Based Medical Consultations: MYCIN, New York: Elsevier/North Holland, (1976)

21. Simmons, R. and Davis, R. Generate, Test, and Debug: Combining Associational Rules and Causal Models, Proceedings of the Tenth International Joint Conference on Artificial Intelligence, (1987) 1071-1078

22. Swartout, W., and Smoliar, S.: On Making Expert Systems More Like Experts, Expert Systems, **4(3)** (1987) 196-207

23. Teach, R. and Shortliffe, E.: An analysis of physician's attitudes, In Rule-Based Expert Systems: The MYCIN Experiments of the Stanford Heuristic Programming Project, Reading, MA: Addison-Wesley, (1984)

24. Thompson, W., Johnson, P., and Moen, J.: Recognition-Based Diagnostic Reasoning, Proceedings of the Eighth International Joint Conference on Artificial Intelligence (1983) 236-238

25. Tong, X., He, Z., and Yu, R.: A Tool For Building Second Generation Expert Systems, Proceedings of the Tenth International Joint Conference on Artificial Intelligence, (1987) 91-96

26. Wick, M. and Thompson, W.: "Reconstructive Expert System Explanation, *Artificial Intelligence Journal* 54 (1992) 33-70.

Part VI

Architectures

Architectural Foundations for Real-Time Performance in Intelligent Agents[1]

Barbara Hayes-Roth

Stanford University
Palo Alto, CA 94304, USA

Abstract. Intelligent agents perform concurrent tasks requiring interaction with a dynamic environment, under real-time constraints. Because an agent's opportunities to perceive, reason, and act exceed its resources, it must determine which operations to perform and when to perform them so as to achieve its most important objectives. Accordingly, we view the problem of real-time performance as a problem in intelligent real-time control. We propose control requirements and present an agent architecture designed to address them. Key features include: parallel perception, action, and cognition processes, limited-capacity I/O buffers with best-first retrieval and worst-first overflow, dynamic control planning, dynamic focus of attention, and a satisficing execution cycle. These features allow an agent to trade quality for speed of response under dynamic goals, resource limitations, and performance constraints. We illustrate the architecture in the Guardian system for intensive care monitoring and contrast it with alternative architectures.

1 Real-Time Performance in Intelligent Agents

Imagine an "errand robot" driving an automobile on its way to some destination. Noticing a yellow traffic light at the next intersection in its path, the robot infers from its current speed, distance to the light, and conservative traffic-light policy that it should stop. The robot immediately releases the accelerator and, after a few seconds,

---

[1] The research was supported by DARPA contract N00039-83-C-0136, NIH contract 5P41-RR-00785, EPRI contract RP2614-48, and AFOSR contract F49620-89-C-0103DEF, and by gifts from Rockwell International, Inc. and FMC Corporation, Inc. The Guardian system is being developed in collaboration with Adam Seiver, Rich Washington, David Ash, Rattikorn Hewett, Anne Collinot, Luc Boureau, Angel Vina, Ida Sim, and Michael Falk. The paper's treatment of real-time requirements reflects discussions with colleagues involved in the AFOSR Program on Intelligent Real Time Problem Solving Systems--especially Stan Rosenschein, Lee Erman, and Yoav Shoham. The paper also benefited from constructive criticism by several anonymous reviewers. Thanks to Ed Feigenbaum for sponsoring the work at the Knowledge Systems Laboratory.

This article is reprinted with the permission of Kluwer Academic Publishers. The article originally appeared in the journal REAL-TIME SYSTEMS, Nos. 1/2, May, 1990. Other than small modifications for formatting purposes, only section 8, "Remarks on Second-Generation Expert Systems," has been added for inclusion in this book.

applies the brake to bring its vehicle to a gradual stop just before entering the intersection. The robot's behavior is satisfactory not simply because it produces the correct result, but because it does so at the right time. If the robot stopped very much before or after reaching the intersection, its behavior would be unsatisfactory and potentially catastrophic.

The errand robot illustrates a class of computer systems, which we call "intelligent agents," whose tasks require both knowledge-based reasoning and interaction with dynamic entities in the environment--such as human beings, physical processes, other computer systems, or complex configurations of such entities. Tasks requiring an intelligent agent occur in diverse domains, such as power plant monitoring [53], process control [10, 41], experiment monitoring [40], student tutoring [38], aircraft pilot advising [47], and intensive care patient monitoring [15, 27].

To perform such tasks, an agent must possess capabilities for: *perception*-- acquiring and interpreting sensed data to obtain knowledge of external entities; *cognition*--knowledge-based reasoning to assess situations, solve problems, and determine actions; and *action*--actuating effectors to execute intended actions and influence external entities. For example, the errand robot perceives signals from which it infers that the traffic light is yellow. It reasons with this perception, its traffic light policies, and other perceptions and knowledge to determine that gradually coming to a stop at the intersection is the desired result and that releasing the accelerator and applying the brake are the appropriate actions. It performs those actions in the appropriate temporal organization, thereby achieving the intended result.

Because external entities have their own temporal dynamics, interacting with them imposes aperiodic hard and soft real-time constraints on the agent's behavior. Following [3] we use the term "aperiodic" to describe tasks having irregular arrival times. Following [16, 50] we use the terms "hard" and "soft" to distinguish between constraints whose violation precludes a successful result versus those whose violation merely degrades the utility of the result. For example, a vehicle that happens to stop in front of the errand robot is an aperiodic event with a hard deadline. The robot must stop in time to avoid colliding with the other vehicle. When that is not possible, the robot should consider alternative actions, such as maneuvering around the stopped vehicle.

In a complex environment, an agent's opportunities for perception, action, and cognition typically exceed its computational resources. For example, in the scenario above, the errand robot has opportunities to perceive the physical features and occupants of other automobiles on the road and the buildings and landscape along the sides of the road. It might reason about any of these perceptions or other facts in its knowledge base. It might perform a variety of actions more or less related to driving its automobile. Fortunately, the robot largely ignores most of these opportunities to focus on matters related to the traffic light. Otherwise, it might fail to perform the necessary perception, reasoning, and actions in time to stop its automobile at the right time. On the other hand, the errand robot cannot totally ignore incidental information without risking the consequences of rare catastrophic events. For example, the robot should notice a child running into its path. In some cases, the robot might benefit from noticing information that is not immediately useful. For example, it might notice a sign posting business hours on a shop window and use that information when planning a subsequent day's errands.

Because an intelligent agent is almost always in a state of perceptual, cognitive, and action overload, it generally cannot perform all potential operations in a timely fashion. While faster hardware or software optimization may solve this problem for selected application systems, they will not solve the general problem of limited resources or obviate its concomitant resource-allocation task [49]. For an agent of any speed, we can define tasks whose computational requirements exceed its resources. Moreover, we seek more from an intelligent agent than satisfactory performance of a predetermined task for which it has been optimized. Rather, we seek satisfactory performance of a range of tasks varying in required functionality and available knowledge as well as real-time constraints. And we seek adaptation to unanticipated conditions and requirements. For example, the errand robot should be able to respond appropriately to traffic signals and other usual and unusual events in a broad range of driving situations. It should drive competently on freeways as well as on surface streets. If it unexpectedly finds itself on surface streets where others are driving at freeway speeds (or, more likely, vice versa), it should adapt its own behavior accordingly. The agent might have other sorts of skills, such as planning its own errands under high-level goals and constraints or learning new routes from experience taking necessary detours. Other things being equal, the broader the range of tasks an agent can handle and the wider the range of circumstances to which it can adapt, the more intelligent it is.

For these reasons, we view real-time performance as a problem in intelligent control. An agent must use knowledge of its goals, constraints, resources, and environment to determine which of its many potential operations to perform at each opportunity. For example, the errand robot might decide to give high priority to perceiving and reasoning about traffic lights so that it can always stop in time for yellow or red lights. When the operations required to achieve an agent's current goals under its specified constraints exceed its computational resources, it may have to modify them as well. For example, if the errand robot finds itself unexpectedly late to an important destination, it might decide to relax its conservative traffic-light policy and drive through selected yellow lights. Because it is situated in a dynamic environment and faces a continuing stream of events, an agent must make a continuing series of control decisions so as to meet demands and exploit opportunities for action as they occur. For example, if the errand robot is making a planned gradual stop at a traffic light and a child runs into its path, the robot should perceive the child and stop immediately. In general, an agent should use intelligent control to produce the best results it can under real-time constraints and other resource (e.g., information, knowledge) constraints.

Our conception of real-time performance in intelligent agents is qualitatively different from conceptions embodied in other sorts of computer systems [3, 7, 16]. In particular, we do not view real-time performance as a provable, guaranteed, universal property of the agent. Nor do we seek real-time performance through effective engineering of the agent for narrowly specified task environments. We feel that these constructs are surely premature and probably unrealistic for the versatile and highly adaptive agents we envision. Rather, we view real-time performance as one of an agent's several objectives, which it will achieve to a greater or lesser degree as the result of interactions between the environment it encounters, the resources available to it, and the decisions it makes. In many cases, the agent will produce timely results for a task only at the expense of quality of result or by compromising the quality or timeliness of its performance of other tasks. Ironically, as the agent's competence expands, so will its need to make such compromises.

From this perspective, real-time performance in intelligent agents depends on an underlying architecture that enables agents to make and apply effective control decisions. Sections 2, 3, and 4 define requirements for real-time control and the architecture we have designed to address the requirements. Section 5 illustrates application of the architecture in the Guardian system for intensive care monitoring. Section 6 discusses alternative approaches to real-time performance in intelligent agents. Section 7 discusses the architecture's emphasis on satisficing methods--dynamically balancing quality and speed of performance. Section 8 briefly discusses a few other issue related to second-generation expert systems.

2 Requirements for Real-Time Control in Intelligent Agents

In section 2.1, we introduce a neutral framework in which to discuss agents and their environments. In sections 2.2 and 2.3, we operationalize environmental characteristics and agent requirements in the terms of the framework and show how the former motivate the latter (see also [12, 30, 31, 34, 42, 46, 49]).

2.1 A Framework

Following [42], we model an intelligent agent as a dynamic embedded system. The overall system is modeled as a time series of states in which instants of time are mapped to a state space of values representing the variables of interest. A change in the value of a state variable is an *event*, *e*. The system's behavior is described with *measurements* defined as functions on state values. Because the system is dynamic, we describe properties of both individual states and time series of states. *Descriptive measurements* represent objective properties, for example the *importance* of an event *e1* or the *latency* of event *e2* following the occurrence of *e1*. *Utility measurements* represent valuational properties, for example the satisfaction of particular constraints on the latency of *e2*.

We partition the system into components representing the intelligent agent, *I*, and the environment, *E*. Each component has dynamic state, which varies as a function of information passed among its internal components and information from the other component. We further partition the agent, *I*, into components for perception, *P*, cognition, *C*, and action, *A*, which similarly manifest events generated internally or by other components. To describe interactions between components, we refer to pairs of *trigger* and *response* events, where both events occur in one component but presumably are mediated by interaction with another component. For example, a trigger-response pair in *E* may be mediated by events in *I*. In some cases, we refer simply to a mediated event, for example an *I*-mediated event in *E*.

2.2 The Environment of an Intelligent Agent

In the terms of our framework, intrinsic characteristics of an agent's environment may be defined as measurements on events in *E*, while characteristics of the relationship between an agent and its environment may be defined as measurements on events in *E* and *I*. Where definitions of environmental characteristics require domain-specific assumptions, we simply indicate the forms such definitions would take.

Data Glut. It is not feasible for the agent to process all potentially interesting events in the environment. That is, the average rate of events in E very much exceeds the maximum rate of E-mediated events in I.

Data Distribution. Important environmental conditions may correspond to configurations of events on different state variables and over variable time intervals. This can be described as particular kinds of many-to-one mappings of events in E to events in I.

Diversity of Events. Environmental conditions vary in importance. This can be expressed as the variability of values on an "importance" attribute of events in E.

Real-Time Constraints. The values of events vary, in part, as a function of when they occur. This can be expressed in terms of utility measurements that incorporate the absolute or relative times of occurrence of events in E.

Multiplicity of Conditions. It is not feasible to enumerate all interesting conditions the agent will encounter, that is, the set of E-mediated events in I that produce criterial values on some measurement.

Predictability. The environment is orderly enough to permit probabilistic prediction of some future events. This can be expressed as descriptive measurements on particular patterns of events in E.

Potential Interactions. Globally coordinated courses of action are sometimes superior to sequences of locally determined actions. This can be expressed as utility measurements on particular patterns of I-mediated events in E.

Underlying Model. Some knowledge of the environment is available. This can be expressed as descriptive measurements on the correspondence between patterns of state values or events in E and I.

Diverse Demands. Multiple interacting demands for interaction with the environment include: interpretation, diagnosis, prediction, reaction, planning, and explanation. These can be expressed as utility measurements on particular types of I-mediated events in E.

Variable Stress. The environment varies in its stressfulness over time. This can be operationalized as descriptive measures involving particular environmental variables, for example, the rate of important events or the number and types of different demands for interaction.

2.3 Agent Requirements

We define the primary objective of an intelligent agent very generally:

To maintain the value of its own behavior within an acceptable range over time.

For a given agent in a given environment, we could formalize this requirement in terms of some utility measurement on I-mediated events in E and also on events in I

if we wish to constrain the agent's management of its own resources. Although we could use this utility measurement to evaluate the agent's behavior in the given context, it would provide little guidance toward the design of effective agents.

We need a more specific set of requirements to constrain the space of possible agent architectures. Below, we define several requirements that we hypothesize will allow an agent to meet its primary objective in the kinds of environments characterized above. (This is a sufficiency hypothesis, not a neccessity hypothesis. There may well be other requirements whose satisfaction would enable an agent to meet its primary objective.) In the terms of our framework, these requirements refer primarily to events in E and to interactions between I and E. In some cases, we extrapolate requirements to interactions among I's components, P, C, and A, in an effort to support satisfaction of the higher-level requirement. Again, where requirements involve domain-specific assumptions, we simply indicate the forms their definitions would take.

Communications. Given the need for I to interact with E, there must be appropriate communications involving I''s components, with information passing at least: from E to P, from P to C, from C to A, and from A to E.

Asynchrony. Given data glut and real-time constraints, the agent must function asynchronously with respect to the environment. That is, the rates of events in I and E must be independent and the rates of events in P, C, and A must be independent.

Selectivity. Given data glut and the diversity of events in the environment, the agent must determine whether and how to perceive, reason about, and act upon different environmental events. Other things being equal, the conditional probability of an I-mediated response event in E, given its trigger event, should be an increasing function of the trigger event's importance. The same holds for events in P, C, and A.

Recency. An agent's sensory information is perishable, the utility of its reasoning degrades with time, and the efficacy of its actions depends upon synchronization with fleeting external events. Therefore, recency is one important selectivity criterion. This can be expressed as a sharply decreasing conditional probability of an I-mediated response event in E, given its trigger event, over time. The same holds for events in P, C, and A.

Coherence. The agent should produce a globally coordinated course of action when that is preferable to a sequence of locally determined actions. That is, we impose utility measurements on certain patterns of I-mediated response events in E, as well as on mediated response events in P, C, and A. Other things being equal, we require a low conditional probability of mediated response events, given associated trigger events, when those response events would not fit an ongoing pattern.

Flexibility. Conversely, the agent must react to important unexpected events in a dynamic environment. Other things being equal, we require a high conditional probability for an I-mediated response event in E, even if it does not fit an ongoing pattern, given a very important trigger event. The same holds for anomalous response events in P, C, and A.

Responsiveness. Other things being equal, the more urgent a situation is, the more quickly the agent should perceive relevant information, perform necessary reasoning, and execute appropriate actions. That is, the latency of an *I*-mediated response event in *E*, following its trigger event, should decrease as the urgency of the trigger event increases. Similar constraints apply to response events in *P*, *C*, and *A*.

Timeliness. Given its dynamic environment, the agent must meet various hard and soft real-time constraints on the utility of its behavior. These may be expressed as utility measurements involving latencies within *I*-mediated pairs of trigger and response events in *E*. Similar measurements could be applied to events in *P*, *C*, and *A*.

Robustness. An agent must adapt to resource-stressing situations by gracefully degrading the utility of its behavior. As environmental stress increases (for example, as event rates increase or required latencies (deadlines) for trigger-response pairs decrease), the global utility of the agent's behavior (for example the rate of *I*-mediated response events in *E*, weighted by importance) should decrease gradually, rather than precipitously. The same holds for interactions among *P*, *C*, and *A*.

Scalability. In the terms of our framework, the agent's satisfaction of the requirements above (but perhaps not its absolute level of performance on any one task) should be invariant over increases in problem size.

Development. An agent must exploit new knowledge to improve the utility of its behavior. As the amount of relevant knowledge in *I* increases, we should observe improvement in the agent's satisfaction of some of the above requirements and, therefore, in the global utility of its behavior.

3 Proposed Agent Architecture

The proposed agent architecture is designed to address the above requirements. Except where noted, the architecture is implemented as described.

3.1 Top-Level Organization

Following the terminology of section 2, we propose an architecture for the agent, I, comprising subsystems for perception, cognition, and action--*P*, *C*, and *A*. The architecture (see Figure 1) partitions each subsystem into smaller components and permits multiple subsystems for different application-specific perception/action modalities. In this figure, curved boxes represent data structures. Rectangular boxes represent parallel processes. Arrows show information flow among data structures and processes. The diagram is hierarchical. Thus, cognition is a process comprising several component processes, data structures, and information flows among them. Arrows that involve compound data structures (e.g., the circle representing the cognitive system's global memory) signify information flow involving all component data structures (e.g., knowledge, reasoning results, control plan).

A *communications interface (CI)* routes data among the I/O buffers of different subsystems. Subsystems function and interact as follows. Signals from the environment enter sensory buffers in *perception subsystems*, which selectively interpret and filter the signals under attentional parameters determined by the cognitive subsystem and place the resulting perceptions in their output buffers. The CI relays these perceptions to input buffers in action subsystems, where they directly drive action execution, or to input buffers in the cognitive subsystem, where they compete with other perceptions and internally generated events for cognitive processing. The *cognitive subsystem* retrieves perceptions from its input buffers for incorporation in its knowledge base, performs all knowledge-based reasoning, and places decisions regarding attentional parameters or intended actions in its output buffers. The CI relays these decisions to the input buffers of appropriate perception/action subsystems. Each *action subsystem* retrieves action descriptions from its input buffers and controls their execution on particular effectors under performance parameters determined by the cognitive subsystem. Executed actions affect entities in the environment.

Subsystems operate in parallel. They do not communicate directly or otherwise interfere with one another. They influence one another only indirectly, by placing information in their own output buffers, from which it is transferred to the input buffers of appropriate other subsystems by the CI. Thus, the architecture limits potential interference to simultaneous efforts to access a subsystem's I/O buffers by the CI and the subsystem itself. Our experiments [32] suggest that, in practice, the architecture provides constant communication latencies among perception, cognition, and action subsystems (the absolute latency being determined by processor speed, network speed, and program optimization) over a wide range of activity levels within each subsystem. Conversely, it provides constant operation latencies within subsystems over a range of levels of communication activities.

The architecture is designed to support graduated reactions. Very fast *peripheral reactions* occur within a perception or action subsystem, producing input-driven attentional shifts or feedback control of action execution. Fast *reflex reactions* occur across perception-action arcs, with information from perception subsystems directly driving the behavior of action subsystems. Slower *cognitive reactions* involve all three kinds of subsystems, with cognition mediating the performance of actions in response to perceived information. Absolute response latencies at each level depend on the architecture's implementation and its instantiation in a particular agent. In our current work, cognitive reactions fall along a latency spectrum, ranging from "immediate" reactions, with latencies under one minute, to "delayed" reactions, with latencies on the order of several minutes or longer. As discussed below, the agent can control the latencies of its cognitive operations in several ways. Although we have not implemented peripheral or reflex reactions, our current implementation could provide latencies on the order of a few seconds.

As mentioned above, *P*, *C*, and *A* subsystems communicate via *I/O buffers*, with the CI, running on a separate process, routing information among them. All I/O buffers have *limited capacity*, with *best-first retrieval* and *worst-first overflow*. Capacity is an architectural parameter that can be defined differently for different agents or for different buffers within an agent. In our current implementation, it is defined in terms of number of items. Best-first and worst-first criteria are defined in terms of four orthogonal attributes of each buffer item: the item's *relevance* to the agent's current reasoning activities; the item's *importance* with respect to the agent's objectives; the *recency* of the item's appearance in the buffer; and the *urgency* of processing the item in order to have the intended effect. Other things equal, buffer items that score higher against these criteria are retrieved earlier, while those that score lower overflow earlier. These attributes are determined and dynamically modified by the agent's reasoning, as discussed below.

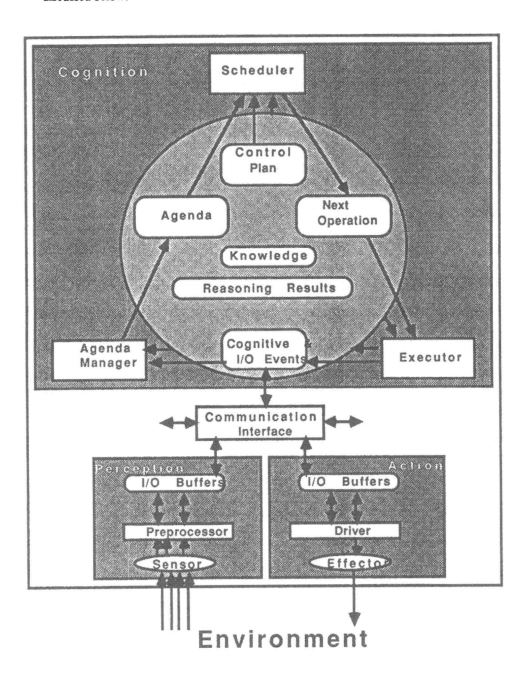

Fig. 1. Overview of the Proposed Agent Architecture.

3.2 Perception Subsystems

Perception subsystems [6, 54], comprising *sensors* and *preprocessors*, acquire information about the dynamic environment as a basis for cognition and action. Each *sensor* acquires signals of a characteristic type, transduces them into an appropriate internal representation, and holds the results in a limited-capacity buffer for retrieval by its associated preprocessor. Each *preprocessor* abstracts, annotates, and filters sensed information and places the results in its output buffer for relay by the CI to the input buffer of the cognitive subsystem or an action subsystem. Abstraction involves interpreting and often compressing sensed data according to current *abstraction forms*. These forms might specify transformations on individual data values (for example, assignment to a value category), on sequences of values (e.g., running averages, trends, modal values), or on patterns of values across multiple variables (for example, co-occurence or temporal succession of related values on different variables). Filtering involves restricting the communication of abstraction results to values that meet current *filtering criteria*. These criteria may be specified for example, as criterial values on particular variables, criterial value changes on particular variables, or deadlines. In our current work, we use a combination of criterial value changes (send a new value when it differs from the last value sent by at least $p\%$) and deadlines (send a new value when at least m seconds have passed since the last value was sent). This allows the agent to bound the variability on data sensed between sent values in the context of some minimum rate. Annotation involves marking and prioritizing abstraction results according to current *standards of relevance, importance, and urgency* (defined above).

All preprocessing parameters--abstraction forms, filtering criteria, and annotation standards--are dynamic. They can change in two ways. The preprocessor can have peripheral reactions, redirecting its own focus of attention in response to sensed data values. For example, a preprocessor might react to a sudden increase in the variability of any sensed data variable by changing its abstraction forms to a finer granularity and weakening its filtering criteria for that variable. The preprocessor also can change its parameters in response to focus of attention instructions from the cognitive subsystem. For example, the cognitive subsystem might instruct the preprocessor to use parameters appropriate for the current reasoning task. Focus of attention is discussed in more detail below.

3.3 Action Subsystems

Action subsystems, comprising *drivers* and *effectors*, retrieve action descriptions from their input buffers, control action execution on effectors, and return feedback to the cognitive subsystem. Each *driver* monitors its input buffer, retrieves intended actions, translates them into executable programs of effector commands, and monitors the execution of those programs by sending successive commands to the appropriate effector at the appropriate times. Each driver also should take into account importance, urgency, and other constraints on performance, but we have not yet implemented these capabilities. For example, a driver might give priority to important and urgent actions over competitors, translate intended actions into different executable forms given their urgency and resource constraints, and if necessary accelerate execution of urgent actions. The driver also should send feedback to the cognitive system regarding the success or failure of action execution. Each *effector* immediately executes commands in its input buffer.

3.4 Cognition Subsystem

The cognition subsystem holds all of an agent's knowledge and performs all of its reasoning. It asynchronously incorporates perceived information, retrieved from its input buffers, into its knowledge base. It performs a variety of knowledge-based reasoning tasks, which vary across different task environments, but typically would include: interpretation of perceived information; detection and diagnosis of exceptional events; reaction to important events; prediction of future events; modeling dynamic external systems; planning longer-term courses of action; explaining its observations, inferences, and plans; explaining its reasoning; learning to improve its behavior based on experience and to adapt its behavior to changing environmental conditions. In addition, it reasons about global control of multiple tasks both to coordinate their interactions and to insure timely achievement of the most important objectives given the available resources. The cognitive subsystem initiates actions by placing descriptions of them in its output buffers.

As shown in Figure 1, the cognition subsystem extends the "dynamic control architecture" [25], previously implemented as the BB1 system. All reasoning operations occur in the context of a *global memory*, which represents all information-*-knowledge* and *reasoning results*--known to the agent, in a conceptual graph formalism [48].

One important kind of knowledge is a repertoire of *reasoning operations* and associated *strategies*, which can be instantiated to perform particular *tasks* (for example, diagnosis, prediction, explanation, or planning) by particular *methods*. For example, an agent might have knowledge of the operations involved in *associative diagnosis*, along with strategies for selecting and applying those operations. It might have similar knowledge of *model-based diagnosis*. It might also have the "meta-knowledge" that model-based diagnosis requires less data, but more knowledge and computation time, and produces more comprehensive and more explanatory results than associative diagnosis.

As discussed above, the global memory contains *input buffers* for perceptions sent by perceptual subsystems and *output buffers* for intended actions to be sent to action drivers and control parameters to be sent to perceptual preprocessors or action drivers. I/O buffers have limited capacity, with best-first retrieval and worst-first overflow.

The global memory also contains information regarding the agent's cognitive behavior (discussed below). A *cognitive buffer* holds cognitive events produced by reasoning operations. An *agenda* holds executable reasoning operations suggested by perceptual or cognitive events. A *control plan* represents the agent's intended course of behavior as determined by reasoning operations. The *next operation* is the reasoning operation that the agent will execute next. Like I/O buffers, the cognitive buffer and the agenda have limited capacity, with best-first retrieval and worst-first overflow. Although our current implementation does not limit the size of the control plan, we intend to impose some sort of limitation.

Finally, the global memory contains the results of reasoning operations: observations, inferences, predictions, and plans. These results are organized in an interval-based time-line representation, with conceptual links to one another and to other knowledge. For example, an agent might record that a diagnosis believed during interval *i2* *explains* an observation that persisted during interval *i1* and that the explanatory relationship between the observation and its diagnosis *instantiates* a known causal relationship within systems of the type under observation.

The cognitive subsystem performs reasoning operations that are suggested by and produce changes to information in the global memory. Its *satisficing cycle* comprises three component processes:

1. The *agenda manager* uses recent perceptual or cognitive events to identify and rate executable reasoning operations, which it records on the agenda. Identification of an executable reasoning operation involves determining that a perceptual or cognitive event satisfies the trigger requirements of a particular type of operation and that other contextual information satisfies its preconditions. On a given cycle, the agenda manager may identify several executable reasoning operations relevant to each of several tasks. Rating an executable operation involves evaluating its importance and urgency against the current control plan, which may include strategic decisions related to different tasks.

2. The *scheduler* determines which of the identified executable operations to execute and when to execute them, based on their ratings, and records each successive one as the next operation.

3. The *executor* executes each next operation as it is recorded. It instantiates the program defined for the chosen operation type, binding program variables to triggering events other contextual information. It then executes the instantiated program, producing associated changes in the global memory. These changes might represent a new inference or conclusion for a new or ongoing reasoning task. They might record new perceptual filters or intended actions in output buffers. They might change the control plan itself by initiating or terminating new tasks or by extending or modifying control decisions for an ongoing task. As discussed below, changes to the control plan change the criteria used to trigger, rate, and schedule operations for execution, from that time forward.

Because control in the cognitive system determines the utility--quality and timeliness--of the agent's perception, reasoning, and action, it is fundamental to the proposed agent architecture, especially to its support for real-time performance. The following sections examine three aspects of control more closely, *dynamic control planning*, by which the agent determines and guides its own reasoning behavior; *focus of attention*, by which the agent parameterizes the behavior of its perception/action subsystems; and the *satisficing cycle* by which the agent controls the time spent on each reasoning cycle.

3.5 Dynamic Control Planning

A *control plan* is a temporally organized pattern of *control decisions*, each of which describes a class of operations the agent intends to perform during some period of time. Control decisions may vary widely in content and specificity, ranging from specific primitive operations intended to be executed at particular moments in time to broad classes of operations intended to be executed during extended time intervals. Control decisions may "stand alone," specifying an independently desirable class of actions. Alternatively, sets or sequences of control decisions may be coordinated to achieve a common objective. Multiple competing, complementary, or independent control decisions regarding a particular time interval may co-exist in the control plan. Multiple constituent plans for performing concurrent tasks may co-exist in the control plan.

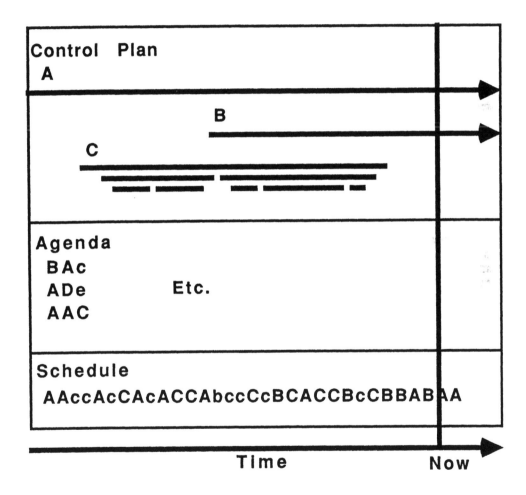

Fig. 2. An Abstract View of Dynamic Control Planning.

For example, Figure 2 gives an abstract view of dynamic control planning. The top panel shows an abstract control plan comprising three constituent plans for tasks A, B, and C, governing the agent's behavior during overlapping time intervals. Plan A is a single, independent, long-term control decision governing behavior prior to, during, and beyond the time period shown. Plan B is another single, independent, long-term control decision governing behavior during a period that begins during the time period shown and continues into the future. Plan C is a local plan, governing behavior during a sub-interval of the time period shown. In addition, Plan C is elaborated in terms of more detailed subordinate decisions at two lower levels of abstraction, which govern behavior during a hierarchically organized sequence of component time intervals. The middle panel of Figure 2 shows the dynamic agenda of executable control (lower case) and task (upper case) operations relevant to tasks A, B, C, D, and E. The bottom panel shows the schedule of control and task operations chosen for execution in accordance with active control plans and agendas during corresponding time intervals.

Control plans can represent not only what task to perform, but also how to perform it given particular policies or resource constraints. In particular, control plans can indicate preferences for reasoning operations that meet time constraints. For example, in Figure 2, Plan C may have been constructed as shown because it will produce a satisfactory outcome within the designated period of time. Alternative control plans may have produced "better" outcomes, but taken longer to do so.

The cognitive system constructs control plans incrementally by means of control operations that generate or modify constituent control decisions. As illustrated in Figure 2, the cognitive system treats control operations (lower case) like other reasoning operations. Control operations are suggested by perceptual or cognitive events, rated and placed on the agenda, and scheduled for execution. Thus, they compete for execution with one another and with all other executable operations.

Different control operations embody different reasoning methods [33]. Some operations generate control decisions bottom up, for example when a perceptual event triggers a decision to respond to the perceived situation. In Figure 2, Plans A and B and the top-most decision of Plan C presumably were generated bottom-up in response to perceived demands or opportunities. Other operations generate decisions top-down, for example when an abstract control decision triggers a sequence of more specific control decisions. In Figure 2, the subordinate decisions in Plan C presumably were generated top-down to elaborate the more general decisions. Other operations generate decisions in a goal-directed fashion, for example when a lack of operations satisfying a prior control decision triggers a decision to perform operations that would trigger such operations. In Figure 2, if no operations on the agenda satisfy Plan A, goal-directed reasoning would generate a decision to perform operations whose results would trigger operations compatible with Plan A.

Control decisions may be generated at any time prior to the time at which they are intended to influence the agent's behavior. Some control decisions are generated and take effect immediately, while others are generated in advance and do not take effect until much later. For example, in Figure 2, Plan C might have been generated in response to a perceived event immediately prior to its initiation point. Alternatively, the agent might have decided much earlier that at that point in time it would follow Plan C. Similarly, the agent has decided that both Plans A and B will persist into the future, governing behavior well beyond the "Now" point.

Regardless of the content or specificity of control decisions, the reasoning methods used to generate them, and the times at which they are generated, all control decisions appear in a single control plan. The agenda manager rates executable operations against all active control decisions whose time intervals include the current time. For example, early in the time interval shown in Figure 2, the agent uses Plan A to rate and schedule reasoning operations. Later, it uses Plans A and C--actually, the current lowest-level decisions of Plan C. Still later, it uses all three Plans, A, B, and C. Following the completion of Plan C, the agent uses Plans A and B to rate and schedule operations for the remainder of the time interval shown and into the future. As mentioned above, we intend to limit the size or complexity of an agent's active control plan during a given time period, but we have not yet implemented such limitations.

In general, the agent can perform operations that change its control plan on any cycle, thereby changing the rating criteria subsequently used by its agenda manager and, as a consequence, the operations subsequently chosen by its scheduler for execution. Dynamic control planning allows the agent to construct strategic plans that are appropriate to an evolving task environment and to follow strategic plans to which it has committed, but also to change those plans as appropriate.

3.6 Focus of Attention

The cognitive subsystem determines the agent's global focus of attention by sending perception/action subsystems control parameters determined by its dynamic control plan and other state information. As discussed above, *perceptual control parameters* are of three types. *Abstraction forms* specify desired transformations on data values. *Filtering criteria* specify conditions under which abstracted data should be sent to the cognitive system. *Annotation standards* specify criteria for determining the *relevance*, *importance*, and *urgency* of perceived data.

The architecture provides three kinds of *perceptual focus operations*, all of which, when executed, place control parameters in output buffers for relay to perceptual preprocessors [6, 54]. *Information-focusing* operations, which are triggered by changes in the agent's control plan, send focus instructions to discriminate among different kinds of input data. For example, if a control decision initiates a new reasoning task, an information-focusing operation will send a perceptual control parameter to increase the relevance, importance, or urgency of the associated data types. Thus, the agent will focus its interpretation of sensed information on those data that are useful to its reasoning. *Resource-focusing* operations, which also are triggered by changes in the control plan, modulate the overall input data rate in anticipation of changing resource demands. For example, if a new task is computationally intensive, a resource-focusing operation will send a parameter that tightens the filtering criteria on all data types in proportion to their relevance and importance. Thus, the agent will focus its perceptual resources on types of data anticipated to be most useful. *Load-balancing* operations, which are triggered by overflow or underflow conditions in the cognitive input buffers, also modulate the overall input data rate, but they do so in response to unanticipated changes in resource demands. For example, if input data arrive faster than the cognitive system can process them, producing repeated input buffer overflows, a load-balancing operation will send a perceptual parameter that tightens filtering criteria. Conversely, if the cognitive system has the capacity to process more frequent input data, a load-balancing oepration will send a parameter to loosen the filtering criteria. Thus, the agent will coordinate its input data rates with its dynamic cognitive capacity to incorporate new input data.

With these operations, the agent focuses its perception of a complex, dynamic environment "top-down," in accordance with its current control plans and available resources. Thus, it protects its cognitive system from being swamped by non-critical inputs. However, the agent remains sensitive to exceptional events outside of its current focus of attention. One way is by instructing perceptual subsystems to relay all data values that fall in critical ranges. In our current work, we "hard-wire" very general forms of these criteria so that the agent is guaranteed to notice extreme events. In addition, preprocessors can potentially redirect their own attention in response to particular patterns of sensed data. Although we have not yet implemented such "peripheral responses," we anticipate that they will play an important role in maintaining an agent's sensitivity to important unanticipated events in a dynamic environment.

As mentioned above, we are studying corresponding sorts of focus operations to set action control parameters related to performance criteria, resource consumption, and side effects.

3.7 The Satisficing Cycle

Let us examine the cognitive system's *satisficing cycle* [28]. Because this cycle is the unit-process underlying all reasoning, bounding and, in fact, controlling its computation time is a prerequisite to controlling computation times for reasoning tasks under real-time constraints. Recall that the cycle comprises three processes: the agenda manager, the scheduler, and the executor. The scheduler's computation time is easily bounded and insignificant. The executor's computation time depends upon the operation it is executing. We currently rely upon programming guidelines to bound operation execution time within acceptable ranges (but see section 5.) Therefore, our efforts to bound and control cycle time have focused on the agenda manager.

As discussed above, the agenda manager identifies and rates executable operations based on cognitive and perceptual events. The time consumed by agenda management is an increasing function of the number of known operations, the number of perceptual and cognitive events, and the number of rating criteria in the control plan. Given the continuous flow of events in the environment and the many tasks and operations an intelligent agent can perform, identification of all executable operations can take a very long time. Given real-time constraints on the agent's behavior, the agenda manager ordinarily cannot identify all currently executable reasoning operations before the agent must execute one of them. Conversely, there is no need to identify the many possible operations that the agent will never execute.

Therefore, the agenda manager is designed to operate in an incremental, non-exhaustive fashion, identifying and rating a subset of the executable operations one at a time and terminating according to current *cycle parameters*. These parameters are of three types. *Criterial operations* describe executable operations that, when identified by the agenda manager, would be "good enough" to execute. *Criterial events* and *deadlines* describe perceptual or cognitive events or specific times whose occurrence requires immediate execution of the "best available" operation. (Criterial events may be viewed as uncertain deadlines.)

Cycle parameters are determined and modified dynamically by the agent's own reasoning in the context of its dynamic control plan. For example, if the current control plan simply specifies operations of a particular type, any executable operation of that type would be "good enough." Other things being equal, a task deadline in the control plan would be translated heuristically into component deadlines for individual reasoning operations.

The occurrence of any condition specified in the current cycle parameters causes the agenda manager to terminate. The scheduler then chooses the highest priority operation on the current, usually incomplete agenda and the executor executes it. In the case of a criterial operation, the highest priority operation will be, by definition, one that is "good enough." In the case of a criterial event or deadline, the highest priority operation will be the "best available" one at that time. We have experimented with cycle parameters that specify criterial operations and deadlines, but not yet with criterial events.

Because the agenda manager is non-exhaustive, the order in which it identifies executable operations is critical. To maximize the speed with which it identifies "good enough" operations and to maximize the priorities of the "best available" operations at those times when it is interrupted by criterial events or deadlines, the agenda manager applies a *heuristic best-first algorithm*. Using whatever criteria appear in the the current control plan, it attempts to instantiate the highest priority operation type for the highest priority event on each iteration. Viewing agenda management as a generate-and-test problem, this algorithm effectively moves some of the test criteria into the generator.

For a given control plan and set of events, the heuristic best-first algorithm identifies executable operations in roughly descending order of priority. How closely it approximates the actual descending order depends on the details of the control plan and the order in which rating criteria are applied. However, because perception and cognition are asynchronous, the agenda manager works with a dynamic set of perceptual events and control decisions, incorporating new ones into its computations as they occur. Thus, it often happens that newly identified executable operations have significantly higher priorities than those already on the agenda.

The agenda manager places each newly identified executable operation on the agenda, ordered by priority. As mentioned above, the agenda has limited capacity, with best-first (highest priority) retrieval by the scheduler and worst-first overflow. Thus, at any point in time, the agenda constitutes a short, ordered list of high priority reasoning operations suggested by recent high-priority events and control decisions.

The satisficing cycle can produce a spectrum of agent behavior, depending on the agent's dynamic control plan and cycle parameters. Control plans are *discriminating* to the degree that they restrict the assignment of high priorities to a smaller set of events and operations. Other things being equal, more discriminating control plans facilitate rapid identification of high-priority executable operations. Cycle parameters are *stressful* to the degree that they reduce the time available for agenda management (lower thresholds for criterial events and operations, short deadlines). Other things being equal, more stressful cycle parameters lead to rapid execution of a large number of operations.

These two factors interact to determine the agent's style of behavior. For example, given a very discriminating control plan and non-stressful cycle parameters, an agent would appear to behave "methodically," executing a small number of very high priority operations per unit time. With more stressful cycle parameters, the agent would appear to behave "purposefully," performing more operations per unit time and perhaps compromising quality by performing some lower-priority operations. With very stressful cycle parameters, the agent could still behave "purposefully" if, for example, its control plan restricted its triggering of executable operations to a very small set of very important operations, categorically excluding less important operations. At the other extreme, given an undiscriminating control plan and very stressful cycle parameters, an agent would appear to "thrash," executing a large number of arbitrary operations per unit time. In fact, given an undiscriminating control plan, the agent's behavior would appear arbitrary regardless of cycle parameters, varying primarily in rate of executed operations.

Ideally, it seems that intelligent agents should perform near the "methodical" end of the spectrum when time and other resources permit and move cautiously along the spectrum when required to do so by time and other resource constraints. In practice, we anticipate that many agents will not often have the luxury of behaving "methodically." However, we are more optimistic about agents' ability to behave "purposefully" by constructing effective control plans. We are exploring these issues.

4 Satisfaction of Real-Time Control Requirements

Let us briefly summarize how the proposed agent architecture is hypothesized to address the requirements introduced in section 2.

Communications. Information passes from the environment to perception subsystems, from perception subsystems to cognition and action subsystems, and from the cognition subsystem to perception and action subsystems.

Asynchrony. Parallel subsystems, with buffered communications, provide asynchronous perception, cognition, action.

Selectivity. Limited-capacity event buffers selectively favor "high priority" inputs that are recent, relevant, important, and urgent. Perception/action subsystems selectively process high priority data and actions. The agenda manager selectively triggers and schedules high priority operations. Dynamic control plans selectively favor high priority reasoning tasks and establish associated focus of attention parameters.

Recency. Limited-capacity buffers with best-first retrieval and worst-first overflow favor recent items, as does the heuristic best-first agenda manager.

Coherence. Dynamic control plans provide a global focus of attention to coordinate perception, cognition, and action over time. They also strategically organize reasoning operations within a task and among concurrent reasoning tasks.

Flexibility. Exceptional events can override global focus of attention in perceptual preprocessors or the cognitive system.

Responsivity. Graduated reactive responses--peripheral, reflex, and cognitive responses--span a range of latencies. Within cognitive responses, additional gradations are supported. The agenda manager can control cycle time. Dynamic control planning can establish deadlines and discriminate among alternative reasoning methods strategies.

Timeliness. Satisfying each of the requirements discussed above contributes to an agent's timely response to the most important events. In addition, dynamic control planning allows an agent to reason explicitly about the time requirements of alternative operations and the time constraints on its behavior.

Robustness. Satisfying many of the requirements discussed above entails trading amount of computation, and therefore, expected quality of response, against latency of response, in a gradual manner.

Scalability. Several aspects of the architecture are designed to accommodate changes in scale. For example, perceptual preprocessing and focus of attention will protect the agent against increasing perceptual overload. Given a discriminating control plan, the satisficing cycle will produce stable cycle times regardless of increases in problem size.

Development. Increases or improvements in knowledge should improve the agent's ability to meet several of these requirements. For example, improvements in its control knowledge should enable it to focus perceptual attention more effectively, improve the strategic control of its reasoning, and execute higher-priority operations more rapidly.

5 The Guardian Application

Because our long-term research goal is to develop a general architecture for intelligent agents, experimental development of agents that operate in diverse domains is a major part of our research. Each new domain tests the sufficiency and generality of the current architecture and presents new requirements for subsequent versions of the architecture. To illustrate how agents are implemented within the proposed architecture, we briefly discuss the Guardian system for intensive care monitoring [27].

5.1 Guardian's Task Environment and Requirements

The sickest surgical patients in the hospital are cared for in the surgical intensive care unit (SICU). Most of these patients have temporary failure of one or more organ systems--usually the lung or the heart--which is treated with life-support devices that assume the fundamental functions of the ailing system until it heals. For example, the ventilator is an artificial breathing machine that augments the patient's own breathing. Life-support devices are adjusted based upon frequent patient observations. Some observations are made continually and automatically, for example, measurements of air pressures and air flows in the patient-ventilator system. Other observations are made intermittently. Blood gases, for example, are measured once every hour or so, while chest xrays are usually taken once or twice a day. Based on patient observations, device settings are adjusted to vary the amount of assistance the device provides. For example, ventilator settings determine the number of breaths delivered to the patient per minute, the volume of air blown into the patient's lungs on each breath, and the amount of oxygen in the air. Other therapeutic actions might include adjusting a ventilator tube, clearing the patient's air passages, administering drugs, etc. The short-term goal of SICU monitoring is to keep the patient as comfortable and healthy as possible, while progressing toward therapeutic objectives. The long-term goal is to withdraw life-support devices gradually so that the patient eventually can function autonomously.

Although we do not anticipate using Guardian in closed-loop mode in a hospital setting, our objectives for it include all of the perception, reasoning, and action necessary for closed-loop control. Thus, Guardian's task instantiates all of the requirements for real-time control discussed earlier in this paper. Because Guardian has access to over one hundred automatically acquired patient data variables, each of them sensed several times per second, and because it can reason about and act upon these observations in many different ways, Guardian must selectively perceive important patient data and perform key reasoning operations that contribute to its performance of the most important actions. Because the patient embodies a dynamic physical process with its own temporal dynamics, Guardian must asynchronously perceive patient data, reason about the patient's condition, and perform therapeutic actions. To insure that its behavior is current, Guardian must "forget" unrealized past opportunities for perception, reasoning, and action in favor of present opportunities. To achieve longer-term therapeutic goals, Guardian must enact a coherent pattern of perception, reasoning, and action over a period of time. On the other hand, uncertain changes in the patient's physiological condition require flexibility and adaptation. Guardian must be responsive to patient conditions of varying urgency; other things being equal, the more urgent the patient's condition is, the more quickly Guardian must perceive the relevant information, perform the necessary reasoning, and execute the appropriate actions. Guardian must satisfy a variety of hard and soft real-time constraints on the utility of its behavior. Because Guardian inevitabably will encounter situations that strain or exceed its capacity--too many important new signs and symptoms, too many important interpretation, diagnosis, prediction, and planning tasks, too many important therapeutic actions--its performance must degrade gracefully and not precipitously. Guardian must maintain the quality of its behavior as we scale up to more realistic problems. Ideally, it should improve the utility of its behavior as it acquires more knowledge.

5.2 Guardian's Current Implementation and Performance

Figure 3 illustrates how Guardian instantiates the proposed agent architecture and how it interacts with a simulation of the patient-ventilator system and hospital laboratories.

A single perceptual preprocessor currently manages Guardian's perception of twenty automatically sensed patient data variables, with an average overall sensed data rate of one data value per second. In addition, Guardian perceives irregularly reported lab results and messages from human users. Each sensed data value, if passed to the cognitive system, would trigger a number of cognitive operations, whose execution would produce a number of cognitive events and trigger new operations. Thus, although this is not a high data rate in absolute terms, it is considerably beyond

Guardian's current cognitive capacity, which is one cognitive operation every two to fifteen seconds with an exhaustive agenda manager and controllable to within a couple of seconds with the heuristic agenda manager. Moreover, we anticipate that, during the next twelve months, Guardian's sensory activity will increase from twenty to one hundred automatically sensed variables, with each of them sensed at least once per second. There will be about twenty irregularly sensed data variables. Finally, as SICU technology advances, Guardian will have access to new data. Thus, Guardian faces significant and growing perceptual overload.

To avoid falling behind real time, Guardian's perceptual preprocessor applies dynamic abstraction, filtering, and annotation parameters sent by the cognitive system. It abstracts numerical data values into value classes and trends. It assigns data values to three levels of importance: life-threatening, abnormal, and other. It distinguishes data that are relevant to ongoing reasoning activities from those that are not relevant. It distinguishes three levels of urgency: events that permit an effective response within four minutes, one hour, or longer. It filters data based on criterial value changes within deadlines. Thus, the cognitive system can bound the variability of unsent intervening values. Using these mechanisms, the preprocessor typicaly reduces sensed data rates by over 90%, maintaining an average overall perception rate of approximately one perceptual input every twenty-two seconds, without reducing solution quality [54]. Additional selectivity is provided by the cognitive system itself. Our preliminary experiments suggest that the proposed approach to perceptual preprocessing will scale up to protect Guardian from overload under the anticipated increase in sensed data rates [6].)

Guardian has a wide range of medical knowledge including: knowledge of meaningful classifications and trends of the twenty-five currently sensed patient data variables; knowledge of a twenty-node hierarchy of respiratory disease conditions, patient data that probabilistically implicate those diseases, and therapeutic actions that correct them; knowledge of the normal structure and function of the respiratory, circulatory, pulmonary exchange, tissue exchange, and tissue metabolism systems; knowledge of the normal structure and function of the ventilator; knowledge of the normal and abnormal structure and function of abstract flow, diffusion, and metabolic systems; knowledge of prototypical therpautic protocols for managing a small number of evolving disease conditions; knowledge of the importance and urgency of particular observations and diagnoses; knowledge of the precondition, results, and time required to perform a number of therapeutic actions.

Guardian also has knowledge about performing several reasoning tasks, including: interpretation of time-varying data, diagnosis of observed signs and symptoms, determination of corrective actions for diagnosed conditions, prediction of future physiological conditions, explanation of observations, diagnoses, and predictions, and dynamic therapy planning. Moreover, for most of these tasks, it has both *associative* and *model-based reasoning methods*. Associative methods capture clinical knowledge and permit quick responses to familiar situations. Model-based methods capture more fundamental biological and physical knowledge and permit more thorough (and time-consuming) responses to both familiar and unfamiliar cases. Each reasoning method is implemented as a set of abstract reasoning operations that are triggered by particular kinds of perceptual or cognitive events, along with control operations that construct resource-bounded control plans in particular contexts. The results of all reasoning activities are recorded in temporally organized episodes in the global memory.

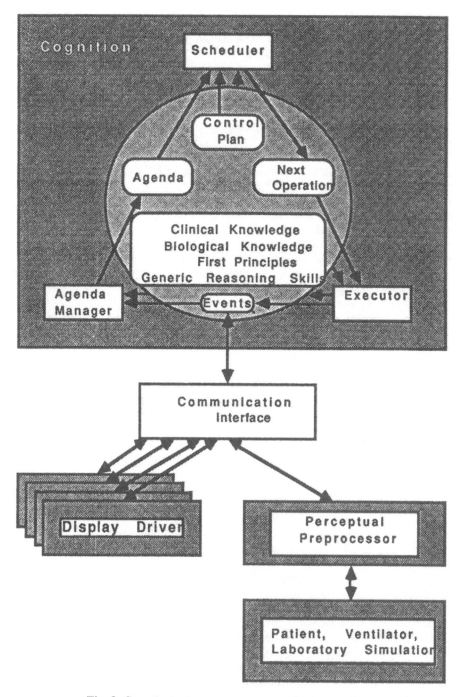

Fig. 3. Guardian's Current Design and Implementation.

Depending upon the circumstances, Guardian may be logically capable of pursuing many different reasoning tasks with both associative and model-based methods. Given the real-time constraints on its behavior, however, Guardian typically must be quite selective about which tasks it pursues and how it allocates reasoning resources among them. Accordingly, it uses strategic knowledge to construct a dynamic global control plan that differentially favors the triggering and scheduling of executable operations involved in competing reasoning tasks.

For example, in one scenario, Guardian observes that a post-operative patient has low body temperature. It makes a global control decision to perform a sequence of reasoning tasks: diagnosing the low temperature; predicting a spontaneous rise in temperature to normal over a period of hours; predicting the undesirable physiological consequences of low temperature; and planning a course of action to be executed over a period of hours to avoid those consequences. Within each of these tasks, Guardian makes local control decisions about whether to apply associative or model-based reasoning methods and how to organize its reasoning within the chosen method. At the same time, Guardian's global control plan also allows it to incorporate new perceptions, but not to reason about most of those perceptions since they are less important than ongoing activities.

As the scenario continues Guardian deviates from this purposeful behavior only when a new perception, very high peak inspiratory pressure, indicates a life-threatening patient condition with a four-minute deadline. Guardian makes a new global control decision to direct all of its resources to correcting this critical condition as quickly as possible. This decision impacts three aspects of Guardian's behavior. Its perceptual preprocessor refocuses to favor patient data relevant to the high peak pressure and to minimize distraction by less important data. Its agenda manager adopts a shorter deadline to insure a quick sequence of responses under a short deadline. And, given the content of the new control decision, its agenda manager and scheduler favor associative reasoning operations (because they have shorter latencies) that diagnose and act to correct the high pressure problem. Given these adaptations, Guardian very quickly (within a minute) performs a sequence of operations to deal with the high peak pressure: diagnoses the immediate problem, inadequate ventilation; increases the breathing rate so the patient will get enough oxygen; diagnoses the underlying problem, a pneumothorax (hole in the lung); performs (on the simulated patient) the appropriate action, inserting a chest tube to relieve the pressure of accumulated air in the chest cavity; reduces the breathing rate now that the pressure is relieved; confirms that the pressure is normal; and confirms that the blood gases are normal. Once the problem is solved, Guardian makes a new global control decision to resume its previous interrupted activities.

Several display drivers manage Guardian's communications with human users. These communications include dynamic graphical displays of: the patient's SICU history; ongoing reasoning and results related to diagnosis, prediction, and therapy planning; structure/function explanations of the patient's condition, diagnosis, prognosis, and therapy; and Guardian's current global control plan. Each of these displays is interactive, permitting the user to pose particular kinds of questions, as well as reviewing previous observations and conclusions.

Guardian can run either closed-loop, executing recommended actions directly on the simulation, or open-loop, simply recommending actions, which human users decide whether or not to execute.

We have developed Guardian's architecture and component capabilities for a small number of characteristic SICU scenarios. Although this knowledge base is far from complete, it allows Guardian to handle a wider set of SICU scenarios than we have actually tested it so far. In addition to extending and refining Guardian's component capabilities, our current work involves collecting a library of new SICU scenarios to identify the limits of Guardian's current knowledge base and to drive extension of the knowledge base. Although our patient simulator provides realistic SICU data, we are interested in evaluating Guardian on real patient data. We have begun collecting patient histories for "re-enactment" studies. We are investigating establishing a direct link between Guardian and computers in the SICU at the Palo Alto Veterans Administration Medical Center.

6 Other Approaches to Intelligent Agents

6.1 Variations on the Proposed Architecture

Designing an agent architecture involves making design decisions in a large space of design features. To put our proposed architecture in perspective, we mention a few of the features we have considered and rejected and a few that we are planning to explore further.

We designed the satisficing cycle and heuristic agenda manager as a replacement for the optimizing cycle and exhaustive agenda manager that we and others have used in the past [9, 13, 25]. This appears essential for real-time performance and probably for efficient performance in large non-real-time systems that have a lot of knowledge and run for many cycles. The present satisficing cycle preserves the sequential nature of the optimizing cycle. However, we are exploring the possibility of allowing agenda management to run continuously, with parallel scheduling and execution of criterial or best available operations. So far, we have finessed the problem of unbounded operation execution times by imposing programming constraints. However, we are studying more flexible approaches that would allow variable computation times for executed operations, with the possibility of interruption by identification of newer, higher-priority next-operations. Depending upon the specification of the operation currently being executed, the executor would either abort execution of the current operation or suspend it and place a rated resumable form of the operation in an appropriate position on the agenda.

Regarding limited-capacity buffers, we have given some thought to introducing spontaneous temporal decay of items in buffers. In a dynamic environment, even very important events are perishable and may not warrant processing after a period of time. Although it has been suggested to us that an agent's buffer capacities might be variable in different contexts, we continue to assume that they are static. However, we are investigating the concept of limited-capacity "back-up buffers" which catch and preserve very important overflow items.

We considered modeling perception and action processes as operations in the cognitive system, but that approach did not provide the desired asynchrony and interfered with timeliness [32].

Finally, we have distributed perception, cognition, and action among parallel processes because they respresent minimally interacting, coarse-grained chunks of knowledge and computation. Therefore, we hypothesize that they can be distributed among parallel processes without incurring excessive communications demands or knowledge redundancy. So far, that hypothesis seems to be correct. Although we have considered distributing cognitive tasks among parallel processes [29], our experience with Guardian suggests that cognitive tasks have many important interactions, including sequential constraints, and associated needs for communication. Operating on a single processor in the context of a single global data structure supports these interactions, so we would favor distribution of cognitive tasks only in a shared-memory architecture.

6.2 Alternative Architectures

A considerable body of research has focused on "classical" planners [17, 44]. Under this model, an agent perceives information from the environment and then constructs a goal-oriented sequence of actions, a plan, which it subsequently executes. Classical planning architectures are not intended to provide comprehensive capabilities for intelligent agents, so it is not surprising that they do not satisfy all of the requirements for real-time control put forth in this paper. Global coherence is the most prominent advantage of classical planners. However, the computational cost of formulating a complete plan by reasoning backward from goals can be excessive [8]. Classical planners do not meet the other requirements.

Relaxing this perceive-plan-act sequence, some researchers allow the agent to interleave planning and execution, either to build the plan incrementally or to modify the plan in response to unanticipated conditions [9, 20, 25, 31, 35]. Other researchers introduced more knowledge intensive and computationally tractable methods for generating partial plans, including: instantiating goal-oriented action schemas [19, 26]; integrating top-down and bottom-up planning methods [24, 33], transferring successful plans to new situations [11, 23]; or successively applying constraints among potential actions [51]). Interleaving planning and execution permits an agent to several real-time requirements. However, their success is limited by unbounded computation times for component processes, especially the match processes that trigger reasoning operations. Although researchers have made progress in developing efficient match algorithms [18, 22], these approaches only speed up the match process. They do not reduce the computational complexity of the process and, more importantly, they do not permit an agent to directly control the amount of time spent on the match process.

By contrast, in an effort to avoid the computational cost of control reasoning and thereby create real-time responsivity, some researchers have turned their attention to the theory, design, and implementation of "reactive agents" [1, 2, 39, 43, 45]. Basically, reactive agents store large numbers of perception-action rules in a computationally efficient form and execute actions invoked by environmental conditions on each iteration of a perceive-act cycle. Thus, they are similar to control theoretic methods [5], where traversal of symbolic networks replaces computation of numerical models. Reactive models often assume synchronization of reactive cycles with the occurrence of events in the environment. Selectivity is achieved to the degree that the system builder has encoded it in the network and flexibility is a natural consequence of the perceive-act cycle. On the other hand, coherence occurs only fortuitously, presumably emerging from the agent's characteristic reactions to events in an orderly task environment. Reactive agents provide responsiveness and robustness only when perception-action networks include context-specific alternative subnetworks. In general, we view the reactive agent model as a good framework for engineering solutions to particular, narrowly defined feedback control tasks for which control-theoretic models are inapplicable--those for which numerical models are either non-existent or intractable. It also might be an appropriate mechanism for low-level perception-action programs that by-pass the cognitive subsystem within the proposed architecture. For example, the proposed architecture might incorporate reactive peripheral programs for focusing perceptual attention or feedback control of actions. However, we suspect that the reactive model is not an appropriate general model for tasks that present challenging requirements for selectivity, global coherence, responsivity, or robustness. And it is not appropriate for complex tasks or for the multiple task behavior expected of generally intelligent agents where enumerating all possible perception-action contingencies and encoding them in a computationally tractable form may be infeasible.

Finally, robotics researchers aim to build "task-level" robot systems (]14, 36]. Unlike robots programmed to perform specific mechanical tasks, task-level robots are intended to accept high-level goals and then determine and perform whatever behaviors are necessary to achieve the goals. They are intended to operate under a variety of incidental contextual conditions, including low-frequency exceptional conditions related to hardware, software, or environmental state. Significant applications of this work include efforts to build autonomous vehicles [21, 37]. Robotics work is similar in spirit to the present research, integrating perception, action, and cognition to achieve goals in a real-time task environment. However, robotics research traditionally has focused on challenging perceptual-motor tasks, only recently beginning to incorporate more cognitive activities, such as goal determination, planning, exception handling, and learning [4]. Conversely, our work grows out of earlier work emphasizing reasoning and problem solving, with new emphases on perceiving and acting in a real-time environment.

7 Limitations of the Proposed Architecture

Despite our interest in the proposed architecture, we must acknowledge that it makes agents vulnerable to errors that do not occur under conventional software architectures. By definition, the architecture's real-time control mechanisms--its perceptual filtering, limited capacity I/O buffers, dynamic control planning, focus of attention, and satisficing cycle--allow an agent to ignore many opportunities to perceive, reason, and act and to perform sub-optimal operations. In general, the agent allocates limited computational resources among competing activities in proportion to their urgency and importance. In many cases, this will not affect the global utility of the agent's performance. In others, it will produce acceptable degration in particular aspects of performance. In extreme cases, however, an agent might decide prematurely to perform costly, ineffective, or counterproductive operations; or it could fail to perform highly desirable operations that are well within its capabilities. Nonetheless, it is our hypothesis that, if we wish to build agents that function well in complex real-time environments, of which the natural environment is a prime example, we must forego optimality in favor of effective management of complexity [52]. Allowing the possibility of occasional, more or less consequential error is a necessary concession toward that end. Formulating control knowledge that allows an agent to meet the most important real-time performance requirements while minimizing the impact of incompleteness and suboptimality is a primary objective of our research.

8 Remarks on Second-Generation Expert Systems

In addition to its support for real-time behavior, which is the focus of the present article, the proposed agent architecture provides a framework for addressing several other features of second-generation expert systems discussed in this book.

First, its generalization of the "blackboard model" allows the architecture to combine reasoning methods within a task, to interleave the operations of multiple tasks, and to share solution elements generated by different methods or tasks. For example, on detecting a new fault condition, Guardian could interleave operations for both associative and model-based diagnosis methods in an effort to get both a quick diagnosis and as much understanding of the underlying causal mechanism as time allows. It could use preliminary hypotheses produced by its associative method to focus its search using the model-based methods, It also could use preliminary hypotheses to constrain ongoing therapy planning for a separate problem in order to avoid undesirable interactions between the planned therapy and the new problem.

Second, the architecture's explicit representation of dynamic control plans provides a data structure in which an agent can reason about which tasks to perform, which methods to use for particular tasks, which strategies to follow in applying particular methods to particular tasks, and how to coordinate its performance interacting tasks over time. For example, in the scenario discussed above, Guardian makes all of these different kinds of decisions to coordinate its performance of several interacting tasks: patient monitoring; diagnosing, predicting, and correcting symptoms of the patient's low temperature; and correcting the patient's urgent low peak inspiratory pressure.

Third, the architecture's concept of control plans also provides a framework for interaction. An agent can *explain* its behavior in terms of the control decisions that actually determined it. For example, Guaridan could explain why it performed a sequence of associative diagnosis operations by citing its decision to "react quickly to the patient's high PIP." An agent can *cooperate* with other agents by incorporating their suggestions as new control decisions. For example, Guardian could accept and follow a nurse's instruction to monitor respiratory data by recording that instruction as a decision in its control plan. An agent can *recognize plans* underlying another agent's behavior by abductively inferring constraints that describe the sequence of actions. For example, having received a sequence of instructions to identify different types of possible causes of an observed condition, followed by instructions to acquire and interpret particular kinds of data, Guardian could infer that the physician who gave the instructions is following a plan to assemble an exhaustive differential diagnosis and then discriminate among competing diagnoses.

Finally, we have extended the architecture with a framework for explicit task-level languages. A task is defined by the types of domain entities it takes as inputs and outputs and the types of abstract roles these entities play within the task. Examples are: diagnosis, planning, and prediction tasks. A method for performing a task is defined by a set of reasoning operations and strategies, along with resource requirements (e.g., knowledge, data, real time, computation) and performance characteristics (e.g., precision, certainty, quality of results). Examples are: associative, model-based, case-based methods. For a given task and method, English-like sentence templates are instantiated to represent particular reasoning operations and

670

strategies within particular domains and contexts. Because these languages are both machine and human interpretable, they substantially enhance the basic architectural capabilities for control and interaction discussed above. In addition, they provide a skeletal framework to guide automatic knowledge acquisition of domain concepts and automatic transfer of strategies among analogous tasks in different domains.[2]

References

1. Agre, P.E., and Chapman, D. Pengi: An implementation of a theory of activity. Proceedings of the National Conference on Artificial Intelligence, 1987.
2. Andersson, R.L. A Robot Ping-Pong Player: Experiment in Real-Time Control. MIT Press, 1988.
3. Baker, T.P., and Shaw, A. The cyclic executive model and Ada. Real-Time Systems, 1:1, 17-26, 1989.
4. Bares, J., Hebert, M., Kanade, T., Krotkov, E., Mitchell, T., Simmons, R., and Whittaker, W. Ambler: An autonomous rover for planetary exploration. Computer, 22:6, 18-28, 1989.
5. Bollinger, J., and Duffie, N. Computer Control of Machines and Processes. 1988.
6. Boureau, L., and Hayes-Roth, B. Deriving priorities and deadlines in real-time knowledge-based systems. Proceedings of the IJCAI89 Workshop on Real-Time Systems, 1989.
7. Brinkley, S., Sha, L., and Lehoczky, J. Aperiodic task scheduling for hard-real-time systems. Real-Time Systems, 1:1, 27-60, 1989.
8. Chapman, D. Planning for conjunctive goals. Artificial Intelligence, 32:3, 333-378, 1987.
9. Corkill, D.D., Lesser, V.R., and Hudlicka, E. Unifying data-directed and goal-directed control: An example and experiments. Proceedings of the National Conference on Artificial Intelligence, 143-147, 1982.
10. d'Ambrosio, B., Fehling, M.R., Forrest, S., Raulefs, P., and Wilbur, M. Real-time process management for materials composition in chemical manufacturing. IEEE Expert, 1987.
11. Daube, F., and Hayes-Roth, B. A case-based mechanical redesign system. Proceedings of the International Conference on Artificial Intelligence, 1989.
12. Dodhiawala, R., Sridharan, N.S., Raulefs, P., and Pickering, C. Real-time AI Systems: A definition and an architecture. Proceedings of the Eleventh International Joint Conference on Artificial Intelligence, 1989.
13. Erman, L.D., Hayes-Roth, F., Lesser, V.R., and Reddy, D.R. The Hearsay-II speech-understanding system: Integrating knowledge to resolve uncertainty. Computing Surveys 12:213-253, 1980.
14. Ernst, H.A. A computer-controlled mechanical hand. PhD Thesis, MIT, Cambridget, MA., 1961.
15. Fagan, L.M. VM: Representing time-dependent relations in a medical setting. PhD Dissertation, Stanford University, 1980.
16. Faulk, S.R., and Parnas, D.L. On synchronization in hard-real-time systems. Communications of the ACM, 31:3, 274-287, 1988.

---

[2] Additional references on task-level languages:

Hayes-Roth, B. Opportunistic control of action in intelligent agents. IEEE Transactions on Systems, Man, and Cybernetics, in press, 1992.

Hayes-Roth, B., Johnson, M.V., Garvey, A., and Hewett, M. Applications of BB1 to arrangement-assembly tasks. Artificial Intelligence in Engineering, 1986, 1, 85-94.

Hayes-Roth, B., Johnson, M.V., Garvey, A., and Hewett, M. A modular and layered environment for reasoning about action. KSL-Technical Report 86-38, 1986.

17. Fikes, R.E., and Nilsson, N.J. STRIPS: A new approach to the application of theorem proving to problem solving. Artificial Intelligence, 2, 198-208, 1971.
18. Forgy, C.L. RETE: A fast algorithm for the many pattern/many object pattern matching problem. Artificial Intelligence, 19, 17-32, 1982.
19. Friedland, P.E. Knowledge-based experiment design in molecular genetics. Technical Report CS-79-71, Stanford University Computer Science Department, 1979.
20. Georgeff, M.P., and Lansky, A.L. Reactive reasoning and planning. Proceedings of the National Conference on Artificial Intelligence, 1987.
21. Goto, Y., and Stentz, A. Mobile robot navigation: The CMU system. IEEE Expert, Volume 2, 4, 44-54, 1989.
22. Gupta, A., Forgy, C., and Newell, A. High-speed implementations of rule-based systems. Technical Report, Carnegie-Mellon University, 1987.
23. Hammond, K. CHEF: A model of case-based reasoning. Proceedings of the National Conference on Artificial Intelligence, 1986.
24. Hayes-Roth, B., Hayes-Roth,, F., Rosenschein, S., and Cammarata, S. Modelling planning as an incremental, opportunistic process. Proceedings of the Sixth International Joint Conference on Artificial Intelligence, 6:375-383, 1979.
25. Hayes-Roth, B. A blackboard architecture for control. Artificial Intelligence, 26:251-321, 1985.
26. Hayes-Roth, B., Buchanan, B.G., Lichtarge, O., Hewett, M., Altman, R., Brinkley, J., Cornelius, C., Duncan, B., and Jardetzky, O. Protean: Deriving protein structure from constraints. Proceedings of the National Conference on Artificial Intelligence, 1986.
27. Hayes-Roth, B., Washington, R., Hewett, R., Hewett, M., and Seiver, A., Intelligent real-time monitoring and control. Proceedings of the Eleventh International Joint Conference on Artificial Intelligence, 1989.
28. Hayes-Roth, B. A multi-processor interrupt-driven architecture for adaptive intelligent systems. Proceedings of the IJCAI89 Workshop on Real-Time Systems, 1989.
29. Hayes-Roth, B., Hewett, M., Washington, R., Hewett, R., and Seiver, A. Distributing intelligence within a single individual. In L. Gasser and M.N. Huhns (Eds.) Distributed Artificial Intelligence, Volume 2. Morgan Kaufmann, 1989.
30. Hayes-Roth, B. Making intelligent systems adaptive. In K. VanLehn (Ed.), Architectures for Intelligence. Lawrence Erlbaum, 1989.
31. Hayes-Roth, B. Dynamic control planning in adaptive intelligent systems. Proceedings of the DARPA Knowledge-Based Planning Workshop, Austin, Texas, 1987
32. Hewett, M., and Hayes-Roth, B. Real-Time I/O in Knowledge-Based Systems. In V. Jagannathan, R.T. Dodhiawala, and L. Baum (Eds.), Current Trends in Blackboard Systems, Morgan Kaufmann, 1989.
33. Johnson, M.V., and Hayes-Roth, B. Integrating diverse reasoning methods in the BB1 blackboard control architecture. Proceedings of the National Conference on Artificial Intelligence, 1987.
34. Laffey, T., Cox, P.A., Schmidt, J.L., Kao, S.M., and Read, J.Y. Real-time knowledge-based systems. AI Magazine, 9:1, 1988.
35. Lesser, V.R., Pavlin, J., and Durfee, E. Approximate processing in real-time problem solving. AI Magazine, 9:1, 49-62, 1988.
36. Lozano-Perez, T., Jones, J.L., Mazer, E., and O'Donnell, P.A. Task-level planning of pick-and-place robot motions. Computer, 22:3, 21-31, 1989.
37. McTamaney, L.S. Mobile robots: Real-time intelligent control. IEEE Expert, 2:4, 55-70, 1989.
38. Murray, W. Dynamic instructional planning in the BB1 blackboard control architecture. In V. Jagannathan, R. Dodhiawala, and L. Baum (eds.), Current Trends in Blackboard Systems, Morgan Kaufman,1989.
39. Nilsson, N. Action Networks. Working Paper, Stanford University Department of Computer Science, 1989.
40. O'Neill, D.M., and Mullarkey, P.W. A knowledge-based approach to real time signal monitoring. Proceedings of the Sixth National Conference on Artificial Intelligence Applications, 1989.

672

41. Pardee, W.J., Shaff, M.A., and Hayes-Roth, B. Intelligent control of complex materials processes. Proceedings of the Workshop on Blackboard Systems, 1989.
42. Rosenschein, S.J., Hayes-Roth, B., and Erman, L. Notes on methodologies for evaluating IRTPS systems. Proceedings of the AFOSR Workshop on Intelligent Real Time Problem Solving Systems. Santa Cruz, 1989.
43. Rosenschein, S.J., and Kaelbling, L.P. The synthesis of digital machines with provable epistemic properties. In J. Halpern (ed.), Proceedings of the Conference on Theoretical Aspects of Reasoning about Knowledge, Morgan Kauffman, 1986.
44. Sacerdoti, E.D. The non-linear nature of plans. Proceedings of the International Joint Conference on Artificial Intelligence, 1975.
45. Schoppers, M. Universal plans for reactive robots in unpredictable environments. Proceedings of the International Joint Conference on Artificial Intelligence, 1987.
46. Shoham, Y., and Hayes-Roth, B. Report on issues, testbed, and methodology for the IRTPS research program. Proceedings of the AFOSR Workshop on Intelligent Real Time Problem Solving Systems. Santa Cruz, 1989.
47. Smith, D.M., and Broadwell, M.M. The pilot's associate - An overview. Proceedings of the Eighth International Workshop on Expert Systems and their Applications.
48. Sowa, J. Conceptual Structures: Information Processing in Mind and Machine. Addition-Wesley, 1984.
49. Stankovic, J.A., Misconceptions about real-time computing: A serious problem for next-generation systems. Computer, 21:10, 10-19, 1988.
50. Stankovic, J.A., and Zhao, W. On real-time transactions. SIGMOD Record, 17, 4-18, 1988.
51. Stefik, M. Planning with constraints. Artificial Intelligence, 16:2, 111-140, 1971.
52. Simon, H.A. The Sciences of the Artificial. MIT Press, 1969.
53. Touchton, R.A. Reactor emergency action level monitor. Technical Report NP-5719, Electric Power Research Institute, 1988.
54. Washington, R., and Hayes-Roth, B. Managing input data in real-time AI systems. Proceedings of the Eleventh International Joint Conference in Artificial Intelligence, 1989.

An Investigation of the Roles of Problem-Solving Methods in Diagnosis*

W.F. Punch[1] and B. Chandrasekaran[2]

[1] AI/Knowledge Based Systems Lab, Computer Science Dept, A714 Wells Hall
Michigan State University, E. Lansing MI 48824
[2] Laboratory for AI Research, Dept. of Computer Science, The Ohio State University
Columbus, OH 43210

Abstract. This work centers on dynamic integration of multiple problem-solvers for the purpose of solving problems with broad and complex domains. A problem-solver based on dynamic integration uses diverse problem solving methods (neural net, rule based, model based etc.) to reason about complex problems. This research is based on a preliminary model called TIPS (Task Integrated Problem Solving). TIPS provides a methodology in which the goal structure of a large-grained problem such as diagnosis is mapped to multiple problem-solving methods. A TIPS diagnosis problem-solver has been constructed in the domain of medical diagnosis (liver and blood disorders) which utilizes a number of different problem-solving methods. This paper will discuss the concept of a task-structure, the TIPS architecture and a medical diagnosis system implemented in TIPS.

1 Introduction

A common (though not universal) definition of the term *diagnosis* in a generic sense is: The mapping of signs and symptoms to malfunctions. Having made this definition, one must immediately note at least two inadequacies.

First, the above definition does not take into account how one may accomplish the diagnostic task. That is, there is no information on how the process of diagnosis should proceed. This is of course due to the fact that there are many views on how diagnosis should be done in the present field of AI. For example, heuristic/empirical/compiled approaches to diagnosis are based on a representation which pre-enumerates the malfunction categories and uses a reasoning method which searches through these categories for those that most clearly account for the observed signs and symptoms [6, 2, 16]. Other approaches which emphasize model-based approaches do not pre-enumerate the categories but determine malfunction based on representations using detailed models of the domain and reasoning methods like design models [9], malfunction/behavior modes[7] or simulation[8, 18].

* Punch would like to acknowledge the support of the Ameritech foundation, Chandrasekaran would like to acknowledge support of AFOSR grants 87-0090 and 89-0250.

The second inadequacy is the lack of inclusion of other aspects of diagnosis which, while not directly concerned with malfunction discovery, are often considered part and parcel of the diagnostic process. For example, the process of therapy is an important part of diagnosis as practiced in the real world. Another would be the process of data validation i.e., providing the diagnostic process with potentially validated data.

The problem seems to be that the generic process of diagnosis is a heterogeneous one. That is, the overall *task* of diagnosis can be decomposed into a structure of subtasks. This *task structure* [4] would be based on:

1. A goal structure for the diagnostic task.
2. A mapping that indicates which of those goals any particular method can achieve.

Thus one might define diagnosis not only in terms of the overall goal (association of signs and symptoms to malfunction), but also in terms of the richness of the subgoals one includes in diagnosis and the types of method used to achieve those goals. A diagnostic system realized in the above terms would have a number of advantages:

1. Such a system would have available multiple approaches for solving a similar problem. Thus the failure of one method does not mean failure for the whole problem-solver.
2. Such a system could potentially have more breadth in the types of diagnostic problems it could successfully solve.
3. The actual problem-solving process of diagnosis would depend on the availability of different types of diagnostic knowledge and on the available data.

Hence we can view diagnosis not only in terms of achieving a simple goal, but also in terms of breadth subgoals it can achieve and breadth of method used to achieve goals. There are a number of advantages to viewing problem-solving using a task structure:

1. It emphasizes problem analysis as an important part of system building. This means that it focuses on a view of the problem based on the various goals and subgoals of a problem and how they interact. The process of mapping goal achievement to various problem-solving methods is left to a later stage, thus concentrating on analysis of the problem and not on how to implement a problem-solver using any one method.
2. Once the goal structure is identified, problem-solving methods can be chosen to achieve the task goals based on their appropriateness for achieving that particular kind of goal. Thus multiple methods, each with a clear designation of what it can do, may be brought together in an integrated problem-solving environment.
3. Various goals may be achieved by a variety of methods. A system built using a task structure analysis allows experimenting with the effectiveness of various methods for achieving a particular goal in a larger problem-solving context.

4. Most importantly, such a task structure can be coupled with an overall control strategy to *dynamically* determine which goal(s) are appropriate to explore. Thus the sequence of method invocation is based on availability of knowledge and the problem-solving state, not on a fixed sequence. For example, if one domain has knowledge which indicates it should explore data validation, then that subgoal may be activated when the need arises. However, another domain may not have such knowledge available, in which case data validation will not be activated and alternate methods will be used to solve the overall problem.

1.1 An Example Task Structure for Diagnosis

One of the most important problems then is the creation of the goal structure for the overall problem. Consider the following medical case as a concrete example (taken from the 1954 case in [10]) of the kinds of goals that can be uncovered in a task such as medical diagnosis.

A 52 year old Italian laborer presents with the following symptoms:

- A series of "palpitations" that had associated chest pains and sweating. No overt signs of heart trouble.
- Blood test indications of anemia (low hematocrit, low rbc and low hemoglobin).
- Increased liver size along with an increase in bilirubin of the indirect (non-conjugated) type along with a slight jaundice, indicating a possible liver disease.

From the perspective of goals in diagnosis, the doctor as a diagnostician has a number of choices in reasoning at this stage:

1. Make the best diagnosis based on the available data, to wit, an unclassified type of liver disease and an anemia, probably *thalassemia minor* based both on the serological data and the patient's heritage[3].
2. Ask for more data that can help further the diagnosis. That is, given the present diagnostic conclusions, what data will give the most leverage in getting a more complete or satisfactory diagnosis? In this case, one could ask for more data about the liver disease, such as biopsy of the organ, or further blood studies to elucidate the kind of anemia.
3. Question data that does not fit in with the present best diagnosis and validate them if necessary. In the subsequent work on this case, the doctor ordered X-rays to confirm the existence of bleeding varices of the esophagus (bleeding from enlarged veins in the throat). Despite the fact that the X-rays were negative, other evidence was sufficient (vomiting of blood, stoppage of bleeding with a Blakemore tube) for confirmation.

---

[3] Thalassemia minor is a common anemia of people with a Mediterranean heritage.

4. Use the present diagnosis as a starting point for consideration of possible causal interactions among the affected organs that would explain the signs and symptoms of the case. In so doing, one may discover a relationship that indicates both a specific disease and data that confirms (or refutes) that disease. This creation of a "causal story" can be a powerful tool in paring down the possible diagnostic situations that need to be examined in more detail. In the case presented, a possible relationship exists between this specific type of anemia, which causes an excess of iron in the blood, and the liver which is responsible for maintaining iron equilibrium. This would suggest diseases of the liver based on overexposure to iron.

The following is an example a goal structure first developed in the domain of medical diagnosis[12] (in particular, Liver and Anemia related diseases). While no claim is made of this being a comprehensive goal structure for diagnosis, it is much broader in scope (in terms of sub-problems addressed) than most other diagnostic systems and is fairly generic is its applicability to other domains. The task structure for diagnosis is displayed in Figure 1.

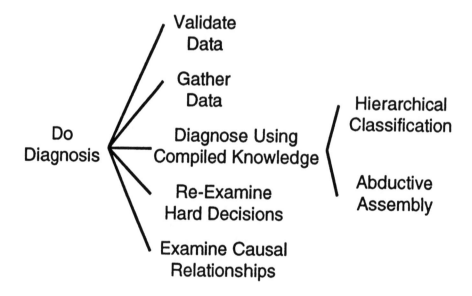

Fig. 1. Task structure of the goals of diagnosis

Those goals are:

– Do Diagnosis: The top level goal is to find a diagnostic explanation that covers all the findings and consists of hypotheses of the most detail possible.

- Diagnose using Compiled Knowledge: A subgoal of Do Diagnosis for creating a diagnostic explanation using compiled knowledge.
- Gather Data: A subgoal of Do Diagnosis for gathering data that facilitates making more detailed diagnostic explanations.
- Validate Data: A subgoal of Do Diagnosis for validating data that appears questionable.
- Re-Examine Hard Decisions: A subgoal of Do Diagnosis to explore alternate diagnostic explanations stemming from difficult hypothesis selections in Diagnose using Compiled Knowledge.
- Examine Causal Relationships: A subgoal of Do Diagnosis to determine the effects of proposed causal interactions between hypotheses in the diagnostic explanation.
- Hierarchical Classification: A subgoal of Diagnose using Compiled Knowledge to explore a pre-enumerated set of malfunction hypotheses that determines which are most plausible given the current problem state.
- Abductive Assembly: A subgoal of Diagnose using Compiled Knowledge to assemble a set of malfunction hypotheses which account for the current diagnostic findings and is causally coherent (i. e. , the hypotheses in the explanation do not conflict causally).

The *goal* of this research is to explore dynamic, task-integrated, problem-solving. The results of this work will be shown in two parts. The first part will discuss the TIPS (Task Integrated Problem Solving) architecture and its usefulness for task-specific integration. The second will briefly discuss a medical diagnosis system implemented in TIPS.

2 Architecture for Using Task Structure Analysis

2.1 Background

The motivation for this work comes from the experience of the authors with the *generic task* [3] approach to system building. Briefly, this view emphasizes the identification of domain-independent, generic approaches to solving particular kinds of high-level problems (classification, routine design). Once a task is identified, the problem is to discover forms of knowledge for both representation and control that are appropriate for that particular task. The promise of such an approach is that once a robust set of tasks have been identified, along with the tools that encode the knowledge for that task, they could form the building blocks of more complex problem solving tasks. That is, complex problem solving could emerge from the proper integration of generic task problem-solvers.

In the first generation of work on using generic tasks to build diagnostic and other complex problem solving systems, the invocation of a GT problem solver was pre-programmed as part of the task-structure. In other words, the invocation of GT problem-solvers had been implicitly "hard-wired" during the programming of the system. We realized that in order to use multiple methods to achieve problem solving goals we needed method selection to occur at run-time based on the state of the problem and availability of knowledge.

Thus the goal was to provide a general purpose architecture that allowed integration of high-level problem-solvers based on a dynamic problem state. The result was a way to analyze complex problems using the task structure (identification of goals in the complex problem and identification of capabilities to meet goals in each sub problem-solver) and an architecture that directly captured that analysis. This architecture is the TIPS architecture.

The TIPS approach to creating dynamically integrated problem-solvers is to provide only enough mechanism to allow monitoring of goal achievement and a mapping of methods that can achieve a goal. How these methods run is left to the designer as long as that conforms to a set of rules that indicate what it has done in terms of achieving its goal. This allows a knowledge engineer to take advantage of "tried and true" software (such as existing generic task problem solvers) without converting it to another format and allows a diversity of method and representation for different kinds of problem solving.

It is worth emphasizing again that the TIPS architecture is a response to the problem of dynamic integration from the point of view of generic tasks. As such, it has features that are particularly well-suited for integration of high-level problem solvers in response to a dynamic problem state. This is not to say that such an architecture could not have been realized in other existing systems. The discerning reader may note, after reading the sections on the actual architecture, some similarities between the TIPS architecture and other systems, in particular general blackboard systems such as BB1 [11] or the problem space architecture of SOAR[15]. This is neither troubling nor surprising.

Both BB1 and SOAR are general architectures and as such have a number of features which we do not need for our goal of integrating generic task problem solvers. Furthermore, as general purpose architectures they do not provide specific constructs/primitives for the knowledge engineer who wishes to construct a system for a high level task. The knowledge engineer must therefore construct/compose these task primitives and as a result is not provided with any task-specific constraints on using them. Recent work in both BB1 and SOAR has been concerned with providing higher level intefaces that hide some of the architecture level details from the knowledge engineer concerned only with programming and integrating high level tasks. TIPS is thus a proposal that shares important ideas with BB1 and SOAR about how to evaluate and choose methods for tasks at run-time. Because of its historical origin, namely the need to integrate generic tasks in a flexible way, its specific proposal for evaluating and selecting methods is somewhat different from those in BB1 and SOAR. The TIPS architecture used for diagnosis in particular makes a specific statement about the task-structure of diagnosis.

Thus we have no quarrel with other architectures. In some sense we have distilled through independent investigation the essential elements necessary to meet the particular problems already stated. In fact, we feel that we have much to give and learn from other designers since our approach to high-level integration dovetails well with research by groups such as SOAR and BB1 which investigate problem solving at an even more generic, broadly applicable though lower levels.

2.2 The TIPS Architecture for Problem Solving

The basis for the representation of control used in TIPS is the Sponsor-Selector system first used in DSPL [1] (Design Specialists and Plans Language). Such a structure is displayed in Figure 2. It consists of a hierarchy of three parts: a *selector*, some number of *sponsors*, and associated with each sponsor a *method invocation*. In short, the available methods are grouped under the selector, where each sponsor provides appropriateness measures for an associated method invocation. At any control choice point (i.e., some point in the flow of problem-solving at which another method could be invoked) the overall control process is to run all the sponsors to rate their associated methods, then have the selector choose the next method to be executed based on the sponsor values and other data.

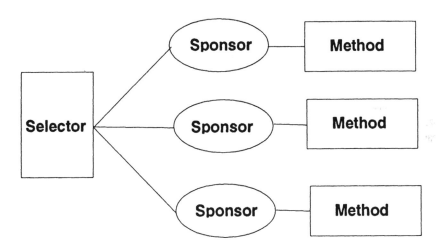

Fig. 2. The structure of a sponsor-selector system.

2.3 Sponsors

Each sponsor contains information about when its associated method is appropriate. The sponsor evaluates this information and yields a discrete value indicating how appropriate the method is. The sponsor's knowledge is represented as a pattern match group similar to the knowledge groups of CSRL [2], the tool used to build hierarchical classification systems. This representation is a table in which each column, except the last one, is a particular query about the problem-solving state of the system. Each row is a combination of answers to each question, a pattern of response. If a row "matches", that is, each pattern element of the row is true for the query with which it is associated, then the last element of the row is the symbolic value for that pattern match group. Thus the last column is a list of the symbolic values that could be potentially returned by the pattern match group. Control of row examination is of the simple "first true" type; that is the rows are evaluated in order until one of them matches. Thus the representation allows a knowledge engineer to investigate knowledge patterns in a specific order. Possible patterns of response are ruled out as the rows are evaluated until a matching pattern is found. If no patterns match and all have been examined, then some default value is returned, usually "unknown".

1) Has the classification method been applied yet?
2) Is the present diagnostic explanation complete?

Query 1	Query 2	Plausibility Value
F	?	3
T	F	1
T	T	-3

Fig. 3. An example match group which determines the classification sponsor appropriateness value

Consider the example pattern match group of Figure 3 for the classification hierarchy sponsor. There are two queries: Query 1 represented by Column 1 is, "Has hierarchical classification been applied yet?" , and Query 2 is, "Is the present diagnostic explanation complete?" (that is, explains all the data). Row 1 represents the pattern of response:

If hierarchical classification has not yet reached completion, represented by the F or false answer to Query 1, then regardless of whether the explanation is complete, represented by the ? or "don't care" answer to Query 2, then return a 3.

The return values can be any discrete range of symbolic values to represent the appropriateness scale; in this case it is one of -3 (for totally inappropriate) to +3 (for totally appropriate).

Note that the pattern information represented in the rows can be more complicated expressions to match the kind of information returned by the queries, not just simple true/false distinctions.

There are two kinds of information available as appropriateness pattern match features:

1. Information about what methods have been applied so far in the problem solving process. These are questions about which methods have run so far, if at all, and when they ran. The architecture provides automatic access to these kinds of questions, such as: "Did the hierarchy run last?", "Has the abductor run in the last 3 cycles?", etc. Query 1 is an example of a query for this type of information.
2. Information concerning goal achievement, such as: "Is the explanation complete?" or, "Has this finding been explained?". This kind of information has to be supplied by the programmer who assembles both the behaviors and the pattern match knowledge and is not part of TIPS. Query 2 is an example of a query for this type of information.

2.4 Selectors

Each group of sponsors and their method invocations are grouped under a selector (see Figure 2). The selector does two things:

1. It organizes the set of methods that are available to be run on each cycle of evaluation.
2. It selects which method is next invoked based on the appropriateness ratings of the sponsors and other knowledge.

If a selector is activated, only the methods under it are available for evaluation on each selection cycle. Other groups of sponsor-selectors may be activated as a result of some method being evaluated, but only one sponsor-selector system at a time is responsible for selecting methods to evaluate.

A selector is responsible for choosing which of its methods to invoke. Its main criterion for so choosing is the appropriateness measures returned from its sponsors, but often this is not enough. The sponsor pattern match information *should* be coded with only local considerations in mind. In other words, it should not be the knowledge engineer's job to have to program each sponsor such that only one should be appropriate under all circumstances. Ideally, each sponsor is coded with little consideration of other sponsors with more global considerations of proper selection left to the selector.

The selector knowledge can be encoded in three ways, as shown in Figure 4.

1. The selection can occur simply based on appropriateness measures. If a clear behavior selection is available, i.e., there is exactly one highly rated behavior, then that method is invoked. If no clear selection is available and no other selection knowledge is available, then a random choice from among the best candidates is selected, i.e., those with the highest plausibility rating.

Associated Sponsors	Hierarchical (Classification Sponsor	Select Finding Sponsor	Select Hypothesis) Sponsor

Ordered Priority List	(Finding, Hierarchy, Hypothesis)

Pattern Match Group	1) Has the classification method been applied yet? 2) Is examination of the hierarchy complete?

Query 1	Query 2	Selected Behavior
No	No	H. Class
Yes	No	Finding

Fig. 4. The internals of a selector

2. If there is a tie among the highest rated methods, tie breaking knowledge in the form of an *ordered priority list* can be used to break the tie. That is, the knowledge engineer can provide knowledge of method priority which determines which method is selected when appropriateness ratings are not enough. If more than one sponsor is marked as appropriate, then the first appropriate method in the priority list will be chosen. As shown in Figure 4, if the hierarchy and the finding-selection sponsors are tied, then findings-selection will be chosen.

3. For special situations, it is possible to override the normal choice mechanism with some pattern match knowledge similar to that found in the sponsors. If the pattern is matched, then the choice indicated in the matching row is used. If no match occurs, then the default priority list choice is used. The advantage of this is the processing time that can be saved to make a specific decision that is already determined by problem-solving analysis. The disadvantage is its inflexibility and narrow applicability. In the figure, if hierarchical classification has never been applied, as opposed to applied but not yet completed, then it should be the selected method. Notice this overrides the priority list.

The overall programming of the TIPS architecture is split into two parts:

1. Local decisions about appropriateness are coded in the sponsor in terms of knowledge about problem-solving progress and history of module activation, i. e. , both success/failure information and information concerning module selection.
2. Global decisions that concern actual choice of module invocation (based on sponsor results and other information) are coded in the selector.

As stated previously, multiple groups of sponsor-selectors can and often do exist, but only one such system is active at a time. Others may be activated by modules of a selector, but that one module-activated selector will remain the only active system until it completes.

Completion of cycling through a sponsor-selector systems is accomplished by a *Return* or *Fail* sponsor. These sponsors do not have any associated modules. Rather, they indicate when that particular sponsor-selector has finished its work or when it has failed to accomplish the task for which it was activated, that is whether the goal associated with the selector has been reached or not. These two sponsors often are at the highest priority since failure or completion are the two exit conditions. Setting of the Return and Failure sponsors are programmed just as any sponsor, by the knowledge engineer.

3 A Medical Diagnosis System in TIPS

In [12] a medical diagnosis system was developed in TIPS to demonstrate its usefulness. The system deals with a broad range of liver and blood diseases and their various interactions. The following briefly summarizes the modules used in the system, their roles and knowledge of when they are appropriate (see [12] for more details).

The diagnosis systems consists of the following modules:

- Compiled knowledge diagnostician. This module is responsible for creating diagnostic explanations using the abductive-assembly/hierarchical-classification architecture found in RED [17, 14]. It is used to meet the Diagnose using Compiled Knowledge goal.

  Briefly, this module has two subgoals, Hierarchical Classification and Abductive Assembly. Hierarchical Classification [2] is a problem solver that examines a hierarchy of (in this case) malfunction categories to determine the plausibility of malfunctions given the present circumstances. This plausibility information is used by the next phase, Abductive Assembly [14], to assemble a subset of the malfunction hypotheses such that the resulting *explanation* is most plausible, consistent and covers the findings.

  When Appropriate: This module is appropriate: as the very first module in a run (to create an initial diagnosis), if more data has been gathered, if a datum value was shown to be invalid and replaced by a validation method, or if causal reasoning has suggested an new malfunction hypothesis to consider for use in the composite explanation.

– Data gathering module. This module gathers evidence that can establish or rule-out pertinent diagnostic hypotheses. It is used to meet the Gather Data goal.

In this particular case, the data that is needed next is determined by the nodes in the hierarchical classifier that suspended due to lack of data. If this data can be made available, then further exploration of the hierarchy is enabled.

When Appropriate: This module is appropriate when: the hierarchical classifier cannot explore leaf level hypotheses due to lack of data, or one of the potential hypotheses in a hard decision (see item "Redoing hard decisions" in this section) has an unanswered question in its specialist.

– Data validation module. This module checks the validity of certain data that have been questioned during the run of the compiled knowledge diagnostician module. It is used to meet the Validate Data goal.

Described in some detail elsewhere (see [5]), the idea is the following. Rather than rely strictly on statistical "averaging" based on multiple sensor readings for one datum, this module uses expectations derived from partial hypotheses already formed by diagnosis. If these expectations are not met (i.e. a partial conclusion of "Liver Disease" requires some change in liver enzyme values and those values report in presently as normal) then there is a potential data problem. These unmet expectations are flagged and further investigated by specific test procedures that validate their value.

When Appropriate: This module is appropriate if, in the process of diagnosis, a plausible composite explanation is generated whose data expectations are not met. Those data that do not meet expectation are noted as questionable and are submitted for validation.

– Re-Examining hard decisions module. This modules examines the assembly of alternate diagnostic explanations stemming from a hard decisions in the compiled knowledge diagnostician module. It is used to meet the Change Hard Decisions goal.

A hard decision is a situation reached in abductive assembly when no clear criteria is available to differentiate among a set of hypotheses that offer to explain a finding. For example, the hypotheses A, B and C all offer to explain finding F and all have the same plausibility. If the only criteria available for differentiating which is the "best" hypothesis to explain F is plausibility, then there is no basis for a choice and a hard decision occurs. Typically the system makes a random choice and goes on but it also records the system state at that point so that the user may later go back and explore other possible solution paths.

When Appropriate: This module is appropriate when a hard decision has resulted during the abductive assembly process.

– Examining Causal Relationships. This module applies the coherence view of causal modeling of [12, 13] to the diagnostic explanations generated by the compiled knowledge diagnostician module. It is used to meet the Do Causal Reasoning goal.

Briefly, associated with each diagnostic hypothesis is some generic knowledge about how the malfunction it represents modifies normal function. These changes are broadly categorized as functional changes (Anemia causes loss of oxygenation function), connective changes (blocked Common Bile duct causes back-up of bile) and structural changes (swelling of pancreas can push on the liver). If a possible link between the elements of a partial abductive assembly hypothesis are found, their relationship is explored using a model of the involved elements to determine some causal results not yet available to the compiled diagnosis component.

Consider the example from Section 1.1. If hemolytic anemia causes a functional increase in iron products in the blood and the liver is responsible for clearing these products, a relationship between hemolytic anemia and the as-of-yet non-specific liver disease can be explored to discern a possible disease process. This can be done by simulating the liver model of "iron-clearing" with an additional parameter of excess iron. The results of this simulation may lead to a better understanding of the liver disease and suggest tests to validate the conclusion.

When Appropriate: The causal reasoning module is appropriate when a possible causal interaction has been noted between hypotheses of the present explanation.

4   An example Case

The following is a brief example of the run of the diagnostic system on the case described in section 1.1. Many details have been left out but the trace is included to give the reader a feel for the type of problem-solving that goes on in the system. Note that depending on the initial data, the system may solve the problem in a completely different way.

The case is taken from a clinicopathological conference at the Albany Medical College (B-56469), May 6, 1954 and cited in Harvey and Bordley [10],

Step 1: Given the data base values and the findings to explain the hierarchical classifier/abductive assembler, which always runs first, comes up with an initial diagnosis of (ThalassemiaMinor Hepatomegaly).

Step 2: The explanation generated is rated via two criteria to determine if it is "good enough". The criteria in this case are that the explanation explain all the findings and that it consist of hypotheses that are most detailed, i.e., come from the leaf level of the hierarchy. This explanation is considered not good enough (the hypothesis elements explained all the findings but were not all at the leaf level of the hierarchy, i. e. , not an explanation of the greatest detail possible), so the sponsor-selector system is invoked. Most method selection will not occur through the action of the sponsor-selector mechanism.

Step 3: The sponsors of the TIPS architecture were evaluated (see Figure 3 for an example sponsor). The ones deemed appropriate this time were Gather More Data and Causal Reasoning, both of which were rated +3 on a scale of +3 (completely appropriate) to -3 (completely inappropriate). Gather More Data was appropriate since the hierarchy was not explored to leaf level. Causal Reasoning was appropriate because a functional relationship was noted between ThalassemiaMinor and Hepatomegaly. The relationship is based on the production of iron by ThalassemiaMinor and the normal liver operation of consuming iron associated with Hepatomegaly. The Causal Reasoning module was selected based on the tie-breaking knowledge of the sponsor's module priority list, shown in Figure 4, since causal reasoning has a higher priority than gathering data

Step 4: The causal reasoning module focuses on the functional relationship of iron, based on `excess-produce-iron` of `ThalassemiaMinor` and the `consume-iron` of `Hepatomegaly`. Note that the latter is a normal function of liver for which there is no evidence of change.

Step 5: Based on the proposed interaction of iron, a search is made for a model of iron-metabolism of liver. It is found in the Liver specialist associated with "iron-metabolism". The liver's iron-metabolism function is simulated on the initial conditions of excess iron, derived from the excess production of iron from `Thalassemia Minor` stored with its interaction knowledge. Note that it also searches for an effect of `consume-iron` on Thalassemia Minor, but finds none. This is important since the interaction could occur in either direction.

Step 6: The simulation yields the state of `iron-deposits-in-liver-cells`, which is noted as abnormal by the data base (the data base stores normal ranges for all data). The causal module searches to see if `iron-deposits-in-liver-cells` is associated with any known disease. It does so by searching another association list of states-to-malfunctions stored in the Liver specialist. An association is discovered between

`iron-deposits-in-liver-cells` and the disease `hemochromatosis`.

Step 7: The causal model runs the compiled knowledge of the hierarchical classifier associated with the disease `hemochromatosis` to determine if there is enough evidence to establish it. Note that this is an example of method invocation bypassing the sponsor-selector system. Such bypassing is appropriate here since the mechanism requires that such potential solutions be confirmed. However, it could also have been programmed through the normal sponsor-selection mechanism with no change in functionality. In any event, the node establishes so the disease `Hepatomegaly` is replaced as a hypothesis for the abductive assembler by `hemochromatosis` since the latter is a particular type of the former and the abductive assembler is trying to create the most detailed explanation possible. The causal reasoning module then returns control to the sponsor-selector.

Step 8: The explanation has not yet changed, the diagnostic explanation is still not "good enough" so the TIPS diagnostic architecture is again invoked. This time, and the Compiled Knowledge Diagnostician Module and the Gather Data Module are the only ones appropriate, both rated at +3. The Compiled Knowledge Diagnostician was appropriate because Causal Reasoning suggested hemochromatosis as a hypothesis for use in the composite explanation. The Gather Data Module is appropriate since the hierarchy was still not explored to leaf level. Since the Compiled Knowledge Diagnostician Module has a higher priority, it is invoked next.

Step 9: The Compiled Knowledge Diagnostician Module creates an alternate explanation with the elements (`ThalassemiaMinor hemochromatosis`). That explanation is complete and detailed, so diagnosis is finished and the case ends.

5   Evaluation

There are two aspects of the TIPS architecture that need to be improved. The first is the lack of any direct representation of the task structure goals. The second is the lack of any standardized guidelines of interaction between the methods and/or goals of a TIPS system.

The first problem is really one of representation. Figure 1 is a direct representation of the goals and their relationship in a problem such as diagnosis. In implementing this in a TIPS system however, those goals are only represented implicitly in the sponsor-selector system. In other words, there is no *direct* representation of the goals or of when the goals become active, or of when a goal has been achieved etc. At present, each sponsor must contain knowledge concerning when its goal(s) are appropriate for exploration and under what conditions its method is appropriate for achieving those goals. Moreover, this lack of clean separation leads to confusion on what gets sponsored. For example, Do Diagnosis is a goal but Hierarchical Classification is more of an approach. This is one of the more pressing problems that needs to be addressed as it does not conform to the task structure analysis.

The second problem is one of standardizing the means by which sponsors can monitor goal status and by which methods can indicate their success, partial success or failure. Likewise, a common means by which problem state information is gathered must be made available. At present, Lisp code specific to the goals and methods in the diagnostic system have been used but this is unacceptable for a general purpose architecture.

In short, we are addressing these problems by modifying the TIPS architecture to directly represent the task structure with a *goal tree*. The goal tree will provide direct representation of the task structure and standardize goal monitoring procedures for sponsors and methods.

References

1. D. C. Brown and B. Chandrasekaran. Knowledge and control for a mechanical design expert system. *IEEE Computer*, 19:92–101, July 1986.
2. T. C. Bylander and S. Mittal. CSRL: A language for classificatory problem solving and uncertainty handling. *AI Magazine*, 7, Summer 1986.
3. B. Chandrasekaran. Towards a functional architecture for intelligence based on generic information processing tasks. In *Proceedings of the International Joint Conference on Artificial Intelligence 87*, pages 1183–1191. International Joint Conference on Artificial Intelligence, 1987.
4. B. Chandrasekaran. Task structures, knowledge acquisition and learning. *Machine Learning*, 4:339–345, 1989.

688

5. B. Chandrasekaran and W. F. Punch III. Data validation during diagnosis, a step beyond traditional sensor validation. In *AAAI87*, pages 778–782, 1987.

6. W. J. Clancey. Heuristic classification. *Artificial Intelligence*, 27(3):289–350, 1985.

7. J. deKleer and B. C. Williams. Diagnosis with behavior modes. In *AAAI89*, pages 1324–1330. Morgan Kaufmann, 1989.

8. P. K. Fink and J. C. Lusth. Expert systsm and diagnostic expertise in the mechanical and electrical domains. *IEEE Trans. on Systems, Man and Cybernetics*, SMC-17(3), May-June 1987.

9. M. R. Genesereth. Diagnosis using hierarchical design models. In *Proceedings AAAI82*, pages 278–284. Morgan Kaufmann, 1982.

10. A. M. Harvey and J. Bordley III. *Illustrative Case I in Liver Diseases*, pages 294–298. W. B. Saunders, 1972.

11. B. Hayes-Roth. A blackboard architecture for control. *Artificial Intelligence*, 26:251–321, 1985.

12. W. F. Punch III. *A Diagnosis System Using a Task Integrated Problem Solving Architecture (TIPS), Including Causal Reasoning.* PhD thesis, The Ohio State University, 1989.

13. W. F. Punch III. Interactions of compiled and causal reasoning in diagnosis. *IEEE Expert*, 1(7):28–35, 1992.

14. J. R. Josephson, B. Chandrasekaran, J. R. Smith, and M. C. Tanner. A mechanisim for forming composite explanatory hypotheses. *IEEE Transactions on Systems, Man and Cybernetics*, SMC-17(3):445–454, 1987.

15. P. S. Rosenbloom, J. E. Laird, and A. Newell. SOAR: an architecture for general intelligence. *Artificial Intelligence*, 33:1–64, 1987.

16. E. H. Shortliffe. *Computer-based Medical Consultations:MYCIN.* Elsevier/North-Holland Inc., 1976.

17. J. W. Smith, J. R. Svirbely, C. A. Evans, P. Strohm, J. R. Josephson, and M. C. Tanner. Red: A red-cell antibody identification expert module. *Journal of Medical Systems*, 9, Issue 3,:121–138, 1985.

18. J. Sticklen. Integrating classification-based compiled level reasoning with function-based deep level reasoning. *Applied Artificial Intelligence*, 3(2), 1989.

Knowledge Architectures for Real Time Decision Support

José Cuena
Departamento de Inteligencia Artificial
Universidad Politécnica de Madrid
Campus de Montegancedo s/n
28660 - Boadilla del Monte
Madrid

Abstract: This chapter deals with the presentation, illustrated by examples, of an architecture aiming to the representation of knowledge for real time decision support for physical systems management. However the proposed approach may be used to deal with other decision support systems where a level of behavior modeling be required.

First, the concept of representation based on knowledge level specification of an agent with subsequent modeling using generic tasks is presented.

Second, the general pattern for reasoning and knowledge structuring of an agent for decision support on physical systems is presented together with some considerations on the alternative approaches for physical behavior modeling.

Third, the example of real time flood management agent is discussed. A knowledge level structure is proposed initially and two symbolic level representations are proposed addressing the specification: the CYRAH and SIRAH architectures. Both approaches are described from the criteria for representation and inference to the operational aspects.

Fourth, to show the possibilities of the approach in a different field the real time traffic management problem is analyzed proposing an architecture adapted to a pattern for reasoning for traffic control strategy real time adaptation to present and emerging problems. This approach is now in course of implementation in several specific projects.

Finally, some comments are proposed on integration of knowledge based approach and conventional software approach suggested by these experiences.

1. INTRODUCTION

The concept of knowledge based systems leaves open, as a design decision, the quality of the knowledge to be introduced in the system. In some cases it is acceptable a very practical knowledge allowing simply to obtain answers for the problems to be solved by the system using a uniform representation such as the rules. In these cases the knowledge based design allows flexibility in the sense that the knowledge may be updated. However in some cases the quality of the knowledge has to be improved because:

- Improved explanation capability is required by the nature of the application. Such is the case of:
  * Education applications, where the student must know the reasons that justify an answer to understand both the right knowledge to be used and the right way to use it. In these cases the quality of the knowledge presented in the explanations is the real quality of the system.
  * Responsibilities associated to the decisions of the system (i.e. in real time emergency systems where important decisions are to be taken with significant socio-economic impacts as opening the valves on a dam or closing a four in the steel industry), the user needs to know the technical reasons for these recommendations, in these cases black box rules compiling technical reasons and expert criteria are not explanatory enough, so models of physical behavior must be included in the knowledge base to get quality enough in the explanation.
- In other cases the nature of knowledge is complex enough to require a deep model to attain an acceptable quality level in the representation. It happens when professional problems are dealt with, in engineering design or management of industrial installations, where it is very difficult to represent the models commonly used by professionals using the rule or frame based approach. Deepening the knowledge through model introduction allows the additional advantages of:
  * Generality and reusability, because the models to be used may be pre-established in existing libraries in such a way that the same model may be used for different applications.
  * Better knowledge acquisition because the knowledge may be obtained guided by the models structure.

A problem of using deep knowledge may be the possible loss of efficiency because more detailed knowledge bases are to be dealt with and several levels of inference may be required. However, the hardware present state of the art allows the operation of such complex systems in acceptable conditions.

When deep knowledge is to be modeled its structure is discovered based on different knowledge components showing that there is a knowledge morphology that may be lost when uniform representations are used. This idea was present in the proposals of [1] for knowledge level specification and [2], [3] for knowledge organization based on a set of generic tasks. As a consequence an evolution in the concept of knowledge based systems has been produced. Now knowledge based systems may be designed as computable analogies of the structure of some specialized intelligence conceived to operate in professional problematic environments.

This chapter deals with a type of such intelligences: the ones oriented to decision support in the management of physical systems. First, an analysis at the knowledge level is presented for this type of agents and, after, two cases of the proposed approach are presented, one dealing with the flood management problem where two alternative symbolic models are discussed and other with the traffic control problem.

2. THE REAL TIME DECISION SUPPORT AGENT

The basic concepts for managing a physical system (natural or artificial) according to [4] are:
- The external actions provoked by:
  * The environment in which the system operates.
  * The decisions of those responsible for the system's management.
- The behavior of the system described by the interaction of some system components on others in such a way that the change of state of one of them has an effect on the others.
- The evaluation for decision purposes of the quality of the system operation, that is, the assessment of the measures of the possible behaviors adjustment to the predefined management goals.

As a consequence, an intelligent agent capable for managing these systems in real time must be able to meet the general goal of maintaining the system behavior according to a set of management conditions predefined by the user. The following subgoals should be met by using the agent knowledge resources:
- Prediction of possible short term external actions scenarios.
- Understanding the possible answers of the system behavior to the different external actions scenarios assuming that the present operation criteria are maintained.
- Identification of actual and foreseeable problems (i.e. differences with respect to final or intermediate management goals).
- Proposal of changes in the current operation strategy to avoid the problems detected as possible.

To meet these subgoals different types of knowledge are required, and different levels for its representation may be conceived. Several knowledge units may be defined for this purpose in a preliminary step:
- A prediction unit to reason about the short term evolution of the external actions, this may be met by a qualitative version of a time series analysis model.
- A simulation unit incorporating models to evaluate the physical behaviors corresponding to the different external actions scenarios.
- A classification unit capable of identification of the type of problems that may happen in the different behavior scenarios.
- A decision unit that allows to reason about the actions to be developed acting on the possible causes of problems or acting on the effects of these problems to be alleviated.

These knowledge units are to be integrated according to the principle of rationality [1] that, in this case, is the use of the different units in the order of presentation in a search tree of the different behavior scenarios. A scenario is defined by a conjunction of values of the attributes characterizing the behavior of the different physical components. Every knowledge unit may be represented at symbolic level by a generic task. The set of component generic tasks, integrated by an inference procedure modeling the principle of rationality, configures a generic task modeling the knowledge of an intelligent decision support agent.

692

As it is shown in the figure 1, a set of feasible short term behavior scenarios may be obtained by the prediction and simulation tasks operation operated sequentially (basic reasoning line in figure 1) using the premises provided by the real time data base. Given that both models are not deterministic, it may happen that this chained task forward reasoning be too expensive because too many scenarios are generated by composition of the partial scenarios generated at each level.

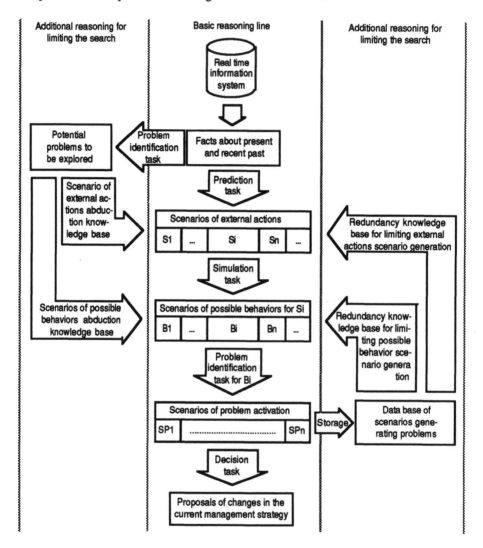

Figure 1: General reasoning for decision support on physical systems management

A real time decision support agent such as this will operate connected with a real time information system about the state of the world in such a way that the present and recent past situation may be known.

Two additional criteria may be introduced to improve this performance by limiting the search spaces:

- *Likelihood.* Scenario ordering based on criteria modeling likelihood. An inertia criterion may be applied if the scenarios are ordered by proximity to the registered trend (i.e. it is more feasible the scenario with minimum differences in its short term behavior changes with respect to the observed trends).
- *Significance.* Knowledge bases may filter at the level of prediction and simulation the possible scenarios by relevance criteria with respect to the management goals. This is an important issue because it may happen that (1) many feasible scenarios be irrelevant from the point of view of the problems to be explored (i.e. if only damage or failure situations are searched the possible short term non problematic behavior scenarios should be pruned). (2) Some behavior scenarios propose situations similar from the point of view of the problems to explore (i.e. the same problems may be presented with the same level of feasibility in different scenarios), producing undesired redundancies.

To meet these objectives additional knowledge must be introduced in the agent:

- To meet the goal of significance a possible solution is the introduction of a shallow behavior representation where adequate constraints for the prediction and simulation tasks may be obtained, by abduction, from the set of possible problems to explore.
- To avoid redundant scenario generation a constraints base may be defined to generate additional limitations to scenario generation taking into account the already deduced scenarios where problems have been detected.

To identify the problems to explore an ad hoc knowledge base, formulated by classification rules, is required for identification of present and potential problems from the information provided by the real time data base about the system state.

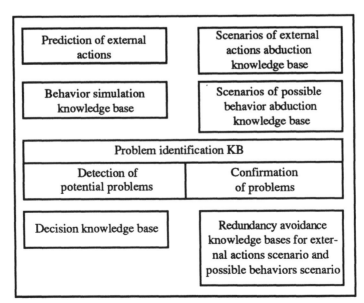

Figure 2: The knowledge components of a decision support agent

694

These additional reasoning activities are shown integrated with the basic reasoning line, commented before, in the figure 1.

The knowledge components of the decision support agent are summarized in the figure 2. This partition of knowledge together with the functional inference relationships to meet the goals of the agent presented in figure 1 show the agent knowledge morphology.

A corresponding generic task may be designed if more specific generic tasks are formulated for the knowledge components and an inference procedure modelling, the general reasoning strategy is formulated. This task is a symbolic level formulation of the agent knowledge, summarized in figure 3.

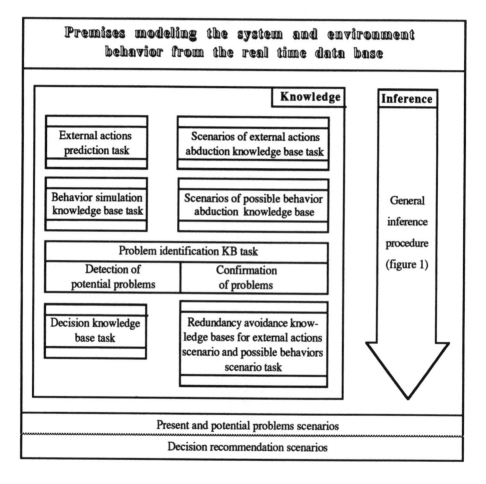

Figure 3: The generic task modeling the decision support agent

All the knowledge bases may be formulated by rules or frames with the exception of the external actions prediction and behavior simulation tasks where the use of existing models must be considered in some way. This requires the discussion of the adequate design approach of the behavior modeling tasks. The following considerations may be established.

Reasoning about prediction of behavior may be symbolized by the macro-rule structure:

$$E(t), A(ti, tn) \Longrightarrow E(tx) \qquad (1)$$

with t, ti, tx, tn representing instants.

t: the present instant.

ti: initial past instant: $ti < t$.

tn: final prediction instant: $t < tn$

tx: intermediate prediction instant: $t \leq tx \leq tn$.

E(z):   physical system state at instant z.

A(ti, tn): External actions between instants ti, tn. These actions may be classified in: (1) registered recent previous actions: A(ti, t) and (2) forecasted, estimated short term actions A(t, tn). This distinction may be interesting when some features of future states may be explained based on past registered actions A(ti, t) which means an economy in uncertainty handling of the predictive aspects of A(t, tn). This is the case of the rainfall-runoff behavior exploration in watersheds where some future flows and water levels are produced by recent, already registered, rainfalls.

The definition of a knowledge based model to explain the relation (1) in physical systems, where complex phenomena may be implied, cannot be approached by the naive method of asking a human expert. The approach to be chosen must take into account that an important amount of work has been done in the field of quantitative simulation models applied to the different engineering problems in such a way that most of the commonsense used by human experts is connected with those existing models. This is the case of predictive hydrology where an important set of models to be applied for the analysis of water behavior problems is available [5]. Those existing models, together with the professional expertise for understanding its use and the problems to be solved, must be the basis for the definition of acceptable knowledge representation approaches.

Three possible modeling strategies may be considered:
- Definition of a common rule based representation of both the physical behavior and the analysis criteria for problem evaluation and decision making.
- Definition of mixed architectures integrating rules, tasks and quantitative models.
- Definition of full qualitative modeling approaches by formulation of qualitative versions of the traditional available quantitative models.

The first option was a reasonable one in the early eighties where qualitative models were just starting. In [6] a general methodology was presented for abstraction of a rule based version of models of physical behavior by using learning techniques based on artificial samples generated previously by quantitative models which were applied to different representative cases.

This approach may produce an important number of rules in order to represent all the possible aspects of behavior with the corresponding effect of lack of insight in the model, given that the rules are as cognitive units too trivial, so in some cases the [7] criticism may be applicable in the sense that huge and not well structured sets of rules may behave as "idiots savants".

This exhaustive rule based approach may be admissible if (1) previous rule format structures are defined by human experts although the rule contents may be obtained by automatic techniques from simulation result samples, (2) the number of rules is manageable and (3) the rules are organized in a modular structure to make them understandable and acceptable by human experts. All these requirements lead to task oriented architectures with rule based knowledge bases created by learning techniques. When this is feasible, this approach may be considered as a good alternative to qualitative modeling.

The second option may have a similar architecture, without requiring the rule-based approximation to models but, rather, the direct use of the existing quantitative models. The main interest of this approach is that the professionals in the field are familiar with the use of the existing quantitative models so it is easy for them to define the knowledge for use and to understand the results provided by these models to solve decision problems.

To make this second option feasible an architecture must be defined for cooperation where knowledge bases for control and generic tasks embodying quantitative models are integrated with general reasoning procedures oriented towards the definition of possible short term behavior patterns.

The inference engine may work in a way similar to the one applied by a human expert with the following steps:

- Reasoning about feasible scenarios of external actions $A(t, tn)$.
- Reasoning about the values of the parameters of the quantitative models.
  These values are usually obtained as a result of the previous work on calibration. The limitations on available data for calibration of the very precise numerical models do not allow a very accurate definition of the parameter values, so usually, a set of value intervals are obtained instead of precise numerical values. The expert's analysis (based on a set of simulation runs) may also define different scenarios of parameter values to be considered according with their perception of the problems to be analyzed (i.e. if a value interval is the domain of feasible values for a parameter they can assume the high values of the interval for some parameters and the low values for others because this is convenient for the objectives of the analysis of a failure).
- Loop of simulation runs of the different alternative scenarios of external actions and parameter values.
- Reasoning about synthesis of the simulation run results, in such a way that qualitative statements may be produced.

The knowledge to build this type of models is available from experts. The main problems of this mixed model is that the number of scenarios to simulate may be significant for efficiency purposes, given that the quantitative simulation runs may require expensive numerical computation

A revised inference procedure may be defined for this second option type of knowledge representation by using additional criteria based on significance pruning as the one proposed before:

- Identification of present and potential short term problems inferred from the registered data with the addition, if possible, of the results of a simulation run of the behavior using as external actions those registered until now (i.e. $A(ti, t)$ in (1)). This additional information from simulation may be interesting when the

process of external actions has inertia enough to make significant the impact of the already registered actions in the short term future behavior.
- Abduction, from the potential problems identified, of present and potential scenario variables domains through the backward processing of a simplified, shallow, model. This makes it possible to constrain the total domains of the scenario variables to the relevant subdomains for the problems to be explored.
- Simulation as in the initial model of the selected, reduced, set of scenarios.

The third behavior representation option is the qualitative simulation approach, a new field developed in the last ten years to deal with physics problems by [8], [9], [10], [11] in already classical papers together with new extensions [12].

A qualitative model generates a set of feasible behaviors in a simulation run and, by application of several runs in some cases, the generation of an envisionment graph as a shallow model of the contiguous behavior relationships is feasible. When complex systems are to be modeled the number of possible behaviors is too large and the number of possible state transitions may be important also, so the envisionment graph is not feasible. A more rational approach is required based on a control knowledge to choose which behavior state transitions must be retained for evaluation and future extension in such a way that only a significant subtree derived from an initial state requires to be analyzed. This is the case in emergency analysis systems where a real time information system provides the initial state and, by qualitative modeling, possible short term problematic future states are to be identified. In those cases the strategic criteria for prediction are represented by control knowledge bases used to recommend choices among the feasible state transitions.

Using qualitative models has as main advantages:
- Advantages in knowledge acquisition. The parameters to be introduced for physical characterization are introduced based on the judgements of the experts that know the physical system. In the quantitative models these qualitative values have to be translated to a set of numerical values representing likely the class represented by a qualitative value.
- Advantages for inference. The qualitative inference procedures (usually constraint satisfaction) are more simple than the numerical ones (usually resolution of huge linear systems) and several numerical computations are required to cover a qualitative domain represented by several numerical values according to the figure 4.
- Advantages for explanation. If the qualitative equations (confluences) are well chosen it is possible to obtain traces for the deduced values of a qualitative model inference step in such a way that the impact of the parameter values and confluences may be understood if necessary. This aspect may not be very significant because, after our experience, the professional expertise of the engineers may understand the meaning of a numerical model results without needing the detailed explanation (useful off line in the model building process) furnished by a qualitative model, in such a way that explanation frames may be activated after the results provided by the quantitative models runs.

The problem of qualitative simulation is the possible generation of spurious behaviors by the inference procedure given that the qualitative knowledge base is more general than the quantitative one. The patterns of predictable behavior obtained by the qualitative branch contain the qualitative generalization of the set of behaviors

698

obtained by the numerical branch as it is shown in the figure 4.

In complex physical systems, such as these, additional heuristics are required to prune the proposals of the qualitative models trying to approach the size of the predictable behavior sets of both branches.

A similar analysis could be done for the external actions prediction task where typical time series analysis techniques are available. Its modeling for real time application may be done by the three possible approaches. An additional model could be added based on a neural network [13] that may be trained off line to obtain a first version and dynamically updated by using the on line information (for instance, in a real time system it could be produced an updated neural net weight values version every hour).

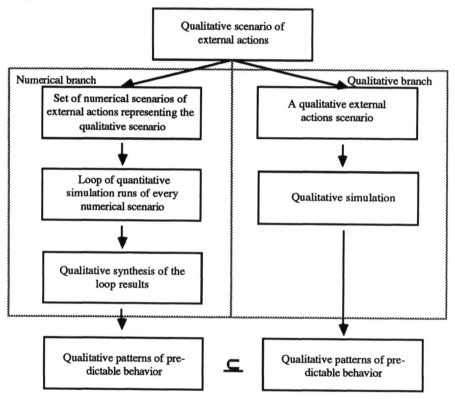

Figure 4: Comparing the two branches of behavior qualitative evaluation

3. THE REAL TIME FLOOD MANAGEMENT PROBLEM

The Spanish Ministry of Public Works has started the SAIH investment program on Automatic Information Systems for Hydrology (Spanish acronym for SAIH). This program has as its main goals the installation of: (1) sensors for rainfall and water levels in the surface of the main Spanish watersheds, (2) a radio network to send the sensor data to the information centre, (3) a software system to give: (a) real time information about water levels and rainfalls, (b) short term prediction of possible problems and recommendable decisions about water control and population information.

The aspect 3.b has been addressed by two architectures for decision support with different approaches for the design of some of its components.

Both models aim to understand the behavior of a set of watersheds under rainfall.

The watershed surface is composed of reception areas that are disjoint surface units with a single outlet for water flow. During rainstorms the outflows drained from reception areas enter the drainage channel network where it can be distinguished the upper basin networks with steep slopes in channels and high water velocities and the final lower river reaches where milder slopes produce slow velocities and possible risk of overflow when storms are present.

Several watersheds may be involved in a flood management problem if they drain to the same floodable river reach in such a way that the flood situations in the reach may be caused by the combined effects of the different watersheds draining on the reach.

According to the general considerations in the paragraph 2, at the knowledge level an agent for flood management may be conceived with the following characteristics:

Goals:
- Prediction of possible short term meteorology scenarios in terms of rainfall in the different areas of the watersheds components of a basin acting on problematic floodable river reaches.
- Prediction of possible behaviors of:
  * Watersheds.
  * Floodable river reaches.
- Identification of present and short term problematic flood situations.
- Proposals of:
  * Dam control actions.
  * Civil defense actions (advice of urban, transport and communication problems).

Knowledge:
- Prediction knowledge based on the understanding of the temporal and spatial structure of the recent registered rainfall.
- Behavior modeling knowledge of (1) the watersheds subject to the predicted rainfall scenarios acting on a known (estimated) physical structure of the watershed, (2) the floodable river reach represented by the water levels along several river reach profiles levels submitted to the watershed draining flows actions.
- Problem identification knowledge, usually of classification type because the possible problems may be known in advance.
- Control decisions knowledge based on the explanation of the predicted problems in the previous step.

The principle of rationality will provide a strategy for using sensibly this knowledge to meet these goal. This may require additional knowledge representing criteria for improving the reasoning effectiveness.

Two symbolic representation approaches have been defined with some common features as the last two items (problem identification and control decision knowledge bases) but with significant differences in prediction and behavior modeling. The CYRAH architecture [14], [15] integrates knowledge based reasoning and quantitative simulation and the SIRAH architecture is based on qualitative modelling.

3.1. The CYRAH Architecture

According to the knowledge level concept of a flood management agent CYRAH proposes the following basic tasks for symbolic level representation:

- A meteorology prediction reasoning task. This task infers the feasible short term rainfall predictions in the different spatial areas considered. The task proposes a set of possible future values affected by a subjective certainty degree.

  The premises for the predictive reasoning are the registered total rainfall in the last 24 hours and the qualitative prediction furnished by the Meteorology Service given to the system by a user dialogue.

  The knowledge base is formulated by rules establishing reasonable spatial and temporal consistency relationships. The rules have been defined summarizing a meteorology study developed for the project. (i.e. if in area A the total rainfall in two hours is X then in the next hour no more than X may be registered or if in the area A the total rainfall during t is X in the neighbour area B, then a rainfall Y may be expected such that Y>15x), together with the personal criteria of experts modeling the strategy for making assumptions in real time flood management.

- Two behavior simulation tasks embedding quantitative models:

  * The SAVEL task uses a physical description data base (figure 5) describing the tree of river reaches (with or without reservoirs embedded in them) for drainage and the set of reception areas where the incidence of rainfall along time is transformed in time series of possible drained flows from every reception area. This physical description includes the parameter values resulting from the calibration previous phase. It may happen that not too precise values be obtained by lack of data so it is possible that some reasoning be required for decision of these parameter values.

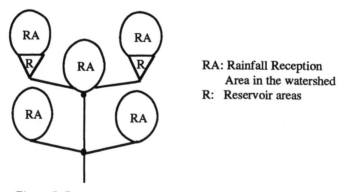

RA: Rainfall Reception
   Area in the watershed
R: Reservoir areas

Figure 5: Drainage structure on a watershed for the SAVEL task

A simulation procedure acts as inference engine when the task is invoked with: (1) a scenario of rainfall time series acting in different reception areas and input flows from upstream basins and (2) an initial state assumption about humidity in areas, and water volume in reservoirs. As a result the predicted flows at the watershed outlet are obtained along time as conclusion of the task.

The inference procedure is based on traditional existing models in the hydrology practice as are the HEC-1 program of US corps of engineers and SWMM of the Environmental Protection Agency (EPA). The theory of this type of models may be found in [5].

* The REBOLSA task uses a physical description of a floodable reach defined by a sequence of profile cross sections and a set of floodable side pockets connected with the main stream by channel links (figure 6).

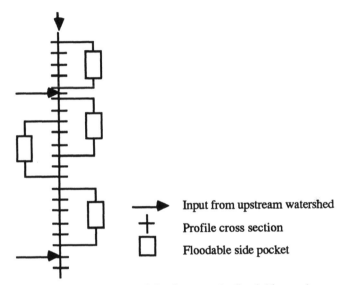

Input from upstream watershed

Profile cross section

Floodable side pocket

Figure 6: The spatial reference of a floodable reach

A simulation procedure acts as inference engine when the task is invoked with (1) a scenario of input flows generated by strategic reasoning about relevant combinations of flows at the outlet of the tributary watersheds from upstream, (2) an initial water level at profiles states and side pockets. As a result the task answers with a short term prediction of the water levels in several significant profiles.

The simulation procedure uses a numerical integration approach to the Saint Venant equations in such a way that every Δt a system of $2n$ linear equations is to be solved (Δt time interval for integration n: no. of profiles). Special equations are developed for floodable side pockets management [5].

- Two interpretation tasks:

    * The input data interpretation task receives as input the time series of measures in the different sensors and produces as output the values of qualitative attributes required for reasoning. This is a large (but simple) knowledge base that generates, for instance, the value of the rainfall in a qualitative scale (low, average, high, very high) based in the rain gages data received as time series. This knowledge base is organized by a set of frames with related attributes, in such a way that some attributes are obtained from measures and others are deduced using methods and rule bases associated with the different slots, modeling consistency and correlation criteria.

    * The problem identification tasks generate the degree of occurrence in different time horizons of several predefined problems types (urban accessibility, road problem, etc.). A knowledge base modeling the general criteria to define every problem prototype and instances of the prototype are generated and complemented for every case. The basic prototype problem frames relating hydrologic behavior attributes such as water levels or flows in river links near to the problem with the attributes about features of the problem are the town and the road link where attributes common to the frame class are defined. At the instance generation step, complementary rules are defined, adapted to the current case study. For the Júcar application 3000 rules for potential problem identification have been defined.

The general reasoning strategy implementing the principle of rationality in the CYRAH generic task has the following steps:

1.- Interpretation of present and recent data received from the real time data base in qualitative form.

2.- Minimal prediction of the near future assuming as external actions the registered rainfall until the present moment with no short term values estimation. To meet this goal a simulation run must be done with the SAVEL task.

3.- Potential problems identification based on the present situation and the minimal prediction defined before. This allows the choice of which of the component basins are to be simulated with future rainfall scenarios: those where present and incipient problems are detected with the minimal prediction.

4.- Simulation of the different selected watersheds: using the SAVEL task with a previous generation of scenarios based on meteorological predictions and the predicted outflows from upstream basins. This generation of scenarios takes into account the relevance for the problems to explore. This step produces as a result a first set of relevant qualitative behaviors of the different watersheds that may be already used for problem evaluation (when only flow values are used in the problem frames) or as input for floodable river reaches simulation (when the floodable river reaches behavior is required).

5.- Simulation of the floodable final river reaches preceded by a reasoning step about relevant watershed inflow combinations (scenarios) generation. As a result of this step the possible behavior in terms of water levels of the floodable river reaches are obtained.

6.- Final problem evaluation, using flows and water levels. The knowledge bases for the different problem types are fired in such a way that possible problems in different time horizons are identified.

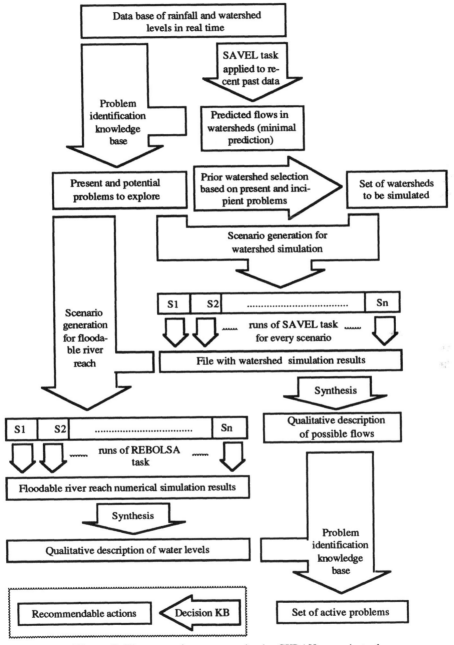

Figure 7: The reasoning strategy in the CYRAH generic task

This reasoning strategy is summarized in figure 7.

The third step is a specific version of the abduction of restrictive criteria for definition of simulation runs based on a previous identification of the relevant problems to be explored. This step of reasoning uses an additional knowledge based task for watershed selection with the following characteristics:

- The premises for the task are the minimal prediction obtained by simulation of past registered rainfalls and the meteorology prediction proposed by the meteorology task.

- A frames and rules knowledge base is defined representing a shallow version of the SAVEL task. The operation of this knowledge base using the premises together with the minimal prediction flow value allows the estimation of short term value range for expected flows at the watershed outlet. If the range of values of the expected flow is below a predefined threshold the watershed will not be retained for simulation.

  This task shows a possible way of cooperation of a shallow version model and the corresponding quantitative model: the shallow version is used for pruning alternatives to be simulated by the quantitative model. The shallow version may be defined by test off-line with the quantitative model in such a way that an adequate filtering criteria be defined.

This approach has as main drawback that once a set of simulation runs is defined the computation of every run may be significantly time consuming and the very precise numerical results are to be synthesized at a qualitative scale. This means a waste of the resources spent in numeric computation. However from the knowledge acquisition point of view this model is quite analog of the professional knowledge state of the art.

Once the concept of representation is specified it is possible the design of a software environment to support the different items of a representation. The figure 8 shows the elements of this environment and the structure of the CYRAH generic task model based on:

- Predefined knowledge units to deal with the knowledge representation and data formulation tasks for model building.

- A set of procedures for knowledge acquisition and inference.

Basic tools for knowledge representation internal to these structures are:

- A rule base management subsystem.

- A subsystem for frame hierarchies management embedding rule bases in the frames for some attributes value definition. The rules are used with backward reasoning with uncertainty management. Every frame may inherit rule bases for attribute value deduction by traversing the hierarchy.

- A relational data base supporting the parameter and structure definition for the simulation tasks.

The general structure of a specific model generic task is presented based on several knowledge unit instantiations and databases representing respectively the criteria for simulation management and problem identification and the data for simulation models.

The user builds a particular instance of a CYRAH model by representing his/her knowledge about the domain using the aforementioned representation tools. Therefore, the user model consists of several instantiations of knowledge units and databases. The watershed model structure consists of a tree-like network, that integrates three types of elements: reception areas, river channels and reservoirs, and an optional floodable reach structure. Watershed description elements are stored in the relational data base structure. These database stores the input data for the simulation tasks and represent the knowledge about the structure of the physical system. Frames are used to characterize objects, such as typical problems, rainfall areas or watersheds, for which some inference has to be done in the different rule bases. These knowledge units represent the criteria for simulation management and problem identification.

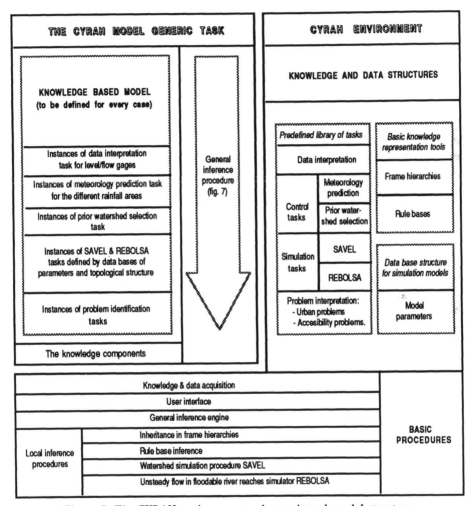

Figure 8: The CYRAH environment and generic task model structure

In figure 8 the set of instances of knowledge units together with the ad hoc complementary rule bases is a version at symbolic level of the knowledge level specification of the intelligent agent for flood management. That means that once such type of modelling is developed the knowledge engineering to build a model is simplified because the environment offers predefined knowledge units near enough to the human experts of the field.

To build a model using the CYRAH environment several additional activities to the traditional approach based on expert interviews are required such as:

- Calibration of quantitative models. Model parameters are estimated in such a way that a convincing representation of basin behavior be obtained. If available, the real-time database information can be used to compare model results with registered data of previous registered flood episodes.
- Based on the quality of the calibration process a first version of the knowledge base for interpretation and control may be defined by traditional knowledge engineering techniques using interviews with human experts.
- The knowledge base for problem identification requires a previous study based on (1) population surveys about the importance of past flood damages and (2) theoretical estimation of potential impacts based on topographical analysis of problem areas subjected to several hypothesis of water levels. These procedures may produce a set of potential impacts connected with the possible water levels or watershed outflows generated by the different simulation runs.

The CYRAH environment was programmed on top of the UNIX operating system in the C language. The implementation required about 80.000 lines of source code. Object oriented design methodology was used in such a way that a primary object library for basic operations on traditional information structures such as strings, list, graphs, etc, was implemented. More advanced objects where formulated to implement the computation of the different generic tasks involved in a model design.

The user interface was developed using X-windows libraries and a data base management system with SQL language was used to keep and manage the data bases of physical structure and model parameters. The simulation models SAVEL and REBOLSA were previously available, written in the FORTRAN language, and only its connection to the data base had to be programmed.

Ten first versions of models have been developed within the CYRAH environment and installed on line with the S.A.I.H. data collection system to be experimented by the Júcar Water Authority of Valencia. Each model corresponds to a group of interrelated watersheds, including several (of the order of twenty) floodable areas with various degrees of complexity.

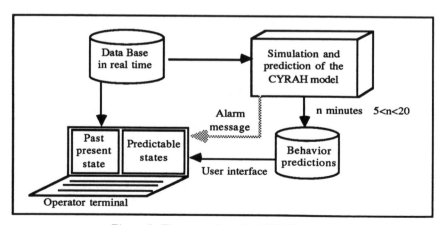

Figure 9: The operation of a CYRAH model

The system operation is fired by operator requests for a specific basin. The corresponding CYRAH model is set to work in background in such a way that every n minutes (5<n<20) a report is produced on the relevant behavior features and problem predictions in the next 4 hours. If the CYRAH model foresees flood problems in the area, it sends an alarm message to an operator terminal. Figure 9 summarizes this operation: At any time the operator can inspect the behaviors and problems predicted as possible by using the operator interface.

Also a specific problem report can be displayed with several screens. Those screens show for several time horizons the villages or cities with possible flood problems, the villages or cities with access problems and the road sections where cuts by water impacts may be expected. Every statement is affected with qualitative uncertainty measures such as "almost certainly", "possibly", "there are signs", etc.

3.2. The SIRAH Architecture

An alternative approach to model at the symbolic level the knowledge functionalities of the flood management agent is to represent the behavior by a set of qualitative models in substitution of the *SAVEL and REBOLSA quantitative models + model management rule base* of the CYRAH approach.

A tree structure of physical components in the sense of [16] may be used to describe the behavior scenarios of a watershed where the stuff flowing between components is water. The tree structure allows to find consistent behavior solutions by a propagation of actions between the models of the different components.

Using qualitative models in this context means that a set of possible behavior scenarios may be obtained from a qualitative reasoning unit that may be input for reasoning about behavior of another physical entity connected with the previous one. Given that qualitative simulation generates sets of feasible state transitions in a physical system it is required, to keep the process on manageable limits, the filtering of the interactions between physical components by using not only units for behavior modeling but also knowledge units for generation of scenarios to be simulated in one component after the predicted behavior of the upstream components, oriented toward the search simplification by definition of goal significant behaviors. .

In summary two basic types of knowledge modules may be defined to deal with the problems of decomposable behavior based on a tree of flows between components:

- *Basic Simulation Tasks* (BST), representing the response of the different physical elements integrating a flow system.
  Every BST module is defined by a task with:
  * The attribute premises for the internal reasoning process (permanent attributes and time variables attributes).
  * The attribute conclusions, set of possible values of state variables to be used for building reasonable scenarios for the next BSTs.
  * A knowledge base defined by rules and constraint confluences for qualitative modeling of behavior.
  * An inference engine to reason, using the knowledge base, from premises to conclusions.

There may be an additional knowledge base to help in the creation phase to infer also advanced characteristics attributes useful for the real time reasoning from more primary attributes given by the user.

- *Scenario Generation Tasks* (SGT), representing the knowledge to generate the input flow scenarios for a given type of BST from the output scenarios generated by the other BSTs upstream. These SGTs have a general structure based on:
  * Attribute premises: possible values of every scenario component and significant values of every pattern of final behavior to be regressed.
  * Attribute results: lists of every feasible combination that makes a scenario.
  * Knowledge bases for: (1) Modeling conditions to constrain the scenarios to be relevant for the final behavior prefixed patterns (i.e. if it is possible to abduce from the problem patterns to be explored, criteria for constraining the scenario generation). (2) Modeling conditions for spatio-temporal consistency of the predictions belonging to the same scenario.
  * An inference engine: for reasoning in two steps: (1) to generate, using its knowledge bases, consistent sets of possible values of every scenario variable. (2) to generate scenarios defined by combinations of the inferred possible values of scenario variables that are consistent with both knowledge bases.

The BST and SGT to be defined depend of the decomposition of the behavior understanding. For the SIRAH system three main BSTs have been considered according to the role of the components of a watershed:

- *Reception area* (RA) to model the behavior of an area submitted to rainfall and producing as a result flows to be drained by the transport network.
- *Upper basin network* (UBN) to model the fast flow river network behavior in the upper basins where the flows generated in the tributary reception areas are concentrated producing surface flows. These flows produce impacts in the low basin floodable river reaches.
- *Floodable river reach* (FRR) to model the water levels behavior in the low basin floodable river reaches submitted to different flows produced by the upper basin networks.

The knowledge of these BST is structured according with the BST general format defined before.

Three SGT types have been defined:

- The *meteorological scenario generation* task to infer possible significant goal combinations of local rainfall predictions acting upon the set of reception areas.
- The *flow transport scenario generation* task to infer the relevant combinations of input flows to the upper basin networks from the reception areas.
- The *floodable river reach scenario generation* task to infer the combination of output flows from the upper basin river networks draining to the floodable river reach.

These general tasks have to be complemented by an ad hoc knowledge for potential problems identification.

The general reasoning procedure for using these basic knowledge units has as main steps:

a) Use of an ad hoc knowledge base for real time data interpretation to identify the present problems and the potential future problems. To explore the feasibility of these future problems this knowledge base defines patterns of final behavior to be explored by the predictive reasoning (i.e. potential problems to be explored may be defined if in some places levels are high but still not problematic levels or they are low but the rate of level change is important etc.)

b) Use of the meteorological scenario generation task to propose possible future rainfall scenarios on the surface of the basin that may be relevant for the problems to be explored generated in a). These scenarios are generated in order of proximity to the existing registered trend and only the first is retained.

c) A depth first search process of qualitative simulations along the different physical elements is produced:

    * The first meteorological scenario is introduced as input to the set of reception area task modules.

    * A first scenario of input flows is generated from the predicted flows drained from the reception areas for the UBNs.

        -. The scenario of upper basin network inflows is introduced as input to the set of river networks in upper basins.

        .- A set of upper basins outflow scenarios relevant for the problem to be explored is generated to be introduced as input to floodable river reach tasks.

    * Simulation of scenarios by the floodable river reach task.

Once a set of behaviors (flows and water levels) is obtained in this process the exploration of the next scenarios for rain or upper basin flows or outflows is decided based on a reasoning step that uses as premises the already obtained behaviors and the current patterns of final behavior to be explored. The knowledge to avoid these redundances may be include in the problem identification knowledge. With the scenarios generated in this way a new depth first traversal is done from b) or c). This process is repeated until some SGT generate no feasible scenarios or a previously defined time period or number of iterations is met.

As in the CYRAH approach a shallow version of the concepts of the models may allow the definition of a model that, by abduction, may obtain the possible values of the premises consistent with the predefined problems to explore. In the figure 10 the relationships of this process at the different levels with the exploration tree of scenario generation and simulation, are shown.

This inference procedure is the representation of the principle of rationality in a generic task with knowledge components of the different task types complemented by ad hoc knowledge base for problem identification. It is in fact an adaptation to the problem specificity of the general concept displayed in the figure 1.

Building a SIRAH knowledge model requires the following steps:

- Formulation of the knowledge bases for problem identification and for definition of the relevant patterns of behavior to be explored at the different levels.

- Formulation of a set of BST modules representing the different physical elements.

- Formulation of the SGT's

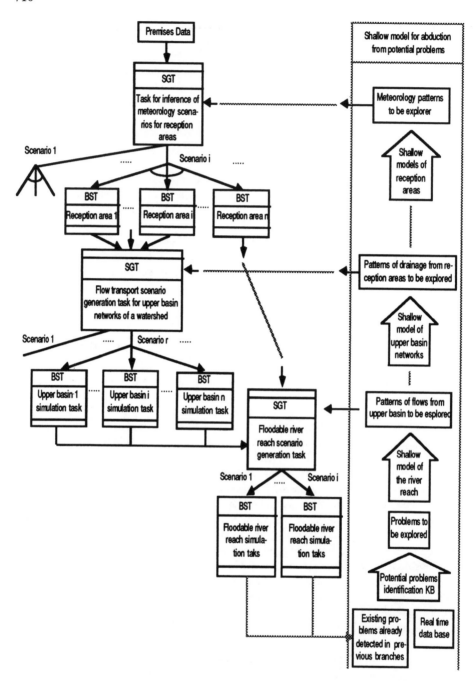

Figure 10: Reasoning tree for SIRAH behavior prediction

- Formulation of the knowledge bases for inference of dams control criteria and civil defense recommendations similar to the ones proposed for the CYRAH models.

To build this type of models given that general features of the knowledge required are known a software SIRAH environment was defined providing predefined elements and procedures to support this building process. The elements provided are:

* A library of task modules for physical behavior modeling of the three types presented before in such a way that it is possible to have different alternative tasks modules in the library to deal with the same concept. These task modules include formal knowledge bases defined by formal constraints and/or rules relating different attributes. The domains of attribute values and the instantiation of the formal rules to specific rules or constraints relating attribute values must be done by the user at the time of building a model for a case study.
* A basic knowledge representation environment (frames, rules and constraints) to allow the definition of the two ad hoc knowledge bases for:
  .- Identification of present problems and patterns of final behavior to explore.
  .- Future problems and control decisions and civil defense recommendations.
  .- Shallow models for abduction of patterns to explore at the different levels of scenario generation.
* A knowledge acquisition procedure to guide the user in the creation of a model.
* A General inference engine for the task reasoning.
* An explanation facility using a trace file generated by the general inference engine if the trace mode execution is used.
* A user interface.

In the figure 11 the structure of a SIRAH generic task model is shown together with the facilities provided by the SIRAH environment. The model structure is a symbolic representation of the knowledge level structure of the flood management agent, in the aspects of physical behavior understanding and problem definition. This structure is a more understandable one than the one provided by CYRAH because the knowledge embodied in the SAVEL and REBOLSA task as a block is now explained by the qualitative models of its components and its relationships.

The modular knowledge architecture such as the one proposed for SIRAH may be computed by object oriented software approach designing for every knowledge module an object to compute its operation and to allow its creation and validation.

4. THE REAL TIME TRAFFIC CONTROL PROBLEM

This is an area where the experimentation with knowledge based systems may produce significant improvements. This is possible because short term congestion may be predicted in such a way that it is possible the introduction of preventive actions such as traffic rerouting or traffic retention when the network structure offers these possibilities.

712

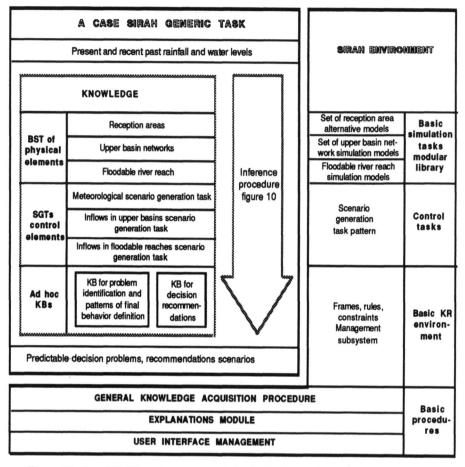

Figure 11: The SIRAH environment and the SIRAH generic task model structure

The knowledge based architecture allows the experimentation with several knowledge base versions of the control criteria to be applied dynamically to the traffic evolution in real time in such a way that a final version be obtained of the knowledge base well fitted to the real time requirements to follow up the traffic evolution in a specific zone.

The traffic control problem is different from the flood management but the same top down methodology may be applied to design a suitable knowledge structure: first a knowledge level description of an ideal agent for solving this type of problems and, after, a symbolic representation is defined in several refinement steps.

The knowledge level characteristics of an agent for decision support in traffic control are the following ones:

Goals:
- Identification of present and potential congestion problems.
- Proposals of changes in the present traffic control strategy.

Knowledge:
- Problem identification knowledge.
- Traffic behavior short term modeling at different levels:
    * Traffic generation in the network areas where traffic may have the origin.
    * Traffic attraction in the areas where traffic may have its destination.
    * Traffic distribution, i.e. the way users choose paths from origins to destinations.
    * Traffic dynamics, when the flow is produced at a high speed (motorways or urban belt-ways) and a real time follow up of the flow dynamic conditions is required.
- Traffic control decisions, based on the present and predictable problem states the agent must be able to generate proposals for changes in the current signal control strategy.

The symbolic representation of these different knowledge types is based on the concepts of [17] with the following modules:

Problem identification tasks

For every problem type a frame may be defined with embodied knowledge for evaluation of the problem frame belief attribute in such a way that, given a traffic data situation defined by the present state and the recent evolution of flows and signals three possible conclusions may be obtained as values of the problem frame belief attribute: (1) the *problem does not happens*, (2) the *problem may happen* and should be confirmed by a deep behavior analysis and (3) *the problem happens*.

Two modes of inference may be considered: (a) the one commented before based on the present situation and recent past evolution and (b) the confirmative mode where attributes of short term predictable behavior obtained from the deep analysis allow a more precise decision.

In the cases where the shallow problem identification model proposes the option (2), once the deep analysis is performed the belief attribute value will be changed to (1) or to a new value: (4) *the problem will happen*.

The knowledge included in the task is a set of facts representing the physical description of the transport infrastructure (i.e. the network) and a shallow model of traffic behavior for the problem identification using as premises the traffic state and the facts representing the network structure.

The conclusion of the task is the value of the problem belief attribute together with the corresponding explanation. The explanation must include causes related to control decisions to be used by the task for traffic control reasoning.

Deep analysis of behavior tasks

The goal of this task type is the prediction of patterns of behavior of a traffic area based on models of the two possible physical systems: a motorway axis or an urban network.

To control a motorway it is required to maintain the fluidity of traffic flow to get a maximum efficiency in the use of these, very expensive, infrastructures. The deep analysis knowledge uses a qualitative model of the dynamic behavior of flows along the motorway axis with the external actions the time series short term prediction modeling of the output and input flow nodes in such a way that congestion sections may be predicted. The reasoning model uses a shock wave numerical model integrated with knowledge bases similar to the CYRAH approach:

- Scenario generation of external actions to be simulated: given the answers of the combination of the different node proposals is a scenario (in the case of not well calibrated parameters in the shock wave model it is possible that parameter scenarios be defined complementarily to those of external actions in such a way that a complementary scenario be a combination of reasonable hypotheses on internal behavior parameters such as capacity or user reaction to signals).
- Scenario simulation. Taking as a basis the initial state and the external actions scenarios a next 20 minutes simulation is computed using the quantitative model, producing the set of behavior scenarios.
- Synthesis of results. Once a significant set of relevant scenarios is simulated, interval values of the flow are chosen for problem evaluation.

An alternative approach has been developed using qualitative modeling of the traffic flow equations in [4].

To control an urban network the dynamic flow fluidity in the car drivers management is not required because the traffic lights produce a stop and go behavior. To increase efficiency it is necessary to allow, by using the signal control, an adequate use of the network by users that may choose alternative paths to their destinations. The reasoning model to be applied has as main steps:

- Identification of the current use of the network paths by the traffic entering the network. This is an abductive reasoning step from the observed flows in the network link and the input and output flows to obtain reasonable consistent assumptions of path choice criteria in the users among the network paths for every couple of origin destination (O-D) nodes.
- Prediction of origins short term traffic generation and destination short term traffic attractions, this may be done by extrapolation of registered trends taking into account the statistics of the previously registered daily structure of traffic. Based on this structure of total traffic predicted in origins and the predicted evolution of attractions an estimate of the O-D matrix may be inferred evaluated by predicted short term value intervals for every couple O-D.
- Short term prediction of behavior assuming as plausible path choices of every couple O-D traffic flow estimate the ones inferred in the first step. As a result interval values of flow in significant links for problem evaluation may be obtained. Also the estimated O-D composition of flow may be obtained that may be used for explanation and subsequent reasoning in traffic control.

If in the motorway a congestion is predicted a similar method (more simple because the graph has no loops in this case) origin structure may be obtained for problem explanation.

In summary, the deep behavior analysis tasks may be designed one for motorways and another for urban networks both of them proposing as a final result the predicted flows with its corresponding explanatory short term O-D structure to be used for traffic control purposes.

Traffic control task

This task receives as input the problems identified together with its plausible explanations (obviously it may happen that a problem has several different explanations). Two possible options for reasoning about traffic control may be considered:

- Design of a set of rules allowing to infer changes in signals with significant effects on the problem causes given by the explanations. These rules will be proposed by experts and tested off line with respect to a simulation model.
- Design of a generate and test loop with the two steps:
    * Use of a rule or constraints base to generate a set of plausible changes in the current strategy.
    * Test of the changes set by a step of qualitative simulation and simplified problem evaluation.

After the loop a more refined set of proposals of changes may be obtained. The models to be used in the test phase may be the same used for the deep analysis of behavior.

The second approach may be necessary when the area structure is too complex for definition in a previous analysis using simulators of the rule set. Again, it is remarkable that in both approaches an adequate modeling of behavior is required. In the first approach it is used off line and in the second approach it is used on line integrated in the reasoning procedure.

The traffic agent modeling

Using these knowledge units a first version of the agent knowledge generic task model may be defined for a given traffic network by the following elements:

- Several problem identification task.
- One deep behavior analysis task for the urban network or for the motorway depending of the type of infrastructure.
- One traffic control task.

The general reasoning strategy of the task uses these knowledge units by a procedure with the following steps:

- Problems identification by calling the different tasks. As a result, a set of problems may be happening, now other set is discarded, and another set is retained for deep analysis because they may happen in the short term.
- If deep analysis is required the corresponding deep behavior task is called and a set of possible short term behavior scenarios is obtained with explanations.

716

- The scenarios proposed by the deep behavior task are introduced as additional premises to the problem tasks retained for deep analysis. As a result it is obtained a final decision for the problems: some of them may be discarded and others will be retained as feasible in short term.
- The set of retained problems together with its potential explanations are introduced as premises in the traffic control task that will produce as conclusion a set of proposals for changes in the current traffic control strategy.

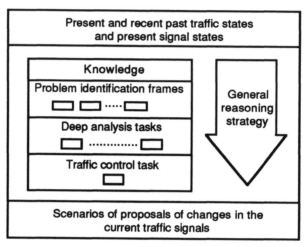

Figure 12: The single area traffic control agent generic task structure

This first version of the agent implementation summarized in figure 12 is acceptable if the knowledge definition to be introduced in the different tasks is feasible. However, if the network is a complex one including belt motorways and urban congestion areas this knowledge structuring may be too flat to embody the understanding of these too complex structures. In these cases a new structuring level should be defined based on local problem areas with a manageable complexity for such type of models. A more adequate model should be based in two type of tasks:

- The Local Problem Area (LPA) task, responsible for understanding the problems and proposing traffic signal changes to solve these local problems.
- The Coordination Task, responsible for reception of the local proposals and reasoning to propose integrated and consistent traffic signal changes scenarios.

The internal structure of a LPA task is the same as the general one proposed before, structured by the following subtasks:

- A set of problem identification subtasks,
- A deep behavior analysis subtask,
- A local traffic control subtask,

with an internal inference engine similar to the one described before for the unique agent approach.

The coordination task includes a constraint knowledge base allowing to generate consistent alternatives of changes in the current strategy. This generation is done by taking into account conditions of spatial continuity and temporal continuity acceptable by the traffic behavior in the total network where the different LPAs subnetworks are embedded. The proposed alternatives of changes are presented in order of level of change implicit in the proposed modifications (i.e. the alternatives with minimal changes with respect the current control strategy state are proposed).

When different tasks propose for a signal contradictory advices the combination of both alternatives is suppressed in favour of alternative options, when no other options are possible from both alternatives the coordination tasks reasons to make a reasonable intermediate choice.

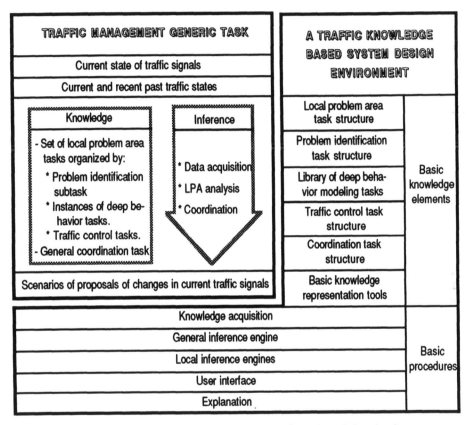

Figure 13: Multi-area traffic management generic task model and software environment required to support its design and operation

An alternative coordination model could be designed based on cooperation among LPAs, in this case the coordination task identifies inconsistencies and informs to the contradictory LPAs that may answer with alternative options.

A new generic task model based on these concepts will be described by:
- A set of LPAs, built by integration of instances, complemented, of the behavior tasks predefined in a library and specific problem identification and traffic control tasks adapted to the physical characteristics of a part of the total traffic network.

This approach allow the use of specialized behavior tasks, some based on motorways and others based on predefined network structure.
- A coordination task modeling the criteria about integration and conflict resolution.
- A general inference engine with the following steps:
    * Reception of data from the network (a possible data validation and completion task may be considered).
    * Call to the different LPAs. Different possible scenarios may be obtained as answers:
        .- Areas without problems where the current strategy may be maintained.
        .- Areas with significant problems (actual or short term) where several local changes scenarios are proposed for the current strategy.
    * Call to the coordination task with the different local proposals. A set of consistent changes may be proposed for the current traffic control strategy to be supervised by human operators or a message passing process according to rules for cooperation may be fired to meet some final consensus proposals.

The structure of models and possible software environment is presented in the figure 15. This type of approach to modeling is being applied in Spain for control in several cities [18] and is now in course of design for the EEC DRIVE program project named KITS [19].

5. CONCLUSIONS

A general methodology to approach the design of knowledge based systems for decision support has been presented.

This approach has emerged after the experience in the design of real world applications where the size of the problems to be addressed has lead to hybrid representations with multilevel reasoning and modular structure for the knowledge with different knowledge representation techniques cooperating to meet the application goals.

The final resulting configuration of models is an integration of data, knowledge and inference procedures at several levels adapted to the problem solving concepts of the cases studied. This may be considered as an alternative approach to software system design, that now may be conceived based on successive abstractions of reasoning level for an agent with the corresponding knowledge structures in the level. This may be also understood as a generalization and improvement of both the traditional computing paradigms based on data + algorithms abstraction and the first knowledge based systems generation approaches based on uniform reasoning single level knowledge structures.

In fact the final implementation of the examples described is being developed by designing an object structured software environment capable of performing the computations required by the operation of the task model showing the correspondance between the Artificial Intelligence approaches to knowledge structuring and the present software approach to computation traditional structuring.

6. REFERENCES

1. Newell A.: "The Knowledge Level" In Artificial Intelligence Vol 18 pp 87-127.

2. Chandrasekaran B.: "Towards a Taxonomy of Problem Solving Types" A.I. Magazine 4 (1) 9-17, 1983.

3. Chandrasekaran, B.: "Generic Tasks in Knowledge Based Reasoning: High Level Building Blocks for Expert Systems Design" IEEE Expert, 1986.

4. Cuena J.: "Knowledge-Based Systems for Aid in Decision-Making: Methodology and Examples" included in "Perspectives in Artificial Intelligence" vol. 1, 73-92. (Campbell J.A., Cuena J. eds.) Ellis Horwood, 1989.

5. Chow V.T., Maidment D.R., Mays L.W.: "Applied Hydrology" Chap. 10. Mc Graw Hill, 1988.

6. Cuena J.: "Building Expert Systems Based on Simulation Models: An Essay on Methodology" included in "Expert System Applications (Bolc, Coombs eds). Springer Verlag, 1988.

7. Winston P.H.: "The commercial Debut of Artificial Intelligence" in "Applications of Expert Systems" Quinlan J.R. (ed) Addison Wesley, 1987.

8. Hayes P.J.: "The Naive Physics Manifesto" in Michie D. (ed) "Expert Systems in the Microelectronic Age". Edinburgh University Press, 1979.

9. De Kleer, J., Brown, S.: "A Qualitative Physics Based on Confluences" Artificial Intelligence 24. Elsevier Science Publishers B.V. (North Holland) 1984, 7-83.

10. Forbus K.D.: "Qualitative Process Theory" Artificial Intelligence 24, 85-108, 1984.

11. Kuipers B.J.: "Qualitative Simulation" Artificial Intelligence 29, 289-338.

12. Weld M., De Kleer J.: "Readings in Qualitative Physics" Morgan Kaufmann, 1990.

13. Weigend A.S., Huberman B.A., Rumelhart D.R.: "Predicting the Future: A Connectionist Approach" Technical Report SSL-90-20, Xerox Palo Alto Research Center (1990).

14. Alonso M., Cuena J., Molina M.: "SIRAH: An Architecture for a Professional Intelligence". Proc.9th European Conference on Artificial Intelligence (ECAI'90). Pitman, 1990.

15. Cuena J., Molina M., Garrote L.: "An Architecture for Cooperation of Knowledge Bases and Quantitative Models: The CYRAH Environment". XI International Workshop on Expert Systems. Special conference on Second Generation Expert Systems. Avignon'91. EC2, 1991.

16. De Kleer, J., Brown, S.: "A Qualitative Physics Based on Confluences" Artificial Intelligence 24. Elsevier Science Publishers B.V. (North Holland) 1984, 7-83.

17. Cuena J.: "Intelligent Systems for Traffic Flow Management: A Qualitative Modeling Approach" International Journal of Intelligent Systems, Vol 7, 133-153, 1992.

18. Cuena J., Martín G., Molina M.: "An Architecture for Knowledge Based Traffic Management for the EXPO-92 Sevilla Urban Ring". Proc. Second International OECD Workshop on Knowledge-Based Expert Systems in Transportation. Montreal, June1992.

19. Cuena J., Ambrosino G., Boero M.: "A General Knowledge-Based Architecture for Traffic Control: The KITS Approach". Proc. International Conference on Artificial Intelligence Applications in Transportation Engineering. San Buenaventura, California. June 1992.

MODEL-K for prototyping and strategic reasoning at the knowledge level

Werner Karbach and Angi Voß

German National Research Institute for Computer-Science (GMD)
AI Research Division
Postfach 1316
D-5205 Sankt Augustin, FRG
e-mail: karbach@gmdzi.gmd.de; avoss@gmdzi.gmd.de

Abstract. To close the gap between knowledge level and symbol level, the MODEL-K language allows to specify KADS conceptual models and to refine them to operational systems. Since both activities may be arbitrarily interleaved, early prototyping is supported at the highest level. Systems written in MODEL-K contain their conceptual model, making them more transparent, easier to communicate to the expert, to explain to the user, and to maintain by the knowledge engineer.
The strategy layer of KADS is supposed to control and possibly repair the activities being modeled by the lower layers. MODEL-K views this kind of strategic reasoning as a meta-activity. In the REFLECT project, we came to view meta-activities like resource-management or competence assessment as ordinary problem solving methods, that in turn can be described using KADS. Correspondingly, we extended MODEL-K to model and operationalize such meta-activities. In particular, the lower three layers and the system they model are automatically kept consistent due to the construction of MODEL-K[1].

1 Motivation

Combining modeling and rapid prototyping In the development of knowledge-based systems there is a recognizable shift from the traditional rapid prototyping approach to model-based approaches. The need for explicit and higher-level descriptions of problem solving methods arose in knowledge acquisition [40] [20], in attempts to reuse knowledge bases [5] and in research on explanations [22] and tutoring [9]. Newell [23] argued that the "knowledge level" is the right level for these purposes.

All model-based approaches to problem solving fall into one of two categories: Either they provide a universal framework to specify arbitrary problem solving

---

[1] This work is part of a research project partially funded by the Esprit Basic Research Programme of the Commission of the European Communities as project number 3178. The partners in this project are the University of Amsterdam (NL), the German National Research Institute for Computer-Science GMD (D), the Netherlands Energy Research Foundation ECN (NL), and BSR-Consulting(D).

methods which are not operational, or they provide a specialized but operational framework (for a detailed comparison see [17]). As a representative of the
first category, KADS [40] [4] proposed a strict separation between knowledge
analysis and implementation. The output of the first phase is a (paper-based) 4-
layered conceptual model describing the expertise. To implement such a model, a
completely separate design model is to be developed. As a consequence, the model of the analysis phase and the implementation are completely disconnected.
Therefore it may be difficult to recognize the model in the system, to transfer
modifications from the model to the system or vice versa, and to explain the
behaviour of the system in terms of the model.

Representatives of the second category are operational systems having an
underlying model of the special task they perform. Examples are SALT, MORE
and others described in [20], the generic task languages CSRL for diagnosis [6]
and DSPL for design [7], shells like MED2/D3 [25] and the knowledge acquisition
tool generator of [21]. As their models are mostly described verbally, it is difficult
to compare the suitability of these systems for the problem at hand. Moreover,
the systems can hardly be adapted or combined, since the paradigms are different
and the knowledge level model is not exactly reflected.

What we need is both, a framework which allows us to conceptualize our
very first ideas on how to approach an arbitrary problem, and to refine these
ideas stepwise to the extent as our pervasion of the problems grows until all
operational details are filled in. Thus an operational model is obtained by successive refinements of the conceptual description. This allows prototyping cycles
as early as any partial model is executable.

The idea of operational descriptions is not completely new. In conventional
software engineering, the executable specifications serve a similar purpose: a very
abstract, formal specification is stepwise refined until an executable algorithmic
specification or rewrite system is obtained [3]. The advantages of prototyping in
software development are described in [13].

The MODEL-K language to be presented in this article allows to model and
operationalize KADS' models of expertise. Several such languages have been put
forward by now. ML^2 [33] and FORKADS [38] are logic-based, KARL [12] maps
into entity relationship descriptions, logic, and an ordinary control language.
OMOS [18], like MODEL-K, translates into BABYLON [8]. Not for KADS, but
for the components of expertise approach, [34] developed an architecture on top
of KRS that establishes a close correspondence between a knowledge level model
and its operationalization. In fact, this approach inspired us to more clearly
distinguish between the conceptual model and its operational refinement.

Strategic and meta-reasoning The need for meta-reasoning in knowledge
based systems was recognized very early in the AI community [31] [10], [11].
Strategic control, assessing and improving one's own competence, detecting deadends in problem solving, tutoring about, or explaining a knowledge based system are typical meta-activities. Although specific systems like HACKER [31],
TERESIAS [11], REASON [28], MOLGEN [30] and PDP [16] were built, a ge-

neral framework for incorporating meta-reasoning into knowledge-based systems is missing.

KADS introduced the strategy layer in its conceptual models in order to cope with this kind of knowledge. However, the notions at this level were so vague that it was hardly ever used and was often mixed up with the task layer. Since the strategy layer dynamically reasons *about*, controls and possibly repairs the lower layers, these layers must be causally connected to their implementation, the so-called object system. A causal connection is a mechanism guaranteeing consistency between the object system and its model. In particular, any progress in the object system must be reflected upwards, and any modifications of the model by the strategic layer must be reflected downwards [19].

An object system built in MODEL-K ideally suits these purposes, since the running system incorporates its own model. Thus consistency between object model and object system is automatically guaranteed by the MODEL-K interpreter.

Other than in computational reflection, the object model consisting of the three lower KADS layers hides any implementation details. They are irrelevant since the kind of meta-reasoning going on at the strategic layer is at the knowledge level [2]. In fact, our work in the REFLECT project [37] [27] revealed that meta-activities like competence assessment and improvement or resource management, although having another computational system as their domain, can be interpreted as generic problem solving methods and can be modeled like any ordinary object level methods. For example, competence assessment can basically be regarded as a diagnosis task.

In the REFLECT project we elaborated these ideas into a framework for "knowledge level reflection". Not only did we extend KADS models of expertise to include a meta-model at the strategy layer, but we also extended MODEL-K to interwovenly specify and implement such meta-models. In fact, the necessary additions were almost straightforward and involved only a few important design decisions.

In the following sections, we will first describe "ordinary MODEL-K" using an office room allocation problem, and later discuss the strategy layer and the meta-level extensions.

2 MODEL-K for object systems

Figure 1 sketches the MODEL-K framework. We distinguish the conceptual model and its operational refinement. Both are described on three layers: domain, inference and control layers. In the conceptual model, the domain layer describes the domain structure in terms of concepts and relations, the inference layer determines the inference structure in terms of knowledge sources, i.e. basic operators and metaclasses, and the control layer specifies the control structure in terms of tasks. In the operational refinement, concepts are supplemented by their instances, relations by their tuples, knowledge sources by their bodies, i.e. executable pieces of code, and tasks by their control statements. For the

724

connection between inference and domain layer, the same distinction is made with built-in default operational refinements. Although syntactically separated, conceptual modelling and operational refinement can be arbitrarily interwoven during knowledge engineering.

Beside the static description of the problem-solver, MODEL-K provides an explicit representation of the dynamic status of system while problem solving: an agenda contains the pending tasks, and the metaclasses contain the variable data that are manipulated by the knowledge sources

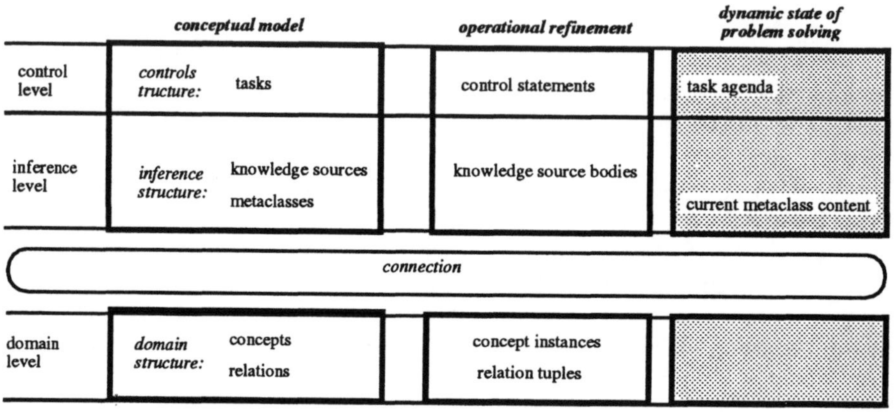

	conceptual model		*operational refinement*	*dynamic state of problem solving*
control level	*controls tructure:*	tasks	control statements	task agenda
inference level	*inference structure:*	knowledge sources, metaclasses	knowledge source bodies	current metaclass content
	connection			
domain level	*domain structure:*	concepts, relations	concept instances, relation tuples	

Fig. 1. The MODEL-K framework.

MODEL-K has strongly been influenced by the conceptual models of the KADS knowledge acquisition methodology [4]. In contrast to KADS, MODEL-K separates the definition of concepts and their specific instances, of relations and their tuples, and of tasks and their control statements. KADS models neither have a precise syntax nor are they executable at all. Consequently, any dynamic aspects of problem solving are ignored either. Like KADS, MODEL-K supports the exchange of individual layers. In particular, splitting off the domain layer yields a generic model or system, respectively. In the Esprit Basic Research Action REFLECT [27] [1] we extended both, KADS models of expertise and MODEL-K to incorporate strategic reasoning at a meta-level. This will be the topic of the second part of this article.

MODEL-K is implemented on top of BABYLON, GMD's hybrid knowledge representation workbench which provides – beside prolog and lisp – rule, frame, and constraint formalisms for the definition of the operational parts [8].

2.1 The office allocation application

Planning the arrangement of employees on a floor is a time-consuming process, especially if personnel movement is high as in research institutes. To reach a

satisfactory solution all criteria for a fertile working climate should be considered, e.g. dense communications between projects, proximity of central services,
equipment requirements and personal characteristics like smoker aversion.

Given a floorplan with a partial assignment of possible rooms to some employees, and a set of requirements, the office allocation task consists of assigning
rooms to all employees satisfying all requirements.

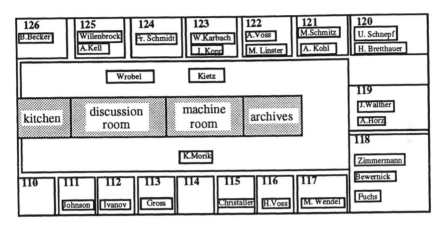

Fig. 2. An office allocation problem.

We treat the problem as an assignment problem where a set of objects, the
employees, have to be assigned to another set, the rooms, so as to satisfy the given requirements. We successively match requirements with employees obtaining
a constraint network with employees as variables and possible rooms as their values. Global propagation followed by a filtering yields all possible solutions, in
case the problem is not overspecified.

The conceptual model of the office allocation problem can be transferred to
other domains. For example, in hotel room reservation, the components are the
guests and the slots are hotel rooms, in hospital bed allocation the components
are the patients and the slots are beds, and in school time table construction,
the components are the instruction units and the slots are time intervals.

2.2 The conceptual model

The control layer

At the control layer the flow of control between the knowledge sources is defined in terms of tasks. Tasks may be decomposed into subtasks and knowledge
sources. For documentation purposes, a precondition and a goal may be specified. The main task of OFFICE-PLAN consists of an initialize step to select the

726

components and slots, a step to generate conditions from the generic requirements and an subtask to solve the conditions. Figure 3 shows the entire task
decomposition tree.

```
(TASK office-plan
    WITH PRECONDITION = true
         GOAL          = find-an-arrangement
         SUBTASKS      = (initialize integrate-component))
```

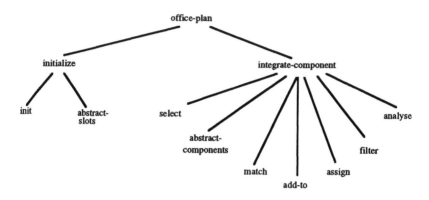

Fig. 3. Task decomposition of OFFICE-PLAN.

The inference layer

At the inference layer, basic inference steps are specified in terms of knowledge
sources operating on metaclasses. Both together constitute a graph, the so-called
inference structure. Figure 4 shows the one for OFFICE-PLAN.

metaclasses describe the roles domain concepts may play during problem solving. In the spirit of KADS, they achieve an abstraction from any specific
domain-layer. Thus, we speak of components instead of employees, and of assignment slots instead of rooms. In MODEL-K, a metaclass can be a structure
composed of domain concepts. "set" is a predefined structure. To define others
like lists, multisets, stacks, queues or trees might is up to the user.

As an example, metaclass **components-to-place** is initially empty, but will
later contain the set of employees that have to be arranged. In other domains, it
might contain guests of hotel rooms, airplanes to gates, or of patients of hospital
beds. The actual relation between a metaclass and possible domain entries is
handled in the connection between inference and domain layer.

```
(METACLASS components-to-place-next-&-their-given-slots
    WITH STRUCTURE       = set)
```

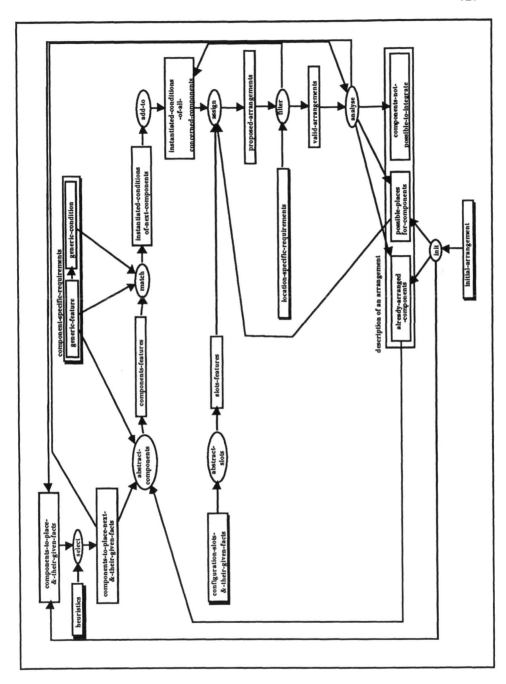

Fig. 4. The inference structure of OFFICE-PLAN.

Knowledge sources describe basic inferences or operations between metacl-asses. They are split into a declaration and a definition part. The former specifies input and output metaclasses and the formal relations used in the body. The formal relations keep the knowledge source domain-independent and will be connected to domain-specific relations by separate connection statements. The definition of a knowledge source, usually being quite implementation-biased, is deferred to the operational refinement stage. For instance, knowledge source **abstract-components** will generate component features given certain requirements without needing any domain relations.

```
(KNOWLEDGE-SOURCE abstract-components
  WITH
  DOCUMENTATION-STRING = ...
  INPUT-METACLASSES    = ((components-to-place-next-&-their-given-slots
                            already-arranged-components
                            component-specific-requirements))
  OUTPUT-METACLASSES   = (components-features))
  REQUIRED-RELATIONS   = nil)
```

In OFFICE-PLAN, there are knowledge sources for **initialization**; to **select** the components to be integrated first according to the given heuristic; to **abstract** essential component and slot features; to **match** the features against the preconditions of requirements in order to instantiate their conditions to constraints; to **add** the newly generated conditions to the constraint network computed formerly; to find all possible **assignments** of components to slots that satisfy the instantiated conditions; to **filter** them by the slot-specific requirements; and to **analyze** the result for proper termination respectively for the next iteration.

The domain connection

One of the aims of KADS is to develop generic inference and task layers which can be connected to different domain layers. MODEL-K provides language constructs for this connection. For example, the metaclass **components-to-place** is connected to instances of the concept **employee**.

```
(CONNECT-MC components-to-place-next-&-their-given-slots
  WITH DOMAIN-OBJECTS = ((employee))
       UPDATE-UP      = static)
```

To allow the synchronization between the contents of a metaclass and the related objects on the domain layer update procedures can be applied at specific points in time. For example, the metaclasses in a system monitoring a chemical plant are kept consistent with the sensor data received at the domain layer via dynamic updating. For office allocation a static connection upwards for initialization is sufficient.

The formal relations of the knowledge sources are always statically connected to domain-specific relations by:

```
(CONNECT-KS-RELATION <formal-relation> WITH
  DOMAIN-RELATION =  <domain-relation>)
```

The domain layer

The domain layer specifies the ontology of the domain. In MODEL-K, the domain-specific information is stated in terms of predefined basic types like string or integer, user-defined enumeration types, concepts and instances, generic and concrete relations. Together, they constitute the domain structure.

Enumeration Types are similar to the scalar types of procedural programming languages. They define discrete sets with a linear ordering.

In OFFICE-PLAN, we use them to specify the **roles, educations, groups, projects, resources** and **themes**. For example, the resources of computing equipment are defined by:

```
(ENUMERATION resources
  WITH values = ((sun macintosh qume symbolics siemens pc)))
```

Concepts are used to represent domain knowledge in an object-oriented way. They may form inheritance hierarchies and describe structural characteristics of domain objects by typed attributes (or slots). In order to suspend the closed-world assumption, the values of a so-called ASSUMABLE attribute may explicitly be specified as to hold, not to hold or to be unknown (see section 2.3 for further details).

In OFFICE-PLAN, **employees, rooms, requirements**, and **conditions** are defined as concepts. For example, an **office-room** is described by its room number, the number of square meters, the research group it belongs to, and the resources it provides. The default value "-" for each slot means that its value is so far unknown.

```
(CONCEPT office-room
  (SLOTS
  (available-resources - :POSSIBLE-VALUES (:SOME-OF-ENUMERATION resources))
  (belongs-to          - :POSSIBLE-VALUES (:ONE-OF-ENUMERATION groups))
  (room-number         - :POSSIBLE-VALUES :NUMBER)
  (size-of-room        - :POSSIBLE-VALUES :NUMBER)
  (ASSUMABLE
  (available-resources size-of-room) :POSSIBLE-VALUES :ANY)))
```

A requirements is declared by a precondition based on features of employees and a condition:

```
(CONCEPT requirement
  (SLOTS (generic-feature   - :POSSIBLE-VALUES :any)
         (generic-condition - :POSSIBLE-VALUES
            (:INSTANCE-OF employee-specific-condition)))))
```

Relations define dependencies between objects of certain types. In the conceptual model, a relation is declared by its arity, i.e. the types of the components in the tuples, and by properties like transitivity or reflectivity. To suspend the closed-word assumption, ASSUMABLE relations allow to specify for which tuples the relation holds, does not hold, or is unknown (more in section 2.3).

The following example declares a non-assumable, symmetric relation `meeting-often` between two employees:

```
(RELATION meeting-often OF RELATION
   WITH PROPERTIES = ((symmetric))
        TYPE       = ((employee employee))
        ASSUMABLE  = false)
```

Generic relations allow to build classes of relations. For instance, the most important relation in OFFICE-PLAN is `arrangement` which describes arbitrary assignments of employees to rooms. As a concrete instance of this generic relation, `init-arranged` describes which employees are initially placed in which rooms, and which employees are in the hall waiting for an assignment. Other arrangement instances like the proposed solutions will be dynamically constructed at the inference layer.

```
(GENERIC-RELATION arrangement
   (SLOTS (TYPE      (room employee))
          (ASSUMABLE false)))

(RELATION init-arranged OF arrangement)
```

2.3   The operational refinement

The conceptual model is not yet operational. Concept instances, relation definitions, knowledge source bodies, control statements ordering the subtasks, and connection procedures still have to be supplied. Being mainly a programming task, this is done in the operational refinement.

The control layer

Control statements: In the control structure, each task specifies its constituent knowledge sources and subtasks. Now the flow of control between them is specified by a control statement which may be composed of sequential, branching and loop statements. For example, the `office-plan` task once executes `initialize` and then repeatedly calls `integrate-component` until there are no more components to arrange.

```
(TASK-BODY office-plan ()
    (SUBTASK initialize)
    (WHILE (> 0 (length (<- components-to-arrange :GET-TRUE 'VALUE)) 0)
        DO ((CALL integrate-component))))))
```

Below we show a trace of the main task in OFFICE-PLAN.

```
(<- office-plan :ACTIVATE :TRACE)

--> activating task 'OFFICE-PLAN'
    it's precondition 'TRUE' is satisfied
    --> STATEMENT
        working on (CALL INITIALIZE)
        --> activating task 'INITIALIZE'
            it's precondition 'TRUE' is satisfied
            --> STATEMENT
                working on INIT
                ==> applying knowledge-source 'INIT' ...
                working on ABSTRACT-SLOTS
                ==> applying knowledge-source 'ABSTRACT-SLOTS' ...
            <-- STATEMENT
        <-- ACTIVATE
            ...
```

The inference layer

Knowledge source bodies: The complexity of KADS knowledge sources may vary considerably, from simple access or test functions to complete problem solvers of their own. And often, they cannot be operationalized without taking efficiency into account. This is why we offer the full BABYLON languages for their definition: prolog, rules, constraints, message passing and lisp. As an example, knowledge source **assign** was implemented to call BABYLON's constraint satisfaction interpreter with the network of instantiated conditions:

```
(KNOWLEDGE-SOURCE-BODY assign ()
  (SATISFY current-net :GLOBALLY :WITH current-varibale-domains))
```

The domain connection

MODEL-K provides default connection procedures for metaclasses and formal relations. If no user-defined connection procedure is given, a metaclass is connected statically. By default, a formal relation is connected to its domain relation by matching the arguments position-wise.

```
(CONNECT-KS-RELATION-BODY <formal-task-name> ()
  <body>)

(CONNECT-MC-UP-BODY <metaclass> ()
  <body>)

(CONNECT-MC-DOWN-BODY <metaclass> ()
  <body>)
```

The domain layer

Instances of concepts describe concrete objects in the domain. They inherit all slots and default values from their concept. For instance, C5-121 is a particular office room. It belongs to group xps, has a number, and has 10 square meters. There are two Macintosh (for simplicity, we did not distinguish between individual machines) and a Sun computer, but definitely no qume terminal. But it is unknown whether there are any siemens terminals, symbolics machines, or pcs.

```
(CONCEPT-INSTANCE C5-121
    OF office-room
    WITH available-resources = (((:TRUE macintosh macintosh sun)
                                 (:FALSE qume)))
        belongs-to = xps
        room-number = 121
        size-of-room = 10)
```

The employee-specific requirements in OFFICE-PLAN are: "The head of group and the secretary should be in next-door rooms." "The head of group and each head of project should be in near rooms." "A smoker and a non-smoker should be in different rooms." "Two persons meeting often should be in different rooms." "Persons with no common themes should be in different rooms." For example, the smoker requirement is modelled by:

```
(CONCEPT-INSTANCE smoker-and-not-smoker-aversion-respected
    OF employee-specific-requirement
    WITH generic-feature = ((smoker-and-not-smoker-pair _em1 _em2))
        generic-condition = should-be-in-different-rooms)
```

Our resource-specific requirements are: "A room should provide enough place to its inhabitants." "A room should provide enough machines to its inhabitants." "Nobody should sit together with more fellow-lodgers than he can bear." For example, the requirement providing each employee with a large enough room is defined by:

```
(CONCEPT-INSTANCE provide-space
    OF resource-specific-requirement
    WITH
    generic-feature = ((needs-space _empl _num))
    generic-condition = should-provide-space)
```

Relations are sets of tuples, which can be defined extensionally by enumeration or intensionally by a characteristic predicate. Both alternatives promote prolog as a suitable definition language. Since MODEL-K is implemented in BABYLON, we use BABYLON's special list-notation for Horn-clauses (c.f. [8, p. 147ff]). For instance, the relation **meeting-often** is defined as follows:

```
(RELATION-BODY meeting-often
  ((meeting-often _em1 _em2) <- (close-friends _em1 _em2))
  ((meeting-often _em1 _em2) <- (are-in-same-projects _em1 _em2))
  (meeting-often john-maier john-mayer))
```

Specifying missing knowledge: As in the example of room C5-121, knowledge may sometimes be incomplete. We definitely know that there are two Macintosh and one Sun in the room. But, under the closed-world assumption that holds for ordinary slots and relations, we cannot express that there definitely is no qume terminal while we do not know anything about the other machines. For such situations, MODEL-K offers the ASSUMABLE attributes and relations. They allow to specify which objects are attribute values or relation tuples, which are not, and which are unknown.

Assumable slots are usually multi-valued. They are interpreted as partial multisets, i.e. as partially defined functions from their POSSIBLE-VALUES domain to the natural numbers. In the example of room C5-121, macintosh is mapped to 2, sun to 1 and qume to 0. To ease the definition of assumable attributes we added abbreviations for cases without unknown values. Moreover, the set of unknown values can always be deduced and need not be specified. To access and modify the values of assumable attributes under a specific truth modality MODEL-K provides predefined methods. For example, after sending the message `(<- C5-121 :add-true 'available-resources '(symbolics))` there will also be a Symbolics in the room. The consistence of the partial multiset is automatically maintained.

Assumable relations are implemented by extending the tuples by a boolean argument. When adding a tuple its status has to be specified in the last component. The example shows the tuples of an assumable relation `close-friends`.

```
(RELATION-BODY
  ((close-friends _em1 _em2 _truth) <- (married _em1 _em2 _truth))
  ((close-friends john-meier john-meyer false)))
```

Again, there are predefined methods to get all true, false or unknown tuples. However, MODEL-K does not provide an interpreter for reasoning under incomplete knowledge so that the knowledge engineer himself must implement the correct inference procedures as was done in the first clause of the example to propagate unknown knowledge.

Switching representation: Since logically the slots of an instance can be viewed as binary relations, MODEL-K provides a uniform PROVE method for both, concept attributes and relations, easing the transition between both representations during development.

For example, (PROVE '(initial-arrangement _X 'C5-121)) finds all persons being seated in room C5-121. And (PROVE '(available-resources _X 'sun)) finds all office-room instances with a sun.

This gives the knowledge engineer the freedom to switch representation formalisms during development without having to change other parts of the description.

2.4 Supporting prototyping

Usually, knowledge sources are called from the control layer. For prototyping, i.e. testing knowledge sources or simulating a not yet existing control layer, it is useful to activate individual knowledge sources by hand. For that purpose, the interpreter can execute (SUBTASK $< task >$) and (KS $< knowledge - source >$) statements for activating tasks and knowledge sources, respectively. For accessing and modifying the status of metaclasses during the development process, a uniform protocol in terms of :GET, :RESET, :ADD and :REMOVE methods is provided to inspect, reset and modify metaclasses.

3 The strategy layer: Meta-reasoning in MODEL-K

The strategy layer in KADS was only vaguely described and has hardly been used in any KADS model. While strategic reasoning is usually concerned with control issues [14], we would like to incorporate some more capabilities at the strategic layer: checking the solvability and difficulty of a problem, predicting and scheduling the resources for problem solving, problem simplification, detecting deadends, and repairing impasses. All these tasks require reasoning *about* the underlying system and thus are meta-activities.

Although the domain of these meta-activities is another knowledge-based system, they can be described in terms of generic problem solving methods like diagnosis, assessment or repair. That means the strategy layer is regarded as another problem solver at the meta-level. Therefore, we can use the same modelling scheme as for the lower three layers, namely another control, inference, and domain layer. Control and inference layers describe the problem solving method to be carried out at the meta-level, for example diagnosing the feasibility of a problem. The domain layer contains the lower three layers to be reasoned about and often special meta-knowledge, like the consistency of data in the object system or necessary conditions to solve a problem.

Since the meta-system reasons about the lower three layers while they are "running", these layers and the object system they model must be kept consistent. Any progress in the object system must be reflected upwards into the model, and any modifications of the model must be propagated downwards into the system. In the terminology of Maes, we need a causal connection, and the object and meta-system together constitute a reflective system [19].

In MODEL-K, we need not worry about the causal connection. Since a system is just an extension of its conceptual model, every object system incorporates its model. You simply cannot change one without the other.

As it turns out, we now have two systems: A meta-system implementing the strategy layer and an object system representing the lower control, inference and domain layers (c.f. figure 5) . This separation has the advantage that meta-systems (and their conceptual models) can be kept generic and reusable for other object systems. For example, predicting the complexity of a problem by estimating the search space is applicable to a wide range of object systems.

In the REFLECT project, we focused on competence assessment, improvement, and resource management. We came up with a range of generic meta-behaviors, most of which we applied to the conceptual model of our office room allocation system. Examples are feasibility studies to detect overcomplex or over-specified problems, relaxing inconsistencies, removing redundancies, controlling time restrictions, etc. [35] [36].

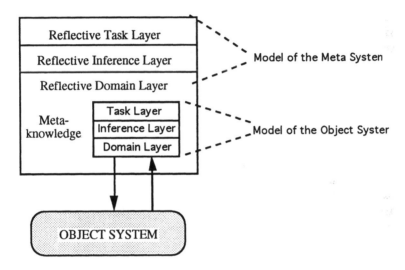

Fig. 5. Knowledge level view of reflective systems.

3.1 Design decisions

Though the idea to use MODEL-K for both, object system and meta-system, seems to be straightforward, a few design decision had to be made which are left open in the conceptual framework. One concerns consistency and the other the control problem of switching between the two systems.

Consistency between the object system and its model

While solving a problem, the object system changes dynamically. For reasons of consistency, these changes must be "reflected" upwards into the model. Vice versa, reflective problem solving operates on its model of the object system, assuming that any changes are "reflected" downwards. (Reflection upwards and downwards are terms introduced by [39] in the context of the logical language FOL). As an example, our time management system repeatedly invokes the assign and filter tasks of OFFICE-PLAN. Based on the number of assignments proposed or filtered, it then decides which task to call next for which time slice. Thus, the number of assignments proposed or filtered has to be repeatedly passed upwards, while the time slices must be passed downwards.

However, such a causal connection is only required if the object model is separated from the object system, which is not the case with MODEL-K. Instead we encounter a similar synchronization problem between the object model and the meta-inference layer. That is because the metaclasses here may contain information from the object model which dynamically changes with the object system. Therefore, the metaclasses at the meta-level must be kept consistent with the object model. An example are the metaclasses for time management which contain the time slices resp. the numbers of solutions. Vice versa, information from meta-level metaclasses may have to be passed downwards into the object model (and thus automatically into the object system).

To maintain consistency, we have three alternatives for both directions. We can lazily update the object system, respectively its model, just before any data item is accessed, we can eagerly propagate all changes directly, or we can propagate them before switching control between the two systems. For MODEL-K we decided to propagate both the changes of the object system to the meta-level metaclasses and vice versa at switching time as a default, reducing the number of update operations. For additional intermediate updates, explicit update statements are provided at the meta-level task layer.

Independently of when we synchronize, we may either update the object system respectively its model completely or incrementally. The former means more copy operations, while the latter requires keeping track of what has changed. For MODEL-K we decided to update incrementally, namely upwards everything that is referenced in a meta-level input metaclass and downwards every output metaclass.

Switching paradigm

Since we have two systems, we have to decide which one should be active and when it should pass over control. For example, for time management we must somewhere state that office planning must proceed up to the assign step. Similarly, the time management system must first perform certain analyses before it can start controlling the assign-filter phase. Afterwards, both systems must be run to completion. In [32] and [27], different switching paradigms were suggested:

Meta-simulation: All control is with the meta-system. Whenever necessary, it has the means to simulate the object system. This alternative requires more knowledge about the object system than we have at the knowledge level.

Asynchronous communication: Meta- and object system run in parallel. Thus it may happen that the conclusions of the meta-part have become obsolete or no longer apply because of the progress in the object system.

Crisis management: The object system operates until it recognizes a crisis. It then passes control to the meta-part, which may modify the object system and then reactivate it. One problem with this paradigm is that the object system must be able to recognize its own crises and deadends. Another problem is, that the meta-system has no chance to prevent any crises.

Reflect-and-act: After each elementary inference step, control is passed from the object system to the meta-system. There the object system may be modified before control is returned. In this paradigm, the elementary inference steps chosen define the grain size for reflection. In the KADS framework, the knowledge sources are natural candidates, since we cannot inspect them any deeper at the knowledge level. Control in the meta-system is necessarily event-driven, which does not readily match with the KADS task structure. As another disadvantage, control is switched more often than necessary.

Subtask management: The meta-system may activate its own tasks as well as tasks in the object system. This paradigm nicely fits into the KADS framework. A meta-task, instead of calling a meta-subtask, would be allowed to call a task in the object system, which could then invoke further object level subtasks. The problem with this alternative is, that there is only one meta-system having exclusive control about the object system.

Instead of having one large meta-system we want to be able to develop small specialists on top of the object system, each tackling an elementary meta-task, like a feasibility expert, a relaxation expert, or a redundancies expert. They should be collected in a library. Given a particular object system, we would like to choose some meta-modules from the library and combine them. The combination should involve minimal changes with the individual meta-systems only.

External switching In order to overcome this problem with subtask management, we came up with a new alternative. We introduced an external scheduler that controls the switches both between the individual meta-specialists and between them and the object system. That means it can call tasks that are defined either at some meta-task layer or in the object system. The task layers of the meta-specialists only contain local tasks. They need not be modified when being combined with other meta-systems. Only the individual scheduling layers must be replaced by a joint one.

Figure 6 shows the resulting scheme of extended MODEL-K. There is one object system with only one model that is accessed from all meta-components. Such a component may have additional meta-domain knowledge, inference and task layers. The individual schedulers are replaced by one common scheduling layer. Examples of meta-domain knowledge may be the pairs of redundant or contradictory constraints, or knowledge about the importance of requirements, constraints, or constraint variables like the employees in office planning.

738

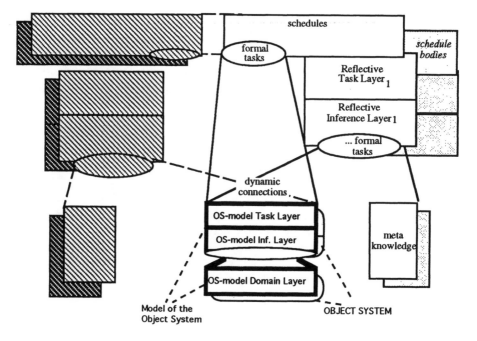

Fig. 6. Schema of extended MODEL-K

Since the scheduler should be generic, it must not directly refer to tasks of the object system. For that reason we introduced formal task names that can be connected to concrete ones when the scheduler is connected to a concrete object system. These formal task names are comparable to the formal relation names we already need in ordinary models. They are used by knowledge sources at the inference layer to generically refer to relations defined at a concrete domain layer.

Calling object system tasks from the scheduler is not always sufficient. Sometimes a meta-knowledge source needs to control certain tasks in the object system exclusively. For instance, the time management system has an inference step invoking the assign and filter steps of the object system with fixed time slices. As for the scheduler, these references are generically made via formal task names.

3.2 Example: Predicting deadends in problem solving

We will motivate why contradictory conditions in office-planning problems can occur at all and how they are removed by the meta-module CONTRA-C.

We will illustrate MODEL-K's meta-approach to strategic reasoning by CONTRA-C, a small competence specialist for OFFICE-PLAN. It prevents the object system from running into a deadend by checking the solvability of a problem in advance and proposing amendments to make the problem solvable. As already said, OFFICE-PLAN transforms requirements, like separate-smoker-and non-smokers into a constraint network. Assume we obtain the following constraints: `same-rooms (Monika, Uli)`, `next-door-rooms (Thomas, Monika)`, `near-rooms(Thomas, Hans)`, `different-rooms (Monika, Uli)`, ... Obviously[2] no consistent assignment can be found because the constraints between Monika and Uli are contradictory.

As shown in figure 7, the task of the meta-module CONTRA-C is decomposed into subtasks for diagnosing (i.e. detecting) and repairing (i.e. removing) contradictory conditions. Diagnosis consists of analyzing the object system and interpreting the obtained findings according to fault categories. Repair consists of proposing repairs and applying them.

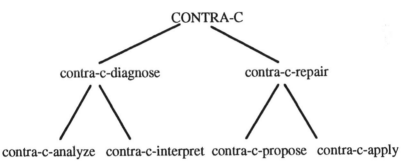

Fig. 7. Task structure of the meta-module

Figure 8 shows the inference structure of CONTRA-C. metaclass `OS-component-conditions` is filled with the relevant information from the object model, which is the constraint network. It is inspected by knowledge source `contra-c-analyze` in order to detect pairs of contradictory conditions. If contradictions have been found knowledge source `contra-c--interpret` adds the fact `(inconsistent-knowledge true)` to metaclass `ml-malfunctions`. `contra-c-propose` then asks the user to remove one condition from each pair of contradiction. The result is passed via metaclass `ml-repairs-remove-contra-c-result` to `contra-c-apply` which removes the chosen conditions from the network.

At its domain layer CONTRA-C needs knowledge about how to detect pairwise contradictory constraints, in its simplest form an opposite relation between pairs of constraints.

We used MODEL-K to model and implement ten competence specialists incorporating strategic knowledge to assess and improve the competence of OFFICE-PLAN: FEASI detects unsolvable problems by comparing available and

---

[2] Although this seems easy to detect for us, we should not forget that the words 'different' and 'same' have no meaning for the object problem solver.

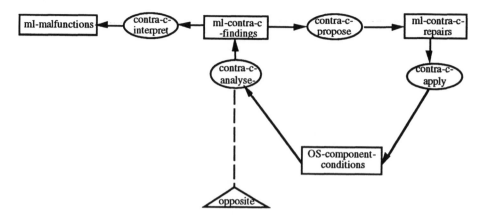

Fig. 8. Inference structure of the meta-module

required resources. CONTRA-R and CONTRA-C detect and remove contradictory requirements from the original problem statement resp. contradictory constraints from the internal representation. RED-R, RED-C, RED-CF, and SIMPLE-D simplify the problem by removing redundancies between generic requirements, between constraints, and by reducing the possible values of constrained variables. COMIC decomposes overcomplex problems and solves them while reusing previously found partial solutions. It can return approximate solutions by suitably composing solved subproblems. TACKLE-TIME allows to limit the time and the number of solutions of the object system by scheduling time slices between a generate and a test subtask (in our case propose and evaluate). One of our partners, BSR-Consulting, built CASY which uses a library of complete cases to shortcut the entire problem solving process.

3.3 Related work

Although our work concerning the strategic layer was influenced by the work on computational reflection [19] [29], it differs in the kind of model used to reflect upon. Whereas languages like KRS or 3-Lisp allow to access the implementation and the run-time environment of programs like class-methods or the interpreter stack, we stress an abstract, implementation-independent model of the underlying object system. We also abandoned the idea of infinite meta-level towers generated by meta-circular interpreters, as we do not see how to acquire knowledge for a third or any higher levels. Work on reflection in logic has shown that a clear separation between object- and meta-level ensures avoidance of paradoxes [24].

ML^2 [33] is a language to formalize KADS knowledge level models. It has been used to explicitly represent the model to be reasoned about. Although ML^2 is in logic and hence more declarative than MODEL-K, the language lacks operational support for the causal connection and the integration of different reflective modules.

The meta-modules developed in MODEL-K are in line with ideas about meta-level reasoning presented in [10], [15], or [37], and recently published work on reasoning under resource limitations [26].

4 Summary

MODEL-K is a language for describing KADS knowledge level models as well as their operational refinements. Since the resulting systems incorporate their conceptual model, this language supports prototyping almost at the knowledge level. Being so close to the knowledge level, the systems are easier to understand by experts and users, they are easier to extend, maintain and explain. But not only knowledge engineers and users profit from this transparency. Knowledge based meta-systems will monitor, assess and improve object systems automatically. The built-in conceptual model in MODEL-K defines the interface for the meta-layer and provides access to the underlying system. Since the meta-system is regarded as another problem solver, the MODEL-K modeling framework can be applied to both, object- and meta-system.

Just like KADS strives at building a large library of knowledge level models, we would like to collect corresponding operationalizations in MODEL-K. Other than generic tasks [6] or the systems of McDermott's group [20], the MODEL-K systems should be easy to adapt and to combine, being written in the same high level language. We are looking forward to results of the KADS II Esprit project, where executable methods shall be developed for the models in the KADS library. Like for object systems, we are aiming at a library of generic meta-systems which can be supplied to classes of object systems.

With its interpretation of the strategic layer, MODEL-K provides a modeling and implementation framework for meta-reasoning systems. To flesh it, more meta-level knowledge and theories have to be acquired. Now the experts are asked –programmers and knowledge engineers– to provide their knowledge *about* how to assess and improve problem solvers.

Acknowledgements

We thank Brigitte Bartsch-Spörl and Hans Voß for comments on earlier versions of this paper, and Ralph Schukey and Uwe Drouven for their cooperation in designing and implementing MODEL-K.

Appendix: The constructs of reflective MODEL-K

〡

SCHEDULER
(SCHEDULE <task-name> WITH <schedule-specification>)

(SCHEDULE-BODY <task-name> () <body>)
    <control-statements>
    (SUBTASK <subtask-name>)
    (RM-TASK <reflective-task-name>)
    (OS-TASK <formal-object-task-name>)

TASK LAYER
(TASK <task-name> WITH <task-specification>)

(TASK-BODY <task-name> () <body>)
    <control-statements>
    (SUBTASK <task-name>)
    (KS <knowledge-source-name>)
    (UPDATE <metaclass> :DOWN)
    (UPDATE <metaclass> :UP)

INFERENCE LAYER
(METACLASS <metaclass-name> <mc-specification>) (KNOWLEDGE-SOURCE <knowledge-source-name> WITH <ks-specification>)
(KNOWLEDGE-SOURCE-BODY <knowledge-source-name> () <body>)   <rules> | <prolog> | <constraints> | <messages>   *(OS-TASK <object-task>)*

DOMAIN CONNECTION
(CONNECT-SCHEDULE-TASK <formal-task-name> WITH <connect-specification>) (CONNECT-MC <metaclass> WITH <connect-specification>) (CONNECT-KS-RELATION <formal-relation> WITH <connect-specification>) *(CONNECT-KS-TASK <formal-task-name> WITH <connect-specification>)*

(CONNECT-SCHEDULE-TASK-BODY <formal-task-name> () <body>)
    (OS-TASK <object-task-name>)
(CONNECT-MC-UP-BODY <metaclass> () <body>)
(CONNECT-MC-DOWN-BODY <metaclass> () <body>)
(CONNECT-KS-TASK-BODY <formal-task-name> () <body>)
    (OS-TASK <object-task-name>)

DOMAIN LAYER
(CONCEPT <concept-name> <concept-specification>) (RELATION <relation-name> OF RELATION WITH <relation-specification>)
(CONCEPT-INSTANCE <name> OF <concept> WITH <instance-specification>) (RELATION-BODY <name> <body>)

Table 1. The constructs of extended MODEL-K. Dotted lines separate conceptual modelling and operational refinement constructs. Constructs which can be used in operational bodies are indented. The constructs of ordinary MODEL-K are printed in normal style, the extensions in italics.

References

1. B. Bartsch-Spoerl, B. Bredeweg, C. Coulon, U. Drouven, F. van Harmelen, W. Karbach, M. Reinders, E. Vinkhuyzen, and A. Voß. Studies and experiments with reflective problem solvers. ESPRIT Basic Research Action P3178 REFLECT, Report IR.3.1,2 RFL/BSR-UvA/II.2/1, REFLECT Consortium, August 1991.

2. B. Bartsch-Sporl, M. Reinders, H. Akkermans, B. Bredeweg, T. Christaller, U. Drouven, F. van Harmelen, W. Karbach, G. Schreiber, A. Voß, and B. Wielinga. A tentative framework for knowledge-level reflection. ESPRIT Basic Research Action P3178 REFLECT, Deliverable IR.2 RFL/BSR-ECN/I.3/1, BSR Consulting and Netherlands Energy Research Foundation ECN, August 1990.

3. C. Beierle, W. Olthoff, and A. Voß. Towards a formalization of the software development process. In *Software engineering 86*, IEE Computing Series 6, London, 1986. PeterPeregrinus Ltd.

4. J. A. Breuker and B. J. Wielinga. Model Driven Knowledge Acquisition. In P. Guida and G. Tasso, editors, *Topics in the Design of Expert Systems*, pages 265–296, Amsterdam, 1989. North Holland.

5. B. Chandrasekaran. Generic tasks in knowledge-based reasoning: High-level building blocks for expert system design. *IEEE Expert*, 1(4):279 – 299, 1986.

6. B. Chandrasekaran. Generic tasks as building blocks for knowledge-based systems: The diagnosis and routine design examples. *The Knowledge Engineering Review*, 3(3):183–210, 1988.

7. D.C. Brownand B. Chandrasekaran. *Design Problem Solving: Knowledge Structures and Control Strategies*. Research Notes in Artificial Intelligence. Pitman, London, 1989.

8. Th. Christaller, F. di Primio, and A. Voß. *The AI Workbench BABYLON: An Open and Portable Development Environment for Expert Systems*. Academic Press, London, 1992.

9. W.J. Clancey. From Guidon to Neomycin and Heracles in twenty short lessons. *The AI Magazine*, 7(3):40–61, August 1986.

10. R. Davis. Applications of meta-knowledge to the construction, maintenance, and use of large knowledge-bases. AI memo 283, Stanford University, Palo Alto, July 1976.

11. R. Davis and B. G. Buchanan. Meta-level knowledge: Overview and applications. In *IJCAI-77*, pages 920 – 927, Cambridge MA, August 1977.

12. D. Fensel, J. Angele, and D. Landes. KARL:: A knowledge acquisition and representation language. In J.C. Rault, editor, *Proceedings of the 11th International Conference Expert systems and their applications*, volume 1 (Tools, Techniques & Methods), pages 513 – 528, Avignon, 1991. EC2.

13. Ch. Floyd. A systematc look at prototyping. In R. Budde, K. Kuhlenkamp, L. Mathiassen, and H. Züllighoven, editors, *Approaches to Prototyping*, pages 1–18. Elsevier, Berlin, 1984.

14. T. R. Gruber. *The acquisition of strategic knowledge*, volume 4 of *Perspectives in artificial intelligence*. Academic Press, Boston, 1989.

15. E. Hudlicka and V.R. Lesser. Meta-level control through fault detection and diagnosis. In *Proceedings of the National Conference on Artificial Intelligence*, pages 153 – 161, Austin, Texas, 1984.

16. W. Jansweijer. *PDP*. PhD thesis, University of Amsterdam, 1988.

17. W. Karbach, M. Linster, and A. Voß. Models, methods, roles and tasks: many labels - one idea? *Knowledge Acquisition journal*, 2:279 – 299, 1990.

18. Marc Linster. Linking modeling to make sense and modeling to implement systems in an operational environment. In Thomas Wetter, Klaus-Dieter Althoff, John Boose, Brian Gaines, Marc Linster, and Franz Schmalhofer, editors, *Current developments in knowledge acquisition: EKAW92*, LNAI, Heidelberg, 1992. Springer.

19. P. Maes. Computational reflection. Technical report 87-2, Free University of Brussels, AI Lab, 1987.

20. S. Marcus, editor. *Automatic knowledge acquisition for expert systems*. Kluwer, 1988.

21. M.A. Musen. *Automated Generation of Model-Based Knowledge-Acquisition Tools*. Pitman, London, 1989. Research Notes in Artificial Intelligence.

22. R. Neches, W. Swartout, and J. Moore. Explainable (and maintainable) expert systems. In *IJCAI-85*, Los Angeles, 1985.

23. A. Newell. The knowledge level. *Artificial Intelligence*, 1982:82–127, 1982.

24. D. Perlis. Languages with self-reference I: Foundations. *Artificial Intelligence*, 25:301–322, 1985.

25. F. Puppe. Med2: How domain characteristics induce expert system features. In H. Stoyan, editor, *GWAI-85*, pages 272–284. Springer-Verlag, 1986.

26. S.J. Russell and S. Zilberstein. Composing real-time systems. In *Proceedings of the 12th International Joint Conference on Artificial Intelligence, Sydney, Australia*, volume 1, pages 212 – 217, San Mateo, 1991. Morgan Kaufmann.

27. G. Schreiber, B. Bartsch-Sporl, B. Bredeweg, F. van Harmelen, W. Karbach, M. Reinders, E. Vinkhuyzen, and A. Voß. Designing architectures for knowledge-level reflection. ESPRIT Basic Research Action P3178 REFLECT, Deliverable IR.4 RFL/UvA/III.1/4, REFLECT Consortium, August 1991.

28. H. E. Shrobe. Dependency directed reasoning in the analysis of programs which modify complex data structures. In *IJCAI-79*, pages 829–835, Tokio, 1979.

29. B. Smith. Reflection and semantics in a procedural language. Technical Report TR-272, MIT, Computer Science Lab., Cambridge, Massachussetts, 1982. Also in: *Readings in Knowledge Representation*, Brachman, R.J. and Levesque, H.J. (eds.), Morgan Kaufman, California, 1985, pp. 31-40.

30. M. Stefik. Planning and meta-planning (molgen: Part 2). *AI journal*, 16:141 – 170, 1981.

31. G. J. Sussman. *A Computer Model of Skill Acquisition*, volume 1 of *Artificial Intelligence Series*. American Elsevier, New York, 1975.

32. F. van Harmelen. *Meta-level Inference Systems*. Research Notes in AI. Pitmann, Morgan Kaufmann, London, San Mateo California, 1991.

33. F. van Harmelen and J. Balder. $(ML)^2$: A formal language for kads models of expertise. *Knowledge Acquisition*, 4, Special Issue in KADS(1):127 – 159, 1992.

34. J. Vanwelkenhuysen and P. Rademakers. Mapping knowledge-level analysis onto a computational framework. In L. Aiello, editor, *Proceedings ECAI'90, Stockholm*, pages 681–686, London, 1990. Pitman.

35. A. Voß, W. Karbach, B. Bartsch-Spoerl, and B. Bredeweg. Reflection and competent problem solving. In Th. Christaller, editor, *GWAI-91, 15th German Workshop on Artificial Intelligence*, pages 206 – 215, London, 1991. Springer Verlag.

36. A. Voß, W. Karbach, C.H. Coulon, U. Drouven, and B. Bartsch-Spoerl. Generic specialists in competent behavior. In *Proceedings of ECAI-92*, 1992.

37. A. Voß, W. Karbach, U. Drouven, and D. Lorek. Competence assessment in configuration tasks. In L.C. Aiello, editor, *Proceedings of the 9th European Conference on Artificial Intelligence*, pages 676 – 681, London, 1990. ECCAI, Pitman.

38. T. Wetter. First-order logic foundation of the KADS conceptual model. In B. Wielinga, J. Boose, B. Gaines, G. Schreiber, and M. van Someren, editors, *Cur-*

rent trends in knowledge acquisition, pages 356–375, Amsterdam, May 1990. IOS Press.

39. R. Weyhrauch. Prolegomena to a theory of mechanized formal reasoning. *Artificial Intelligence*, 13, 1980. Also in: *Readings in Artificial Intelligence*, Webber, B.L. and Nilsson, N.J. (eds.), Tioga publishing, Palo Alto, CA, 1981, pp. 173-191. Also in: *Readings in Knowledge Representation*, Brachman, R.J. and Levesque, H.J. (eds.), Morgan Kaufman, California, 1985, pp. 309-328.

40. B. Wielinga and J. Breuker. Models of expertise. In *Proceedings ECAI'86*, pages 306–318, Brighton, 1986.

A Framework for Integrating Heterogeneous Learning Agents

Bernard Silver, John Vittal, William Frawley, Glenn Iba, Tom Fawcett,
Susan Dusseault, and John Doleac

GTE Laboratories Incorporated, 40 Sylvan Road,
Waltham MA 02254, USA

Abstract. Machine Learning is a rapidly growing subfield of Artificial
Intelligence, and a large variety of learning algorithms have been reported in the literature. However, no one algorithm provides a totally
satisfactory solution to a wide range of problems.

This chapter describes our domain-independent Integrated Learning System (ILS), and one application, which learns how to control a telecommunications network. Our approach includes a framework for combining
various learning paradigms, integrating different reasoning techniques,
and coordinating distributed cooperating problem-solvers.

The current implementation has five learning paradigms (agents) that
cooperate to improve problem-solving performance. ILS also includes a
central controller, called *The Learning Coordinator* (TLC), which manages control flow and communication between the agents. The agents
provide TLC with advice. TLC chooses which suggestion to adopt and
performs the appropriate actions. At intervals, the agents can inspect the
results of the TLC's actions and use this feedback to learn, improving
the value of their future advice.

1 Introduction

This chapter describes our implementation of a domain-independent, distributed
Integrated Learning System (ILS). The first application of ILS learns, through
experience, how to control a telecommunications network. This ongoing work addresses issues involved in combining various learning paradigms, integrating different reasoning techniques, and coordinating distributed cooperating problem-
solvers.

Traditional programs, including most expert systems, cannot respond to
changes in their operating environment or in their requirements, and they cannot learn from experience. For example, if a program produces the wrong answer
once on certain input, it will continue to give the same wrong answer each time it
receives that input, until it is programmed to act differently. Such behavior lacks
a key feature of intelligence: adaptability. This inability to adapt both knowledge and advice based on that knowledge carries a high cost in post-production
debugging and development of a program. One of the goals of Machine Learning
is to produce software, not necessarily expert system software, that can improve

autonomously. Such software can learn from experience, adapt to changing situations and requirements, and refine its knowledge-base, perhaps leading to a level of expertise beyond that of human experts. In some cases, the knowledge can be learned from scratch; in others, it is better to start with an existing knowledge base.

Machine Learning is a rapidly growing subfield of Artificial Intelligence and a large variety of learning algorithms have been reported in the literature. (See, for example, [6, 16, 17, 22, 20, 1].) However, no one algorithm is adequate for a wide range of problems. Our approach is to create a framework that integrates several algorithms. Our hope is that the resulting program can be used (like a shell) across a range of problems.

ILS provides a framework for integrating heterogeneous learning agents, written in various languages and executing on various platforms that cooperate to improve problem-solving performance. It also includes a central controller called *The Learning Coordinator* (TLC) which manages control flow and communication among the agents, using a high-level communication protocol. The agents provide TLC with expert advice concerning the current problem; TLC then chooses which suggestion to adopt, and performs the appropriate actions. The agents compete by offering potentially differing advice to TLC, and cooperate to overcome gaps in their individual knowledge. At intervals, the agents can inspect the results of the TLC's actions and use this feedback to learn. As they learn, either autonomously or cooperatively, the quality of advice given to TLC increases, leading to better performance.

The original ILS integrates implementations of three learning paradigms, called agents, and TLC. The learning paradigms are: inductive (FBI), macro-learning (MACLEARN), and knowledge-based learning (NETMAN). Experimental results have been obtained using this configuration of the ILS. Recently, two additional agents have been added: feature-learning (ZENITH) and reactive-planning (DYNA).

Figure 1 shows the current ILS architecture; the box beneath each agent indicates the type of data used by that agent. The solid lines represent TLC-initiated communication, the dashed line represents inter-agent communication.

The agents are heterogeneous in that they each have a different:

− model of the domain
− area of expertise
− learning paradigm

In addition, TLC, each agent, and the domain simulator can execute in parallel on different machines.

The heterogeneous approach distinguishes ILS from systems such as SOAR [15], which uses one learning paradigm (chunking) for all learning tasks, and others like THEO [2], which uses one representation framework (frames) for all learning tasks.

In the remainder of this chapter, Section 2 discusses the domain of experimentation, telecommunications network traffic control, and a realistic simulator

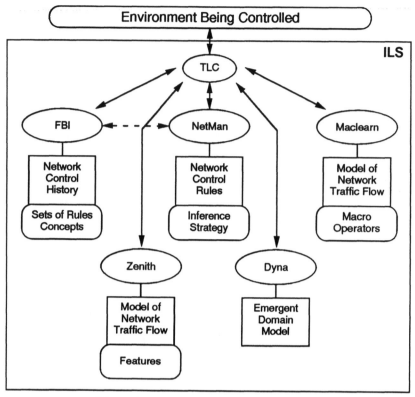

Fig. 1. The Integrated Learning System

called NEMACS. Section 3 describes the learning paradigms and their specific realizations as agents in ILS. Section 5 discusses the operation of TLC. Section 6 describes the inter-agent cooperation implemented in the present version of ILS. Section 7 describes our preliminary results. Section 8 discusses the short-term future direction of the work.

2 Application Domain: Network Traffic Control

A circuit-switched telecommunications network consists of switches connected by trunk groups of varying call-carrying capacities. Each switch has a *routing table* which specifies how calls arriving at that switch bound for any given destination switch should be handled. The routing table specifies which trunk group a call should use to go to the *next* switch, and contains a prioritized list of trunk groups to consider. Under normal circumstances, the switch tries the trunk groups in order, attempting to find a free trunk. Once a free trunk is found, the call is routed along it to the next switch. If no free trunks are available in any of the trunk groups, the call fails and is cancelled. That is, there is no back-up-and-retry, just as in present day telephone systems: a caller may receive a message

"All circuits are busy, please hang up and try your call later".

The effect of the routing tables can be modified by placing *controls* on the switches and trunk groups. These controls can cause calls to be cancelled or to traverse a path other than the paths specified in the routing table.

The Network Traffic Control problem is to "optimize" the behavior of a network by intelligently placing controls. Traffic Managers, the people who put the controls on the network, generally judge a network to be performing satisfactorily if the ratio of network completed calls to network offered calls is 0.99 or higher.

A Traffic Manager obtains feedback from the network via *switch statistics*. Every five minutes each switch produces many statistics concerning the calls it has processed in the previous five minutes. They include:

1. Completed calls from each switch, in total, and broken down by destination and by destination-and-trunk-group.
2. Attempted calls from each switch, in total, and broken down by destination.
3. Current usage of each trunk group.

Network Traffic Management is of great economic importance to service providers because customers are not charged for calls that fail to complete. Some calls, such as those to a number which is busy, will inevitably fail. Other calls will be cancelled by a control or because they fail to find a trunk. Some of these calls might have been completed if traffic had been routed differently. A call that is *unnecessarily* cancelled is lost revenue.

A Traffic Manager's job is difficult, partly because of the huge amount of data produced and its time-varying nature. There is some reliance on *preplans*; standard procedures for predictable occurrences, such as Mother's Day, which is the busiest calling day of the year. However, unpredictable problems arise, and they cause the major difficulty. One example is the partial or total failure of a network element (a trunk group or a switch) which may cause some unavoidable denial of service to some users. However, effective traffic management can greatly improve the situation, for example, by rerouting traffic around the failed element.

Any automated system needs to know not only how to recognize that a failure has occurred, but also, based on the situation, how to try to "fix" the problem. No Traffic Manager has a complete understanding of how to do this; indeed it is likely that no group of Traffic Managers have together a complete understanding of how the system works, all of the situations that will arise, and how to control the network in these cases. Many Artificial Intelligence techniques have been applied to this task, including Case-Based Reasoning [13] and traditional Expert Systems (*e.g.* [14]). The knowledge bases used by these systems are incomplete. These approaches suffer from the inflexibility of all non-learning programs: an inability to learn from experience and thereby to grow their model of the network and to improve their control of it over time.

As can be imagined, it is impractical to experiment on a commercial network. As a result, ILS uses a fine-grained realistic network simulator, called NEMACS [3], to provide a realistic environment to evaluate the learning paradigms.[1] NEMACS, written in C, performs a relatively fine-grained simulation of a user-defined network. The simulation is carried out at the level of individual calls, and embodies statistical models of call generation and call duration. The switches produce many statistics so that network performance can be monitored.

Most of the experiments use a network consisting of ten switches. NEMACS simulates five minutes of behavior in this network in about ninety seconds of real time. The network produces about 30 kilobytes of data every five simulated minutes.

One property of this domain is its complexity. In ongoing experiments on the simulation of a ten-switch, sixteen-trunk network there are always at least 3000 individual controls that could be placed. Moreover, in most cases it is reasonable to impose several controls simultaneously, increasing the number of allowable control options considerably.

3 The Learning Agents

This section describes five learning paradigms and their implementations in ILS: inductive (FBI), search-based (MACLEARN), knowledge-based (NETMAN), feature discovery (ZENITH) and reactive planning (DYNA). FBI, MACLEARN and DYNA are written in Lisp, ZENITH and NETMAN are written in Prolog. ILS is completely distributed. Communication among instances of the agents and TLC is via TCP/IP streams with a text-based protocol, and is described in Sections 4 and 5.

3.1 Inductive Learning

FBI Function-Based Induction, [9], is an extension of Quinlan's ID3, [21]. FBI learns decision trees from large numbers of examples. Trees both compress and generalize the experience represented by sets of examples; the trees completely describe the examples. A decision tree can be expanded into a set of rules, one for each leaf of the tree, so that this approach generates classification rulesets from examples.

ID3 is an *attribute-based* induction system. Attributes can be viewed as the fields in a record of a data-base. ID3 treats all attributes equally and conjoins them in a decision tree (or set of rules) using statistical measures (see [21] for details) without regard for the semantics of the attributes involved. This approach may allow interesting rules to be discovered without the user having to know very much about a domain. However, in other cases ID3 is unable to build a satisfactory decision tree because the desired concept cannot be adequately expressed in terms of conjunctions and disjunctions of the basic attributes.

FBI extends ID3 by allowing arbitrary *functions* of attributes. This allows the easy incorporation of domain knowledge into the induction task. Frawley

---

[1] NEMACS has replaced an earlier simulator, NETSIM, [10]. NEMACS can simulate more facets of the domain.

[9] gives a simple example concerning a personnel database. The database contains attributes such as name, age, seniority, salary and Social Security number. Suppose that the goal is to construct a decision tree to classify individuals as *pensionable* or not. On such a database, ID3 produces a very large tree, which may not generalize to new examples. In contrast, if FBI is provided the domain knowledge that the sum of age and seniority is an important concept in this domain, it produces a very small tree that will generalize.

FBI is also able to discover potentially useful concepts that are combinations of existing functions by examining a tree and finding paths that lead to identical subtrees. The discovered concepts are then used to simplify the existing decision tree and are made available as building blocks in the construction of other decision trees.

Often the concepts discovered in this way are useful because they reflect genuine features of the domain. In other cases, the concepts discovered are artifacts caused by random patterns in the example set. FBI could ask other elements of ILS, in particular NETMAN, to assess the utility of a discovered concept. This is discussed in Section 6.4.

3.2 Search-based Learning

MACLEARN [12, 11] currently performs *best-first search* (see, for example, [19]) in order to learn *macro-operators*, or *macros*, which are useful combinations of operators that can be subsequently treated as a single operator. Macro-learning is a form of chunking which can improve search performance by enlarging the set of operators available for the search. The availability of a good set of macros will often drastically reduce the combinatorially explosive nature of a search problem.

Macros reduce search in two general ways. The first is to take larger steps in the search space. Since a macro actually represents a number of primitive operators, the application of a single macro can result in moving a greater distance through the search space. A problem that may require hundreds of primitive steps to solve, may be solvable more quickly by only tens of applications of macro steps.

The second is to provide synergistic combinations of operators. Applying a set of operators as a group may be beneficial, whereas applying any operator alone may make things worse. In such a case, it may be difficult for a search to discover the combination; but once it has been discovered it is best to remember it in order to avoid having to duplicate the lengthy search in subsequent similar situations. Thus macro learning can be viewed as a kind of encapsulation of experience.

However, there is a cost associated with creating macros. Macros enable larger steps through the search space, but they increase the number of possible branches at each step. This increased branching factor will tend to slow down the search. In order for macros to prove beneficial, the advantages must more than compensate for the disadvantages. Thus a key issue in macro learning is to be highly selective in choosing which macros to keep. MACLEARN uses various heuristic criteria to perform the filtering process, as is discussed in [11, 12].

On complex problems, MACLEARN may encounter a combinatorial explosion as the search space of possible operators becomes too large. MACLEARN becomes bogged down in the search and may be unable to find a satisfactory solution. Other agents within ILS can provide assistance to MACLEARN by constraining the search and indicating which part of the search space should be examined. This is discussed further in Section 6.3.

3.3 Knowledge-Based Learning

NETMAN, [25], is an example of a knowledge-intensive learning system. Such systems have a large amount of knowledge of the domain, similar to the knowledge base of an expert system. This contrasts with the data-driven *empirical* approach of algorithms, such as ID3, which have little or no knowledge of possible relationships between attributes.

Knowledge-intensive systems, also called *analytic* systems, generally use a variation of the algorithm called *explanation-based learning* (EBL), [5, 18, 23]. EBL systems can learn a great deal from a single example, and if the domain theory (and the explanation) is correct, any generalizations produced by the system are guaranteed to be right. This again contrasts with the ID3 class of algorithms, where a generalization produced from the training set may well be incorrect when tested against more examples.

On the other hand, EBL systems require a great deal of knowledge, which is not available in many domains. If no such strong theory of the domain of interest is known, one possibility is to discard the entire EBL approach and use a purely data-driven empirical method. However, even if there is no strong theory, people often possess heuristics about the domain, and such heuristics can be viewed as forming a weak theory. Such weak theories will not be powerful enough to support full explanation-based learning. However, it may be possible to supplement the theory using an empirical learning technique. This is the approach used by NETMAN within ILS.

NETMAN has a large amount of domain knowledge. However, the knowledge need be neither complete nor totally accurate. As a result, NETMAN can make mistakes. (Human experts suffer from the same limitation, of course.) In EBL terms, the domain theory is incomplete and computationally intractable, and so NETMAN uses a heuristic approximation.

The domain knowledge in NETMAN is encoded as rules. The rules are partitioned into two types:

1. **Diagnostic/Treatment Rules**: These rules are used to diagnose what may be wrong with the network. Some of the rules also suggest what action should be performed to correct the problem.
2. **Selection Rules**: These rules choose between the actions proposed by the treatment rules.

NETMAN learns three major types of information from experience:

1. *Stored caches*: NETMAN stores as a macro the sequence of rule firings that led to advice that worked.
2. *Support List*: The support list indicates how successful or unsuccessful a particular action proved to be. Those that have proved valuable in the past are more likely to be used in the future.
3. *Possible Bugs*: When an action fails to have the expected effect, NETMAN can classify the cause and severity of this failure. This information is stored and will affect future use of the action.

When actions have unexpected effects, NETMAN attempts to explain the cause of the unpredicted behavior. This analysis allows NETMAN to discover that sometimes an action will fail due to a *bug*. NETMAN is able to classify the type of bug, and associate this type with the action. Note that the action may often work successfully; bugs may occur only in certain situations.

Ideally, NETMAN would be able to distinguish accurately between situations in which an action will be successful and those in which it fails with a bug. Unfortunately, the computation involved, and the stochastic nature of the domain, make this impossible to do precisely. Instead, NETMAN heuristically differentiates the cases by calling on another component of ILS, FBI. Section 6.1 describes this interaction.

3.4 Feature Learning

Like MACLEARN, ZENITH is a search-based problem solver that performs best-first search in the space of possible network states. An operator is the application of a control to a switch in the network; each network state comprises a network, the controls that have been applied to it, and the resulting performance data. ZENITH is given a fixed amount of time to search, in which it tries to find a network state that is able to complete the maximum number of calls placed.

ZENITH's search is guided by an evaluation function that determines the relative worth of states. The evaluation function is a linear combination of *features*, each feature being a numeric-valued measurement of a network state. For example, one feature might be the total number of calls completed by the network in a five minute period, and another might be the number of calls that could be routed from one switch to another. Each feature represents some aspect of the network that is presumably important to the problem solver in directing its search.

ZENITH learns new features so that it may construct better evaluation functions from them. ZENITH generates features using a set of transformations. The original feature is based on the goal of the performance system (in this case, to maximize call completions in a network), and successive features are created by transforming existing ones. ZENITH employs four different kinds of transformations: goal regression, abstraction, specialization and decomposition [8]. In creating new features, the transformations use both a domain theory of telecommunication networks and indirect feedback from problem solving, so this approach is a hybrid of analytical and empirical learning.

Because ZENITH iteratively improves the set of features that its evaluation function can use, the evaluation function improves over time. However, ZENITH must also consider the expense of its evaluation function. Every feature incurs a computational cost when it is applied to a state. ZENITH is given a limit on the amount of time that it can spend evaluating a single state, so the combined costs of the features that it chooses for its evaluation function must not exceed this limit. A feature selection method is used that attempts to produce the most accurate evaluation function possible within the time limit imposed.

3.5 Reactive-Planning

DYNA [27, 7] embodies both reinforcement learning and planning. These two methodologies combine to form one process which operates alternately on the domain and a model of the domain. When the system functions in the real world, it is learning a good set of reactions (in this case, network controls) from trial and error. The world model enables the system to plan using information learned from hypothetical experience. DYNA's two core abilities, *policy function* and *evaluation function*, closely parallel those required by the ILS. The policy function takes as input a state and proposes an action which will bring the system closer to its goal. The evaluation function formulates the potential of a given state and action pair to achieve the system's goal. DYNA must repeatedly perform a given action in a given state in order to adequately learn their relationship to the derived outcome (the measure of which is called a *Q-value*).

Due to the complexity of the domain and the corresponding amount of learning required, DYNA must generalize and have a fast and dynamic data structure. DYNA classifies a state by the largest connected subgraph of overflowing trunk groups in the network. With this classification system, DYNA obtains a degree of specialization without sacrificing the benefits of a knowledge-poor system. This partial representation of the state space allows for a many-to-one mapping of states to state descriptors. The underlying data structure is composed of two layers of *Red-Black trees* (self-balancing binary trees; see, for example, [4]) which enable $O(lg\ n)$ access time and an evolving information storage system. The first layer indexes over state space instances. The underlying layer is composed of two Red-Black trees which share one data set, the first indexes over actions and the second over *Q-values*.

4   The ILS Protocol

Within ILS, agents interact using a communication protocol consisting of the six message (request) types enumerated below. Any agent may access any other agent using ILS language primitives or any other calls understood by the target agent.

1. The `INITIALIZE` message is a request for an agent to initialize itself and set up communication with other agents. This message includes information specifying the current host machine for each of the other agents. The

response to this message is simply an acknowledgment that system and communication initialization is complete.

2. The **ADVISE** message is a request for advice on what to do in the current state of the external domain to be controlled. An agent responds to this message by examining the current state and deciding what actions would be best for improving the this state. A vote (in the range 1-5) accompanies each recommendation, indicating how beneficial the agent predicts this advice is likely to be. If the agent is unable to come up with advice that improves the situation, it may respond with the reply **UNKNOWN**.

3. The **CRITIQUE** message is a request for an agent to provide its opinion of advice offered by other agents. The specific pieces of advice other agents have proposed is passed along as part of this message. The response to this request is a set of votes (again in the range 1-5) reflecting the value of each piece of advice as viewed by the responding agent. A vote of **UNKNOWN** is given for those pieces of advice that an agent is not able to meaningfully critique. Agents are also required to critique their own advice. Currently an agent is constrained to critique its own proposal with the same vote as it gave when it proposed the action (in response to the **ADVISE** message).

4. The **DATA-AVAILABLE** message has two purposes: Firstly it tells the agents which of the suggested set of actions was taken. Secondly, it informs the agents that a sufficient period of time has passed to allow domain data to reflect those actions. In response to this message, agents can gather feedback from the domain in order to learn. Finally, they send back an acknowledgment that they have finished processing the current data.

5. The **RECORD** message is sent between agents that maintain their own histories of past cases. One agent asks another to record additional information about a given case for later recall or processing. The major use for this message in the current implementation is between NETMANand FBI. NETMAN sends the message to FBI to record that certain cases have properties of interest to NETMAN. See Section 6.1 below for more details.

6. The **CLASSIFY** message is a request for an agent to classify the current state of the external domain with regard to a particular predicate used in a previous **RECORD** message. For example, NETMAN uses this message to ask FBI to classify the current state using data from states that have been RECORDed.

5   The Learning Coordinator

In its current state, the ILS relies on a Learning Coordinator (TLC). TLC manages the control flow between the agents, TLC, and the simulated domain. The basic loop, repeated every five simulated minutes, is as follows:

1. TLC asks the agents to propose actions to control the network. Each agent returns a list of possible actions, and associates with each action a *vote*, indicating the agent's perception of the value of that action.

2. TLC then asks the agents to critique the proposals of the other agents. Each agent returns a vote for each proposed action.

3. Now TLC has a list of proposed actions, and each action has, at present, a set of up to five votes associated with it. TLC has to choose between these actions. There are several possible techniques that can be used for this selection process, some of which are described below. As currently implemented, TLC averages the critique votes for each proposal and executes the action with the highest average score, thus adding and/or removing controls from NEMACS.

4. Five simulated minutes later new switch statistics are produced. The agents inspect these statistics and thus obtain feedback on the success or failure of the chosen action, allowing them to learn appropriately to affect their future problem-solving performance. The following sections discuss the individual steps in more detail, using the NEMACS domain.

5.1 Proposing Controls

The agents individually obtain network statistics from TLC via TCP/IP streams. Each agent then examines the statistics and attempts to produce an ordered list of actions that the agent believes will improve the network state. An action may remove some controls already in place and/or impose some new controls.

Alternatively, an agent can suggest taking no action, if it believes that the current state of the network is satisfactory, or can indicate that it does not know what to do. In the last case, no further processing is performed.

No agent will propose actions that appear to make the situation worse. If an agent cannot find an action that will improve a bad network state, it will indicate that it does not know what to do.

Each agent must also calculate a *vote* for each proposed action; in other words, determine how much it believes in the action that it is proposing.

MACLEARN and ZENITH calculate their advice using simplified simulators. Each performs best-first search for good actions on its own simulator and returns the best one found within a time limit. To calculate the vote, each agent compares the simulated outcome with the current network state, giving a very high vote if the action appears to greatly improve the situation, and a somewhat lower vote if the action promises only a small improvement.

FBI calculates its advice using its database of previous examples. An example consists of descriptions of an initial network state, a set of actions, and the network state that results from taking those actions and running the network for an additional period of simulated time. Two preferred subsets are maintained, one of examples whose rankings are *very high*, and one of examples whose rankings are *high*. Learned decision trees defined over these map an initial state to a set of actions: the advice provided is either a *very high* set of actions, a *high* set, or none. FBI's vote depends on success ratios of similar actions in the database.

NETMAN calculates its vote using both past experience and its domain theory. The domain theory models the likely effect of controls. For example, an action receives credit if it contains controls that move traffic from overflowing trunks to non-overflowing ones. NETMAN calculates the vote for a proposal by combining the vote based on past experience (if available) with the vote based on domain knowledge.

When advising the TLC of the best action to take in a given situation, DYNA finds the state descriptor in the first layer Red-Black tree, steps to the Q-value tree in the second layer and retrieves the action with the highest associated Q-value. The magnitude of the Q-value determines the vote.

5.2 Critiquing Suggestions of Others

In general, an agent critiques a proposal using the same mechanism used to produce a vote. Thus MACLEARN and ZENITH use their internal simulators to simulate the effect of the proposed controls, FBI uses a decision tree, computed over all examples, mapping pairs of initial states and actions into rankings to evaluate the expected effect of a proposed action. When criticizing another agent's advice, DYNA simply indexes over the state and then the control set to retrieve the associated Q-value, which is then scaled appropriately. NETMAN uses a domain model and previous experience to estimate the effectiveness of the proposal. NETMAN also performs a series of "sanity checks" on the proposal. For example, rerouting traffic to a trunk that it is currently non-operational is a bad mistake, and a proposal containing such a reroute will receive a poor score. Such checks are an important part of the critiquing cycle as other agents may not be able to detect that various network elements have failed.

In some cases an agent may indicate that it has no opinion on a proposal. This can happen if the agent has no knowledge or experience concerning a particular control or set of controls. Such critiques are discarded.

5.3 Choosing between the Proposals

As indicated above, currently ILS chooses the action with the highest average critique score. This appears to work quite well. Some other alternatives include:

- Choose the action with the highest *raw* score; in other words ignore the effects of critiquing.
- Choose the action that is highly scored by the majority of the agents.
- Choose the action proposed by the agent that has proved most reliable in the past.
- Weight the votes of an agent in proportion to its past performance.

These and other strategies are currently being examined.

The last two suggestions above require that TLC keeps track of the performance of each agent, and thus itself *learn* to choose among the various proposals. Section 8.1 describes how this might be implemented.

5.4 Obtaining Feedback

One interesting feature of the ILS architecture is that some agents can learn even when another agent's action is the one that is chosen. In the case of FBI and DYNA, the mechanism is particularly simple; the whole cycle is just another example, consisting of a before state, an action and an after state. FBI stores the example, DYNA updates the Q-value tree to reflect the newly acquired knowledge. NETMAN is able to learn if the action chosen is sufficiently similar (according to a complex metric) to an action it proposed.

At present, ZENITH and MACLEARN do not make use of the feedback.

6 Inter-agent Cooperation

Section 5.2 described one level of cooperation between the agents: the ability to critique the actions of each other. This section further describes our ongoing work on some of the ways in which the various agents interact to improve the performance of individual agents.

6.1 Concept Formation

Ideally, NETMAN would be able to distinguish accurately between situations in which an action will be successful and those in which it fails in a certain way. However, the complexity and stochastic nature of the domain make this an unrealistic target. Instead, NETMAN heuristically differentiates the cases by calling on another component of ILS, FBI.

FBI is given, via the RECORD message, two classes of examples: in one class are all the examples where the failure mode occurred, in the other are the cases where the action worked. FBI is used to produce a function that heuristically classifies network states as likely to suffer from that failure mode or not. If NETMAN is considering performing the action, it asks the inductive learning program for its classification, using the CLASSIFY message. If the current state is classified as likely to fail, and the failure mode has proved sufficiently severe, NETMAN does not propose the action. In effect, the classification step is added as a precondition to the treatment rule that proposes the action.

6.2 Detecting Unreliable Data

Within the ILS, agents generally assume that all changes in the domain are caused by controls being added or removed in preceding cycles. This assumption is not always valid in the scenarios used in our experiments.

Unless the changes in the domain can be recognized, agents may incorrectly attribute credit or blame to the last action taken. This may interfere with future learning by adding "noise" to the data (an action appears good in one episode, and bad in another almost identical episode). Not all agents can recognize these changes. However, NETMAN is able to detect major fluctuations and can inform other agents. Currently, NETMAN tells FBI when these situations occur, and FBI marks such episodes specially, so that they can be discounted in the future.

6.3 Reducing the Search Space

MACLEARN can be overwhelmed by a combinatorial explosion on complex networks. We are investigating ways in which the other agents in ILS can help MACLEARN by giving it *constrained* search problems. The advice can come from FBI or NETMAN detecting important features of the current network state. The search can be constrained in various ways:

- Reduced operator sets: MACLEARN is told to consider only certain types of controls.
- Constrained areas of application: MACLEARN is told to consider placing controls only on the specified network elements.
- New starting state: MACLEARN is told to assume that certain controls must be present

Constraining the search space helps MACLEARN derive a satisfactory solution to the current problem state and possibly also search more deeply (in a constrained part of the search space), making it more likely to discover useful *macros* (see [12] for details). In this case, other agents can help MACLEARN solve a problem that it cannot otherwise solve. In addition, with the help of learned macros, MACLEARN may now be able to solve other similar problems without help from other agents.

6.4 Assessing Discovered Concepts

As described in Section 3.1, FBI can automatically discover potentially interesting concepts that are combinations of other existing functions. Often the concepts discovered in this way are useful because they reflect genuine features of the domain. In other cases, the concepts discovered are artifacts caused by random patterns in the example set.

A knowledge-based agent, such as NETMAN, can heuristically classify a concept as useful or not useful. When FBI proposes a new concept, it could ask NETMAN if there is any domain knowledge that combines the functions contained in the concept. If NETMAN does have such domain knowledge, the concept is probably a genuine one. If not, the concept may be an artifact, although perhaps NETMAN is missing some domain knowledge.

This kind of interaction between FBI and NETMAN has not yet been implemented.

7 Results

Our initial experiments, run with FBI, MACLEARN, and NETMAN, are encouraging: ILS as a whole can out-perform each individual learning program.

An experiment, run on a well-engineered circuit-switched network consisting of ten end offices connected by sixteen trunk-groups, was made up of four distinct episodes involving different kinds of network overload plus one period of normal traffic. The amount of overload was sufficient to ensure that not all calls could be completed. In each case, 6,600 telephone calls were placed during the seventy minutes of network simulation. Uncontrolled, the network fails to complete seven percent (465) of the 6,600 offered calls. The learning agents attempt to reduce this loss. Table 1 reflects the number of the 6,600 calls that were not completed for the uncontrolled network, the average for the learning agents working individually, and when all three agents are working in concert. The third column shows the percentage of the 465 calls that were completed for each of these three scenarios.

	Number of Lost Calls	Percent Improvement
(No controller)	465	0.0
Average agent	387	16.8
All three Agents	322	30.8

Table 1. Experimental Results

Other experiments with slightly different scenarios gave approximately the same results. We are now performing further experiments using networks that more closely simulate the topologies found in typical metropolitan areas.

8   Further Work

8.1   Meta-Learning

As indicated above, the ILS chooses the action with the highest average score. One problem with this technique is that the advice of each agent is given the same weight, even though experience may show that one agent performs better than another agent in a certain type of situation. It may be desirable for the system to *learn* the reliability of the individual agents. We call this type of learning *meta-learning*.

Central Control One possible solution is for TLC to keep track of the performance of each agent, and thus learn the reliability of the agents and use this information to choose among the various proposals. This can be done with varying degrees of sophistication.

The simplest method is to increase the perceived reliability of an agent when its choice is selected and causes improvement, and to decrease the perceived reliability if its action makes the network worse. Then, when TLC comes to choose between various proposals, the vote of an agent is weighted by its perceived reliability. Thus, the vote of an agent deemed unreliable would count for very little, reducing the probability that its preferred action would be selected. The reliability of an agent can also be evaluated with respect to critiques. If an agent gave a low score to an action that was in fact successful, TLC can decrease its perceived reliability and similarly in the other cases.

Learning the global reliability of an agent is somewhat crude. Rather than discovering that one agent is generally more reliable than another, it is more useful to discover the reliability of *agent/situation* pairs. For example, it may be valuable to learn that agent A is very good at solving situations involving a large amount of traffic flowing to one switch, but less good than agent B in situations involving failed network elements. However, this approach requires that TLC has a certain amount of knowledge (to distinguish the states) and, perhaps, a fairly sophisticated learning algorithm. This conflicts with the goal of putting most of the interesting behavior in the agents and keeping TLC simple.

Distributed Control An alternative approach is to distribute most of the tasks of TLC to the agents. In this scheme, which is currently being implemented, TLC is basically a bulletin board and a global clock. Agents post proposals and critiques to the board for other agents to read. Each agent is free to build a model of the reliability of other agents, using any technique that it possesses.

An agent can, if it desires, raise or lower its critique of a proposal of another agent. For example, when asked to critique action A proposed by agent B, another agent may believe that there is a heavily overloaded switch in the current network state, and that agent B is particularly good at dealing with such situations. The agent may then increase its vote for A, based on its understanding of the reliability of B in this situation. NETMAN adopts this approach in the current implementation.

Problems with Meta-Learning One problem with these approaches to meta-learning is that neither TLC nor the individual agents can know whether a successful action was the best of all of the suggested actions; this is inherent in every scheme that does not perform a total search. Thus an agent may be rewarded when the untried suggestion of another agent would have caused greater improvement. However, experience suggests that this problem is not very critical, but further experiments have to be performed to verify this. Another difficulty with these methods is that the agents are learning, so that an agent that originally provided poor advice may now produce effective suggestions. One way of correcting this problem is to discount earlier performance, giving more weight to recent experience.

8.2 Extending the Proposal Cycle

One weakness of the current implementation is that each agent only has one opportunity per cycle to suggest useful actions. During the critique phase, an agent may decide that an action proposed by another agent is superior to any proposed by itself. In such a case, the agent will give the superior action a high vote. However, an agent might detect that its proposal could be usefully combined with that of another agent if the two proposals are sufficiently independent.

ILS currently contains no mechanism for synthesizing new proposals from existing ones in this way. From the viewpoint of TLC, proposals are atomic, and exactly one is chosen and imposed on the simulator.

One avenue for further research is to extend our current proposal cycle to be iterative, examining independent proposals, and proposing combined actions. Such an approach, reflecting that of more mainstream distributed AI (DAI), should produce better quality advice leading to better problem-solving performance and learning.

9   Conclusions

This paper has described ILS, a framework for integrating several distributed heterogeneous learning agents that cooperate to improve problem-solving performance. The agents learn both independently and cooperatively.

Each agent has been tested independently using telecommunications traffic control as a domain, and each has demonstrated that it can learn by interacting with that domain. At present, ILS is being extensively tested using the same domain. One focus of the current research is the relative utility of various TLC selection strategies. Simple strategies appear to be effective.

Detailed experiments will be performed to evaluate the ILS framework. At a minimum, to be successful, ILS must demonstrate:

- *Enhanced problem-solving performance*: The ILS as a whole must do better than each of its constituent parts.
- *Improved Learning*: The learning of each agent will be accelerated within ILS, and each agent's knowledge will be adjusted to be more effective.

The intent is ultimately to develop a *domain independent* ILS.

Acknowledgments

Many past and present members of GTE Laboratories provided the project with both useful information concerning the network traffic control domain, and with interesting discussions in machine learning and associated fields: Oliver Selfridge, Alvah Davis, Mark Adler, Alan Lemmon, Ralph Worrest, Robert Weihmayer, Rich Brandau and Ludmila Kopeikina. Kelly Bradford implemented much of TLC. Rich Sutton, Marty Hiller, and Philip Chan assisted the integration of DYNA into the ILS. Discussions with Paul Utgoff were helpful in the design and implementation of ZENITH. Tom Fawcett's work on ZENITH was funded in part by the Office of Naval Research through a University Research Initiative Program under contract N00014-86-K-0764.

References

1. L.A. Birnbaum and G.C. Collins, editors. *Proceedings of the 8th International Machine Learning Workshop*. Morgan Kaufmann, 1991.
2. J. Blythe and T.M. Mitchell. On becoming reactive. In A. Segre, editor, *Proceedings of the 6th International Machine Learning Workshop*, pages 255–257. Morgan Kaufmann, 1989.

3. R. Chipalkatti, S. Kheradpir, and W. Stinson. NEMACS: The NEtwork MAnagement and Control Simulator. Technical Memorandum TM 0299-08-90-465-01, GTE Laboratories Incorporated, August 1990.

4. T.H. Cormen, C.E. Leiserson, and R.L. Rivest. *Introduction to Algorithms*. MIT Press, 1990.

5. G. DeJong and R. Mooney. Explanation-based learning: An alternative view. *Machine Learning*, 1(2):145–176, 1986.

6. T.G. Dietterich, R. London, K. Clarkson, and G. Dromey. Learning and inductive inference. In P.R. Cohen and E.A. Feigenbaum, editors, *The Handbook of Artificial Intelligence, Volume 3*, chapter XIV. Pitman Books Ltd, 1982.

7. S.E. Dusseault. DYNA in ILS: An overview. Technical Correspondence TC-0179-03-92-506, Computer and Intelligent Systems Laboratory, GTE Laboratories Incorporated, 1992.

8. T.E. Fawcett and P.E. Utgoff. Automatic feature generation for problem solving systems. In D. Sleeman and P. Edwards, editors, *Proceedings of the 9th International Machine Learning Workshop*, pages 144–153, 1992.

9. W.J. Frawley. Using functions to encode domain and contextual knowledge in statistical induction. In G. Piatetsky-Shapiro and W.J. Frawley, editors, *Knowledge Discovery in Databases*. AAAI Press, 1991.

10. W.J. Frawley, T.E. Fawcett, and K. Bradford. NETSIM: An object-oriented simulation of the operation and control of a circuit-switched network. Technical Report TN 88-506.1, Computer and Intelligent Systems Laboratory, GTE Laboratories Incorporated, 1988.

11. G. Iba. The application of heuristic search and discovery of macro-operators to network traffic control. Technical Memorandum TM-0062-10-88-506, Computer and Intelligent Systems Laboratory, GTE Laboratories Incorporated, 1988.

12. G. Iba. A heuristic approach to the discovery of macro-operators. *Machine Learning*, 3(4):285–317, 1989.

13. L. Kopeikina, R. Brandau, and A. Lemmon. Case based reasoning for continous control. In J Kolodner, editor, *Proceedings of a Workshop on Case-Based Reasoning*, pages 250–259. Morgan Kaufmann, 1988.

14. P. Kosieniak, V. Mathis, M. St Jaques, and D. Stevens. The Network Control Assistant (NCA), a real-time prototype expert system for network management. In *Proceedings of First International Conference on Industrial and Engineering Applications of Artificial Intelligence and Expert Systems*, pages 367–377. Association for Computing Machinery, 1988.

15. J.E. Laird, A. Newell, and P.S. Rosenbloom. Soar: An architecture for general intelligence. *Artificial Intelligence*, 33(1):1–64, 1987.

16. R.S. Michalski, J.G. Carbonell, and T.M. Mitchell, editors. *Machine Learning: An Artificial Intelligence Approach Vol 1*. Tioga Press, 1983.

17. R.S. Michalski, J.G. Carbonell, and T.M. Mitchell, editors. *Machine Learning: An Artificial Intelligence Approach Vol 2*. Morgan Kaufmann, 1986.

18. T.M. Mitchell, R.M. Keller, and S.T. Kedar-Cabelli. Explanation-based generalization: A unifying view. *Machine Learning*, 1(1):47–80, 1986.

19. N.J. Nilsson. *Principles of Artificial Intelligence*. Tioga Pub. Co., Palo Alto, California, 1980.

20. B. Porter and R. Mooney, editors. *Proceedings of the 7th International Machine Learning Conference*. Morgan Kaufmann, 1990.

21. J.R. Quinlan. Induction of decision trees. *Machine Learning*, 1(1):81–106, 1986.

22. A Segre, editor. *Proceedings of the 6th International Machine Learning Workshop.* Morgan Kaufmann, 1989.

23. B. Silver. *Meta-Level Inference.* Number 1 in Studies in Computer Science and Artificial Intelligence. North Holland, 1986.

24. B. Silver. A hybrid approach in an imperfect domain. In G. DeJong, editor, *Proceedings of AAAI Symposium on Explanation-Based Learning.* American Association for Artificial Intelligence, 1988.

25. B. Silver. *NetMan:* A learning network traffic controller. In M. Matthews, editor, *Proceedings of Third International Conference on Industrial and Engineering Applications of Artificial Intelligence and Expert Systems,* pages 923–931. Association for Computing Machinery, 1990.

26. B. Silver, W. Frawley, G. Iba, and J. Vittal. An architecture for self-improving distributed heterogeneous agents. In J. Bezdek, editor, *Proceedings of Fourth International Conference on Industrial and Engineering Applications of Artificial Intelligence and Expert Systems.* Association for Computing Machinery, 1991.

27. R.S. Sutton. Integrated architectures for learning, planning, and reacting based on approximating dynamic programming. In B. Porter and R. Mooney, editors, *Proceedings of the 7th International Machine Learning Conference,* pages 216–224. Morgan Kaufmann, 1990.

Made in the USA
Middletown, DE
08 February 2017